■ Absolute Music

Absolute Music

The History of an Idea

Mark Evan Bonds

OXFORD
UNIVERSITY PRESS

Oxford University Press is a department of the University of
Oxford. It furthers the University's objective of excellence in research,
scholarship, and education by publishing worldwide.

Oxford   New York
Auckland   Cape Town   Dar es Salaam   Hong Kong   Karachi
Kuala Lumpur   Madrid   Melbourne   Mexico City   Nairobi
New Delhi   Shanghai   Taipei   Toronto

With offices in
Argentina   Austria   Brazil   Chile   Czech Republic   France   Greece
Guatemala   Hungary   Italy   Japan   Poland   Portugal   Singapore
South Korea   Switzerland   Thailand   Turkey   Ukraine   Vietnam

Oxford is a registered trademark of Oxford University Press
in the UK and certain other countries.

Published in the United States of America by
Oxford University Press
198 Madison Avenue, New York, NY 10016

Library of Congress Cataloging-in-Publication Data
Bonds, Mark Evan, author.
Absolute music : the history of an idea / Mark Evan Bonds.
pages; cm
Includes bibliographical references and index.
ISBN 978-0-19-934363-8 (hardback)—ISBN 978-0-19-934365-2 (updf)—
ISBN 978-0-19-934364-5 (online content)   1. Absolute music.
2. Music—Philosophy and aesthetics.   I. Title.
ML3854.B66 2014
781.1'7—dc23
2013033095

This volume is published with the generous support of the Joseph Kerman Endowment of the American
Musicological Society, funded in part by the National Endowment for the Humanities and the Andrew W.
Mellon Foundation.

9 8 7 6 5 4 3 2 1
Printed in the United States of America
on acid-free paper

To Gilbert T. Sewall

◼ CONTENTS

List of Figures		*ix*
List of Abbreviations		*xi*
Acknowledgments		*xiii*
Introduction		1
PART I ◼ **Essence as Effect: To 1550**		17
1	Orpheus and Pythagoras	19
2	Isomorphic Resonance	30
PART II ◼ **Essence and Effect: 1550–1850**		39
3	Expression	41
	The Separation of Powers	41
	Music and Language	48
	Music as Language	58
	Mimesis	69
4	Beauty	79
5	Form	90
	Form as Number	91
	Form as Content	98
6	Autonomy	103
	Material Autonomy	103
	Ethical Autonomy	108
7	Disclosiveness	112
	The Composer as Oracle	112
	Beautiful Insights	118
	Cosmic Insights	121

PART III ■ Essence or Effect: 1850–1945   127

8   Wagner's "Absolute" Music   129

9   Hanslick's "Pure" Music   141
    Terminology   143
    Hanslick's Early Aesthetics   151
    Hanslick the Conventional   157
    Hanslick the Radical   173
    Hanslick the Ambivalent   183

10   Liszt's "Program" Music   210

11   Polemics   219

12   Reconciliation   237

13   Qualities Recast   250
    Expression   251
    Beauty   268
    Form   269
    Autonomy   284
    Disclosiveness   290

Epilogue: Since 1945   297

Appendix: Hanslick's Vom Musikalisch-Schönen: Early
    and Selected Later Responses   301
Works Cited   317
Index   353

1	Orpheus	20
2	Pythagoras	24
3	The Macrocosm	27
4	The Microcosm	28
5	The Three Manifestations of Music	33
6	Wagner Assaults the Ear	174
7	Hanslick Worships at the Altar of Brahms	175
8	Chladni's Acoustical Figures	197
9	Chladni Demonstrates his Acoustic Figures	198
10	Seebeck's Entoptic Figures	202
11	Hans Christian Ørsted	203
12	Modern Aesthetics, 1877	270

LIST OF ABBREVIATIONS

19CM	*19th-Century Music*
AfMw	*Archiv für Musikwissenschaft*
AmZ	*Allgemeine musikalische Zeitung* (Leipzig)
GSD	Richard Wagner, *Gesammelte Schriften und Dichtungen*. Ed. Wolfgang Golter. 11 vols. Berlin: Bong, 1913.
JAAC	*Journal of Aesthetics and Art Criticism*
JAMS	*Journal of the American Musicological Society*
JHI	*Journal of the History of Ideas*
JM	*Journal of Musicology*
JMT	*Journal of Music Theory*
JRMA	*Journal of the Royal Musical Association*
M&L	*Music & Letters*
MQ	*Musical Quarterly*
MR	*Music Review*
NZfM	*Neue Zeitschrift für Musik*
OMB	Eduard Hanslick, *On the Musically Beautiful*. Trans. Geoffrey Payzant. Indianapolis: Hackett, 1986.
PW	Richard Wagner, *Prose Works*. Trans. William Ashton Ellis. 8 vols. London: K. Paul, Trench, Trübner, 1893–99.
VMS	Eduard Hanslick, *Vom Musikalisch-Schönen*. Ed. Dietmar Strauß. 2 vols. Mainz: Schott, 1990.

■ ACKNOWLEDGMENTS

For research fellowships that gave me the time needed to complete this book, I am grateful to the American Council of Learned Societies, the National Endowment for the Humanities, the William N. Reynolds Foundation, and the College of Arts and Sciences at the University of North Carolina at Chapel Hill. I am also grateful to the University of California Press for permission to use, in chapter 9, material that had previously appeared in a slightly different form as "Aesthetic Amputations: Absolute Music and the Deleted Endings of Hanslick's *Vom Musikalisch-Schönen*," in *19th-Century Music* 36 (2012): 1–23.

Ready access to the resources of the University Libraries of the University of North Carolina at Chapel Hill made my work far easier than it might otherwise have been. The staff of the Music Library (Philip Vandermeer, Diane Steinhaus, Bradshaw Lentz, and Carrie Monette) was unfailingly helpful. Thank you.

A number of friends and colleagues were kind enough to offer comments on all or parts of the manuscript at various stages of its development: Tim Carter, James Davis, J. Samuel Hammond, Kevin Karnes, Tomas McAuley, Michael Morse, James Parsons, Jeremy Yudkin, and Nick Zangwill. Their suggestions were invaluable. My thinking also benefited from conversations along the way with Karol Berger, Katherine Bergeron, Calvin Bower, Keith Chapin, Annegret Fauser, Lydia Goehr, Nicole Grimes, James Hepokoski, Stefan Litwin, Robert Nosow, Massimo Ossi, Sanna Pederson, Karen Painter, Jann Pasler, Elaine Sisman, Noel Verzosa, and William Weber. For help with some finer points of translation, I am grateful to Annegret Fauser (French) and Tim Carter and Massimo Ossi (Italian).

At Oxford University Press, my editor, Suzanne Ryan, helped shape the project at every step along the way. Jessen O'Brien provided expert help with the book's images. And I am especially grateful to my copy editor, Barbara Norton, for her keen eye. For the index: Thank you, Sam.

Thanks, too, to my family: Dorothea, Peter, and Andrew have helped in ways that they may not themselves realize. But I do.

Finally, my debt of longest standing is to Gilbert T. Sewall, an inspiring teacher. He gave me a kick-start when I needed it most.

■ Absolute Music

Introduction

What is music and why does it move us? From antiquity to the present, writers have answered these questions in many ways, but they have almost always treated them in tandem, for how we identify the essence of music—what it is—inevitably shapes our accounts of its effect—what it does—and vice versa. We cannot, after all, explain how music works without first establishing its identity, which is to say, without first conceiving of it in isolation, apart from all else, consisting only of itself.

This book traces the history of the idea of music's essence as autonomous, self-contained, and wholly self-referential. "Absolute music" is the most common of several terms used to convey this conception, which manifests itself most clearly in compositions that have no text to be sung and no titles or accompanying descriptive terms that might in some way suggest what a particular work might be "about."

By this definition, the concept of absolute music might seem straightforward enough. We can readily distinguish between the nature of a piano sonata by Mozart and Berlioz's *Symphonie fantastique*, with its elaborate prose program describing an "episode in the life of an artist," or between a two-part invention by Bach and Dukas's *L'apprenti sorcier*, whose title compels us to recall the tale of the magician-in-training who oversteps his bounds. Yet the idea of absolute music has proven to be a flashpoint of musical aesthetics, particularly since the middle of the nineteenth century. Some have rejected the premise that music can function exclusively within its own sphere, while others have insisted that it can do nothing more. Few concepts in the aesthetics of music have evoked such polarizing reactions.

The polemics erupted shortly after the term "absolute music" itself first appeared. This was no mere coincidence, for the term was purposefully burdened with ideological baggage from the start. It was coined in 1846 by none other than Richard Wagner, who used it as a pejorative in his efforts to expose the limitations of purely instrumental music, thereby providing a justification for his own theory of opera.[1] To Wagner's mind, a self-contained art of pure form could serve no useful purpose in society: it was "absolute" in the sense that it was isolated, sterile, and irrelevant to life. Within a few years, Wagner was calling into question the plausibility of his own neologism, dismissing the

---

1. Richard Wagner, "Programm zur 9. Symphonie von Beethoven" (1846), *GSD*, 2:61; *PW*, 7:252. On the early history of the term and its cognates, see Sanna Pederson, "Defining the Term 'Absolute Music' Historically," *M&L* 90 (2009): 240–62.

idea of an "absolute artwork" as a "non-thing," a "specter of aesthetic fantasy," a "hobgoblin in the brain of our aesthetic critics."² The notion of an artwork wholly unconnected to the world around it, Wagner declared, was quite literally inconceivable.

In an ironic twist, those who considered music to be autonomous and entirely self-referential appropriated the very term Wagner had used to denigrate that conception of the art. The most important figure on this side of the debate was the Viennese music critic Eduard Hanslick, who in his brief treatise *Vom Musikalisch-Schönen* (*On the Musically Beautiful*, 1854) celebrated precisely those qualities of abstraction and isolation so repugnant to Wagner.

The controversy that ensued transcended the narrow world of musical aesthetics because it went to the heart of two long-standing issues about the nature of all the arts. The first concerned the relationship between form and content. As the least material and most inherently abstract of all the arts, music had long been acknowledged as different in kind. Unlike a poem, a drama, a novel, a painting, or a sculpture, a work of purely instrumental music did not have to be *about* anything at all. (If a composer happened to provide some verbal clue as to a work's import, as for example in the case of Dukas's *L'apprenti sorcier*, that information was not actually heard in performance and could therefore be considered as standing apart from the work itself.) And while philosophers and critics had always acknowledged the importance of form as an aesthetic category, the idea of an art consisting entirely and exclusively of form, without representational content of any kind, posed a conceptual challenge. At a time when the term "abstract art" did not yet exist, only music offered the possibility of an art of pure form. But commentators were slow to accept the implications of such a high degree of abstraction. They responded to music in a variety of ways: some remained content to treat it simply as an exception, which often meant marginalizing it, while most attempted to rationalize its place within the broader spectrum of all the arts by downplaying its abstract nature and emphasizing its capacity to represent human passions. This necessarily entailed a distinction between the form of a work and its content, which could be an object, an event, an idea, or an emotion. It was not until the early years of the nineteenth century that any significant number of critics began to argue that that music's form *is* its content. The proponents of absolute music eventually advanced to the forefront of those who saw the identity of form and content as the highest aesthetic ideal.

---

2. Wagner, *Eine Mitteilung an meine Freunde* (1851), GSD, 4:234, 235: "Das absolute Kunstwerk...ist ein vollständiges Unding, ein Schattenbild ästhetischer Gedankenphantasie...das Spukgebild im Hirne unserer ästhetischen Kritiker." Unless otherwise noted, all translations are my own. Additional citations to William Ashton Ellis's English-language edition of Wagner's *Prose Works* (PW) are offered throughout to facilitate comparison to a different translation; in this case, see PW, 1:274, 275.

By 1877, the novelist and literary critic Walter Pater could famously declare that "all art constantly aspires towards the condition of music."[3]

Vom Musikalisch-Schönen also spoke to the central issue of art's role in society. Because of its wholly self-contained essence, Hanslick argued, music in its purest form could not engage with the vicissitudes of life; this in turn allowed it to function as a refuge of pure beauty from the realm of the mundane. Hanslick's motives were at least in part political: writing in the wake of the Revolutions of 1848–49, he wanted to provide a theoretical justification for insulating music from the turmoil of social and political change. In this respect, his attitude toward music was actually far more radical than that of Wagner, who considered music (and art in general) as a means of revolution. Wagner's idea was scarcely novel: the socially disruptive potential of music had been recognized long before by Socrates, who in Plato's *Republic* declares that "the guardians of the state must beware of changing to a new form of music, since it threatens the whole system.... The musical modes are never changed without change in the most important of a city's laws."[4] Hanslick's view of music as a wholly self-contained art, by contrast, would figure prominently in several currents of modernist aesthetics in the early twentieth century. Serial composition and the aesthetics of "New Objectivity" (*Neue Sachlichkeit*), both of which emerged in the 1920s, owed much to the premise of music as an art of pure form, even if figures like Schoenberg, Stravinsky, and Hindemith had no desire to be associated with a critic from a previous generation whose reputation was that of a hard-boiled reactionary. By the middle decades of the twentieth century, critics were routinely interpreting abstract painting and sculpture as the visual counterparts of absolute music. Formalism would become a particularly contested issue on the Cold War's cultural front: the East denounced it as an aesthetic that promoted the production of artworks lacking in social value, even as the West endorsed it for precisely the same reason. Seen from a distance, then, it is Hanslick and not Wagner who emerges as the more forward-looking of the two, though not in ways that Hanslick himself could have anticipated. As Jean-Jacques Nattiez has rightly noted, *Vom Musikalisch-Schönen* is a text "fundamental to musical modernity."[5]

The notion of "the music itself"—a phrase often invoked in the context of music analysis—and the related constructs of "purity" and "autonomy" continue

3. Walter Pater, "The School of Giorgione," *Fortnightly Review* 22 (October 1877): 528. Pater would later incorporate this essay, with some revisions, into the third edition of Pater, *The Renaissance: Studies in Art and Poetry* (London: Macmillan, 1888). For further commentary on Pater's dictum, see p. 271–73.

4. Plato, *Republic* 424c, trans. G. M. A. Grube, rev. C. D. C. Reeve, in Plato, *Complete Works*, ed. John M. Cooper (Indianapolis: Hackett, 1997), 1056.

5. Jean-Jacques Nattiez, "Hanslick: The Contradictions of Immanence," in Nattiez, *The Battle of Chronos and Orpheus: Essays in Applied Musical Semiology*, trans. Jonathan Dunsby (New York: Oxford University Press, 2004), 105.

to function as ideals in discussions about music. These concepts are deeply problematic, however, for they imply that we can somehow hear, contemplate, and discuss music entirely on its own terms. As Richard Taruskin has pointed out on many occasions, such claims isolate music from the humans who write, perform, and listen to it and who never do these things—and never *could* do these things—in a sphere somehow cordoned off from everyday existence.[6] The claims of purity and autonomy, qualities closely associated with absolute music, frequently mask their own ideological premises. We always listen to or think about music within a specific historical moment and cultural context, and the idea of "pure" music is itself an abstraction, for the "purely musical experience" is never purely musical. Ethnomusicologists have developed an entire discipline based on this premise.

Indeed, every work of music inevitably reflects its historical and cultural context to at least some degree, no matter how "absolute" it might seem. Bach's inventions and Mozart's sonatas, to return to our earlier examples, are what they are for reasons that go beyond purely musical considerations. We know that one of Bach's purposes in writing his two- and three-part inventions was pedagogical: this is evident in the order and increasing contrapuntal sophistication of these works in the collection of inventions he composed for members of his family and for what he called "amateurs of the keyboard." In the prefatory note to a manuscript set of these pieces, assembled in 1723, Bach described these inventions as works of "straightforward instruction" for composing as well as performing, first in two voices, then in three, by means of which those who applied themselves diligently might arrive "above all...at a *cantabile* manner in playing, all the while acquiring a strong foretaste of composition."[7] And we know from Mozart's correspondence that the style of at least one of his late piano sonatas owes much to personal and economic circumstances. When he asked his friend and fellow Freemason Michael Puchberg for a loan in the summer

---

6. See Richard Taruskin, "A Myth of the Twentieth Century: *The Rite of Spring*, the Tradition of the New, and 'The Music Itself,'" *Modernism/Modernity* 2 (1995): 1–26, republished in Taruskin, *Defining Russia Musically: Historical and Hermeneutical Essays* (Princeton, NJ: Princeton University Press, 1997), 360–88; Taruskin, "Is There a Baby in the Bathwater?" *AfMw* 63 (2006): 163–85, 309–27; Taruskin, "Back to Whom? Neoclassicism as Ideology," in Taruskin, *The Danger of Music* (Berkeley and Los Angeles: University of California Press, 2009), 382–405; and Taruskin, "Afterword: *Nicht blutbefleckt?*," *JM* 26 (2009): 274–84. Susan McClary has also argued this point on more than one occasion; see her "Narrative Agendas in 'Absolute' Music: Identity and Difference in Brahms's Third Symphony," in *Musicology and Difference: Gender and Sexuality in Music Scholarship*, ed. Ruth Solie (Berkeley and Los Angeles: University of California Press, 1993), 326–44; and *Conventional Wisdom: The Content of Musical Form* (Berkeley and Los Angeles: University of California Press, 2000).

7. Johann Sebastian Bach, title page to a manuscript collection of inventions (1723), in *Schriftstücke von der Hand Johann Sebastian Bachs*, ed. Werner Neumann and Hans-Joachim Schulze (Kassel: Bärenreiter, 1963), 220–21: "Auffrichtige Anleitung, wormit denen Liebhabern des Clavires...gezeiget wird...mit 2 Stimmen reine spielen zu lernen...[und] mit dreyen obligaten Partien richtig und wohl zu verfahren, anbey auch zugelich gute *inventions*...zu bekommen,...am allermeisten aber eine *cantable* [*sic*] art im Spielen zu erlangen, und darneben einen starcken Vorschmack von der

of 1789, Mozart assured him that he was already in the process of doing all he could to earn the money to repay the loan, including writing a set of six "easy" (*leichte*) sonatas to be published and sold to the market of musical amateurs in Vienna.[8] In the end, Mozart wrote only one of these, the Sonata in D Major, K. 576, and this work does in fact stand out for its unusually modest demands on the performer. When we listen to these compositions by Bach and Mozart, we can choose to hear them as autonomous and self-contained works of art, or we can choose to hear them as manifestations of specific personal, institutional, political, and economic circumstances; we are most likely to hear them as some combination of the two. But that is a choice we make and not a quality inherent in the works themselves. Neither mode of listening is superior to the other, and the notion that we can hear them in exclusively one way or the other is in any case deeply suspect.

The purpose of this book, then, is not to argue for or against the legitimacy of the idea of absolute music, but rather to trace the history of this idea and its consequences. This account goes up to but does not incorporate the recent lively philosophical debate about music's connections (or lack thereof) to the world around it. In many respects, contemporary philosophers like Lydia Goehr, Peter Kivy, Jerrold Levinson, Jenefer Robinson, Kendall Walton, and Nick Zangwill are addressing the same questions that exercised Wagner and Hanslick more than 150 years ago: Is music by itself capable of expressing emotions or ideas? If so, how? If not, what—if anything—*does* music express?[9] This debate often draws on historical sources, to be sure: Kivy and Zangwell, in particular, have offered important insights into Hanslick's arguments in *Vom Musikalisch-Schönen* to support their own (divergent) views about what music can and cannot express. I have largely avoided engaging with these more recent lines of discussion, in part to keep the present study within manageable bounds, and in part because my purpose is not to advocate any particular philosophical point of view but rather

Composition zu überkommen." Translation from Laurence Dreyfus, *Bach and the Patterns of Invention* (Cambridge, MA: Harvard University Press, 1996), 1.

8. Letter of 12 July 1789 to Michael Puchberg in Mozart, *Briefe und Aufzeichnungen*, 7 vols., ed. Wilhelm A. Bauer and Otto Erich Deutsch (Kassel: Bärenreiter, 1962–75), 4:93; English version in *The Letters of Mozart and his Family*, ed. and trans. Emily Anderson (New York: W. W. Norton, 1989), 930.

9. See, for example, Lydia Goehr, *The Quest for Voice: Music, Politics, and the Limits of Philosophy* (Berkeley and Los Angeles: University of California Press, 1998); Peter Kivy, *Music Alone: Reflections on the Purely Musical Experience* (Ithaca, NY: Cornell University Press, 1990); Kivy, *Antithetical Arts: On the Ancient Quarrel between Literature and Music* (Oxford: Clarendon Press, 2009); Jerrold Levinson, *Music, Art, and Metaphysics: Essays in Philosophical Aesthetics* (New York: Oxford University Press, 2011); Jenefer Robinson, *Deeper than Reason: Emotion and Its Role in Literature, Music, and Art* (Oxford: Clarendon Press, 2005); Kendall L. Walton, "What Is Abstract about the Art of Music?" *JAAC* 46 (1988): 351–64; Walton, "Listening with Imagination: Is Music Representational?" *JAAC* 52 (1994): 47–61; Nick Zangwill, *The Metaphysics of Beauty* (Ithaca, NY: Cornell University Press, 2001); and Zangwill, "Against Emotion: Hanslick Was Right about Music," *British Journal of Aesthetics* 44 (2004): 29–43.

to examine how others in the past have used the construct of absolute music to promote their own ideas about what music is and how it works. Philosophers of art both past and present have tended to treat absolute music as a constitutive concept, a quality or set of qualities that are (or are not) inherent within music and that we may (or may not) perceive in listening to music; I prefer to approach absolute music as a regulative concept, a premise that can be neither proven nor disproven but that provides a framework for discussing other ideas, most important among them the relationship between music's perceived essence and its effect. In practice, constitutive and regulative constructs can overlap considerably, and regulative constructs used in the past can enrich current thinking about the essence of music, even if the reverse is not always the case.

If we approach absolute music as a regulative construct, we can move outside the framework in which its history is conventionally cast. Almost every account to date presents it as an aesthetic concept that emerged toward the end of the eighteenth century, even while acknowledging that it did not acquire its own distinctive term until the middle of the nineteenth.[10] For the most part, however, these narratives perpetuate the terminology and conceptual framework laid down in the polemics between Wagner and Hanslick in the middle of the nineteenth century. Surprising as it may seem, the two agreed about the nature of absolute music; they differed only on its value. Or to put this another way: they agreed on its essence but disagreed about its effect. Wagner equated absolute music with sterility, Hanslick with purity, but its "absoluteness" in the sense of its separation from all other realms of art and of life, was never in dispute. The two also constructed remarkably similar narratives to explain its origins in the instrumental repertory of what we now think of as the "Classical" era, which reached its high point in the music of Haydn, Mozart, and early Beethoven. Wagner praised these composers for having elevated purely instrumental music to its fullest potential, but he regarded that potential as necessarily limited. For Wagner, instrumental music was a historically superseded mode of expression. He pointed to the finale of Beethoven's Ninth Symphony as a harbinger of the future: it was here that even Beethoven, the great symphonist, had recognized the limitations of purely musical expression and had dared to incorporate words into what until that time (1824) had been an otherwise purely instrumental genre. Hanslick, by contrast, equated instrumental music with the essence of music itself: the legacy

10. See, for example, Hugo Riemann, *Die Elemente der musikalischen Aesthetik* (Berlin and Stuttgart: W. Spemann, 1901), 204–05; Carl Dahlhaus, *Die Idee der absoluten Musik* (Kassel: Bärenreiter, 1978); Daniel K. L. Chua, *Absolute Music and the Construction of Meaning* (Cambridge: Cambridge University Press, 1999); Roger Scruton, "Absolute Music," in *The New Grove Dictionary of Music and Musicians*, 2nd ed., 29 vols. (London: Macmillan, 2000); Wilhelm Seidel, "Absolute Musik," in *Die Musik in Geschichte und Gegenwart*, 2nd ed., 27 vols. (Kassel: Bärenreiter, 1994–2008); and Ruth Katz, *A Language of Its Own: Sense and Meaning in the Making of Western Art Music* (Chicago: University of Chicago Press, 2009), 166, 187, 208 and passim.

of Haydn, Mozart, and early Beethoven was something to be preserved and extended. He considered the Ninth an anomaly in Beethoven's output, a one-time experiment. As a critic, Hanslick embraced vocal music enthusiastically, but as a philosopher, he insisted that music, without the aid of a sung text or verbal cues, was entirely self-sufficient.

The polemics between Wagner and Hanslick and their surrogates extended across the remainder of the nineteenth century. Music became a cultural battlefield that pitted defenders of the past—Haydn, Mozart, and Beethoven, or at least the Beethoven of the first eight symphonies—against the advocates of the "Music of the Future," who hailed the finale of Beethoven's Ninth as the fountainhead of the new music of Wagner and Liszt. The direct critical response to *Vom Musikalisch-Schönen* was both intense and protracted. (The more significant early reviews and commentaries are discussed in chapter 11; see also the Appendix.) Each new edition of the treatise through the eighth (1891) provoked reactions from supporters and detractors alike. By the time of the last authorial edition (the tenth, 1901), it had been translated and published in Spanish (1865), French (1877), Italian (1883), Danish (1885), Russian (twice: 1885 and 1895), English (1891), and Dutch (1892). The text gave opponents of Wagner, Liszt, and self-styled "progressives" a philosophical basis by which to justify their resistance to the "Music of the Future" on something more than merely personal dislike of this new music or an aversion to change in general. By the same token, *Zukunftsmusiker*, the "Musicians of the Future," could now attack their opponents on grounds that went beyond the charge of garden-variety conservatism. Hanslick's treatise claimed philosophical standing in the world of ideas and as such provided a useful target of opportunity. Nor did these two sides talk past each other, for they agreed, as noted, on the basic terms of the debate. Wagner had good reason to coin a new term ("absolute music") when he did, and Hanslick had good reason to accept Wagner's understanding of what it meant. Their self-serving yet oddly congruent arguments will be examined in detail in chapters 8 and 9; for the moment, suffice it to say that their mutually reinforcing accounts of the nature and history of absolute music (or "pure" music—*reine Musik*—as Hanslick preferred to call it) established the framework in which scholars have examined this idea from the middle of the nineteenth century down to the present day.

From a historical perspective, this framework is hopelessly myopic. Both Wagner and Hanslick all but ignored a long tradition of debate about the essence of music, and to the extent that they took account of this earlier discourse at all, they distorted it to their own ends. Their narratives of music history are based on the premise that music is a wordless language that had managed to "emancipate" itself from conventional language toward the end of the eighteenth century. But the idea of "pure" music is far older than this. It has occupied a central position in commentary on the art since antiquity and dates back to the time of Pythagoras, that quasi-mythical figure of the sixth century BCE who is said to have discovered the arithmetic ratios of musical intervals and who considered music to be the audible manifestation of number. This connection of sound to number carried implications far beyond the measurement of music, for it demonstrated an even more fundamental connection between the realms of the visible and invisible, between the world of the senses and the world of the mind. Small wonder, then, that Pythagorean thought exercised such a profound influence two centuries later on Plato, who identified Pythagorean proportions as the basis of that which harmonizes the universe and everything in it.[11] For Plato, no other human endeavor is as deeply embedded in the construction of the universe as music, the most abstract and pure of all the arts, lacking in tangible substance. By this line of thought, the physical senses cannot be trusted: the ear can hear music as sound, but only the mind can penetrate its true essence as number. This Pythagorean-Platonic conception of music would be transmitted to the Middle Ages through the writings of Boethius (ca. 480-ca. 524), who classified music as one of the arts of number in the quadrivium, along with arithmetic, geometry, and astronomy.

This belief in a relationship between the essence of music and the essence of the cosmos never disappeared entirely. Hanslick himself would invoke it at the very end of *Vom Musikalisch-Schönen*, without actually citing Pythagoras by name:

> It is not merely and absolutely through its own intrinsic beauty that music affects the listener, but rather at the same time as a sounding image of the great motions of the universe. Through profound and secret connections to nature, the meaning of tones elevates itself high above the tones themselves, allowing us to feel at the same time the infinite in works of human talent. Just as the elements of music—sound, tone, rhythm, loudness, softness—are found throughout the entire universe, so does one find anew in music the entire universe.[12]

11. Plato, *Timaeus*, 35b–36b, trans. Donald J. Zeyl, in Plato, *Complete Works*, ed. Cooper, 1239. See Francis Macdonald Cornford, *Plato's Cosmology: The Timaeus of Plato* (London: Kegan Paul, 1937); Ernest G. McClain, *The Pythagorean Plato: Prelude to the Song Itself* (Stony Brook, NY: N. Hays, 1978); and Francesco Pelosi, *Plato on Music, Soul and Body*, trans. Sophie Henderson (Cambridge: Cambridge University Press, 2010).

12. Eduard Hanslick, *VMS*, 1:171: "Ihm wirkt die Musik nicht blos und absolut durch ihre eigenste Schönheit, sondern zugleich als tönendes Abbild der großen Bewegungen im Weltall. Durch tiefe und geheime Naturbeziehungen steigert sich die Bedeutung der Töne hoch über sie selbst hinaus und läßt uns in dem Werke menschlichen Talents immer zugleich das Unendliche fühlen. Da die Elemente der Musik: Schall, Ton, Rhythmus, Stärke, Schwäche im ganzen Universum sich finden, so findet der Mensch wieder in der Musik das ganze Universum." Unless otherwise noted, all quotations from *VMS* are taken from the first edition (1854). This passage does not appear in the translations by Cohen or Payzant (*OMB*), which are based on the seventh (1885) and eighth (1891) editions, respectively.

The concepts and the language are unmistakably Pythagorean: music is an audible microcosm, a "sounding image" of the "great motions of the universe" through which we can perceive that which is infinite, inaccessible, and ultimately beyond human comprehension. Hanslick would delete this final paragraph in later editions of his treatise for reasons to be considered in detail in chapter 9. What is important to recognize for the moment is that the roots of his thought are to be found in an intellectual tradition that reaches back long before his time.

The first edition of *Vom Musikalisch-Schönen* (1854) marks a pivotal moment in the history of the idea of absolute music. It articulates an aesthetic of autonomy that looks forward to the twentieth century, yet its conclusion looks backward to the much older traditions of antiquity that had endowed music with cosmic significance, both literally and figuratively. Hanslick's subsequent decision to delete these cryptic final sentences reflects his eventual turn toward a more austere variety of autonomy that would enjoy its greatest aesthetic and philosophical prestige in the first three-quarters of the twentieth century.

The original closing paragraph nevertheless offers a window on what would remain the central questions of *Vom Musikalisch-Schönen* through all its ten authorial editions: What is the essence of music, and how does this essence relate to its effect? Hanslick subtitled his treatise "A Contribution toward a Revision of the Aesthetics of Music," and what needed revising, he maintained, was the "decayed aesthetics of feeling."[13] For Hanslick, the essence of music had nothing to do with its effect and everything to do with the quality of what he called "specifically musical beauty," a kind of beauty to be found in music and in no other art. The perception of musical beauty, in turn, demanded a detached, contemplative mode of attention. Music that affected only the emotions and not the intellect was in this sense not really music at all. Hanslick acknowledged music's ability to generate emotional responses, but he characterized these effects as mere by-products of the aesthetic experience and not as constitutive of the art itself. Individual responses to music, he maintained, were in any case too variable to figure into any account of the true—which is to say, pure and immutable—essence of music.

It is this insistence on a strict separation between essence and effect that was genuinely radical in Hanslick's thought. At no point in the earlier history of aesthetics had anyone ever thought to cordon off the two so profoundly. We cannot grasp the radical nature of the concept of absolute music as it emerged in the middle of the nineteenth century without considering in some detail the long history of thought leading up to this categorical distinction between music's essence and effect.

13. *VMS*, 1:9: "verrottete Gefühlsästhetik." This passage, from the preface to the first edition, does not appear in *OMB*.

The structure of the present book reflects three broad stages in the history of this relationship. Part One ("Essence as Effect") surveys the period from antiquity through the middle of the sixteenth century when music's essence was understood as the direct cause of its effect. This relationship is exemplified by the complementary and at times overlapping figures of Orpheus and Pythagoras. The latter was credited with having discovered the essence of music—what it is—while the former was hailed as the supreme practitioner of the art, demonstrating the full extent of its magical hold over humans, beasts, objects and even gods—in short, what music does. Orpheus was the paradigmatic musician who used his art to tame animals, move stones, and even cross back and forth between the realms of the living and dead. Pindar, Aeschylus, Euripides, Apollonius Rhodius, Virgil, and Ovid, among others, describe these miracles in many different ways, but not one of them questions or explains the mechanism of how Orpheus's music could overwhelm all within its range, from sirens to the guardians of the underworld, from wild beasts to inanimate objects. For all these writers, the power of music lay in its very essence: a skilled musician could tap into the inner structure of the universe, both animate and inanimate, and Orpheus was the most skilled of all musicians. Pythagoras was no musician, Orpheus no philosopher, yet their perspectives on music complement each other, even while reflecting fault lines that run the entire length of the history of music: theory vs. practice, being versus doing, contemplation versus action, mind versus body, the immutable versus the contingent, abstraction versus sensation. It is all the more remarkable, then, that throughout the immense lore and commentary surrounding both of these figures, their perspectives on music were never perceived as contradictory in any way. Quite the opposite: as we shall see in chapter 2, many ancient accounts link these two and relate Pythagoras's abstractions to the miraculous powers exercised by Orpheus. At times in fact the two figures become virtually indistinguishable, for the perceived essence of music—the arithmetically harmonic proportions of the cosmos—was understood to be the source of its effect.

When the Pythagorean-Platonic conception of the cosmos began to lose its hold around the middle of the sixteenth century, writers sought alternative models to explain the correlation between music's nature and its power. Part Two ("Essence and Effect") traces these efforts in the period between roughly 1550 and 1850. Orpheus's miracles, though still recounted, no longer enjoyed the status of literal truth, and empirical science had revealed that Pythagoras's reputed calculations relating sound to number did not in fact square with the harmonies actually produced. The ear, along with the senses in general, began to challenge the mind as a source of knowledge.

For humanists of the sixteenth century, Plato's definition of *melos* in *The Republic* offered a more attractive starting point for discussions about the nature of music than his speculations on the order and nature of the universe in *Timaeus*. In

Marsilio Ficino's widely used Latin translation, first published in Venice in 1491, the key passage in *The Republic* (398d) reads: "music consists of three things: oration, harmony, and rhythm" (*melodiam ex tribus constare, oratione, harmonia, rhythmus*), with the admonition that "the harmony and rhythm must conform to the oration" (*atqui harmonia et rhythmus orationem sequi debent*), which is to say, to the words and their delivery. This alliance of music and speech allowed writers to explain music's power by conceiving of it as an essentially expressive art, without the necessity of recourse to theories of cosmic harmony or the World Soul.

The principle of expression did not altogether supplant the Pythagorean principle of number, which, with its emphasis on structure, would eventually come to be thought of as form. Indeed, many of the best minds of the seventeenth and eighteenth centuries, from Leibniz to Rameau, used concepts based on number and form to explain the innermost nature of music. Over the course of the eighteenth century, beauty emerged as yet another quality by which to explain music's effect: it became the *sine qua non* of what were coming to be known as the fine arts or the "arts of beauty," as they were called in French and German (*les beaux-arts, die schönen Künste*). Still another group of Enlightenment writers gave central prominence to music's autonomy, pointing to its self-sufficiency as its defining feature among the arts, operating entirely within its own circumscribed sphere and on its own terms. And with the rise of idealist thought toward the end of the eighteenth century, a growing number of authors conceived of music primarily in terms of its capacity to reveal higher truths that would otherwise remain unknowable. This perceived quality of disclosiveness shaped the increasingly widespread conception of music as an art of transcendence, a means of insight into a higher realm.

From the middle of the sixteenth century until the middle of the nineteenth, commentators on music generally perceived these various qualities—expression, form, beauty, autonomy, disclosiveness—as mutually reinforcing. Individual writers might well emphasize the significance of one or two of these qualities in their accounts of music's essence but in so doing felt no need to disprove or deny the validity of any of the others. And while some of these qualities enjoyed greater prestige at different times and in different places, each of them contributed to an understanding of the nature of music and the arts in general. Beauty, for example, had played a role in discussions about the arts from Plato onward, but it did not begin to assume central importance as a defining criterion of art in the minds of most critics until the eighteenth century. And the capacity of music to disclose truths about the structure of the universe, although implicit in Pythagorean thought, did not assume widespread significance until the early nineteenth century. To single out any one of these qualities as the central criterion behind the concept of absolute music would be to ignore the multiple sources of the idea.

The terms of the debate changed sharply around the middle of the nineteenth century when Hanslick decoupled the essence of music from its effect. He acknowledged that music could produce a powerful response in listeners, but he considered this response unrelated to the fundamental nature of the art. In this respect, he was an essentialist: his treatise is an attempt to define what music *is* without regard to what it *does*, deeming the latter irrelevant to the former. At no point did Hanslick ever assert the aesthetic superiority of purely instrumental music: he even conceded that the union of music and poetry "extends the power of music," but he insisted that this union does not extend the "boundaries" of the art.[14] Hanslick's purpose, then, was to define the limits of music and valorize the art within those carefully circumscribed limits. Wagner's purpose, by contrast, was to lay out a blueprint by which a composer—Wagner—could maximize music's effect by uniting it with the "fertilizing seed" of the word.[15] Franz Liszt's 1855 neologism of "program music" polarized the discussion more strongly still by positing absolute and program music as mutually exclusive categories of instrumental music.

Part Three ("Essence or Effect") outlines the course of this debate from the middle of the nineteenth century to the middle of the twentieth. Wagner, Hanslick, and Liszt—especially Hanslick—receive more scrutiny than any other figures, for together they established a new discursive practice (to use Foucault's term): their terminology, perspectives, and rhetorical strategies became so deeply embedded in everday parlance that they were eventually no longer associated with their original authors.[16] By aligning the age-old idea of "pure" music with a specific repertory—instrumental, non-programmatic music—these three figures together changed the framework of the debate about the relationship between music's essence and effect. Hanslick, in particular, made purity the hallmark of "true" music and considered its effect a mere by-product of its essence, not an inescapable consequence.

In the middle of the nineteenth century, absolute music was a new term applied to old music; by the early decades of the twentieth century, it had become an old term more likely to be associated with new music, its aesthetics evident in the compositions and commentaries of such diverse modernists as Schoenberg, Webern, Busoni, and Stravinsky. Yet not one of these composers aligned himself with Hanslick. They adopted his central ideas and even elements of his terminology but never mentioned him once by name, even in passing. The line from Hanslick to the aesthetics of early modernism was circuitous: much of it, as outlined in chapter 13, passed through discourse about the visual arts in the

14. *VMS*, 1:53: "Die Vereinigung mit der Dichtkunst erweitert die Macht der Musik, aber nicht ihre Gränzen." For a different translation, see *OMB*, 15.

15. Wagner, *Oper und Drama, GSD*, 4:103: "dieser zeugende Samen." *PW*, 2:236. On the sources and implications of Wagner's imagery, see Thomas S. Grey, *Wagner's Musical Prose: Texts and Contexts* (Cambridge: Cambridge University Press, 1995), 141–43, 264.

16. Michel Foucault, "What Is an Author," in *Textual Strategies: Perspectives in Post-Structuralist Criticism*, ed. Josué V. Harari (Ithaca, NY: Cornell University Press, 1979), 154.

last quarter of the nineteenth century. The notion that a painting might consist largely or even solely of line and color—form—with little or no regard to its object of representation helped pave the way for a profound change in attitudes toward the role of form in music. The abstract nature of music, long acknowledged but rarely celebrated, was now the central element of its prestige.

Both as an idea and as a repertory, absolute music enjoyed its greatest esteem in the middle decades of the twentieth century, particularly in the West during the era of the Cold War. As recently as 1993, Susan McClary could open her influential essay "Narrative Agendas in 'Absolute' Music: Identity and Difference in Brahms's Third Symphony" with the observation that "of all the sacrosanct preserves of art music today, the most prestigious, the most carefully protected is a domain known as 'Absolute Music': music purported to operate on the basis of pure configurations, untainted by words, stories, or even affect."[17] Though no one would make such a claim today, the statement was true enough at the time. In the second half of the twentieth century, absolute music was such a widely accepted—and therefore generally unspoken—premise of high art music that it resists isolation as a topic of discourse. It was foundational to mainstream of European-American musical aesthetics, and to trace its history in these years would be to survey the era's musical aesthetics in general. For this reason, my survey of the idea ends around the middle of the twentieth century. Its more recent fortunes must await a separate study.

* * *

For all its importance in the musical aesthetics, the history of the idea of absolute music has never been adequately documented. The most important study to date is Carl Dahlhaus's *Die Idee der absoluten Musik*, first published in 1978 and issued in an outstanding English translation in 1989.[18] Dahlhaus begins his brief monograph by rightly distinguishing between absolute music as an intellectual construct—an idea, as his title makes clear—and as a type of music. The "idea of 'absolute music'... consists of the conviction that instrumental music purely and clearly expresses the true nature of music by its very lack of concept, object, and purpose." Two sentences later, however, this idea, this conviction, becomes a repertory with its own agency and immanent qualities: "Detached from the affections and feelings of the real world," absolute music "forms a 'separate world for itself.'"[19] In conflating an idea and an object, Dahlhaus commits the fallacy of reification,

17. McClary, "Narrative Agendas in 'Absolute' Music," 326.

18. Dahlhaus, *Die Idee der absoluten Musik* (Kassel: Bärenreiter, 1978), translated by Roger Lustig as *The Idea of Absolute Music* (Chicago: University of Chicago Press, 1989).

19. Dahlhaus, *Die Idee der absoluten Musik*, 13; translation from *Idea of Absolute Music*, 7. The internal quotation is from Ludwig Tieck's essay "Die Töne," in *Phantasien über die Kunst, für Freunde der Kunst*, ed. Ludwig Tieck (Hamburg: Heinrich Perthes, 1799), 241: "eine abgesonderte Welt für sich selbst." A modern edition is available in Wilhelm Heinrich Wackenroder, *Sämtliche Werke und Briefe*,

or as the philosopher Alfred North Whitehead called it in another context, the "Fallacy of Misplaced Concreteness," the "error of mistaking the abstract for the concrete."[20] This tendency to turn "ideas into objects" is what Richard Taruskin has identified as the "essential modernist fallacy."[21] Dahlhaus was neither the first nor the last to fall into this trap. Wagner applied his own self-invented term inconsistently, and in the latest edition of *The New Grove Dictionary of Music and Musicians*, Roger Scruton similarly blurs concept and object: he begins his entry on absolute music by identifying it as an idea but in the middle of second paragraph shifts, without notice, to treating it as a specific type of music. This failure to distinguish between the older idea of absolute (or "pure") music as a concept and the later idea of it as a repertory has led to seriously flawed readings of the historical record, readings that ascribe an unwarranted degree of stability to a protean concept.

Dahlhaus, moreover, based his arguments on a highly selective range of historical sources, ignoring many relevant commentaries both within and beyond writings devoted to music.[22] Two subsequent studies have since addressed this shortcoming to at least some extent: John Neubauer's *The Emancipation of Music from Language* (1986) and Anselm Gerhard's *London und der Klassizmus in der Musik* (2002), both of which survey an impressive array of authors from a variety of fields.[23] Neubauer's study is especially valuable for its emphasis on the continuing importance of Pythagorean thought in the eighteenth century and the ongoing friction between verbal (semantic) and mathematical (syntactic) conceptions of music. His account of the aesthetics of musical autonomy in the eighteenth century is rather less satisfactory. He argues that the "inversion" in the hierarchical relationship between language and music at that time was "induced by the emergence of classical instrumental music." This "new music"—a repertory of sonatas, symphonies, and chamber music—"forced an aesthetic revaluation of major import, whose implications went well beyond the confines of music proper."[24] Just how or why the instrumental music of this era might

ed. Silvio Vietta and Richard Littlejohns, 2 vols. (Heidelberg: Carl Winter Universitätsverlag, 1991), 1:236. On the authorship of the individual essays in this collaborative volume, see the commentary to Wackenroder's *Sämtliche Werke*, 1:368–72.

20. Alfred North Whitehead, *Science and the Modern World* (New York: Macmillan, 1925), 74–75.

21. Richard Taruskin, *Text and Act: Essays on Music and Performance* (New York: Oxford University Press, 1995), 24.

22. For a brief but insightful commentary on Dahlhaus's *Die Idee der absoluten Musik*, see Ulrich Tadday, *Das schöne Unendliche: Ästhetik, Kritik, Geschichte der romantischen Musikanschauung* (Stuttgart and Weimar: J. B. Metzler, 1999), 122–24. Sanna Pederson, in "Defining the Term 'Absolute Music' Historically," rightly notes the tendency of Dahlhaus and others to treat absolute music as a monolithic idea.

23. John Neubauer, *The Emancipation of Music from Language: Departure from Mimesis in Eighteenth-Century Aesthetics* (New Haven: Yale University Press, 1986); and Anselm Gerhard, *London und der Klassizismus in der Musik: Die Idee der "absoluten" Musik und Muzio Clementis Klavierwerk* (Stuttgart: Metzler, 2002).

24. Neubauer, *The Emancipation of Music from Language*, 2.

have altered opinions about the nature of music in general remains unclear (its quality? quantity? style?). The writers of the time most frequently called upon to testify about changing attitudes toward the art—Kant, Schiller, Friedrich and August Wilhelm Schlegel, Novalis, Wackenroder, and Tieck—are in any case frustratingly vague or silent about the specific repertories of music they might have had in mind.[25] Neubauer's study, in any event, stops at 1800 and makes no attempt to connect eighteenth-century debates with the positions of later writers like Wagner and Hanslick. Gerhard, in turn, rightly emphasizes the contributions of English-language philosophers and aestheticians to the nascent conception of instrumental music as an autonomous art, and he uses aesthetics to remind us that musical "classicism" in the late eighteenth and early nineteenth centuries was by no means centered on Vienna in the persons of Haydn, Mozart, and Beethoven.[26] Implicit in this position, however, is the problematic premise that aesthetic autonomy can manifest itself as an audible feature of a musical style.

Daniel Chua, in his provocative *Absolute Music and the Construction of Meaning* (1999), mixes historical observations with philosophical arguments, at times offering contradictory hypotheses in the spirit of the Romantic irony that figures so prominently in his account. In a series of brief and largely self-contained chapters, he emphasizes the paradoxes inherent in the concept itself. Absolute music, he asserts, has no history, "for an absolute by definition cannot have a history": it has always been there. "To write a history of absolute music is to write against it."[27] Chua of course recognizes that the *idea* has a history, but his mosaic-like approach obscures issues of chronology and important changes in attitudes toward the nature of "pure" music over time. Like Dahlhaus, he tends to treat absolute music as a monolithic concept, minimizing the profound differences between the aesthetics of 1800 and 1850.

It is only in the last twenty years or so that scholars have begun to expose the social, political, economic, and ideological implications of absolute music. James Hepokoski, Susan McClary, Anne Shreffler, and Richard Taruskin, among others, have revealed the value-laden premises that for so long contributed to its prestige.[28] The need to trace the changing historical attitudes toward the idea

---

25. See Mark Evan Bonds, *Music as Thought: Listening to the Symphony in the Age of Beethoven* (Princeton: Princeton University Press, 2006), 23.

26. Gerhard, *London und der Klassizismus in der Musik*; see especially 123–50 and 297–331. In Gerhard, "Leonhard Euler, die Französische Gemeinde zu Berlin und die ästhetische Grundlegung der 'absoluten Musik,'" *Schweizer Jahrbuch für Musikwissenschaft*, neue Folge 17 (1997): 15–28, Gerhard also makes a case for Berlin as a center of thought that laid the groundwork for the concept of absolute music.

27. Chua, *Absolute Music*, 3, 7.

28. James Hepokoski, "The Dahlhaus Project and Its Extra-musicological Sources," *19CM* 14 (1991): 221–46; McClary, "Narrative Agendas"; Anne Shreffler, "Berlin Walls: Dahlhaus, Knepler, and Ideologies of Music History," *JM* 20 (2003): 498–525. On Taruskin's contributions, see n. 6.

thus becomes all the more pressing. As Taruskin points out about regulative concepts in general, "What is important and distinctive is not the thing or the concept itself, but the value placed on it, and its status as a regulative ideal," to which he adds: "Our modern concept of 'absolute music' is not completely or even accurately defined if we do not emphasize the supreme value placed on it as an art-experience, since the nineteenth century, by musicians who have inherited the German Romantic aesthetic."[29]

In spite of its declining prestige in recent decades, the idea of absolute music remains an unavoidable and in many respects still useful construct. Those who deny its existence evoke it as a foil by which to explicate the socially constructed parameters in which music is produced and consumed. And as Leo Treitler has pointed out, even the most contextually sensitive interpreters of a given composition must at some point come to terms with the notes on the page and at least temporarily entertain the isolated—absolute—conception of music they might otherwise reject.[30] In this sense, the idea of absolute music reflects the enduring Western tendency to juxtapose mind and body, reason and emotion, the spiritual and the material. "What truly organizes music in the West," as McClary observes, "is the tension between the inescapable body and the...deep-seated need to control or transcend that body through intellectual idealism."[31]

In the end, absolute music stands as one of the most influential concepts in the history of Western musical aesthetics. From Pythagoras to the present, it has shaped basic conceptions of what music is and how we respond to it. For some, it captures the very essence of the art. For others, it isolates music in ways that ignore the art's inescapable power. *Absolute Music: The History of an Idea* outlines the history of this contested construct.

29. Taruskin, "Is There a Baby in the Bathwater?," 175.

30. Leo Treitler, "The Historiography of Music: Issues of Past and Present," in *Rethinking Music*, ed. Nicholas Cook and Mark Everist (Oxford: Oxford University Press, 1999), 370. For a spirited defense of "purely musical" analysis, see Giles Hooper, "An Incomplete Project: Modernism, Formalism and the 'Music Itself,'" *Music Analysis* 23 (2004): 311–29.

31. Susan McClary, "Music, the Pythagoreans, and the Body," in *Choreographing History*, ed. Susan Leigh Foster (Bloomington: Indiana University Press, 1995), 83. See also Carolyn Abbate, "Music—Drastic or Gnostic?" *Critical Inquiry* 30 (2004): 505–36.

PART I

Essence as Effect: To 1550

The figures of Orpheus and Pythagoras embody two fundamentally different perspectives on music that together circumscribe the foundation of Western attitudes toward the art. As a musician, Orpheus demonstrated music's effect; as a philosopher, Pythagoras explained its essence. Until at least the sixteenth century, and often beyond, Pythagoras was credited with having discovered music's essence—what it *is*—while Orpheus was hailed as the paradigmatic musician, a performer able to demonstrate the fullest extent of music's effect—what it *does*. These contrasting figures were never perceived in opposition to each other, however, nor even as two sides of the same coin. Their relationship was understood as one of mutual reinforcement: Pythagoras's explanation of music's essence was at the same time an explanation for its effect, as realized through the skill of Orpheus.

1   Orpheus and Pythagoras

Orpheus is the most prominent of several mythical figures who embody the power of music.[1] Countless narratives tell of his abilities to tame wild beasts, make rocks move, and divert rivers, all entirely through music (see Figure 1). As one of Jason's Argonauts, Orpheus alone could overwhelm the competing song of the sirens, the same creatures Odysseus would later be able to resist only by having himself bound to the mast of his ship and the ears of his crew plugged with wax. In the most spectacular of all his musical feats, Orpheus used music to overwhelm the guardians of Hades and move back and forth between the realms of the living and dead. The many and varied retellings of that tale agree that Orpheus sang and played the lyre, yet it was not his words that moved these spirits. Virgil gives no account of Orpheus's verbal pleas, observing instead that the hearts of Hades' monarchs did not know how to be softened by human prayer, which is to say, by words. The more garrulous Ovid provides the text Orpheus sang in spite of its utter predictability.[2] Charon, Pluto, and Persephone had heard such requests many times before: Euridice was scarcely the first human to die before the fullness of her time, nor was Orpheus the first to become a widower on his wedding day. Had it been Orpheus's words that moved, his plea would have become a paradigm of rhetorical prowess. As it is, none of the poetry attributed to him ever achieved the kind of prestige accorded the work of such figures as Homer or Pindar. By their very nature, the poets of antiquity were poet-musicians: Orpheus, Homer, and Pindar are invariably depicted with lyre in hand, which makes it more striking still that the myths of Orpheus focus so squarely on his music. Wild beasts, stones, and rivers have no understanding of language at all, after all, and in later times it would be musicians, not poets, who sought to emulate Orpheus.

Orpheus was not the only miraculous musician of antiquity: Amphion is said to have moved stones and built the citadel of Thebes entirely through the sound of his lyre; and Arion, like Orpheus, transcended the divide between humans and animals, using his lyre to summon a pair of dolphins to bring him safely to shore from what would otherwise have been a sure death by drowning. Timotheus, a

---

1. Among the many studies devoted to the myths of Orpheus, see Ivan M. Linforth, *The Arts of Orpheus* (Berkeley and Los Angeles: University of California Press, 1941); W. K. C. Guthrie, *Orpheus and Greek Religion: A Study of the Orphic Movement*, rev. ed. (New York: Norton, 1966); John Block Friedman, *Orpheus in the Middle Ages* (Cambridge, MA: Harvard University Press, 1970); and John Warden, ed., *Orpheus: The Metamorphoses of a Myth* (Toronto: University of Toronto Press, 1982).

2. Virgil, *Georgics*, book 4, 470; Ovid, *Metamorphoses*, book 10.

Figure 1. Orpheus
In this early third-century CE mosaic from Sicily, Orpheus tames the wild beasts
through the power of wordless—that is, instrumental—music. In his right hand he
holds an oversized plectrum with which to pluck the strings of his lyre.
Source: Museo archeologico regionale "Antonio Salinas" di Palermo; Erich Lessing
Photo and Fine Arts Archive, Vienna.

musician who played at a victory banquet for Alexander the Great, could arouse and calm the most powerful ruler on earth through music, manipulating him like a puppet simply by changing the nature of the music he played and sang. This legend would be transmitted to the Middle Ages through Saint Basil's *Ad adolescentes* and to still later generations through John Dryden's ode *Alexander's Feast* (1697), the basis of the text set to music by Handel in 1736.

Ultimately, however, it is Orpheus who takes center stage in the inevitable *laudes musicae* that introduce discussions of music throughout the Middle Ages and Renaissance. The figure of Orpheus would become a touchstone for composers as well: those compared to him include such diverse luminaries as, in England, John Dowland, Henry Purcell, and George Frideric Handel; in Germany, Andreas Hammerschmidt, Ludwig Senfl, Johann Adolph Hasse, and Wolfgang Amadeus Mozart; in Italy, Niccolò Jommelli; and in France, Jean-Baptiste Lully and Jean-Philippe Rameau. Johann Matthias Gesner, rector of the Thomasschule in Leipzig from 1730 to 1734, went so far as to say that Johann Sebastian Bach "outshone Orpheus many times," and the composer Bernhard Romberg (1767–1841) dubbed Haydn the "Orpheus of the Danube."[3] In the nineteenth century the comparison of specific composers to Orpheus became commonplace.[4]

It was not necessary to believe in the literal truth of the Orpheus myths to recognize their broader basis in music's capacity to move the human spirit. Cassiodorus (ca. 490–526) dismissed the legend of Orpheus and the sirens as a fable, yet wholeheartedly accepted the story of David curing Saul of melancholy "by the discipline of wholesome melody," as well as reports that Asclepiades, the renowned physician of antiquity, had used music to restore a patient from frenzy to his former self.[5] Belief in the curative powers of music, moreover, transcends Western culture.[6] With or without the figure of Orpheus, music's power has never been questioned.

It has, however, been feared. Music can be used for evil as well as for good, after all. "The guardians of the state," Socrates asserts in Plato's *Republic*, "must beware of changing to a new form of music, since it threatens the whole system. As Damon says, and I am convinced, the musical modes are never changed without change

---

3. Christoph Wolff, *Bach: Essays on his Life and Music* (Cambridge, MA: Harvard University Press, 1991), 39; Horst Walter, "Haydn gewidmete Streichquartette," in *Joseph Haydn: Tradition und Rezeption*, ed. Georg Feder, Heinrich Hüschen, and Ulrich Tank (Regensburg: Gustav Bosse, 1985), 45.

4. See Arnfried Edler, *Studien zur Auffassung antiker Musikmythen im 19. Jahrhundert* (Kassel: Bärenreiter, 1970); and Edler, "'Die Macht der Töne': Über die Bedeutung eines antiken Mythos im 19. Jahrhundert," in *Musik in Antike und Neuzeit*, ed. Michael von Albrecht and Werner Schubert (Frankfurt am Main: Peter Lang, 1987), 51–65.

5. Flavius Magnus Aurelius Cassiodorus, *Fundamentals of Sacred and Secular Learning*, trans. William Strunk, Jr., and Oliver Strunk, rev. James McKinnon, in *Source Readings in Music History*, rev. ed., ed. Oliver Strunk and Leo Treitler (New York: Norton, 1998), 148.

6. See Benjamin D. Koen, ed., *The Oxford Handbook of Medical Ethnomusicology* (New York: Oxford University Press, 2008).

... ...e most important of a city's laws." Those assembled agree with Socrates, who goes on to observe that music is particularly dangerous precisely because it *seems* like mere play; this is the reason it must be monitored carefully in the education of youth.[7] Aristotle similarly recognized the ethical effects of music, outlining in his *Politics* the qualities of the various modes and observing that "in melodies themselves there are representations of characters." Music "has the power to produce a certain quality in the character of the soul ... That is why many of the wise say that the soul is a harmony and others say that it has a harmony."[8]

That harmony, as so many writers since Plato and Aristotle have observed, can be disrupted all too easily. Orpheus's power was immediate and for that very reason dangerous: it bypassed, in effect, the faculty of reason, giving priority to the emotional over the rational, the physical over the mental, the body over the mind. The fear that the senses—the body—might overwhelm the intellect—the mind—lies at the heart of Western attitudes toward the arts in general but particularly toward music, which more than any other art exposes the division between the mind and the senses. The danger of being overpowered by music is as old the tale of the sirens: those seduced by the pleasure of sound are doomed, and fatally drawn away from duty and from the very necessities of survival.

Pleasure alone was an insufficient reason for cultivating music and indeed a source of unending anxiety. In his account of David curing Saul, Saint Augustine (354–430) was quick to emphasize that although "David was a man highly skilled in songs, a man who loved the harmony of music," he was "not the ordinary man for whom music is merely for pleasure; for him it served the purpose of his faith. He used it in the service of his God, the true God, by giving a mystical prefiguration of a matter of high importance. For the concord of different sounds, controlled in due proportion, suggests the unity of a well-ordered city, welded together in harmonious variety."[9] Augustine's "merely for pleasure" marks one of the great dividing lines in discourse about music. At the end of the eighteenth century Immanuel Kant would call this purely physical response to art "pathological," a term he used to describe a spontaneous, unreflective, prerational reaction to beauty. The implication of disease in an inherent vulnerability of the emotions to external forces was already present in his time and would become all the more prominent in the decades that followed. The poet and critic Heinrich

7. Plato, *Republic* 424c; see p. 3. On the significance of the reference to Damon in this passage, see Warren D. Anderson, "Damonian Theory in Plato's Thought," *American Philological Association Transactions* 86 (1955): 88–102. On the ethics of music in antiquity, see Anderson, *Ethos and Education in Greek Music: The Evidence of Poetry and Philosophy* (Cambridge, MA: Harvard University Press, 1966); and Edward A. Lippman, *Musical Thought in Ancient Greece* (New York: Columbia University Press, 1964), 45–86.

8. Aristotle, *Politics*, book 8, 1340a38 and 1340b10, in Aristotle, *Politics, Books VII and VIII*, ed. and trans. Richard Kraut (Oxford: Clarendon Press, 1997), 43–44.

9. Saint Augustine, *Concerning the City of God against the Pagans*, trans. Henry Bettenson (London: Penguin Books, 2003), 744 (book 17, chapter 14).

Heine, observing an audience's tumultuous response to a piano recital by Franz Liszt in Paris in 1844, mused that the phenomenon was "perhaps more a matter of pathology than of aesthetics."[10] Eduard Hanslick, too, adopted Kant's terminology and consigned listening that bypassed the mind to the realm of the "pathological."[11] In practice, however, such simple dichotomies between thought and emotion or between body and spirit have proved difficult to sustain,[12] and from antiquity to the present many of those who have attempted to describe the nature of music have felt obligated to reconcile the rational and emotional elements of the art.

While the myths of Orpheus tell of music's power, they do not explain its source. For that, the ancient Greeks turned to the teachings of Pythagoras, that shadowy personage of the sixth century BCE about whom so little is known and to whom so much is ascribed. The undisputed biographical evidence is scant, and by the time Plato wrote about him he was already largely a mythical figure whose teachings had inspired a cult following. Pythagoras's theories of music are known to us today entirely through the writings of later authors, including Plato, Aristotle, Plutarch, Nicomachus of Gerasa, Claudius Ptolemy, and Aristides Quintilianus.[13] Lost sources, forgeries, interpolations, and misattributions make it all but impossible to distinguish between the thought of Pythagoras the individual and the ideas attributed to him as a mythic figure. In the account that follows, then, "Pythagoras" and "Pythagoreanism" stand for a perceived individual and the teachings associated with him.

Pythagoras was more interested in music's structure than in its actual sound. He and his followers maintained that the entire universe was ordered and governed by number, and that music was the audible manifestation of number. One of the most famous of the many legends he inspired tells of

10. Heinrich Heine, "Musikalische Saison von 1844," in Heine, *Werke, Briefwechsel, Lebenszeugnisse: Säkularausgabe*, vol. 11, *Lutezia: Berichte über Politik, Kunst und Volksleben*, ed. Lucienne Netter (Berlin: Akademie-Verlag; Paris: Editions du CNRS, 1974), 251: "Was ist aber der Grund dieser Erscheinung? Die Lösung der Frage gehört vielleicht eher in die Pathologie als in die Ästhetik." For similar reactions from other nineteenth-century critics, see James Kennaway, *Bad Vibrations: The History of the Idea of Music as a Cause of Disease* (Aldershot: Ashgate, 2012), 49–51; and Robert Michael Anderson, "Polemics or Philosophy? Musical Pathology in Eduard Hanslick's *Vom Musikalisch-Schönen*," *Musical Times* 154, no. 1924 (Autumn 2013): 65–76.

11. *VMS*, 1:29; *OMB*, 5.

12. See Karol Berger, "Musicology According to Don Giovanni, or: Should We Get Drastic?" *JM* 22 (2005): 490–501.

13. On Pythagoras and early Pythagoreans, see Walter Burkert, *Lore and Science in Ancient Pythagoreanism*, trans. Edwin L. Minar Jr. (Cambridge, MA: Harvard University Press, 1972); Andrew Barker, ed., *Greek Musical Writings*, 2 vols. (Cambridge: Cambridge University Press, 1984-89), vol. 2, chapter 1; and Christoph Riedweg, *Pythagoras: His Life, Teaching, and Influence*, trans. Steven Rendall (Ithaca, NY: Cornell University Press, 2005). Two useful collections of early sources are Kenneth Sylvan Guthrie and David R. Fideler, eds., *The Pythagorean Sourcebook and Library* (Grand Rapids, MI: Phanes Press, 1987); and Joscelyn Godwin, ed., *The Harmony of the Spheres: A Sourcebook of the Pythagorean Tradition in Music* (Rochester, VT: Inner Traditions International, 1993).

his discovery of the relationship between number and sound. Passing by a forge one day, Pythagoras observed that the blacksmiths' hammers produced pitches of different intervals, some consonant with each other, some dissonant (see Figure 2). On further investigation, he found that these pitches were proportional to the weight of the hammers, and that these weights and pitches could be correlated arithmetically. A ratio of 2:1 produced pitches at the interval of an octave; a ratio of 3:2 produced the interval of a perfect fifth; 4:3 produced a perfect fourth, and so on. By linking sound to both number and physical properties, Pythagoras was able to put the science of acoustics on a rational basis. The earliest recorded version of this legend dates from some eight centuries after Pythagoras's lifetime, and the specifics of the calculations would undergo later refinement, but the underlying principle that explained sounding intervals in terms of ratios was correct, and this was enough to ensure the centrality of Pythagorean thought in accounts of music until well into the early modern era. The relationship of sound, number, and matter, moreover, transcended the realm of music because it demonstrated an even broader connection between the corporeal and the abstract, between the worlds of the visible and the invisible.

Figure 2. Pythagoras
This detail from the frontispiece to Athanasius Kircher's *Musurgia universalis* (1650) shows Pythagoras gesturing with one hand to the theorem that bears his name and with the other to the smiths whose hammers of different weights, according to legend, had revealed to him the mathematical relationship of musical intervals. Note the musical instruments at his feet: it is Pythagoras who provided the conceptual conduit linking sound, number, and music.
Source: Athanasius Kircher, *Musurgia universalis* (Rome: Corbelletti, 1650).

Pythagorean concepts occupy the core of Plato's cosmology. For Plato, the World Soul provided a template for both the cosmos and human souls, the latter derived from the "leftovers" of the World Soul. The microcosm of the human soul is for this reason impure. Nevertheless, it rests on the same basic proportions as the macrocosm, the same proportions made audible through music. The arithmetic is complicated, but the depth of this correlation manifests itself in the exact identity of the smallest unit within the World Soul—the improbable fraction of 256/243—and the ratio of the Pythagorean diatonic semitone.[14] Plato drew on Pythagorean teachings again in the myth of Er, presented in the last book of *The Republic* (614–18). There he describes the cosmos as consisting of eight concentric orbits for the stars, the planets, the sun, and the moon; each of these orbits is associated with a siren who sings a specific pitch proportionate to its distance from the center, and together these sirens create a harmonious sound, the harmony of the spheres, theoretically audible to humans but unnoticed because of its omnipresence.

Later cosmologies indebted to Pythagorean thought and the proportions of musical intervals appear in the writings of Aristotle (*On the Heavens*), Cicero (*The Dream of Scipio*, first century BCE), Ptolemy (*Harmonics*, mid-second century CE), Boethius (*De institutione musica*, early sixth century), Gioseffo Zarlino (*Istitutioni harmoniche*, 1558), and as late as the seventeenth century in the works of Robert Fludd (*Utriusque cosmi maioris scilicet et minoris metaphysica, physica atque technica historia*, 1617–19), Johannes Kepler (*Harmonices mundi*, 1619), and Athanasius Kircher (*Musurgia universalis*, 1650). These accounts differ considerably in their particulars—Aristotle, for example, rejected the notion of a sounding music of the spheres—but they all posit a direct congruence of cosmic, human, and musical harmony.[15] For almost two millennia these proportional similarities were understood not merely as analogical but as morphological: the harmony of musical intervals manifests the harmony of the universe, and number alone reveals these relationships. "Harmony" was a remarkably broad and malleable concept for as long as it was precisely because it was perceived to signify a perceptible manifestation of cosmic order (see Figures 3 and 4).[16]

14. See Richard L. Crocker, "Pythagorean Mathematics and Music," *JAAC* 22 (1963–64): 189–98, 325–35; and Lippman, *Musical Thought in Ancient Greece*, 22–27.

15. For a representative selection of writings on this theme, see Godwin, *The Harmony of the Spheres*. See also Claude V. Palisca, "Harmonies and Disharmonies of the Spheres," in Palisca, *Humanism in Italian Renaissance Musical Thought* (New Haven: Yale University Press, 1986), 161–90; Ann E. Moyer, *Musica Scientia: Musical Scholarship in the Italian Renaissance* (Ithaca, NY: Cornell University Press, 1992); and Penelope Gouk, "The Role of Harmonics in the Scientific Revolution," in *The Cambridge History of Western Music Theory*, ed. Thomas Christensen (Cambridge: Cambridge University Press, 2002), 223–45.

16. See Thomas J. Mathiesen, "Problems of Terminology in Ancient Greek Theory: 'APMONÍA,'" in *Festival Essays for Pauline Alderman: A Musicological Tribute*, ed. Burton L. Karson (Provo, UT: Brigham Young University Press, 1976); and Lippman, *Musical Thought in Ancient Greece*, 1–44.

The early church fathers went to great lengths to incorporate Pythagorean thought into Christian doctrine. They sometimes substituted the figures of David or Jubal for the pagan Pythagoras but fully embraced the idea of a numerical—and therefore musical—congruence of micro- and macrocosm. Clement of Alexandria, Saint Ambrose, Saint Jerome, Saint Chrysostom, and Saint Augustine all promulgated this line of thought. The last of these declared number as fundamental to God's creation; for humankind, it was a means by which to mediate between the changing realm of the senses and the unchanging realm of truth.[17]

By the time of Boethius (ca. 480–ca. 524), the arts of number had coalesced into the quadrivium, the four disciplines devoted to the study of essences unchanged by material form. Arithmetic, astronomy, music, and geometry offered a fourfold path to the realm of immutable knowledge. Perceptions might deceive, but the logically demonstrable law of number offered the surest means by which to discover that which is impervious to change and to the imperfections of the senses. Boethius endorsed the Pythagorean-Platonic conception of music, and the revival of his writings in the ninth century ensured the continuing authority of this tradition throughout the Middle Ages. Early on in his *De institutione musica* he observes that

> what Plato rightfully said can likewise be understood: the soul of the universe was joined together according to musical concord. For when we hear what is properly and harmoniously united in sound in conjunction with that which is harmoniously coupled and joined together within us and are attracted to it, then we recognize that we ourselves are put together in its likeness.[18]

The theme of cosmic harmony reverberates throughout the scholastic and theological thought of the Middle Ages. Sounding music is but one manifestation of the deeper proportions that structure the cosmos and all within it. "Without music," Isidore of Seville (ca. 599–636) declared, "no discipline can be perfect for there is nothing without it. The very universe, it is said, is held together by a certain harmony of sounds, and the heavens themselves are made to revolve

17. On the Christianization of Pythagorean lore and its profound influence in the Middle Ages and Renaissance, see S. K. Heninger Jr., *Touches of Sweet Harmony: Pythagorean Cosmology and Renaissance Poetics* (San Marino, CA: Huntington Library, 1974), 201–33; Christiane L. Joost-Gaugier, *Measuring Heaven: Pythagoras and His Influence on Thought and Art in Antiquity and the Middle Ages* (Ithaca, NY: Cornell University Press, 2006); and Joost-Gaugier, *Pythagoras and Renaissance Europe: Finding Heaven* (Cambridge: Cambridge University Press, 2009). On the often wildly speculative efforts to reconcile the musical legacies of Athens and Jerusalem, see James W. McKinnon, "Jubal vel Pythagoras, quis sit inventor musicae?" *MQ* 64 (1978): 1–28.

18. Anicius Manlius Severinus Boethius, *De institutione musica*, 1.1.180, ed. Claude V. Palisca, trans. Calvin M. Bower as *Fundamentals of Music* (New Haven: Yale University Press, 1989), 2. On the Platonic basis of Boethius's views on music, see Anja Heilmann, *Boethius' Musiktheorie und das Quadrivium: Eine Einführung in den neuplatonischen Hintergrund von "De institutione musica"* (Göttingen: Vandenhoeck & Ruprecht, 2007).

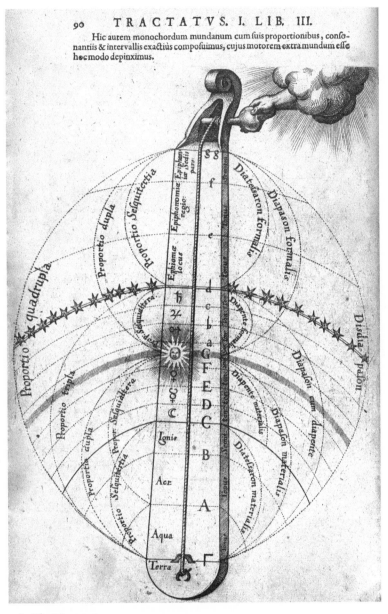

Figure 3. The Macrocosm
The "Divine Monochord" from the first volume of Robert Fludd's *Utriusque cosmi…historia* (1617). The structure of the universe is likened to an enormous monochord, its proportions governed by the same relationships that manifest themselves in musical intervals, such as the diapason (octave), diapente (fifth), and diatesseron (fourth).
Source: Robert Fludd, *Utriusque cosmi maioris scilicet et minoris metaphysica, physica atque technica historia,* 2 vols. (Oppenheim: de Bry, 1617–19), 1:90. David M. Rubenstein Rare Book & Manuscript Library, Duke University.

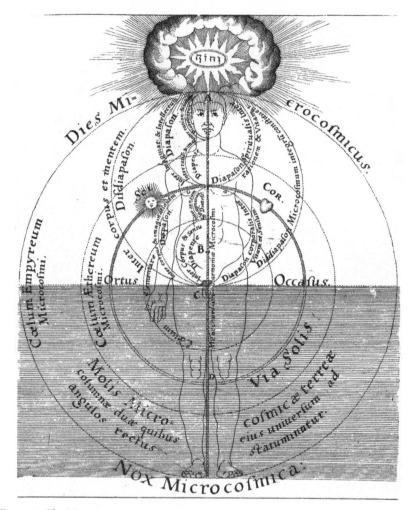

Figure 4. The Microcosm
The "Harmonic Monochord of the Microcosm" is the string that extends down the
length of the human body. As in the cosmic monochord, proportions are represented
through musical intervals.
Source: Robert Fludd, *Utriusque cosmi maioris scilicet et minoris metaphysica, physica
atque technica historia*, 2 vols. (Oppenheim: de Bry, 1617–19), 1:275. David
M. Rubenstein Rare Book & Manuscript Library, Duke University.

by the modulation of harmony."[19] Saint Bonaventure (ca. 1217–1274) similarly emphasized the close relationship of harmony and number. "Beauty and delight do not exist without proportion, and since proportion exists primarily in numbers, all things are subject to number." Number, he maintained, is "the principal vestige leading to Wisdom."[20] Thomas Aquinas (1225–1274) also incorporated key elements of Pythagorean-Platonic cosmology into his thought, pointing out that the harmony of the universe rested upon the same ratios as musical intervals. Like other theologians before and after, he understood the Holy Trinity as a harmony, a synthesis of different entities that retained their identity even when merged into a single whole.

Efforts to place Pythagoras within the Judeo-Christian tradition continued well into the Renaissance. Marsilio Ficino (1433–1499) appealed to the authority of Saint Ambrose to support his conclusion that Pythagoras's father was Jewish, while Giovanni Pico della Mirandola (1463–1494) proposed that Pythagoras received the doctrine of monotheism from none other than Moses himself.[21] The frontispiece of Ralph Cudworth's *The True Intellectual System of the Universe* (1678) shows Pythagoras as the most prominent of three theists (along with Socrates and Aristotle) at the altar of religion, all three standing beneath the laurel wreath of "Victory" over and against three visibly discouraged atheists (Anaximander, Epicurus, and Strato), whose collective wreath of "Confusion" hangs broken in two.[22]

From the Middle Ages onward Pythagorean thought dominated much of what we now conceive of as music theory. The calculation of intervals, the tuning of scales, and the distinction between consonance and dissonance could all be reduced ultimately to number, and the conceptual similarity of mathematics and music has remained a constant in Western thought ever since.[23]

19. Isidore of Seville, *Etymologies*, book 3, trans. William Strunk Jr. and Oliver Strunk, rev. James McKinnon, in Strunk and Treitler, *Source Readings in Music History*, rev. ed., 150.

20. Saint Bonaventure, *Itinerarium mentis in Deum*, II.10, ed. Stephen F. Brown and trans. Philotheus Boehner as *The Journey to the Mind of God* (Indianapolis: Hackett, 1993), 16.

21. Heninger, *Touches of Sweet Harmony*, 201–2.

22. Heninger, *Touches of Sweet Harmony*, 201; the frontispiece is reproduced on page 249 of Heninger's book.

23. For an accessible summary of these parallels, see Edward Rothstein, *Emblems of the Mind: The Inner Life of Music and Mathematics* (New York: Random House, 1995). The legacy of Pythagoreanism is summarized in Catherine Nolan, "Music Theory and Mathematics," in *The Cambridge History of Western Music Theory*, ed. Thomas Christensen (Cambridge: Cambridge University Press, 2002), 272–84.

2   Isomorphic Resonance

Ancient retellings of the feats of Orpheus never identify the source of music's power for the simple reason that no such explanation was necessary: music's effect was understood to emanate from its very essence. Pythagoreanism explains the effect of music as the product of what might be called isomorphic resonance: the ratios that govern the intervals of music are the same ratios that govern the structure of the universe at every level, from that of the individual human to that of the cosmos as a whole. This tripartite morphological congruence, when set in motion through sound, creates a resonance that reverberates within humans, beasts, and even stones. This resonance also accounts for the varying degrees of music's power in the hands of different musicians: Orpheus's music is more perfectly tuned to the structure of the cosmos, the music of ordinary mortals less so.

In one sense this model would seem to transcend the division between body and mind that is so basic to Western thought in all things, including attitudes toward music. Yet the concept of number, which is what drives this explanation of music's power, is itself an abstraction, a construct of the mind. The model of isomorphic resonance, in other words, rests on premises originating in the mind and not in the body. More extreme manifestations of Pythagoreanism rejected the senses altogether. In the dialogue on music long attributed to Plutarch (ca. 45–120), Soterichus observes to the general approval of his audience that "the grave Pythagoras rejected the judging of music by the sense of hearing, asserting that its excellence must be apprehended by the mind. This is why he did not judge it by the ear, but by the scale based on the proportions."[1] From the Pythagorean perspective, to experience music as sound was to perceive through the senses that which lay beyond the realm of the senses: the very structure of the cosmos itself.

Recent scholarship has repeatedly and rightly characterized the Western tendency to privilege reason over the senses as a suppression of the body.[2] This should not, however, obscure the positive motivations behind this prejudice.

---

1. Plutarch, *De musica*, 1144, trans. B. Einarson and P. H. De Lacy as *On Music* (Cambridge, MA: Harvard University Press; London: William Heinemann, 1967), 441.

2. In addition to McClary, "Music, the Pythagoreans, and the Body," and Abbate, "Music—Drastic or Gnostic?," see in particular Bruce W. Holsinger, *Music, Body, and Desire in Medieval Culture: Hildegard of Bingen to Chaucer* (Palo Alto, CA: Stanford University Press, 2001).

Essence resides in qualities that are both demonstrable and stable. Hearing is by its very nature subjective and variable, and in their accounts of music, ancient and medieval commentators tended to emphasize the priority of the mind because they viewed mathematical calculations as indisputable, unchanging, and for this reason more real than impressions acquired through sensory perception. The notion of music's essence in number rather than audible sound would endure for more than two millennia, and its influence is evident in later modes of thought that include Neoplatonism and the various forms of idealism that flourished in the late eighteenth and early nineteenth centuries.

Not all the ancients accepted an a priori subordination of the senses to reason in the realm of music. Aristoxenus (ca. 375/360 BCE–?) was the most prominent of the early philosophers to question Pythagorean attitudes toward the sense of hearing. A pupil of Aristotle, Aristoxenus approached music primarily as an experience rather than as an object: his writings minimize (but do not deny) the role of mathematics and favor the perceptions of the ear over the calculations of the mind.[3] Theophrastus (ca. 371–287 BCE), also a pupil of Aristotle, similarly conceded the importance of number as necessary for comparing different pitches but questioned whether this could account for all the qualities of music, including what we now think of as timbre. Moreover, he distinguished between the analysis of individual pitches and the way in which these pitches might function within a melody. Whereas Pythagoreans emphasized the identification and description of music's constituent parts, Theophrastus attended to the ways in which these parts—individual pitches—might function together as a whole. He concluded that "music has but one nature: the motion of the soul that arises from the release of evils brought about by the passions; if there were not this motion, there would be no nature of music."[4] For Aristoxenus and Theophrastus, the essence of music could not be defined without reference to its effect.

In the conflict between the mind and the senses—mirroring in a very broad way the differences between Plato and Aristotle—a consensus eventually coalesced around the writings of Ptolemy (after 83–161), who reconciled the two positions by granting the ear at least some role in the discussion of intervals and ratios. Music and astronomy, he maintained, both employ arithmetic and geometry "as instruments of indisputable authority, to discover the quantity and quality of the primary movements; and they are as it were cousins, born of the sisters, sight and hearing, and brought up by arithmetic and geometry as children most closely related in their

3. On Aristoxenus, see Thomas J. Mathiesen, *Apollo's Lyre: Greek Music and Music Theory in Antiquity and the Middle Ages* (Lincoln: University of Nebraska Press, 1999), 294–344.

4. Theophrastus, as quoted in Porphyrius's *In Ptolemaei Harmonica commentarium*; translation from Mathiesen, *Apollo's Lyre*, 519.

stock."[5] Yet for another thousand years, few (including Ptolemy himself) were prepared to question the ultimate authority of number.

This hierarchical distinction between the mind and the senses reveals itself with special clarity in the threefold classification of music in Boethius's *De institutione musica*. Two of the three categories he identifies are inaudible to the human ear:

- *Musica mundana*, the harmony of the spheres, imperceptible to humankind;
- *Musica humana*, the harmony of the human soul, perceptible within the mind of the individual;
- *Musica instrumentalis*, sounding music, perceptible through the senses; *instrumentalis* is used here in the sense of instrumentality, not in the sense of instrumental music.

In a vivid thirteenth-century depiction of these three manifestations (see Figure 5), *musica mundana* occupies pride of place at the top: the wand held by the figure of Musica extends from her hand to a point just short of an orb that joins the four elements of earth, water, air, and fire. In the middle panel, her wand just barely crosses the divide that separates her from *musica humana*, represented by four humans. And in the bottom panel, her wand stays entirely on her side of the boundary that separates her from *musica instrumentalis*; she has even transferred her wand to her left hand so that she can admonish the performing musician with a wag of her right index finger. The function of this image as the frontispiece to a large and important collection of early polyphony was intended at least in part to remind users that even the complex two-, three-, and four-part polyphony of this collection—*musica instrumentalis*—is but a distant approximation of the higher forms of music.[6]

This image also captures the distinction between what Boethius called "knowledge offered by the senses" and "the more certain things of the intellect." The "mind's eye," he maintained in *De institutione arithmetica*, is "composed of many corporeal eyes and is of higher dignity than they"; only through the processes of the intellect can truth be "investigated and beheld." This "mind's eye" is "submerged and surrounded by the corporeal senses" but is nevertheless "illuminated by the disciplines of the quadrivium." Arithmetic is the foundational discipline within the quadrivium because "God, the creator of the massive structure of the world, considered this first discipline as the exemplar of his own thought and established all things in accord with it."[7]

5. Ptolemy, *The Harmonics*, 3.3; translation by Andrew Barker in Barker, *Greek Musical Writings*, 2:373. See also Barker, "Mathematical Beauty Made Audible: Musical Aesthetics in Ptolemy's *Harmonics*," *Classical Philology* 105 (2010): 403–20.

6. See Tilman Seebass, "Lady Music and Her Protégés, from Musical Allegory to Musicians' Portraits," *Musica Disciplina* 42 (1988): 27–29.

7. Anicius Manlius Severinus Boethius, *De institutione arithmetica*, ed. and trans. Michael Masi as *Boethian Number Theory* (Amsterdam: Rodopi, 1983), 73–74.

Figure 5. The Three Manifestations of Music
In this frontispiece to a large collection of early-medieval polyphony, ca. 1245–54, the figure of Musica gestures to each of the three manifestations of music. In the top panel, her wand extends across a boundary toward the four elements (earth, water, air, fire), representing the highest category of music, *musica mundana*. In the middle panel, her wand still penetrates the barrier but not by as much, pointing to *musica humana*, the harmonizing force that unites body, spirit, and matter. In the bottom panel, her wand remains on her own side of the barrier, and she point an admonishing finger at a man playing the viol, a manifestation of *musica instrumentalis*, the only variety audible to humans.
Source: Florence, Biblioteca Medicea Laurenziana, plut. 29.1.

The tendency of medieval writers to prioritize thought over action and intellect over experience found its most celebrated musical manifestation in the distinction between *musicus* and *cantor*. Aurelian of Réôme (fl. mid-ninth century) was the first to articulate the difference, but it was made most memorable by Guido of Arezzo (ca. 991/2–after 1033), who turned it into a verse that, as Calvin Bower observes, would "be repeated *ad infinitum* by music theorists for centuries to come."

> Musicorum et cantorum, magna est distantia
> isti dicunt, illi sciunt, quae componit musica.
> Nam qui facit quod non sapit, diffinitur bestia.

> Great is the difference between musicians and singers,
> The latter *say*, the former *know* what music comprises.
> And he who does what he does not know is defined as a beast.[8]

Here the hierarchical relationship between knowing and doing lies beyond all doubt: the *musicus* comprehends that which is abstract; the *cantor* merely realizes these abstractions without understanding them. Only later would the term *musica* and its cognates come to be applied to both the theoretical and the practical sides of the art.

Until roughly the middle of the sixteenth century, the dual perspectives of music as an object and music as an experience rarely came into conflict, for sounding music was understood to be the perceptible manifestation of what was in essence an abstraction. The cosmos, the human body, and music were all conceived as structured—"tuned," to use the prevailing image of earlier times—according to the same basic proportions. For the ancient world, and well into the early modern era, the miraculous powers of Orpheus (music's effect) could be explained by appealing to the insights of Pythagoras (music's essence). Multiple accounts repeatedly connect Pythagoras and his followers to the cults of Orpheus, and at least some of Pythagoras's supposed writings were disseminated under Orpheus's name.[9] Even the two figures' paternal origins became conflated at one point: although Orpheus was often identified as the son of Apollo, the Neoplatonist Iamblichus, writing in the late third or early fourth century, felt it necessary to deny the report, apparently current at the time, that

---

8. Guido of Arezzo, *Regule rithmice* 2:8–10, as transcribed and translated by Calvin M. Bower, "The Transmission of Ancient Music Theory into the Middle Ages," in *The Cambridge History of Western Music Theory*, ed. Thomas Christensen (Cambridge: Cambridge University Press, 2002), 163.

9. See Karl Kerényi, *Pythagoras und Orpheus: Präludien zu einer zukünftigen Geschichte der Orphik und des Pythagoreismus*, 3rd ed. (Zürich: Rhein-Verlag, 1950), especially 41; E. R. Dodds, *The Greeks and the Irrational* (Berkeley and Los Angeles: University of California Press, 1951), 148–49; Walter Burkert, *Greek Religion: Archaic and Classical*, trans. John Raffan (Oxford: Basil Blackwell, 1985), 296–301; and Riedweg, *Pythagoras*, 7–9, 58–59, 88–89. Riedweg points out that while later connections may be fanciful, sources dating from as early as the fifth century BCE connect the two.

Apollo was also the father of Pythagoras. Iamblichus goes on to assure his readers, however, that Apollo was the father of Pythagoras's *soul*.[10]

The two figures approach a point of near-convergence in the profusion of Orpheus-like miracles ascribed to Pythagoras. Iamblichus credited Pythagoras with the ability to tame wild animals and to shape human behavior through music,[11] while Cicero (106–43 BCE) and Quintilian (ca. 35–ca. 100 CE) told different versions of a story in which Pythagoras uses music to prevent a crime. Boethius transmitted the tale thus:

> It is common knowledge that song has many times calmed rages, and that it has often worked great wonders on the affections of bodies or minds. Who does not know that Pythagoras, by performing a spondee, restored a drunk adolescent of Taormina incited by the sound of the Phrygian mode to a calmer and more composed state? One night, when a whore was closeted in the house of a rival, this frenzied youth wanted to set fire to the house. Pythagoras, being a night owl, was contemplating the courses of the heavens (as was his custom) when he learned that this youth, incited by the sound of the Phrygian mode, would not desist from his action in response to the many warnings of his friends; he ordered that the mode be changed, thereby tempering the disposition of the frenzied youth to a state of absolute calm.[12]

"Pythagoras...contemplating the courses of the heavens (as was his custom)": This seemingly irrelevant detail—why should it matter what Pythagoras happened to be doing when he learned of the impending conflagration?—is in fact essential to Boethius's larger point: that understanding the movements of the celestial bodies enhances one's understanding of the human soul, of music, and of music's effect on the human soul.

The tendency to fuse the images of Orpheus and Pythagoras grew even stronger in the Renaissance. Drawing on Iamblichus's *Life of Pythagoras*, Pico stated in his celebrated *Oratio de hominis dignitate* (1486) that "Pythagoras had the Orphic theology as the model after which he molded and formed his own philosophy. In fact, they say that the words of Pythagoras are called holy only because they flowed from the teachings of Orpheus: thence as from their primal source flowed the secret doctrine of numbers, and whatever Greek philosophy had that was great and sublime."[13] And in his *De poeta* of 1559, the Italian poet and prelate Antonio Minturno (1500–1574) traced the doctrine of numbers in

---

10. See Dominic J. O'Meara, *Pythagoras Revived: Mathematics and Philosophy in Late Antiquity* (Oxford: Clarendon Press, 1989), 36–37.

11. Iamblichus of Chalcis, "The Life of Pythagoras," in Guthrie and Fideler, *The Pythagorean Sourcebook and Library*, 70–71, 84–86. See also Vladimir L. Marchenkov, *The Orpheus Myth and the Powers of Music* (Hillsdale, NY: Pendragon Press, 2009), passim.

12. Boethius, *De institutione musica*, book 1, ed. Palisca, trans. Bower, 5.

13. Giovanni Pico della Mirandola, *Oratio de hominis dignitate* (1486), trans. Charles Glenn Wallis as *On the Dignity of Man* (Indianapolis: Hackett, 1998), 33.

a direct line that "flowed from the Orphic spring to Pythagoras and in succession on to Plato," all of whom "constructed the universe on musical principles."[14] Antoine Busnoys's motet *In hydraulis* (ca. 1467), with a text presumably by the composer himself, opens with a laudation of Pythagoras as the founder of music and ends with an acclamation of Busnoys's teacher, Johannes Ockeghem, who is acclaimed as the "new Orpheus."[15]

These perceived similarities between Pythagoras and Orpheus underscore their essentially similar approaches to music: both used it to change human behavior. If in Boethian terminology Orpheus was the *cantor* and Pythagoras the *musicus*, both acted with equal effect in a universe governed by harmony. As Boethius observed:

> From all these accounts it appears beyond doubt that music is so naturally united with us that we cannot be free from it even if we so desired. For this reason the power of the intellect ought to be summoned, so that this art, innate through nature, may also be mastered, comprehended through knowledge. For just as in seeing it does not suffice for the learned to perceive colors and forms without also searching out their properties, so it does not suffice for musicians to find pleasure in melodies without also coming to know how they are structured internally by means of ratio of pitches.[16]

Once again, however, pleasure is the sticking point. If comprehended by the intellect, it is acceptable; if it remains at the level of the purely sensuous— "pathological," to use the term Kant and Hanslick would apply much later—it is capable of overthrowing the soul and therefore undesirable. The danger here is a loss of control, a surrendering of the self (willingly or unwillingly) to the physical power of sound. Plato, sensing this danger, had limited music's proper use to a form of therapy, as a means of restoring order to a disordered soul:

> And harmony, whose movements are akin to the orbits within our souls, is a gift of the Muses, if our dealings with them are guided by understanding, not for irrational pleasure, for which people nowadays seem to make use of it, but to serve as an ally in the fight to bring order to any orbit in our souls that has become unharmonized, and make it concordant with itself. Rhythm, too, has likewise been given us by the Muses for the same purpose.[17]

---

14. Antonio Minturno, *De poeta* (Venice: Franciscus Rampazetus, 1559), 91: "Doctrina autem, ac sapientia illa, quae a fonte Orpheo ad Pythagoram, ac deinceps ad Platonem permanavit, mundum musica ratione constituit." Translation from Christopher Butler, *Number Symbolism* (London: Routledge, 1970), 105.

15. On the significance of number in actual compositions of this era, see Reinhard Strohm, "*De plus en plus*: Number, Binchois, and Ockeghem," in *Citation and Authority in Medieval and Renaissance Musical Culture: Learning from the Learned*, ed. Suzannah Clark and Elizabeth Eva Leach (Woodbridge, UK: Boydell Press, 2005), 160–73.

16. Boethius, *De institutione musica*, book 1, ed. Palisca, trans. Bower, 8.

17. Plato, *Timaeus* 47d–e, trans. Donald J. Zeyl, in Plato, *Complete Works*, ed. Cooper, 1250.

Music used for "irrational pleasure," by implication, decenters the soul and takes it to places it otherwise cannot—and should not—go. This was literally true in the case of Orpheus, who in descending to the underworld to retrieve his dead bride used music to serve his own personal pleasure and in ways that go beyond the laws of nature. That it all ends so badly suggests that this is (among other things) a cautionary tale about the uses of music. In commanding his crew to plug their ears with wax and lash him to the mast of his ship, Odysseus was wiser: he knew that he could endure the song of the sirens only if he suppressed his spontaneous, natural, and bodily responses to it. This, too, is a cautionary tale, albeit one with a happier outcome.

There is, in the end, something both delightful and disturbing about music's power to sway us. As the critic and theologian Jeremy Collier (1650–1726) put it in his essay "On Musick" from 1694:

> Though the Entertainments of Musick are very Engaging; though they make a great Discovery of the Soul; and shew it capable of strange Diversities of Pleasure: Yet to have our Passions lye at the Mercy of a little Minstrelsy; to be Fiddled out of our Reason and Sobriety; to have our Courage depend upon a *Drum*, or our Devotions on an *Organ*, is a Sign we are not so great as we might be. If we were proof against the charming of Sounds; or could we have the Satisfaction without the Danger; or raise our Minds to what pitch we pleas'd by the Strength of *Thinking*, it would be a nobler Instance of Power and Perfection.[18]

"Satisfaction without the Danger": this captures the dilemma Odysseus faced thousands of years before. In the end, any attempt to explain music's power is driven by a desire to assert control over it, overcome its danger, and quell our anxiety that we are in fact not so great as we might be.

As long as the Pythagorean-Platonic conception of the universe held sway, few questioned the causal mechanism of music's effect. With the gradual recovery of the writings of Aristotle in the late Middle Ages, particularly from the thirteenth century onward, new models of the cosmos—and music—began to take hold. Aristotle's lost treatise on music would never resurface, but his surviving remarks elsewhere make it clear that he was far more inclined to treat music as belonging to the study of the natural sciences—that is, as sound—than to mathematics. He did not reject the mathematical elements of music, but he did distinguish clearly between mathematical and acoustical harmony.[19]

---

18. Jeremy Collier, "Of Musick," in Collier, *Essays upon Several Moral Subjects*, 3rd ed. (London: R. Sare & H. Hindmarch, 1698), 24. For a later but very similar expression of revulsion at the raw power of music without words, see Johann Gottfried Herder, *Briefe zur Beförderung der Humanität*, 83rd letter, in Herder, *Werke*, 10 vols., ed. Martin Bollacher, vol. 7, *Briefe zur Beförderung der Humanität*, ed. Hans Dietrich Irmscher (Frankfurt am Main: Deutscher Klassiker Verlag, 1991), 462–66.

19. Aristotle, *Posterior Analytics*, 79a 1–2.

Advances in empirical science brought further pressure on the Pythagorean-Platonic conception of music and the cosmos. This new way of thinking about the structure of the universe was aided by the emerging concept of the *scientie medie*, those realms of knowledge seen to occupy a middle ground between the immutable and the contingent. This line of thought provided a framework for reconciling the philosophies of Plato and Aristotle, and it was promoted in the late Middle Ages by such leading philosophers as Albertus Magnus (ca. 1206–1280) and Thomas Aquinas (1225–1274). Aquinas, for one, acknowledged the dual nature of music by drawing on the distinction between the Aristotelian categories of music's formal cause (arithmetic proportions) and its material cause (physical sound). By the early fifteenth century, as Joseph Dyer observes, "physical science, not mathematics, was considered best capable of explaining musical phenomena."[20] In the sixteenth century the astronomical observations and theories of Nicolaus Copernicus, Kepler, Galileo Galilei, and Tycho Brahe, among others, rendered the theory of isomorphic resonance largely unsustainable. These new conceptions of the universe generated new conceptions of music's essence, which in turn demanded new explanations for the mechanism of its effect.

20. Joseph Dyer, "The Place of *Musica* in Medieval Classifications of Knowledge," *JM* 24 (2007): 46.

PART II

Essence and Effect: 1550–1850

By the middle of the sixteenth century humanist writers had begun to raise serious questions about music as a sounding manifestation of number. Faced with a growing body of empirical evidence, particularly from the realm of astronomy, they could no longer accept the Pythagorean-Platonic model of the cosmos. This in turn created a demand for explanations of music's power that went beyond the principle of isomorphic resonance. Even those who saw the essence of music in number had cause to doubt this as the source of music's effect. It was also becoming increasingly clear that Pythagorean ratios, the basis of just intonation, could not be applied in any wholly consistent way in modern musical practice. While intervals based on the simple ratios of 2:1, 3:2, and 4:3—the octave, fifth, and fourth—continued to serve perfectly well in monophonic music, including plainchant, they posed serious difficulties in polyphonic works, because intervals that worked melodically did not necessarily produce harmonic consonances when sung or played against other melodic lines. The so-called—and very common—"imperfect" consonances of the major and minor third proved especially troublesome. The arithmetic calculations that worked so well on paper produced audible consequences unsatisfactory to the ear. In the ongoing battle between Pythagoreans, who favored reason, and Aristoxenians, who favored the senses, the latter gradually achieved parity and in some circles superiority.[1] Belief in Pythagorean principles suffered yet another blow when Vincenzo Galilei (late 1520s–1591), father of the famed mathematician and astronomer, was able to demonstrate that Pythagoras's reputed method of weighing the blacksmiths' hammers to explain the ratios of musical intervals could not have led to the results it was alleged to have produced.[2]

The basic principle of a relationship between sound and number never disappeared entirely, but the Pythagorean-Platonic idea of isomorphic resonance eventually gave way to a narrower concept of music as a sounding art that achieved its effects by other means. Having deprived number of its central role in

---

1. See Claude V. Palisca, "Aristoxenus Redeemed in the Renaissance," in Palisca, *Studies in the History of Italian Music and Music Theory* (Oxford: Clarendon Press, 1994), 189–99.

2. See Claude V. Palisca, ed. and trans., *The Florentine Camerata: Documentary Studies and Translations* (New Haven: Yale University Press, 1989), 163, 183–85. See also William Jordan, "Galileo and the Demise of Pythagoreanism," in *Music and Science in the Age of Galileo*, ed. Victor Coelho (Dordrecht: Kluwer Academic, 1992), 129–39; and Daniel K. L. Chua, "Vincenzo Galilei, Modernity and the Division of Nature," in *Music Theory and Natural Order from the Renaissance to the Early Twentieth Century*, ed. Suzannah Clark and Alexander Rehding (Cambridge: Cambridge University Press, 2001), 17–29.

the cosmos, philosophers could not leave music metaphysically orphaned, and so they developed other models to preserve music's status as an art of the mind and not merely of the senses. In the period between roughly 1550 and 1850, the most important of the qualities used to explain the connection between the nature and power of music were:

- **Expression**, which placed fundamental importance on music's ability to convey and arouse ideas or emotions;
- **Form**, which gave priority to the structure of music;
- **Beauty**, which privileged that quality as central to the art;
- **Autonomy**, which emphasized the independence of music from all other forms of art, from the world at large, or both; and
- **Disclosiveness**, which valued music as an organon of knowledge, a means by which to gain access to truth.

These qualities are neither exhaustive nor mutually exclusive, but they are the ones that figure most often in discussions about the relationship between music's essence and effect. The conceptual dichotomy that emerged in the middle of the nineteenth century between "absolute" and "program" music would literally change the terms of the debate about the essence and effect of the art. For the preceding three centuries, however, commentators used these qualities in varying configurations and with varying degrees of emphasis to explain the relationship between the nature and the power of music.

3   Expression

The idea of music as an art of expression seems so self-evident that it is easy to overlook the premises behind this assumption. Expression of any kind, musical or otherwise, posits a distinction between that which is expressed (such as an emotion or an idea) and the means by which it is expressed (such as language, music, or language and music together). This distinction is not addressed in the theory of isomorphic resonance, which offers an explanation for the effect of any kind of music, with or without a sung text. Ancient writers nevertheless agreed that certain kinds of texts could be appropriately sung to certain kinds of music but not others, depending on the occasion and the audience. Plato, for example, identifies music in the Dorian mode as suitable for warriors, while music in the Ionian and Lydian modes are more suitable for drinking-parties.[1] This same kind of concern for matching music with text is evident throughout the Middle Ages. The first of the precepts for composing a chant or song given by the early twelfth-century writer known variously as Johannes Afflighemensis, John Cotton, or simply John recommends that the music should be crafted "according to the meaning of the words." The melodist must use the right mode and tempo and take the nature of the audience into account: a song composed for young people should be "youthful and playful," as opposed to one written for "old folk," which should be "slow and staid."[2]

■ THE SEPARATION OF POWERS

It was precisely this concern for matching words and music that reflects a conceptual separation between the power of music and the power of the text. Plainchant itself was largely understood as a form of enhanced speech, a way of projecting the words that heightened both their audibility and their import.[3] In theory it was easy enough to accord priority to the liturgical text of a plainchant melody; in practice it was difficult to deny the power of the melody, a power so significant that it might even overshadow the import of the words.

---

1. Plato, *Republic*, 398d–99b.

2. John, *De musica*, chapter 18, in *Hucbald, Guido, and John on Music: Three Medieval Treatises*, ed. Claude V. Palisca, trans. Warren Babb (New Haven: Yale University Press, 1978), 137.

3. For a recent summary of the relevant literature on this point, see Blair Sullivan, *The Classical Analogy between Speech and Music and Its Transmission in Carolingian Music Theory* (Tempe: Arizona Center for Medieval and Renaissance Studies, 2011).

Nowhere is this fear of music's power over the mind more evident than in the writings of Saint Augustine, who in his *Confessions* famously describes his conflicted responses to the singing of psalms in early Christian liturgy. He recognized that when sung, the words took on greater force than when merely recited. Yet he feared that this response constituted a "contentment of the flesh," and he considered it a sin to "be more moved with the voice than the words sung."[4] Nor was Augustine alone in his concerns about the capacity of music to draw attention away from the text. He recalled how Athanasius, bishop of Alexandria, had "made the reader of the psalm utter it with so slight inflection of voice that it was nearer speaking than singing." Augustine found this approach equally problematic, however, for it robbed the church of a potent means of inspiring devotion:

> When I remember the tears I shed at the Psalmody of Thy Church, in the beginning of my recovered faith; and how at this time I am moved, not with the singing, but with the things sung, when they are sung with a clear voice and modulation most suitable, I acknowledge the great use of this institution. Thus I fluctuate between peril of pleasure and approved wholesomeness; inclined the rather (though not as pronouncing an irrevocable opinion) to approve of the usage of singing in the church; that so by the delight of the ears, the weaker minds may rise to the feeling of devotion. Yet when it befalls me to be more moved with the voice than the words sung, I confess to have sinned penally, and then had rather not hear music.[5]

Augustine's solution to overcoming the "delights of the ear" (*voluptates aurium*) was to "repose briefly" in the sounds but then to "rise up" though a "force of will" (*ut surgam cum volo*) to place his central focus on the words being sung.[6] This approach emphasizes the responsibility of the listener to subordinate the pleasures of the senses to the rationality of the mind. This oppositional relationship between body and spirit is entirely consistent with church teachings but is not to be found in the Pythagorean-Platonic concept of music's essence and effect. Plato consistently attributes the ethical effects of music to the specific nature of the music itself; for him, listening is an essentially passive activity. If a certain piece of music produces unsatisfactory behavior, it is the fault of the music, not the listener. The wrong mode, the wrong rhythm, or the wrong timbre have the potential to bring the soul out of equilibrium and create an inappropriate or unwanted reaction. Pythagoras's ability to change the

---

4. Saint Augustine, *The Confessions*, ed. Temple Scott, trans. Edward B. Pusey (New York: E. P. Dutton, 1900), 267, 268. On the struggle in medieval thought between mind and body in response to music, see Holsinger, *Music, Body, and Desire in Medieval Culture.*

5. Saint Augustine, *The Confessions*, trans. Pusey, 268.

6. Saint Augustine, *Confessiones*, book 10, XXXIII, 49: "Voluptates aurium tenacius me implicaverant et subiugaverant; sed resolvisti et liberasti me. Nunc in sonis quos animant eloquia tua, cum suavi et artificiosa voce cantantur, fateor, aliquantulum acquiesco, non quidem ut haeream, sed ut surgam cum volo."

behavior of the outraged youth determined to commit arson-murder simply by ordering a nearby musician to play in a particular mode illustrates what might be called an allopathic conception of music's ethical powers: specific kinds of music can be counted on to elicit specific responses.

Augustine, by contrast, calls into question not the nature of the music that at times overpowers him, but rather his reaction to it. What he resolves to change, in other words, is not the music he hears but the way he hears it. He would doubtless have held strong views about what kinds of music would be appropriate or inappropriate for singing the Psalms of David, and he could easily have prescribed (and proscribed) specific types of melody as a solution to his dilemma. But the only music he explicitly rejects is the kind favored by Athanasius, a style in which the words are projected in a manner "nearer to speaking than singing." Augustine is struggling here with essentials: what torments and delights him goes beyond certain melodies or kinds of melody to the very phenomenon of music itself. He wants to hear the singing of the psalms but at the same time feels obliged to restrain his response. Odysseus had overcome the music of the sirens by physical restraint, by having his crew lash him to his ship's mast; Augustine performs the mental equivalent, tying down the sensuous side of his interior self so that he might "rise above" the "delights of the ears."

By subordinating his senses to the faculties of reason, then, Augustine makes a sharp distinction between words and music and places the two in opposition. This approach marks the beginning of a fissure in Western conceptions of music that undermined the perceived unity of the micro- and macrocosm. On the one hand, Augustine accepts, as do other fathers of the church, the parallels between musical proportions and the structure of a harmonious cosmos. But when he moves from speculating on the abstract nature of music to describing his personal experience of actual sounding music, he finds cosmic structures inadequate to explain his response and comes to the realization that music has its own means of expression that lie outside of—and, more important, go beyond—the capacity of language. In his commentary on Psalm 99 (100), "Jubilate Domino omnis terra," he observes that "one who jubilates does not speak words":

> It is rather a sort of sound of joy without words, since it is the voice of a soul poured out in joy and expressing, as best it can, the feeling, though not grasping the sense. A man delighting in his joy, from some words which cannot be spoken or understood, bursts forth in a certain voice of exultation without words, so that it seems he does indeed rejoice with his own voice, but as if, because filled with too much joy, he cannot explain in words what it is in which he delights.[7]

7. Saint Augustine, *In Psalmum XCIX*, in *Patrologiae cursus completus, Series Latina*, ed. J.-P. Migne, 221 vols. (Paris: Migne, 1844–55), 37:1272: "Qui jubilat, non verba dicit, sed sonus quidam est laetitiae

And elsewhere, in his explication of Psalm 32 (33), he returns to the idea of "jubilation" as a form of musical expression:

> What is it to sing in jubilation? To be unable to understand, to express in words, what is sung in the heart. For they who sing, either in the harvest, in the vineyard, or in some other arduous occupation, after beginning to manifest their gladness in the words of songs, are filled with such joy that they cannot express it in words, and turn from the syllables of words and proceed to the sound of jubilation. The *jubilus* is something which signifies that the heart labors with what it cannot utter. And whom does jubilation befit but the ineffable God? For he is ineffable whom you cannot speak. And if you cannot speak him, yet ought not to be silent, what remains but that you jubilate; so that the heart rejoices without words, and the great expanse of joy has not the limits of syllables? "Sing well unto him in jubilation" (Ps. 32:3).[8]

Whether or not Augustine's comments relate to what would later be called the *jubilus* of the Alleluia—the extended and often quite elaborate melisma of the closing syllable of the word "Alleluia"—is a matter of contention among chant scholars but not immediately relevant to what is at issue here, namely, the categorical distinction between giving expression through singing with or without words. Augustine acknowledges his inability to explain the effect of music without a text and in so doing foreshadows, long before Wilhelm Heinrich Wackenroder, Ludwig Tieck, and E. T. A. Hoffmann in the late eighteenth and early nineteenth centuries, the topos of instrumental music's ineffability.[9]

Later writings that refer unambiguously to the *jubilus* of the Alleluia do in any case reinforce Augustine's concept of jubilation as an expression of joy that transcends language. Amalar of Metz (d. ca. 850) observes that "this jubilation, which cantors call the 'sequence,' leads our minds into that state when speaking in words will no longer be necessary and when mind will manifest itself to mind

---

sine verbis: vox est enim animi diffusi laetitia, quantum potest, exprimentis affectum, non sensum comprehendentis. Gaudens homo in exultatione sua, ex verbis quibusdam quae non possunt dici et intelligi, erumpit in vocem quamdam exsultationis sine verbis: ita ut appareat eum ipsa voce gaudere quidem, sed quasi repletum nimio gaudio, non posse verbis explicare quod gaudet." Translation by James McKinnon in James McKinnon, ed., *Music in Early Christian Literature* (Cambridge: Cambridge University Press, 1987), 158.

8. Augustine, *In Psalmum XXXII*, in *Patrologiae cursus completus*, ed. Migne, 36:283: "Quid est in jubilatione canere? Intelligere, verbis explicare non posse quod canitur corde. Etenim illi qui cantant, sive in messe, sive in vinea, sive in aliquo opere ferventi, cum coeperint in verbis canticorum exsultare laetitia, veluti impleti tanta laetitia, ut eam verbis explicare non possint, avertunt se a syllabis verborum, et eunt in sonum jubilationis. Jubilum sonus quidam est significans cor parturire quod dicere non potest. Et quem decet ista jubilatio, nisi ineffabilem Deum? Ineffabilis enim est, quem fari non potes: et si eum fari non potes, et tacere non debes, quid restat nisi ut jubiles; ut gaudeat cor sine verbis, et immensa latitudo gaudiorum metas non habeat syllabarum? *Bene cantate ei in jubilatione*." Translation by James McKinnon in McKinnon, *Music in Early Christian Literature*, 156–57.

9. As Lawrence Kramer points out in "Oracular Musicology; or, Faking the Ineffable," *AfMw* 69 (2012): 101–9, postmodern assertions about the ineffability of music fail to take into account the long history of this perspective and say more about the shortcomings of language than they do about music.

by thought alone."[10] The imagery evokes the thirteenth chapter of Saint Paul's first epistle to the Corinthians, which describes a future state of revelation in which the expression of thought has no need of language and will be far clearer than anything that can be communicated by words. Hugh of Saint Victor, writing in the twelfth century, similarly observed that the melismatic passages found in "the Alleluia and in other chants of few words, signify the *jubilus*, which happens when the mind is so fixed upon God at times and in a certain ineffable sweetness, that it is not able to express fully what it feels."[11] Aquinas, too, interpreted the *jubilus* in much the same way, as a nonverbal expression of spiritual joy.[12]

In short, the idea of what a much later era would call "purely musical" expression, independent of words—and at least potentially superior to them—was not unknown to the medieval church. This is not to suggest that composers of the Middle Ages were unconcerned with issues of text-setting or the ideal of moving the spirit through an artful conjunction of words and music.[13] But attempts to explain the effect of music without recourse to the meaning of any words being sung and without recourse to the model of isomorphic resonance mark the early stages of an important categorical division in the history of musical aesthetics.

The difficulty of identifying the sources of music's power emerges with special clarity toward the end of the *Musica enchiriadis*, a widely distributed ninth-century treatise on the elements of music in general and of plainchant in particular. The author—probably a monk or priest—transmits the standard account of music as sounding number, its intervals the aural manifestation of arithmetic ratios. Having covered the obligatory topics on mode, melody, and so on, the author concludes with the story of Orpheus and Euridice. He recounts the tale at some length and frames it as an allegory of the futility of understanding the essence of music in all its fullness. The names of the characters, in keeping with the tradition of speculative etymology, reflect their essential qualities: Aristeus, "which may be translated as 'good man,'" is in love with Euridice,

---

10. As quoted in Calvin Bower, "From Alleluia to Sequence: Some Definitions of Relations," in *Western Plainchant in the First Millennium: Studies in the Medieval Liturgy and Its Music*, ed. Sean Gallagher (Aldershot: Ashgate, 2003), 367: "Haec iubilatio, quam cantores sequentiam vocant, illum statum ad mentem nostram ducit, quando non erit necessaria locutio verborum, sed sola cogitatione mens menti monstrabit quod retinet in se." Translation slightly modified from Paul K. Raftery, "Amalar of Metz on the Mass: A Translation of Book III, Chapters 1–18 of the *Liber officialis*" (Licentiate in Sacred Theology, Jesuit School of Theology at Berkeley, 2010), 95–96.

11. Hugh of Saint Victor, *De officiis ecclesiasticis*, as quoted and translated in James McKinnon, "The Patristic Jubilus and the Alleluia of the Mass," in *Cantus Planus: Papers Read at the Third Meeting, Tihany, Hungary, 19–24 September 1988*, ed. László Dobszay (Budapest: Hungarian Academy of Sciences, 1990), 70.

12. See Hermann-Josef Burbach, *Studien zur Musikanschauung des Thomas von Aquin* (Regensburg: Gustav Bosse, 1966), 120.

13. See John Stevens, *Words and Music in the Middle Ages: Song, Narrative, Dance, and Drama, 1050–1350* (Cambridge: Cambridge University Press, 1986); and Fritz Reckow, "Zwischen Ontologie und Rhetorik: die Idee des *movere animos* und der Übergang vom Spätmittelalter zur frühen Neuzeit in der

"whose name means 'deep discernment.' "[14] She is the wife of Orpheus, "whose name—*oreo phone*—means 'excellent voice.' " Aristeus pursues Euridice across a field but is "unable to hold her completely." At this moment she is bitten by a serpent, "by divine prudence, as it were."

> But when again through Orpheus—that is through the most excellent sound of song—she is summoned from her secret places and from the lower regions, like some phantom she is led even into the ears of this state of being, yet at the moment when she seems to be seen, she is lost; for truly among those things which at present we know in part and within an enigma, even this discipline by no means holds theory capable of penetrating in this life.[15]

Like Augustine, the author of the *Musica enchiriadis* pays allegiance to the theoretical basis of music in number and yet at the same time cannot quite accept the idea that this provides an entirely sufficient explanation for what he actually experiences in sound. He too perceives music's effect as something that cannot be explained by its essence in number. Through the allegory of Orpheus (the singer), Euridice (wisdom, "deep discernment": she has been bitten by the serpent), and Aristeus (who pursues the embodiment of knowledge in Euridice), he suggests that trying to understand the nature of music is like trying to understand the divine: in this life we cannot fully comprehend either. There are many aspects of music within our grasp here on earth, such as the construction of melody, the appropriateness of a given mode to a certain text, and the reduction of intervals to numerical ratios that correspond to consonance and dissonance. And we can judge the appropriateness of a melody for any given text based on the content of the words being sung. There are nevertheless "many more things which lie hidden from us because of rather mysterious causes." The closing chapter of the treatise moves back and forth between that which can be understood about music and that which cannot. In one particularly remarkable statement, the author affirms the congruence of music and the microcosm and in the same breath questions the capacity of this congruence to explain the true nature of the art and its effects on the human spirit: "Yet how music maintains with our souls such a communion and union—even if we do know that we are

Musikgeschichte," in *Traditionswandel und Traditionsverhalten,* ed. Walter Haug and Burghart Wachinger (Tübingen: Max Niemeyer, 1991), 145–78.

14. It is in Virgil's telling of the story (*Georgics,* book 4) that Aristeus is held at least indirectly responsible for Euridice's death.

15. Anonymous, *Musica enchiriadis:* "Sed dum rursus per Orpheum, id est per optimum cantilenae sonum, a secretis suis acsi ab inferis evocatur, imaginarie perducitur usque in auras huius vitae dumque videri videtur, amittitur, scilicet quia inter cetera, quae adhuc ex parte et in enigmate cernimus, haec etiam disciplina haud ad plenum habet rationem in hac vita penetrabilem." This reading of the text and Calvin Bower's translation are both from " '*Adhuc ex parte et in enigmate cernimus…*': Reflections on the Closing Chapters of *Musica enchiriadis,*" in *Music in the Mirror: Reflections on the History of Music Theory*

joined with music through a certain likeness—we are not capable of explaining clearly."[16] The author of the *Musica enchiriadis* ends his treatise by praising the knowledge gained "through the painstaking scrutiny of the ancients," and he lauds Boethius for having "disclosed many marvelous things about music theory, clearly demonstrating all things by the authority of numbers." But this obeisance to standard authority cannot eliminate his lingering doubts about the sufficiency of number to explain the effects of music. At the end of the treatise, as Calvin Bower has pointed out, the author both accepts and resists the Pythagorean tradition as transmitted by Boethius and ultimately adopts the Pauline perspective of seeing "though a glass darkly." As Bower notes, the author "clearly admires Boethius's mathematical demonstrations but finds reduction of basic elements of his art to numerical ratios and the arrogant epistemological position espoused by Boethius essentially foreign to his monastic spirituality." [17]

This struggle of medieval writers to reconcile the legacies of ancient music theory and the more recent repertory of Christian chant is not in itself unusual: a great deal of early medieval theory, as Richard Crocker has pointed out, is driven by the attempt to rationalize sacred chant—a functional, sounding repertory—on the basis of a theoretical apparatus inherited from late antiquity.[18] What sets the ending of the *Musica enchiriadis* apart from other treatises of its time is the extent to which it questions the ability of mathematics to explain music's capacity to elevate the spirit. Its author tries to deal with the music quite apart from its text but in the end seems more convinced that music's power is the result of an ineffable spiritual quality not unlike that of a faith which itself claimed to pass all understanding.

The doubts articulated in the *Musica enchiriadis* would nevertheless remain very much in the minority for another half millennium. Even writers like Johannes de Grocheo (fl. ca. 1300) and Johannes Tinctoris (ca. 1435–1511), who shared Aristotle's skepticism about whether the harmony of the spheres involved actual sound, ascribed the ethical effects of music to the congruence of number in the micro- and macrocosm.[19] By the middle of the sixteenth century, however, more and more commentators were beginning to question the

and Literature for the 21st Century, ed. Andreas Giger and Thomas J. Mathiesen (Lincoln: University of Nebraska Press, 2002), 31.

16. Anonymous, *Musica enchiriadis,* ed. and trans. in Bower, " '*Adhuc ex parte,*' " 32: "Quomodo vero tantam cum animis nostris musica commutationem et societatem habeat, etsi scimus quadam nos similitudine cum illa compactos, edicere ad liquidum non valemus."

17. Bower, " '*Adhuc ex parte,*' " 43.

18. Richard L. Crocker, "*Musica rhythmica* and *Musica metrica* in Antique and Medieval Theory," *JMT* 2 (1958): 2.

19. See the excerpts from Aristotle's *Metaphysics* in Barker, *Greek Musical Writings,* 2:32–33, and Hermann Abert, *Die Musikanschauung des Mittelalters und ihre Grundlagen* (Halle: Niemeyer, 1905), 153–54. For a detailed discussion of the issues as they played out around the concept of consonance

theory of isomorphic resonance, and they sought alternative models to explain the sources of music's power.

■ MUSIC AND LANGUAGE

With the new attitude toward music as a sounding art of expression came a new sense of what lay at its core. In the preface to his translation of Pseudo-Plutarch's *De musica*, published in Brescia in 1507, Carlo Valgulio proposed a decidedly nonmathematical assessment of music's essence:

> I believe there is no one in the world so insensitive, so leaden, that he is not moved by song. Theophrastus rightly said in the second book on music that the essence of music is the movement of the soul, which drives away evils from the soul invaded by confusion. If music did not have this effect of drawing the soul where it wants, it would become, in essence, nothing.[20]

The contrast with Platonic-Pythagorean thought could not be more striking. If music did not sound and move the soul, it would be *nothing*. There is an entirely new spirit here, one that reflects a fundamental shift in attitudes about the essence of music. Valgulio focused his attention on the response of the human spirit to physical sound, not on the resonance of that spirit with the supposedly congruent structures of music and the cosmos.

Another driving force behind this conceptual reconfiguration of music was humanism's ongoing program to reconcile reason and the senses. Once writers began to question the actual mechanism by which the legendary musicians of antiquity had achieved their miracles, they no longer felt obligated to begin their treatises on music with a discussion of number. Sounding music—*musica instrumentalis*, to use Boethius's term—begins to take precedence over *musica mundana* and *musica humana*. Mathematics continued to function as a way of measuring music—its pitches, intervals, and rhythms—but it was no longer accepted unquestioningly as that which defined its essence because it could no longer explain music's effect.

Nicola Vicentino's *L'antica musica ridotta alla moderna prattica* (Rome, 1555) is among the most important of the early treatises that reflect a new approach to the relationship between music and language. In it Vicentino (1511–ca. 1576), a composer who had studied under Adrian Willaert in Venice, dispenses with

---

ca. 1300, see Frank Hentschel, *Sinnlichkeit und Vernunft in der mittelalterlichen Musiktheorie: Strategien der Konsonanzwertung und der Gegenstand der "musica sonora" um 1300* (Stuttgart: Franz Steiner, 2000).

20. Carlo Valgulio, "Proem on Plutarch's *Musica* to Titus Pyrrhinus," as translated by Claude V. Palisca in *The Florentine Camerata*, 32. Palisca (ibid., 13) considered Valgulio's *Proemium* one the most important and widely read documents of musical humanism in the early sixteenth century.

the usual rehearsal of the three types of music and the theory of harmonic ratios. Instead, he opens by endorsing a judicious blend of reason and the senses:

Very diverse...are the opinions of philosophers concerning the origins and goals of music. It is well known that many philosophers discovered many things; however, by searching, calculating, disputing, and likewise opposing each other's opinion, they have bequeathed uncertainty instead of theory or practice to mankind. Aristoxenus, who depended solely on sense, denied reason, whereas the Pythagoreans...governed themselves solely by reason, not sense. Ptolemy more sanely embraced both sense and reason, and his opinion has satisfied many people up to now.[21]

This sort of appeal to a middle ground between reason and the senses was nothing new: Boethius had advocated a similar approach long before. But by the middle of the sixteenth century, the search for a causal relationship between the two began in earnest. In the alliance of reason and the senses, Vicentino maintained, the presence of a text to be sung compels composers to give language—which is to say, reason—the upper hand. "Music set to words has no other purpose than to express in harmony the meaning of the words, their passion and their effects."[22] This connection of music with the verbal arts of poetry and rhetoric, as Claude Palisca observed, "was as characteristic of the Renaissance as it was typical of the Middle Ages to ally music with the mathematical sciences."[23]

One indicator of this increasing desire to "express in harmony the meaning of the words" was the growing attention that mid-sixteenth-century composers, scribes, and publishers gave to issues of text underlay in their manuscripts and editions. What in earlier times had often seemed a matter of indifference now became an issue of clear concern.[24] While it is difficult to generalize—practices

21. Nicola Vicentino, *L'antica musica ridotta alla moderna prattica* (Rome: Antonio Barre, 1555), fol. 3r: "Molto varie...sono state l'oppinioni de Filosofi intorno all'origine e fine della Musica. Conciosia cosa che molti, molte cose habbino ritrovate, nondimeno cercando; calculando, disputando, e parimente al parere l'uno dell'altr' opponendosi, hanno lasciato à mortali più di dubbio, che di scienza o prattica. Aristosseno, accostandosi solo al senso, negava la ragione, quando per il contrario li Pittagorici si governavano solamente con la ragione, e non per il senso. Ma Tolomeo più sanamente abbraccio il senso, e la ragione insieme, di cui l'oppinione fin' hora è piaciuta à molti." Translation from Vicentino, *Ancient Music Adapted to Modern Practice*, ed. Claude V. Palisca, trans. Maria Rika Maniates (New Haven: Yale University Press, 1996), 6.

22. Vicentino, *L'antica musica*, fol. 86r: "La musica fatta sopra parole, non è fatta per altro se non per esprimere il concetto, et le passioni, et gil effetti di quelle con l'armonia." Translation by Maria Rika Maniates in Vicentino, *Ancient Music*, 270.

23. Claude V. Palisca, "A Natural New Alliance of the Arts," in Palisca, *Humanism in Italian Renaissance Musical Thought*, 333.

24. See Don Harrán, *Word-Tone Relationships in Musical Thought from Antiquity to the Seventeenth Century* (Neuhausen-Stuttgart: Hänssler, 1986). Warwick Edwards, "Text Treatment in Motets around 1500: The Humanistic Fallacy," in *The Motet around 1500: On the Relationship of Imitation and Text Treatment?*, ed. Thomas Schmidt-Beste (Turnhout: Brepols, 2012), 113–38, points out that the idea of the "primacy of the text" in musical settings becomes credible only from the 1540s onward.

varied by region, composer, genre, scribe, and editor—it is easy to sense in the written record a growing conviction that certain words had to be aligned with certain notes and that their musical articulation could not be left entirely to the discretion of performers. The sixteenth century was, after all, the age in which the genre of the madrigal enjoyed its greatest prestige and popularity throughout Europe, and composers vied with one another—often setting the same texts—to show the different ways in which the expressivity of poetry could be heightened by music. The move toward recitative and homophonic texture in the closing decades of the sixteenth century made the projection of sung texts even more central: words previously distributed across equal-voice polyphonic textures could now be projected by a single voice, supported by a strong bass line and harmonies generated by the basso continuo.

Gioseffo Zarlino's *Istitutioni harmoniche* (1558) plays a pivotal role in this shifting alliance between music and language. Zarlino (1517–1590) juxtaposes the older conception of music as a sounding manifestation of number with the newer ideal of music as an art of expression but makes no attempt to synthesize or reconcile the two. The leading musical theorist of his day and a highly regarded composer in his own right, Zarlino held the prestigious position of *maestro di cappella* at San Marco in Venice from 1565 until his death; a generation later, that position would be occupied by none other than Claudio Monteverdi. Zarlino devotes the first two parts of his *Istitutioni*—fully a quarter of his text—to establishing the mathematical basis of the art. Because it rests on the foundation of number, music is "noble and certain." He points to the constancy of the heavens—the courses of the planets and the seasonal movements of the stars, based on astronomical observations—as evidence of the incontestable nature of the mathematical sciences. "Music is nothing other than harmony," Zarlino declares early on, and "the subject of music" is "sounding number."[25] Such conventional ideas provide the backdrop for an equally conventional review of *musica mundana* and *musica humana*.[26]

For the remainder of his treatise, however, Zarlino adopts Plato's dictum that *melos*—which he translates as *melodia*, following Ficino's Latin (see 00)—is a combination of oration, harmony, and rhythm, and he grants explicit precedence to the first of these. "Although it seems that in such a combination no one of these things is prior to another," he explains, "Plato grants primacy to the oration and makes the other two parts subservient to it, for after he has shown the whole by means of the parts, he says that harmony and rhythm ought to follow the oration, and that the oration should not follow either the rhythm or

25. Gioseffo Zarlino, *Le istitutioni harmoniche* (Venice: [F. de Franceschi], 1558), 10 (book 1, chapter 5): "musica non è altro che Harmonia." Ibid., 29 (book 1, chapter 18): "il Sogetto della Musica è il Numero sonoro."

26. Zarlino's account of the harmony of the spheres in book 1, chapter 6, of *Le istitutioni harmoniche* is available in English in Godwin, *The Harmony of the Spheres*, 206–13.

harmony. And this is the obligation."[27] Zarlino acknowledges the power of harmony, but only up to a point—for music, as he had observed earlier in his treatise, cannot reach its fullest potential without the aid of rhythm and above all speech in the form of oration (*oratione*):

> Although harmony on its own possesses a certain power to dispose the spirit and to make it happy or sad, and although its power can double itself through rhythm, these two elements together are nevertheless insufficient to generate any extrinsic passions in any subject in the manner described above. Such power is achieved, however, through the oration, which expresses a variety of deportments.[28]

Zarlino further reminds his readers that the "choice of a harmony and a rhythm" must project not only the meter and rhythm of the words but also their import. The composer must

> take care to accompany each word in such a way that, if it denotes harshness, hardness, cruelty, bitterness, and other things of this sort, the harmony will be similar, that is, somewhat hard and harsh, but so that it does not offend. In the same way, if any word expresses complaint, grief, affliction, sighs, tears, and other things of this sort, the harmony will be full of sadness.[29]

The key phrase here is "so that it does not offend" (*di maniera...che non offendi*). This wholly subjective criterion would become the sticking point in the pamphlet war that erupted in the first decade of the seventeenth century between the Bolognese theorist and composer Giovanni Maria Artusi (ca. 1540–1613) and Claudio Monteverdi (1567–1643), the leading composer of his generation. Both agreed with Zarlino that the music of any vocal work should bring out and enhance the sense of the text being sung; their differences stemmed from the extent to which the composer could be granted license in pursuit of this end to

27. Zarlino, *Le istitutioni harmoniche*, 339 (book 4, chapter 32): "& pari che in tal compositione l'una di queste cose non sia prima dell'altra; tuttavia avanti le altre parti pone la Oratione, come cosa principale; & le altre due parti, come quelle, che serveno a lei: Percioche dopo che hà manifestato il tutto col mez[z]o delle parti dice, che l'Harmonia, & il Numero debbeno seguitare la Oratione, & non la Oratione il Numero, ne l'Harmonia. Et ciò il dovere." Translation slightly modified from that by Oliver Strunk in Strunk and Treitler, *Source Readings in Music History*, rev. ed., 457, where Strunk translates "oratione" as "speech."

28. Zarlino, *Le istitutioni harmoniche*, 72 (book 2, chapter 7): "Percioche se bene l'Harmonia sola hà una certa possanza di dispor l'animo, & di farlo allegro, o mesto; et che dal Numero posto in atto le siano raddoppiate le forze; non sono però potenti queste due cose poste insieme di generare alcuna passione estrinseca in alcun soggetto, al modo detto: conciosia che tal possanza acquistano dalla Oratione, che esprime alcuni costumi."

29. Zarlino, *Le istitutioni harmoniche*, 339 (book 4, chapter 32): "Et debbe avertire di accompagnare in tal maniera ogni parola, che dove ella dinoti asprezza, durezza, crudeltà, amaritudine, & altre cose simili, l'harmonia sia simile a lei, cioè alquanto dura, & aspra; di maniera però, che non offendi. Simigliantemente quando alcuna delle parole dimostrarà pianto, dolore, cordoglio, sospiri, lagrime, & altre cose simili; che l'harmonia sia piena di mestitia." Translation slightly altered from by Oliver Strunk

bend or even break the generally accepted conventions of melodic and contrapuntal writing. The *prima pratica*, to use Monteverdi's terminology, remained
within established musical practices; the *seconda pratica*—the "new" practice—reserved the right to violate those conventions as needed to set a text in
the most effective manner possible. Artusi and Monteverdi disagreed not about
the contrapuntal rules codified by Zarlino, but rather about the extent to which
one might take liberties with them. The fact that Zarlino himself has since come
to be associated with the *prima pratica* is something of an anachronism, for his
treatise first appeared more than forty years before Artusi launched his attack
against Monteverdi. His posthumous association with the *prima pratica*, moreover, has obscured the fact that he was one of the earliest and most prominent
figures to place the relationship of text and music at the forefront of compositional technique.

The polemics of the *seconda pratica* have been examined elsewhere on many
occasions, and with good reason: the dispute between Artusi and Monteverdi
encapsulates major aesthetic and stylistic issues at a crucial moment in music
history.[30] Artusi objected to Monteverdi's treatment of certain dissonances
and went so far as to include musical examples from some of the composer's
still-unpublished madrigals to support his case. Monteverdi responded briefly
in a commentary published in his *Fifth Book of Madrigals* (1605) and then at
greater length but indirectly through the mouthpiece of his brother, Giulio
Cesare Monteverdi, in an extended gloss on this earlier text in the preface to the
Scherzi musicali (1607).

While the dispute may have centered on issues of style, the differences between Artusi and Monteverdi ultimately derive from conflicting premises regarding the very nature of music. The polemics between Rameau and Rousseau
in the eighteenth century and between Wagner and Hanslick in the nineteenth, as
we shall see, would follow a similar pattern. Monteverdi, Rousseau, and Wagner
all viewed expression as the essence of music, inseparable from any means necessary to realize that expression, whereas Artusi, Rameau, and Hanslick viewed
music's essence more narrowly, in terms of its material substance. Artusi's musical examples from Monteverdi's madrigals famously reproduce the notes but
not the words sung to those notes. The assumption that music and text should

---

in Strunk and Treitler, *Source Readings in Music History*, rev. ed., 458. On Zarlino's attitudes toward the
relationship of text and music, see Harrán, *Word-Tone Relations in Musical Thought*, 189–95.

30. See, for example, Claude V. Palisca, "The Artusi–Monteverdi Controversy," in *The New
Monteverdi Companion*, ed. Denis Arnold and Nigel Fortune (London: Faber, 1985), 127–58, repub-
lished in Palisca, *Studies in the History of Italian Music and Music Theory* (Oxford: Clarendon Press, 1994),
54–87; Tim Carter, "Artusi, Monteverdi, and the Poetics of Modern Music," in *Musical Humanism and
Its Legacy: Essays in Honor of Claude V. Palisca*, ed. Nancy Kovaleff Baker and Barbara Russano Hanning
(Stuyvesant, NY: Pendragon Press, 1992), 171–94; Massimo Ossi, *Divining the Oracle: Monteverdi's
Seconda Prattica* (Chicago: University of Chicago Press, 2003); and Karol Berger, "Concepts and

work in close coordination was never an issue: that had been established long before the *seconda pratica*. The real question in the years around 1600 was whether the demands of expressive text-setting trumped what later critics would call "purely musical considerations," such as voice-leading and the treatment of dissonance. No one writing at the turn of the seventeenth century used this particular term or anything like it, but one of the paradoxes of the growing alliance between words and music in the sixteenth century is that it helped sharpen awareness of their categorical differences by emphasizing the capacities of what each could and could not do.

This conceptual realignment of music away from number and toward language allowed the art to maintain and in some respects even enhance its standing among the disciplines of the seven liberal arts. Having lost its status as a sounding manifestation of the structure of the cosmos, music could now appeal for philosophical prestige to the rationality of language. Zarlino reconciles these two approaches to at least some degree in his *Dimostrationi harmoniche* (1571) by defining music in terms of the Aristotelian categories of cause: material (sound), formal (number), and final ("to change the feeling...and to induce in us diverse passions").[31] He distinguishes between definition and description and criticizes those who—all too often, in his opinion—confuse music's essential and accidental features. Mathematics, he maintains, applies solely to the formal cause of music, not to its purpose.[32] This marks a significant shift in thinking, one taken up by most subsequent theorists: mathematics remains an element of music, but within the scheme of the liberal arts, music's closest companion would now be rhetoric, one of the arts of the trivium. In theory, at least, music remained within the quadrivium as an art of number. In practice, it would be treated more and more as an art of language and, more specifically still, as an art of persuasion, which is to say, as an art of rhetoric.

The applicability of rhetorical concepts to music had been recognized long before. The author of the ninth-century *Musica enchiriadis*—the same writer who had questioned the ability of number alone to explain music's effect—begins his treatise by pointing out that letters, syllables, nouns, and verbs are analogous to the "the coupling of *soni*," which are "the first foundations of chant." He later compares marks of punctuation with cadences and observes that the "lesser parts" of melodies "are the *cola* and *commata* of singing, which mark off the song at its endings."[33] In the twelfth century the writer known as John drew attention to the formal parallels

Developments in Music Theory," in *European Music, 1520–1640*, ed. James Haar (Woodbridge: Boydell, 2006), 304–28.

31. Gioseffo Zarlino, *Dimostrationi harmoniche* (Venice: Francesco dei Franceschi Senese, 1571), 10: "il mutare il senso:...& anco di indurre in noi passioni diverse."

32. Zarlino, *Dimostrationi harmoniche*, 11: "il Mathematico...dimostra solamente per la cagione formale."

33. See Harold S. Powers, "Language Models and Musical Analysis," *Ethnomusicology* 24 (1980): 49.

of melody and language in much the same way, comparing punctuation marks of varying weight (colon, comma, period) to what we now call melodic cadences.[34] Leading rhetoricians of antiquity, for their part, had encouraged orators to study the principles of music as a means of perfecting their own art. In his *Institutio oratoria*, Quintilian points out the related powers of the voice that sings and the voice that speaks, characterizing music as an art that has the power to excite or soothe human emotions.[35] Cicero, in turn, compares the delivery of the ideal orator to that of the musician. "Every emotion," he says, "has its own facial expression, tone of voice, and gesture." The voice itself is "stretched taut like the strings of an instrument, to re-spond to each and every touch, to sound high, low, fast, slow, loud, and soft," and the orator must be able to draw on a full range of pitches, dynamics, and tone color.[36]

The discipline of rhetoric, which examines the technical means of persuasion through speech, offered musical theorists of the Renaissance a rich source of concepts and terminology that could be applied, *mutatis mutandis*, to music. The recovery and eventual publication of ancient rhetorical treatises in the fifteenth and early sixteenth centuries laid the groundwork for an investigation into the ways in which the human mind and passions could be persuaded—moved—by music as well as by words.[37] In 1599 the German composer and theorist Joachim Burmeister (ca. 1564–1629) reversed the process when he published an anal-ysis of Orlande de Lassus's (1530 or 1532–1594) six-voice motet *In me tran-sierunt* that compared the musical work to an oration.[38] Burmeister describes the form of the motet as consisting of a beginning, middle, and end, a structural template drawn from classical rhetoric. These sections correspond to the nine phrases of the text: the *exordium* and *epilogue* present the first and last, respec-tively, while the *confirmatio* presents the *corpus carminis*, the "body of the song." To demonstrate the musical means by which Lassus enhances the meaning of the words being sung, Burmeister draws on a wide range of rhetorical figures (metalepsis, hypotyposis, hyperbole, etc.) and maps these onto Lassus's motet. Scholars have read the particulars of Burmeister's approach—and for that matter its underlying legitimacy—in different ways, but the important point for present

34. See John, *De musica*, in Palisca, *Hucbald, Guido, and John on Music*, 116–17.
35. Quintilian, *Institutio oratoria*, I.10.22–33.
36. Cicero, *De oratore*, III.216–17, trans. James M. May and Jakob Wise as *On the Ideal Orator* (New York: Oxford University Press, 2001), 292.
37. On the recovery of texts by Aristotle, Cicero, Quintilian, and others, see George A. Kennedy, *Classical Rhetoric and Its Christian and Secular Tradition from Ancient to Modern Times*, 2nd ed. (Chapel Hill: University of North Carolina Press, 1999). See also Blake McDowell Wilson, "*Ut oratoria musica* in the Writings of Renaissance Music Theorists," in *Festa Musicologica: Essays in Honor of George J. Buelow*, ed. Thomas J. Mathiesen and Benito V. Rivera (Stuyvesant, NY: Pendragon Press, 1995), 341–68.
38. Burmeister presented different forms of the same basic analysis in three publications from 1599, 1601, and 1606; the last of these, in his *Musica poetica* (Rostock: S. Myliander), would become the best-known. For a translation of that treatise, see *Musical Poetics*, trans. Benito V. Rivera (New Haven: Yale University Press, 1993). For overviews of musical rhetoric in the Renaissance and baroque, see Claude V. Palisca, "*Ut oratoria musica*: The Rhetorical Basis of Musical Mannerism," in Palisca,

purposes is that his analysis reflects a significant change in thinking about music as a language. Burmeister stops short of explicitly calling music a language in its own right, but his analogical approach, applying the premises and elements of verbal rhetoric systematically to a specific work of music, laid the basic foundation for a metaphor that would become basic to discourse about music, particularly in the eighteenth century (see 000).

The venerable tradition of the poet-musician helped reinforce this view of music as a rhetorical art. Zarlino justified the close connections of words and music on the grounds that in ancient times there had been no essential distinction between poets and musicians, citing as examples not only Orpheus but such diverse figures as Demodocus, Amphion, Terpander, Arion, Hesiod, Pindar, and King David.[39] The reconceptualization of music as an art of rhetoric, as opposed to an art of number, thus revived ancient wisdom and practice in a way that favored Orpheus at the expense of Pythagoras.

This growing concern with issues of practice as opposed to theory can be traced through the increasingly narrow conception of the term "harmony" in writings about music. In his *Discorso ... sopra la musica antica, e 'l cantar bene* (ca. 1578), Giovanni de' Bardi (1534–1612), one of the key participants in the circle that would later come to be known as the Florentine Camerata, acknowledges that "harmony" had long been used as an overarching concept by Pythagoras, and that Plato had maintained that "the world was composed of it." But Bardi enjoins his readers to "come to the concrete" and focus more specifically on harmony as sound, as a "proportion of low, high, and intermediate [pitches] and of words with rhythm."[40]

Bardi's appeal to actual practice captures the growing tendency of his time to give priority to issues of application over issues of theory. And the key question of actual practice for composers of his time—related to Aristotle's and Zarlino's "final cause"—was how to move listeners. The primary goal of the composer thus gradually came into alignment with the goal of the poet and, in performance, the orator. Bardi urged composers to emulate the poet-musicians of antiquity by striving

> above all to arrange the verse well and to make the words comprehensible, not letting yourself be led astray by counterpoint like a poor swimmer who lets himself be carried away by the current, not reaching the other side of the river as he intended.

Studies in the History of Italian Music and Music Theory (Oxford: Clarendon Press, 1994), 282–311; and Patrick McCreless, "Music and Rhetoric," in *The Cambridge History of Western Music Theory,* ed. Thomas Christensen (Cambridge: Cambridge University Press, 2002), 847–79.

39. Zarlino, *Le istitutioni harmoniche,* 67–70 (book 2, chapter 6).

40. Giovanni de' Bardi, *Discorso mandato a Giulio Caccini detto romano sopra la musica antica,* trans. by Claude Palisca as "Discourse Addressed to Giulio Caccini, Called the Roman, on Ancient Music and Good Singing," in Palisca, ed. and trans., *Florentine Camerata,* 93: "Ma venghiamo al particolare ... è adunque l'Armonia proportione di grave, d'acuto, e di mezano; e di parole con ritmo."

Keeping in mind that just as the soul is nobler than the body, so the text is nobler than the counterpoint, and just as the mind should rule the body, so the counterpoint should receive its rule from the text. Would it not seem to you comical if, while in the square, you saw a servant followed by and commanding his master, or a child giving instruction to his parent or teacher?[41]

Bardi's comparison of words to the soul and counterpoint to the body reflects nothing less than an aesthetic revolution. Until this moment, number (audible as sounding music, in this instance as counterpoint) had always been assumed to hold the upper hand on the basis of its immutability: it was the ideal of which sounding music was simply one perceptible manifestation. Bardi, however, wastes little time on the essence of music or any ideal behind it; his principal concern is with music's actual practice and realization. He does not dispute the importance of harmony as a concept that orders the cosmos, but he calls attention to the fact that he intends to treat harmony strictly as sound.

Vincenzo Galilei, a protégé of Bardi's, argued along much the same lines a few years later, maintaining that the differing effects of "ancient" and "modern" music revolve around the issue of textual intelligibility.[42] Galilei has "Bardi," the principal interlocutor of the dialogue, observe that the shortcomings of modern music lie in its failure to emulate rhetorical practices of ancient times and deliver its verbal content in a clear and moving manner: Galilei cites on his behalf Isocrates and Corax, two prominent rhetoricians of ancient Greece. While modern music's sole aim is "to delight the hearing," that of ancient music was "to lead others by its means into the same affection as one felt oneself."[43] The "rules of modern contrapuntists, observed as inviolable laws"—Galilei almost certainly has Zarlino, his erstwhile teacher, in mind here—"are all directly contrary to the perfection of the optimal and true melodies and songs." For "contrapuntists in our time" use "artful mannerisms" (*maniere d'artificio*) that are "not

---

41. Bardi, *Discorso…sopra la musica antica*, trans. Palisca, 115: "Però componendo sopra tutto v'ingegnerete che il verso ben regolato, e la parola quanto più si possa ben intesa sia, no lasciando traviarvi dal contrapunto quasi cattivo notatore che dalla corrente trasportar si lasci, ne arrivi oltre al fiume, la ove eglli proposto s'haveva, tenendo per costante che così come l'anima del corpo è più nobile, altresì le parole più nobili del contrapunto sono, e come il corpo dall'anima regolato esser debbe, così il contrapunto dalle parole dee prender norma: Hor no vi parebbe egli cosa ridicola s'andando in piazza vedeste 'l servo del suo Signore esser seguito, e ad esso commandare: o fanciullo che al Padre, o pedagogo suo ammaestramento dar volesse?"

42. Vincezo Galilei, *Dialogo della musica antica, et della moderna* (Florence: Giorgio Mareschotti, 1581). Palisca called Galilei's text "surely the most influential music treatise of the late sixteenth century"; see his edition and translation, *Dialogue on Ancient and Modern Music* (New Haven: Yale University Press, 2003), xvii; Karol Berger, in turn ("Concepts and Developments in Music Theory," 311), calls the treatise "the Camerata's main theoretical statement."

43. Galilei, *Dialogo*, 89: "non altro il fine di questo che il diletto dell'udito, & di quella il condurre altrui per quel mezzo nella medesima affettione di se stesso." Translation from *Dialogue*, 224.

only of supreme hindrance but the worst poison to the expression of ideas and to impressing affections on the listener."[44]

In Galilei's dialogue, "Bardi" points out that contrapuntal rules do nothing more than "make the harmony varied and full," and this "does not always—rather never—suit the expression of any conceit of a poet or orator." He proposes an original but scarcely credible thesis that these rules of counterpoint had originally been developed in ancient times for "the simple sound of artificial wind and stringed instruments" and not for the projection of a text and its attendant ideas.[45] Dubious as "Bardi's" theory may be, it exposes another conceptual divide that would grow over time: the unequal expressive capacities of instrumental and vocal music.

By the end of the sixteenth century writers no longer felt it sufficient merely to repeat ancient accounts about the miraculous effects of music: they now sought to identify the means by which such effects might actually have been realized. Some, like Nicola Vicentino, experimented with extreme chromaticism in an attempt to recreate the chromatic and enharmonic genera of ancient Greek music. These efforts were no mere essays in antiquarianism but rather, as Karol Berger has argued, part of a broader attempt to increase the emotional expressivity of music.[46] In the years around 1600, however, the general consensus was that the miraculous powers of ancient Greek music lay in its ability to enhance the meaning and affect of a sung text. The new genre that would later come to be known as opera was the product of an attempt to recreate the performance and effect of ancient Greek drama. This demanded a new approach to the setting of texts, one that would accommodate solo singing (one singer portraying a single character on stage), which in turn would allow the text being sung to be understood by listeners instead of getting lost in a thicket of contrapuntal voices. Composers and singers were eager to demonstrate the potential of this new style in staged dramatic performances, and the role of Orpheus proved the ideal vehicle for this. The mythic musician figures prominently in several of these early staged works: Jacopo Peri's *Euridice* (1600), Giulio Caccini's *Euridice* (1602), and most famously Monteverdi's *L'Orfeo* (1607).[47] In the preface to his *Le nuove musiche* of 1602, a collection of homophonic songs, Caccini (1551–1618)

44. Galilei, *Dialogo*, 81; 87: "l'un & l'altre delle qalli, all'espressione de concetti per imprimer gli affetti nell'uditore, non solo sono di sommo impedimento, ma pessimo veleno." Translations from *Dialogue*, 201, 216–17.

45. Galilei, *Dialogo*, 85: "Imperò che elle sono atte non ad altro, che à fare il concento vario & pieno, la qual cosa non sempre anzi mai, conviene all'espressione di qual sia concetto de Poeta & dell'Oratore." Ibid., "per il semplice suono degli artifitiali strumenti & di fiato & di corde." Translations from *Dialogue*, 212.

46. Karol Berger, *Theories of Chromatic and Enharmonic Music in Late 16th-Century Italy* (Ann Arbor, MI: UMI Research Press, 1980), 121.

47. F. W. Sternfeld, *The Birth of Opera* (Oxford: Clarendon Press, 1993), 2, provides a table showing more than twenty productions with music (including ballets and masques) between 1599 and 1698

proudly drew attention to his participation in Bardi's Camerata and thanked "the most knowledgeable gentlemen" of that group for convincing him

> with the most lucid reasoning… not to esteem that sort of music which, preventing any clear understanding of the words, shatters both their form and their content, … but rather to conform to that manner so lauded by Plato and other philosophers (who declared that music is naught but speech, with rhythm and tone coming after; not vice versa) with the aim that it enter into the minds of men and have those wonderful effects admired by the great writers.[48]

In the postface to his *Fifth Book of Madrigals* (1605), Monteverdi similarly emphasized the role of reason in this "modern manner of composition" and promised to deliver a defense of it in a way that would satisfy reason and sense. He never followed through on this, but the direction of his thought is clear enough. Language—the texts Artusi had suppressed in criticizing Monteverdi's treatment of dissonance—provided the bridge that could connect the mind with the ear. What for so long had been ignored in most accounts of Orpheus's deeds—the words he sang—was now the key to explaining the miraculous effects of his music.

■ MUSIC AS LANGUAGE

The centrality of language in the new ideal of musical expression did nothing to enhance the prestige of instrumental music, which continued to be regarded as inferior in kind to vocal music. Vincenzo Galilei, for one, belittled the artificial nature of instruments and the music they produced:

> The goal of modern practitioners is… to delight the sense of hearing with the variety of consonances, if this capacity to tickle the ear, which cannot truly be called delight, can reside in a simple piece of concave wood over which are strung four, six, or more strings from the gut of one brutish animal or other, disposed according to the nature of harmonic numbers, or in a similar number of natural reeds or pipes artificially made of wood, metal, or other material, divided in proportionate and suitable sizes in which little spirals of air circulate when they are touched or struck by a coarse and

---

on the legend of Orpheus. For an even more extensive listing, see Reinhard Kapp, "Orpheus Settings," in *Talismane: Festschrift Klaus Heinrich zum 70. Geburtstag*, ed. Sigrun Anselm and Caroline Neubaur (Basel: Stroemfeld, 1998), 425–57.

48. Giulio Caccini, preface ("Ai lettori") to his *Le nuove musiche* (Venice: I Marescotti, 1602): "Questi intendissimi gentilhuomini m'hanno sempre confortato, e con chiarissime ragioni convinto à non pregiare quella sorte di musica, che non lasciando bene intendersi le parole, guasta il concetto, et il verso … ma ad attenermi à quella maniera cotanto lodata da Platone, et altri Filosofi, che affermarono la musica altro non essere che la favella, e 'l rithmo, et il suono per ultimo, e non per il contrario, à volere, che ella possa penetrare nell'altrui intelletto, e fare quei mirabili effetti, che ammirano gli Scrittori." Translation by H. Wiley Hitchcock from his edition of *Le nuove musiche*, 2nd ed. (Madison, WI: A-R Editions, 2009), 3.

unschooled hand of some vile idiot. Leave to such instruments this goal of delighting with the variety of their chords, since, devoid of sense, motion, intellect, speech, discourse, reason, and soul, they are incapable of anything more. But humans, who have been endowed by nature with all their beautiful, noble, and excellent parts, seek with their means not only to delight, but, as imitators of the good ancients, also to benefit, because they are fit to do this and if they did otherwise they would be acting against nature and the ministry of God.[49]

Such misgivings about the ethics of instrumental music stretch back to antiquity. In the middle of a lengthy discussion about music in Plato's *Laws*, one of the interlocutors points out that when music is performed "by stringed instruments and pipes on their own without singers," it becomes "extraordinarily difficult to know what the rhythm and harmony without speech are supposed to signify and what worthwhile object they imitate and represent. The conclusion is inevitable: such practices appeal to the taste of the village idiot."[50] The early church, for its part, was deeply ambivalent about instrumental music. Although sanctioned in many biblical passages, particularly the Psalms, it provoked suspicion in many quarters on the grounds that it could arouse pleasure without necessarily uplifting the soul. Saint Jerome (ca. 347–420), in his letter on the education of a Christian girl, assured her that she need know nothing of instruments or their music.[51] Much later but along similar lines, Thomas Aquinas, who approved of singing in sacred services, deemed musical instruments inappropriate on the grounds that they "usually move the soul to pleasure rather than create a good disposition in it."[52]

Those who defended instrumental music could not argue for its equality with vocal music; at best, they could argue for its similarity. In his *Fontegara* (1535), a manual aimed at amateurs who wanted to learn how to play the recorder,

---

49. Galileo, *Dialogo*, 86: "che se il fine de moderni parttici è … il dilettare con la diversità delle consonanze il senso dell'udito, & se tal proprietà di solleticarlo, che si può ne anco con verità chiamare diletto altramente, l'ha un semplice pezzo di legno concavo, sopra il quale siano tese quattro, sei, ò piu corde d'intestini di bruto animale ò d'altro; disposte secondo la natura degli harmonici numeri; overamente una tal quantità di canne naturali, ò pure artifitiosamente fatte di legno, di metallo, ò d'altro; divise in proportionate & convenienti misure, dentro le quali spiri qualche poco d'aria, mentre che elle sono poscia tocche & percosse da rozza & indotta mano di qual si voglia vile & idiota huomo; lascisi questo fine del dilettare con la diversità de loro accordi ad essi strumenti; perche sendo privi di senso, di moto, d'intelletto, di parlare, di discorso, di ragione, & d'anima; non sono di piu oltre capaci: ma gli huomini che sono dalla natura stati dotati di tutte queste bellé nobili, & eccellenti parti, cerchino col mezzo di esse non solo di dilettare, ma come imitatori de buoni antichi, di giovare insieme, poiche acciò sono atti; perche altramente facendo, fanno contro la natura, che è ministra di Dio." Translation from Galilei, *Dialogue*, 215. See also Berger, "Concepts and Developments in Music Theory," 312–13.

50. Plato, *Laws*, 670, trans. Trevor J. Saunders, in Plato, *Complete Works*, ed. Cooper, 1360.

51. See Kathi Meyer-Baer, *Music of the Spheres and the Dance of Death: Studies in Musical Iconology* (Princeton: Princeton University Press, 1970), 272–73.

52. Thomas Aquinas, *The Summa Theologica*, trans. Fathers of the English Dominican Province, 22 vols. (New York: Benziger Brothers, 1920-25), 12:166 (Question 91, Article 2).

Silvestro di Ganassi urged instrumentalists to imitate the voice and offered specific advice about how to achieve this effect by varying the pressure of breath and by shaping the tone through subtleties of fingering. Skilled instrumentalists, he has heard it said, can cause listeners to "perceive words to their music, so that one might well say that with this instrument only the form of the human body is absent, just as one says of a fine painting that only breath is lacking."[53]

On the whole, however, Ganassi's contemporaries were reluctant to address the expressive qualities of a repertory unconnected to language, in part because it was still too easy for them to fall back on traditional theories of number. The controversies around the *seconda pratica* in the early seventeenth century, in turn, centered on the treatment of texts more than issues of style per se: the words to be set could be used to justify almost any style, old or new. In the case of music written expressly and exclusively for instruments, there was no text to justify (or prohibit) melodic motion or part-writing that did not follow conventional procedures. Once monody, recitative, and the basso continuo had become standard features in the early decades of the seventeenth century, the theoretical underpinnings of the *seconda pratica* dried up quickly: the treatise promised by Monteverdi in his *Fifth Book of Madrigals* (and again in his brother's gloss on that statement two years later) never materialized. By the 1620s, in any case, the debate about old and new styles had largely played itself out.[54] Still, the paucity of aesthetic commentary on instrumental music around this time remains puzzling, particularly in light of the enormous upsurge of music written and published specifically for instruments alone. The style of writing for instruments was becoming increasingly idiomatic, and there was clearly a market for this repertory.[55]

And here, in the minds of at least some commentators, the absence of words could actually work to the benefit of instrumental music. Though his father had complained about the artificial nature of instruments, Galileo Galilei (1564–1642) marveled at their ability to convey and arouse the passions precisely because of their artificiality. In a private letter of 1612, he pointed out that sculpture approximates the objects it portrays more closely than painting by virtue of its three-dimensionality. But this is not necessarily to the credit of that art, for

53. Silvestro Ganassi, *Opera intitolata Fontegara* (Venice: n.p., 1535; reprint, Bologna: Forni, 1969), unnumbered page in chapter 1: "& audito da altri sonatori farsi intendere con il suo sonar le parole di essa cosa che si poteva ben dire a quello instrumento non mancarli altro che la forma dil corpo humano si come si dice ala pintura ben fatta non mancarli solum il fiato."

54. See Andrew Dell'Antonio, *Syntax, Form and Genre in Sonatas and Canzonas, 1621–35* (Lucca: Libreria Musicale Italiana, 1997), 291–93.

55. One revealing index of the marked increase in the publication of instrumental music around this time is the inventory in Warwick Edwards, "Sources of Instrumental Ensemble Music," in *The New Grove Dictionary of Music and Musicians*, 2nd ed., ed. Stanley Sadie (London and New York: Macmillan, 2001), which stops at 1630.

the farther removed the means by which one imitates are from the thing to be imitated, the more worthy of wonder the imitation will be. In ancient times those actors who could tell a whole story exclusively by means of movements and gestures were more highly appreciated than those who expressed it *viva voce* in tragedy or comedy, because the former used a means very different and a mode of representation quite divergent from the actions represented. Will we not admire a musician who moves us to sympathy with a lover by representing his sorrows and passions in song much more than if he were to do it by sobs? And this we do because song is a medium not only different from but opposite to the [natural] expression of pain while tears and sobs are very similar to it. And we would admire him even much more if he were to do it silently [*sic*], with an instrument only, by means of dissonances and passionate musical accents; for the inanimate strings are [of themselves] less capable of awakening the hidden passions of our soul than is the voice that narrates them.[56]

Although very much in the minority in his own day on this point (as on others), Galileo hints here at an attitude that would become more common over time. The ability of instrumental music to suggest rather than to state would eventually become a cornerstone of early romantic aesthetics. And even in the seventeenth century we can detect indirect signs of this outlook in practice. It is no coincidence, as Andrew dell'Antonio points out, "that the most ineffable moment of the Mass, the Elevation, was accompanied in the Italian *seicento* not by a motet but by an instrumental toccata or sonata."[57]

The idea that instrumental music was by its very nature inferior to vocal music would nevertheless remain the standard view until the beginning of the nineteenth century; only at that point did any significant number of critics and philosophers begin to entertain the notion that instrumental music's freedom from the constraints of language and representation might actually make it a superior mode of expression. In the meantime, instrumental music moved to the forefront of the debate about the essence of the art, aided by the new conception that music—and now for the first time in the specific sense of instrumental music—constituted a

56. Galileo Galilei, lettter of 26 June 1612 to Lodovico Cigoli, in Erwin Panofsky, *Galileo as a Critic of the Arts* (The Hague: Nijhoff, 1954), 33–34: "perciocchè quanto più i mezzi, co' quali si imita, son lontani dalle cose da imitarsi, tanto più l'imitazione è maravigliosa. Era anticamente molto più stimata quella sorta d'istrioni che co' movimenti soli e co' cenni sapevano recitare una intera storia o favola, che quelli che con la viva voce l'esprimevano in tragedia o in commedia, per usar quelli un mezzo diversissimo et un modo di rappresentare in tutto differente dalle azioni rappresentate. Non ammireremmo noi un musico, il quale cantando e rappresentandoci le querele e le passioni d'un amante ci muovesse a compassionarlo, molto più che se piangendo ciò facesse? e questo, per essere il canto un mezzo non solo diverso, ma contrario ad esprimere i dolori, e la lagrime et il pianto similissimo. E molto più l'ammireremmo, se tacendo, col solo strumento, con crudezze et accenti patetici musicali, ciò facesse, per esser le inanimate corde meno atte a risvegliare gli affetti occulti dell'anima nostra, che la voce raccontandole." The translation is from Panofsky, *Galileo as Critic of the Arts*, 36–37.

57. Dell'Antonio, *Syntax, Form and Genre*, 301.

language in its own right, a language capable of giving voice to emotions in ways that conventional language could not.

This new way of thinking about music as the "language of the heart" or "the language of feelings" was made possible by shifting attitudes not only toward music but toward language itself. The key concept in this debate was the distinction between universal and arbitrary signs.[58] The connections between most words and the ideas or objects they indicated were considered arbitrary: the word for "dog," for example, varied widely from language to language (*chien* in French, *Hund* in German, etc.). Nonverbal sounds indicating emotions, on the other hand, were more natural, less variable, and therefore universal.[59] As early as 1629, René Descartes had made this case in a letter to the Jesuit polymath Marin Mersenne, arguing that the inarticulate utterances of the passions transcended the differences among various verbal languages and thus constituted a universal language of their own. This led Mersenne to conclude that the closest approximation of a "natural" language was to be found in music, which operates independently of words.[60] Reversing the admonitions of Cicero and Quintilian, Mersenne urged musicians to learn "the art of the harmonic orator, who must know all the degrees, rhythms, movements, and proper accents to excite everything he wishes in his audiences." Composers, in turn, should "imitate harangues in all their phrases, divisions, and periods, and use all kinds of figures and harmonic embellishments, as does the orator, so that the art of composing melodies will concede nothing to rhetoric."[61] But Mersenne stopped short of calling music a language in its own right and ultimately fell back on the more conventional definition of song as "nothing more than a discourse embellished and elevated by an

---

58. For a concise overview of this debate, see Nicholas Hudson, "Theories of Language," in *The Cambridge History of Literary Criticism*, vol. 4, *The Eighteenth Century*, ed. H. B. Nisbet and Claude Rawson (Cambridge: Cambridge University Press, 1997), 335–48. See also Downing A. Thomas, *Music and the Origins of Language: Theories from the French Enlightenment* (Cambridge: Cambridge University Press, 1995); and Andrew Bowie, *Music, Philosophy, and Modernity* (Cambridge: Cambridge University Press, 2007), chapter 2, "Music, Language, and the Origins of Modernity."

59. See, for example, Moses Mendelssohn, "Über die Hauptgrundsätze der schönen Künste und Wissenschaften" (1757), in Mendelssohn, *Schriften zur Philosophie, Aesthetik und Apologetik*, 2 vols., ed. Moritz Brasch (Leipzig: Leopold Voss, 1880), 2:163; and Johann Jakob Engel, *Ueber die musikalische Malerey* (Berlin: Christian Friedrich Voss und Sohn, 1780), 6–7.

60. Marin Mersenne, *Harmonie universelle, contenant la théorie et la pratique de la musique*, 3 vols. (Paris, 1636–37; reprint, Paris: CNRS, 1963), 2:12–13, 69–70. See Dean T. Mace, "Marin Mersenne on Music and Language," *JMT* 14 (1970): 15.

61. Mersenne, *Harmonie universelle*, 2:365: "qui doivent en quelque façon imiter les Harangues, afin d'avoir des membres, des parties, & des periodes, & d'user de toutes sortes de figures & de passages harmoniques, comme l'Orateur & que l'Art de composer des Airs, & le Contrepoint ne cede rien à la Retorique." Translation by David Allen Duncan, "Persuading the Affections: Rhetorical Theory and Mersenne's Advice to Harmonic Orators," in *French Musical Thought, 1600–1800*, ed. Georgia Cowart (Ann Arbor, MI: UMI Research Press, 1989), 153. See also Penelope Gouk, "Music and the Sciences," in *The Cambridge History of Seventeenth-Century Music*, ed. Tim Carter and John Butt (Cambridge: Cambridge University Press, 2005), 145.

excellent harmony." For Mersenne, language remained the dominant force in music, in spite of his concern with both the emotional and mathematical side of the art.

Subsequent writers—most notably John Locke (1632–1704), Giambattista Vico (1668–1744), Jean-Baptiste Dubos (1670–1742), Jean-Jacques Rousseau (1712–1778), Étienne Bonnot de Condillac (1715–1780), Moses Mendelssohn (1729–1786), and Michel Paul Gui de Chabanon (1730–1792)—developed the idea of music as a language in various ways. In his influential *Réflexions critiques sur la poésie et sur la peinture* of 1719, Dubos argued that the musician imitates "the tones, the accents, the sighs, the inflections of the voice, in short, any sound that nature herself uses to express its sentiments and passions." Music's sounds are thus "the signifiers of passion, instituted by nature, from which they receive their energy, in place of articulate words, which are the arbitrary signifiers of passion." Words take their sense from human institutions and are not universally comprehensible.[62] Rousseau emphasized the differences between spoken and written language, insisting that ideas were best expressed in writing, feelings in the act of speech:

> In writing, one is forced to use all the words according to their conventional meaning. But in speaking, one varies the meanings by varying one's tone of voice, determining them as one pleases. Being less constrained to clarity, one can be more forceful.... To say everything as one would write it would be merely to read aloud.[63]

Like Vico before him, Rousseau saw speech as having descended from song, the primordial source of all audible expression. Music was the original human language, capable of expressing assent, disagreement, tenderness, anger, and many other emotions, all without words. In humankind's fall from grace, verbal language had replaced these preverbal, "musical" sounds with a system that was more refined yet also less immediate. This original music, although "inarticulate," to use Rousseau's term, was "vivid, ardent, passionate" and had "a hundred

---

62. Jean Baptise Dubos, *Réflexions critiques sur la poésie et sur la peinture*, 2 vols. (Paris: Jean Mariette, 1719), 1:634–35: "Le Musicien imite les tons, les accens, les soûpirs, les infléxions de voix, enfin tous ces sons, à l'aide desquels la nature même exprime ses sentimens & ses passions. Tous ces sons, comme nous l'avons déja exposé, ont une force merveilleuse pour nous émouvoir, parce qu'ils sont les signes des passions, instituez par la nature dont ils ont reçû leur énergie, au lieu que les mots articulez ne sont que des signes arbitraires des passions. Les mots articulez ne tirent leur signification & leur valeur que de l'institution des hommes qui n'ont pû leur donner cours que dans un certain pays."

63. Jean-Jacques Rousseau, *Essai sur l'origine des langues*, ed. Jean Starobinski (Paris: Gallimard, 1990), 79: "En écrivant on est forcé de prendre tous les mots dans l'acception commune; mais celui qui parle varie les acceptions par les tons, il les détermine comme il lui plait; moins gêné pour être clair, il donne plus à la force ... En disant tout comme on l'écriroit on ne fait plus que lire en parlant." Translation from Jean-Jacques Rousseau, *Essay on the Origin of Language*, trans. John H. Moran, in *On the Origin of Language*, ed. John H. Moran and Alexander Gode (New York: Frederick Ungar, 1966), 21–22. The *Essai* was not published until 1781, three years after Rousseau's death, and it is unclear when Rousseau wrote it; see Thomas, *Music and the Origins of Language*, 83–86.

times more energy than speech itself." What language gained in precision over time, it lost in expressivity.[64]

Rousseau's most revealing comments about instrumental music appear, oddly enough, in the entry "Opera" in his *Dictionnaire de musique* (1768). At some unspecified point fairly early in the history of the genre, he says, composers began to realize that music, independent of any text, "was not indifferent to that which they had to say" and that "the effect of melody alone" could go "directly to the heart," surpassing even the capacity of words, which often conveyed these ideas "badly." Melody, separated from its text "by necessity," assumed for itself "beauties" that were "absolute and purely musical." Harmony "discovered or perfected new paths to please and move" listeners, and rhythm, "freed from the constraint of poetic meter," could develop on its own, unbound to anything but itself. Music thus became its own language, independent of poetry: "The symphony itself acquired the ability to speak without words and often projected sentiments from the orchestra that were no less vital than those that came out of the mouths of the actors."[65]

Johann Georg Sulzer's entry "Gesang" (in the sense of "melody" rather than "song") in his *Allgemeine Theorie der schönen Künste* (1771–74) summarizes the late eighteenth century's conventional wisdom on this point succinctly:

> The tones of speech are designative tones that originally served to awaken a mental image of things that sound like them or like something similar to them. Now they are mostly indifferent tones or arbitrary signs. Passionate tones are natural signs of the sentiments. A succession of indifferent tones characterizes speech, and a succession of passionate tones characterizes melody.[66]

---

64. See Thomas, *Music and the Origins of Language*; Gary Tomlinson, "Vico's Songs: Detours at the Origins of (Ethno)musicology," *MQ* 83 (1999): 344–77.

65. Jean-Jacques Rousseau. "Opéra," in *Dictionnaire de musique* (Paris: Veuve Duchesne, 1768), 343–44: "Bientôt on commença de sentir qu'indépendamment de la déclamation musicale, que souvent la Langue comportoit mal, le choix du Mouvement, de l'Harmonie & des Chants n'étoit pas indifférent aux choses qu'on avoit à dire, & que, par conséquent, l'effet de la seule Musique borné jusqu'alors au sens, pouvoit aller jusqu'au cœur. La Mélodie, qui ne s'étoit d'abord séparée de la Poésie que par nécessité, tira parti de cette indépendance pour se donner des beautés absolues & purement musicales: l'Harmonie découverte ou perfectionnée lui ouvrit de nouvelles routes pour plaire & pour émouvoir; & la Mesure, affranchie de la gêne du Rhythme poétique, acquit aussi une sorte de cadence à part, qu'elle ne tenoit que d'elle seule.

"La Musique … eut bien-tôt son langage, son expression, ses tableaux, tout-à-fait indépendans de la Poésie. La Symphonie même apprit à parler sans le secours des paroles, & souvent il ne sortoit pas des sentimens moins vifs de l'Orchestre que de la bouche des Acteurs." Rousseau uses *symphonie* here in the sense of any piece for an instrumental ensemble.

66. Johann Georg Sulzer, "Gesang," in Sulzer, *Allgemeine Theorie der schönen Künste*, 2 vols. (Leipzig: M. G. Weidemanns Erben & Reich, 1771–74), 1:460: "Die Töne der Rede sind zeichnende Töne, die ursprünglich dienten, Vorstellungen von Dingen zu erwe[c]ken, die solche oder ähnliche Töne hören lassen. Itzt sind sie meistens gleichgültige Töne, oder willkührliche Zeichen: die leidenschaftlichen Töne sind natürliche Zeichen der Empfindungen. Eine Folge gleichgültiger Töne

Critics thus came to perceive instrumental music's inarticulateness as both its strength and its weakness: its emotional power was what made it rationally inadequate, and its rational shortcomings were what made it emotionally powerful. The parallels with oratory are instructive once again. The precepts of rhetoric dictated that a speaker appeal to both the reason *and* the emotions of an audience. The duty of an orator, as laid down by such authorities as Quintilian and Cicero and repeated endlessly in manuals of rhetoric, is to inform, please, and move listeners, to which Cicero adds that while instruction is a duty and pleasure a gift (*honorarium*) to the audience, moving that audience is a necessity.[67] In oratory, however, moving the passions was a means to a higher end— to lead, to teach, to inform—and not an end in its own right. In vocal music, this higher end was self-evident in the text being sung; the question for instrumental music was whether it could do more than simply move the passions. When the assumed superiority of language came under question toward the end of the eighteenth century, at least some critics would propose that it was in fact instrumental music that could best serve as an organon of truth, a vehicle of disclosure (see chapter 7). For the moment, however, instrumental music had achieved a toehold within the realm of language, broadly conceived, which in turn contributed greatly to its eventual acceptance as an autonomous art (see chapter 6).

As in earlier times, music's emotional power was considered something best experienced in moderation. Moving the passions simply for the sake of moving the passions was not always considered a good or terribly sophisticated thing. Chabanon, for example, noted in 1785 that the elemental and natural force of music could be readily demonstrated by observing its powers over animals, babies, and "savages."[68] These effects, he observed, derived from instinct, not thought. And though the English critic Daniel Webb (1718 or -19–1798) accorded a greater power of expression to music than to language, he seems distressed to have arrived at this conclusion:

> Now, though the imitations of verse may be applied to the purposes either of expression or of description, it is not the same thing with regard to music, the effects of which are so exquisite, so fitted by nature to move the passions, that we feel ourselves

bezeichnet die Rede, und eine Folge leidenschaftlicher Töne, den Gesang." For a different translation, see Nancy K. Baker and Thomas Christensen, eds. and trans., *Aesthetics and the Art of Musical Composition in the German Enlightenment: Selected Writings of Johann Georg Sulzer and Heinrich Christoph Koch* (Cambridge: Cambridge University Press, 1995), 93.

67. Cicero, *De optimo genere oratorum*, I, 3–4, ed. and trans. H. M. Hubbell (Cambridge, MA: Harvard University Press, 1949), 356: "Optimus est enim orator qui dicendo animos audientium et docet et delectat et permovet. Docere debitum est, delectare honorarium, permovere necessarium."

68. Michel Gui de Chabanon, *De la musique considérée en elle-même et dans ses rapports avec la parole, les langues, la poésie, et le théâtre* (Paris: Pissot, 1785), 45–46.

hurt and disappointed, when forced to reconcile our sensations to a simple and unaffecting coincidence of sound or motion.[69]

Webb's dismay at the discrepancy of cause ("a simple ... coincidence of sound or motion") and effect ("exquisite") epitomizes the struggles of Enlightenment thought to reconcile the power of music with its essence, its pleasures with its apparent lack of conceptual content.

In the midst of all this theorizing about the relationship of words and music, thought and emotion, the composer and critic Johann Mattheson (1681–1764) addressed the expressive capacities of instrumental music on a more technical level, proposing that music was a language with its own syntax and semantics. He conceded that numbers reflect the proportions of its intervals but vehemently rejected any suggestion that they constituted its essence. He insisted that he was not so foolish as to mistake the form of a thing for its essence, its bones for its flesh.[70] He scoffed at the presumption of mathematics as anything more than an auxiliary branch of knowledge, a handmaiden to other disciplines: "Throw out the maid (mathematics), along with her son (number)," he implored, "for calculation is our servant!"[71] Simply because music makes use of mathematics, he argued, does not mean that it is beholden to it, any more than a king is beholden to those who have mined the gold that goes into his crown. In and of themselves, sounds "are neither good nor bad, but they become good or bad according to how they are used," and these distinctions of usage are not to be found in the arts of measurement or counting. Number theory is to musical practice as a nautical chart is to an actual voyage of a ship: on a chart one can measure everything with compass and rule, whereas at sea there are many unexpected turns, rocks, and irregular winds, against all of which "more is required than contemplation." Addressing mathematics as if it were a person and resorting to neologism, Mattheson declares that "you, my pious man, with your large mathematicoterie, are certainly no longer the hero you perhaps were under the reign of Pythagoras!"[72]

Mattheson's vitriol reflects the enduring force of Pythagorean thought in the eighteenth century. He regrets that "repugnant, foolish, tasteless" mathematical doctrines have persisted down to the present and have not yet been

69. Daniel Webb, *Observations on the Correspondence between Poetry and Music* (London: J. Dodsley, 1769), 139–40.

70. Johann Mattheson, *Der vollkommene Capellmeister* (Hamburg: Herold, 1739), preface (*Vorrede*), section 6 ("Von der musikalischen Mathematik"), 16–22, 19.

71. Johann Mattheson, *Das forschende Orchestre* (Hamburg: Schillers Wittwe, 1721), 253: "Stoß die Magd (Mathematicam) hinaus mit ihrem Sohn (Numerum). Denn Rechen-Kunst ist (per anagramma) Unser Knecht!" Mattheson uses *Rechen-Kunst* (calculation) as an anagram for *unser Knecht* (our servant).

72. Mattheson, *Das forschende Orchestre*, 253, 277: "Derowegen, mein frommer Mann, numerosissime domine Mathematicotere, du bist lange der Held nicht mehr, der du in der Pythagorischen Regierung hättest seyn können!"

expunged from the teaching of harmony, a term he uses only in its specifically musical sense as it concerns the consonance or dissonance of sounding intervals.[73] Mattheson grants no metaphysical import to what the monochord can demonstrate, pointing out that the instrument is incapable of revealing "a single musical truth" and only "a few... of middling significance" as far as harmony is concerned.[74] Musicians sympathetic to Pythagorean ideals, in the end, are nothing more than "simplistic, uncultivated, cold, senseless *Harmonici*" who do not understand their true craft.[75]

Mattheson defines music not as an object but as a practice, the "science and art of setting out adroit and pleasing sounds wisely, joining them correctly, and presenting them delightfully, so that through their euphony God's honor and all virtues might be promoted." This definition, he notes, encompasses "the material, the form, and the final cause of our entire system of music."[76] He gives a brief nod toward the concepts of *musica mundana* (*Welt-Music*) and *musica humana* (*Mensch-Music*) but announces that his treatise will be about *Werck-Music*—literally, "work music"—his term for the kind of music perceived through the sense of hearing, "for there is nothing in the mind that did not enter it earlier by means of the senses."[77]

Expression is everything: "All that occurs [in music] without praiseworthy affects says nothing, does nothing, is good for nothing."[78] Sounds (*Klänge*) are to music what words are to speech (*Rede*), and song is a *Klang-Rede*, an "oration in musical sound" in which the music elevates the sense and affect of the words being sung. An instrumental melody, as he points out, "can dispense with actual words but not with moving the psyche."[79] For a composer of vocal music, the affect or passion (*Leidenschaft*) is given in advance by the poet; a composer of instrumental music has the more challenging task of imagining the specific affect

73. Mattheson, *Das forschende Orchestre*, 347. The terms Mattheson uses are *garstig, närrisch,* and *abgeschmackt.*

74. Mattheson, *Der vollkommene Capellmeister*, preface (*Vorrede*), 17: "Das liebe Monochord vermag keine einzige musikalische Wahrheit darzuthun; wo[h]l aber einige harmonikalische von mittelmäßiger Wichtigkeit."

75. Mattheson, *Das forschende Orchestre*, 349: "einfältige, ungeschickte, kahle, Sinn-lose *Harmonici*."

76. Mattheson, *Der vollkommene Capellmeister*, 5: "Musica ist eine Wissenschafft und Kunst, geschickte und angenehme Klänge klüglich zu stellen, richtig an einander zu fügen, und lieblich heraus zu bringen, damit durch ihren Wo[h]llaut Gottes Ehre und alle Tugenden befördert werden. In diesen Worten zeigen sich die Materie, die Form und der Endzweck unsrer gantzen Ton-Lehre."

77. Mattheson, *Der vollkommene Capellmeister*, 6: "Denn es ist gar nichts im Verstande, was nicht vorher in die Sinne gefallen ist." On the Aristotelian origin and long history of this formulation, see Paul F. Cranefield, "On the Origin of the Phrase 'Nihil est in intellectu quod non prius fuerit in sensu,'" *Journal of the History of Medicine and Allied Sciences* 25 (1970): 77–80.

78. Mattheson, *Der vollkommene Capellmeister*, 146: " Alles was ohne löbliche Affecten geschiehet, heißt nichts, thut nichts, gilt nichts."

79. Mattheson, *Der vollkommene Capellmeister*, 207: "daß die Spiel-Melodie zwar der eigentlichen Worte, aber nicht der Gemüthsbewegung entbehren kan[n]." On the term *Gemüt*, see p. 150–51.

to be represented and expressing it through music without the aid of an external stimulus.[80]

Mattheson's analysis of an aria by Benedetto Marcello (1686–1739) is particularly revealing in this regard, for he ignores the text altogether.[81] In breaking down this aria into its component parts, he applies many of the rhetorical terms and concepts that were now being associated more and more with music: invention, disposition, elaboration, decoration, sentence, and theme. Mattheson maps the six parts of a classical oration onto the music (*exordium, narratio, propositio,* etc.) in an attempt to show the parallels between the structure of a verbal and musical "oration."[82] His failure to give even so much as a textual incipit is no mere oversight, for the purpose of his analysis is to demonstrate the ways in which the musical elements of the aria function in relation to one another, not in relation to any text. In a way, then, his account represents the first attempt to analyze what amounts to a work of instrumental music. This kind of analysis had no doubt occurred before in private lessons as part of the oral tradition by which the craft of composition was passed down from master to pupil, but Mattheson's account marks the first time such an approach found its way into print. By tracing each successive transformation of the principal musical idea—its *Spiel-Melodie* (instrumental melody), as he calls it elsewhere—Mattheson shows aspiring composers how to construct a movement of music from the ground up, using the metaphor of the oration as a conceptual framework for the presentation of ideas that are exclusively musical.

The image of music as a language plays a central role in the writings of such distinguished figures from the second half of the eighteenth century as Johann Joachim Quantz (1697–1773), Carl Philipp Emanuel Bach (1714–1788), and Johann Nicolaus Forkel (1749–1818).[83] But the metaphor of language suggests at least some degree of semantic content, and the task of deciphering music's meaning would remain a challenge throughout the eighteenth century and beyond. Even Hanslick would declare in *Vom Musikalisch-Schönen* that "music is a language we

---

80. Mattheson, *Der vollkommene Capellmeister,* 127.

81. Mattheson first published his account of Marcello's aria in his *Kern melodischer Wissenschaft* (Hamburg: C. Herold, 1737), 127–39, and then again in *Der vollkommene Capellmeister,* 235–42. To this day the aria has eluded identification, for it is not otherwise preserved among that composer's known works.

82. For a more detailed discussion of Mattheson's analysis and critical responses to it, see Mark Evan Bonds, *Wordless Rhetoric: Musical Form and the Metaphor of the Oration* (Cambridge, MA: Harvard University Press, 1991), 85–90.

83. Johann Joachim Quantz, *Versuch einer Anweisung die Flöte traversiere zu spielen* (Berlin: J. F. Voss, 1752), 102–3; Forkel, *Allgemeine Geschichte der Musik,* 2 vols. (Leipzig: Schwickert, 1788–1801), introduction to vol. 1; and C. P. E. Bach, review of the first volume of Forkel's *Allgemeine Geschichte der Musik* in the *Hamburgische unpartheyische Correspondenten,* 9 January 1788, republished in full in C. H. Bitter, *Carl Philipp Emanuel und Wilhelm Friedemann Bach und deren Brüder,* 2 vols. (Berlin: Wilhelm Müller, 1868), 2:109–11.

speak and understand and yet are unable to translate."[84] If music was a language, then what, exactly, did it communicate?

■ MIMESIS

Mimesis offered yet another means by which to explain instrumental music's powers to express and arouse emotions. A protean concept, mimesis has been applied to the arts since ancient times. The Greek *mimesis* is most often translated as "imitation," but it is more than this. For Plato, it was a metaphysical concept that addressed the relationship between objects and ideas.[85] Aristotle, in turn, emphasized its role in the arts and conceived of it as a concept that governed the way in which objects might be represented not simply as they are but rather as they ought to be.[86] Both of these understandings suggest a strong degree of idealization that moves well beyond the act of merely copying an object in nature. Neoplatonists held that the object of imitation could include an idea in the artist's mind, which is to say, an imitation of something internal and intangible.[87] It is easy to see why, over time, mimesis eventually became almost indistinguishable from expression itself.[88]

The earliest mimetic theories of music posited a cause-and-effect relationship between the physics of sound and the physical and mental constitution of the listener: because music resembled ("imitated") in some way the emotions of the soul, it could thereby evoke a corresponding emotional response—a resonance, as it were—in the mind, body, and soul of the listener. Mersenne recommended that those who wanted to discover "the reason of the effects of each movement"—that is, rhythm—"must themselves study to recognize the movements of the passions, the blood, and the other humors... because it appears that there is no more powerful means for arousing the passions of hearers than using the same times and movements by which the same passions are produced in those who are moved by them."[89]

84. *VMS*, 1:78: "Sie ist eine Sprache, die wir sprechen und verstehen, jedoch zu übersetzen nicht imstande sind." *OMB*, 30.

85. Paul Oskar Kristeller, "The Modern System of the Arts: A Study in the History of Aesthetics," *JHI* 12 (1951): 504.

86. See Richard Kraut, commentary to his translation of Aristotle, *Politics, Books VII and VIII*, 193–94.

87. M. H. Abrams, *The Mirror and the Lamp: Romantic Theory and the Critical Tradition* (London: Oxford University Press, 1953), 43–46.

88. In addition to Abrams's *Mirror and the Lamp*, see Gunter Gebauer and Christoph Wulf, *Mimesis: Culture, Art, Society*, trans. Don Reneau (Berkeley and Los Angeles: University of California Press, 1995); Walter Serauky, *Die musikalische Nachahmungsästhetik im Zeitraum von 1700 bis 1850* (Münster: Helios-Verlag, 1929); and Edward A. Lippman, *A History of Western Musical Aesthetics* (Lincoln: University of Nebraska Press, 1992), chapter 6, "Imitation and Expression."

89. Mersenne, *Harmonie universelle*, 2:402–3: "Ceux qui desirent passer outre pour trouver la raison des effects de chaque mouvement... doivent s'estudier à connoistre les mouvemens des passions, du sang & des autres humeurs, qui se suivent & s'accompagnent ordinairement, car il semble qu'il n'y a

Athanasius Kircher (1601–1680), a native of Fulda who spent most of his adult life in Rome as a professor of mathematics, physics, and Eastern studies at the Collegio Romano, was particularly fascinated by the physical properties of sound, and he devoted large portions of his wide-ranging *Musurgia universalis* (1650) to what we now think of as acoustics. He endorsed the idea of cosmic harmony but tried to explain the affective powers of music in mechanistic terms as well. Harmony and rhythm together have the power to "move" and "excite" spirit and body alike; the addition of words only strengthens these powers. *Musica pathetica* is the category of music whose goal is to arouse all sorts of affects in the spirit of the listener.[90]

René Descartes (1596–1650) ignored the principles of cosmic harmony altogether and considered music part of a mechanistic universe. He emphasized aural experience to an unprecedented degree and was by far the most influential of those many seventeenth-century writers who investigated the interplay of the senses and perception. Descartes helped shift the center of aesthetic debate from rationalism to sensualism, from Pythagoras to Orpheus. Like others before him, he distinguished between the efficient and the final causes of music. The object of music is sound; its goal is to "please and to move in us the various passions."[91] How it does this is an issue for natural philosophers (*physici*), who must "study the quality of sound, from which body it [i.e., sound] is produced, and under which conditions it may be most pleasing." The study of music's effects, in turn, "depends on a perfect knowledge of the motions of the soul."[92]

In the opening sentence of his *Traité des passions de l'âme*, Descartes announces his refusal to conform to the received wisdom of the past. "The defectiveness of the science we inherit from the ancients," he declares, "is nowhere more apparent than in what they wrote about the passions."[93] He says little specifically about music in this treatise, but his taxonomy of emotions suggests that certain kinds of music could elicit certain specific responses by way of the bodily

nul moyen plus puissant pour exciter les passions des Auditeurs que d'user des mesmes temps & mouvemens dont se servent les mesmes passions dans ceux qui en sont touchez." Translation from Mace, "Marin Mersenne on Music and Language," 21.

90. Athanasius Kircher, *Musurgia universalis*, 2 vols. (Rome, 1650; reprint, Hildesheim: Olms, 1999), 1:550–51, 578.

91. René Descartes, *Compendium musicae* (Utrecht: G. Zjill, 1650), 5: "Finis, ut delectet, variosque in nobis moveat affectus." Written in 1618, the *Compendium musicae* was not published until 1650.

92. Descartes, *Compendium musicae*, 5: "de ipsius soni qualitate, ex quo corpore & quo pacto gratior exeat, agunt Physici." Ibid., 10: "pendet ab exquisita cognitione motuum animi." Translations from Paolo Gozza, "Renaissance Mathematics: The Music of Descartes," in *Number to Sound: The Musical Way to the Scientific Revolution*, ed. Paolo Gozza (Dordrecht: Kluwer, 1999), 161, 157.

93. Descartes, *Traité des passions de l'âme*, ed. Geneviève Rodis-Lewis (Paris: J. Vrin, 2010), 97: "Il n'y a rien en quoi paraisse mieux combien les sciences que nous avons des Anciens sont défectueuses, qu'en ce qu'ils on écrit des Passions." Translation from *The Passions of the Soul*, trans. Stephen H. Voss (Indianapolis: Hackett, 1989), 18.

humors. As one later historian would note, "It is probably no coincidence that Pavlov had a bust of Descartes on his mantelpiece."[94]

This model of cause and effect lay at the heart of much mimetic theory throughout the late seventeenth and eighteenth centuries. Commentators were quick to align the human passions with specific kinds of musical figures and gestures. There was no consistent or systematic theory that warranted the twentieth-century designation of *Affektenlehre* (doctrine of the affects), but eighteenth-century authors agreed on the underlying principle that certain varieties of music were conducive to producing certain emotional responses in listeners.[95] This was nothing new in and of itself: the ancient Greeks had posited specific responses to specific modes of music, and later writers extended this tradition to the system of major and minor keys. But the more modern system also included melodic and rhythmic gestures, and theorists were quick to produce elaborate (if at times widely divergent) accounts of musical figures matched to their corresponding rhetorical tropes, illustrating once again the broader belief in music's capacity to function as a language of emotion.[96]

Mimesis also proved important as a feature—and for some writers, *the* feature—common to all the arts. In his influential *Les beaux-arts réduits à un même principe* of 1746, Charles Batteux identified mimesis as the unifying principle for all the fine arts. Every work of art, he maintained, had to imitate or represent an object drawn from nature. The artist was obliged to give this object a stylized form, to be sure, but every poem or painting or piece of sculpture had to represent something tangible, be it a person, a historical event, or a scene in nature. This principle could be applied easily to vocal music, whose object of representation could be located in the text being sung. But what might instrumental music represent? Here Batteux and other critics struggled. This was an art form that used neither images nor words: it lay outside the realm of language, at least in any conventional sense of the term, and its sole visible manifestation, notation, used a system of wholly arbitrary, self-contained signs that could not be applied to any other purpose. The idea that a work of fine art might consist solely of form, without an object, was simply inconceivable at the time. The consensus that emerged over the course of the eighteenth century was that human passions were what instrumental music could imitate or represent best: love, anger, tenderness, melancholy, and the like. Critics also recognized a

---

94. Charles Kent, introduction to René Descartes, *Compendium of Music*, ed. Charles Kent, trans. Walter Robert (S.l.: American Institute of Musicology, 1961), 9.

95. See George J. Buelow, "Johann Mattheson and the Invention of the *Affektenlehre*," in *New Mattheson Studies*, ed. George J. Buelow and Hans Joachim Marx (Cambridge: Cambridge University Press, 1983), 393–407.

96. See Rita Steblin, *A History of Key Characteristics in the Eighteenth and Early Nineteenth Centuries*, 2nd ed. (Rochester, NY: University of Rochester Press, 2002); and Dietrich Bartel, *Musica poetica: Musical-Rhetorical Figures in German Baroque Music* (Lincoln: University of Nebraska Press, 1997).

secondary kind of imitation in certain sounds of nature that could be transferred to an instrument or an ensemble of instruments, such as birdcalls or waterfalls or thunder. But commentators invariably considered this literalistic sort of imitation to be of a lesser kind. Human passions, on the other hand, could be imitated—represented—in music.

But emotions can be hard to pin down, and Batteux labored to apply the principle of mimesis to music lacking a text. He proceeded from the a priori assumption that because it is an art, "all music...must have a meaning." He rejected as nonsensical the idea of an art that might signify—that is, imitate—nothing at all and accepted instead the metaphor of music as a language of emotions, a "language of tones," which must conform to the same artistic principles as an oration or painting:

> If I were to say that I could derive no pleasure from a lecture that I did not understand, my confession would in no way seem strange. But if I ventured to say the same of a piece of music, people would ask whether I considered myself enough of a connoisseur to appreciate the merits of so carefully constructed and fine a composition. I would dare to reply yes, for it is a matter of feeling. I do not [while listening to music] pretend in any way to calculate the sounds, their interrelationships or their connection with the ear. I am speaking here neither of oscillations, string vibrations, nor mathematical proportions. I leave such speculations to learned theorists; these are akin to the grammar and dialectic of a lecture which I can appreciate without going into such details. Music speaks to me in tones: this language is natural to me. If I do not understand it, art has corrupted nature rather than perfected her. A musical composition must be judged in the same way as a painting. In the painting I find shapes and colors that I can comprehend; it charms and touches me. What would we think of a painter who was content to throw on the canvas bold shapes and masses of the liveliest color without reference to any known object? The same argument can be applied to music.[97]

97. Charles Batteux, *Les beaux-arts réduits à un même principe* (Paris: Durand, 1746), 260: "Toute Musique...doit avoir une signification, un sens." Ibid., 262–63: "Si je disois que je ne puis me plaire à un Discours que je ne comprends pas, mon aveu n'auroit rien de singulier. Mais que j'ose dire la même chose d'une piéce de musique; vous croyez-vous, me dira-t'on, assez connoisseur pour sentir le mérite d'une musique fine & travaillée avec soin? J'ose répondre: oui, car il s'agit de sentir. Je ne prétends point calculer les sons, ni leurs rapports, soit entre eux, soit avec notre organe: je ne parle ici, ni de trémoussemens, ni de vibrations de cordes, ni de proportion mathématique. J'abandonne aux savans Théoristes, ces spéculations, qui ne sont que comme le grammatical fin, ou la dialectique d'un Discours, dont je puis sentir le mérite, sans entrer dans ce détail. La Musique me parle par des tons: ce langage m'est naturel: si je ne l'entends point, l'Art a corrompu la nature, plutôt que de la perfectionner. On doit juger d'une musique, comme d'un tableau. Je vois dans celui-ci des traits & des couleurs dont je comprends le sens; il me flatte, il me touche. Que diroit-on d'un Peintre, qui se contenteroit de jetter sur la toile des traits hardis, & des masses des couleurs les plus vives, sans aucune ressemblance avec quelque objet connu? L'application se fait d'elle-même à la Musique." Translation slightly modified from Peter Le Huray and James Day, eds., *Music and Aesthetics in the Eighteenth and Early-Nineteenth Centuries* (Cambridge: Cambridge University Press, 1981), 48–49.

The principle of mimesis helped promote the emerging genre of what we now think of as program music, a repertory that began to flourish around 1700, when a growing number of composers and critics alike embraced the idea of purely instrumental music as a language capable of representing something outside of itself, without the aid of a sung text.[98]

The effort to specify—and thus rationalize—the object of purely instrumental music is in this sense an Enlightenment phenomenon. Johann Kuhnau's *Musicalische Vorstellung einiger Biblischer Historien* (1700), a set of six of suites for harpsichord, offers a relatively early example of this approach to composition. In each of these "musical representations of stories from the Bible," Kuhnau (1660–1722), J. S. Bach's immediate predecessor at the Thomaskirche in Leipzig, used descriptive titles and running commentaries in the score to leave no doubt about the events he portrayed through his music. In "The Battle between David and Goliath," for instance, he annotated his score with detailed verbal explanations of what was happening at any given moment: we are told that a sudden upward sweeping figure corresponds precisely to the point at which David slings a stone toward the giant, and that the loud, low chord that follows—it sounds very much like a thud—represents "the fall of Goliath." The subsequent fugue is labeled the "Flight of the Philistines," and the gigue-like movement that follows is the "Joy of the Israelites." The suite ends with a "Concert of Music in Honor of David." Such annotations, Kuhnau pointed out in his prefatory letter to the set, were needed in purely instrumental music if the listener was to be moved by "the appropriate affect."[99]

Other examples of program music from the first half of the eighteenth century include Vivaldi's *Le quattro stagioni*, a set of four concertos for violin and strings that when first issued in print in 1725 were accompanied by a series of four poems, one for every season, each with stanzas corresponding to the movements of the individual concertos. In one particularly graphic instance of early program music, Marin Marais (1656–1728) used the resources of only a viola da gamba and basso continuo to depict an operation to remove a kidney stone.[100] François Couperin often gave clues to what inspired his character pieces. In the preface to the first book of his *Pièces de clavecin* (1713), he noted that he had

98. On programmatic works of the seventeenth century, mostly for keyboard, see David Fuller, "Of Portraits, 'Sapho' and Couperin: Titles and Characters in French Instrumental Music of the High Baroque," *M&L* 78 (1997): 149–74.

99. Johann Kuhnau, *Musicalische Vorstellung einiger Biblischer Historien* (Leipzig: Immanuel Tietzen, 1700; reprint, Florence: Studio per Edizioni Scelte, 2000), fourth unnumbered page of the prefatory letter to the reader: "Wo aber die blosse Instrumental-Music den gehörigen Affect bewegen soll / so wird es ohne Zweiffel was mehrer[e]s zu thun setzen."

100. Marin Marais, *Pièces de viole*, book 5: "Le tableau de l'opération de la taille," in Marin Maris, *The Instrumental Works*, vol. 5, *Pièces de viole: Cinquème livre* (1725), ed. John Hsu (New York: Broude Trust, 2000), 175–76.

"always had an object in composing all these pieces; different occasions gave them to me. Thus the titles correspond to ideas I have had: I may be excused for not giving an account of them."[101] Along similar lines, Emanuel Bach endorsed the idea of using verbal indications that went beyond mere markings of tempo or mood to convey the "true content" of a work so that performers might play it with the "appropriate affect."[102] The critic, theorist, and composer Friedrich Wilhelm Marpurg (1718–1795) agreed but expressed his views on the matter from the perspective of the listener rather than that of the composer or performer. Music, he maintained, will engage one's understanding if it has an object, and for this reason instrumental music should give listeners the ability to think about something other than "noise" (Getöse). An orator always makes known the topic of his discourse; why should musicians be hesitant to do the same?[103]

Paradoxically, mimesis both enhanced and undermined the aesthetic status of instrumental music. It made plausible the idea that music without words could convey something beyond itself. Yet the practice of indicating "content" for some pieces but not for others raised problems of its own. This dilemma is epitomized in Rousseau's 1768 anecdote about the philosophe Bernard Le Bovier de Fontenelle (1657–1757), who during a concert of instrumental music found himself "worn out by these endless symphonies" and "in a transport of impatience cried out quite loudly: 'Sonate, que me veux-tu?'"[104] Fontenelle's outburst—"Sonata, what do you want of me?"—would be quoted over and over again for the next hundred years, in Germany as well as in France, invariably in connection with the question of what instrumental music that carried only a generic title like sonata or symphony might "mean."[105]

---

101. François Couperin, Pièces de clavecin, book 1 (Paris: Author, 1713), unnumbered first page of the preface: "J'ay toûjours eu un objet en composant toutes ces piéces; des occasions différentes me l'ont fourni, ainsi les Titres répondent aux idées que j'ay eües; on me dispensera d'en rendre compte."

102. C. P. E. Bach, Versuch über die wahre Art das Clavier zu spielen, 2 vols. (Berlin: C. F. Henning; Berlin: G. L. Winter, 1753–62), 1:124: "Indem man also ein jedes Stück nach seinem wahren Inhalte, und mit dem gehörigen Affecte spielen soll; so thun die Componisten wohl, wenn sie ihren Ausarbeitungen ausser der Bezeichnung das Tempo, annoch solche Wörter vorsetzen, wodurch der Inhalt derselben erkläret wird." On C. P. E. Bach's character pieces, see Darrell M. Berg, "C. P. E. Bach's Character Pieces and his Friendship Circle," in C. P. E. Bach Studies, ed. Stephen L. Clark (Oxford: Clarendon Press, 1988), 1–32; Joshua S. Walden, "Composing Character in Musical Portraits: Carl Philipp Emanuel Bach and L'Aly Rupalich," MQ 91 (2008): 379–411.

103. Friedrich Wilhelm Marpurg, "Anmerkungen über vorhergehendes Schreiben," Historisch-kritische Beyträge zur Aufnahme der Musik 1 (1754): 34–35.

104. Rousseau, Dictionnaire de musique, 452 ("Sonate"): "Je n'oublierai jamais la saillie du célèbre Fontenelle, qui se trouvant excédé de ces éternelles Symphonies, s'écria tout haut dans un transport d'impatience: Sonate, que me veux-tu?"

105. On this tradition in France, see Maria Rika Maniates, "'Sonate, que me veux-tu?' The Enigma of French Musical Aesthetics in the 18th Century," Current Musicology 9 (1969):117–40. On Germany, see Mary Sue Morrow, German Music Criticism in the Late Eighteenth Century: Aesthetic Issues in Instrumental Music (Cambridge: Cambridge University Press, 1997), 4–18.

But there is more to this episode than its punch line. The paradox of musical mimesis becomes more pronounced when we compare Rousseau's version of the story with the earlier yet less well-known account given by the philosophe Jean Leronde d'Alembert (1717–1783). Rousseau and d'Alembert agree in their essentials (including the wording of Fontenelle's rhetorical question) but differ sharply in their premises and conclusions. To judge by his "Preliminary Discourse" (1751) to Diderot's *Encyclopédie*, d'Alembert was predisposed to sympathize with Fontenelle's impatience, offering this comment on instrumental music in general:

> In its origins, music was destined to represent only noise, but little by little it has become a kind of discourse, even a language through which one expresses the different sentiments of the soul, or rather, its different passions. But why reduce this expression to the passions alone and not extend them, insofar as possible, to the sensations themselves?...All music that does not depict something is only noise, and without the habit of custom (which distorts everything), it would create little more than the pleasure given by a succession of harmonious and sonorous words stripped of all order and connection.[106]

In his later "De la liberté de la musique" (1758), d'Alembert addressed Fontenelle's question directly:

> All this purely instrumental music, without purpose and without aim, speaks to neither the mind nor the soul and deserves the question posed to it by Fontenelle: "Sonate que me veux-tu?" Composers who write instrumental music will produce nothing but trifling noise unless they have in mind to paint an event or an expression [of feeling], as in the case of the celebrated Tartini, for example. Some sonatas, if only rather few, have this advantage that is so desirable and so necessary to render themselves agreeable to persons of taste. We would cite here one that has the title *Didone abbandonata*. It is a very beautiful monologue; one sees in rapid succession and in a very distinct manner *sorrow, hope, despair*—in different degrees and following various nuances—and one could easily turn this sonata into a very animated *scena* full of pathos. But similar pieces are rare. It must be acknowledged that in general one cannot sense the full expression of a work of music unless it is

---

106. Jean Leronde d'Alembert, "Discours préliminaire" (1751), in *Discours préliminaire de l'Encylopédie et articles de l'Encyclopédie*, ed. Martine Groult (Paris: Champion, 2011), 94–95: "La musique, qui, dans son origine n'étoit peut-être destinée à représenter que du bruit, est devenue peu à peu une espece de discours et même de langue, par laquelle on exprime les différens sentiments de l'ame, ou plûtôt ses différentes passions: mais pourquoi réduire cette expression aux passions seules, & ne pas l'étendre, autant qu'il est possible, jusqu'aux sensations mêmes?...Toute musique qui ne peint rien n'est que du bruit; et sans l'habitude, qui dénature tout, elle ne feroit guere plus de plaisir qu'une suite de mots harmonieux et sonores dénués d'ordre et de liaison."

linked to words or to dance. Music is a language without vowels; it is up to the action to supply them.[107]

The key distinction here is whether or not the composer draws our attention explicitly to some sort of "action," an object, idea, or narrative that stands outside what we actually hear. And on this point Rousseau is not so sympathetic to Fontenelle's reaction. Like d'Alembert, Rousseau conceives of music as a language, but as the language of the heart, a language that needs no vowels or consonants because it is, by its very nature, passionate rather than rational. Here is the fuller context of Rousseau's account of Fontenelle:

> To understand what all the tumult of sonatas by which one is overwhelmed might want to say, we would have to follow the lead of the crude artist who was obliged to write underneath that which he had drawn such statements as "This is a tree," or "This is a man," or "This is a horse." I shall never forget the witticism of the celebrated Fontenelle, who found himself worn out by these ceaseless symphonies and in a transport of impatience cried out quite loudly: "Sonate, que me veux-tu?"[108]

To Rousseau's mind, music was immediate and elemental, and to identify its associated emotions defeated the purpose of expressing those emotions in the first place. Without identifying d'Alembert by name, Rousseau takes him to task for demanding a degree of specificity that is more than music can bear.

Perhaps the most remarkable point about Fontenelle's outburst is that he asked the question at all. It is easy enough to see the humor in it—Rousseau calls it a witticism, a *saillie*—but the best witticisms provide genuine insight as well as amusement. Fontenelle's question resonated for as long as it did because it goes beyond issues about the differences between vocal and instrumental music, or between instrumental music that does or does not reveal its extramusical

---

107. Jean Leronde d'Alembert, "De la liberté de la musique" (1758), from his *Oeuvres*, 5 vols. (Paris: Belin, 1821–22), 1:544: "Toute cette musique purement instrumentale, sans dessein et sans objet, ne parle ni à l'esprit ni à l'âme, et mérite qu'on lui demande avec Fontenelle, *sonate que me veux-tu?* Les auteurs qui composent de la musique instrumentale ne feront qu'un vain bruit, tant qu'ils n'auront pas dans la tête, à l'exemple, dit-on, du célèbre Tartini, une action ou une expression à peindre. Quelques sonates, mais en assez petit nombre, ont cet avantage si désirable, et si nécessaire pour les rendre agréables aux gens de goût. Nous en citerons une qui a pour titre *Didone abbandonata*. C'est un très-beau monologue; on y voit se succéder rapidement et d'une manière très-marquée, *la douleur, l'espérance, le désespoir*, avec des degrés et suivant des nuances différentes; et on pourrait de cette sonate faire aisément une scène très-animée et très-pathétique. Mais de pareils morceaux sont rares. Il faut même avouer qu'en général on ne sent toute l'expression de la musique, que lorsqu'elle est liée à des paroles ou à des danses. La musique est une langue sans voyelles; c'est à l'action à les y mettre."

108. Rousseau, *Dictionnaire de musique*, 452 ("Sonate"): "Pour savoir ce que veulent dire tous ces fatras de *Sonates* dont on est accablé, il faudroit faire comme ce Peintre grossier qui étoit obligé d'écrire au-dessous de ses figures; *c'est un arbre, c'est un homme, c'est un cheval*. Je n'oublierai jamais la saillie du célèbre Fontenelle, qui se trouvant excédé de ces éternelles Symphonies, s'écria tout haut dans un transport d'impatience: Sonate, que me veux-tu?"

sources. These are important points, to be sure, but even more fundamental is the act of listening itself: in order to feel "overwhelmed" by instrumental music, Fontenelle had to be listening to it with some degree of attentiveness in the first place. This may seem painfully obvious to us today, but in the context of the eighteenth century, his question marks a profound shift in attitudes toward listening in general. Indeed, it might well be said to mark the beginning of modern listening, the idea that members of a concert audience have an obligation to come to terms with the music, to understand the trajectory of its argument and the passions it expresses. Fontenelle, in his time, could have very easily made the choice *not* to listen. At some point in the late eighteenth or early nineteenth century, audiences around Europe began to fall silent during performances and exhibit the kind of concert decorum we are used to today; but in the middle of the eighteenth century, members of almost any audience had the option of listening or chatting, or perhaps listening *and* chatting. The iconographic evidence here is overwhelming: images of concert or operatic performances from before 1800 routinely show a mixed audience of listeners and nonlisteners.[109] The very fact that Fontenelle became agitated by a performance of instrumental music is significant in its own right, for he did not consider conversation an option in that particular moment. He seems instead to have felt an obligation to listen, to *try* to understand the work at hand. But he had nothing outside of musical sound to which he could apply his imagination, hence his bon mot.

The metaphor of music as a language—with or without vowels—carries the corollary that music is a mode of communication a listener may or may not understand. Composers and musicians, including amateurs such as Castiglione's courtier, had always been expected to study and cultivate their craft, but before the middle of the eighteenth century the idea that listeners would have to make an active effort to achieve even a minimal level of skill—the musical equivalent of linguistic competency—scarcely existed.[110] Toward the end of the eighteenth century, we begin to see the first trickle of what would soon become a flood of journals and books aimed at these listeners, the equivalent of today's "how-to-listen-to-music" books. Johann Nicolaus Forkel's *Ueber die Theorie der Musik, insofern sie Liebhabern und Kennern nothwendig und nützlich ist* (1777), is one of the earliest such publications. It outlines a series of public lectures he proposed to give in Göttingen "on the theory of music, insofar as is necessary

---

109. For a summary of the evidence, both visual and verbal, see William Weber, "Did People Listen in the 18th Century?" *Early Music* 25 (1997): 678–91. See also James H. Johnson, *Listening in Paris: A Cultural History* (Berkeley and Los Angeles: University of California Press, 1995).

110. On listening practices in the eighteenth century, see Matthew Riley, "Johann Nikolaus Forkel on the Listening Practices of 'Kenner' and 'Liebhaber,'" *M&L* 84 (2003): 414–33; Riley, *Musical Listening in the German Enlightenment: Attention, Wonder and Astonishment* (Aldershot: Ashgate, 2004); and Martin Kaltenecker, *L'oreille divisée: Les discours sur l'écoute musicale aux XVIIIe et XIXe siècles* (Paris: MF, 2010). Andrew Dell'Antonio traces the role of listening in contexts of sacred devotion in the

and useful for amateurs and connoisseurs." Forkel used live musical examples to accompany his talks, drawing on the resources of the university's collegium musicum, which he conducted. In his published prospectus for these lectures, he pointed out that anyone who listens to a speech must at the very least comprehend the meaning of the words and their syntax. He argued that music, in turn, has its own "words"—notes—and its own syntax, and that anyone listening to a symphony or concerto must similarly grasp at least the basics of that syntactic structure.[111] Without such knowledge, the listener can neither enjoy nor judge an oration, be it verbal or purely musical.

Forkel never published his lectures, but we know from contemporary reports that they attracted an attentive audience eager to learn how to listen to music. Had he lived a generation later, Fontenelle might well have benefited from those lectures. Denis Diderot (1713–1784), born almost half a century after Fontenelle, experienced a similar frustration with purely instrumental music yet seems to have enjoyed engaging his imagination with such works. In an essay written in 1771, he acknowledged that "beautiful chords, well connected and sequenced, flatter my ear," but he insisted that "in all truth, I would not listen long to a piece of music that had only this merit. I have never listened to a beautiful symphony [i.e., an instrumental work], above all an adagio or andante, without interpreting it, sometimes so happily that I have recognized precisely what the composer had proposed to depict."[112]

By the second half of the eighteenth century, however, mimesis began to give way to another, more abstract quality that would place even greater demands on the attentiveness and taste of listeners: beauty.

seventeenth century in Dell'Antonio, *Listening as Spiritual Practice in Early Modern Italy* (Berkeley and Los Angeles: University of California Press, 2011).

111. Johann Nicolaus Forkel, *Ueber die Theorie der Musik, insofern sie Liebhabern und Kennern nothwendig und nützlich ist: Eine Einladungsschrift zu musikalischen Vorlesungen* (Göttingen: Wittwe Vandenhoeck, 1777), 8–11.

112. Denis Diderot, "Lettre au sujet des observations du Chevalier de Chastellux sur le Traité du mélodrame" (1771), in Diderot, *Oeuvres complètes*, 20 vols., ed. J. Assézat (Paris: Garnier frères, 1875–77), 8:508: "De beaux accords, bien suivis, bien enchaînés, flattent mon oreille...je n'écouterais pas longtemps une musique qui n'aurait que ce mérite. Je n'ai jamais entendu de bonne symphonie, surtout *adagio* ou *andante*, que je ne l'aie interprétée, et quelquefois si heureusement, que je rencontrais précisément ce que le musicien s'était proposé de peindre."

4 Beauty

When Hanslick set out to make a "contribution to a revision of the aesthetics of music" in the middle of the nineteenth century, he made beauty the titular focus of his argument. He had good reason to do so, for the concept of beauty served his purposes well. In the wake of Immanuel Kant, beauty was a quality closely associated with reflection, contemplation, and thought, all activities that privilege the intellectual and spiritual elements of the aesthetic experience over the merely sensuous. The perception of beauty, according to this line of thought, is predicated on personal detachment, abstraction, and the faculty of imagination (what Hanslick would call *Phantasie*, the equivalent of Kant's *Einbildungskraft*), all of which helped reinforce the case for music as an art of *Geist*—that is, an art of mind or spirit—rather than an art of expression. "Musical beauty alone is the goal of the musician," he declared. "We acknowledge no beauty without *Geist*."[1]

Beauty had always played a role in commentary on the arts, but it was not until the eighteenth century that it became the defining element of a new category: the fine arts. The "arts of beauty," as they were called in French and German (*les beaux-arts, die schönen Künste*) made beauty the quality that distinguished art from craft, artistry from artisanship. One essential attribute of any beautiful object was its lack of practical function. To be considered a work of fine art, it should exist solely for the sake of its own beauty: the beholder must attend to the work at hand without any expectations of utility.[2] A table, for example, might be exquisitely wrought, but its utility as a table—as a functional object—diminishes its status as a work of fine art. If put on display in a museum, the table's utility would be effectively eliminated, and in this setting it could be more readily appreciated as an example of fine art. These contrasting scenarios

---

1. *VMS*, 1:125: "Musikalische Schönheit allein ist das Ziel des Tonkünstlers." The translation in *OMB*, 57, is based on the different wording of the eighth edition. From the second edition (1858) onward, Hanslick had substituted "die wahre Kraft" for "das Ziel." *VMS*, 1:78: "Denn wir anerkennen keine Schönheit ohne Geist." Again, the translation in *OMB*, 30, is based on a different wording in the eighth edition ("keine Schönheit ohne jeglichen Antheil von Geist") and in any case inexplicably renders *Geist* as "ideality." For more on Hanslick's use of the term *Geist*, see p. 148–50.

2. See M. H. Abrams, "From Addison to Kant: Modern Aesthetics and the Exemplary Art," in *Studies in Eighteenth-Century British Art and Aesthetics*, ed. Ralph Cohen (Berkeley and Los Angeles: University of California Press, 1985), 21–25; Abrams, "Art as Such: The Sociology of Modern Aesthetics," in Abrams, *Doing Things with Texts* (New York: W. W. Norton, 1989), 135–57; and Larry Shiner, *The Invention of Art: A Cultural History* (Chicago: University of Chicago Press, 2001).

illustrate the importance of the beholder's attitude of disinterested contemplation and the distinction between utility and contemplation.

The idea of the fine arts helped establish another new conceptual sphere: aesthetics. This, too, was a neologism, coined by the German philosopher Alexander Baumgarten (1714–1762) in 1735, though the "denomination of the field," as the historian of philosophy Paul Guyer points out, was in many respects an "adult baptism," for the nature of beauty and its relation to the senses had been a focus of attention since antiquity.[3] Baumgarten defined aesthetics as the "science of sensory cognition," the goal of which is "the perfection of sensory cognition as such," and he explicitly equated this perfection with beauty (*pulcritudo*).[4] Baumgarten's focus was thus on knowledge gained through perception, as opposed to knowledge gained by logic, and though he considered the mind superior to the senses, he insisted that the rule of reason should not be tyrannical.[5] He also emphasized the role of imagination in making the products of cognition as rich and varied as possible: aesthetic perception was an active experience, not a passive one.[6] Above all, aesthetics differentiated itself from poetics by approaching art from the perspective of the beholder, not that of the creative artist.

From the very start, then, the study of aesthetics centered on beauty, which Baumgarten and others regarded as the point at which the senses and the mind worked together most intensively. It was in the judgment of beauty that the faculties of perception and reason confronted each other most fully and completely—or, to use Baumgarten's term, perfectly. "Taste" and "judgment" became key terms in the debate about the relationship between the senses and the mind, and beauty was the most prestigious, revealing, and contested point in this relationship, the litmus test of judgment. The purpose of Kant's *Kritik der Urteilskraft* (1790), as its title makes clear, is to examine the power or faculty of judgment, which in turn reveals itself most tellingly through the perception and contemplation of beauty. The main body of the treatise opens with the words "In order to decide whether or not something is beautiful...."[7] An investigation of

---

3. Paul Guyer, "Free Play and True Well-Being: Herder's Critique of Kant's Aesthetics," *JAAC* 65 (2007): 353.

4. Alexander Baumgarten, *Aesthetica* (Frankfurt am Oder: Johann Christian Kleyb, 1750), 1 (sec. 1): "Aesthetica...est scientia cognitionis sensitivae"; ibid., 6 (sec. 14): "Aesthetices finis est perfectio cognitionis sensitivae, qua talis. Haec autem est pulcritudo."

5. See Ernst Cassirer, *The Philosophy of the Enlightenment*, trans. Fritz C. A. Koelln and James P. Pettegrove (Princeton: Princeton University Press, 1951), 347.

6. See Paul Guyer, *Values of Beauty: Historical Essays in Aesthetics* (Cambridge: Cambridge University Press, 2005), 29.

7. Immanuel Kant, *Kritik der Urteilskraft*, ed. Heiner F. Klemme (Hamburg: Felix Meiner, 2001), 47 (§1, B3): "Um zu unterscheiden, ob etwas schön sei oder nicht." Translation by Paul Guyer and Eric Matthews in Kant, *Critique of the Power of Judgment*, ed. Paul Guyer (Cambridge: Cambridge University Press, 2000), 89.

beauty, Kant believed, would address one of the enduring problems of philosophy: the relationship between the perceiving subject and the perceived object.

In taste as in law, judgment had to be impartial and removed from any hint of personal self-interest. This had not always been the case. For Plato, beauty had been inseparable from desire; Aristotle associated it with virtue; and Aquinas had considered it a theological concept, inseparable from the idea of God. For critics of the eighteenth century, by contrast, beauty became an increasingly abstract quality capable of being recognized only in the absence of longing, morality, divinity, or any other consideration beyond the quality of beauty itself.[8] Thus, although someone who is hungry might well perceive a table covered with tasty dishes as beautiful, this sight could not qualify as an object of aesthetic beauty, whereas a still-life of the same bounty might.

Anthony Ashley Cooper, the third Earl of Shaftesbury (1671–1713), is generally regarded as the first to have established disinterestedness as a predicate of aesthetic experience. Joseph Addison, George Berkeley, Francis Hutcheson, David Hume, Edmund Burke, and Kant would all expand on this principle, describing it as an attitude that entails a satisfying engagement of mental powers.[9] Shaftesbury used mathematics to illustrate this mode of attention. Anyone familiar with even the most basic principles of mathematics, he argued,

> has found that in the exercise of his mind on the discoveries he there makes, though merely of speculative truths,... receives a pleasure and delight superior to that of sense. When we have thoroughly searched into the nature of this contemplative delight, we shall find it of a kind which relates not in the least to any private interest of the creature, nor has for its object any self-good or advantage of the private system. The admiration, joy or love turns wholly upon what is exterior and foreign to ourselves.[10]

This absence of desire became the *sine qua non* of aesthetic judgment for most (though not all) Enlightenment thinkers and helped separate the fine arts from all other products of human endeavor. "There is a beautiful art of passion," Schiller declared; "but a beautiful passionate art is a contradiction in terms, for the inevitable effect of beauty is freedom from passion."[11] The net result was the cultivation of an aesthetic attitude that promoted reflection, detachment,

8. See Alexander Nehamas, *Only a Promise of Happiness: The Place of Beauty in a World of Art* (Princeton: Princeton University Press, 2007), especially 7–8.

9. See Jerome Stolnitz, "On the Origins of 'Aesthetic Disinterestedness,'" *JAAC* 20 (1961–62): 131–43; and Paul Guyer, *Kant and the Experience of Freedom: Essays on Aesthetics and Morality* (Cambridge: Cambridge University Press, 1993), chapters 2 and 3.

10. Anthony Ashley Cooper, third Earl of Shaftesbury, *Characteristics of Men, Manners, Opinions, Times* (1713), ed. Lawrence E. Klein (Cambridge: Cambridge University Press, 1999), 202.

11. Friedrich Schiller, *Über die ästhetische Erziehung des Menschen*, ed. Elizabeth Wilkinson and L. A. Willoughby (Oxford: Clarendon Press, 1967), 156 (Letter 22): "Eine schöne Kunst der Leidenschaft gibt es; aber eine schöne leidenschaftliche Kunst ist ein Widerspruch, denn der unausbleibliche Effekt

self-awareness, and an increasing sense of distance between the realm of art and the world around it. In the second quarter of the nineteenth century, this attitude would eventually lead to an ideology known as *l'art pour l'art*, which actively sought to insulate art from society (see chapter 6).

Because of its inherently more detached and reflective nature, the pleasure afforded by beauty was regarded as superior to the pleasure afforded by the senses alone. In this respect, the newly launched field of aesthetics continued the enduring tradition of Western philosophy that values mind over body. Aesthetics may have been committed to explaining the relationship between reason and the senses, but old habits die hard, and no critic of the time was prepared to grant equal footing to the senses. Some, like Johann Gottfried Herder (1744–1803), argued that there was no reason to eliminate desire from the aesthetic equation: he maintained that Kant's division between the agreeable and the beautiful was both artificial and unnecessary. Even Herder, however, subscribed to the traditional notion that beauty, whether desired or not, had the capacity to elevate the spirit, thereby reinforcing the traditional priority of intellectual pleasure.

This is precisely the approach Hanslick would recommend for listeners in the middle of the nineteenth century. What was at stake for him was nothing less than the question of whether music was an art of the mind and spirit—*Geist*—or a merely sensory entertainment, pleasurable and even moving but not intellectual. Beauty was the key to this distinction, as Enlightenment philosophers had argued. That Hanslick would virtually ignore this philosophical tradition, preferring instead to excoriate those who had argued for the essence of music as an art of expression, will be explored more fully in chapter 9.

But exactly what were the criteria of beauty? Enlightenment philosophers were for the most part either unable or reluctant to define it in any meaningful way. A long-standing tradition—what the philosopher and art historian Władysław Tatarkiewicz called the "Great Theory" of European aesthetics—had located beauty in a pleasing proportional relationship between a whole and its parts.[12] Pythagoras equated proportion with the order of the universe, which was considered inherently beautiful. For Aquinas, beauty resided within the proportions of the object itself. And Leon Battista Alberti (1404–1472), in his treatise on architecture, defined beauty as "a form of sympathy and consonance of the parts within a body, according to a definite number, outline, and position, as dictated by *concinnitas*, the absolute and fundamental rule in Nature."[13] In the eighteenth

des Schönen ist Freiheit von Leidenschaften." The bilingual edition from which this passage is taken offers a different translation (157).

12. Władysław Tatarkiewicz, *A History of Six Ideas: An Essay in Aesthetics*, trans. Christopher Kasparek (Warsaw: Polish Scientific, 1980), 125–29. Tatarkiewicz provides an excellent summary of the basic issues in chapters 4 ("Beauty: History of the Concept"), 5 ("Beauty: History of the Category"), and 6 ("Beauty: The Dispute Between Objectivism and Subjectivism").

13. Leon Batista Alberti, *De Re Aedificatoria* (1485), book 9, chapter 5, trans. Joseph Rykwert, Neil Leach, and Robert Tavernor as *On the Art of Building* (Cambridge, MA: MIT Press, 1988), 303.

century "unity in variety" and "variety in unity" would become popular slogans by which to explain beauty. But it is easy to sense a certain lack of conviction in such vague and readily producible qualities as "order" and "proportion."

The more common approach to the definition of beauty was to declare it ineffable, passing all understanding, and therefore by its very nature resistant to definition. No less an artist than Albrecht Dürer (1471–1528) had frankly admitted that he did not know what beauty was, and commentators were using phrases like *non so che* and *je ne sais quoi* routinely from the seventeenth century onward.[14] Hume averred that "beauty, like wit, cannot be defin'd, but is discern'd only by a taste or sensation."[15] Even Kant, the great definer of philosophical concepts, conceded in a marginal annotation to his copy of Baumgarten's *Metaphysica* (1739) that "beauty must remain ineffable. We are not always able to say what we think."[16] In his own *Kritik der Urteilskraft*, Kant would conclude that "aesthetic ideas" were those that could not be reduced to concepts (which could be articulated through words) and that beauty could not be defined or described in a series of rules or characteristics. Herder, too, considered beauty an experience that defied verbal description.[17]

Beauty's ineffability made the question of its location all the more difficult: was it in the perceived object, as had for so long been maintained under the Great Theory, or in the mind of the perceiving subject, as newer theories suggested? The subjective-objective debate was consistently framed in terms of the interaction between lower (sensory) and higher (mental) faculties, an interplay between relative (variable) and absolute (immutable) qualities. George Berkeley (1685–1753), for example, had one of the characters in a dialogue assert (with the assent of his interlocutor) that "proportions... are not, strictly speaking, perceived by the sense of sight, but only by reason through the means of sight.... Consequently beauty... is an object, not of the eye, but of the mind."[18] Hume similarly observed that "beauty is no quality in things themselves: it

---

14. See Albrecht Dürer, *Schriftlicher Nachlass*, 3 vols., ed. Hans Rupprich (Berlin: Deutscher Verein für Kunstwissenschaft, 1956–69), 2:100: "Waß aber dy schonheit sey, daz weis jch nit." On the long history of this trope, see Richard Scholar, *The Je-Ne-Sais-Quoi in Early Modern Europe: Encounters with a Certain Something* (New York: Oxford University Press, 2005).

15. David Hume, *A Treatise of Human Nature* (1739–40), ed. L. A. Selby-Bigge, rev. P. H. Nidditch (Oxford: Clarendon Press, 1978), 299.

16. Kant, "Reflexionen zur Ästhetik, als Randbemerkungen zu A. G. Baumgartens *Psychologia empirica*" in Kant, *Schriften zur Ästhetik*, 62: "Daß die Schönheit müsse unaussprechlich sein. Was wir denken, können wir nicht immer sagen." The annotation probably dates from the mid- to late 1760s.

17. Kant, *Kritik der Urteilskraft*, §49 (B192–93); *Critique of the Power of Judgment*, ed. Guyer, 191–2; and Herder, *Kritische Wälder: Viertes Wäldchen* (1769), in Herder, *Werke*, 10 vols., ed. Martin Bollacher, vol. 2, *Schriften zur Ästhetik und Literatur, 1767–1781*, ed. Gunter E. Grimm (Frankfurt am Main: Deutscher Klassiker Verlag, 1998), 264–65.

18. George Berkeley, *Alciphron: or, The Minute Philosopher*, 2nd ed., 2 vols. (London: J. Tonson, 1732), 1:175.

exists merely in the mind which contemplates them; and each mind perceives a different beauty."[19] A circle, as he pointed out elsewhere by way of example, is not beautiful in and of itself. For even though Euclid "has fully explained every quality of the circle," he "has not, in any proposition, said a word of its beauty. The reason is evident. Beauty is not a quality of the circle.... It is only the effect, which that figure produces upon a mind, whose particular fabric or structure renders it susceptible to such sentiments."[20] Beauty is "nothing but a form, which produces pleasure, as deformity is a structure of parts, which conveys pain."[21] Hume was particularly insistent on the subjective nature of beauty. "Each mind," he declared, "perceives a different beauty":

> One person may even perceive deformity, where another is sensible of beauty; and every individual ought to acquiesce in his own sentiment, without pretending to regulate those of others. To seek the real beauty, or real deformity, is as fruitless an inquiry, as to pretend to ascertain the real sweet or real bitter. According to the disposition of the organs, the same object may be both sweet and bitter; and the proverb has justly determined it to be fruitless to dispute concerning tastes. It is very natural, and even quite necessary, to extend this axiom to mental as well as bodily taste; and thus common sense, which is so often at variance with philosophy, especially with the sceptical kind, is found, in one instance at least, to agree in pronouncing the same decision.[22]

Kant came to much the same conclusion. He regarded beauty as a sensation rather than as a quality of any given object, an experience elicited by our pleasure at the "harmonious play of our faculties of cognition."[23]

Within the specific field of music, the basic outlines of a subjective aesthetic of beauty are evident as early as 1741 in the highly influential *Essai sur le beau* by the French mathematician and philosopher Yves Marie André (1675–1704).[24] At one point in his treatise, André interviews a fictitious music-lover who has just heard a "magnificent concert" and asks him what was beautiful about it. After listening to a long account about the size of the orchestra, its pleasing sounds, the harmonious blending of voices, the precision of the ensemble, André interrupts:

19. David Hume, "Of the Standard of Taste" (1757), in Hume, *Selected Essays*, ed. Stephen Copley and Andrew Edgar (New York: Oxford University Press, 1993), 136–37.

20. Hume, "The Sceptic" (1742), in Hume, *Selected Essays*, ed. Copley and Edgar, 100.

21. Hume, *A Treatise of Human Nature*, 299.

22. Hume, "Of the Standard of Taste," 136–37.

23. Kant, *Kritik der Urteilskraft*, 68 (B29): "Harmonie der Erkenntnisvermögen"; *Critique of the Power of Judgment*, trans. Guyer and Matthews, 103. On Kant's theories of the formative power of the mind in relation to aesthetics, see David Summers, "'Form,' Nineteenth-Century Metaphysics, and the Problem of Art Historical Description," *Critical Inquiry* 15 (1989): 372–93.

24. Yves Marie André, *Essai sur le beau* (Paris: Guerin, 1741). The treatise was translated into German in 1753 and again in 1757 and appeared in dozens of subsequent editions in both French and German over the next 70 years.

Very well. Order, regularity, proportion, precision, propriety, concord: I begin to understand what is beautiful in your music. But all this is neither the sound that struck your ear, nor the pleasant sensation it aroused in your soul, nor is it the satisfaction that followed in your heart upon reflection. What would you conclude from this? I conclude that in a concert there is a pleasure more pure than the sweetness of the sounds you hear there, a beauty that is not an object of the senses, a beauty that charms the mind and which the mind alone perceives and judges.[25]

André then proceeds to delineate the distinction between sensuous and intellectual pleasure and emphasizes the primacy of the latter:

That is to say, Sir, that during the time this large ensemble of voices and sonorous instruments was impressing your ear with pleasurable harmonies, you sensed deep down within you an interior *Maître de musique* who beat time, if I may dare to put it this way, to show you how precise the music was, who revealed to you its principle by means of a light superior to that of the senses, in the idea of order, in the beauty of succession in the outline of the piece; in the idea of sonorous numbers, the rule of proportions and harmonic progressions of which they are essential likenesses; in the idea of propriety, a sacred law that prescribes each part its position, its conclusion, and the proper path by which to arrive there. In other words, while all those who were performing were each reading their notated parts on paper, you were also reading yours, written in eternal and ineradicable notes in the great book of reason, which is open to all attentive spirits. This is to say, in short, that we must either refuse music the name of harmony (which it has carried without contradiction from the first concert ever given down to the present) or we must acknowledge that there is a musical beauty, essential and absolute, which must be an inviolable rule. This is a fundamental truth that we must establish at the outset for the honor of so beautiful an art.[26]

André's approach accommodates both the sensory and the spiritual, the latter in the sense of *esprit*, which, like its German counterpart, *Geist*, connotes an intellectual experience that suggests (without necessarily imposing) elements of the divine. We perceive beauty through the senses, but it does not end there.

25. André, *Essai sur le beau*, 246–47: "Fort bien. Ordonnance, régularité, proportion, justesse, décence, accord; je commence à voir du Beau dans votre Musique. Mais tout cela n'est pas le son qui vous frappoit l'oreille, ni la sensation agréable qui en résultoit dans votre âme, ni la satisfaction réfléchie qui la suivoit dans votre cœur. Que voulez-vous conclure de là? Je conclus que dans ce concert il y a un agrément plus pur, que la douceur des sons que vous y entendez; un Beau, qui n'est pas l'objet des sens; un certain Beau qui charme l'esprit, que l'esprit seul y apperçoit & dont il juge." The translation in Le Huray and Day, *Music and Aesthetics*, 29, is based on the text of a later edition of the treatise.

26. André *Essai sur le beau*, 248–50: "C'est-à-dire, Monsieur, que pendant que tant de voix et d'instrumens sonores vous frappoient l'oreille par des accords agréables, vous sentiez au dedans de vous-même un Maître de Musique intérieur qui battoit la mesure, si j'ose ainsi parler, pour vous en marquer la justesse; qui vous en découvroit le principe dans une lumiere supérieure aux sens; dans l'idée de l'ordre, la beauté de l'ordonnance du dessein de la piéce; dans l'idée des nombres sonores, la régle

Along similar lines, Forkel maintained in the introduction to the first volume of his *Allgemeine Geschichte der Musik* (1788) that there are two different kinds of beauty, the first "absolute," appealing to the *Geist*, the second "relative," appealing to the heart.[27] To Forkel's mind, the two were not mutually exclusive; in fact, the ideal artwork combines both:

> In all the fine arts and sciences, there are in general two kinds of beauty, namely, one for the *Geist*, the other for the heart, or sentiment. Beauty for the *Geist* is based primarily on correctness in the combination of artistic expressions, on clarity, distinctness, order, and the unity of diverse parts. Because this kind of beauty is immutable for all times and for all peoples who have ascended to the necessary degree of culture, and because it is acknowledged as beauty in general, it is called absolute beauty, or that beauty that pleases the human *Geist* under all circumstances; it may not be lacking in any way in a work of art. The second kind of beauty, namely, beauty for the heart, is based on the diverse moods in the sentiments of individual persons and of nations; for just this reason it is quite diverse and variable. It is called relative beauty, or that beauty which arouses pleasure and delight or sympathetic sentiments according to the sentiments expressed in different ways by various nations and individuals. The highest that a work of art is capable of presenting is the union of these two kinds of beauty, which for this reason would be capable of arousing the most general pleasure for both the *Geist* and heart at one and the same time.
>
> *Absolute* beauty rests on the general laws of reason and sentiment on which all persons agree; it is the foundation of *relative* beauty, which is to say: without correctness in the combination of [artistic] expressions and unity of the individual parts, no beauty of any kind at all is possible.[28]

The limitations of Forkel's argument are obvious: absolute beauty is "immutable for all times and for all peoples"—provided those peoples have ascended to some essential but unspecified degree of culture, presumably one that happens

---

des proportions & des progressions harmoniques, dont ils sont les images essentielles; dans l'idée de la décence, une loi sacrée, qui prescrivoit à chaque partie son rang, son terme, & la route légitime pour y arriver; c'est-à-dire, que pendant que tous vos Concertans lisoient sur le papier chacun sa tablature, vous lisiez aussi la vôtre écrite en notes éternelles & ineffaçables dans le grand livre de la Raison, qui est ouvert à tous les esprits attentifs. C'est-à-dire, en un mot, qu'il faut, ou refuser à la Musique le nom d'harmonie, qu'elle a toujours porté sans contradiction depuis le premier concert qu'elle a donné au monde jusqu'à notre siécle, ou convenir qu'il y a un Beau musical, essentiel & absolu, en quoi en doit être la régle inviolable. Vérité fondamentale, que nous devions d'abord établir pour l'honneur d'un si bel art." The translation in Le Huray and Day, *Music and Aesthetics*, 29–30, is based on the text of a later edition of the treatise.

27. Forkel, *Allgemeine Geschichte der Musik*, 1:64–65 (§131–32). For further commentary on this passage, see Frank Hentschel, *Bürgerliche Ideologie und Musik: Politik der Musikgeschichtsschreibung in Deutschland, 1776–1871* (Frankfurt am Main: Campus, 2006), 44–48.

28. Forkel, *Allgemeine Geschichte der Musik*, I, 64 (§131–32):

In allen schönen Wissenschaften und Künsten giebt es vorzüglich zweyerley Arten von Schönheit, ne[h]mlich eine für den Geist, und die andere für das Herz, oder die Empfindung. Die Schönheit für

to coincide with the standards of eighteenth-century Europe. His observations nevertheless acknowledge the extent to which cultural distinctions can cause the same music to elicit contrasting responses, making beauty itself—or at least "beauty for the heart"—culturally contingent.

Kant distinguished between the beautiful and the agreeable (*das Angenehme*): the latter derived from an unmediated physical ("pathological") pleasure based on the senses alone. and involved no concepts (*Begriffe*). Unlike beauty, then, the agreeable could not serve as an object of judgment: one simply liked something or not, such as a particular color.[29] But instrumental music posed a problem. No one, including Kant, denied its power over human emotions; the dispute centered on the extent to which it also engaged the mind. In his *Kritik der Urteilskraft*, he followed convention in calling music a "language of sensations," describing it (along with *Farbenkunst*, the art of colors) as "the art of the beautiful play of sensations."[30] He conceded that it could provoke ideas but dismissed these as the effects of what might be compared to a "mechanical association."[31] Unlike the literary or visual arts, music speaks entirely through sentiments, without concepts, and thus leaves nothing on which the mind can reflect. In this respect, it belongs, like the nonrepresentational patterns of wallpaper, to the "agreeable" arts (*angenehme Künste*), pleasing but lacking in beauty.

---

den Geist gründet sich hauptsächlich auf Richtigkeit in der Zusammensetzung der Kunstausdrücke, auf Klarheit, Deutlichkeit, Ordnung und Einheit der mannigfaltigen Theile. Da diese Art von Schönheit, zu allen Zeiten, und von allen Menschen, die bis zu dem dazu gehörigen Grad von Kultur hinaufgestiegen sind, unveränderlich ist, und allgemein für Schönheit erkannt wird, so nennt man sie das *absolute Schöne*, oder diejenige Schönheit, die unter allen Umständen dem menschlichen Geiste Vergnügen macht, und auf keine Weise einem Kunstwerke mangeln darf. Die zweyte Art von Schönheit, ne[h]mlich die Schönheit für das Herz, gründet sich auf die mannichfaltigen Stimmungen in den Empfindungen einzelner Menschen und Nationen, ist folglich eben deswegen sehr vielseitig und veränderlich. Man nennt sie das *relative Schöne*, oder diejenige Schönheit, die nur nach dem Maß Wohlgefallen und Vergnügen, oder sympathetische Empfindung erregt, als sie den Empfindungen entspricht, die sich auf sehr verschiedene Weise bey Nationen und einzelnen Menschen äußern. Die Vereinigung dieser beyden Arten von Schönheit ist das höchste, was ein Kunstwerk hervorzubringen vermag, und eben daher auch im Stande, das allgemeinste Wohlgefallen für Geist und Herz zugleich zu erregen.

Das *absolute Schöne* beruht auf allgemeinen Grundsätzen der Vernunft und Empfindung, worin alle Menschen mit einander übereinstimmen, und ist die Grundlage des *relativen*, das heißt, ohne Richtigkeit in der Zusammensetzung der Ausdrücke, in der Ordnung und Einheit der einzelnen Theile, ist überhaupt keine Schönheit möglich.

29. Kant, *Kritik der Urteilskraft*, §5.

30. Kant, *Kritik der Urteilskraft*, 223 (§53, B218): "Sprache der Empfindungen"; 216 (§51, B211): "die Kunst des schönen Spiels der Empfindungen." *Critique of the Power of Judgment*, trans. Guyer and Matthews, 206, 201. *Empfindungen* is a word closely related to and often rendered as "sentiments."

31. Kant, *Kritik der Urteilskraft*, 222 (§53, B218): "das Gedankenpiel, was nebenbei dadurch erregt wird, ist bloß die Wirkung einer gleichsam mechanischen Assoziation." *Critique of the Power of Judgment*, trans. Guyer and Matthews, 205.

Kant wavered at this point, however: he was reluctant to assign such a low status to so powerful an art. In the end, he declared music without words to rank as either the lowest of the fine arts or the highest of the agreeable arts, more a matter of pleasure than culture (*mehr Genuß als Kultur*), but culture to at least some degree nevertheless.[32]

Hegel was even more severe in minimizing the status of instrumental music, calling it "empty and meaningless" on the grounds that it "lacks a principal feature of all art—spiritual content [*geistiger Inhalt*] and expression." On this basis, indeed, it could hardly be considered to have risen to the level of art at all. Hegel nevertheless argued that "the fundamental task of music" is to "give resonance not to objectivity but rather to the manner in which the innermost self is essentially moved according to its subjectivity and the ideal nature of the soul."[33] In this way, by treating instrumental music as an art different in kind—nonrepresentational and nonconceptual—Hegel left the door open for it to do things that other arts could not.

Instrumental music faced an additional obstacle in that it could be absorbed passively, or even against one's will: one cannot avert one's ears in the way one can turn one's eyes away from a work of literature, a painting, or a sculpture. Kant compared listening in this respect to the sense of smell: the scent of a perfumed handkerchief, he observed, imposes itself on others whether they like it or not.[34] And though the spoken arts of poetry and drama also used the medium of sound, they entailed an attendant comprehension of language, which in turn demanded mental processes not imposed by purely instrumental music.

These associations of instrumental music with passive sensation further reinforced the general notion that music was in the end an art of sentiment rather than thought, more a matter of the senses than of judgment. For there is no judgment—no reflection, no thought, no *Geist*—associated with sensory perception alone. "All sentiment is right," Hume famously declared,

> because sentiment has a reference to nothing beyond itself, and is always real, wherever a man is conscious of it. But all determinations of the understanding are not

---

32. Kant, *Kritik der Urteilskraft*, 222 (§53, B218); *Critique of the Power of Judgment*, trans. Guyer and Matthews, 205.

33. Georg Wilhelm Friedrich Hegel, *Vorlesungen über die Ästhetik*, ed. Eva Moldenhauer and Karl Markus Michel, 3 vols. (Frankfurt am Main: Suhrkamp, 1970), 3:148–49: "Dann bleibt aber die Musik leer, bedeutungslos und ist, da ihr die eine Hauptseite aller Kunst, der geistige Inhalt und Ausdruck abgeht, noch nicht eigentlich zur Kunst zu rechnen." Ibid., 3:135: "Die Hauptaufgabe der Musik wird deshalb darin bestehen, nicht die Gegenständlichkeit selbst, sondern im Gegenteil die Art und Weise widerklingen zu lassen, in welcher das innerste Selbst seiner Subjektivität und ideellen Seele nach in sich bewegt ist." Hegel's treatise on aesthetics, first published posthumously in 1835, is based on lectures given in Berlin the 1820s.

34. Kant, *Kritik der Urteilskraft*, 225 (§53, B222); *Critique of the Power of Judgment*, trans. Guyer and Matthews, 207.

right; because they have a reference to something beyond themselves, to wit, real matter of fact; and are not always conformable to that standard. Among a thousand different opinions which different men may entertain of the same subject, there is one, and but one, that is just and true; and the only difficulty is to fix and ascertain it. On the contrary, a thousand different sentiments, excited by the same object, are all right; because no sentiment represents what is really in the object.[35]

If purely instrumental music was to be counted among the arts of beauty, then passive sentiment had to be reconciled with the act of judgment, which in turn was predicated on active listening. Once again, Forkel's conviction that listening to music demands certain skills comes into play. Understanding music, he argued—and by this he implicitly meant music of all kinds, including strictly instrumental music—is like understanding an oration: one must know the meaning of a language's words and its syntax; otherwise one will be swayed by nothing more than gestures and facial expressions. Forkel quotes Shaftesbury—in English—on this point:

A Taste or Judgment can hardly come ready form'd with us into the World. Whatever Principles or Materials of this Kind we may possibly bring with us; a legitimate and just Taste can neither be begotten, made, conceiv'd, or produc'd without the antecedent Labour and Pains of Criticism.[36]

This contradicts the trope of music as consisting of "natural" signs, in contrast to the "arbitrary" signs of a verbal language. And while it must be recognized that Forkel was trying to drum up business for a series of lectures on how to listen to music—he was not a disinterested observer—the fact that he correctly perceived a need for such lectures is a good indication that the "natural" signs of music may in fact not have been as natural in practice as they were in theory.

35. Hume, "Of the Standard of Taste," 136.
36. Forkel, *Ueber die Theorie der Musik*, 9. Forkel's quotation condenses through silent omission lengthy portions of Shaftesbury's original statement, found in vol. 3, chapter 2, of Shaftesbury, *Characteristics of Men, Manners, Opinions, Times* (1713).

5   Form

For many writers in the period between 1550 and 1850, form was the central quality by which to relate music's essence to its effect. Most adhered to the principles of Pythagoreanism, in either a "hard" version based on the theory of isomorphic resonance or a "soft" version that related the fundamental nature of music to number without necessarily equating it to the structure of the micro- and macrocosms. In its more extreme manifestations, formalism denies the category of expression altogether: a work does not "express" anything other than its form, and there is no idea "in" or "behind" the music to be expressed in the literal sense of being made external. A more accommodating line of thought acknowledged music's capacity to reflect ideas or emotions in some manner—often unspecified—through the element of form.

All of these accounts approach music more as an object than as an experience, and they give priority to those elements considered pure and immutable. To perceive music as an art of expression or of beauty was to venture into realms that necessarily differed from performance to performance and from listener to listener. To perceive music as an art of form was to treat it as a stable object based on enduring principles that lay behind whatever appearances it might take on at any given moment.

Ironically, "form" itself is a notoriously slippery concept. Two of its most common usages are utterly contradictory. On the one hand, we routinely speak of the form of a work when we talk about such large-scale structural conventions as sonata form, rondo, ABA, theme and variations, and so on. Form in this sense amounts to features common to a great many works. On the other hand, we routinely use the very same term to talk about what makes the structure of any given work unique. Form can also operate on many levels, from the smallest gesture to the shape of an entire movement or even an entire cycle of movements. In every instance, form amounts to an abstraction of some kind, a mental reduction of that which is visible (in the score) or audible (in performance). Form—no matter how one defines the term—is always present in a work but cannot be perceived or identified as such without some intermediary step of reflection and thought.

To think about form, then, is to approach music in a way that emphasizes abstraction. If beauty engages both the senses and the mind, form lies one step removed from the senses, perceived through them but recognized and understood only by the intellect. It is for this very reason that Western writings on music have traditionally favored form over material substance. Zarlino's

Istitutioni harmoniche, published near the start of the period under consideration here, is typical in this regard. Zarlino pauses at one point to consider whether music, as "sounding number" (*numero sonoro*), is fundamentally a science of physics (*scienza naturale*)—that is, sound—or mathematics (number). Sound provides the material, he points out, and number provides the form. But "because we must judge all things by their noblest qualities, it makes more sense to call music a mathematical rather than a physical science, for form is more noble than material."[1]

■ FORM AS NUMBER

"Hard" Pythagoreanism continued throughout the seventeenth and eighteenth centuries, especially in northern Europe. In his *Synopsis musicae novae* (1612), the Alsatian theologian and music theorist Johannes Lippius (1585–1612) juxtaposes a description of the latest developments in musical style (triads as the basic building blocks of harmony, a more vertically oriented harmonic idiom, the fundamental role of the bass line) with a renewed validation of the structural congruence of music, the soul, and the cosmos. He opens his "synopsis of new music" with an encomium to harmony as the force that holds together the disparate elements of the universe, a force that through its sounding manifestation in music "penetrates the human structure," where it "often succeeds in awakening, establishing, and eliciting man's internal harmony." For Lippius, music is a "mathematical science... dealing with the artful and prudent composition of a harmonic piece, with a view towards moving man forcefully to moderation, for the glory of God. More briefly, music is a mathematical science that deals with the making of a harmonic piece."[2]

The astronomer Johannes Kepler (1571–1630) used the more modern sense of harmony—that is, as a concordance of vertically arranged pitches rather than the more linear, scale-like proportions expounded by writers from Plato through Zarlino—to demonstrate that recent musicians had achieved an unprecedented approximation of the audible harmony of the spheres.[3] In his *Harmonices mundi* (1619), Kepler describes a system that aligns planetary orbits with ratios

1. Zarlino, *Le istitutioni harmoniche*, 31 (book 1, chapter 20): "Ma perche dalla scienza naturale il Musico hà la ragione della materia della Consonanza, che sono i Suoni & le Voci, & dalla Mathematica hà la ragione della sua forma; cioè della sua proportione; però dovendosi denominare tutte le cose dalla cosa più nobile; più ragionevolmente diciamo la Musica essere scienza mathematica, che naturale: conciosia che la forma sia più nobile della materia." The reference to music as *numero sonoro* is from book 1, chapter 18.

2. Johannes Lippius, *Synopsis of New Music* (*Synopsis musicae novae*), trans. Benito V. Rivera (Colorado Springs: Colorado College Music Press, 1977), 3, 7–8.

3. See D. P. Walker, "Kepler's Celestial Music," *Journal of the Warburg and Courtauld Institutes* 30 (1967): 228–29. See also Eric Werner, "The Last Pythagorean Musician: Johannes Kepler," in *Aspects of Medieval and Renaissance Music*, ed. Jan LaRue (New York: W. W. Norton, 1966), 867–92.

corresponding to musical intervals. He entreats Urania, the muse of astronomy, to summon

> a grander sound, while I ascend by the harmonic stair of the celestial motions to higher things, where the true archetype of the fabric of the world is laid up and preserved. Follow me, modern musicians, and attribute it to your arts, unknown to antiquity: in these last centuries, Nature, always prodigal of herself, has at last brought forth, after an incubation of twice a thousand years, you, the first true offprints of the universal whole. By your harmonizing of various voices, and through your ears, she has whispered of herself, as she is in her innermost bosom, to the human mind, most beloved daughter of God the Creator.[4]

Kepler had an excellent knowledge of music and seems to have been partial to the works of Lassus, even going so far as to cite specific polyphonic motets by that composer.[5] The English physician and polymath Robert Fludd (1574–1637) shared Kepler's view of a harmonic universe, even if he disagreed with the astronomer's ideas about its more precise structure. Fludd was one of the last to embrace with apparently unreserved conviction the categories of *musica mundana*, *musica humana*, and *musica instrumentalis*; he refers to Boethius as if that writer had lived only a generation or two before. The images in Fludd's various publications are nevertheless unusually vivid in conveying what he perceives to be an intimate relationship among music, the microcosm, and the macrocosm (see Figures 3 and 4).[6]

For the North German composer and theorist Andreas Werckmeister (1645–1706), music is sounding number (*numeros sonoros*) and one of the means by which the Creator reveals himself to mankind: the ratios by which God created the universe are the same ratios inherent in the musical intervals that move listeners' spirits.[7] Werckmeister concedes that a listener moved by music will most likely not understand the mechanism by which numbers can

4. Johannes Kepler, *Harmonices mundi* (1619), book 5, chapter 7. Translation from Johannes Kepler, *The Harmony of the World*, trans. E. J. Aiton, A. M. Duncan, and J. V. Field (Philadelphia: American Philosophical Society, 1997), 441.

5. See Peter Pesic, "Earthly Music and Cosmic Harmony: Johannes Kepler's Interest in Practical Music, Especially Orlando di Lasso," *Journal of Seventeenth-Century Music* (http://www.sscm-jscm.org/v11/no1/pesic.html). See also Michael Dickreiter, *Der Musiktheoretiker Johannes Kepler* (Bern: Francke, 1973); Bruce Stephenson, *The Music of the Heavens: Kepler's Harmonic Astronomy* (Princeton: Princeton University Press, 1994); and Siglind Bruhn, *The Musical Order of the World: Kepler, Hesse, Hindemith* (Hillsdale, NY: Pendragon, 2005). On Renaissance beliefs surrounding the harmony of the spheres see also Gary Tomlinson, *Music in Renaissance Magic: Toward a Historiography of Others* (Chicago: University of Chicago Press, 1993), chapter 3, "Modes and Planetary Song: The Musical Alliance of Ethics and Cosmology."

6. See Peter J. Ammann, "The Musical Theory and Philosophy of Robert Fludd," *Journal of the Warburg and Courtauld Institutes* 30 (1967): 198–227.

7. Andreas Werckmeister, *Musicalische Paradoxal-Discourse* (Quedlinburg, 1707; reprint, Hildesheim: Olms, 1970), 28–29.

have such a powerful effect and cites as his authorities on this point Boethius, Augustine, and Luther.[8] This does not, however, diminish the primacy of reason. In the dedication to his *Erweiterte und vermehrte Orgelprobe* (1698), he points out that while we may not think about the mathematical basis of music during the act of listening, we perceive it nevertheless, for the sense of hearing is like a servant who obediently responds, "Yes, sir," to "that which is built on a solid foundation"—in this case, number.[9] Vincenzo Galilei had used the same imagery much earlier in his *Dialogo della musica antica, et delle moderna* (1581), arguing that the senses are the servants and not the masters of reason.[10]

Werckmeister's writings were almost certainly known to Johann Sebastian Bach, whose personal circle included at least two other individuals who promulgated Pythagoreanism: the composer and organist Johann Gottfried Walther (1684–1748) and the physician and mathematician Lorenz Christoph Mizler (1711–1778). In a compositional treatise written in 1708, Walther calls music "a heavenly-philosophical science based specifically on mathematics and dealing with sound, in so far as a good and artful harmony or concord can be brought out of the same."[11] He reiterates this idea in the opening of the treatise's second part ("Musicae poeticae") and rehearses the Platonic-Pythagorean conception of the micro- and macrocosm: man is a harmonic being whose bodily parts and soul consist of musical proportions, "as Plato and Pythagoras maintained, and with them many Christian philosophers and *Musici Mathematici.*" Because man is himself a "musical formula," he delights when presented with his corresponding image in sound, through musical proportions.[12]

Mizler, who knew Bach personally in Leipzig, founded the Societät der musikalischen Wissenschaften in 1738. Its goal was to promote the understanding of music, which Mizler defined as a "mathematical science" but whose cultivation

8. Werckmeister, *Musicalische Paradoxal-Discourse*, 25.

9. Andreas Werckmeister, *Erweiterte und vermehrte Orgel-Probe* (Quedlinburg, 1698; reprint, Kassel: Bärenreiter, 1970), "Dedicatio der ersten Edition," [5]: "Das Gehör ist nur gleich als ein Ja-Herr / bewilliget und belustiget sich an dem / was durch ein gut Fundament geschlossen und erbauet ist." On Werckmeister's view of the relations between music and the cosmos, see David Yearsley, *Bach and the Meanings of Counterpoint* (Cambridge: Cambridge University Press, 2002), 18, 20, 57.

10. Galilei, *Dialogo*, 84; *Dialogue*, 209. On the perceived relationship between reason and the sense of hearing around this time, see Michael Fend, "The Changing Function of *Senso* and *Ragione* in Italian Music Theory of the Late Sixteenth Century," in *The Second Sense: Studies in Hearing and Musical Judgment from Antiquity to the Seventeenth Century*, ed. Charles Burnett, Michael Fend, and Penelope Gouk (London: Warburg Institute, 1991), 199–221.

11. Johann Gottfried Walther, *Praecepta der musicalischen Composition*, ed. Peter Benary (Leipzig: Breitkopf & Härtel, 1955), 13: "eine himmlisch-philosophische, und sonderlich auf Mathesin sich gründende Wißenschaft, welche umgehet mit dem Sono, so fern aus selbigen eine gute und künstl[iche] Harmonie oder Zusammenstimmung hervor zubringen."

12. Walther, *Praecepta*, 75: "wie Plato und Pythagoras, und mit ihnen viele Christl[iche] *Philosophi* und *Musici Mathematici*...ein rechtes Formular der Music."

as such had been neglected. Future generations, he predicted, would be "aston-ished that musical knowledge remains so meager in spite of the heights mathe-matical knowledge has achieved in our times."[13] Perhaps the pleasure that music gives, he speculated, had obscured its fundamental nature. The musician must be well versed in *Weltweisheit*, particularly mathematics, as well as in the physics of sound, anatomy (especially of the ear), Latin, Greek, and other languages. He must have extensive practical experience in music as well, for a mathematician cannot write music. By the same token, the greatest composer cannot demon-strate the inner reasons for the coherence of even two successive measures of music. Theoretical and practical knowledge must be blended, and it was to this end that Mizler established his Society.

In his outline of the organization, Mizler announced that it would not ac-cept as members those whose knowledge of music is merely practical. Musicians versed in theory, on the other hand, would be accepted even if they are not terribly knowledgeable about musical practice, for they "can perhaps discover something useful in mathematical measurements." The ideal members of the society, Mizler declared, would be those who are equally adept at both theory and practice.[14] Bach was admitted in 1746 on the basis of his six-part Canonic Variations on *Vom Himmel hoch*, BWV 769, a work that demonstrates precisely such a combination of theoretical knowledge and practical ability.

Paradoxically, this attempt to reconcile theory and practice led to growing fric-tion between the two: whereas in previous times they could be conceived of as wholly separate spheres—ships passing in the night, as it were—they now had to be configured in such a way as to accommodate each other. A practically-minded composer and musician like Mattheson could not tolerate Mizler's Pythagorean orientation, which approached music first and foremost as an object and only secondarily as an experience. Mattheson railed against the supposed mathemat-ical essence of music on more than one occasion, beginning in *Das forschende Orchester* of 1721 and continuing with even great force in a six-page assault in *Der vollkommene Capellmeister* of 1739. As the organist and scholar Jakob Adlung noted almost twenty years later, Mizler "is a Pythagorean and for that reason contradicts Herr Mattheson quite brazenly."[15] The fact that Adlung felt no need to elaborate on this statement speaks to the enduring strength of the Pythagorean tradition: the premises of Pythagoreanism were still known well enough, even in the middle of the eighteenth century, to require no particular explanation.

13. Mizler, "Vorrede" to his *Neu-eröffnete Musikalische Bibliothek* 1 (1739), part 1, fols. 4r and 4v.

14. Mizler, "Gesetze der correspondirenden Societät der musikalischen Wissenschaften in Deut-schland," *Neu-eröffnete musikalische Bibliothek* 3 (1746), 349.

15. Adlung, *Anleitung zu der musikalischen Gelahrtheit* (Erfurt: J. D. Jungnicol, 1758), 35: "Mizler... ist ein Pythagoräer; derowegen er dem Herrn Mattheson hierinnen ganz dreyste widerspricht."

It would therefore be mistaken to cast the likes of Werckmeister, Walther, and Mizler as conservatives, relics of an outmoded tradition of thought. Indeed, the rising prestige of mathematics as an organon of all knowledge from the late sixteenth century onward ensured that the concept of music as sounding number would do more than merely endure during this time: it would actually gain in strength. Mathematics was seen as occupying a sphere of knowledge that lay beyond the vagaries of the senses and as such was understood to be the key that could unlock the laws of physics, including the physics of sound. The period's intense engagement with mathematics as a means by which to solve the riddle of the universe, Alfred North Whitehead would later observe, makes the history of seventeenth-century science "read as though it were some vivid dream of Plato or Pythagoras."[16] While we routinely view Aristotle as the ancient model for the newer empirical science, the contemporaries of Copernicus and Galileo were just as likely to see recent advances as a revival of teachings ascribed to Pythagoras.[17]

The connection between form and number was further reinforced by the image of God the Creator as a geometer-mathematician. The key scriptural passage in this regard comes from the apocryphal Book of Wisdom 11:21 in the Vulgate (also known as the Wisdom of Solomon or the Liber Sapientiae): "Omnia in mensura et numero et pondere disposuisti" (Thou hast ordered all things in measure and number and weight). This passage was one to which Augustine had turned his attention often, and it would be cited by such diverse later writers as Kircher, Leibniz, and Gottsched.[18] For Gottsched, "the beauty of an artful work... has its solid and necessary foundation in the nature of things. God has created everything according to number, measure, and weight.... The source of all beauty is the exact proportion, order, and proper balance of all the parts that constitute a thing."[19] In his landmark history of music, published in 1776, John Hawkins pointed to the Book of Wisdom to justify his belief that the principles of music "are founded in geometrical truth, and seem to result from some general and universal law of nature, so its excellence is intrinsic, absolute, and

---

16. Whitehead, *Science and the Modern World*, 46. On the rise of mathematics as an explanatory branch of knowledge, see Timothy Reiss, *Knowledge, Discovery, and Imagination in Early Modern Europe: The Rise of Aesthetic Rationalism* (Cambridge: Cambridge University Press, 1997).

17. Burkert, *Lore and Science*, 1.

18. See W. Beierwaltes, "Augustins Interpretation von Sapientia 11, 21," *Révue des Etudes Augustiniennes* 15 (1969): 51–61; Walter Blankenburg, "Der Hamonie-Begriff in der lutherisch-barocken Musikanschauung," *AfMw* 16 (1959): 44; and Ulrich Leisinger, *Leibniz-Reflexe in der deutschen Musiktheorie des 18. Jahrhunderts* (Würzburg: Königshausen & Neumann, 1994), 20–23.

19. Johann Christoph Gottsched, *Versuch einer critischen Dichtkunst*, 3rd ed. (Leipzig: Bernhard Christoph Breitkopf, 1742), 132: "Die Schönheit eines künstlichen Werkes... hat ihren festen und nothwendigen Grund in der Natur der Dinge. Gott hat alles nach Zahl, Maaß und Gewicht geschaffen.... Das genaue Verhältniß, die Ordnung und das richtige Abmessung aller Theile, daraus ein Ding besteht, ist die Quelle aller Schönheit."

inherent, and, in short, resolvable only into his will, who has ordered all things in number, weight, and measure."[20]

The period after 1750 witnessed a move toward a somewhat less rigid variety of Pythagoreanism, one that maintained the importance of number for the essence of music without a corresponding belief in the theory of isomorphic resonance. Forkel, in the first volume of his history of music, published in 1788, observed that no one really still believed in the harmony of the spheres; he nevertheless insisted that this ancient idea revealed an awareness of some sort of connection between the laws of nature and the laws of music. For those interested in pursuing this line of thought, Forkel recommended the writings of Kepler.[21]

The allure of number as demonstrable, rational, and impervious to change did not conflict with the perceived abilities of music to capture a variety of moods. Johann Kuhnau, for example, who had depicted through music stories from the Bible in great detail ("The Fall of Goliath," "The Flight of the Philistines," etc.), held fast to the idea that music is a fundamentally mathematical art. The monochord, he observed in the preface to his "musical representations of stories from the Bible," has the power to demonstrate "in a tangible and marvelous way" what may or may not be perceptible to the "deceptive sense of hearing."[22] Thus even a composer committed to music as an overtly representational art could point to number as the basis of its true, unchanging essence.

The idea of using mathematics to explain the expressive powers of music may seem counterintuitive today, but it lay at the heart of a good deal of early and mid-eighteenth-century commentary on all the arts. Leibniz, Christian Wolff, and Johann Christoph Gottsched, among others, believed that each art could be reduced to a series of rational, codifiable, and demonstrable rules. Kuhnau's double-barreled insistence on expressivity within an essentially mathematical framework is but one manifestation of this broader mode of thought.[23]

Mathematics certainly lay at the core of the aesthetics of Gottfried Wilhelm Leibniz (1646–1716), who in an oft-quoted formulation called music "the hidden arithmetical exercise of a mind unconscious that it is calculating."[24] Calculations are a function of the mind, and for Leibniz, no pleasure surpassed

20. John Hawkins, *A General History of the Science and Practice of Music*, 5 vols. (London: T. Payne and Son, 1776), 1:iv.

21. Forkel, *Allgemeine Geschichte der Musik*, 1:225.

22. Kuhnau, *Musikalische Vorstellung einiger Biblischer Historien*, prefatory letter to the reader, [4]: "handgreifflich und zur Verwunderung"; "nicht bloß auff dem betrüglichen *sensu Auditus*."

23. On the confluence of mathematics and poetics in the Enlightenment, see Frederick Beiser, *Diotima's Children: German Aesthetic Rationalism from Leibniz to Lessing* (New York: Oxford University Press, 2009), especially 49–50; and Joachim Birke, *Christian Wolffs Metaphysik und die zeitgenössische Literatur- und Musiktheorie: Gottsched, Scheibe, Mizler* (Berlin: de Gruyter, 1966).

24. Letter to the mathematician Christian Goldbach, 17 April 1721, in Leibniz, *Epistolae ad diversos*, 4 vols. (Leipzig: Bernhard Christoph Breitkopf, 1734–42), 1:241: "Musica est exercitium arithmeticae

that of the intellect.[25] This ideal, moreover, was not entirely disinterested: it satisfied a type of desire different from (and superior to) merely sensuous desire, but it was desire nevertheless. Leibniz's thought is very much in line with that of Werckmeister, who in his *Musikalische Paradoxal-Discourse* (1707) had observed that "when a well-disposed person hears music, his psyche [*Gemüt*] perceives the delightfulness intended by the Creator, but he does not know the cause, which without numbers would never have taken him there."[26]

The composer and theorist Jean-Philippe Rameau (1683–1764) also emphasized the importance of mathematics in music, even though he was not a Pythagorean: he believed that numbers could measure sound but were not themselves the source of sound. Rameau based his theories instead on the physical manifestations of the *corps sonore*, a "sounding body" whose resonance produces tones that can be measured according to precise mathematical proportions. Music, as Rameau asserts in the preface to his *Traité de l'harmonie* (1722), is

> a science which should have definite rules; these rules should be drawn from an evident principle; and this principle cannot really be known to us without the aid of mathematics. Notwithstanding all the experience I may have acquired in music from being associated with it for so long, I must confess that only with the aid of mathematics did my ideas become clear and did light replace a certain obscurity of which I was unaware before.... It is not enough to feel the effects of a science or an art. One must also conceptualize these effects in order to render them intelligible.[27]

Once again, reason explains what the senses perceive. Rameau does not trust the senses entirely and uses mathematical calculations to justify them. He makes no attempt to explain the mechanism by which music works its power over listeners, even though he acknowledges that "the true goal of music...should be the expression of thought, sentiment, passions."[28]

occultum nescientis se numerare animae." On the resonance of this observation in the eighteenth century, see Leisinger, *Leibniz-Reflexe*, 43–58.

25. See Beiser, *Diotima's Children*, 37.

26. Werckmeister, *Musikalische Paradoxal-Discourse*, 25: "Wenn nun ein wohlgesinneter Mensch eine Music höret / so empfindet sein Gemüthe zwar die Lieblichkeit / so der Schöpfer geordnet / aber er weiß doch nicht die Uhrsache / wo ihn nicht die Zahlen dahin gebracht hätten."

27. Jean-Philippe Rameau, *Traité de l'harmonie reduite à ses principes naturels* (Paris: Ballard, 1722), [iii]: "La Musique est une science qui doit avoir des regles certaines; ces regles doivent être tirées d'un principe évident, & ce principe ne peut gueres nous être connus sans le secours des Mathematiques: Aussi dois-je avoüer que, nonobstant toute l'experience que je pouvois m'être acquise dans la Musique, pour l'avoir pratiquée pendant une assez longue suite de temps, ce n'est cependant que par le secours des Mathematiques que mes idées se sont debroüillées, & que la lumiere y a succedé à une certaine obscurité, dont je ne m'appercevois pas auparavant.... Il ne suffit donc pas de sentir les effets d'une Science ou d'un Art, il faut de plus les concevoir de façon qu'on puisse les rendre intelligibles." Translation from Rameau, *Treatise on Harmony*, ed. and trans. Philip Gossett (New York: Dover, 1971), xxxv.

28. Rameau, *Code de musique pratique* (Paris: Imprimerie royale, 1760), 170: "En un mot, l'expression de la pensée, du sentiment, des passions, doit être le vrai but de la Musique." See Thomas

Diderot, too, subscribed to an aesthetic that accepted Pythagorean principles of audible proportions without their cosmic implications. In his "Principes généraux de la science du son" (1748), he praises Pythagoras for having developed the "first foundations of the science of sounds" and for discovering that the perception of them was the "source of musical pleasure." These pleasing proportions, moreover, govern not only music but the arts in general: we experience pleasure through our perceptions of relationships in "poetry, painting, architecture, moral philosophy, and all sciences" as well. "A beautiful machine, a beautiful painting, a beautiful portico please us only through the relationships we discern in them; could this not even be said of a beautiful view as much as of a beautiful concerto? The perception of relationships is the unique foundation of our admiration and pleasure; and it is from this point that we must explain the most subtle phenomena offered to us by the sciences and the arts."[29]

■ FORM AS CONTENT

The relationship of form and content has always been an uneasy one in the Western aesthetic tradition, and nowhere more so than in music. The growing distinction between the two eventually gave rise to formalism, which in its broadest sense encompasses any theory that equates a work's form with its content. Schiller, Goethe, and a number of other writers from late eighteenth and early nineteenth centuries made the case for a formalist approach to music long before Hanslick. In his *Über die ästhetische Erziehung des Menschen* (1795), Schiller identifies music as the one art whose form transcends its material, which in turn provides a model for all other arts. He considers material as something the artist must "overcome" (*überwinden*) through form.

Christensen, *Rameau and Musical Thought in the Enlightenment* (Cambridge: Cambridge University Press, 1993), 238–40.

29. Denis Diderot, *Mémoires sur différens sujets de mathématiques* (1748), in Diderot, *Œuvres complètes: Édition critique et annotée*, ed. Herbert Dieckmann, Jean Fabre, and Jacques Proust, vol. 2, *Philosophie et mathématique: Idées I*, ed. Arthur M. Wilson (Paris: Hermann, 1975), 256: "Le plaisir en général consiste dans la perception des rapports: ce principe a lieu en poésie, en peinture, en architecture, en morale, dans tous les arts & dans toutes les sciences. Une belle machine, un beau tableau, un beau portique, ne nous plaisent que par les rapports que nous y remarquons; ne peut-on pas même dire, qu'il en est en cela d'une belle vie [recte: vue] comme d'un beau concert? La perception des rapports est l'unique fondement de notre admiration & de nos plaisirs; & c'est de-là qu'il faut partir pour expliquer les phénomenes les plus délicats qui nous sont offerts par les sciences & les arts." The translations in Christensen, *Rameau and Musical Thought*, 240, and in Enrico Fubini, ed., *Music & Culture in Eighteenth-Century Europe: A Source Book*, ed. Bonnie J. Blackburn, trans. Wolfgang Freis, Lisa Gasbarrone, and Michael Louis Leone (Chicago: University of Chicago Press, 1994), 152, both of which are based on this most recent critical edition of Diderot's works, perpetuate the typographical error of "une belle vie" from page 52 of the first edition (Paris: Durand,1748). The correct (and far less obscure) reading of "une belle vue" appears in later editions of the work, as for example in the *Mémoires sur différens sujets de mathématiques* (Amsterdam: n.p., 1772), 73.

Music, at its most noble, must become an organized whole [*Gestalt*] and affect us with the serene power of antiquity; the visual arts at their most accomplished, must become music and move us through their unmediated sensuous presence; poetry, most fully developed, must grip us like music, but at the same time, as with the visual arts, surround us with serene clarity. Perfect style reveals itself thus in every art, that it knows how to remove the art's specific limitations without at the same time sacrificing its specific advantages, thereby endowing, through a wise use of its individual peculiarities, a more general character.[30]

"In a truly beautiful work," Schiller declares, "content should do nothing, the form everything":

> For it is through form alone that the whole of the human being is affected; content affects only discrete capacities. Thus the content of a work, no matter how sublime or expansive, always affects the *Geist* in a delimiting manner; only through form can we expect true aesthetic freedom. Herein, then, resides the real artistic secret of the master, *that he eradicates the material through form*. And the more imposing, assertive, and seductive the material is in its own right, the more autonomously it promotes its effect, or the more the beholder is inclined to engage with it directly, then all the more triumphant is that art which repels its material and asserts dominion over it.[31]

Schiller maintains a distinction between form and content, even if the difference between the two in music becomes virtually indistinguishable at times. In his review of a volume of poetry by Friedrich von Matthisson, he asserts that "although the *content* of emotions cannot be represented" in any work of art, "the *form* certainly can be." There is, moreover, one art, "universally beloved and

---

30. Schiller, *Über die ästhetische Erziehung des Menschen*, 154 (Letter 22): "Die Musik in ihrer höchsten Veredlung muß Gestalt werden und mit der ruhigen Macht der Antike auf uns wirken; die bildende Kunst in ihrer höchsten Vollendung muss Musik werden und uns durch unmittelbare sinnliche Gegenwart rühren; die Poesie in ihrer vollkommensten Ausbildung muss uns, wie die Tonkunst, mächtig fassen, zugleich aber, wie die Plastik, mit ruhiger Klarheit umgeben. Darin eben zeigt sich der vollkommene Stil in jeglicher Kunst, dass er die spezifischen Schranken derselben zu entfernen weiss, ohne doch ihre spezifischen Vorzüge mit aufzuheben, und durch eine weise Benutzung ihrer Eigentümlichkeit ihr einen mehr allgemeinen Charakter erteilt." For a different translation, see Wilkinson and Willoughby's edition, 155.

31. Schiller, *Über die ästhetische Erziehung des Menschen*, 154, 156 (Letter 22): "In einem wahrhaft schönen Kunstwerk soll der Inhalt nichts, die Form aber alles tun; denn durch die Form allein wird auf das Ganze des Menschen, durch den Inhalt hingegen nur auf einzelne Kräfte gewirkt. Der Inhalt, wie erhaben und weitumfassend er auch sei, wirkt also jederzeit einschränkend auf den Geist und nur von der Form ist wahre ästhetische Freiheit zu erwarten. Darin also besteht das eigentliche Kunstgeheimnis des Meisters, *dass er den Stoff durch die Form vertilgt*; und je imposanter, anmassender, verführerischer der Stoff an sich selbst ist, je eigenmächtiger derselbe mit seiner Wirkung sich vordrängt, oder je mehr der Betrachter geneigt ist, sich unmittelbar mit dem Stoff einzulassen, desto triumphierender ist die Kunst, welche jenen zurückzwingt und über diesen die Herrschaft behauptet." Emphasis in original. For a different translation, see Wilkinson and Willoughby's edition, 155, 157.

powerful, that has no other object than the form of these emotions. This art is *music*."[32]

Goethe, too, recognized the unique nature of form in music. In an aphorism that would be quoted repeatedly throughout the nineteenth century, he observed that "the dignity of art appears most eminently in music, because it has no material that would have to be taken into account. It is entirely form and substance [*Gehalt*] and elevates and ennobles everything it expresses."[33]

Like Schiller, Goethe was no hard-edged formalist. In regarding art as a "conveyor of the ineffable," he acknowledged a distinction between form and content but regarded any attempt to translate this content into words as "folly," even if the effort occasionally paid modest rewards.[34] Goethe himself was certainly not immune to the temptation of making such associations. When Felix Mendelssohn played a transcription of Bach's Overture in D Major, BWV 1068, for him on the piano in 1830, the elderly poet told him that he found the very beginning "so majestic and refined" that "one could properly see a procession of elegantly attired people descending a grand staircase."[35]

In his commentaries on music, the polymath Johann Gebhard Ehrenreich Maaß (1766–1823) betrays a similarly ambivalent attitude toward form. A noted lexicographer of the German language, Maaß lectured on philosophy, rhetoric, and mathematics at the University of Halle. He agreed with Kant that the "beauty of a thing resides in its form" and that there is a difference between the

32. Schiller, "Über Matthissons Gedichte" (1794), in Schiller, *Werke und Briefe*, 12 vols., ed. Klaus Harro Hilzinger, vol. 8, *Theoretische Schriften*, ed. Rolf-Peter Janz (Frankfurt am Main: Deutscher Klassiker Verlag, 1992), 1023: "Zwar sind Empfindungen, *ihrem Inhalte nach*, keiner Darstellung fähig; aber *ihrer Form nach* sind sie es allerdings, und es existiert wirklich eine allgemein beliebte und wirksame Kunst, die kein anderes Objekt hat, als eben diese Form der Empfindungen. Diese Kunst ist die *Musik*." Emphasis in original.

33. Goethe, "Betrachtungen im Sinne des Wanderer," in book 2 of *Wilhelm Meisters Wanderjahre* (1829), in Goethe, *Werke: Hamburger Ausgabe*, 14 vols., ed. Erich Trunz, vol. 8, *Romane und Novellen III*, ed. Erich Trunz (Munich: Beck, 1981), 290: "Die Würde der Kunst erscheint bei der Musik vielleicht am eminentesten, weil sie keinen Stoff hat, der abgerechnet werden müßte. Sie ist ganz Form und Gehalt und erhöht und veredelt alles, was sie ausdrückt." Goethe's aphorism would not always be quoted accurately. In a lecture delivered at the London Institution in 1864, for example, the composer William Sterndale Bennett quotes Goethe as saying that music "is wholly form and power," misreading *Gewalt* (power) for the original *Gehalt* (substance); see William Sterndale Bennett, *Lectures on Musical Life*, ed. Nicholas Temperley (Woodbridge: Boydell Press, 2006), 87. This mistaken rendition would also be quoted by John Sullivan Dwight in Dwight, "The Intellectual Influence of Music," *Atlantic Monthly*, 19 November 1870, 621.

34. Goethe, *Aphorismen*, 1.238, in Goethe, *Werke*, vol. 1, book 3, 39: "Die Kunst ist eine Vermittlerin des Unaussprechlichen; darum scheint es eine Thorheit, sie wieder durch Worte vermitteln zu wollen; doch indem wir uns darin bemühen, findet sich für den Verstand so mancher Gewinn, der dem ausübenden Vermögen auch wieder zu gute kommt."

35. Felix Mendelssohn to Carl Friedrich Zelter, letter of 22 June 1830, in Mendelssohn, *Sämtliche Briefe*, ed. Helmut Loos and Wilhelm Seidel (Kassel: Bärenreiter, 2008–), 1:559: "Über die Ouvertüre von Seb. Bach aus d dur mit den Trompeten…hatte er eine große Freude; 'im Anfange gehe es so

agreeable and the beautiful. In a 1792 essay on instrumental music, he observed that a work could have "true, genuine beauty without expressing anything, even a sentiment or passion, but entirely as an embodiment of tones. Why should this be any less possible with an audible object than a visible one? A rose is beautiful. At the same time, it is not an expression of an emotion or a passion."[36] Hanslick would make a similar analogy in *Vom Musikalisch-Schönen* in his attempt to decouple beauty and expression when he pointed out that "the rose has a fragrance, but its 'content' is certainly not 'the representation of fragrance.' "[37] Yet Maaß, again following Kant, notes that while works of music do not *have* to express an emotion, those that do are inherently superior to those that do not. A composition whose beauty resides exclusively in its tones "is like a body without a soul." Returning to his earlier image, Maaß compares the beauty of a flower to the beauty of "a human face in which a noble *Geist* is reflected." It is the *Geist* that gives life to the animate object, and while many objects may be beautiful, the one that projects a soul is the more moving of the two.[38]

This same sort of soft formalism, once again influenced by Kant, comes through in the writings of Christian Friedrich Michaelis (1770–1834), who heard lectures by Schiller and Karl Reinhold in Jena and who was in direct contact with the circle of philosophers who gathered there in the second half of the 1790s. Although his attempts at a career in academic philosophy proved largely unsuccessful, he played an important role in transmitting Kantian philosophy to a music-loving public through his journalistic writings.[39] Like Maaß, Michaelis accords value to musical works "not merely for what they *represent* or *signify*, but for what they themselves *are*, in their own incomparable *essence*." At the same time, he allows that music can express feelings that "arouse circumstances and ideas in us" and "*symbolically* indicate and portray what our spirit beholds or thinks."[40] Music can please either of its own accord or through imitation and

---

pompös und vornehm zu, man sehe ordentlich die Reihe geputzter Leute die von einer großen Treppe herunterstiegen.' "

36. Johann Gebhard Ehrenreich Maaß, "Ueber die Instrumentalmusik," *Neue Bibliothek der schönen Wissenschaften* 48 (1792): 6: "daß alle Schönheit eines Dinges in seiner Form angetroffen wird." Ibid., 22: "Es geht also daraus hervor, daß ein Tonstück wahre, ächte Schönheit haben könne, ohne irgend etwas, also auch ohne eine Empfindung oder Leidenschaft auszudrücken, bloß als ein Inbegriff von Tönen. Warum sollte das auch bey hörbaren Objekten weniger möglich seyn, als bey sichtbaren? Eine Rose ist schön. Gleichwohl ist sie auf keine Art ein Ausdruck einer Empfindung oder Leidenschaft."

37. Preface to the second edition (1858) of *VMS*, 1:10: "Die Rose duftet, aber ihr 'Inhalt' ist doch nicht 'die Darstellung des Duftes.' " This passage does not appear in *OMB*.

38. Maaß, "Ueber die Instrumentalmusik," 27: "Es bleibt gleichsam ein Körper ohne Seele, und verhält sich zu einer Musik, die Empfindungen ausdrückt, wie eine schöne Blume zu einem schönen menschlichen Gesichte, worin ein edler Geist sichtbar sich spiegelt."

39. See Lothar Schmidt, "Nachwort" to Christian Friedrich Michaelis, *Ueber den Geist der Tonkunst und andere Schriften*, ed. Lothar Schmidt (Chemnitz: Gudrun Schröter Verlag, 1997), 297–301.

40. Christian Friedrich Michaelis, "Ueber das Idealische der Tonkunst," *AmZ* 10 (1808): 450: "Vollendete musikalische Werke haben ihren Werth nicht etwa blos darin, dass sie etwas

expression; Michaelis grants equal validity to both and dismisses only literalistic tone painting in his taxonomy of musical options.

> Music can *in the first place* be independent. This independent, pure music pleases through its self, without meaning, without depicting, without imitating or expressing anything specific.... This music steps forth as self-sovereign and subordinate to no other art.... *Second*, music can imitate, depict, and express. In this case, it also pleases through the attractiveness of its meaning, through the truth of its depiction, through the depth of its expression. And here it appears in two regards. *Either* it seeks to express in tones inner human nature, the changes of feeling, the motions of the heart, the disposition of feelings, affects, or passions. *Or* it seeks to paint phenomena of external nature.... Musical painting must guard against copies that are small-gaited, unworthy, or wide of the mark, as well as against playful triflings.[41]

Schiller and Michaelis, as James Garratt points out, "neutralize music's pathological effect."[42] The agenda is as old as Augustine and Aquinas. In the polemics of the 1850s, however, all these earlier musings on the role of form in music's essence would be largely ignored or forgotten.

---

anders *vorstellen*, etwas anders *bedeuten*, sondern in dem, was sie selbst *sind*, in ihrem eigenen unvergleichlichen *Wesen*." Ibid., 452: "sie [die Musik] kann die eignen *Gefühle* ausdrücken, welche gewisse Gegenstände und Ideen in uns erregen, sie kann *sinnbildlich* andeuten und schildern, was unser Geist anschaut oder denkt." Emphasis in original.

41. C. F. Michaelis, "Ein Versuch, das innere Wesen der Tonkunst zu entwickeln," *AmZ* 8 (30 July 1806): 691–92: "Die Musik kann *erstens* selbstständig seyn. Diese selbstständige reine Musik gefällt durch sich selbst, ohne Bedeutung, ohne zu schildern, ohne nachzuahmen oder etwas Bestimmtes auszudrücken....Diese Musik tritt als Selbstherrscherin auf und ist keiner andern Kunst unterthan. *Zweitens* kann die Musik nachahmen, schildern, ausdrücken. Sie gefällt dann auch durch das Anziehende ihrer Bedeutung, durch die Wahrheit ihrer Schilderung, durch die Tiefe ihres Ausdrucks. Und hier erscheint sie in zweifacher Beziehung. *Entweder* sucht sie in Tönen die innere menschliche Natur, die Gemüthsveränderungen, die Bewegungen des Herzens, die Stimmung des Gefühls, Affekte und Leidenschaften auszudrucken. *Oder* sie sucht Erscheinungen der äusserlichen Natur für die Phantasie innerlich zu malen....Die musikalische Malerei hat sich nur vor kleinlichen, unwürdigen oder verfehlten Kopieen und vor Spielereien zu hüten." Emphasis in original.

42. James Garratt, *Music, Culture and Social Reform in the Age of Wagner* (Cambridge: Cambridge University Press, 2010), 30.

6 Autonomy

Autonomy is a quality that manifests itself in a variety of ways in discourse about music. It figures prominently in arguments that emphasize either or both of two closely related concepts: the unique nature of music's material elements among all the arts, and the freedom of music from any moral or social purpose.

■ MATERIAL AUTONOMY

The conviction that each art has its own strengths and limitations is as old as aesthetic speculation itself. In the eighteenth century, the emerging concept of the fine arts provoked a flood of commentary on how beauty could manifest itself through various media. By far the most important such account was Gotthold Ephraim Lessing's *Laokoön, oder: Über die Grenzen der Malerei und Poesie* (1766), which laid out sharp distinctions between the verbal and visual arts: the former operate through time, the latter through space, and their materials are not altogether compatible.[1] In these efforts to isolate, define, and classify, music posed more challenges than any other art. Lacking words, it was nonconceptual; and lacking images, it was invisible. Mimesis, the most important principle among various eighteenth-century attempts to explain beauty and the arts of beauty did not map onto instrumental music particularly well, as critics of the time were quick to point out. Even Johann Adolf Schlegel (1721–1793), who had translated Batteux's *Les beaux-arts réduits à un même principe* into German in 1751 and was otherwise sympathetic to its argument, felt compelled to question the applicability of mimesis to all music. In his heavily annotated translation of the text, Schlegel agreed that "tones can and do serve expressions," but he questioned whether *all* music necessarily does this or whether tones might not "at times also be manipulated simply as tones, according to their relationship to one another and thus in this manner also capable of pleasing a musical ear."[2]

1. See Herbert M. Schueller, "Correspondences between Music and the Sister Arts, According to 18th Century Aesthetic Theory," *JAAC* 11 (1953): 334–59; James S. Malek, *The Arts Compared: An Aspect of Eighteenth-Century British Aesthetics* (Detroit: Wayne State University Press, 1974); and David E. Wellbery, *Lessing's Laocoon: Semiotics and Aesthetics in the Age of Reason* (Cambridge: Cambridge University Press, 1984).

2. Charles Batteux, *Einschränkung der schönen Künste auf einen einzigen Grundsatz*, 3rd ed., 2 vols., ed. and trans. Johann Adolf Schlegel (Leipzig: Weidmanns Erben und Reich, 1770; reprint, Hildesheim: Olms, 1976), 1:403: "Daß die Töne zu Ausdrücken dienen können und wirklich dienen, das ist wohl kein Zweifel. Es beruhet daher alles darauf, ob die Töne allezeit nothwendig, als Ausdrücke,

Friedrich Justus Riedel (1742–1785), who would later become professor of philosophy in Vienna, harbored similar doubts. He noted in 1767 that the "artificial turns" Batteux had executed to "defend his favored position" had led to "nothing useful."[3] Sulzer maintained that the theory of mimesis was limited to the visual arts.[4]

The difficulty of applying mimesis to music encouraged philosophers to think of music as a wholly autonomous art that operated independent of image, word, or gesture. The Scottish philosopher and poet James Beattie, for one, questioned whether the alleged mimetic qualities of music are actually audible in performance. In his 1762 "Essay on Music and Poetry," he gave an extended account of what we now think of as program music, including this commentary on Arcangelo Corelli's Concerto Grosso op. 6 no. 8, which bears the subtitle "Fatto per la notte di Natale" and was widely known in English-speaking lands as his *Christmas* Concerto:

> I have heard, that the *Pastorale* in the eighth of Corelli's *Concertos* (which appears by the inscription to have been composed for the night of the Nativity) was intended for an imitation of the song of angels hovering above the fields of Bethlehem, and gradually soaring up to heaven. The music, however, is not such as would of itself convey this idea: and, even with the help of the commentary, it requires a lively fancy to connect the various movements and melodies of the piece with the motions and evolutions of the heavenly host; as sometimes flying off, and sometimes returning; singing sometimes in one quarter of the sky, and sometimes in another; now in one or two parts, and now in full chorus. It is not clear, that the author intended any imitation; and whether he did or not, is a matter of no consequence; for the music will continue to please, when the tradition is no more remembered. The harmonies of this *pastorale* are indeed so uncommon, and so ravishingly sweet, that it is almost impossible not to think of heaven when one hears them. I would not call them imitative; but I believe they are finer than any imitative music in the world.

betrachtet werden müssen; ob sie nicht zu weilen auch bloß als Töne, nach ihrem Verhältnisse untereinander, bearbeitet werden können, und auch in so fern ein musikalisches Ohr zu reizen fähig sind." Hugo Goldschmidt, *Die Musikästhetik des 18. Jahrhunderts und ihre Beziehungen zu seinem Kunstschaffen* (Zurich and Leipzig: Rascher, 1915), 134, mistranscribes the passage, substituting "zuweilen als bloße Töne" for the original "zu weilen auch bloß als Töne" and attributes it not to Johann Adolf Schlegel (who was the father of Friedrich and August Wilhelm) but rather to his older brother, Johann Elias (1719–1749). Lippmann's translation in his *History of Western Musical Aesthetics*, 117, is based on Goldschmidt's faulty transcription and perpetuates the misattribution to J. E. Schlegel.

3. Friedrich Just Riedel, *Theorie der schönen Künste und Wissenschaften* (Jena: Cuno, 1767), 146: "Die gekünstelten Wendungen, in welchen Batteux sich drehet, um diese seine Lieblings-Meinung zu vertheidigen, läßt uns schon nichts vortheilhaftes dafür vermuthen."

4. Sulzer, "Nachahmung," in Sulzer, *Allgemeine Theorie der schönen Künste*, 2:796.

Beattie concluded that "sounds in themselves can imitate nothing directly but sounds, nor in their motions any thing but motions. But the natural sounds and motions that music is allowed to imitate, are but few."[5]

In the decades that followed, mimesis would lose much of its appeal in all the arts, supplanted by ideas of genius, originality, and self-expression.[6] Lessing, Goethe, Herder, and others continued to acknowledge nature as a point of reference, but the emphasis now shifted to imitating the process rather than the products of creation. The earliest form of poetry, as Herder argued, was man's act of naming things in relation to himself, as related in the book of Genesis. The poet functions as an imitator of the godhead, a "second creator."[7]

The decline of mimesis as an aesthetic theory helped elevate the status of purely instrumental music. The Scottish philosopher and political economist Adam Smith (1723–1790) wrote with particular eloquence on this point. "The effect of instrumental Music upon the mind," he observed, "has been called its expression... [but] whatever effect it produces is the immediate effect of that melody and harmony, and not of something else which is signified and suggested by them: they in fact signify and suggest nothing."[8] Music, Smith argues,

> seldom means to tell any particular story, or to imitate any particular event, or in general to suggest any particular object, distinct from that combination of sounds of which itself is composed. Its meaning, therefore, may be said to be complete in itself, and to require no interpreters to explain it. What is called the subject of such Music is merely... a certain leading combination of notes, to which it frequently returns, and to which all its digressions and variations bear a certain affinity. It is altogether different from what is called the subject of a poem or a picture, which is always something which is not either in the poem or in the picture.[9]

Instrumental music, moreover,

> presents an object so agreeable, so great, so various, and so interesting, that alone, and without suggesting any other object, either by imitation or otherwise, it can occupy, and as it were fill up, completely the whole capacity of the mind, so as to leave

5. James Beattie, "An Essay on Poetry and Music, as They Affect the Mind" (1762), in Beattie, *Essays* (Edinburgh: William Creech, 1776), 442–43.

6. See Abrams, *The Mirror and the Lamp*; John Boyd, *The Function of Mimesis and Its Decline*, 2nd ed. (New York: Fordham University Press, 1980); and Klaus L. Berghahn, "German Literary Theory from Gottsched to Goethe," in *The Cambridge History of Literary Criticism*, vol. 4, *The Eighteenth Century*, ed. H. B. Nisbet and Claude Rawson (Cambridge: Cambridge University Press, 1997), 522–45.

7. Herder, *Vom Geist der ebräischen Poesie, zweiter Theil* (1783), in Herder, *Werke*, 10 vols., ed. Martin Bollacher, vol. 5, *Schriften zum alten Testament*, ed. Rudolf Smend (Frankfurt/Main: Deutscher Klassiker Verlag, 1993), 963: "Nachahmer der Gottheit, der zweite Schöpfer."

8. Adam Smith, "Of the Nature of That Imitation Which Takes Place in What Are Called the Imitative Arts" (1795), in Smith, *Essays on Philosophical Subjects* (London: T. Cadell & W. Davies, 1795), 173–74.

9. Smith, "Of the Nature of That Imitation," 173.

no part of its attention vacant for thinking of any thing else. In the contemplation of that immense variety of agreeable and melodious sounds, arranged and digested, both in their coincidence [i.e., harmony] and in their succession [i.e., melody], into so complete and regular a system, the mind in reality enjoys not only a very great sensual, but a very high intellectual pleasure, not unlike that which it derives from the contemplation of a great system in any other science.[10]

Smith's valorization of the "intellectual pleasure" afforded by music emphasizes the act of contemplation in ways that prefigure nineteenth-century debates about the aesthetic perception of the art.[11]

This line of thought helped promote the conceptualization of music as an autonomous art, one that did not have to (and indeed could not) follow the precepts of any other art, given the intangible, nonconceptual nature of its material. In *Kalligone* (1800), Herder argued that music, in its primordial state, had been wholly independent and had preceded language. Pan, the "awakener and herald of the music of the universe," had no need of word or gesture; Apollo, through his lyre alone, became the "founder of all choruses of the muses"; and Orpheus moved Orcus, god of the underworld, "solely through the language of his string-playing," for the "the Eumenides would not have obeyed the words of a mortal."[12] Over time, however, mankind had somehow lost faith in music's innate capacities, and "the slow course of music's history demonstrates how difficult it has been for music to separate herself from word and gesture, her sisters, and develop as an art in her own right." Music, Herder insisted, "must have its own freedom to speak for itself alone," for it "has developed itself into an art of its *own* kind, without words, through itself and in itself."[13]

10. Smith, "Of the Nature of That Imitation," 172.
11. On Smith, see James S. Malek, "Adam Smith's Contribution to Eighteenth-Century British Aesthetics," *JAAC* 31, no. 1 (1972): 49–54. Wilhelm Seidel, in "Absolute Musik und Kunstreligion um 1800," in *Musik und Religion*, 2nd ed., ed. Helga de la Motte-Haber (Laaber: Laaber-Verlag, 2003), 135–38, considers Smith the first writer to have proposed an aesthetic of absolute music; see also Seidel, "Zählt die Musik zu den imitativen Künsten? Zur Revision der Nachahmungsästhetik durch Adam Smith," in *Die Sprache der Musik: Festschrift Klaus Wolfgang Niemöller zum 60. Geburtstag*, ed. Jobst Peter Fricke (Regensburg: G. Bosse, 1989), 495–511.
12. Herder, *Kalligone* (1800), in Herder, *Werke*, 10 vols., ed. Martin Bollacher, vol. 8, *Schriften zu Literatur und Philosophie, 1792–1800*, ed. H. D. Irmscher (Frankfurt am Main: Deutscher Klassiker Verlag, 1998), 818: "Pan, Aufrufer und Verkündiger der Musik des Universum. Apollo, der die Leier erfand, als ihm der Schwan allein horchte, ward durch sich und diese Leier Stifter aller Musenchöre. Orpheus durch die Sprache des Saitenspiels bewegte den Orkus; Worten eines Sterblichen hätten die Eumeniden nicht gehorchet." E. T. A. Hoffmann repeats the image of Orpheus's lyre at the portals of Orcus in his 1810 review of Beethoven's Fifth Symphony, immediately after emphasizing that the true nature of music manifests itself only in instrumental music; see p. 144.
13. Herder, *Kalligone*, 818: "Wie schwer es der Musik worden sei, sich von ihren Schwestern, Worten und Gebärden zu trennen, und für sich selbst als Kunst auszubilden, erweiset der langsame Gang ihrer Geschichte.... Auch die Musik muß Freiheit haben, allein zu sprechen.... Ohne Worte, bloß durch und an sich, hat sich die Musik zur Kunst *ihrer* Art gebildet." Emphasis in original. On Herder's

Autonomy, as Herder suggests, is closely related to purity, an aesthetic quality with its own long history. Its roots go back at least to Aristotle, that great proponent of classification who maintained that the most potent manifestation of any phenomenon is to be found in its purest state. Enlightenment thinkers in general, given their predilection for taxonomies and hierarchies—one need think only of Kant here—were fundamentally suspicious of mixtures and valued purity all the more. As Joshua Reynolds noted in 1786, "no art can be engrafted with success on another art. For though all profess the same origin, and to proceed from the same stock, yet each has its own peculiar modes both of imitating Nature, and of deviating from it, each for the accomplishment of its own particular purpose. These deviations...will not bear transplantation to another soil."[14]

The idea of purity plays a central role in Johann Karl Friedrich Triest's survey of the history of German music in the eighteenth century, published serially in the *Allgemeine musikalische Zeitung* of Leipzig in 1801. In this lengthy essay, Triest divides music into the categories of "pure" and "applied" that do not, however, correspond to instrumental and vocal music. Vocal music whose text "says nothing" but serves instead as a vehicle for the voice belongs to the category of *reine Musik*, a definition that anticipates Wagner's idea of "absolute melody," which can be found even in opera whenever the words are subordinated to the music.[15] Triest assigns "characteristic" works of instrumental music, on the other hand—what we now think of as program music—to the category of "applied" music. He acknowledges that he has borrowed these concepts from the field of mathematics, which is divided into pure and applied branches, and that this same distinction between functional and nonfunctional music can be applied to all the arts.[16] The playwright and essayist Ludwig Tieck (1773–1853) accorded special value to purity in music. In his essay "Symphonies" (1799), he laments that instrumental and vocal music "have not yet sufficiently differentiated themselves," which in turn has prevented each from "moving on its own footing. They are still regarded too much as a unity, and it is for this reason that music itself is often regarded merely as a complement to poetry."[17] The composer and theorist Heinrich Christoph Koch (1749–1816) evoked the

efforts to reconcile art—particularly music—and nature, see Neubauer, *The Emancipation of Music from Language*, 159–63.

14. Joshua Reynolds, *Discourses on Art*, ed. Robert R. Wark (New Haven: Yale University Press, 1975), 240.

15. Johann Karl Friedrich Triest, "Bemerkungen über die Ausbildung der Tonkunst in Deutschland im achtzehnten Jahrhundert," *AmZ* 3 (1 January 1801): 227. For an English version of Triest's text, see his "Remarks on the Development of the Art of Music in Germany in the Eighteenth Century," trans. Susan Gillespie, in *Haydn and His World*, ed. Elaine Sisman (Princeton: Princeton University Press, 1997), 321–94. On Wagner, see chapter 8.

16. Triest, "Bemerkungen," 227n.; "Remarks," 387n.

17. Tieck, "Symphonien," in Wackenroder and Tieck, *Phantasien über die Kunst, für Freunde der Kunst* (1799), in Wackenroder, *Sämtliche Werke und Briefe*, 1:242: "Vorzüglich scheint mir die Vokal- und Instrumentalmusik noch nicht genug gesondert, und jede auf ihrem eigenen Boden zu wandeln,

concepts of "pure" and "applied" in a slightly different fashion in the brief edition of his music dictionary, published in 1807, using the former to describe what we would now think of as the theory and aesthetics of music, the latter to describe actual works of music, including pieces listened to "for entertainment."[18]

In each of these instances, purity is an abstraction that reveals the essence of music, and it is a concept Hanslick would invoke repeatedly in *Vom Musikalisch-Schönen: rein* (pure) and *Reinheit* (purity) are words he uses over and over throughout his text. He was not opposed to the mixture of words and music, but he insisted that musical beauty was different in kind from all other manifestations of beauty, and that it could not be identified without first being isolated. Robert Schumann, as Hanslick observed in a footnote added to the sixth edition of his treatise (1881), had "fostered a good deal of harm" with his assertion that "the aesthetic of one art is the aesthetic of others; only the medium differs.'"[19]

■ ETHICAL AUTONOMY

The concept of the fine arts rested on the conviction that the arts of beauty should serve no purpose other than to be contemplated for their own sake. This belief, which first gained currency in the eighteenth century, would eventually become what Richard Taruskin has called "the dominant regulative concept of both art-theory and art-practice for more than two centuries."[20] The intense debate on this point in the first half of the nineteenth century helped lay the groundwork for a musical aesthetic that supported the idea of an art which was ethically as well as materially autonomous.

Aesthetic autonomy developed as late as it did because earlier critics had routinely viewed beauty in relation to ethics: the beautiful and the good were long considered virtually synonymous. Shaftesbury, for example, had held that "the admiration and love of order, harmony and proportion, in whatever kind, is

---

man betrachtet sie noch zu sehr als ein verbundenes Wesen, und daher kömmt es auch, daß die Musik selbst oft nur als Ergänzung der Poesie betrachtet wird."

18. Heinrich Christoph Koch, "Reine Musik," in Koch, *Kurzgefasstes Lexicon* (Leipzig: Johann Friedrich Hartknoch, 1807), 293: "Unterhaltungstonstücke." There is no comparable entry in Koch's earlier and larger *Musikalisches Lexikon* (Frankfurt am Main: August Hermann d. J., 1802).

19. *VMS*, 1:23: "R. Schumann hat viel Unheil angestiftet mit seinem Satz...: 'Die Ästhetik der einen Kunst ist die der andern, nur das Material ist verschieden.'" *OMB*, 2. In its original context, the statement is an aphorism from the pen of Schumann's fictional "Florestan." See Schumann, *Gesammelte Schriften und Dichtungen*, 5th ed., ed. Martin Kreisig, 2 vols. (Leipzig: Breitkopf & Härtel, 1914), 1:26.

20. Taruskin, "Is There a Baby in the Bathwater?," 163. Whether it is actually possible for any art to function exclusively as an object of contemplation has been discussed elsewhere at length. In addition to Taruskin's essay, see Martha Woodmansee, "The Interests of Disinterestedness: Karl Philipp Moritz and the Emergence of the Theory of Aesthetic Autonomy in Eighteenth-Century Germany," *Modern Language Quarterly* 45 (1984): 22–47; and Michael Einfalt, "Autonomie," in *Ästhetische Grundbegriffe: Historisches Wörterbuch*, ed. Karlheinz Barck (Stuttgart: Metzler, 2000–5), 1:431–79.

naturally improving to the temper, advantageous to social affection, and highly assistant to virtue, which is itself no other than the love of order and beauty in society."[21] Over the course of the eighteenth century, however, critics began to draw distinctions between art and morals. Francis Hutcheson was among the first to do so in his *Inquiry into the Original of Our Ideas of Beauty and Virtue* (1725), which he divided into two separate sections, the first "Concerning Beauty, Order, Harmony, Design," the second "Concerning Moral Good and Evil." As Paul Guyer points out, such a distinction between the beautiful and the good would never have occurred to Shaftesbury or earlier critics.[22] In his *Kritik der Urteilskraft*, Kant would argue that the beautiful is at most a *symbol* for the morally good but does not itself constitute the good. The beautiful in and of itself, he insisted, could offer nothing in the way of moral instruction.[23] By the early nineteenth century, critics had generally accepted the idea that while truth and morality might intersect with art in certain respects, these were not necessary elements of it.

Arguments for music's social autonomy also arose as a reaction against the growing use of the art as a means of social manipulation. The nobility and aristocracy had long employed music and all the arts as a means by which to project cultural power. In the wake of the French Revolution, that power was now extended toward—and to at least some extent even placed in the hands of—entire populations.[24] The French governments of the 1790s recognized the potential of music to inspire citizens of the new republic to the cause of national unity and incorporated mass song into the rituals of their public festivals.[25] These post-Revolutionary festivals were part of a broader program to democratize the arts, and they coincided with the establishment of the Louvre as the first public art museum. This was also the era in which public concerts, though by no means new, began to enjoy popularity on an unprecedented scale throughout Europe.[26]

---

21. Shaftesbury, *Characteristics* (1711), ed. Klein, 191.

22. Guyer, *Values of Beauty*, 13.

23. Kant, *Kritik der Urteilskraft*, §17, §59. On the ethical dimension of Kant's *Kritik der Urteilskraft*, see Guyer, *Values of Beauty*, chapter 8. See also J. M. Bernstein, *The Fate of Art: Aesthetic Alienation from Kant to Derrida and Adorno* (University Park: Pennsylvania State University Press, 1992), 1–16; and Woodmansee, "The Interests of Disinterestedness."

24. See T. C. W. Blanning, *The Culture of Power and the Power of Culture: Old Regime Europe, 1660–1789* (Oxford: Oxford University Press, 2002); Tim Blanning, *The Triumph of Music: The Rise of Composers, Musicians, and Their Art* (Cambridge, MA: Harvard University Press, 2008); and Garratt, *Music, Culture and Social Reform in the Age of Wagner*.

25. See Mona Ozouf, *Festivals and the French Revolution*, trans. Alan Sheridan (Cambridge, MA: Harvard University Press, 1988); and Laura Mason, *Singing the French Revolution: Popular Culture and Politics, 1787–1799* (Ithaca, NY: Cornell University Press, 1996).

26. On the arts in France, see Shiner, *Invention of Art*, 169–86; on the rise of public concerts, see William Weber, *The Great Transformation of Musical Taste: Concert Programming from Haydn to Brahms* (Cambridge: Cambridge University Press, 2008).

Such developments made all the more acute the distinction between art as a means to an end and art as an end in its own right. The former ran the risk of compromising the integrity of art, while the latter attracted accusations of elitism, a charged notion in the wake of the French Revolution. What, then, was the proper role of art in society? This question became increasingly urgent during the second quarter of the nineteenth century. The Saint-Simonian movement in France, which flourished in the 1820s and '30s and attracted followers in Germany as well, openly promoted the arts as a catalyst of social change.[27] This "democratization" of art elicited a counterreaction from those determined to insulate the arts within their own privileged, nonfunctional space. As the French critic Gustave Planche described the situation in 1835:

> We are called upon to choose between the champions of pure art and the apostles of social reform. It seems so far that both sides take pleasure in confusing the issues. The poets cry until they are hoarse: "Poetry by itself is complete and independent, having no other mission than its own caprice, no other law than its own good pleasure: its sole legitimate purpose is to make its imaginings come to life." The moralists repeat every day: "Fantasy that serves only itself is useless in any case and often dangerous. To create just to create: That is monstrous egoism, criminal dissoluteness."[28]

Those who argued for art's ethical autonomy adopted the slogan *l'art pour l'art*. The term has a murky history that reflects the secondhand and largely garbled transmission of Kant's notion of "disinterested interestedness" to France via such figures as Benjamin Constant, Madame de Staël, and Victor Cousin.[29] As Gene H. Bell-Villada observes in his history of the concept, *l'art pour l'art*

27. See E. M. Butler, *The Saint-Simonian Religion in Germany: A Study of the Young German Movement* (Cambridge: Cambridge University Press, 1926); Ralph P. Locke, *Music, Musicians, and the Saint-Simonians* (Chicago: University of Chicago Press, 1986); and Neil McWilliam, *Dreams of Happiness: Social Art and the French Left, 1830–1850* (Princeton: Princeton University Press, 1993). For an excellent summary of the idea of literature as a means of social critique in nineteenth-century Germany, with special emphasis on the influence of Hegel, see John Walker, "Two Realisms: German Literature and Philosophy, 1830–1890," in *Philosophy and German Literature, 1700–1900*, ed. Nicholas Saul (Cambridge: Cambridge University Press, 2002), 102–49.

28. Gustave Planche, "Histoire et philosophie de l'art, VI: Moralité de la poésie," *Revue des deux mondes* 19 (1835): 241: "Entre les champions de l'art pur et les apôtres de la réforme sociale, il faut choisir et se décider. Mais il semble jusqu'ici que chacun des deux partis prenne plaisir à embrouiller la question. Les poètes crient à s'enrouer: La poésie est par elle-même une chose complète, indépendante, n'ayant d'autre mission que son caprice, d'autre loi que son bon plaisir; son but unique et légitime est de réaliser sa fantaisie. Les moralistes répètent chaque jour: La fantaisie livrée à elle-même est inutile dans tous les cas, et souvent dangereuse. Créer pour créer, c'est un monstrueux égoïsme, un dérèglement coupable." The translation is largely from John Wilcox, "The Beginnings of l'Art pour l'Art," *JAAC* 11 (1953): 375.

29. See Wilcox, "The Beginnings of l'Art pour l'Art," 360–77. Kant's writings were for all practical purposes inaccessible to French readers for many years: the *Kritik der Urteilskraft* was not translated into French until 1846. See Gene H. Bell-Villada, *Art for Art's Sake: How Politics and Markets Helped Shape the Ideology & Culture of Aestheticism, 1790–1990* (Lincoln: University of Nebraska Press, 1996), 36.

had been "basically inconceivable to the Western mind before the early nineteenth century," and it met enormous resistance when it entered public debate in France in the years around 1830. Before then, art had routinely been viewed as a social act: it was the belief that it could withdraw into its own self-contained sphere that was new.[30]

In any event, the ideology of *l'art pour l'art* reinforced the importance of both beauty and form. As Théophile Gautier pointed out in 1847, "*L'art pour l'art* means not form for form's sake, but rather form for the sake of the beautiful, apart from any extraneous idea, from any detour to the profit of some doctrine or other, from any direct utility."[31] He praised the paintings of Jean-Auguste-Dominique Ingres as "the ultimate example of art's autonomy" and declared that "*l'art pour l'art* signifies, for its adherents, a work disengaged from all other preoccupation than that of the beautiful in itself." In this same essay, Gautier speaks of the "aesthetic effect of absolute beauty."[32]

But a place of refuge can also become a place of isolation. Heinrich Heine criticized the followers of Goethe for regarding art as "an independent, second world which they rank so highly that all the doings of humankind—its religion, its morality, changing and mutable—goes along beneath it all."[33] The doctrine of *l'art pour l'art* would soon come to be linked with notions of either conservatism or apoliticism, both of which served the sociopolitical status quo.[34] Wagner, who lived in Paris from September 1839 until April 1842, witnessed this debate at first hand, and his attack on the "absolute artwork" in his Zurich writings, as we shall see, was less an attack on formalism per se than on the idea that music should exist for its own sake and not for the sake of some broader social purpose.

30. Bell-Villada, *Art for Art's Sake*, 3–4. See also Elizabeth Prettejohn, *Beauty and Art, 1750–2000* (Oxford: Oxford University Press, 2005), 97.

31. Théophile Gautier, "Du beau dans l'art," *Revue des deux mondes* 19 (1847): 901: "L'art pour l'art veut dire non pas la forme pour la forme, mais bien la forme pour le beau, abstraction faite de toute idée étrangère, de tout détournement au profit d'une doctrine quelconque, de toute utilité directe." Translation from Prettejohn, *Beauty and Art*, 98.

32. Gautier, "Du beau dans l'art," 900: "L'art pour l'art signifie, pour les adeptes, un travail dégagé de toute préoccupation autre que celle du beau en lui-même." Translation from Prettjohn, *Beauty and Art*, 97. Ibid., 900: "l'effet esthétique du beau absolu."

33. Heinrich Heine, *Die romantische Schule* (Hamburg: Hoffmann und Campe, 1836), 81: "Indem die Goetheaner von solcher Ansicht ausgehen, betrachten sie die Kunst als eine unabhängige zweite Welt, die sie so hoch stellen, dass alles Treiben der Menschen, ihre Religion und ihre Moral, wechselnd und wandelbar, unter ihr hin sich bewegt."

34. See Bell-Villada, *Art for Art's Sake*, 39.

7   Disclosiveness

On 16 March 1804 the composer and conductor Carl Friedrich Zelter (1758–1832) wrote from Berlin to Joseph Haydn in Vienna:

> Your *Geist* has penetrated the holy sphere of divine wisdom. You have brought fire from heaven and with it you warm and illuminate earthly hearts and lead them to the infinite. The best that we others can do consists merely in this: to honor with thanks and joy God, who has sent you so that we might recognize the wonders that he has revealed through you in art.[1]

We are more likely today to think of Beethoven as Prometheus, not Haydn. But Zelter's letter reflects the growing conviction at the turn of the nineteenth century that music had the capacity to disclose the "wonders" of the universe in ways that words could not, and that the greatest composers were in effect oracles, intermediaries between the divine and the human. By this reckoning, music's greatest value is formative, in that it helps us perceive the world in ways we otherwise would not.[2] Theories of music centered on its disclosive capacities do not deny the qualities of expression, form, beauty, or autonomy of the art, but they place primary emphasis on music's potential to shape our understanding of the world around us. Even Hanslick, at the very end of the first edition of *Vom Musikalisch-Schönen*, had to acknowledge music's ability to reveal higher truths, though he struggled mightily with this admission, as we shall see in chapter 9.

■ THE COMPOSER AS ORACLE

Over the course of the eighteenth century, as noted in chapter 3, instrumental music achieved the status of a language by analogy, nonconceptual but all the more powerful in its ability to express emotions. Toward the end of the century, however, changing conceptions of verbal language itself precipitated a

---

1. Joseph Haydn, *Gesammelte Briefe und Aufzeichnungen*, ed. Dénes Bartha (Kassel: Bärenreiter, 1965), 438: "Ihr Geist ist in das Heiligthum göttlicher Weisheit eingedrungen; Sie haben das Feuer vom Himmel geholt, wo mit Sie irdische Herzen erwärmen und erleuchten und zu dem Unendlichen leiten. Das Beste, was wir Andern können, besteht bloß darin: mit Dank und Freude Gott zu verehren, der Sie gesandt, damit wir die Wunder erkennen, die er durch Sie in der Kunst geoffenbaret hat."

2. See Lawrence Kramer, "The Mysteries of Animation: History, Analysis and Musical Subjectivity," *Music Analysis* 20 (2001): 153–54; and Bowie, *Music, Philosophy, and Modernity*.

fundamental rethinking of this analogy. Writers such as Herder, Johann Georg Hamann, Friedrich Schleiermacher, and Wilhelm von Humboldt, began to put forward the idea that language plays a basic role in the way in which we perceive our surroundings. From this perspective, language is not an a priori tool that can be used to designate objects and ideas (what Foucault would later call a "spontaneous grid for the knowledge of things"); rather, by its own nature it is constitutive, in that it shapes the way in which we apprehend the world around us.[3] By the early decades of the nineteenth century, philosophers no longer assumed that verbal language was the highest vehicle of human thought and expression.[4]

This new attitude toward the nature of verbal language greatly enhanced the status of instrumental music, which, as a "language" in its own right, also came to be seen as ontologically constitutive. No longer was there any need to apologize for its supposed inadequacies. For the novelist Wilhelm Heinse, writing in the mid-1790s, music was an art that expresses in universal terms what language can "indicate only rawly and clumsily." By the early 1820s, the poet and playwright Franz Grillparzer was stating a commonplace when he asserted that "where words no longer suffice, tones speak."[5] According to this line of thought, as Andrew Bowie has observed more recently, music "exemplifies how our self-understanding can never be fully achieved by discursive articulation. If all we are can be stated in words, why does our being also need to be articulated in music, as every known human culture seems to suggest?"[6] Bowie points to a passage in Friedrich Schlegel's lectures of 1805 as an exemplary articulation of the limitations of verbal language and the disclosive potential of music. Feeling, Schlegel argues, is the root of subjectivity and consciousness; yet language, for all its richness, falls short in conveying the richness of human emotion. This "fundamental deficiency" of language must be "supplemented" by another means of communication: music. As a "philosophical language"—not

3. Michel Foucault, *The Order of Things: An Archaeology of the Human Sciences* (New York: Vintage, 1994), 304.

4. Among the many commentaries on the linguistic turn of the late eighteenth and early nineteenth centuries, see Charles Taylor, *Human Agency and Language* (Cambridge: Cambridge University Press, 1985), especially 227–47; Andrew Bowie, *From Romanticism to Critical Theory: The Philosophy of German Literary Theory* (London: Routledge, 1997), chapters 1–3; Cristina Lafont, *The Linguistic Turn in Hermeneutic Philosophy*, trans. José Medina (Cambridge, MA: MIT Press, 1999), chapters 1–2; and Kurt Mueller-Vollmer, "Romantic Language Theory and the Art of Understanding," in *The Cambridge History of Literary Criticism*, vol. 5, *Romanticism*, ed. Marshall Brown (Cambridge: Cambridge University Press, 2000), 162–84.

5. Wilhelm Heinse, *Hildegard von Hohenthal*, in Heinse, *Sämmtliche Werke*, 10 vols., ed. Carl Schüddekopf (Leipzig: Insel-Verlag, 1902–25), 6:39. Franz Grillparzer, "Der Freischütz, Oper von Maria Weber" (1821), in Grillparzer, *Sämmtliche Werke*, 4th ed., 16 vols. (Stuttgart: Cotta, 1887), 11:217: "Wo Worte nicht mehr hinreichen, sprechen die Töne."

6. Andrew Bowie, *Aesthetics and Subjectivity from Kant to Nietzsche*, 2nd ed. (Manchester: Manchester University Press, 2003), 3.

as a representational art—music in fact stands "high above art in general," for "feeling and will often go far beyond thought. Music, as inspiration, as the language of feeling, which agitates consciousness at its source, is the only universal language and the only ideal for any language that would justify itself by acting upon the innermost heart of consciousness. To be sure, feeling does not take precedence as the ruler of consciousness, though in terms of priority and origin it does."[7]

Against this background, a composer of instrumental music could be seen as something of an oracle, using a language that operates on principles beyond words, reason, and concepts. Oracles disclose: they do not explain what they say, and what they say is often cryptic and obscure. How much we can glean something from them depends on our efforts as listeners to come to terms with their utterances.

This reconfigured perception of music as an oracular language appeared around the same time that a handful of composers—most notably Haydn, Mozart, and Beethoven—were beginning to be hailed as geniuses, as Promethean figures with access to divine insights that they could convey, through music, to mere mortals. The genius of individual composers had been recognized long before, to be sure, but it was understood as a faculty, not as an identity. The letters of Mozart and his family speak of Wolfgang's genius, but at no point does anyone in his family ever refer to him *as* a genius. Usage changed rapidly in the decades around 1800, however, when critics began to hail Beethoven as the paradigmatic genius of music.

Mattheson's image of the composer as orator, engaging listeners in a manner that is both pleasing and intelligible, had by this point become a distant memory. The composer is now an oracle who speaks in tones that cannot be translated into words: rhetoric gives way to revelation.[8] The effective orator leads listeners step by step, compelling them toward a particular point of view, a specific and ineluctable conclusion. An oracle, by contrast, reveals truth in an oblique

---

7. Friedrich Schlegel, *Kritische Friedrich-Schlegel-Ausgabe*, ed. Ernst Behler, vol. 13, *Philosophische Vorlesungen, 1800–1807*, ed. Jean-Jacques Anstett (Munich: Ferdinand Schöningh, 1964), 57–58: "Dieses geschieht durch die Musik, die aber hier weniger als darstellende Kunst zu betrachten ist, wie als philosophische Sprache, und eigentlich noch weit höher liegt, als die bloße Kunst.... Fühlen und Wollen geht oft weit über das Denken hinaus; die Musik, als Begeisterung, als Sprache des Gefühls, die das Bewußtsein in seiner Urquelle aufregt, ist die einzige universelle Sprache, und das einzige Ideal für dieselbe, das sich rechtfertigen läßt, indem sie eben in das innerste Herz des Bewußtseins eingreift. Das Gefühl hat allerdings nicht als Beherrscherin des Bewußtseins den Vorrang, wohl aber in Rücksicht der Priorität und des Ursprungs." Bowie's discussion of this passage (*Music, Philosophy, and Modernity*, 101–2) offers a different translation.

8. On the decline of rhetoric in the early nineteenth century as an explanatory model for music, see Bonds, *Wordless Rhetoric*, 141–49; on the decline of rhetoric in general around this time, see David Wellbery, "The Transformation of Rhetoric," in *The Cambridge History of Literary Criticism*, vol. 5, *Romanticism*, ed. Marshall Brown (Cambridge: Cambridge University Press, 2000), 185–202.

manner: listeners struggle to understand, and they disagree about the import of what they have heard. The effective orator sweeps listeners along, while an oracle requires—demands—interpretation. This shift in the presumptions of a listener's responsibilities one of the most significant of all the many changes that took place in music in the years around 1800. Listening moves from a largely passive experience to an activity of mind, and in this nonconceptual mode of thought, insight comes only with effort. The onus is now on the listener to come to terms with the music, hence the explosion of publications aimed at its consumers: periodicals; Forkel's public lectures, aimed at amateurs who wanted to understand music better; and above all, biographies of composers. The expression "understanding music" begins to take hold around this time.[9] In the decades around 1800, a substantial industry of decipherment arises to meet the demands of this increasingly oracular art.

And here, the absence of concepts in purely instrumental music enhances its perceived ability to reveal a higher sort of reality. Obscurity becomes a virtue. In his *Philosophical Enquiry into the Origins of our Ideas of the Sublime and Beautiful* (1756), Edmund Burke (1729–1797) had praised the power of that which lies beyond our comprehension, equating clarity with smallness, obscurity with greatness.

> It is one thing to make an idea clear, and another to make it *affecting* to the imagination. If I make a drawing of a palace, or a temple, or a landscape, I present a very clear idea of those objects; but then...my picture can at most affect only as the palace, temple, or landscape would have affected in the reality. On the other hand, the most lively and spirited verbal description I can give raises a very obscure and imperfect *idea* of such objects; but then it is in my power to raise a stronger *emotion* by the description than I could do by the best painting.
>
> ...I think there are reasons in nature why the obscure idea, when properly conveyed, should be more affecting than the clear. It is our ignorance of things that causes all our admiration, and chiefly excites our passions. Knowledge and acquaintance make the most striking causes affect but little.... The ideas of eternity, and infinity, are among the most affecting we have, and yet perhaps there is nothing of which we really understand so little, as of infinity and eternity.... Hardly any thing can strike the mind with its greatness, which does not make some sort of approach towards infinity; which nothing can do whilst we are able to perceive its bounds; but to see an object distinctly, and to perceive its bounds, is one and the same thing. A clear idea is therefore another name for a little idea.[10]

9. Frieder Zaminer, "Über die Herkunft des Ausdrucks 'Musik verstehen,'" in *Musik und Verstehen: Aufsätze zur semiotischen Theorie, Ästhetik und Soziologie der musikalischen Rezeption*, ed. Peter Faltin and Hans-Peter Reinecke (Cologne: Arno Volk, 1973), 314–19.

10. Edmund Burke, *A Philosophical Enquiry into the Origins of Our Ideas of the Sublime and Beautiful* (1756), rev. ed., ed. James T. Boulton (Oxford: Basil Blackwell, 1987), 60, 61, 63.

The early romantic philosophers were quick to associate beauty with the infinite, the obscure, and the impenetrable. These ideas filtered down to a broader public through periodicals like the semiweekly *Allgemeine musikalische Zeitung,* whose contributors included Friedrich Rochlitz (the journal's first editor), Christian Friedrich Michaelis, and above all E. T. A. Hoffmann (1776–1822). In his 1810 review of Beethoven's Fifth Symphony, Hoffmann declares that while Haydn and Mozart lead us into higher realms of the spirit, it is the music of Beethoven that opens up to us "the realm of the monstrous and immeasurable. Burning rays of light shoot through the deep night of this realm, and we become aware of giant shadows that surge back and forth." The imagery evokes Plato's Cave, a site in which we gain knowledge by becoming aware of the limitations of our knowledge.[11] This scenario is routinely associated with theories of the sublime, but it is also—and, more importantly—an indication of the new alliance between instrumental music and insight: the symphony is now a vehicle of disclosure about the nature of the universe.

The idea of the artist as oracle was not entirely new, of course: the concept of *furor poeticus* as a form of divine madness is as old as antiquity. The rules of art defied codification because artistic creation demanded a transcendence of reason and logic. For Socrates, it required a kind of madness "that is possession by the Muses, which takes a tender virgin soul and awakens it to a Bacchic frenzy of songs and poetry.... If anyone comes to the gates of poetry and expects to become an adequate poet by acquiring expert knowledge of the subject without the Muses' madness, he will fail, and his self-controlled verses will be eclipsed by the poetry of men who have been driven out of their minds."[12] Elsewhere, in *Ion,* Socrates points out that

> a poet is an airy thing, winged and holy, and he is not able to make poetry until he becomes inspired and goes out of his mind and his intellect is no longer in him. As long as a human being has his intellect in his possession he will always lack the power to make poetry or sing prophecy.... You see, it's not mastery that enables them [poets] to speak those verses, but a divine power.... The god takes their intellect away from them when he uses them as his servants... the god himself is the one who speaks, and he gives voice through them to us.... In this more than anything, then, I think, the god is showing us... that these beautiful poems are not human, not even *from* human beings, but are divine and from gods; that poets are nothing but representatives of the gods, possessed by whoever possesses them.[13]

11. E. T. A. Hoffmann, review of Beethoven's Fifth Symphony, *AmZ* 12 (4 July 1810): 632–33: "das Reich des Ungeheueren und Unermesslichen. Glühende Strahlen schiessen durch dieses Reiches tiefe Nacht, und wir werden Riesenschatten gewahr, die auf- und abwogen." On Hoffmann's review as it relates to contemporaneous theories of epistemology, see Bonds, *Music as Thought,* 44–59.

12. Plato, *Phaedrus* 245a, trans. Alexander Nehamas and Paul Woodruff, in *Complete Works,* ed. Cooper, 523.

13. Plato, *Ion* 533e–34e, trans. Paul Woodruff, in Plato, *Complete Works,* ed. Cooper, 941–42. On the concept of genius and inspiration as applied to major composers of the eighteenth and early nineteenth

Before the early decades of the nineteenth century, however, few if any critics had applied such thinking to composers, least of all to composers of instrumental music. Music's primary obligation up to this point had been to serve the cause of beauty; the new expectations of metaphysical revelation called into question even this most basic assumption. Beethoven was one of the first to suffer at the hands of listeners and critics who had not yet accepted this new approach to the art. His "pure" and "autonomous instrumental music," the Swiss conductor and pedagogue Hans Georg Nägeli (1773–1836) observed in defense of Beethoven, still during the composer's lifetime, had confused many listeners, especially those who expected to hear lyrical melody (*Cantabilität*).

> Whenever his novelty is admired and praised, one hears often enough the question: But is it beautiful? Must the novel not also be beautiful? And one was justified to ask this when lyricism was a condition of beauty. For this is what Beethoven counterattacked, like an artistic hero of battle. In his music it is not a human voice but a spirit-voice that predominates. But this kind of voice belongs to a higher organism than that which possesses a human throat. How he used it to address, seize, and penetrate the psyches of others—all the larger cities of Europe and many smaller ones, including my Zurich—bear witness to this.[14]

Such pronouncements would soon become a commonplace of Beethoven criticism. For the critic Eduard Krüger (1807–1885), Beethoven was "the most recent son of the Titans" to whom "human songs" were "distant" and whose instrumental works could lead listeners into a far-off realm.[15] "With Beethoven's symphonies," the journalist and literary critic Julian Schmidt observed in 1853, "we have the feeling that we are dealing with something very different from the usual alternations of joy and sorrow through which wordless music ordinarily moves us. We intuit the mysterious abyss of a spiritual world, and we torment ourselves in an effort to understand it."[16]

---

centuries, see Peter Kivy, *The Possessor and the Possessed: Handel, Mozart, Beethoven, and the Idea of Musical Genius* (New Haven: Yale University Press, 2001).

14. Hans Georg Nägeli, *Vorlesungen über Musik, mit Berücksichtigung der Dilettanten* (Stuttgart and Tübingen: Cotta, 1826), 188: "Oft genug hörte man, wo seine Neuheit bewundert und gepriesen wurde, die Frage: aber ist denn das schön? muß das Neue nicht auch schön seyn? und man hatte ganz recht, so zu fragen, wenn man die Cantabilität zur Bedingung der Schönheit machte. Denn das war es eben, womit Beethoven, wie ein künstlerischer Schlachtheld, in Gegenstoß gerieth. In seiner Musik weht nicht eine Menschenstimme, sondern eine Geisterstimme. Diese aber hat einen höhern Organismus, als der ist, welcher in der menschlichen Kehle wurzelt. Wie er damit die Gemüther ansprach, ergriff, durchdrang, davon können alle größern Städte Europa's, und viele kleinere, wie auch mein Zürich, zeugen." Nägeli dedicated his published *Vorlesungen* to Archduke Rudolph of Austria (1788–1831), Beethoven's patron and composition pupil.

15. Eduard Krüger, *Beiträge für Leben und Wissenschaft der Tonkunst* (Leipzig: Breitkopf & Härtel, 1847), 164.

16. Julian Schmidt, *Geschichte der deutschen Nationalliteratur im neunzehnten Jahrhundert*, 2 vols. (Leipzig: Herbig, 1853), 2:410: "Bei Beethoven's Symphonien haben wir das Gefühl, es handle sich

■ BEAUTIFUL INSIGHTS

The sublime—that which surpassed comprehension—was not the only means by which the arts could disclose the nature of the universe. Beauty, according to many of the leading philosophers of the eighteenth century, could provide such insights as well. Moses Mendelssohn stressed the potential of beauty to reveal the innermost nature of the human spirit when he observed in 1757 that the fine arts are "an occupation for the virtuoso, a source of pleasure for the amateur, and a school of teaching for the world-wise." The "deepest secrets of our soul" are hidden in the "rules of beauty," and "every rule of beauty is a discovery in the theory of the soul."[17] And in his influential essay *Über die bildende Nachahmung des Schönen* (1788), Karl Philipp Moritz (1756–1793) maintained that "every beautiful whole from the hand of the visual artist is thus in miniature a reflection of the highest form of beauty in the great wide realm of nature."[18] August Wilhelm Schlegel would quote Moritz's assertion approvingly in his 1802 Berlin lectures on the fine arts, first published in 1805 and reissued frequently.[19] Goethe, too, was drawn to this observation and would make a modified extract of it in his digest of Moritz's work. "The vivid poetic contemplation of a limited situation," as he observed on another occasion, "elevates an individual object to a delineated yet boundless All, so that in a small space we believe we see the entire world."[20] And in a dialogue on truth and plausibility in art, Goethe has the more intelligent of the two participants observe that "a consummate work of art is a work of human *Geist* and in this sense also a work of nature." The beholder,

---

um etwas ganz Anderes, als um den gewöhnlichen Wechsel von Lust und Schmerz, in welchem sich die wortlose Musik sonst bewegt. Wir ahnen den geheimnißvollen Abgrund einer geistigen Welt, und quälen uns um das Verständniß." Further documentation of this kind is available in Hans Heinrich Eggebrecht, *Zur Geschichte der Beethoven-Rezeption*, 2nd ed. (Laaber: Laaber-Verlag, 1994).

17. Moses Mendelssohn, "Über die Hauptgrundsätze der schönen Künste und Wissenschaften," in Mendelssohn, *Schriften zur Philosophie, Aesthetik und Apologetik*, 2:143: "Die schönen Künste und Wissenschaften sind für den Virtuosen eine Beschäftigung, für den Liebhaber eine Quelle des Vergnügens, und für den Weltweisen eine Schule des Unterrichts. In den Regeln der Schönheit, die das Genie des Künstlers empfindet und der Kunstrichter in Vernunftschlüsse auflöst, liegen die tiefsten Geheimnisse unserer Seele verborgen. Jede Regel der Schönheit ist zugleich eine Entdeckung in der Seelenlehre."

18. Karl Philipp Moritz, *Über die bildende Nachahmung des Schönen* (1788), in Moritz, *Werke*, ed. Heide Holmer and Albert Meier, 2 vols. (Frankfurt am Main: Deutscher Klassiker Verlag, 1997), 1:969: "Jedes schöne Ganze aus der Hand des bildenden Künstlers ist daher im Kleinen ein Abdruck des höchsten Schönen im großen Ganzen der Natur."

19. August Wilhelm Schlegel, *Vorlesungen über Ästhetik I (1798–1803)*, ed. Ernst Behler (Paderborn: Ferdinand Schöningh, 1989), 259.

20. Goethe, review of *Des Knaben Wunderhorn* in the *Jenaische Allgemeine Literaturzeitung* (1806), republished in Goethe, *Werke: Hamburger Ausgabe*, vol. 12, *Schriften zur Kunst*, ed. Erich Trunz and Hans Joachim Schrimpf (Munich: Beck, 1981), 282: "Das lebhafte poetische Anschauen eines beschränkten Zustandes erhebt ein Einzelnes zum zwar begrenzten, doch unumschränkten All, so daß wir im kleinen Raume die ganze Welt zu sehen glauben."

through repeated contemplation, gains a sense that he "must be able to elevate himself to a higher existence."[21]

Schiller also considered beauty disclosive, a synthesis of the senses and intellect, body and mind. "Only through the morning-portal of beauty / Shall you press into the land of insight," he wrote in his poem *Die Künstler* (1789).[22] Along these same lines, Wackenroder would maintain that it is "in the mirror of tones" that "the human heart gets to know itself," using the German verb *kennenlernen*—figuratively, "to meet," or literally, "to learn to know." Music's tones "give living consciousness to many a dreaming spirit in the hidden corners of the psyche."[23]

Wackenroder and his collaborator Tieck are often dismissed as overly emotional enthusiasts and not "true" philosophers: *schwärmerisch*—rhapsodic and hypersensitive, tinged with irrationality—is a word critics seem incapable of avoiding when talking about these two. But this attitude denies the potential of an unconventional style of prose to articulate ideas already in the philosophical mainstream, including the belief that a musical work can represent an alternative, interior world, which in turn possesses the capacity to disclose otherwise inaccessible features of the experienced world. From this perspective, music is not an escapist realm of dream: it is an art that helps us better comprehend the earthly reality in which we live. The paradigmatic expressions of romantic musical criticism—the writings of Wackenroder, Tieck, and Hoffmann—are in the end at least as much about disclosure and intellect as they are about expression and emotion.[24]

The idea of art as a means of disclosure is basic to the early philosophy of Friedrich Wilhelm Schelling (1775–1854). Art is "the one true and eternal organon and at the same time document of philosophy," he declared in his widely read *System des transzendentalen Idealismus* (1800), for it "constantly makes known that which philosophy cannot present externally, namely, the primordial unity of the conscious and unconscious."[25] In this treatise, Schelling dwells

21. Johann Wolfgang Goethe, "Über Wahrheit und Wahrscheinlichkeit der Kunstwerke: Ein Gespräch" (1798), in Goethe, *Werke: Hamburger Ausgabe*, 14 vols., ed. Erich Trunz, vol. 12, *Schriften zur Kunst, Schriften zur Literatur, Maximen und Reflexionen*, ed. Erich Trunz and Hans Joachim Schrimpf (Munich: Beck, 1981), 72: "Ein vollkommenes Kunstwerk ist ein Werk des menschlichen Geistes, und in diesem Sinne auch ein Werk der Natur." "Er fühlt, daß er...sich selbst dadurch eine höhere Existenz geben müsse."

22. Schiller, "Die Künstler," in Schiller, *Werke und Briefe*, ed. Klaus Harro Hilzinger, 12 vols., vol. 1, *Gedichte*. ed. Georg Kurscheidt, 208: "Nur durch das Morgentor des Schönen / Drangst du in der Erkenntnis Land."

23. Wilhelm Heinrich Wackenroder, "Das eigentümliche innere Wesen der Tonkunst, und die Seelenlehre der heutigen Instrumentalmusik" (1799), in Wackenroder, *Sämtliche Werke und Briefe*, 1:220: "In dem Spiegel der Töne lernt das menschliche Herz sich selber kennen"; "sie geben vielen in verborgenen Winkeln des Gemüths träumenden Geistern lebendes Bewußtweyn."

24. On the relationship of Wackenroder, Tieck, and Hoffmann to early romantic idealist philosophy, see Bonds, *Music as Thought*, 5–43.

25. Friedrich Wilhelm Joseph von Schelling, *System des transzendentalen Idealismus* (1800), ed. Horst D. Brandt and Peter Müller (Hamburg: Felix Meiner, 1992), 299: "So versteht sich von selbst, daß die Kunst das einzige wahre und ewige Organon zugleich und Dokument der Philosophie sei,

at length on the idea of art as the highest form of thought available to the philosopher. Art "opens, as it were, the holiest of holies.... When a great painting comes into being it is as though the invisible curtain that separates the real from the ideal world is raised."[26] In his lectures on the philosophy of art delivered a few years later in Jena, Schelling would evoke Pythagoras and Kepler at various junctures, stating at one point that "rhythm, harmony, and melody... are the first and purest forms of motion in the universe." "The forms of music," he declared, "are the forms of eternal things in so far as they can be considered from the perspective of the material world," and music is "nothing other than the perceived rhythm and harmony of the visible universe itself."[27] Sound and tone play an especially important role in this regard, for "in the battle between the spiritual and the physical, music alone can be an image of primordial nature and its motion, as its entire essence consists of circulation."[28]

Hegel accepted the disclosive capacity of the arts in general when he defined beauty as the sensuous manifestation of the Idea.[29] But he did not accord any particularly disclosive capacity to music and least of all to instrumental music, on the grounds that it was non-conceptual. In this respect, Hegel followed very much in the footsteps of Kant.

Over time, however, more and more writers acknowledged music as the most disclosive of all the arts. Ferdinand Gotthelf Hand, in one of the first extended philosophical treatises devoted solely to the aesthetics of the music (1837-41), saw beauty as a manifestation of infinity: "the idea becomes a perceptible *Gestalt*, in that the human soul reveals itself in its highest degree of purity; in that through the presentation of the unconditioned, the perfect, that which is pure *Geist*, as

---

welches immer und fortwährend aufs neue beurkundet, was die Philosophie äußerlich nicht darstellen kann, nämlich das Bewußtlose im Handeln und Produzieren, und seine ursprüngliche Identität mit dem Bewußten." On the importance of art in Schelling's philosophy, see Dieter Jähnig, *Schelling: Die Kunst in der Philosophie*, 2 vols. (Pfullingen: Neske, 1966–69), especially vol. 2, *Die Wahrheitsfunktion der Kunst*.

26. Schelling, *System des transzendentalen Idealismus*, 299: "Die Kunst ist eben deswegen dem Philosophen das Höchste, weil sie ihm das Allerheiligste gleichsam öffnet.... Jedes herrliche Gemälde entsteht dadurch gleichsam, daß die unsichtbare Scheidewand aufgehoben wird, welche die wirkliche und idealische Welt trennt, und ist nur die Öffnung, durch welche jene Gestalten und Gegenden der Phantasiewelt, welche durch die wirkliche nur unvollkommen hindurchschimmern, völlig hervortreten."

27. Schelling, *Philosophie der Kunst* (1802-3), ed. K. F. A. Schelling (Stuttgart: Cotta, 1859; reprint, Darmstadt: Wissenschaftliche Buchgesellschaft, 1976), 503: "Rhythmus, Harmonie und Melodie... sind die ersten und reinsten Formen der Bewegung im Universum." Ibid., 501: "Die Formen der Musik sind Formen der ewigen Dinge, inwiefern sie von der realen Seite betrachtet warden... demnach die Musik nichts anderes als der vernommene Rhythmus und die Harmonie des sichtbaren Universums selbst."

28. Schelling, *Die Weltalter: Fragmente in den Urauffassungen von 1811 und 1813*, ed. Manfred Schröter (Munich: Beck, 1966), 43: "Weil Klang und Ton allein in eben jenem Kampf zwischen Geistigkeit und Körperlichkeit zu entstehen scheinen: so kann die Tonkunst allein ein Bild jener uranfänglichen Natur und ihrer Bewegung seyn, wie denn auch ihr ganzes Wesen im Umlauf besteht."

29. Hegel, *Vorlesungen über die Ästhetik*, 1:151: "So ist *Schönheit* und *Wahrheit* einerseits dasselbe;... das sinnliche Scheinen der Idee." Emphasis in original.

no object of everyday experience offers, intimations of the soul are awakened that go beyond the boundaries of conditioned finitude and transport us to an invisible and inaudible world."[30] A work of art has achieved its goal "when it finds in the well-ordered structure of sensuously perceptible forms the reflection of a hidden infinity and awakens in the beholder the consciousness of a unity of finite and eternal existence in both the small and large scale, which transport him to the region of an unconditioned freedom and of a pure peace of the soul."[31]

■ COSMIC INSIGHTS

The idea that music might provide insight into the structure of the cosmos is as old as Pythagoreanism, a mode of thought that many philosophers and critics working around 1800 found attractive for its holistic perspective. Johann Friedrich Hugo von Dalberg (1760–1812) was one of several writers of his generation who endorsed an essentially Pythagorean conception of music. A Protestant cleric and polymath, Dalberg was an accomplished pianist who had studied composition with Ignaz Holzbauer in Mannheim. Music provides the soul (a "world in miniature") with a glimpse of a "higher world," and he quoted with approval Leibniz's description of music as an "ongoing calculation of the soul."[32] His *Blicke eines Tonkünstlers in die Musik der Geister* (1787) posits a latter-day *musica humana* in which humans act "according to the laws of music" in all matters.[33]

By the lights of early romantic philosophy, the disclosive capacities of music were just as important as its expressive capacities. No one perceived these qualities as contradictory in any way. Lockmann, the fictional composer and conductor in Wilhelm Heinse's novel *Hildegard von Hohenthal* (1795–96), spends a great deal of time emoting about music's ability to convey feelings, yet he also

30. Ferdinand Gotthelf Hand, *Aesthetik der Tonkunst*, 2 vols. (Leipzig: Hochhausen und Fournes; Jena: Carl Hochhausen, 1837–41), 1:271–72: "Das Unendliche aber kömmt im Schönen zur Erscheinung, und die Idee wird zur sinnlicherfaßbaren Gestalt, indem die Seele des Menschen in ihrer höchsten Reinheit sich offenbart; indem durch die Darstellung des Unbedingten, des Vollkommenen, des Reingeistigen, wie kein Gegenstand der gewöhnlichen Erfahrung es darbietet, Ahndungen der Seele erweckt werden, welche über die Schranken der bedingten Endlichkeit hinausführen und in eine unsichtbare und unhörbare Welt versetzen."

31. Hand, *Aesthetik*, 2:43: "Erreicht hat das Kunstwerk seinen Zweck, wenn der Abglanz eines verborgenen Unendlichen in dem wohlgeordneten Aufbau sinnlich erfaßbarer Formen Raum findet und das Bewußtweyn einer Einheit des endlichen und ewigen Daseyns im Kleinen, wie im Großen, dem Beschauer Ahndungen weckt, die ihn in die Region einer unbedingten Freiheit und eines reinen Seelenfriedens versetzen."

32. Johann Friedrich Hugo von Dalberg, *Vom Erfinden und Bilden* (Frankfurt am Main: Johann Christian Hermann, 1791), 39: "eine Welt im kleinen"; "eine höhere Welt." Ibid., 9: "eine fortwährende Rechenkunst der Seele."

33. Johann Friedrich Hugo von Dalberg, *Blicke eines Tonkünstlers in die Musik der Geister* (Mannheim: Neue Hof- und akademische Buchhandlung, 1787), 7.

holds forth repeatedly on the connections between music, number, and the universe. "Oh, if only I were Pythagoras!" he cries out in frustration at one point. "I could demonstrate to you and cause you to feel in sufficient depth the enchanting perfection of all primordial creation in the mysterious relations of 1, 2, 3, 4, and 5."[34] In a footnote to his own text, Heinse notes that Pythagoras was the inventor of the monochord, which is "undoubtedly the entryway to the realm of holiness."[35] On another occasion, Lockmann declares that the height, depth, strength, weakness, duration, succession, and connection of tones constitutes "pure music" (die reine Musik), which we perceive not simply with our ears but with our entire bodies: "Our feeling itself is nothing other than an inner music, the constant vibration of our life nerves."[36] Appropriately enough, an image of Pythagoras seated at his monochord graces the frontispiece of the first volume of the novel's first edition.

The idea of listening with the entire body appears in Herder's Kalligone (1800) as well. In a remarkable passage, Herder notes that as a "participant in the universe," every human being is an Akroatiker. This apparent neologism is derived from akroasis, a term used in ancient Greek pedagogy to identify the process of learning through listening, as opposed to seeing (aisthesis). More specifically within the pedagogy of rhetoric, akroasis was an exercise in which students listened to an oration with an ear toward memorizing it and absorbing its structure.[37] To understand the structure of the cosmos, Herder says, we must listen attentively to the "voice of the universe." The interiority of the ear is an indicator of the depth of listening, both literally and figuratively, and we listen "almost with our entire body."[38] Thus, the act of listening unites the sense of hearing and the mind at the deepest possible level, with the mind simultaneously analyzing, as

---

34. Heinse, Hildegard von Hohenthal, in Heinse, Sämmtliche Werke, 6:20: "O, wär' ich Pythagoras, um Ihnen die entzückende Vollkommenheit aller Urgeschöpfe in den geheimnißvollen Verhältnissen von 1, 2, 3, 4 und 5 tief genug auszuempfinden und zu schildern!" For an excellent summary of the musical ideas in Heinse's novel, see Neubauer, The Emancipation of Music from Language, 163–66.

35. Heinse, Hildegard von Hohenthal, in Heinse, Sämmtliche Werke, 5:71: "Gewiß ist das Monochord der Eingang ins Heiligthum."

36. Heinse, Hildegard von Hohenthal, in Heinse, Sämmtliche Werke, 5:24: "Der ganze Mensch erklingt gleichsam.... Unser Gefühl selbst ist nichts anders, als eine innere Musik, immerwährende Schwingung der Lebensnerven."

37. See Hans Kayser, Akróasis: Die Lehre von der Harmonik der Welt (Basel: Benno Schwabe, 1946); and Günther Wille, Akroasis: Der akustische Sinnesbereich in der griechischen Literatur bis zum Ende der klassischen Zeit, 2 vols. (Tübingen: Attempto, 2001).

38. Herder, Kalligone, 811–12: "Wir fanden, daß auch hier der Mensch ein allgemeiner Teilnehmer, ein Akroatiker des Universums sei, daß er jedem erregten Wesen, dessen Stimme zu ihm gelangt, sein Mitgefühl leihen müsse. Beobachtungen gemäß reicht sein von außen verborgenstes Gehörorgan am tiefsten ins Innere des Haupts, dem empfindenden Gemeinsinn zunächst sich nahend, und so verbreitet, daß, wie Erfahrungen zeigen, wir fast mit unserm ganzen Körper hören." Edward Lippman, in his translation of this passage, renders Akroatiker simply as "auditor"; see Lippman, ed., Musical Aesthetics: A Historical Reader, 3 vols. (Stuyvesant, NY: Pendragon Press, 1985–90), 2:34.

it were, the structure of what it hears.[39] Elsewhere in *Kalligone*, Herder observes that the spectrum of colors and the scale of notes, each in its own way, reveals the order of the universe (*Weltordnung*), one visibly, the other audibly.[40]

Novalis (the pseudonym of Friedrich von Hardenberg [1772–1801]) was equally convinced of a close relationship between music and the cosmos. In music, he observed, mathematics manifests itself in a perceptible manner "as revelation, as creative idealism.... All pleasure is musical and, as such, mathematical."[41] "Musical relationships," he remarked on another occasion, "seem to me in fact to be the fundamental relationships of nature."[42] The harmony of the spheres also figures in a number of novels by Jean Paul (Johann Paul Friedrich Richter [1763–1825]).[43]

Early on in his *Ideen zu einer Ästhetik der Tonkunst* (written in the mid-1780s but not published until 1806), the composer and critic Christian Friedrich Daniel Schubart (1739–1791) declares that his treatise will revolve around "two great questions: What is the musically beautiful? And how is this beauty brought forth?"[44] Schubart praises Newton, the "confidant of the Creator," for having placed so much emphasis on the role of musical intervals in the structure of the cosmos: we see reflections of the musical triad (root, third, and fifth) everywhere around us in nature. "This profound observation comprises the entire theory of music in indescribable brevity and opens up at the same time miraculous perspectives on το παν."[45] The idea of *en to pan* manifests itself in the Western tradition as some variation on the concept that "the all is one" or "the one is all."

Nor were such pronouncements confined to the early decades of the nineteenth century. Hand used similar language in his *Aesthetik der Tonkunst* to describe music's ability to convey the "presentiment of a higher world."

39. On Herder's conception of *Harmonie* as it relates to cosmology, see Walter Wiora, "Herders Ideen zur Geschichte der Musik," in *Im Geiste Herders*, ed. Erich Keyser (Kitzingen: Holzner, 1953), 73–128. For further commentary on this passage, see Watkins, *Metaphors of Depth in German Musical Thought*, 31–32.

40. Herder, *Kalligone*, 706.

41. Novalis, *Schriften*, ed. Paul Kluckhohn and Richard Samuel, 3rd ed. (Stuttgart: W. Kohlhammer, 1977–), 3:593: "In der Musik erscheint sie förmlich, als Offenbarung—als schaffender Idealism.... Aller Genuß ist musikalisch, mithin mathematisch." See Martin Dyck, *Novalis and Mathematics* (Chapel Hill: University of North Carolina Press, 1959).

42. Novalis, *Schriften*, 3:564: "Die musikalischen Verhältnisse scheinen mir recht eigentlich die Grundverh[ältnisse] der Natur zu seyn."

43. See Julia Cloot, *Geheime Texte: Jean Paul und die Musik* (Berlin: de Gruyter, 2001), 212–17.

44. Schubart, *Ideen zu einer Ästhetik der Tonkunst* (Vienna: J. V. Degen, 1806), 2: "Um die zwey großen Fragen: Was ist das musikalische Schöne? Wie wird dieß Schöne hervorgebracht? soll sich die ganze Abhandlung drehen." Hanslick knew Schubart's treatise (which was reissued in a new edition in 1839 by Scheible of Stuttgart) and describes as *ergötzlich* (amusing, delectable, comical) Schubart's account of Johann Stamitz's Andante movements as a "natural consequence" of the composer's "feeling-filled heart" (*VMS*, 1:105; *OMB*, 46) but makes no acknowledgment of Schubart's broader efforts to relate the musically beautiful with the structure of the cosmos—which, as we shall see, is exactly what Hanslick would attempt to do at the end of the first edition of *Vom Musikalisch-Schönen*.

45. Schubart, *Ideen* (1806), 256–57: "Diese tiefsinnige Bemerkung enthält die ganze Lehre von der Tonkunst in unbeschreiblicher Kürze und öffnet zugleich wunderbare Aussichten ins το παν."

The articulation of something spiritual and nonsensuous, and the unity of *Geist* with nature: it is this in music that pleases, delights, and makes us blissful and awakens in us an inkling of something infinite yet related to us. The beautiful thus radiates the reflection of eternal essence in some unknown way. This speaks to us as a counterimage of our selves and satisfies in us, insofar as is possible in earthly life, the desire to become one with the infinite.[46]

Hand stipulates three varieties of beauty, all of which must be accounted for if a given work is to be deemed beautiful: formal beauty (structure), characteristic beauty (expression), and ideal beauty. The last of these requires that the artwork elevate us, as listeners, to a higher realm, and it is here, in ideal beauty, that we glimpse the infinite.[47] An anonymous review of the first volume of Hand's treatise praises these insights and ascribes the "unique impression" of Beethoven's symphonies to their inner nature as "images of cosmic harmony in rejuvenated measure, in which we reverberate, purely or impurely, moved by an invisible hand."[48]

Gustav Schilling's *Versuch einer Philosophie des Schönen in der Musik, oder Aesthetik der Tonkunst* (1838) makes similar claims for music's connections to the cosmos. Schilling expounds at length on the importance of motion in music and throughout the universe, including the realm of the human spirit. He devotes a section of his treatise to the "Beauty of Motion" (*Schönheit der Bewegung*) and says that "all actions of the soul carry with them the concept of motion, and not only those that we call motions of the psyche (*Gemüthsbewegungen*) but also those carried out without passion....All the fine arts are based irrefutably in motion."[49] It seems almost certain that Hanslick would have known this work: treatises

46. Hand, *Aesthetik der Tonkunst*, 1:154: "die Ahndung einer höheren Welt." Ibid., 153: "Die Aussprache eines Geistigen, Nichtsinnlichen und die Einstimmung des Geistes mit der Natur ist's, was in der Musik gefällt, ergötzt und beseligt, und was die Ahndung eines Unendlichen, aber uns Verwandten weckt. So strahlt das Schöne das ewige Wesen, auch unerkannt auf welche Weise, wieder; dies spricht uns als ein Gleiches an und befriedigt, sofern dies im irdischen Leben möglich ist, das Verlangen Eins zu werden mit dem Unendlichen."

47. Hand, *Aesthetik der Tonkunst*, 1:271–72.

48. Anonymous, review of Hand, *Aesthetik der Tonkunst*, vol. 1, in *Blätter für literarische Unterhaltung*, no. 147 (27 May 1838): 598: "Darum machen die Beethoven'schen Symphonien auf den Gebildeten einen so einzigen Eindruck. Sie sind Bilder der Weltharmonie in verjüngtem Maßstabe, in denen wir selbst, von einer unsichtbaren Hand berührt, reiner oder unreiner mitklingen." Hanslick, as we shall see, would reject the idea of characteristic beauty, or at best subordinate it to formal beauty; but he could not reject entirely what Hand calls ideal beauty, though he was clearly uncomfortable with the concept.

49. Gustav Schilling, *Versuch einer Philosophie des Schönen in der Musik, oder Aesthetik der Tonkunst*, 2 vols. (Mainz: B. Schott's Söhne, 1838), 1:106: "Alle Handlungen der Seele führen den Begriff der Bewegung mit sich; und zwar nicht die allein, welche wir Gemüthsbewegungen nennen, sondern auch Handlungen ohne Leidenschaft....Alle schönen Künste...[sind] unabweislich begründet in der Bewegung." In 1840 Carl Ferdinand Becker would expose large sections of Schilling's treatise, including the passage quoted above, as a plagiarism of Carl Seidel's *Charinomos: Beiträge zur allgemeinen Theorie und Geschichte der schönen Künste*, 2 vols. (Magdeburg: Ferdinand Rubach, 1825–28). See Becker, "Die zu frühe Rezension," *NZfM* 13 (14 November 1840): 158–59. The passage in question is found on pages 81–82 of the first volume of Seidel's treatise. Further plagiarisms by Schilling in his *Polyphonomos* (1839), in which he copied large portions of Johann Bernhard Logier's *System der Musikwissenschaft*

devoted exclusively to the aesthetics of music were rare enough in his youth, and a few years after its publication Schilling would dedicate his *Geschichte der heutigen oder modernen Musik* (1841) to Hanslick's piano and theory teacher in Prague, the composer Václav Tomášek (Wenzel Tomaschek, 1774–1850)—an event that cannot help but have made an impression on the fifteen-year-old Hanslick.[50] Tomášek himself, in an installment of his German-language memoirs published in Prague in 1846, spoke disparagingly of those composers who, like Gioachino Rossini, evinced no concern for harmony, counterpoint, or aesthetics, and who believed that music's sole purpose was pleasure and that the ear alone is the recipient of music, not the mind.[51]

Pythagorean tendencies are also evident in yet another aesthetics of music from 1838, Karl Friedrich Krause's posthumously published *Anfangsgründe der allgemeinen Theorie der Musik nach Grundsätzen der Wesenlehre.* Krause (1781– 1832), who studied at various times with Schelling, Hegel, and Fichte, was an acquaintance of Arthur Schopenhauer at the time the latter was writing the first volume of his *Die Welt als Wille und Vorstellung* and is said to have helped deepen Schopenhauer's understanding of Eastern philosophy. Like Schopenhauer, Krause emphasized the cosmic nature of music and specifically extolled the power of "pure music" over language. In his *Anfangsgründe* he praises "our modern music for large orchestra" as "the true triumph of music as such, in its completely pure and self-sufficient power and magnificence."[52]

Theodor Mundt's general *Aesthetik* (1845) makes many of these same points. By virtue of its elemental nature, sound points to the order of the cosmos. Through sound, matter is set into motion, and other bodies in nature sense this vibration. It is thus, through motion, that nature is brought into harmony; this includes the harmony of the solar system. In nature, however, sound remains a merely physical phenomenon. Only through the intervention of man, in music, is it imbued with *Geist*, for music derives "exclusively from the harmony of the human soul."[53] Out of the "motions and vibrations of self-consciousness," man

---

und der praktischen Composition (1827), would be exposed by Heinrich Dorn in "G. Schilling," *NZfM* 14 (1841): 9–11, 13–14, 17–20, 21–26. Schilling nevertheless carried on a reasonably successful career as a journalist until 1857, when, hounded by creditors, he fled to the United States. He died on his son's farm in Crete, Nebraska.

50. On Tomášek's prominent position in the musical life of Prague, see Verne Waldo Thompson, "Wenzel Johann Tomaschek: His Predecessors, His Life, His Piano Works" (Ph.D. diss., University of Rochester, 1955).

51. Wenzel Tomaschek, "Selbstbiographie," *Libussa: Jahrbuch für 1846,* 349–50.

52. Karl Christian Friedrich Krause, *Anfangsgründe der allgemeinen Theorie der Musik nach Grundsätzen der Wesenlehre,* ed. Victor Strauss (Göttingen: Dieterich, 1838), 136: "[D]ie reine Musik in ihrer ganzen Wesenheit umfasst beiweitem mehr, als durch irgend Worte angezeigt oder erschöpft werden mag, und unsere moderne grosse Orchestermusik ohne Worte ist der eigentliche Triumph der Musik als solcher in ihrer ganzen reinen selbständigen Macht und Herrlichkeit." August Kahlert, in his *System der Aesthetik* (1846), 367, recommended Krause's book as offering "deep insights into the innermost essence of music" (*tiefe Blicke in das innerste Wesen der Tonkunst*).

53. Theodor Mundt, *Aesthetik: Die Idee der Schönheit und des Kunstwerks im Lichte unserer Zeit* (Berlin: M. Simion, 1845), 360–63. Ibid., 364: "Der Schall erlebt...nur durch den Menschen seine

produces an objective creation of his own, thereby satisfying his striving for revelation (*Offenbarungsdrang*).[54]

In his *Aesthetik* (1847), the noted philosopher Friedrich Theodor Vischer (1807–1887) concurred that music has much to reveal about the structure of the cosmos, for it is an art that rests on a "concealed relationship of numbers."[55] Form is essentially a relationship of elements, and to conceive of the universe as form is to recognize that nothing lies outside of it. After quoting Leibniz's dictum that music is an unconscious mathematical exercise of the mind, Vischer declares music to be "ideality itself, the revealed soul of all arts, the mystery of all form, an intimation of the laws that structure the cosmos."[56]

* * *

Eduard Hanslick turned twenty-nine only a few weeks before the first edition of *Vom Musikalisch-Schönen* went to press in 1854, and we know from the sources he cites in his treatise, along with comments in his later memoirs, that he read voraciously in the field of music aesthetics while in his twenties. He was well acquainted with the Pythagorean strain in the writings of Schubart, Hand, Schilling, Tomášek, Krause, Mundt, and Vischer, and in fact admired Vischer's work so much that he sent him a copy of his new treatise only days after its publication.[57] Pythagoreanism's underlying belief in a congruity of structure between music and the cosmos appealed to Hanslick because it shielded "pure" music—which is to say, instrumental music—from the charge that it consisted merely of form, and was therefore without import. He recognized that the parallels between the motions of the universe and the motions of music offered a means by which to give music context without content. The Pythagorean essence of music, sanctioned by no less a figure than Vischer, allowed Hanslick to ascribe (at least obliquely) the effect of music to its essence, and he made his case for this in the original final paragraph of his treatise. In the end, however, that paragraph did not survive beyond the work's second edition, and he eventually chose to treat the essence of music as a thing wholly apart from its effect.

Vergeistigung und Vervollständigung zur Musik. In der Natur selbst verbleibt er ein Schall.... Die Musik selbst ist daher geistigen Wesens, weil sie in ihrer höchsten Ausbildung nur aus der Harmonie der menschlichen Seele stammt."

54. Mundt, *Aesthetik*, 351: "innere Bewegungen und Schwingungen des Selbstbewußtseins."

55. Friedrich Theodor Vischer, *Aesthetik, oder Wissenschaft des Schönen*, 3 vols. (Reutlingen and Leipzig: C. Mäcken, 1846–57), vol. 2, part 1, *Die Lehre vom Naturschönen* (1847), 353 (§396): "als es gewiß ist, daß alle Musik auf verborgenen Zahlenverhältnissen beruht."

56. Vischer, *Aesthetik*, vol. 3, *Die Kunstlehre*, 820–23 (§762), 826 (§764): "Sie [die Musik] ist das Ideal selbst, die blosgelegte Seele aller Künste, das Geheimniß aller Form, eine Ahnung weltbauender Gesetze."

57. The preface to the first edition bears the date 11 September 1854 (Hanslick's twenty-ninth birthday), and when he sent a copy of the book to Vischer on 2 October 1854, he refers to it as having "just appeared" (*soeben erschienen*), which sets a publication date of at least several days before to allow for the author's copies to have been shipped from Leipzig to Hanslick in Vienna. See the facsimile, transcription, and translation of Hanslick's letter to Vischer in Barbara Titus, "Conceptualizing Music: Friedrich Theodor Vischer and Hegelian Currents in German Music Criticism, 1848–1887" (Ph.D. diss., Oxford University, 2005), 192–97; and in Titus, "The Quest for Spiritualized Form: (Re) positioning Eduard Hanslick," *Acta musicologica* 80 (2008): 90–97.

PART III

Essence or Effect: 1850–1945

For at least three hundred years prior to the middle of the nineteenth century, writers had sought to explain the essence of music by emphasizing one or more of the art's characteristic qualities: expression, beauty, form, autonomy, and the capacity to disclose higher truths. In the 1840s and '50s, Wagner and Liszt continued in this vein, extolling music's ability to express emotions but emphasizing its corresponding inability to convey concepts. To remedy this shortcoming, they advocated a union of music with the other arts, particularly the verbal arts, either in the form of a sung text (Wagner) or, in the case of instrumental music, a program or evocative title of some kind (Liszt) that could suggest what a given work might be "about." They considered music without such content to be overly abstract, lacking in social utility, and isolated from the world around it—"absolute," to use Wagner's term.

These were conventional arguments in many respects. Zarlino, Bardi, and Vincenzo Galilei had all made similar points in the second half of the sixteenth century when they posited the projection of a text as the "final cause" of music. Galilei, like Wagner almost three centuries later, excoriated those who believed that music's sole aim was "to delight the hearing." Wagner, like Galilei, pointed to the sung dramas of ancient Greece as a model art that combined words and music in a perfect synthesis.

Hanslick conceded that music could accommodate and enhance sung texts, but he saw this as an option, not a necessity. To counter long-standing prejudices against music's isolation from the world and its inability to articulate concepts, he rejected or drastically altered every one of the categories that until his time had been used to explain the essence of the art. He denied music the capacity to express or disclose anything other than itself, and while he conceded that it could arouse emotions, he considered listeners' responses far too variable to be factored into any account of its essence. For Hanslick, autonomy extended to every element of music: its particular form could not be related to any other kind of form, and its beauty could not be related to any other kind of beauty. *Vom Musikalisch-Schönen* is not about beauty as its manifests itself in music, but about specifically musical beauty. The distinction is critical. Only in the final paragraph of his treatise did Hanslick attempt to relate musical beauty to any broader concept or manifestation of beauty, and by the third edition (1865) he had eradicated even this eleventh-hour attempt. The severance of essence and effect was complete. Hanslick was the first to define the essence of music in exclusively musical terms.

Wagner, Liszt, and Hanslick did agree on one point, however. All three aligned the essence of music with its purest manifestation, and they agreed that its purest manifestation was to be found in a very specific repertory: nonprogrammatic instrumental music. For the first time music's essence became reified. "Pure" music, once an idea, was now an object with its own distinct name ("absolute music") and, by 1855, thanks to Liszt, a counterpart ("program music") that could further distinguish between subcategories of instrumental music. That all three of them would adopt a rhetoric of purity has had profound implications, from their own time down to the present.

8 Wagner's "Absolute" Music

Wagner's Zurich writings and Hanslick's *Vom Musikalisch-Schönen* appeared within a span of only five years after the Revolutions of 1848–49, a time of deep polarization between self-proclaimed "progressives" and "conservatives" throughout German society. Wagner was only one of many social critics who saw art as a catalyst of social and political reform; Hanslick, in turn, represented those determined to keep art sheltered from the turmoils of life.

The early stages of this political-aesthetic polarization had been evident at least a decade before with the ascendency of realism, a mode of philosophical thought that encouraged attitudes which engaged society, politics, and the material world more directly: the community took precedence over the individual.[1] The failed Revolutions of 1848–49 accelerated the demand for an aesthetic more immediately applicable to social issues. In a long essay published in the *Neue Zeitschrift für Musik* in early July 1848, the Magdeburg critic and jurist Carl Kretschmann (1826–1897) dismissed romanticism as an aesthetic that had led merely inward, toward contemplation rather than change. He called for an end to "dreaming" and the isolation of the self: "The times are serious, and the arena of spiritual creation is no longer the 'I' alone."[2] That same year the poet, literary historian, music critic, and professor of philosophy August Kahlert (1807–1864) declared that the "political gravity of the present has thoroughly defeated the romantic worldview. There is no longer time in which to lose oneself in dreams." Kahlert pointed out that the political activists Arnold Ruge and Georg Gottfried Gervinus had argued a full ten years before that romanticism had "sapped the political energy of the German nation" and that "every newspaper reader now understands that order without freedom gives rise to despotism, and that

---

1. See Sanna Pederson, "Romantic Music under Siege in 1848," in *Music Theory in the Age of Romanticism*, ed. Ian Bent (Cambridge: Cambridge University Press, 1996), 57–74; Martin Geck, *Zwischen Romantik und Restauration: Musik im Realismus-Diskurs der Jahre 1848 bis 1871* (Stuttgart: Metzler, 2001); James Garratt, "Inventing Realism: Dahlhaus, Geck, and the Unities of Discourse," *M&L* 84 (2003): 456–68; and Garratt, *Music, Culture and Social Reform*. In "Inventing Realism," Garratt rightly emphasizes the extent to which much of this dissatisfaction was already palpable well before the Revolutions of 1848–49.

2. Carl Kretschmann, "Romantik in der Musik," *NZfM* 29 (1 July 1848): 3–4, 10: "Die Zeit ist ernst, der Schauplatz geistigen Schaffens ist nicht mehr das Ich allein." For further commentary on Kretschmann's essay, see Geck, *Zwischen Romantik und Restauration*, 20–23, and Garratt, *Music, Culture and Social Reform*, 130–31. On the growing dissatisfaction with abstraction, see Thomas S. Grey, *Wagner's Musical Prose: Texts and Contexts* (Cambridge: Cambridge University Press, 1995), 111–12.

freedom without order gives rise to anarchy." Works of art, he asserted, ran the risk of degenerating either into "dead mechanisms" or "expressions of insanity."[3] The either/or nature of Kahlert's argument is characteristic of its time, for this was an era that liked to think in terms of binaries: dream and reality, abstract and concrete, individual and community.

One did not have to be a barricade-storming radical in the middle of the nineteenth century to sympathize with the need for a new kind of music to match the spirit of the age. As Robert Schumann confessed in a private letter to the critic Franz Brendel in June 1849:

> Ah, yes—to speak of the pains and joys that move the present: this, I feel, has been granted to me above many others. And that you sometimes point out to people just how strongly my music in particular is rooted in the present and seeks something beyond mere euphony and pleasant entertainment: this brings me joy and encourages me to higher aspirations.[4]

Even A. B. Marx, famous for his codification of musical forms, emphasized that art does not exist for its own sake but must always function in a mutual relationship with the "full substance" of humanity.[5] In the years leading up to the Revolutions of 1848–49, and even more in the years immediately following, there was a growing sense that music could not remain isolated in its own sphere. Just how it might engage with the world around it, however, was far from means clear.

Wagner *was* a barricade-storming radical, and he had an outstanding warrant for his arrest to prove it. The manifestos he issued during his years of

3. August Kahlert, "Ueber den Begriff der klassischen und romantischen Musik," *AmZ* 50 (3 May 1848): 295: "Der politische Ernst der Gegenwart hat die romantische Weltansicht zu Boden geschlagen. Es ist nicht mehr Zeit, sich in Träume zu verlieren, denn Gesetz und Ordnung zur vollen Giltigkeit überall zu bringen, das ist die Losung, nachdem seit zehn Jahren Männer wie *Gervinus* und *Ruge* den Beweis geführt, dass die Romantik die politische Kraft der deutschen Nation gebrochen habe. Jetzt begreift jeder Zeitungsleser, dass Ordnung ohne Freiheit den Despotismus, und Freiheit ohne Ordnung Anarchie hervorbringt, Kunstwerke können bis zum todten Mechanismus oder zum Ausdrucke der Verrücktheit herabsinken, dies ist dasselbe." For a different translation of an extended excerpt from this essay, see Le Huray and Day, *Music and Aesthetics*, 559–65.

4. Robert Schumann, letter to Franz Brendel, 17 June 1849, in *Briefe: Neue Folge*, ed. F. Gustav Jansen (Leipzig: Breitkopf & Härtel, 1904), 306: "Ach ja—von den Schmerzen und Freuden, die die Zeit bewegen, der Musik zu erzählen, dies, fühl ich, ist mir vor vielen Andern zuertheilt worden. Und daß Sie es den Leuten manchmal vorhalten, wie stark eben meine Musik in der Gegewart wurzelt und etwas ganz anderes will als nur Wohlklang und angenehme Unterhaltung, dies freut mich und muntert mich auf zu höherem Streben." On Schumann and the Revolution, see John Daverio, "Sounds without the Gate: Schumann and the Dresden Revolution," *Il saggiatore musicale* 4 (1997): 87–112.

5. Adolph Bernhard Marx, *Die Musik des 19. Jahrhunderts und ihre Pflege* (Leipzig: Breitkopf & Härtel, 1855), 491–92: "Kunst ist ebenfalls nichts durchaus für sich Bestehendes, sie ist nur eine Seite des ganzen Menschenthums, nicht loszulösen vom Leben der Menschheit sondern in steter Beziehung und Wechselwirkung mit dessen gesammtem Gehalt." Liszt, "Marx und die Musik des neunzehnten Jahrhunderts," *NZfM* 42 (11 May 1855): 217, quotes this passage approvingly.

refuge in Zurich identify social change as the primary justification for the arts in general and music in particular. The perspective throughout *Die Kunst und die Revolution* (1849), *Das Kunstwerk der Zukunft* (1849, published 1850), *Oper und Drama* (1850–51, published 1852), and *Eine Mitteilung an meine Freunde* (1851) is Hegelian: Wagner conceives of the essence of any phenomenon in terms of its unfolding over time. His conception of music is based on its history, and Wagner's history of music follows Rousseau's fall-of-man narrative, in which music and language, once indistinguishable, had become increasingly specialized, with language giving voice to ideas, music to emotions. For Wagner, however, the lost paradise was not Rousseau's watering hole of pre-verbal man, but Periclean Athens, where tone, gesture, and poetry had all been united in the *mousike* of ancient Greek drama. In an open letter of 1854 to Franz Brendel, he observed that

> we have grown accustomed to understanding the term "music" [*Musik*] as only the art of tone [*Tonkunst*], or nowadays even as the mere artifice of tones [*Tonkünstelei*]. We know that this is an arbitrary assumption, for the people who invented the name "music" understood it to mean not only poetry and the art of tone but rather all artistic expression of the inner man in general, in so far as he could communicate his feelings and intuitions in their most compelling manifestation through the organ of sounding speech.[6]

It was during his years of exile that Wagner returned to the term *absolute Musik*, which he had coined in his 1846 commentary on Beethoven's Ninth Symphony (see p. 1–2). At the time, he had introduced the term without fanfare and used it only once. Still, its implications had been clear enough from the start: instrumental music by itself offers a means of expression that is emotionally powerful yet conceptually vague and therefore limited in what it can convey. Wagner points to the finale of the Ninth Symphony as the pivotal moment in the history of music, for it was here that Beethoven found the means by which to overcome the expressive limitations of purely instrumental music.[7] Early in

6. Richard Wagner, "Ein Brief an den Redacteur der Neuen Zeitschrift für Musik," *NZfM* 36 (6 February 1852), 60; published in *GSD* under the title "Über musikalische Kritik: Brief an den Herausgeber der 'Neuen Zeitschrift für Musik,'" 5:59–60: "Wir haben uns gewöhnt, unter 'Musik' nur noch die Tonkunst, jetzt endlich sogar nur noch die Tonkünstelei, zu begreifen: daß dies eine willkürliche Annahme ist, wissen wir, denn das Volk, welches den Namen 'Musik' erfand, begriff unter ihm nicht nur Dichtkunst und Tonkunst, sondern alle künstlerische Kundgebung des inneren Menschen überhaupt, in soweit er seine Gefühle und Anschauungen in letzter überzeugendster Versinnlichung durch das Organ der tönenden Sprache ausdrucksvoll mitteilte." *PW*, 3:68. For further commentary on this passage, see Dieter Borchmeyer, *Richard Wagner: Theory and Theatre*, trans. Stewart Spencer (Oxford: Clarendon Press, 1991), 107–8.

7. Wagner was not the first to make the argument that the Ninth represents a historical move toward specificity in the genre of the symphony: A. B. Marx had made this point as early as 1829. See Grey, *Wagner's Musical Prose*, 44–45.

the finale, the instruments take on a speaking quality of their own, which in turn introduces—or as Wagner puts it, demands—the medium of the voice.

> With this beginning of the finale Beethoven's music takes on a decidedly more speaking character: it abandons the character of pure instrumental music to which it had adhered in the first three movements, the character of pure instrumental music, which manifests itself in infinite and indeterminate expression. The continuation of the musical poetry demands resolution, a resolution that can be articulated only in human speech. We marvel at how the Master prepares the entrance of language and the human voice as a necessity to be expected through this stirring recitative of the instrumental basses, which, already having almost abandoned the confines of absolute music, confronts the other instruments with powerful, emotional speech, demanding resolution, and which at last changes into a lyrical theme that in its simple moving flow, as if in solemn joy, carries the other instruments along with it and thus swells to a powerful height. This seems like the final attempt to express through instrumental music alone a secure, well-defined, and unalloyed sense of joy. This intractable medium [i.e., instrumental music], however, appears inadequate to sustain such limitation; like the raging sea, it foams up, sinks back down again, and the wild, chaotic scream of unsatiated passion assaults our ears more strongly than before. At this point, a human voice confronts the rage of the instruments with the clear and confident expression of speech, and we do not know whether to admire the Master's keen inspiration or his naïveté when he has the voice cry out to the instruments:
>
> "Oh Friends, not these tones! Let us instead tune ourselves more agreeably and joyfully!"
>
> With these words, light appears in the chaos. A definite, specific expression has been achieved, through which we may hear articulated clearly and precisely that which had been carried along by the now-restrained medium of the instruments.[8]

Given the pervasiveness of the term "absolute" in German critical thought from the late eighteenth century onward, both as an adjective (*absolut*) and as a noun

8. Wagner, "Programm zur 9. Symphonie von Beethoven" (1846), *GSD*, 2:60–62: "Mit diesem Beginne des letzten Satzes nimmt Beethovens Musik einen entschieden sprechenderen Charakter an: sie verläßt den in den drei ersten Sätzen festgehaltenen Charakter der reinen Instrumentalmusik, der sich im unendlichen und unentschiedenen Ausdrucke kundgibt; der Fortgang der musikalischen Dichtung dringt auf Entscheidung, auf eine Entscheidung, wie sie nur in der menschlichen Sprache ausgesprochen werden kann. Bewundern wir, wie der Meister das Hinzutreten der Sprache und Stimme des Menschen als eine zu erwartende Nothwendigkeit mit diesem erschütternden Rezitativ der Instrumentalbässe vorbereitet, welches, die Schranken der absoluten Musik fast schon verlassend, wie mit kräftiger, gefühlvoller Rede den übrigen Instrumenten, auf Entscheidung dringend, entgegentritt, und endlich selbst zu einem Gesangsthema übergeht, das in seinem einfachen, wie in feierlicher Freude bewegten Strome, die übrigen Instrumente mit sich fortzieht und so zu einer mächtigen Höhe anschwillt. Es erscheint dies wie der letzte Versuch, durch Instrumentalmusik allein ein sicheres, festbegrenztes und untrübbares freudiges Glück auszudrücken: das unbändige Element scheint aber dieser Beschränkung nicht fähig zu sein; wie zum brausenden Meere schäumt es auf, sinkt wieder zurück, und stärker noch als vorher dringt der wilde, chaotische Aufschrei der unbefriedigten Leidenschaft an unser

(*das Absolute*), it is remarkable that critics had applied it to music so infrequently. The fact that *absolute Musik* as a specific term did not appear until 1846 is all the more striking when we consider that Schelling had articulated the concept of the "absolute artwork" as early as 1800, in his *System des transzendentalen Idealismus*, as an imagined, single, unitary work of art that could exist in multiple different exemplars, each capable in its own way of embodying the infinite Absolute. "There is no work of art," Schelling maintained, "that does not present the infinite directly or at the very least a reflection of it."[9] For Schelling, the Absolute was a "point of non-difference" (*Indifferenzpunkt*) in which no distinction could be made between subject and object, being and knowing, perception and content.

Hegel agreed with Schelling that the Absolute is a state of complete self-consciousness, the "identity of identity and non-identity" achieved through an overcoming of all distinctions between subject and object. In the Absolute, the material world is both subsumed and transcended—or *aufgehoben*, to use that famously supple term that conveys at once the ideas of being canceled, preserved, elevated, and transformed. But Hegel famously dismissed Schelling's a priori notion of the Absolute as "the night... in which all cows are black" and insisted that it should constitute the result rather than the starting point of thought.[10]

With its promise of representing the highest possible state of consciousness— and to some, nothing less than the mind of God—the Absolute exercised an almost talismanic power over several generations of German thinkers, including Wagner. He confessed in his autobiography to having been particularly fascinated by the concept in the mid-1840s, at a point in his life when he returned to Hegel's writings and Schelling's *System des transzendentalen Idealismus*, discovered the philosophy of Ludwig Feuerbach, and began an intense study of Beethoven's Ninth Symphony.[11] This convergence of intellectual pursuits suggests why Wagner introduced the term "absolute music" when he did, though it

---

Ohr. Da tritt eine menschliche Stimme mit dem klaren, sicheren Ausdruck der Sprache dem Toben der Instrumente entgegen, und wir wissen nicht, ob wir mehr die kühne Eingebung oder die große Naivität des Meisters bewundern sollen, wenn er diese Stimme den Instrumenten zurufen läßt:

'Ihr Freunde, nicht diese Töne! Sondern laßt uns
angenehmere anstimmen und freudenvollere!'

Mit diesen Worten wird es Licht in dem Chaos; ein bestimmter, sicherer Ausdruck ist gewonnen, in dem wir, von dem beherrschten Elemente der Instrumentalmusik getragen, klar und deutlich das ausgesprochen hören dürfen."
PW, 7:251–52.

9. Schelling, *System des transzendentalen Idealismus*, 298: "So gibt es eigentlich auch nur *ein* absolutes Kunstwerk, welches zwar in ganz verschiedenen Exemplaren existiren kann, aber doch nur *eines* ist.... Es ist nichts ein Kunstwerk, was nicht ein Unendliches unmittelbar oder wenigstens im Reflex darstellt."

10. Georg Wilhelm Friedrich Hegel, *Phänomenologie des Geistes* (1807), ed. Eva Moldenhauer and Karl Markus Michel (Frankfurt am Main: Suhrkamp, 1970), 22: "die Nacht...worin...alle Kühe schwarz sind."

11. Richard Wagner, *Mein Leben* (1870–80), 2 vols. (Munich: F. Bruckmann, 1911), 1:507.

does not explain why no one else had done so earlier. After all, Hegel, Schelling, Feuerbach, and Beethoven were scarcely obscure figures. How had other writers on music managed without the term for so long?

We can begin to answer this question by recognizing that "absolute music" is a retronym, a two-word neologism created to distinguish between older and newer varieties of a particular phenomenon, typically in response to technological or historical developments.[12] Retronyms include such formations as ancien régime, acoustic guitar, analog watch, conventional weapons, manual typewriter, optical microscope, Summer Olympics, and World War I. A retronym does not emerge until something new creates a need for it. Until the advent of the electric typewriter, all typewriters were manual, and so the word "typewriter" alone sufficed. And before the appearance of the electron microscope, it would have been pointless to draw attention to the fact that the microscope was an optical instrument. Each of the nouns listed above, without a modifier, was at one time sufficient to identify the object in question in its full range of manifestations.

The novelty Wagner perceived when he created the retronym "absolute music" in 1846 was not "program music." That particular term would not appear in print until 1855, and the phenomenon itself was already known by any number of comparable designations ("characteristic music," "painterly music," "representational music," etc.).[13] Wagner was responding instead to an increasingly widespread aesthetic attitude that conceived of music as an entirely autonomous art, existing for its own sake and serving no broader social purpose. The doctrine of l'art pour l'art, as noted earlier, had been attracting increasing numbers of adherents since the 1830s, particularly in France, and Wagner would have been well aware of this intellectual movement from his earlier years in the French capital (1839–42), when he worked as a part-time critic and essayist. He recognized in this outlook an impediment to his utopian vision of a world in which the political, the social, and the artistic would all work in harmony at every level of society and indeed be virtually indistinguishable from one another. This ideal was shared to varying degrees by the Saint-Simonians, Pierre-Joseph Proudhon, and especially Ludwig Feuerbach, the dedicatee of Wagner's Das Kunstwerk der Zukunft, the opening sentence of which declares: "As humankind is to nature, so is art to humankind."[14]

Wagner needed a shorthand term to designate a type of music that served no broader purpose beyond itself. "Instrumental music" did not suffice, because Wagner considered a great deal of vocal music—including opera—to be

---

12. See "Retronym," in *The Concise Oxford Companion to the English Language*, ed. Tom McArthur (Oxford: Oxford University Press, 2005).

13. For an overview of terminological options in the generation before Wagner and Liszt, see Richard Will, *The Characteristic Symphony in the Age of Haydn and Beethoven* (Cambridge: Cambridge University Press, 2002), 4–9.

14. Wagner, *Das Kunstwerk der Zukunft*, GSD, 3:42: "Wie der Mensch sich zur Natur verhält, so verhält die Kunst sich zum Menschen." *PW*, 1:69.

equally isolated and self-serving, its text a mere pretext for melody. "Absolute" was his preferred term to convey this state of isolation, and he applied it in the philosophical sense of that which is conditioned by nothing outside of itself. Wagner seems to have applied this sense of the term to any artwork whose entire being is autonomous through and through, both materially and ethically. By the end of the 1840s he had come to consider the absolute manifestation of any object deficient on the grounds of its excessive abstraction and separation from its surroundings, from the "absolute melody" of Rossinian opera (whose words Wagner dismissed as a mere vehicle for the music) to its political analogue, "absolute monarchy."[15] To Wagner and to the later adherents of the New German School, music and all the arts were means to the end of human progress: their value could be fully measured only in relation to their effect on society. The "absolute artist" is one who looks only inward and is absorbed in his own circumscribed "world of art," a sphere "wholly separated from life" in which "art plays with its own self, withdrawing hypersensitively from any contact with reality."[16]

"Absolute music," by this line of thought, has to do with the function of a work: whether that work is vocal or instrumental is beside the point. Wagner's neologism thus originated not as a designation for a particular repertory of music, but for any kind of music (instrumental or vocal) that was socially disengaged and existed merely for its own sake. Wagner called works of this kind *unfrei* (not free), on the grounds that they were consigned to a sort of aesthetic solitary confinement. For the arts as well as for humankind, only the communal—that which exists in the absence of boundaries—is truly free.[17]

The philosophical stature of the Absolute gave Wagner a self-made target of attack prestigious enough to warrant a frontal assault. The very term "absolute music," moreover, though new enough in its own right, reeked of the past. By the middle of the nineteenth century, the Absolute was a concept closely associated with the prevailing philosophical tendencies of an earlier generation perceived to have been more concerned with abstraction than action. Realism was the new order of the day, and the resonance of *absolute Musik* reinforced the idea that any music connected with this concept was more likely to be conservative than progressive. Moreover, although any number of earlier critics had pointed out the abstract nature of music, no one had treated this in relation to the issue of music's social function. By using politically charged terminology, Wagner was able to align absolute music with an implicitly conservative aesthetic.

15. Wagner, *Oper und Drama, GSD*, 3:255; *PW*, 2:45. On Wagner's low estimation of anything "absolute," see Borchmeyer, *Richard Wagner: Theory and Theatre*, 108–9; and Grey, *Wagner's Musical Prose*, chapter 1.

16. Wagner, *Eine Mitteilung an meine Freunde, GSD*, 4:247: "sie [die Kunst] ist die vom Leben schlechtweg abgesonderte Kunstwelt, in welcher die Kunst mit sich selbst spielt, vor jeder Berührung mit der Wirklichkeit…empfindlich sich zurückzieht." *PW*, 1:287.

17. Wagner, *Das Kunstwerk der Zukunft, GSD*, 3:68: "Der Einsame ist unfrei, weil beschränkt…der Gemeinsame frei, weil unbeschränkt." *PW*, 1:96.

But Wagner did not use the term consistently in this sense. On a number of occasions he simply equated it with instrumental music, thereby mapping an aesthetic attitude—*l'art pour l'art*—onto a specific repertory. In *Das Kunstwerk der Zukunft* he railed against those composers who continued to write symphonies as if Beethoven's Ninth had never existed, ignoring the imperatives of history and its dialectic:

> As soon as Beethoven had written his last symphony, every musical guild could patch and stuff as much as it liked in its effort to create a man of absolute music. But it was just this and nothing more: a patched and stuffed imaginary man. No sensate, natural man could emerge from such a workshop any longer. After Haydn and Mozart, a Beethoven could and had to appear. The spirit of music necessarily demanded him, and without waiting, there he was. Who would now be to Beethoven what Beethoven was to Haydn and Mozart in the realm of absolute music? The greatest genius could do nothing more here, precisely because the spirit of absolute music no longer has need of him.[18]

In this same tract, Wagner also confronts (without citing it explicitly) the idea of "infinite longing" evoked by Hoffmann in his review of Beethoven's Fifth Symphony. For Hoffmann and others in the orbit of idealist thought in the early decades of the century, longing was not simply an emotional state but a mode of thought, a way of knowing.[19] By the end of the 1840s, however, the epistemological claims of longing had been either forgotten or rejected. Wagner compares Beethoven to an explorer who sets out to discover new worlds, likening him to a mariner who loves the sea and yet is also weary of it and seeks safer anchorage from the "blissful storm of wild tempestuousness." Though "glad of this ineffably expressive capacity of speech" that operates in an "absolute language of tone" (*absolute Tonsprache*), Beethoven suffers from an "endless longing" that can be vanquished only by its absorption into an object. Even in its most exalted manifestation, the object of "absolute music," expressive though it might be, is in the end only "feeling," a feeling "associated with the deed" but not the deed itself. As such, absolute music lacks "moral will." And in the end, no one felt "more dissatisfied with this victory" of the Fifth Symphony than Beethoven himself. A "mindless herd" of

18. Wagner, *Das Kunstwerk der Zukunft, GSD*, 3:100–101: "Sobald, mit einem Wort, Beethoven seine letzte Symphonie geschrieben hatte,—konnte alle musikalische Zunftgenossenschaft flicken und stopfen, wie sie wollte, um einen absoluten Musikmenschen zu Stande zu bringen: eben nur ein geflickter und gestopfter scheckiger Phantasiemensch, kein nervig stämmiger Naturmensch konnte aus ihrer Werkstatt mehr hervorgehen. Auf Haydn und Mozart konnte und mußte ein Beethoven kommen; der Genius der Musik verlangte ihn mit Notwendigkeit, und ohne auf sich warten zu lassen, war er da; wer will nun auf Beethoven das sein, was dieser auf Haydn und Mozart im Gebiete der absoluten Musik war? Das größte Genie würde hier nichts mehr vermögen, eben weil der Genius der absoluten Musik seiner nicht mehr bedarf." *PW*, 1:130–31. On Wagner's relationship to the history of the symphony, see Bonds, *Music as Thought*, 105–7.

19. See Bonds, *Music as Thought*, chapter 3, "Listening to Truth: Beethoven's Fifth Symphony."

subsequent composers would nevertheless bring forth "endless victory festivals of major-mode jubilation after having endured minor-mode tribulations." Not until the Ninth Symphony would Beethoven discover the means by which to satisfy his sense of endless longing.[20] Wagner argued along much the same lines in *Oper und Drama*, again pointing to Beethoven as the composer who had pushed beyond the boundaries of absolute music. Conveniently, this provided Wagner's own theory of the *Gesamtkunstwerk* with an unassailable pedigree.[21]

In his *Eine Mitteilung an meine Freunde*, on the other hand, Wagner turned against his own neologism in an apparent fit of exasperation, dismissing the "absolute artwork" as a "non-thing" (*Unding*), a "conservative phantasm," an "apparition in the brain of our aesthetic critics" that is "bound to neither place nor time, nor presented by specific individuals under specific circumstances to individuals who are themselves specific and to whom the work is meant to be intelligible." Belief in the absolute artwork, Wagner maintained, had caused aesthetics to devolve

> into a truly art-murderous activity, driven to dogmatic cruelty in that it seeks to sacrifice with reactionary zeal the reality of the natural disposition toward new works of art on the altar of the conservative phantasm of an absolute artwork (which can never be realized for the simple reason that its realization already lies far behind us in the past)....As something merely thought, the absolute—that is, the unconditioned—artwork is naturally bound to neither time nor place, nor to specific circumstances. It can have been written for Athenian democracy two thousand years ago, for example, and performed today at the Prussian Court in Potsdam; yet in the imagination of our aestheticians, it must have altogether the same value and altogether the same essential characteristics, regardless of here or there, today or yesterday. To the contrary, our aestheticians actually imagine that such an artwork, like certain varieties of wine, improves through a process of aging and can be understood fully and correctly only here and now.[22]

Having dismissed the "absolute artwork" as unimaginable, Wagner continued to condemn it. In an open letter on Liszt's symphonic poems (1857), he declared that as far as its manifestation in actual life is concerned, "nothing is less

20. Wagner, *Das Kunstwerk der Zukunft*, GSD, 3:92–99; PW, 1:125–29.

21. Wagner, *Oper und Drama*, GSD, 3:279; PW, 1:72–73.

22. Wagner, *Eine Mitteilung an meine Freunde*, GSD, 4:234–35:

> Das absolute Kunstwerk, das ist: das Kunstwerk, das weder an Ort und Zeit gebunden, noch von bestimmten Menschen unter bestimmten Umständen an wiederum bestimmte Menschen dargestellt und von diesen verstanden werden soll,—ist ein vollständiges Unding, ein Schattenbild ästhetischer Gedankenphantasie. Von der Wirklichkeit der Kunstwerke verschiedener Zeiten hat man den Begriff der Kunst abgezogen: um diesem Begriffe eine wieder gedachte Realität zu geben, da man ohnedem ihn sich selbst in Gedanken nicht faßlich vorstellen konnte, hat man ihn mit einem eingebildeten Körper bekleidet, der als absolutes Kunstwerk, eingestandener oder nicht

absolute than music.... The champions of an absolute music apparently do not know what they are talking about."[23]

Wagner thus defined absolute music at various times in at least three different ways: (1) as any music that served no purpose beyond itself; (2) as purely instrumental music; (3) as a kind of music that could not be imagined, much less realized, in practice. The critic Theodor Uhlig (1822–1853), one of Wagner's most articulate early disciples, tended toward the first of these usages. He distinguished between absolute music and "depictional, representational, descriptive music" but disapproved of both, calling the latter a hybrid genre (*Zwittergattung*) that carried within it the seeds of its own destruction. Although Beethoven had explored this approach in works like the *Pastoral* Symphony, he had realized the error of his ways by the time of the Ninth Symphony.[24] On another occasion, Uhlig used the term "absolute music" to include vocal music that takes no notice of its words.[25] The composer Joachim Raff (1822–1882) also used the term in its broadest sense, referring at one point in his polemical *Die Wagnerfrage* (1854) to Palestrina's polyphonic art as the "high point of absolute music" in its time. Elsewhere in the same tract he refers to *absolute Instrumentalmusik* and *absolut-musikalische Formen*.[26]

On the whole, however, most writers simply equated absolute music with instrumental music and rarely felt any need to explain or justify their use of the term in this sense.[27] Typical of such accounts is Richard Pohl's report on the

eingestandenermaßen, das Spukgebild im Hirne unserer ästhetischen Kritiker ausmacht. Wie dieser eingebildete Körper alle Merkmale seiner gedachten sinnlichen Erscheinung nur den wirklichen Eigenschaften der Kunstwerke der Vergangenheit entnimmt, so ist der ästhetische Glaube an ihn auch ein wesentlich konservativer, und die Bethätigung dieses Glaubens daher an sich die vollständigste künstlerische Unfruchtbarkeit....

Hierdurch geräth die ästhetische Wissenschaft in eine wahrhaft kunstmörderische, bis zur dogmatischen Grausamkeit fanatisierte Tätigkeit, indem sie dem konservativen Wahngebilde eines absoluten Kunstwerkes, das sie aus dem einfachen Grunde nie verwirklicht sehen kann, weil seine Verwirklichung bereits in der Geschichte längst hinter uns liegt, die Wirklichkeit der natürlichen Anlagen zu neuen Kunstwerken mit reaktionärem Eifer aufgeopfert wissen will....Das absolute, d.i. unbedingte Kunstwerk ist, als ein nur gedachtes, natürlich weder an Zeit und Ort, noch an bestimmte Umstände gebunden: es kann z.B. vor zweitausend Jahren für die athenische Demokratie gedichtet worden sein, und heute vor dem preußischen Hofe in Potsdam aufgeführt werden; in der Vorstellung unserer Ästhetiker muß es ganz denselben Werth, ganz dieselben wesenhaften Eigenschaften haben, gleichviel ob hier oder dort, heute oder damals: im Gegenteile bildet man sich wohl gar noch ein, daß es, wie gewisse Weinsorten, durch Ablagerung gewinne, und erst heute und hier so recht und ganz verstanden werden könne."
PW, 1:274.

23. Wagner, "Über Franz Liszts symphonische Dichtungen," *GSD*, 5:191: "Nichts ist (wohlgemerkt: für seine Erscheinung im Leben) weniger absolut, als die Musik, und die Verfechter einer absoluten Musik wissen offenbar nicht, was sie meinen." *PW*, 3:247.

24. Theodor Uhlig, "Die Instrumentalmusik," *Deutsche Monatsschrift für Politik, Wissenschaft, Kunst und Leben* 2, no. 1 (1851): 173: "malende, schildernde, beschreibende Tonkunst."

25. Uhlig, "Zur Kritik des Liedes," *NZfM* 36 (4 June 1852), 253–55.

26. Joachim Raff, *Die Wagnerfrage* (Braunschweig: Vieweg und Sohn, 1854), 76; 52 (*absolute Instrumentalmusik*); 92 (*absolut-musikalische Formen*).

27. See, for example, Louis Köhler, *Die Melodie der Sprache in ihrer Anwendung besonders auf das Lied und die Oper* (Leipzig: J. J. Weber, 1853), 1; Friedrich Hinrichs, *Richard Wagner und die neuere Musik*

Karlsruhe Music Festival of October 1853, which captures the intensity of the struggle between traditionalists and the adherents of the "Music of the Future." In a series of articles published shortly after the event in the *Neue Zeitschrift für Musik*, Pohl (1826–1896), writing under the pen name of "Hoplit," hailed the festival as a "celebration of modern art's entry into southern Germany." Soon afterward he would reissue his account as a separate publication with an appendix of three essays by Wagner, each a manifesto in its own right, on *Tannhäuser, Lohengrin*, and Beethoven's Ninth Symphony, the last of which had included the first use of the term *absolute Musik*.[28] Pohl associates the "one-sided conservatism in music" with "static formalism" and decries the sterility of the "the absolute musician" and "empty formalism." It was Beethoven, Pohl maintained, who had moved beyond "abstract aesthetics," which had been tied to " 'absolute' forms" (the scare quotes are Pohl's).[29] Privately, Raff conceded that Liszt and his followers in Weimar, including Pohl, Cornelius, and Raff himself, had not laid the aesthetic groundwork for the festival sufficiently in the local press, and that the event had succeeded merely in antagonizing the opposition.[30]

Paradoxically, Wagner's opponents embraced the term "absolute music" with equal zeal, and they equated it consistently from the start with purely instrumental music. As early as 1850 the anti-Wagnerian Ludwig Bischoff (1794–1867), founder of the influential *Rheinische Musik-Zeitung*, called instrumental music "autonomous or absolute music."[31] He pointed to Haydn as a composer whose "fully developed artistic nature" made "everything seem musical to him." Haydn's "own feeling is music." In a passage that reads like a paragraph from *Vom Musikalisch-Schönen* four years before its publication, Bischoff says of Haydn:

> He does not think philosophy, aesthetics, history, romanticism, etc.; he thinks music. His outlook and perceptions, his thoughts and fantasies are music and must from inner necessity create musical forms. All of nature appears to him as music; he hears within himself no language other than music, and thus it is quite natural that he speaks no other language.[32]

(Halle: Schrödel und Simon, 1854), 48, 81; Ernst Gottschald, *Beethoven's Symphonien nach ihrem idealen Gehalt* (Dresden: Adolph Brauer, 1854), 24; and Johann Christian Lobe, "Briefe über Richard Wagner an einen jungen Komponisten," *Fliegende Blätter für Musik* 1 (1855): 419.

28. Hoplit [i.e., Richard Pohl], "Das Karlsruher Musikfest" *NZfM* 39 (1853), 160–62; 166–71; 178–80; 187–90; 211–14. Hoplit, *Das Karlsruher Musikfest im Oktober 1853* (Leipzig: Bruno Hinze, 1853), 75: "Die Feier des Einzuges der modernen Kunst in Süddeutschland."

29. Pohl, *Das Karlsruher Musikfest*, 14: "einseitig conservative Richtung in der Musik...starrer Formalismus"; 26: "der absolute Musiker"; 28: "leerer Formalismus"; 46: "die abstrakte Aesthetik," " 'absolute' Formen."

30. See James Deaville, "Die neudeutsche Musikkritik: Der Weimarer Kreis," in *Liszt und die Neudeutsche Schule*, ed. Detlef Altenburg (Laaber: Laaber-Verlag, 2006), 62–63.

31. Ludwig Bischoff, "Joseph Haydn's Musik," *Rheinische Musik-Zeitung* 1 (23 November 1850): 162: " die Instrumentalmusik, die selbstständige oder absolute Musik."

32. Bischoff, "Joseph Haydn's Musik," *Rheinische Musik-Zeitung* 1 (1 February 1851): 242: "Einer so vollendeten künstlerischen Natur, wie Joseph Haydn's, erscheint alles musikalisch: seine eigene

In his enthusiastic 1855 review of *Vom Musikalisch-Schönen*, Bischoff would in fact cite this very essay to illustrate the way in which his own viewpoints had presented "in an aphoristic manner" the more extended and systematic argument Hanslick would later make.[33]

Conservatives like Bischoff and progressives like Pohl, working from opposite ends of the aesthetic spectrum, agreed more or less on the nature of absolute music, and this made their differences about its value all the more intense. The new term precipitated a rhetoric of alterity from both sides of the ideological divide. At its core, the debate came down to whether there was one kind of music that manifested itself in many ways, or two different kinds of music that manifested themselves in two distinct repertories, one instrumental, the other vocal. The high ground in this debate, as both Wagner and Hanslick realized, lay in defining the essence of music.

Empfindung ist Musik, er denkt nicht Philosophie, nicht Aesthetik, nicht Geschichte, nicht Romantik u.s.w., er denkt Musik; seine Anschauungen und Vorstellungen, seine Gedanken und Phantasien sind Musik und müssen sich aus innerer Nothwendigkeit eine musikalische Form schaffen. Die ganze Natur erscheint ihm als Musik, er hört in sich keine andere Sprache als Musik, und so ist es denn auch ganz natürlich, dass er keine andere redet."

33. Ludwig Bischoff, "Eduard Hanslick," *Niederrheinische Musik-Zeitung* 3 (24 Feburary 1855): 57.

9   Hanslick's "Pure" Music

It was partly in response to attacks by Wagner and others on the self-sufficiency of music that Hanslick issued his *Vom Musikalisch-Schönen* in the autumn of 1854. The treatise addresses all of the qualities—expression, beauty, form, autonomy, disclosiveness—that had for so long figured prominently in discussions about the relationship between music's essence and effect but radically partitions these two spheres. The effect of music, Hanslick insists, has nothing to do with its essence, and vice versa. He does not deny music's capacity to move us, but our response has nothing to do with the fundamental nature of the art. The essence of music lies in an autonomous and specifically musical (*Musikalisch-*) manifestation of beauty (*-Schönen*); its sole content, to quote the treatise's most celebrated phrase, consists of *tönend bewegte Formen*, "tonally animated forms." It is the partitioning of essence from effect that constitutes the primary "contribution to the revision of musical aesthetics" promised in the book's subtitle.

Hanslick presents his argument in seven chapters, moving from a negative thesis (what music is not) to a positive one (what it is).

1. THE AESTHETICS OF FEELING[1]

Musical aesthetics has focused for too long on the role of feelings in music. But feelings differ from individual to individual and are in any case a by-product of listening to music, not the essence of music itself. What is needed is an "objective" aesthetics of the art that will establish the immutable nature of specifically musical beauty. Music's goal has routinely been defined as the expression or arousal of emotion, and emotion has too often been erroneously equated with its content, as witnessed by a long list of quotations from earlier writers from the 1730s to as recently as 1853.

2. FEELINGS ARE NOT THE CONTENT OF MUSIC

Music has emotional power but not emotional content. It does not express feelings, though it does project the dynamics of feelings. Any assertions about the essence of music must be applicable to purely instrumental

---

1. Chapter 1 has no title in the first edition. When he added the title "Die Gefühlsästhetik" for the second edition, Hanslick eliminated two subheadings that had appeared in the table of contents (but not in the body of the text) of the first edition: (1) "The Hitherto Unscientific Perspective of Musical Aesthetics" (*Unwissenschaftlicher Standpunkt der bisherigen musikalischen Aesthetik*); and (2) "Feelings Are Not the Goal of Music" (*Die Gefühle sind nicht Zweck der Musik*).

music, which is the "pure, absolute art of tone." Instrumental music by itself can convey neither concepts or emotions. The addition of a sung text makes no difference: the same music can be (and on many occasions has been) sung to very different texts, which demonstrates the autonomous nature of the art.

3. THE MUSICALLY BEAUTIFUL

Beauty in music is specifically musical, independent of any content that might come from another source. The ideas a composer expresses in music are purely musical ideas. Music's content consists entirely and solely of "tonally animated forms" (*tönend bewegte Formen*), which are based on elements of melody, harmony, rhythm, and timbre. These forms have no representational content and might best be compared to a "living arabesque" or the shifting patterns of a kaleidoscope, which are beautiful in and of themselves. The composer's intentions or the circumstances surrounding the composition of a given work are irrelevant to what is actually in the work itself. The act of musical composition is a "working of *Geist* in material capable of incorporating *Geist*."[2] By its very nature, then, musical beauty is endowed with *Geist*, a quality that is both intellectual and spiritual.

4. ANALYSIS OF THE SUBJECTIVE IMPRESSION OF MUSIC

Imagination (*Phantasie*), not emotion, is the true "organ" of aesthetic perception. The alleged miraculous effects of music, reported from Pythagoras down to the present, cannot be replicated. Neither physiology nor psychology can explain the precise mechanism by which we perceive and respond to music. Our subjective impressions of the art are compounded by the fact that the composer's score must be performed in order to be heard: this introduces yet another layer of variability into the aesthetic experience.

5. THE AESTHETIC PERCEPTION OF MUSIC CONTRASTED WITH THE PATHOLOGICAL

There are two ways of listening to music: the aesthetic manner contemplates it attentively and engages the imagination, while the pathological manner bypasses *Geist* and responds in a purely physical fashion.

6. THE RELATIONSHIP OF MUSIC TO NATURE

Nature is full of sound (*Klang*) but only music uses tone (*Ton*). There is no music in nature: birdsong, for example, does not make use of tones. The two realms of sound cannot be reconciled. The imitation of natural sounds in music,

---

2. *VMS*, 1:79: "Componieren ist ein Arbeiten des Geistes in geistfähigem Material." *OMB*, 31, renders this as: "Composing is a work of mind upon material compatible with mind." On the problematic nature of the term *Geist*, see p. 148–50.

as in Haydn's *Seasons* or Beethoven's *Pastoral* Symphony, are not intended for the sake of their beauty but simply to evoke a poetic idea at a particular moment. Only *Ton* is imbued with *Geist*, and music is thus capable of incorporating *Geist* in a way that nature is not.

7. THE CONCEPTS OF "CONTENT" AND "FORM" IN MUSIC

Music's content is its form. The composer thinks and poeticizes in tones, which are removed from all phenomena of the external world. The resulting forms constitute the work. Music has content, but that content cannot be conveyed through words or any other medium. Music does not "speak" through tones, it speaks only *in* tones. In the mind of the listener, musical beauty unites with all other great and beautiful ideas and provides a sonic reflection of the cosmos. (This final sentence reflects the substance of the last paragraph of the first edition of the text; Hanslick later deleted it in stages, as we shall see later in this chapter.)

■ TERMINOLOGY

Hanslick's case revolves around a handful of key terms that demand careful scrutiny. Some of them, such as *Geist* and *tönend bewegte Formen*, pose special problems of their own when rendered in translation.

"Absolute Tonkunst"

The term *absolute Musik* never appears in *Vom Musikalisch-Schönen*, and Hanslick uses the phrase *absolute Tonkunst* only once. Given the charged nature of Wagner's neologism and the speed with which it had entered musical discourse, the relevant passage in *Vom Musikalisch-Schönen* is worth quoting in detail.

> We have purposefully chosen *instrumental movements* as examples. For only that which can be asserted about instrumental music applies to music as such. If some general assertion about music is to be examined—anything that characterizes its essence and nature or determines its boundaries and tendencies—then only instrumental music can be considered. It ought never be said that music can do anything of which *instrumental* music is incapable, for only instrumental music is a pure, absolute art of tone [*reine, absolute Tonkunst*]. If one wanted to give precedence to vocal or instrumental music as far as value and effect is concerned—an unscientific and largely arbitrary procedure—one would always have to concede that the concept of an "art of tone" [*"Tonkunst"*] could not be applied in any pure way to a musical piece composed to the words of a text. In a vocal composition the effect of the tones can never be separated precisely from the effect of the words, the plot, or the scenery in such a way that would allow for a strictly differentiated calculation of the various arts. We

must reject here even those musical works that bear specific headings or programs about the "content" of the music. Union with poetry extends the power of music but not its boundaries.[3]

This passage resonates with E. T. A. Hoffmann's review of Beethoven's Fifth Symphony from more than forty years before, when Hoffmann had declared that to speak of music as an autonomous art meant to speak of instrumental music, which alone gives voice to the true essence of music by virtue of avoiding admixture with any other art.[4] It also responds to Wagner, who rejected Hoffmann's interpretation of Beethoven's Fifth as mere "longing."[5] Wagner goes unnamed here but was clearly one of those who sought to "give precedence" to vocal music "as far as value and effect is concerned" and who had forcefully sought to extend "the power of music" through a union with poetry. Even though the words *Musik* and *Tonkunst* are ordinarily interchangeable in German, Hanslick goes out of his way to avoid Wagner's term (*absolute Musik*)—in part so as not to give the appearance of sanctioning it, in part to emphasize the essence of music as an art (*Kunst*) that consists specifically and solely of musical tone (*Ton*). This point, central to the sixth chapter of the treatise, stands in direct opposition to Wagner's understanding of music as an art that in its original (and superior) form had integrated tone, gesture, and word. As to his evocation of the Absolute, Hanslick was too familiar with its implications in German philosophy to have used the term unthinkingly. The fact that he left this passage unaltered throughout all ten authorial editions of his treatise speaks to the care with which he had chosen his words at this juncture.

On an even more fundamental level, Hanslick resisted the term *absolute Musik* on the grounds that it was redundant. To his mind, music was by its very nature absolute. He perceived no need for Wagner's retronym because the essence of music, as he conceived it, could not be qualified in any way. Certain

---

3. *VMS*, 1:52–53: "Wir haben absichtlich *Instrumentalsätze* zu Beispielen gewählt. Denn nur was von der Instrumentalmusik behauptet werden kann, gilt von der Tonkunst als solcher. Wenn irgend eine allgemeine Bestimmtheit der Musik untersucht wird, etwas so ihr Wesen und ihre Natur kennzeichnen, ihre Gränzen und Richtung feststellen soll, so kann nur von der Instrumentalmusik die Rede sein. Was die *Instrumentalmusik* nicht kann, von dem darf nie gesagt werden, die *Musik* könne es; denn nur sie ist reine, absolute *Tonkunst*. Ob man nun die Vocal- oder die Instrumentalmusik an Werth und Wirkung vorziehen wolle,—eine unwissenschaftliche Procedur, bei der meist flache Willkür das Wort führt—man wird stets einräumen müssen, daß der Begriff 'Tonkunst' in einem auf Textworte componirten Musikstück nicht rein aufgehe. In einer Vocalcomposition kann die Wirksamkeit der Töne nie so genau von jener der Worte, der Handlung, der Decoration getrennt werden, daß die Rechnung der verschiedenen Künste sich streng sondern ließe. Sogar Tonstücke mit bestimmten Ueberschriften oder Programmen müssen wir ablehnen, wo es sich um den 'Inhalt' der Musik handelt. Die Vereinigung mit der Dichtkunst erweitert die Macht der Musik, aber nicht ihre Gränzen." *OMB*, 14–15.

4. E. T. A. Hoffmann, Review of Beethoven's Fifth Symphony, *AmZ* 12 (4 July 1810): 630.

5. See Bonds, *Music as Thought*, 106–07.

kinds of music might tolerate or even require a modifier of some sort (characteristic music, dramatic music, vocal music), but the need for such modifiers simply confirmed the paradigmatic essence of instrumental music. The union of music and poetry, he observed, could "extend the powers of music but not its boundaries." Absolute music, for Hanslick, could be indicated quite simply in a single word: music.

In another key passage, also in chapter 2, Hanslick asserts that music can provide an "intimation of the Absolute," thereby connecting the act of listening with a transcendental experience. Again, the fuller context of this use of the term makes the paragraph worth quoting in full:

> The ideas that the composer puts forward are first and foremost purely *musical* ideas. A beautiful melody appears in his imagination. It has no purpose other than to be itself. But just as every concrete manifestation points toward its conceptually higher kind, toward the idea it most immediately fulfills, and so on, ever higher and higher to the absolute idea, so it is with musical ideas as well. Thus it is that *this* gentle, harmonious Adagio can manifest the idea of the gentle and harmonious *in general*. Imagination as a whole, which gladly places the ideas of art in relation to those of the self—to those of the life of the human soul—will perceive this sound still higher, e.g., as the expression of mild resignation of a spirit reconciled with itself, and from there ascend to an intimation of the Absolute.[6]

The passage is deeply indebted to Hegel, who viewed art in general as the sensuous, perceptible manifestation of Idea and a means by which to ascend (at least in theory) to a higher plane of consciousness.[7] Even as he insists (yet again) that music exists entirely for its own sake, Hanslick acknowledges that it can function disclosively and even provide an "intimation" of the highest idea of all, the Absolute. Music's beauty, he suggests, is both immanent and transcendent. But Hanslick had second thoughts about this passage and changed the end of the final sentence in the second edition of 1858 to read: "still higher, e.g., as the expression of mild resignation of a spirit reconciled with itself, and can perhaps from there ascend to an intimation of an eternal transcendent

---

6. *VMS*, 1:45–46: "Die Ideen, welche der Componist darstellt, sind vor Allem und zuerst rein *musikalische*. Seiner Phantasie erscheint eine bestimmte schöne Melodie. Sie soll nichts Anderes sein, als sie selbst. Wie aber jede concrete Erscheinung auf ihren höheren Gattungsbegriff, auf die sie zunächst erfüllende Idee hinaufweist, und so fort immer höher und höher bis zur absoluten Idee, so geschieht es auch mit den musikalischen Ideen. So wird z.B. *dieses* sanfte, harmonisch ausklingende Adagio die Idee des Sanften, Harmonischen *überhaupt* zur schönen Erscheinung bringen. Die allgemeine Phantasie, welche gern die Ideen der Kunst in Bezug zum eigenen, menschlichen Seelenleben setzt, wird dies Ausklingen noch höher z.B. als den Ausdruck milder Resignation eines in sich versöhnten Gemüthes auffassen, und so fort bis zur Ahnung des Absoluten steigen." *OMB*, 10.

7. His protestations notwithstanding, Hanslick owed much to Hegel; see Paul Bruchhagen, "Hanslick und die spekulative Ästhetik," *Zeitschrift für Ästhetik und allgemeine Kunstwissenschaft* 30 (1936): 270–76.

peace."[8] Whether or not these higher spheres might be equated with a concept explicitly identified as the Absolute is in fact less important than his acknowledgment of a process by which the mind is led upward, above and beyond the realm of tone. Such careful (and revealing) changes make it all the more likely that Hanslick used—and retained—the phrase *absolute Tonkunst* later in the same chapter from the first edition onward as an implicit rebuttal of Wagner's excoriation of the idea.

Hanslick's preferred terms in his journalistic criticism were always "pure music" (*reine Musik*) and "pure instrumental music" (*reine Instrumentalmusik*). He rarely used "absolute music," and then only much later in his career, having apparently recognized that the term had become part of the standard critical vocabulary and was in any case no longer connected so directly in the public's memory with the figure of Wagner.[9] On at least one occasion, however, he used the term in Wagner's original sense, applying it to the relationship of words and music in Italian opera, where "absolute music and the virtuosity of the singers are so fundamentally essential that attention to language falls almost entirely by the wayside."[10]

"Ton"

Hanslick identifies tone (*Ton*) as the most basic element of music, and he places great importance on the distinction between tone, a quintessentially human product, and sound (*Schall* or *Klang*), a product of nature. This was a long-standing distinction found in commentaries by a wide range of writers that included Rousseau, Forkel, Krause, Mundt, and Kahlert. As Rousseau put it, "Birds whistle; man alone sings."[11] In an argument that strongly anticipates the sixth chapter of *Vom Musikalisch-Schönen*, Mundt praises music as the "remarkable production of an infinite world that exists nowhere else" and emanates "from human *Geist* and its insatiable desire for revelation." Only humans can produce tones, and therefore only humans can produce

---

8. *VMS*, 1:46: "z.B. als den Ausdruck milder Resignation eines in sich versöhnten Gemüthes auffassen, und kann vielleicht so fort bis zur Ahnung eines ewigen jenseitigen Friedens aufsteigen." *OMB*, 10.

9. Sanna Pederson, "On the Musically Beautiful and 'Absolute Music,'" paper presented at the annual meeting of the American Musicological Society, Philadelphia, 2009. I am grateful to Professor Pederson for providing me a copy of her text.

10. Eduard Hanslick, "Richard Wagner über das Hofoperntheater," *Die Presse*, 18 October 1863, 2: "Die absolute Musik und die Virtuosität der Sänger sind hier so sehr das Wesentliche, daß fast jede Aufmerksamkeit auf die Sprache…hinwegfällt."

11. Rousseau, *Essai sur l'origine des langues*, 132: "Les oiseaux sifflent, l'homme seul chante"; *Essay on the Origin of Language*, trans. Moran, 64. Forkel, *Allgemeine Geschichte der Musik*, 2–3; Krause, *Anfangsgründe der allgemeinen Theorie der Musik*, 39–53; Mundt, *Aesthetik*, 348–51; and Kahlert, *System der Aesthetik* (1846), 386–87.

music: the song of the nightingale reminds us that man alone is capable of bringing sounds together in tones as an "intellectual-spiritual whole" (*ein geistiges Ganzes*).[12]

"Tönend bewegte Formen"

Like a well-turned phrase from a poem, Hanslick's *tönend bewegte Formen* defies straightforward translation. It is most often rendered as "tonally moving forms" or "tonally moved forms," but neither of these captures the sense of agency played by tones. "Tonally animated forms" comes somewhat closer to the mark. Hanslick's "forms" (*Formen*) are set in motion (*bewegt*) by "sounding tones" (*tönend*), "tones" being the elemental units of music, as noted above.[13] The sound of humanly produced tones, in other words, creates forms that move through time.

Formen is no less problematic, for the German word is even more capacious than its English cognate. In music, *Formen* can be used to describe conventional structural patterns (sonata form, theme and variations, rondo, ABA, etc.), entire genres, or musical units of any kind and any size beyond a single tone, from a brief gesture to a two-measure phrase to a melody to a complete movement or even an entire multimovement work. In the context of Hanslick's celebrated phrase, however, *Formen* is perhaps best understood in the even more general sense of "manifestations" or "configurations." The concept of form in music, Hanslick emphasizes, is unlike that in any other art. Tonal forms "are not empty but filled, not mere linear outlines of a vacuum but rather *Geist* that shapes itself from within."[14] Tone is imbued with *Geist*, and forms are the larger manifestations of the *Geist* inherent in tone.

We can get some sense of just how broadly the term *Formen* could be used in Hanslick's time by considering its application in a treatise he openly admired. In early 1855 Hanslick sent a copy of his newly published work to the noted philosopher and physician Hermann Lotze (1817–1881), along with a letter of gushing admiration for Lotze's *Medicinische Psychologie*, which, as Hanslick told its author, was especially important to him in writing the fourth and fifth

---

12. Mundt, *Aesthetik*, 351: "Die wundersame Produktion einer unendlichen, sonst nirgend gegenständlich vorhandenen Welt, welche die Musik unternimmt, sie tritt daher rein aus dem menschlichen Geiste selbst und dessen unersättlichem Offenbarungsdrange heraus." Ibid., 366.

13. Geoffrey Payzant considers various other possible translations of the phrase in Payzant, "Hanslick, Sams, Gay, and 'Tönend bewegte Formen,'" *JAAC* 40 (1981): 41–48. On the philosophical implications of *Bewegung*, see Lydia Goehr, "*Doppelbewegung*: The Musical Movement of Philosophy and the Philosophical Movement of Music," in *Sound Figures of Modernity: German Music and Philosophy*, ed. Jost Hermand and Gerhard Richter (Madison: University of Wisconsin Press, 2006), 19–63; and Goehr, *Elective Affinities: Musical Essays on the History of Aesthetic Theory* (New York: Columbia University Press, 2008), 6–11 and passim.

14. *VMS*, 1:78: "Die Formen, welche sich aus Tönen bilden, sind nicht leere, sondern erfüllte, nicht bloße Linienbegrenzung eines Vacuums, sondern sich von innen heraus gestaltender Geist." *OMB*, 30.

chapters of *Vom Musikalisch-Schönen.*[15] Lotze's book includes a chapter titled "Von den verschiedenen Formen des Seelenlebens," which suggests a meaning of *Formen* that more nearly approximates that of words such as "manifestations" or (in the medical sense) "presentations." In an earlier essay on aesthetics, Lotze, echoing Goethe, had recognized music's advantage of being more capable than any other art of "express[ing] entirely through the play of forms all the essential aspects of beauty."[16]

"Geist"

Geist, a ubiquitous concept in German-language writings of the nineteenth century, is another term that is notoriously difficult to translate: it can mean spirit, mind, or a combination of the two—hence the English-language renditions of Hegel's *Phänomenologie des Geistes* sometimes as *Phenomenology of Mind,* sometimes as *Phenomenology of Spirit.* Neither is wholly satisfactory: one emphasizes intellect too much, the other too little. In any case, *Geist* is always a good thing to have: an individual, a society, a work of art, indeed a statement of any kind cannot claim intellectual or spiritual depth if it lacks *Geist.* The concept is perhaps best captured by the Latin *anima,* connoting the vital principle of life, of the soul, an animating force.

In his lectures on aesthetics, published posthumously in 1835, Hegel had followed Kant in minimizing the status of instrumental music, calling it "empty and meaningless" on the grounds that it "lacks a principal factor of all art—spiritual-intellectual content [*der geistige Inhalt*] and the expression of *Geist.*" On this basis, indeed, "it could hardly be considered an art at all."[17] Hegel conceded that music could rise to the level of "a true art" only if it could incorporate—with or without a text—*Geist* "through the sensuous medium of tones and their diverse combinations."[18] Music's "fundamental task" is to "give resonance not to objectivity but rather to the manner in which the innermost self is essentially moved

---

15. Hermann Lotze, *Medicinische Psychologie, oder, Physiologie der Seele* (Leipzig: Weidmann, 1852); for Hanslick's letter, see Hermann Lotze, *Briefe und Dokumente,* ed. Reinhardt Pester (Würzburg: Königshausen & Neumann, 2003), 263–64. Lotze would publish a mixed review of Hanslick's treatise in July 1855 (see Appendix); see Franz Michael Maier, "Lotze und Zimmermann als Rezensenten von Hanslicks *Vom Musikalisch-Schönen,*" *AfMw* 70 (2013): 209–26. I am grateful to Dr. Maier for sharing a copy of his essay in advance of its publication.

16. Lotze, *Ueber Bedingungen der Kunstschönheit* (Göttingen: Vandenhoeck und Ruprecht, 1847), 33–34: "Keine Kunst ist so sehr wie sie geeignet, in dem blossen Spiele der Formen alle wesentlichen Seiten der Schönheit auszudrücken."

17. Hegel, *Vorlesungen über die Ästhetik,* 3:148–49.

18. Hegel, *Vorlesungen über die Ästhetik,* 3:149: "Erst wenn sich in dem sinnlichen Element der Töne und ihrer mannigfaltigen Figuration Geistiges in angemessener Weise ausdrückt, erhebt sich auch die Musik zur wahren Kunst."

according to its subjectivity and the ideal nature of the soul."[19] Hegel pointed out that in "recent times," music in particular had "retreated into its own medium," thereby compromising "its power over the whole of inner life." The "pleasure it offers" had becoming increasingly restricted to the "purely musical" aspect, which appeals primarily to connoisseurs and not to the interests of a broader audience.[20]

The kinds of things the general public *did* respond to—to the dismay of countless critics—were virtuosity and special orchestral effects.[21] Mere technical skills in performance or orchestration, however, did not ensure the quality of depth so many critics (especially German ones) considered essential.[22] By the middle of the nineteenth century, the presence (or absence) of *Geist* in purely instrumental music had become a matter of intense debate. The "life-question for our art," as A. B. Marx put it in 1841, "is simply this: *whether its spiritual* [geistige] *or sensuous side shall prevail.*"[23]

Hanslick realized that without *Geist*, his *tönend bewegte Formen* would amount to little more than an empty play of sensuous forms, and this is why he went to such great lengths to argue that the music's *Geist* or *geistiger Gehalt* (substance) resides in forms constructed of tones (*Tonformen*).[24] His extended case in chapter 6 against the origins or presence of music in nature is crucial to his position that music, as an object created through *Geist*, a human quality, is itself imbued with *Geist*. Forms in and of themselves did not ensure the presence of *Geist*: this is a point Hanslick would make repeatedly in his journalistic criticism. He attributes the success of fugues by Bach and Handel, for example, to the ability of those composers to "think polyphonically." For them, the fugal style

19. Hegel, *Vorlesungen über die Ästhetik*, 3:135: "Die Hauptaufgabe der Musik wird deshalb darin bestehen, nicht die Gegenständlichkeit selbst, sondern im Gegenteil die Art und Weise widerklingen zu lassen, in welcher das innerste Selbst seiner Subjektivität und ideellen Seele nach in sich bewegt ist."

20. Hegel, *Vorlesungen über die Ästhetik*, 3:145: "In neuerer Zeit besonders ist die Musik…in ihr eigenes Element zurückgegangen, doch hat dafür auch desto mehr an Macht über das ganze Innere verloren, indem der Genuß, den sie bieten kann, sich nur der einen Seite der Kunst zuwendet, dem bloßen Interesse nämlich für das rein Musikalische der Komposition und deren Geschicklichkeit, eine Seite, welche nur Sache der Kenner ist, und das allgemeine menschliche Kunstinteresse weniger angeht."

21. See Dana Gooley, "The Battle Against Instrumental Virtuosity in the Early Nineteenth Century," in *Franz Liszt and His World*, ed. Christopher H. Gibbs and Dana Gooley (Princeton: Princeton University Press, 2006), 75–111; and Fritz Reckow, "'Wirkung' und 'Effekt': Über einige Voraussetzungen, Tendenzen und Probleme der deutschen Berlioz-Kritik," *Die Musikforschung* 33 (1980): 1–36.

22. See Holly Watkins, *Metaphors of Depth in German Musical Thought: From E. T. A. Hoffmann to Arnold Schoenberg* (Cambridge: Cambridge University Press, 2011).

23. Marx, *Die alte Musiklehre im Streit mit unserer Zeit* (Leipzig: Breitkopf & Härtel, 1841), vi: "Die Lebensfrage für uns[e]re Kunst…ist einfach die: *ob ihre geistige, oder sinnliche Seite vorwalten…soll.*" Emphasis in original. Bernd Sponheuer, *Musik als Kunst und Nicht-Kunst: Untersuchungen zur Dichotomie von "hoher" und "niederer" Musik im musikästhetischen Denken zwischen Kant und Hanslick* (Kassel: Bärenreiter, 1987), traces in detail the role of *Geist* in music criticism between ca. 1790 and ca. 1860 as the quality that separated "high" from "low" art, or what later generations would identify as "classical" and "popular" repertories.

24. *VMS*, 1:78; *OMB*, 30.

was a "perfectly natural language." In the hands of later composers such as Verdi, by contrast, the fugue had "shriveled to a mere formalism."[25]

Geist was also inextricably linked to beauty. Kant had pointed to *Geist* as the central quality that elevated the beautiful above the merely agreeable, and this distinction remained a fundamental premise of aesthetics throughout the nineteenth century. In Gustav Schilling's *Geschichte der heutigen oder modernen Musik* (1841)—the work dedicated to Tomášek, who at the time was Hanslick's piano and theory instructor in Prague—we read such statements as:

> The sensuous in a work of art should exist only in so far as it exists for the *Geist* of humankind and not for its own sake. The form of a work of art should be not merely…pleasing to the senses as a pleasing (tasteful) whole; it must be a form that is *rich in Geist*, one that is *Geist-filled* and *Geist-filling*.[26]

Both in spite and because of its centrality, *Geist* was a term whose import no one felt compelled to spell out clearly. Like the Absolute, it possessed its own quasi-mystical aura in the minds of German-language authors. Only its prestige remained beyond question, and many critics, including Hanslick, may well have relied at times on its nimbus to convince their readers of the profundity of their subject matter.

"Gemüt"

From the 1730s onward, *Gemüt* (also spelled *Gemüth*) was for many German-language writers the locus of music's spiritual and psychological effect. *Gemüt* is closely related to *Geist* in that it entails a combination of both intellect and spirit but with the added element of feeling as well. It is perhaps best translated as "psyche." Kant treated it as a faculty of the mind, the site of "the animating principle of *Geist*."[27] Hegel, in a moment of tautological virtuosity, called music "the art of *Gemüt* that addresses itself directly toward the *Gemüt* itself."[28] In his monograph on the aesthetics of music published in 1830, Wilhelm

25. Hanslick, "Verdi's Requiem" (1879), in Hanslick, *Musikalische Stationen* (Berlin: A. Hofmann, 1880), 8: " polyphon denkt "; " eine vollkommen natürliche Sprache"; "Später ist die Fuge immer mehr zum bloßen Formalismus eingeschrumpft."

26. Gustav Schilling, *Geschichte der heutigen oder modernen Musik* (Karlsruhe: Christian Theodor Groos, 1841), 9: "Das Sinnliche eines Kunstwerks soll nur Daseyn haben, in sofern es für den Geist des Menschen, nicht aber in sofern es selbst als Sinnliches für sich existirt; die Form eines Kunstwerks muß nicht blos eine…den Sinnen allenfalls noch wohlgefällige (geschmackvolle) Gestalt, sondern eine *geistreiche, geisterfüllte* und *erfüllende* Form seyn." Emphasis in original.

27. Kant, *Kritik der Urteilskraft*, §49 (B192), 201: "Geist, in ästhetischer Bedeutung, heißt das belebende Prinzip im Gemüte." Guyer and Matthews, in their translation, render *Gemüt* as "mind"; see *Critique of the Power of Judgment*, 191–92.

28. Hegel, *Vorlesungen über die Ästhetik*, 3:135: "die Kunst des Gemüts, welche sich unmittelbar an das Gemüt selber wendet."

Christian Müller identified the *Gemüt* as the "organ of *Poesie* and of aesthetics."[29] August Kahlert opened his *System der Aesthetik* of 1846 with the observation that "the mysterious effect that works of fine art exercise on the human *Gemüt* is an eternal riddle scholarship is constantly being challenged to solve."[30] It is usages of this kind that had prompted Goethe to suggest in 1826 a moratorium on the word: "Germans should not utter the word *Gemüt* for thirty years; it might then regenerate itself. For the moment, it indicates merely an indulgence with weaknesses—of one's self and of others."[31]

Hanslick jumped Goethe's proposed moratorium by two years when he used the term or some variant of it repeatedly throughout *Vom Musikalisch-Schönen*. The most important of these passages appears in first edition's final paragraph. It is in the *Gemüt*, he declares, that the listener combines the "intellectual-spiritual substance" (*geistiger Gehalt*) of music with "all other great and beautiful ideas."[32] *Gemüt* could accommodate emotions as well as ideas. Once again, however, this conceptual intersection of the material and spiritual would prove deeply problematic for Hanslick, and he would eventually delete the sentence altogether.

■ HANSLICK'S EARLY AESTHETICS

For all its terminological subtleties, Hanslick's treatise won nearly universal praise for the clarity of its prose. In German-speaking lands, philosophy in general and aesthetics in particular had long been burdened with a tradition of linguistic density that many perceived as obscurity. But even Hanslick's most severe critics deemed his treatise accessible, clear, and occasionally even witty. It appeared at a time, moreover, when few voices were speaking out in opposition to Wagnerism and the "Music of the Future." The more conservative *Allgemeine musikalische Zeitung* of Leipzig had ceased publication in 1848; it would start up again in the 1860s, but for the moment, no major journal stood in opposition to the *Neue Zeitschrift für Musik*, which under the editorship of Franz Brendel (1811–1868) had become a mouthpiece for Wagner, Liszt, and what would soon come to be called the New German School, a term Brendel himself would

---

29. Wilhelm Christian Müller, *Aesthetisch-historische Einleitungen in die Wissenschaft der Tonkunst*, 2 vols. (Leipzig:Breitkopf & Härtel, 1830), 1:6.

30. Kahlert, *System der Aesthetik*, 3: "Die geheimnißvolle Wirkung, welche auf das menschliche Gemüth Werke der schönen Kunst ausüben, ist eines jener ewigen Räthsel, zu deren Lösung die Wissenschaft immer wieder aufs Neue aufgefordert wird."

31. Goethe, *Kunst und Alterthum*, vol. 5, part 3 (1826), in Goethe, *Werke*, vol. 1, part 3, *Sprüche in Prosa*, ed. Harald Fricke (Frankfurt am Main: Deutscher Klassiker Verlag, 1993), 35: "Die Deutschen sollten in einem Zeitraume von dreyßig Jahren das Wort Gemüth nicht aussprechen, dann würde nach und nach Gemüth sich wieder erzeugen; jetzt heißt es nur Nachsicht mit Schwächen, eignen und fremden."

32. *VMS*, 1:171: "Dieser geistige Gehalt verbindet nun auch im Gemüth des Hörers das Schöne der Tonkunst mit allen andern großen und schönen Ideen." See below, p. 184.

coin in 1859. For those who opposed Wagner and his music, Hanslick's treatise provided an intellectual rallying point, a philosophical justification that went beyond matters of mere style or personal taste.

Hanslick came to his own aesthetic convictions by fits and starts. He grew up in a household filled with both philosophy and music. His father, Joseph Adolf Hanslik (1785–1859), who spelled his name without a "c," was a librarian by profession but a philosopher by inclination. He had studied for a time with the philosopher and aesthetician Johann Heinrich Dambeck (1774–1820) and even substituted for him at the University of Prague for a year during one of his teacher's illnesses; he would later edit and see into print Dambeck's lectures on aesthetics. In his memoirs, Eduard Hanslick noted that the book his father had edited "was highly valued in its time, i.e., when Kantian philosophy was still being cultivated." Hanslik also published his own tabular "Overview of Logical Forms as an Aid to Public and Self-Instruction" and made excerpts from philosophical works for his children to study.[33]

After finishing his studies in piano and theory with Tomášek—who happened to be a close personal friend of Dambeck—the younger Hanslick pursued a degree in law, first in Prague (until the end of 1846) and then in Vienna, where he completed his studies in 1849.[34] It was during his student years that Hanslick began writing music criticism. His opinions about the self-contained nature of the art were already in place by April 1847 when he published a review of a concert that featured works by Alfred Julius Becher (1803–1848), a Viennese composer and fellow music critic. At the very end of his review, Hanslick contrasts Becher with Berlioz:

> The characteristic individuality of Berlioz's music consists of this: that in his compositions, music is not an end in itself, not music in the strict sense, i.e., a free play of tones in beautiful form that make audible in tones a certain sentiment, but rather a means for the expression of a *poetic* ideal. B[ernhard] Gutt said rightly that Berlioz does not *compose* but rather poeticizes with musical elements. Because of the inability of music to replicate anything concrete in combinations of tones, Berlioz's music—which nevertheless aspires to this—requires a primer for the listener, a

---

33. Johann Heinrich Dambeck, *Vorlesungen über Aesthetik,* ed. Joseph A. Hanslik, 2 vols. (Prague: Carl Wilhelm Enders, 1822–23); and Joseph Adolph Hanslik, *Uibersicht* [sic] *der logischen Formen, als Hilfsmittel beim öffentlichen und Selbstunterricht* (Prague: Enders, 1822). Eduard Hanslick, *Aus meinem Leben,* 2 vols. (Berlin: Allgemeiner Verein für deutsche Litteratur, 1894), 1:4: "ein Lehrbuch, das seinerzeit, d.h., als so lange die Kantsche Philosophie noch Pflege fand, sehr geschätzt war." Ibid., 1:8. On Hanslick's early education, see Ines Grimm, *Eduard Hanslicks Prager Zeit: Frühe Wurzeln seiner Schrift Vom Musikalisch-Schönen* (Saarbrücken: Pfau, 2003). On Joseph Adolph Hanslik, see I. J. Hanus, *Zusätze und Inhalts-Verzeichnisze* [sic] *zu Hanslik's Geschichte und Beschreibung der k. k. Prager Universitäts-Bibliothek* (Prague: Hanuś, 1863), vii–viii.

34. On the personal connections between Tomášek and Dambeck, see Thompson, "Wenzel Johann Tomaschek," 90–91.

reverse translation of the music into words. For this reason, all of Berlioz's compositions have programs and headings, and they need to have them. Becher, by contrast, does not compose from this perspective: his compositions are music in the strict sense, music that through the most profound intellectual-spiritual content suffices as such. To be sure, Becher allows his music to stream out of definite feelings, as did Beethoven, but he does not put forward a specific image in the way Berlioz does. Becher's music thus belongs in no way to "descriptive" music.[35]

What is of special interest here is Hanslick's distinction between the way in which Berlioz "expresses" (*ausdruckt*) ideas or emotions while Becher "entones" his (*austönt*). This difference in formulation was to play a critical role in *Vom Musikalisch-Schönen*, where Hanslick would argue that while a composer may be moved by a particular feeling to write a work of music, the way in which that feeling is made manifest—or at least *should* be made manifest—is purely musical and cannot be translated verbally or in any other way.

The tumultuous events of March 1848 caused Hanslick to forget this distinction momentarily. He heard political elements not only in the operas of the day— he cites Auber's *La muette de Portici*, Meyerbeer's *Les Huguenots*, and Wagner's *Rienzi* by name in one of his reviews—but in instrumental music as well. "Do not Hungarian sabers rattle in the finale of Schubert's C Major Symphony? And when you play Chopin's mazurkas, do you not feel the mournfully oppressive air of Ostrolenka?"[36] He declared music, religion, and philosophy to be "merely

35. Hanslick, "Für Musik: Dr. Alfred Julius Becher," in Hanslick, *Sämtliche Schriften: Historisch-kritische Ausgabe*, ed. Dietmar Strauß (Vienna: Böhlau, 1993–), I/1:118–19, originally published in the *Sonntagsblätter* (Vienna), 11 April 1847: "Die karakteristische Eigenthümlichkeit Berlioz's besteht darin, daß ihm in seinen Kompozizionen die Musik nicht Selbstzweck ist, nicht Musik im strengen Sinne, d.i. ein freies Spiel mit Tönen in schöner Form, das irgend eine Stimmung oder Empfindung austönt, sondern Mittel des Ausdru[c]kes zur Darstellung eines *poetischen* Ideals. B. Gutt sagte richtig, Berlioz *komponire* nicht, sondern dichte mit musikalischen Elementen. Wegen des Unvermögens der Musik, ein Konkretes in Tonkombinazionen wiederzugeben, braucht Berlioz's Musik, welche dieß dennoch anstrebt, einen Leitfaden für den Zuhörer, einer Rü[c]kübersetzung der Musik in das Wort. Deßhalb haben alle Kompozizionen Berlioz's Programme und Ueberschriften, und müssen sie haben. Becher hingegen komponirt nicht von diesem Standpunkte aus, seine Kompozizionen sind Musik im strengen Sinne, Musik, die, bei dem tiefsten geistigen Inhalte, sich als solche genügt. Becher läßt seine Musik wo[h]l aus einem bestimmten Gefühle ausströmen, wie Beethoven, stellt aber nicht ein bestimmtes Bild dar, wie Berlioz.—Becher's Musik gehört also keineswegs zur 'deskriptiven.'" Emphasis in original. In his partial translation of this passage, Payzant ("Eduard Hanslick and Bernhard Gutt," *MR* 50 [1989]: 131) translates *ein freies Spiel mit Tönen in schöner Form* as "a spontaneous play of tones in beautiful configuration," a reading that suppresses the key word *Form*, equates "free" with "spontaneous," and overlooks the antecedents of the concept of *freies Spiel* in the writings of Kant, Schiller, Nägeli, and others. Payzant does, however, correctly point out the strong similarities between this passage and one written by Gutt in January 1846, noting that such unacknowledged borrowings were "more common and less objectionable" at the time than they would be today.

36. Eduard Hanslick, "Censur und Kunst-Kritik," in Hanslick, *Sämtliche Schriften*, vol. 1, part 1, 157; originally published in the *Wiener Zeitung*, 24 March 1848: "Klirren nicht Ungarische Säbel in dem Finale von Schubert's C-dur-Symphonie? Und wenn ihr Chopin's Mazuren [*sic*] spielt, fühlt ihr sie

different refractions of the same ray of light," arguing that "the works of the great tone-poets are more than music: they are mirror images of the *philosophical, religious,* and *political* worldviews of their time. Does not the proud majesty and the painful skepticism of German philosophy permeate the late works of Beethoven and the works of Berlioz?"[37] When Hanslick witnessed the violence of the revolution in Vienna firsthand, however, he turned to an aesthetic that saw art as a refuge from change, not as a means to promote it. In his memoirs, published in 1894, he recalled his horror at seeing the corpse of the assassinated minister of war, Theodor Graf Baillet de Latour, strung up on a lamppost in Vienna at the beginning of the October Uprising in 1848:

> The mob had lit the gas flame above the head of the murder victim and shouted and hooted around the corpse, at times setting it swinging back and forth with a push. Shuddering inwardly, I forced my way out of the crowd, which by now filled the entire square, and I ran, almost unconscious, back to my abode. There I lit my lamp and opened a volume of Goethe, in order to wash myself clean from the vision.[38]

From this point on, Hanslick came to see art increasingly as a refuge from politics—and the more pure the art, the more solid the refuge. *Rein*—"pure" or "clean"—is a word that appears over and over in *Vom Musikalisch-Schönen.*

For at least several years after this incident, Hanslick struggled with the conceptual division between expression and form. In his 1849 review of a newly published anthology of keyboard music from earlier times—four pieces each by Bach and Handel, one by Mozart, and one by Domenico Scarlatti—he praises their composers' "remarkable realization of the *purely musical* element" and their formal design. This leads him to declare the keyboard music of the previous century superior to that of the present. He goes on to note, however, that the "great advance of more recent (romantic) piano composition" lies in "its *poetic spiritualization.*" This has allowed composers since Beethoven to move beyond the demands of constructing a pleasing, self-contained work and respond to "a higher calling for music: the artistic representation of human feelings, moods, and passions." Composers of the present day give priority to content, while

nicht, die klagend schwüle Luft von Ostrolenka?" The defeat of Polish forces in the Battle of Ostrolenka was a pivotal moment in the Polish-Russian War of 1830–31.

37. Hanslick, "Censur und Kunst-Kritik," in Hanslick, *Sämtliche Schriften,* vol. 1, part 1,157; originally published in the *Wiener Zeitung,* 24 March 1848: "Die Werke der großen Tondichter sind mehr als Musik, sie sind Spiegelbilder der *philosophischen, religiösen* und *politischen* Weltanschauungen ihrer Zeit. Webt nicht in Beethovens letzten Werken, und in Berlioz die stolze Hoheit und die schmerzliche Scepsis der Deutschen Philosophie?" Emphasis in original.

38. Hanslick, *Aus meinem Leben,* 1:135–36: "Der Pöbel hatte die Gasflamme über dem Haupte des Ermordeten angezündet und schrie und johlte um die Leiche herum, setzte sie auch zeitweilig durch einen Stoß in schaukelnde Bewegung. Ich drängte mich, im Innersten schauernd, aus der Menge heraus, welche den ganzen Platz anfüllte und rannte fast bewußtlos nach Hause. Da zündete ich meine Lampe an und schlug einen Band Goethe auf, um mich rein zu waschen von dem Gesehenen."

their predecessors had devoted themselves to issues of form. At this point, however, Hanslick could make this contrast without coming down in favor of one or the other.[39]

Having received his degree in law, Hanslick accepted a position as a civil servant, first in Klagenfurt (1850–52) and then in Vienna. In his memoirs he recalled that his duties allowed him sufficient leisure to increase his knowledge of music and musical aesthetics, and it was during this time that he conceived the idea of writing a treatise on the aesthetics of music.

To this end, I went almost regularly to the Hofbibliothek [in Vienna] for months on end... and read scores and books there until being told it was closing time. The scores were largely of earlier operas, which always interested me the most. The books were primarily on the aesthetics and history of music. Heavens, to think of all that I read and made excerpts from there! Throughout this study, I relied entirely on myself and had no one to whom I could turn for advice. With the exception of two or three evenings a week devoted to social events or visits to the theater, I regularly studied at home with a glass of beer at my side, or when drowsiness threatened to overcome me, a cup of tea. These studies helped my musical criticism and vice versa. I may at any rate testify on my behalf that I was not unproductive.

Reading so many books dealing with musical aesthetics that all posited the essence of music in the "feelings" aroused by it, and that ascribed to it a very precise capacity of expression, had long since awakened in me feelings of doubt and opposition. At the same time the first enthusiastic voices for Wagner's operas and Liszt's program symphonies were beginning to arise, noisily. I let my own ideas on the matter develop and ripen within myself until they took shape as the well-known treatise *Vom Musikalisch-Schönen*.[40]

In the summer of 1853 and spring of 1854, he published two extended essays— which would later become chapters 4, 5, and 6 of his treatise—in the *Österreichische Blätter für Literatur und Kunst*, a supplement to the *Wiener Zeitung*, for which he

---

39. Hanslick, "Classische Studien für das Pianoforte," in Hanslick, *Sämtliche Schriften*, vol. 1, part 2, 88, originally published in the *Beilage zum Morgenblatte der Wiener Zeitung*, 16 June 1849: "man muß sich klare Rechenschaft legen, worin die Claviermusik des vorigen Jahrhunderts die des gegenwärtigen überragt? Die Antwort lautet: 'In der bewunderungswürdigen Ausführung des *rein musikalischen Elements.*'" Ibid., 89: "Der große Fortschritt der neueren (romantischen) Claviercomposition ist die *poetische Beseelung.* Sie hat...über den Standpunkt erhoben, von welchem eine Tondichtung nur als ein in sich vollkommen construirtes, wohlgefälliges Klangwerk erscheint, sie erkennt ein Höheres für die Aufgabe der Musik. Die künstlerische Darstellung der menschlichen Gefühle, Stimmungen und Leidenschaften." Emphasis in original.

40. Hanslick, *Aus meinem Leben*, 1:236–37: "Zu diesem Behufe ging ich durch Monate fast regelmäßig...in die Hofbibliothek und las da Partituren und Bücher, bis man uns zum Fortgehen läutete. Partituren größtenteils von alten Opern, die mich stets am meisten interessierten. An Büchern hauptsächlich Ästhetik und Geschichte der Musik. Himmel, was habe ich da alles zusammengelesen und exzerpiert! Bei diesem Studium war ich ganz allein auf mich angewiesen, hatte niemand, bei dem ich mir Rats erholen konnte. Die Abende, bis auf zwei oder drei, welche Gesellheit oder Theater in

was writing musical criticisms. He had difficulty finding a publisher for the completed manuscript of his full treatise, but with the help of the art historian Rudolf von Eitelberger, editor of the *Österreichische Blätter*, he secured a contract from the firm of Rudolph Weigel in Leipzig, which published *Vom Musikalisch-Schönen* in late September 1854.[41]

In keeping with the conventions of aesthetic polemics, Hanslick was careful not to identify his target by name. He could easily have focused his attack on Wagner alone, whose writings include many of the kinds of assertions paraded in Hanslick's extensive list of writers who had deemed expression as the essence of music. In *Das Kunstwerk der Zukunft*, for example, Wagner had claimed that even in its highest form, absolute music is "only feeling."[42] By not referring to Wagner or the "Music of the Future" explicitly, Hanslick could maintain the appearance of objectivity, even going so far at one point as to claim that his thesis contained "not even a hint of partisanship."[43]

By the time of the work's second edition (1858), Hanslick realized that there was no point in trying to maintain any pretense of nonpartisanship.[44] The year before, in his review of the Viennese premiere of *Tannhäuser*, he had publicly and explicitly attacked Wagner's aesthetics and in the process had referred readers to his own *Vom Musikalisch-Schönen* for a more detailed discussion of the relevant aesthetic issues.[45] His review makes it clear that he was well acquainted not only with Wagner's writings but also with those by Brendel, Raff, and others. Having

Anspruch nahmen, verbrachte ich regelmäßig studierend zu Hause bei einem Glas Bier, oder wenn sich Schläfrigkeit einzustellen drohte, bei einer Tasse Thee. Die Studien kamen meinen Musikkritiken zu gute und diese wiederum den ersteren. Ich darf mir wenigstens das Zeugnis geben, nicht unfleißig gewesen zu sein Die Lektüre so vieler Bücher musik-ästhetischen Inhalts, die alle das Wesen der Musik in die durch sie erregten 'Gefühle' setzten, und ihr eine sehr bestimmte Ausdrucksfähigkeit zuschrieben, hatten längst Zweifel und Opposition in mir wach gerufen. Gleichzeitig erhoben sich lärmend die ersten enthusiastischen Stimmen für Wagners Opern und Liszts Programm-Sinfonien. Ich ließ meine eigenen Ideen über die Sache in mir arbeiten und reifen, bis sie sich zu der bekannten Abhandlung 'Vom Musikalisch-Schönen' gestalteten."

41. For the publishing history of the work, see Strauß's commentary in *VMS*, 2:66–67; see also Hanslick, *Aus meinem Leben*, 1:237–38. Eitelberger (1817–1885), the first professor of art history at the University of Vienna, was a proponent of the scientific, "objective" study of art history and as such would have been immediately drawn to Hanslick's approach to music; see Matthew Rampley, "The Idea of a Scientific Discipline: Rudolf von Eitelberger and the Emergence of Art History in Vienna, 1847–1873," *Art History* 34 (2011): 54–79.

42. Wagner, *Das Kunstwerk der Zukunft*, *GSD*, 3:93: "Sie [i.e., *die absolute Musik*] ist, in ihrer unendlichsten Steigerung, doch immer nur Gefühl." *PW*, 1:123.

43. *VMS*, 1:92: "Unsere Thesis also enthält auch nicht die Andeutung einer Parteinahme." *OMB*, 38.

44. Although the title page bears the date "1858," the second edition was actually issued in the first half of December 1857; see the advertisement ("soeben erschienen") in the *Wiener Zeitung*, 15 December 1857, 3541. Hanslick's preface is dated 9 November 1857.

45. Hanslick, "Ein Vorwort zu R.Wagners 'Tannhäuser,'" *Die Presse*, 28 August 1857, republished in *Sämtliche Schriften*, vol. 1, part 4, 152–56. On Hanslick's views about the "Music of the Future," see Dietmar Strauß, "Eduard Hanslick und die Diskussion um die Musik der Zukunft," in Hanslick, *Sämtliche Schriften*, vol. 1, part 4, 407–25.

tipped his hand, Hanslick openly acknowledged the polemical origins and nature of his tract in the preface to the new edition of *Vom Musikalisch-Schönen*. He noted that at the time he had written his treatise, the "spokesmen of the Music of the Future" were "at their loudest," which "had to incite persons of my belief to react." In the years since the appearance of the treatise's first edition, Wagner's writings had been supplemented by "Liszt's program symphonies, which succeed in abdicating more completely than ever the autonomous significance of music."[46] In light of these developments, Hanslick asked the readers of his second edition to indulge him for not having abbreviated or mollified "the polemical element of my treatise":

> To the contrary, it seemed to me all the more necessary to point relentlessly to that which is indivisible and immutable in music, to musical beauty, as observed by our masters Bach, Haydn, Mozart, Beethoven, and Mendelssohn, and which will continue to be cultivated by all genuine musical innovators throughout the future.[47]

At the same time, Hanslick's argument is no mere period piece, for it engaged a long-standing debate about the relative status of texted and untexted music. Hanslick was trying to rescue instrumental music from the charge leveled by Kant, sustained by Hegel, and intensified by Wagner that, although music without words could express emotions, it could not convey concepts or embody *Geist*. Hanslick was not, however, the first to make this case.

■ HANSLICK THE CONVENTIONAL

In spite of its subtitle—*A Contribution to the Revision of Musical Aesthetics*—*Vom Musikalisch-Schönen* was not nearly as original as Hanslick wished his readers to believe. Most of its central arguments would have been familiar to attentive critics of the day. Its broader philosophical premises owed much to the writings of Johann Friedrich Herbart, Bernard Bolzano, and Robert Zimmermann, among others, and almost all its claims relating specifically to music were in circulation long before in the writings of such authors as Hans Georg Nägeli, Christian Hermann Weisse, and Ferdinand Hand.

46. *VMS*, 1:10: "Als ich diese Abhandlung schrieb, waren die Wortführer der Zukunftsmusik eben am lautesten bei Stimme und mußten wohl Leute von meinem Glaubensbekenntniß zur Reaction reizen. Nun, wo ich die 2. Auflage zu veranstalten habe, sind zu Wagners Schriften noch Liszt's Programm-Symphonien hinzugekommen, welche vollständiger, als es bisher gelungen ist, die selbstständige Bedeutung der Musik abdanken." This passage does not appear in *OMB*.

47. *VMS*, 1:11: "Man möge es mir zu Gute halten, wenn ich Angesichts solcher Zeichen keine Neigung fühlte, den polemischen Theil meiner Schrift zu kürzen oder abzuschwächen. Vielmehr däuchte es mir um so nothwendiger, rücksichtslos auf das Eine und Unvergängliche in der Tonkunst, auf die musikalische Schönheit hinzuweisen, wie sie unsere Meister Bach, Haydn, Mozart, Beethoven und Mendelssohn gefeiert haben, und echt musikalische Erfinder sie auch in aller Zukunft pflegen werden." This passage does not appear in *OMB*.

Herbart (1776–1841) was Kant's successor in the chair of philosophy at the university in Königsberg (1809); he later moved to the University of Göttingen (1835).[48] He had no professional or personal connections to Austria, yet his writings exerted an enormous influence there because they offered an alternative to the various strands of idealism and speculative philosophy that dominated the northern portions of German-speaking lands.[49] Unlike Kant and Hegel, he was not perceived as overtly Protestant in his outlook. The Catholic opposition to Kant had found its voice as early as 1788 in *Anti-Kant*, a treatise by the Jesuit theologian Benedikt Stattler, who argued that while Christian Wolff's philosophy could be accommodated within Catholic doctrine, Kant's could not. In 1827, the Vatican would place the Italian edition of the *Kritik der reinen Vernunft* on its Index of Prohibited Books. The offensive against Kant was still going on as late as 1850 with the *Neuer Anti-Kant* by Franz Prihonsky, a pupil of Bolzano.[50]

In the wake of the events of 1848–49, the writings of philosophers such as Kant and Hegel were widely seen as having encouraged revolutionary ideals in the *Vormärz*. Partly in response to this, a more "objective" brand of philosophy gained ground in the decade that followed, particularly in Austria, where the ministry of

48. On Herbart's aesthetics, see Michael Podro, *The Manifold in Perception: Theories of Art from Kant to Hildebrand* (Oxford: Clarendon Press, 1972), 61–79; *Herbarts Kultursystem: Perspektiven der Transdisziplinarität im 19. Jahrhundert*, ed. Andreas Hoeschen and Lothar Schneider (Würzburg: Königshausen & Neumann, 2001), particularly the essays by Andreas Hoeschen ("Gegenstand, Relation und System im 'ästhetischen Formalismus,'" 297–316), Lothar Schneider ("Realismus und formale Ästhetik: Die Auseinandersetzung zwischen Robert Zimmermann und Friedrich Theodor Vischer als poetologische Leitdifferenz im späten neunzehnten Jahrhundert," 259–81), and Lambert Wiesing ("Formale Ästhetik nach Herbart und Zimmermann," 283–96); and *Formalismes esthétiques et héritage herbartien: Vienne, Prague, Moscou*, ed. Céline Trautmann-Waller and Carole Maigné (Hildesheim: Olms, 2009).

49. For an overview of Herbart's influence in Austria, see William M. Johnston, *The Austrian Mind: An Intellectual and Social History, 1848–1938* (Berkeley and Los Angeles: University of California Press, 1972), 281–86. For a more detailed account, see Georg Jäger, "Die Herbartianische Ästhetik— ein österreichischer Weg in die Moderne," in *Die österreichische Literatur: Ihr Profil im 19. Jahrhundert (1830–1880)*, ed. Herbert Zeman (Graz: Akademische Druck- u. Verlagsanstalt, 1982), 195–219.

50. Franz Prihonsky, *Neuer Anti-Kant, oder: Prüfung der Kritik der reinen Vernunft nach den in Bolzano's Wissenschaftslehre niedergelegten Begriffen* (Bautzen: Weller, 1850). On anti-Kantian and anti-idealist sentiment in Austria in general, see Roger Bauer, *Der Idealismus und seine Gegner in Österreich* (Heidelberg: Carl Winter, 1966). The most penetrating work on Hanslick's own intellectual background has been carried out in a series of publications by Christoph Landerer, who situates him in a specifically Austrian context. See Landerer's "Eduard Hanslicks Ästhetikprogramm und die österreichische Philosophie der Jahrhundertmitte," *Österreichische Musikzeitschrift* 54/9 (1999): 6–20; "Ästhetik von oben? Ästhetik von unten? Objektivität und 'naturwissenschaftliche' Methode in Eduard Hanslicks Musikästhetik," *AfMw* 61 (2004): 38–53; *Eduard Hanslick und Bernard Bolzano: Ästhetisches Denken in Österreich in der Mitte des 19. Jahrhunderts* (Sankt Augustin: Academia, 2004); and "Eduard Hanslick und die österreichische Geistesgeschichte," in *Eduard Hanslick zum Gedenken: Bericht des Symposions zum Anlass seines 100. Todestages*, ed. Theophil Antonicek, Gernot Gruber, and Christoph Landerer (Tutzing: Schneider, 2010), 55–63. Important earlier studies include Rudolf Schäfke, *Eduard Hanslick und die Musikästhetik* (Leipzig: Breitkopf & Härtel, 1922), and Werner Abegg, *Musikästhetik und Musikkritik bei Eduard Hanslick* (Regensburg: Bosse, 1974).

education promoted an approach that favored the examination of formal structures. With a mandate from Franz Joseph, the new emperor, the Austrian government enacted wide-ranging institutional and curricular reforms, and it promoted the work of Herbart and his followers as a counterweight to the legacies of Kant and Hegel.[51] It was around this time that a number of key Austrian thinkers—including Bolzano, Zimmermann, and Franz Serafin Exner (1802–1853)—openly aligned themselves with Herbart. Exner was one of only two non–music teachers Hanslick praised by name in his memoirs when recalling his early years in the Bohemian capital.[52]

As a midlevel bureaucrat in the ministry of education, and no doubt following the advice of his close personal friend Zimmermann, Hanslick recognized that it would be to his advantage to declare himself a Herbartian. When he petitioned the University of Vienna in 1856 to accept Vom Musikalisch-Schönen as his Habilitationsschrift, he pointed out that his philosophical approach to music kept him "almost entirely removed from purely metaphysical discussions"— which is to say, Kant and Hegel—and that he considered himself closest to "the philosophical system of Herbart, which as a favored student of Exner's I had the opportunity to learn quite thoroughly." In the same document he also drew attention to a passage in Ambros's Die Grenzen der Musik und Poesie that aligns Vom Musikalisch-Schönen with Herbart.[53]

At least some of Hanslick's contemporaries questioned his Herbartian credentials. The philosopher and psychologist Moritz Lazarus (1824–1903) tempered his praise of Vom Musikalisch-Schönen with the observation that it is a "pity that Hanslick was not familiar with the achievements of Herbart; otherwise his work would have been more thorough and fruitful."[54] In later years, Zimmermann

---

51. See Kurt Blaukopf, Pioniere empiristischer Musikforschung: Österreich und Böhmen als Wiege der modernen Kunstsoziologie (Vienna: Hölder-Pichler-Tempsky, 1995); and Kevin Karnes, Music, Criticism, and the Challenge of History (New York: Oxford University Press, 2008), 30–33, with references to further literature. For a particularly vivid account of just how vicious Austrian academic politics could be at this time, see Eduard Winter's introduction to his Robert Zimmermanns philosophische Propädeutik und die Vorlagen aus der Wissenschaftslehre Bernard Bolzanos: Eine Dokumentation zur Geschichte des Denkens und der Erziehung in der Donaumonarchie (Vienna: Österreichische Akademie der Wissenschaften, 1975), 7–35. On Herbart's influence on Hanslick specifically, see Grimm, Eduard Hanslicks Prager Zeit, 146–52.

52. On Exner, see Deborah R. Coen, Vienna in the Age of Uncertainty: Science, Liberalism, and Private Life (Chicago: University of Chicago Press, 2007), chapter 1; and Hanslick, Aus meinem Leben, 1:22.

53. Hanslick, "Habilitationsgesuch," transcribed in VMS, 2:145: "Mein Prinzip, die aesthetischen Grundsätze einer Kunst aus deren eigenster, spezifischer Natur zu gewinnen, hält mich von rein metaphysischen Erörterungen fast gänzlich fern. Am nächsten stehe ich jedoch dem philosophischen System Herbarts, das ich als bevorzugter Schüler Exners genau kennen zu lernen Gelegenheit hatte." On the politics surrounding Hanslick's appointment, see Karnes, Music, Criticism, and the Challenge of History, 21–37. On the importance of formalism in the Austrian academy at this time, see Barbara Boisits, "Formalismus als österreichische Staatsdoktrin? Zum Kontext musikalischer Formalästhetik innerhalb der Wissenschaft Zentraleuropas," Muzikološki zbornik / Musicological Annual 40 (2004): 129–36.

54. Moritz Lazarus, Das Leben der Seele in Monographien über seine Erscheinungen und Gesetze, 2 vols. (Berlin: Heinrich Schindler, 1856–57), 2:314: "Schade daß H. die Leistungen Herbarts nicht gekannt hat; seine Arbeit würde dann gründlicher und fruchtbarer geworden sein."

himself would observe that Hanslick was neither a philosopher nor a Herbartian, even after having conceded on another occasion that Hanslick's views on music were entirely consistent with Herbartian thought.[55]

The Herbartian elements of *Vom Musikalisch-Schönen* claimed by Hanslick, recognized by Ambros, and acknowledged (eventually) by Zimmermann can be summarized thus:

(1)   Herbart insisted that each art must be understood on its own specific terms and not in relation to any other art, an approach basic to *Vom Musikalisch-Schönen*.[56]

(2)   Herbart drew a sharp distinction between the essence of an art and its effect. In his review of Carl Seidel's *Charinomos* (1825–28), a treatise on the "General Theory and History of the Fine Arts," for example, he noted that Seidel had committed the common error of confusing "the effects of the beautiful on feeling with the beautiful itself. Herein lies the vacuousness of aesthetics as commonly practiced."[57] Hanslick would make the same point repeatedly in his treatise on musical aesthetics.

(3)   Herbart viewed philosophy as the clarification of concepts and believed in the principle of noncontradiction, tendencies that pervade *Vom Musikalisch-Schönen*.[58] Neither Herbart nor Hanslick was sympathetic to the possibility that two apparent opposites might be equally and simultaneously valid, a mode of thought that characterizes a great deal of speculative philosophy, whose metaphysics depended on the willingness (and capacity) of the mind to accept what its opponents perceived as outright contradictions (e.g., the unity of subject and object, identity and nonidentity), incompleteness (the fragment), and the ungraspable (infinity). The opponents of idealism—including Herbart, Bolzano, Zimmermann, and Hanslick—insisted on verifiable results and noncontradiction.

(4)   Herbart regarded technical construction as central to the essence of each art, including music. The only indispensable element is beauty;

---

55. Robert Zimmermann, "Abwehr," *Zeitschrift für exacte Philosophie im Sinne des neuern philosophischen Realismus* 4 (1864): 199–206; Zimmermann, *Aesthetik*, 2 vols. (Vienna: Wilhelm Braumüller, 1858–65), 1:784n.

56. See Herbart, *Allgemeine praktische Philosophie* (Göttingen: Justus Friedrich Danckwerts, 1808), 25–26.

57. Herbart, Review of Carl Seidel, *Charinomos: Beiträge zur allgemeinen Theorie und Geschichte der schönen Künste*, vol. 1 (Magdeburg, 1825), first published in the *Leipziger Literatur-Zeitung*, 1826, no. 316; republished in Herbart's *Sämtliche Werke*, vol. 12, ed. Otto Flügel, (Langensalza: Hermann Beyer & Söhne, 1907), 342: "Diesem Schema [Seidel's] liegt der so häufig begangene Fehler zum Grunde, *daß die Wirkungen des Schönen aufs Gefühl verwechselt werden mit dem Schönen selbst*. Darin liegt die Leerheit der Ästhetik, wie sie gewöhnlich behandelt wird." Emphasis in original.

58. See Frederick Charles Copleston, *A History of Philosophy*, vol. 7, *Modern Philosophy: From the Post-Kantian Idealists to Marx, Kierkegaard, and Nietzsche* (New York: Doubleday, 1994), 250–52.

signification is irrelevant. "Consider how much Haydn undertook to paint in his *Creation* and *Seasons!*" Herbart urged his readers. "Fortunately his music needs no text; at best, one wants to know out of curiosity what he his depicting, for his music is music and it has no need to mean anything at all in order to be beautiful."[59] He even pointed to Johann Georg Albrechtsberger's *Gründliche Anweisung zur Composition* (1790)—a nuts-and-bolts manual for aspiring composers that consists largely of musical examples and exercises—as a paradigm of what a treatise on musical aesthetics should look like, acknowledging that this would be "a shock for all those who want only to create an effect."[60] In the sixth edition of *Vom Musikalisch-Schönen* (1881), Hanslick added an extended quotation from Herbart's *Kurze Encyklopädie* on this point:

> Down to this day, even connoisseurs of music repeat the statement that music expresses feelings, as if the feeling aroused perchance through music...somehow originated in the general rules of simple and double counterpoint, rules on which the true essence of that music rests. What did the old artists who developed the possible forms of the fugue intend to express? They wanted to express nothing at all; their thoughts did not go outward but rather into the essence of the arts. Those who on the other hand rely on signification betray their diffidence toward the interior of things and their predilection for external appearances.[61]

Hanslick laments that Herbart did not develop this "brilliant" (*glänzende*) idea, which had not received the attention it deserved. Hanslick tempers his praise, however, by noting that the earlier philosopher had on other occasions made "some strange comments" about music. By

59. Herbart, *Kurze Encyklopädie der Philosophie aus praktischen Gesichtspuncten* (Halle: C. A. Schwetschke & Sohn, 1831), 124: "Was hat nicht Haydn in seiner Schöpfung und in den Jahreszeiten durch Töne zu malen unternommen! Glücklicherweise braucht seine Musik keinen Text; man verlangt höchstens aus Neugier zu wissen, was er eben schildern will, denn seine Musik ist Musik, und sie braucht gar Nichts zu bedeuten, um schön zu seyn."

60. Johann Georg Albrechtsberger, *Gründliche Anweisung zur Composition* (Leipzig: J. G. I. Breitkopf, 1790); 3rd ed. (Leipzig: Breitkopf & Härtel, 1821). See also Herbart, *Kurze Encyklopädie der Philosophie*, 126: "zum Schrecken für Alle, die nur Effect machen wollen."

61. *VMS*, 1:37–38, quoting Herbart, *Kurze Encyklopädie der Philosophie*, 124–25: "So wiederholen, bis auf den heutigen Tag, selbst gute Musikkenner den Satz, die Musik drücke Gefühle aus, als ob das Gefühl, das [in Herbart's original: was] durch sie etwa erregt wird...den allgemeinen Regeln des einfachen oder doppelten Contrapuncts zum Grunde läge, auf denen ihr wahres Wesen beruht. Was mögen doch die alten Künstler, welche die möglichen Formen der Fuge entwickelten...auszudrücken beabsichtigt haben? Gar Nichts wollten sie ausdrücken; ihre Gedanken gingen nicht hinaus, sondern in das innere Wesen der Künste hinein; diejenigen aber, die sich auf Bedeutungen legen, verrathen ihre Scheu vor dem Innern, und ihre Vorliebe für den äußern Schein." Payzant, in his translation, moves Hanslick's discussion and quotation of Herbart from chapter 1 to a one-page appendix in *OMB* (p. 85).

1881, Hanslick was secure enough in his professional position at the University of Vienna that he had no need to be counted within or outside the Herbartian tradition.[62]

(5) Herbart, like Hanslick after him, considered the sensuous side of art as a portal to the intellect.

(6) Formalism is central to Herbart's aesthetics: he understood beauty to reside in the structural relationship of the various elements of a work of art, and he rejected Hegel's notion that beauty is a harmony of form and content.[63]

The influence of Bernard Bolzano (1781–1848) is also evident in Hanslick's work. A native of Prague, Bolzano was one of the most renowned mathematicians and logicians of his era; he was also a Catholic priest and for a time professor of philosophy at the university there. A Leibnizian, he opposed Kant and believed that objects, truths, and propositions existed independently of mind.[64] Like several of his Austrian contemporaries, including Ignaz Jeitteles (1783–1843), and Wilhelm Hebenstreit (1774–1854), and like Hanslick after him, Bolzano believed that aesthetics, the philosophy of beauty, could be pursued on a rational, objective basis, independent of any emotional response to art. These thinkers, along with Zimmermann and Hanslick in the next generation, promoted what has been characterized as a distinctively Austrian line of aesthetic thought in the second quarter of the nineteenth century.[65] Zimmermann, one of Bolzano's students, noted in his memorial lecture that his teacher was constantly striving for "naked, transparent, objective truth" and that logic constituted the principal organon of knowledge, which in turn had driven Bolzano's tendency to carefully reduce every individual concept to its smallest constituent elements.[66]

62. *VMS*, 1:38: "manche schiefe Bemerkungen." *OMB*, 85.

63. See Johnston, *The Austrian Mind*, 283.

64. See Johnston, *The Austrian Mind*, 275–76; and Boisits, "Formalismus," 130. On Bolzano as anti-Kantian, see Bauer, *Der Idealismus und seine Gegner in Österreich*, 37–60. On Bolzano's influence on the nascent discipline of musicology, see Kurt Blaukopf, "Im Geiste Bolzanos und Herbarts: Ansätze empiristischer Musikforschung in Wien und Prag," in *Bolzano und die österreichische Geistesgeschichte*, ed. Heinrich Ganthaler and Otto Neumaier (Sankt Augustin: Academia, 1997), 237–64. On the implications of "objective" philosophy for aesthetics, see Kurt Blaukopf, "Kunstforschung als exacte Wissenschaft," in *Elemente moderner Wissenschaftstheorie: Zur Interaktion von Philosophie, Geschichte und Theorie der Wissenschaften*, ed. Friedrich Stadler (Vienna and New York: Springer, 2000), 177–211.

65. See Blaukopf, "Kunstforschung als exacte Wissenschaft." On the connections between Bolazno's work and *VMS*, see Karnes, *Music, Criticism, and the Challenge of History*, chapter 1; and Landerer, "Eduard Hanslicks Ästhetikprogramm," 17–18.

66. Robert Zimmermann, "Über den wissenschaftlichen Charakter und die philosophische Bedeutung Bernhard [sic] Bolzanos. Gastvortrag in der Sitzung vom 17. Oktober 1849," *Sitzungsberichte der kaiserlichen Akademie der Wissenschaften: Philosophisch-historische Classe*, Jahrgang 1849, 2. Abteilung (Vienna: Hof- und Staatsdruckerei, 1849), 173–74, 167.

Zimmermann was a professor of philosophy, first at the University of Prague and then after 1861 at the University of Vienna. He too promoted the idea that aesthetics could and should be pursued on an entirely objective basis. In an essay published in February 1854 under the title "Die spekulative Aesthetik und die Kritik," he argued for objective standards of beauty on the grounds that if anyone could consider any given object as beautiful, then the concept of beauty carried no meaning at all. He bemoaned the growing gap between artists and critics, the one creating and the other responding to art on a strictly individual basis, without regard for the objective standard that should unite them.

> Each goes his own way, and the necessary consequence of this is a true spiritual anarchy.... The spirit of bare, naked individualism dominates art as it does criticism. The artist follows his subjective tendency, the critic his personal whim.... This condition is sad because it is demoralizing. Anarchy in the world of art, as in life, is barbarism.... The aesthetic creed must be social, like the political and religious creed, because there must be a law for beauty, just as there is a law for justice and truth....
> The duty of aesthetics is to create a common ground of criticism and art in the recognition and judgment of beauty.[67]

Elsewhere in the same essay, Zimmermann observes that it was the "romantic school"—he names Clemens Brentano and Achim von Arnim specifically—that turned away from "objective beauty" in favor of its own "subjective preferences," replacing consensus with personal taste. Implicit in this critique is the myth of a lost golden age. "The idealistic subject dethroned objectivity; egoism became the principle of art, the principle of criticism, and the principle of life."[68] This leads Zimmermann to condemn in the broadest terms all speculative aesthetics, from Kant through Fichte and Schelling and on to Hegel. He takes Kant to task for his assertions in the *Kritik der Urteilskraft* that that there are no objective rules of taste and that to seek a criterion of beauty is a futile undertaking.[69]

---

67. Robert Zimmermann, "Die spekulative Aesthetik und die Kritik," *Oesterreichische Blätter für Literatur und Kunst* 6 (6 February 1854), 37:

> Jeder handelt auf eigene Faust und die nothwendige Folge ist eine wahre Geisteranarchie.... Der Geist des baaren nackten Individualismus beherrscht die Kunst wie die Kritik. Der Künstler folgt seinem subjektiven Hang, der Kritiker seiner persönlichen Grille.... Dieser Zustand ist traurig, weil er demoralisirend ist. Anarchie auf dem Kunst- wie auf dem Lebensgebiete ist Barbarei.... Das ästhetische Credo muß gemeinschaftlich sein, wie das politische und religiöse, weil es einen Kanon für das Schöne geben muß, wie es einen für das Recht und die Wahrheit gibt....
> Den gemeinsamen Boden in der Kritik, wie in der Kunst, in der Erkenntnis und der Beurtheilung des Schönen herzustellen, ist die Aufgabe der Aesthetik.

68. Zimmermann, "Die spekulative Aesthetik und die Kritik," 37: "Das idealische Subjekt stieß die Objektivität vom Thron, das Prinzip der Kunst, der Kritik wie das des Lebens ward der Egoismus."

69. The passage to which Zimmermann alludes is from the *Kritik der Urteilskraft*, §17 ("Vom Ideale der Schönheit").

Zimmermann even goes so far as to implicate speculative aesthetics with polit-ical and social unrest, for its method "makes revolution permanent" by declaring beauty to be the product of history. In the face of this "spiritual anarchy," the critic has a responsibility to identify the beautiful as a universal quality, indepen-dent of its time and place.[70]

In his later and more temperate *Aesthetik* (1858-65), Zimmermann endorses Herbart's approach to issues of taste, which focuses on the object rather than the perceiving subject. Because form alone pleases or displeases, aesthetics is therefore a "pure science of form," which is to say, a "morphology of the beau-tiful." Beauty is a function of structural proportions, and aesthetics has no other purpose than to identify that which is beautiful.[71]

Within the more specific field of musical aesthetics, many of Hanslick's arguments had also been put forward by earlier writers. A comparison of *Vom Musikalisch-Schönen* with three well-known treatises, each of a decidedly dif-ferent kind, will suffice to illustrate the extent to which Hanslick incorporated the conventional thought of his time, even if he rarely acknowledged it: (1) Hans Georg Nägeli's *Vorlesungen über Musik, mit Berücksichtigung der Dilettanten* (1826), a series of lectures aimed at a lay audience; (2) Christian Hermann Weisse's *System der Ästhetik als Wissenschaft von der Idee der Schönheit* (1830), a two-volume treatise on aesthetics in general, with an extensive discussion of music; and (3) Ferdinand Gotthelf Hand's *Aesthetik der Tonkunst* (1837-41; 2nd ed. 1847), one of the first most comprehensive aesthetic treatises devoted exclusively to music and written by a major philosopher.

Hanslick's intellectual debt to Nägeli's lectures is far more extensive than the two passing citations in *Vom Musikalisch-Schönen* would suggest.[72] A number of passages in Nägeli's treatise sound remarkably Hanslickian *avant la lettre*. Nägeli equates "pure" music with "autonomous instrumental music."[73] He calls play (*Spiel*) the characteristic essence (*das eigentümliche Wesen*) of the art and places great em-phasis on the movement (*Bewegung*) of tones. He identifies motion as the "founda-tional element of music" and rejects the idea that instrumental music is an imitation of vocal music, or that the origins of music lie in the voice.[74] Music "has no content,

---

70. Zimmermann, "Die spekulative Aesthetik und die Kritik," 39–40.

71. Zimmermann, *Aesthetik*, 1:772; ibid., 2:30: "Die Aesthetik als reine Formwissenschaft ist eine Morphologie des Schönen. Indem sie zeigt, dass nur Formen gefallen und missfallen, legt sie unter Einem dar, dass Alles, was gefällt oder missfällt, durch Formen gefallen und missfallen müsse." Zimmermann, *Aesthetik*, 1:746.

72. *VMS*, 1:109 and 147. From the eighth edition onward, Hanslick dropped the first reference to Nägeli, and so this passage does not appear in Payzant's translation; for the second of the two references, see *OMB*, 69. On Hanslick's underacknowledged indebtedness to Nägeli, see Felix Printz, *Zur Würdigung des musikästhetischen Formalismus Eduard Hanslicks* (Borna-Leipzig: R. Noske, 1918), 11–17.

73. Nägeli, *Vorlesungen über Musik*, 187: "die 'reine' Musik, die selbstständige Instrumentalkunst."

74. Nägeli, *Vorlesungen über Musik*, 37–38: "das Grundelement der Tonkunst." See also 41. On the importance of the concept of motion to Nägeli's aesthetics of music and to nineteenth-century aesthetics

as is usually maintained and in spite of anything that might be ascribed to it. It has only forms, ordered concatenations of tones and series of tones that constitute a whole."[75] The forms of the visual arts that most resemble music are the arabesque and Gothic architecture, which in their play of interpenetrating lines create an effect that might be called "an anticipated surrogate of the pure instrumental music that emerges much later."[76] Nägeli consistently uses *Formen* in same broad sense that Hanslick would three decades later.

Hanslick acknowledges none of this. This is not in itself unusual: his attitude toward other authors might charitably be described as uncharitable: he rarely cites the work of predecessors with approval and often quotes or paraphrases in ways that misrepresent their positions. Both the terminology and the core of Hanslick's argument are nevertheless already present in Nägeli's lecture.

Christian Hermann Weisse's *System der Ästhetik als Wissenschaft von der Idee der Schönheit* (1830) is another source well-known in its time that goes unacknowledged by Hanslick. Weisse (1801–1866) was a Protestant theologian and professor of philosophy at the University of Leipzig from 1845 until his death. His pupils included Lotze, whose writings Hanslick admired, as well as Franz Brendel, editor of the *Neue Zeitschrift für Musik*, whose writings Hanslick did not admire. The title of Weisse's treatise reflects the Hegelian outlook characteristic of his early career, even if his attitude toward music is far more sympathetic than Hegel's.[77] Like Herbart, Weisse emphasizes the technical aspects of each individual art, pointing out that it is difficult to separate the spiritual and technical elements of beauty, which together derive from the technical manipulation of the material (*Stoff*)—an indifferent medium (*gleichgültiger Mittel*) in any art. He stresses the importance of *Phantasie* in the perception of art and maintains that every domain of art exhibits its own particular kind of beauty.[78]

in general, see Rafael Köhler, *Natur und Geist: Energetische Form in der Musiktheorie* (Stuttgart: Franz Steiner, 1996), 65–80 and passim.

75. Nägeli, *Vorlesungen über Musik*, 32: "Sie [die Musik] hat...keinen Inhalt, wie man sonst meinte, und was man ihr auch andichten wollte. Sie hat nur Formen, geregelte Zusammenverbindung von Tönen und Tonreihen zu einem Ganzen."

76. Nägeli, *Vorlesungen über Musik*, 45–46: "So sind kunsthistorisch sowohl Arabeske als Gothische Baukunst, ihrer Wirkungsart nach, so zu sagen, als anticipirte Surrogate der viel später erfundenen reinen Instrumentalmusik zu betrachten." For an overview of the long history of the arabesque in aesthetic discourse, see Günter Oesterle, "Arabeske," in *Ästhetische Grundbegriffe: Historisches Wörterbuch*, 7 vols., ed. Karlheinz Barck (Stuttgart: Metzler, 2000–05), 1:272–86. On Hanslick's use of the term, see Lothar Schmidt, "Arabeske: Zu einigen Voraussetzungen und Konsequenzen von Eduard Hanslicks musikalsichem Formbegriff," *AfMw* (1989): 91–120.

77. On Weisse's musical-aesthetic outlook in relation to Hegel's, see Nicole Grimes, "In Search of Absolute Inwardness and Spiritual Subjectivity? The Historical and Ideological Context of Schumann's 'Neue Bahnen,'" *International Review of the Aesthetics and Sociology of Music* 39 (2008): 144–46.

78. Weisse, *System der Ästhetik als Wissenschaft von der Idee der Schönheit*, 2 vols. (Leipzig: E. H. F. Hartmann, 1830), 2:7–9 (material); 2:18–19 and passim (*Phantasie*); 2:13–14 (each art has its own beauty).

Weisse focuses on three broad areas of art—music, the visual arts, and the verbal arts—and divides each of these into three subcategories. In contrast to vocal or dramatic music, he considers instrumental music "true" music because the "mechanical" nature of its tones allows it to operate in a sphere "purified" of "all contingent, finite meaning" that would otherwise "disturb and darken" the quality of that which is *geistig* and absolute.[79] The very artificiality of instrumental music, in other words, allows it transcend the realm of the mundane. Weisse denies that music exists to give expression to feelings and emphasizes instead its abstract beauty. He accords far greater importance to music than do earlier philosophers precisely on the grounds of its immateriality and non-representational quality. Long before the sixth chapter of *Vom Musikalisch-Schönen*, Weisse insists that *Ton* is the elemental unit of music and not to be found in nature. It exhibits instead a "purity of motion" (*Reinheit der Bewegung*) and defines itself exclusively in relationship to other tones.[80] Like Hanslick after him, Weisse consistently emphasizes the primacy of melody, and he devotes scarcely a word to issues of expression or emotion. His primary concern is to identify the essence of music, which, as he insists, has nothing to do with expression or with the imitation of nature; music is an autonomous and nonreferential art whose essence is abstract form.[81]

Yet another important source for Hanslick's aesthetics is the *Aesthetik der Tonkunst* (1837–41) by Ferdinand Gotthelf Hand (1786–1851), a professor of philosophy in Jena and director of the academic concerts there.[82] In his autobiography Hanslick acknowledged having studied Hand's work carefully and cites it explicitly in his own treatise, even if his treatment of the earlier writer is far from generous.[83]

Hand bemoans the increasing polarization of opinion between those who consider music without a text to be little more than a play of pleasing tones and those who believe it possesses some underlying significance in spite of the absence of words. The first opinion, he observes, denies the possibility of any intellectual process in an art of pure form, and the latter denies the possibility that beauty by itself may suffice in a work of art, that art has no need of understanding and rational reflection. Music, Hand asserts, is the representation of beauty through tones, and beauty is the singular goal of all art in such a way that

---

79. Weisse, *System der Ästhetik*, 2:49: "Der Begriff der Musik...ist unmittelbar zunächst der Begriff der Instrumentalmusik. Die Töne...werden durch mechanische Kunst hervorgebracht...um von aller besondern, endlichen Bedeutung sie zu reinigen, die als ein fremdartiger Inhalt den absolut geistigen, der in sie hineingebildet werden soll, stören und trüben würde."

80. Weisse, *System der Ästhetik*, 2:53; 2:24.

81. Weisse, *System der Ästhetik*, 2:52–54.

82. See Matthias Tischer, *Ferdinand Hands Aesthetik der Tonkunst: Ein Beitrag zur Inhaltsästhetik der ersten Hälfte des 19. Jahrhunderts* (Sinzig: Studio, 2004).

83. Hanslick, *Aus meinem Leben*, 1:39–40.

"*Geist*-imbued life in its free form can satisfy and please" the spirit of the perceiving subject, who is similarly imbued with *Geist*.[84] Because it has no connection to any of the other arts, music is the purest of all the arts and therefore the one most readily capable of presenting ideal beauty. A work of music becomes a work of art through beauty, and this beauty resides not in its material but in the form given to it by the composer. The work of art is its own singular goal, and its only purpose is to be beautiful.[85]

Like Nägeli before and Hanslick after him, Hand places central importance on the idea of motion (*Bewegung*) in music. He speaks of music's "pure forms of motion" and says that "the inner movement of life articulates itself in tones that move through time.... The form of tonal movement is also the form of the inner movement of life."[86] The formulation is not as pithy as Hanslick's *tönend bewegte Formen*, but the idea is substantially the same.

Hand views instrumental music as the purest manifestation of the art and stresses the inherent presence of *Geist* in music for instruments alone.[87] He returns repeatedly to the concept of music's *geistiger Inhalt*—its intellectual-spiritual content—over and against Nägeli's formalism, which, he maintains, has no content: "Without the expression of an intellectual-spiritual content, music would cease to be human and beautiful."[88] And music is decidedly human: the "music of nature," including birdsong, is dictated by the necessities of survival and reproduction, whereas human music is characterized by beauty, which is a product of *Geist* and thus premised on the absence of necessity. Hand does not use the term "pathological listening," but the concept conforms to his distinction between listening with *Geist* and listening for the sake of "merely sensuous pleasure."[89]

Hanslick takes issue with Hand only on the matter of expression, yet even here the differences are not nearly as great as Hanslick makes them out to be. Hand considered beauty to be the governing concept of all aesthetic experience: even our emotional responses to music are ultimately a function of beauty, just as all reason is governed by the idea of truth. Not everything we feel is necessarily beautiful; but the quality of *Geist* is a necessary element of the beautiful. Moreover, feelings are not limited to the here and now but extend to a higher

84. Hand, *Aesthetik der Tonkunst*, 1:9–10; ibid., 2:7, 9: "In allen ihren Productionen aber verfolgt die Kunst nur den einen Zweck für das Schöne, damit geistiges Leben in seiner freien Form den beschauenden Geist befriedige und ihm gefalle."

85. Hand, *Aesthetik der Tonkunst*, 2:10, 21, 39.

86. Hand, *Aesthetik der Tonkunst*, 1:112: "reine Formen der Bewegung." Ibid., 1:30: "In den Tönen... spricht sich innere Lebensbewegung als durch das in der Zeit Bewegte aus....Die Form der Tonbewegung [ist] auch die Form der inneren Lebensbewegung."

87. Hand, *Aesthetik der Tonkunst*, 1:85.

88. Hand, *Aesthetik der Tonkunst*, 1:85. Ibid., 1:96: "Ohne Ausdruck eines geistigen Inhalts hörte die Musik auf, menschlich und schön zu seyn."

89. Hand, *Aesthetik der Tonkunst*, 2:42–45: "blos sinnliche Ergötzung" (42).

world through the contemplative life of the soul.[90] Hand's definition of feeling, then, goes beyond standard accounts of the emotions; yet Hanslick's portrayal of the earlier writer's work conveys nothing of this.

Hand's approach to instrumental music is far more wide-ranging than Hanslick's: he is committed to explaining the full range of listeners' responses, both emotional and intellectual, whereas Hanslick is content to regard emotional responses as operating at a lower level, unrelated to the essence of music, and therefore unworthy of serious consideration. Hand even goes so far as to suggest a kind of latter-day *Affektenlehre* in which "every feeling and mood has in music its specific tone and rhythm, just as every concept has its specific word"; but he concedes that these feelings and moods cannot be readily codified in any kind of "theoretical semiotics of music" because verbal language cannot match the emotional capacities of musical language.[91] In the end, Hand subordinates all aspects of expression to the quality of beauty, in contrast to Hanslick, who dismisses expression as irrelevant to it. Hand in fact anticipates this very approach by confronting an aesthetic position that would later be attributed to Hanslick:

> It has lately been maintained that everything beautiful in music resides in its form, and that what affects the psyche [*Gemüt*], such as the graceful, the sublime, the frightful, must be separated from the work in such a way that all lively expression must be actively ignored…in order that the aesthetic judgment might apply itself to the pure form. The basis for such an error lies in a misunderstanding of the nature of beauty.[92]

Whereas Hanslick mentions Nägeli only in passing and ignores Weisse altogether, he goes out of his way to misrepresent Hand. In what Geoffrey Payzant fittingly dubbed a "rogues' gallery of quotations from writers who upheld the 'feeling-theory' of music,"[93] Hanslick quotes Hand (with unacknowledged omissions) in such a way as to give the impression that Hand is but one of many in a long line of commentators who simply state that music expresses feelings.[94] The "quotation" from Hand's *Aesthetik* is presented without context of any kind, and the unsuspecting reader might well believe that it reflects Hand's opinion on the relationship between music and feeling. It does not. Hand's treatment of the issue, as noted, is lengthy and nuanced, and while he does not deny a connection

90. Hand, *Aesthetik der Tonkunst*, 1:78. Ibid., 1:92.

91. Hand, *Aesthetik der Tonkunst*, 1:85–88. Ibid., 1:89: "eine theoretische Semiotik der Musik."

92. Hand, *Aesthetik der Tonkunst*, 2:40: "Man hat neuerdings freilich, namentlich in Bezug auf Musik gelehrt, es beruhe beim Schönen Alles in der Form, und was dabei noch besonders auf das Gemüth wirke, wie das Anmuthige, das Erhabene, das Furchtbare, müsse gesondert und aus dem Musikstücke…der lebenvolle Ausdruck hinweggedacht werden, damit das ästhetische Urtheil die reine Form behandeln könne. Der Grund eines solchen Irrthums liegt in der Verkennung des Wesens der Schönheit."

93. *OMB*, 86.

94. *VMS*, 1:40; *OMB*, 86. On Hanslick's mangling of Hand's text, see Payzant's commentary in *OMB*, 90.

between music and the emotions, he emphasizes (just as Hanslick would later) the subordination of expression to the all-embracing qualities of beauty and *Geist*.

In chapter 6 of his treatise, Hanslick gives full play to his uncharitable tendencies. He acknowledges that Hand denies any artistic quality to the sounds of nature but then proceeds to criticize him for saying that some sounds "must also be called music 'in certain respects.'" The qualifying phrase "in certain respects" (*gewissermaßen*) sends Hanslick into a fit of indignation: "When it comes to questions of principle, there is no 'in certain respects': what we hear in nature either *is* music or it is *not* music."[95] Here once again Hanslick distorts Hand's subtleties. Hand rejects birdsong and other seemingly musical sounds of nature as music on the grounds that they are motivated by the twin needs of survival and procreation; this "music" is instinctive, not free, and therefore lacks *Geist*, the quality in music on which Hanslick places such importance. Hand allows that while birdsong *might* be called music (not "must," as Hanslick's account would have it), it is "not music in the human sense," and he concludes from this that "the tones of nature, aside from those of humans, are therefore not musical tones.... We cannot speak of a music of nature."[96] For Hand, whether or not birdsong constitutes music depends on how one defines music, and he proposes a definition that excludes it. This is all too subtle for Hanslick, who approaches the question with a blunt instrument: birdsong either *is* or is *not* music. Again, Hanslick creates the impression of a wholly incompetent predecessor.

Nor does Hanslick's mean-spiritedness stop there. He attacks Hand for placing emphasis throughout his discussion of music in nature on "spiritual animation."[97] This is willfully misleading. Having dismissed birdsong as music in any human sense, Hand extends the discussion to ask why it should nevertheless please us. At the end of his account he offers this:

> We read a spiritual animation into it [i.e., birdsong] and ascribe to the nightingale the feeling of longing, or we perceive in the call of the quail a religious cry. In this symbolization, nature provides our life with ideas, but it is we ourselves and we alone who apprehend these images in foreign nature and draw them closer to us.[98]

Far from "placing emphasis throughout" on *geistige Beseelung*, Hand raises the idea briefly in order to reject it.

---

95. *VMS*, 1:151: "Wo es sich aber um Principienfragen handelt, da gibt es kein 'gewissermaßen'; was wir in der Natur vernehmen, *ist* entweder Musik, oder ist *keine* Musik." Emphasis in the original. *OMB*, 72.

96. Hand, *Aesthetik*, 1:40–41, 42: "Die Töne der Naturwesen außer dem Menschen sind also nicht die musikalischen.... [S]o können wir auch nicht von einer Musik der Natur sprechen."

97. *VMS*, 1:151: "Hand legt den Nachdruck überall auf die 'geistige Beseelung.'" *OMB*, 72.

98. Hand, *Aesthetik der Tonkunst*, 1:44: "Wir legen da wo[h]l auch eine geistige Beseelung unter, und ertheilen der Nachtigall das Gefühl der Sehnsucht, oder vernehmen in dem Schlag der Wachtel einen

Hanslick's "rogues' gallery of 'feeling-theorists'" runs from Johann Mattheson (*Der vollkommene Capellmeister*, 1739) to Fermo Bellini (*Manuale di musica*, 1853), yet he could just as easily have presented a series of quotations from at least some of these same authors *supporting* his notion of musical beauty. Hanslick takes Michaelis to task, for example, for calling music "the art of the expression of feelings through the modulation of tones," yet he ignores Michaelis's later observation (in the readily accessible *Allgemeine musikalische Zeitung* of 1808) that musical works have value not only in what they might mean, but also in "that which they *are* themselves, in their own incomparable *essence*."[99] Hanslick also ignores an entire category of commentators whose authority would have undermined the very credibility of his argument: composers. He would have been hard-pressed to maintain that composers did not know the nature and purpose of music, and so he turns his back on them altogether. Carl Philipp Emanuel Bach, for example, comments repeatedly on the importance of expression in music in his treatise on keyboard playing (1753) and urges composers to indicate the "true content" of a piece through some verbal cue beyond the tempo so that musicians might bring out the "appropriate affect" in performance.[100] Rameau, as noted earlier, had identified the "the true goal of music" to be "the expression of thought, sentiment, passions."[101] And Beethoven had famously called his *Pastoral* Symphony "more the expression of feeling than depiction," a comment Hanslick could have known from any number of sources at the time, including Hand's *Aesthetik*.[102]

Even Hanslick's central idea, that music's sole content is its form, was in no way novel (see above, pp. 98–102). This equation was already something of a commonplace in discussions of the arts in general in the first half of the nineteenth century. In a formulation that would be quoted repeatedly by others, Hegel declared that "*content* is nothing but the *transformation of form* into content, and *form* is nothing but the *transformation of content* into form."[103] Writers

---

religiösen Aufruf. In dieser Symbolisi[e]rung dient die Natur unserem Leben in Ideen, wir sind es aber selbst und allein, deren Bild wir in der fremden Natur auffassen und näher ziehen."

99. *VMS*, 1:39; *OMB*, 87. The offending quotation is from Michaelis's *Ueber den Geist der Tonkunst*, 2 vols. (Leipzig: Schäfer, 1795–1800; reprint, Brussels: Culture et Civilisation, 1970), 2:29: "Sie [die Musik] ist die Kunst des Ausdrucks von Empfindungen durch Modulation der Töne." Michaelis, "Ueber das Idealische der Tonkunst," *AmZ* 10 (1808): 450. See above, p. 101. Ines Grimm identifies a number of parallels between *VMS* and Michaelis's writings in her *Eduard Hanslicks Prager Zeit*, 153–60.

100. C. P. E. Bach, *Versuch über die wahre Art das Clavier zu spielen*, 1:124. For the original wording, see above, p. 74.

101. Rameau, *Code de musique pratique* (1760); see above, p. 97.

102. "Mehr Ausdruck der Empfindung als Mahlerei." Hand, *Aesthetik*, 2:166. See also Elliot Forbes, *Thayer's Life of Beethoven*, rev. ed. (Princeton: Princeton University Press, 1967), 436; and Lewis Lockwood, *Beethoven: The Music and the Life* (New York: Norton, 2003), 225–26.

103. Hegel, *Encyklopädie der philosophischen Wissenschaften im Grundrisse*, 2nd ed. (Heidelberg: August Oßwald, 1827), 135 (§133): "so daß *der Inhalt* nichts ist, als das *Umschlagen der Form* in Inhalt, und die *Form* nichts, als *Umschlagen des Inhalts* in Form." Emphasis in original.

on musical aesthetics took up this line of thought repeatedly, as even Hanslick had to acknowledge, though he was quick to point out that Rousseau, Kant, Hegel, Vischer, and Kahlert were "almost all philosophers," as if this somehow vitiated the value of their observations.[104] By this logic the word of composers should have carried all the more weight. Moreover, the idea had already appeared repeatedly in books and journals aimed specifically at musicians and music-lovers. Kahlert, for example, had noted in *Cäcilia* in 1834 that in music, "form takes the place of content."[105] And Gustav Schilling, in the treatise dedicated to Tomášek, Hanslick's piano teacher in Prague, deemed "the highest calling of form" in music to be its "identity with the content."[106] In one particularly striking passage that appeared in the *Wiener allgemeine Musik-Zeitung* in 1846, a journal in which Hanslick's own criticisms had already begun to appear, the critic Julius Wend speaks of "pure instrumental music" as "the true center of musical expression, that is, as the absolute form in which music as such—liberated from any heterogeneous elements—manifests its innermost meaning, its most essential self." It is in the symphony, music's "most magnificent flowering," Wend asserts, that the "absolute autonomy of tone" presents itself "in an artistic manner" and that the "unique essence of music" is most readily apparent.[107] Later in this same essay, Wend points to the arabesque and kaleidoscope as useful images to describe the fantasy-like nature of Berlioz's symphony *Roméo et Juliette*.[108]

The Russian critic Alexandre Oulibicheff (1794–1858), who published his writings in French, identified "pure music" (*la musique pure*) as the highest category of the art more than a decade before *Vom Musikalisch-Schönen*. Pure music follows its own internal laws and subjects itself to no considerations outside itself. "Applied music" (*musique appliquée*), by contrast, subordinates itself to nonmusical elements, such as a text to be sung or a scene to be represented on the

104. *VMS*, 1:160; *OMB*, 77.

105. August Kahlert, "Ueber die Bedeutung des Romantischen," *Cäcilia* 16 (1834): 244: "Bei der Musik ist es nun aber die Form, die die Stelle des Stoffes vertritt." In this context, *Stoff* is the subject of a painting Kahlert had discussed in the previous paragraph.

106. Schilling, *Geschichte der heutigen oder modernen Musik*, 16: "die höchste Aufgabe der Form... Identität mit dem Inhalte."

107. Julius Wend, "Berlioz und die moderne Symphonie: Ein Beitrag zu einer Philosopie der Musik," *Wiener allgemeine Musik-Zeitung* 6 (1846): 157: "die reine Instrumentalmusik als das eigentliche Centrum der musikalischen Ausdrucksweise, also die absolute Form, in der die Tonkunst als solche— abgelöst von jedem heterogenen Elemente—ihrer innersten Bedeutung, ihrem eigensten Wesen nach zur Existenz gelangt.... [S]o sehen wir... in der reinen Instrumentalmusik und ihrer herrlichsten Blüte 'der Symphonie' das absolute Selbstgenügen des Tones... kunstvoll zur Wirklichkeit herausgestaltet. In der Symphonie erst hat sich die tönende Kunst... zu ihrer höchsten idealen Bedeutung, zur absoluten Selbstständigkeit, zur Würde und dem Selbstgenügen des Ideals entfaltet.... Wir behaupten hier... daß das eigenthümliche Wesen der Musik als solcher, dem formellen Ausdrucke nach, in der Symphonie am reinsten ausgesprochen, und am unvermischtesten durchgeführt erscheine."

108. Wend, "Berlioz und die moderne Symphonie," 169.

stage. In his three-volume biography of Mozart (1843), Oulibicheff notes that in *musique pure*

> every musical idea presents above all a signification based on itself, which is to say, a purely musical signification.... Music does not conform to the indications of some relative or indirect sense or to a program or to an afterthought of some kind; it proceeds and orders itself solely according to the conventions and logic that are proper to it, according to the absolute sense of the musical ideas, such as melody and harmony. And this is what we call pure music.[109]

One final example of Hanslick the Conventional: Otto Gumprecht's essay "Geist und Musik," published in the *Deutsches Museum* in 1852, anticipates *Vom Musikalisch-Schönen* on almost every principal point: music is altogether different in kind from the other arts and cannot be judged according to their standards; musical form and content are inseparable; there is no precedent for music in nature; the principle of music is motion (*Bewegung*); instrumental music has a content (*Inhalt*) imbued with *Geist*.[110] One can well understand the cryptic comment toward the end of entry on "Aesthetics" in Julius Schladebach's *Neues Universal-Lexikon der Tonkunst* of 1855 that Hanslick's *Vom Musikalisch-Schönen* is "not nearly as new as one might be tempted to believe."[111] Even Guido Adler, Hanslick's longtime assistant and eventual successor at the University of Vienna, would remark that while his predecessor may have been the best-known proponent of *tönend bewegte Formen*, he was not the first to have proposed such a theory.[112]

---

109. Alexandre Oulibicheff, *Nouvelle biographie de Mozart*, 3 vols. (Moscow: Auguste Semen, 1843), 2:161: "Toute idée musicale présente, avant tout, une signification fondée en elle-même, c'est-à-dire une signification purement musicale, sans quoi l'idée n'en serait pas une.... Or, quand le compositeur a adopté quelques unes de celles-là pour base de son travail, la musique ne se règle plus sur les indications d'un sens relatif et détourné, d'un programme ou d'une arrière-pensée quelconques; elle marche et s'arrange uniquement d'après les convenances et la logique qui lui sont propres, d'après le sens absolu que les idées musicales ont comme mélodie et comme harmonie. Et c'est ce que nous appelons de la musique pure." The book was later translated into German as *Mozart's Leben* (Stuttgart: Becher, 1847).

110. Otto Gumprecht, "Geist und Musik," *Deutsches Museum: Zeitschrift für Literatur, Kunst und öffentliches Leben* 2 (1852): 597–609, 801–14. Wagner mentions Gumprecht's essay disparagingly in a postscript to a letter to Theodor Uhlig dated 15 July 1852 with the comment: "Es ist unglaublich, was für ein schönes Ding es um die absolute Musik ist!" See his *Sämtliche Briefe*, ed. Gertrud Strobel and Werner Wolf (Leipzig: Deutscher Verlag für Musik, 1967–), 4:409.

111. Julius Schladebach, ed., *Neues Universal-Lexikon der Tonkunst*, 3 vols. (Dresden: Robert Schaefer, 1855–61), 1:83: "keineswegs vollständig neu ist, wie man zu glauben versucht sein könnte." Schladebach's preface is dated April 1855; after the release of the first few installments (including the entry "Aesthetik"), he transferred editorship of the work to Eduard Bernsdorf.

112. Guido Adler, *Der Stil in der Musik* (Leipzig: Breitkopf & Härtel, 1911), 16.

▓ HANSLICK THE RADICAL

While many of Hanslick's arguments were less novel than he made them out to be, others were far more radical than he cared to acknowledge. One of the greatest obstacles to understanding the historical context of *Vom Musikalisch-Schönen* is the enduring perception of it is as an inherently "conservative" work, as a treatise that sought to preserve the aesthetic of an earlier era against the encroaching "Music of the Future."

Public opinion often defines individuals on the basis of their opponents, and in the middle of the nineteenth century, even the most casual music-lover would have been aware that Hanslick's opponents were Wagner and Liszt, the avatars of music's future; from there it was but a short step to the assumption that Hanslick must therefore be an advocate of the music's past, which indeed he was. He extolled the works of Haydn, Mozart, and Beethoven, and championed among contemporary composers the music of Brahms (see Figure 7), who was perceived at the time—rightly or wrongly—as a musical conservative on the grounds that he cultivated traditional genres such as the symphony and string quartet and for the most part avoided writing program music, or at least did not openly acknowledge any programs that might have inspired his works.[113]

Wagner, moreover, was not merely *a* musical radical but *the* musical radical of his time. Through his chromaticism and alleged "formlessness," he assaulted the mid-nineteenth-century musical ear with as much gusto as he had assaulted the political status quo during the Revolution in 1849 (see Figure 6). Wagner himself would contribute to the notion of Hanslick not merely as a conservative but as a full-fledged reactionary by skewering him in the character of Beckmesser, the pedantic and rule-obsessed judge of the song contest in Wagner's *Die Meistersinger von Nürnberg*. At an early stage in the development of the libretto, in fact, Wagner had called this character "Veit Hanslich."[114]

Hanslick, for his part, seems to have been quite happy to serve as the figurehead of musical conservatism in Vienna: he did nothing to discourage this image and quite a bit to promote it. He was in all respects a creature of the establishment throughout his entire adult life, first as a bureaucrat, then as a university professor. *Vom Musikalisch-Schönen* received the imperial

---

113. On Brahms and Hanslick, see Constantin Floros, "Das Brahms-Bild von Eduard Hanslick," in Floros, *Johannes Brahms: "Frei aber einsam": Ein Leben für eine poetische Musik* (Zurich and Hamburg: Arche, 1997), 225–38. An English-language translation of this essay is available in "Hanslick's Image of Brahms," in Floros, *Johannes Brahms: "Free but Alone": A Life for a Poetic Music*, trans. Ernest Bernhardt-Kabisch (Frankfurt am Main: Peter Lang, 2010), 194–202.

114. See Thomas S. Grey, "Masters and Their Critics: Wagner, Hanslick, Beckmesser, and *Die Meistersinger*," in *Wagner's "Meistersinger": Performance, History, Representation*, ed. Nicholas Vazsonyi (Rochester, NY: University of Rochester Press, 2003), 165–89.

Figure 6. Richard Wagner
This 1869 caricature by the French artist André Gill (1840–1885) reflects the
perception of Wagner as a revolutionary, his music a violent affront to established
standards.
Source: L'Eclipse 2 (18 April 1869).

imprimatur when Emperor Franz Josef awarded it a Gold Medal for Arts and
Letters in 1858.[115]

When viewed from the perspective of aesthetic theory, however, the roles of
Wagner and Hanslick are not nearly so clear-cut. A radical is, by definition, someone
who stands in the minority, and a small minority at that. By this criterion, Wagner
can scarcely count as one. He enjoyed the support of a great many fellow composers and music critics of the day, including Franz Liszt and Franz Brendel. By the
late 1840s the *Neue Zeitschrift* had become the unofficial mouthpiece of what was
widely characterized at the time as the "Musical Left," which was deeply influenced
by the writings of Feuerbach and other so-called Left Hegelians. Wagner may have
been an *enfant terrible*, but he had too much support in the mainstream press to
qualify as a true radical. Furthermore, his ideas about music and the arts as vehicles
of social change were, as noted before, scarcely novel.

By contrast, not a single composer, critic, or prominent musician of any
standing came to the defense of Hanslick. Brahms, for one, refused to take a

115. *Neue Berliner Musik-Zeitung* 12 (3 February 1858): 47: "Se. Majestät der Kaiser hat dem
Privatdocenten Dr. Hanslick für sein Werk 'Aesthetik der Tonkunst' die goldene Medaille für Kunst und
Wissenschaften verliehen."

Figure 7. Eduard Hanslick
Hanslick worships at the altar of Brahms, who quite literally stands on a pedestal.
The critic's archaic garb reflects what many perceived to be his conservative tastes in
music and may be a play on Wagner's thinly veiled caricature of him in the figure of
Beckmesser in *Die Meistersinger von Nürnberg*.
Source: T.Z., "Karikaturen-Winkel: Dr. Eduard Hanslick," *Figaro: Humoristisches
Wochenblatt*, 15 March 1890.

public stand on *Vom Musikalisch-Schönen*, even though he and the author eventually became close acquaintances. He wrote disparagingly to Clara Schumann
in 1856 (before he knew Hanslick personally) that although he had wanted to
read the treatise, he "set it down" after glancing through it, because he noticed
"so much that was stupid."[116] Brahms was rather more generous if decidedly cir-
cumspect in comments to Hanslick himself in a letter written in the summer of
1863, thanking the author for the gift of an inscribed copy.[117]

116. Brahms to Clara Schuman, letter of 15 January 1856, in *Clara Schumann und Johannes
Brahms: Briefe aus den Jahren 1853–1896*, ed. Berthold Litzmann, 2 vols. (Leipzig: Breitkopf & Härtel,
1927), 1:168: "Sein Buch 'Vom Musikalisch-Schönen'…wollte ich lesen, fand aber gleich beim
Durchsehen so viel Dummes, daß ich's ließ." Brahms makes a word-play here on *ließ*, the homophonic
imperfect of both *lassen* (to set aside, put down) and *lesen* (to read).
117. The text of the 1863 letter was first published in the *Neue freie Presse*—the Viennese newspaper for which Hanslick was the chief music critic—in July 1897, a few months after Brahms's death.

The most radical elements of *Vom Musikalisch-Schönen* are to be found not in its conclusions but in its premises and methods. Hanslick's first radical move was to isolate musical beauty from all other manifestations of beauty. Writers on aesthetics had always acknowledged that each art operates in its own distinctive way according to its materials, capacities, and limitations, but they had invariably framed their accounts within a broader concept of beauty in general. Music had proven consistently problematic in this regard: its nonrepresentational nature made it resistant to such explanations (see pp. 69–78). As Theodor Mundt noted in his *Aesthetik* (1845), the "incomprehensible beauty of music" posed an obstacle to those philosophers who wanted to rationalize art in every detail. Painting and sculpture had their corporeal models, but a "vacillating world of tones" conveyed through and dissipating in air resembled "swarms of drunken bees that fly up and disperse," offering no point of entry to philosophers of art.[118] Mundt and others nevertheless persisted in their attempts to find common ground between beauty and musical beauty.

Hanslick did not. He treated musical beauty as a quality apart from all else, and at no point did he ever address the question of what constitutes beauty in general. No one before had pursued such an exclusive—or, as his detractors complained, blinkered—approach to music. His single-minded focus on musical beauty is itself part of a broader strategy to make musical aesthetics more "objective" by concentrating entirely on the object of attention, the musical work. Whatever might be said about any given composition, he maintained, has to be audible within the work itself and not dependent upon concepts, theories, or systems of thought outside of music—including, it seems, the concept of beauty itself.

The second radical element in Hanslick's treatise is not his theory of formalism—many others had put forward this idea before—but his strategy of essentialism. As a mode of thought, essentialism privileges autonomy at the expense of interaction, stasis at the expense of change. Hanslick treats music as an object, not a practice, and the primary goal of *Vom Musikalisch-Schönen* is to define what music is, not how it works. He does this by focusing on music's intrinsic qualities and excluding from consideration the various ways in which a musical work might be realized by performers, perceived by listeners, or used in social contexts.

See Christiane Wiesenfeldt, "Johannes Brahms im Briefwechsel mit Eduard Hanslick," in *Musik und Musikforschung: Johannes Brahms im Dialog mit der Geschichte*, ed. Wolfgang Sandberger and Christiane Wiesenfeldt (Kassel: Bärenreiter, 2007), 282; and Styra Avins, ed., *Johannes Brahms: Life and Letters* (New York: Oxford University Press, 1997), 284.

118. Mundt, *Aesthetik* (1845), 355: "eine in der Luft entstehende und mit dem Schall verschwebende Welt von Tönen, die gleich trunkenen Bienenschwärmen aufflattern und wieder auseinanderstieben, scheint der philosophirenden Betrachtung der Kunst auch gar keinen Anknüpfungspunkt zu bieten."

Because of its fundamentally ahistorical nature, essentialism allowed Hanslick to isolate musical beauty as a timeless quality of all music; indeed, the ability of an artwork to transcend its particular time and place was one indicator of its inherent beauty. It was on this basis that Hanslick claimed to stand above the polemical fray of his time. Musical beauty, he maintained, was a quality applicable to all music, past and present, and not limited to "Classical" or "Romantic" works. It is, instead,

> equally applicable to both, governing the music of *Bach* as well as *Beethoven*, the music of *Mozart* as well as *Schumann*.... Our thesis thus contains not even a hint of partisanship. The entire thrust of the present investigation does not seek to express any sense of what *should* be, but considers only what *is*. No one *particular* musical ideal can be reduced to the truly beautiful; all we can do is merely demonstrate what the beautiful is, even in the most diametrically opposed schools of composition.[119]

This claim to nonpartisanship, as noted earlier, was disingenuous, as Hanslick himself acknowledged soon enough in the preface to the second edition of his treatise. His essentializing, ahistorical approach to art was precisely the attitude Wagner had excoriated in his dismissal of the very idea of an "absolute artwork," as something that "can have been written for Athenian democracy two thousand years ago ... and performed today at the Prussian Court in Potsdam," yet retain, in the "imagination of our aestheticians ... altogether the same value and altogether the same essential characteristics, regardless of here or there, today or yesterday."[120] Hanslick sought to rise above partisanship—or at least give the appearance of rising above it—by placing music outside of history. He recognized that he could not stem the tide of the "Music of the Future," and so instead he attacked the basic premise that there could even *be* such a thing as a music of the future. Beauty, by Hanslick's lights the most basic element of music, was a quality unrelated to a work's social context. He did not deny that a composition might reflect its historical milieu and even praised the value of recognizing such connections, but he drew a sharp distinction between the historical context and aesthetic value. Spontini's operas, he conceded, may well be an "expression of the French Empire," and Rossini's operas may be said to reflect an era of "Political Restoration," but such assertions have nothing to do with the presence or absence of musical beauty in these works. He acknowledged that no art exhausts as many forms and idioms as quickly as music and that composers were constantly

---

119. Hanslick, *VMS*, 1:91–92: "Es gilt sowohl in der einen als der andern Richtung, beherrscht *Bach* so gut als *Beethoven*, *Mozart* so gut als *Schumann*....Unsere Thesis also enthält auch nicht die Andeutung einer Parteinahme. Der ganze Verlauf der gegenwärtigen Untersuchung spricht überhaupt kein *Sollen* aus, sondern betrachtet nur ein *Sein*; kein *bestimmtes* musikalisches Ideal läßt sich daraus als das wahrhaft Schöne deduciren, sondern blos nachweisen, was in jeder auch in den entgegengesetztesten Schulen in gleicher Weise das Schöne ist." Emphasis in original. *OMB*, 38.

120. Wagner, *Eine Mitteilung an meine Freunde, GSD*, 4: 234–35.

seeking new ways of writing modulations, cadences, and melodic and harmonic progressions, so much so that a great many works might legitimately be said to have been beautiful at one time.[121] But it is precisely such transitory issues of musical style that occlude the deeper quality of immutable beauty.

This distanced, "objective" attitude found a welcoming readership in its time, and Hanslick's essentializing seemed to place him above the fray at a moment when bitter partisanship was the order of the day. Hanslick was not arguing for a particular type or style of music, as he emphasized repeatedly (if insincerely); instead, he was seeking to identify the true nature of musical beauty in terms that were timeless and purely musical. The argument is circular, for it creates a closed system of definition, and at least some of his critics took note of this. Eduard Krüger, for one, called Hanslick's reasoning tautological: if music is only music, then we can never really say anything about it. "A thing," Krüger maintained, "is not merely an 'it'; it is also a 'something.'"[122]

Hanslick's essentialism, moreover, merely claims to stand outside of history, for in spite of his denials ("*Bach* as well as *Beethoven*, the music of *Mozart* as well as *Schumann*"), the instrumental, nonprogrammatic repertory he valorizes as music in its purest—and therefore, for him, highest—form is in fact associated with a relatively brief span in the history of the art. Hanslick had little interest in music before Bach and once confessed publicly (though late in life) that he would rather see all the music of Schütz, Palestrina, and even the concertos and sonatas of Bach "go up in flames" than lose Brahms's *Deutsches Requiem* (over and against Schütz), the works of Mendelssohn (at the expense of Palestrina), or the quartets of Schumann and Brahms (vs. Bach). He expressed respect for these earlier composers from the perspective of their technique and historical significance but admitted that he did not respond to their music in the same way that he did to later composers, for the work of these earlier artists reflected a "circle of ideas" that had long since been "shattered." Their music was not, as he put it in a conversation with his friend Theodor Billroth, "flesh of our flesh, blood of our blood."[123] This late and private confession of prejudice is inscribed, covertly, on the pages of *Vom Musikalisch-Schönen*.

The tendentiousness of this approach is nowhere more evident than in the one passage of the treatise in which Hanslick abandons his ahistorical posturing momentarily to confront Beethoven's Ninth Symphony, the work Wagner had hailed as the turning point in the history of music. Hanslick acknowledges that the Ninth marks a divide between "two streams of opposing convictions." He

---

121. *VMS*, 1:92–93, 86–87; *OMB*, 39, 35–36.

122. Eduard Krüger, *System der Tonkunst* (Leipzig: Breitkopf & Härtel, 1866), 63: "Das Ding ist aber nicht bloß Es, es ist auch Etwas."

123. Hanslick, *Aus meinem Leben*, 2:304, 305: "einem längst zersprungenen Ideenkreise"; "Sie sind nicht Fleisch von unserem Fleisch, nicht Blut von unserem Blut."

praises the first three movements for their beauty. But because the finale adds voices and oversteps the boundaries of its genre, he deems it "not beautiful"—*unschön*—and thus outside the realm of debate about what constitutes the musically beautiful.[124] Even within his favored span of music history, Hanslick is highly selective in the composers and works he chooses to discuss. If one's knowledge of music history were somehow limited exclusively to *Vom Musikalisch-Schönen*, one would never know that program music had existed before the nineteenth century, or that Haydn's depiction of "Chaos" through instruments alone in *The Creation* was an object of nearly universal praise in its time. He mentions Beethoven's *Pastoral* Symphony only once, in passing, in order to dismiss the birdcalls at the end of the second movement as having been included merely for their symbolic quality, not for their beauty; indeed, Hanslick claims that they cannot strictly be considered music at all.[125]

In the end, both Wagner and Hanslick subscribed to—and reinforced—a common narrative of music history that served two opposing purposes. Wagner wanted a past epoch of pure form from which to trace music's rise through its union with other arts. Hanslick wanted an era of pure form from which to trace music's decline through its union with other arts. Given the polemical nature of their debate, it is perhaps not all that surprising that Wagner and Hanslick should have created tendentious histories to serve their own ideological ends. What is surprising is the extent to which these histories converge and the extent to which their accounts continue to resonate through subsequent histories of music. The retrospective imposition of formalism onto earlier eras—either the empty formalism described by Wagner or the *Geist*-imbued formalism described by Hanslick—offered an attractive means for both sides of the ideological divide to characterize the musical era extending from Bach and Handel through Haydn and Mozart in purely musical terms, unconnected to any broader cultural or political influences. The same basic narrative is evident in two highly influential histories of music from the second half of the nineteenth century written from opposite ends of the philosophical-aesthetic spectrum: Franz Brendel's *Geschichte der Musik in Italien, Deutschland und Frankreich*, which went through eight editions between 1852 and 1903, and Heinrich Adolf Köstlin's *Geschichte der Musik im Umriß*, which went through six editions between 1875 and 1910.

Brendel's and Köstlin's accounts are strikingly similar in their methodologies and conclusions. The history of music amounts to a history of the great composers, and Beethoven is the pivotal figure who divides Old from New. But even the "great man" school of history needed its context, particularly if one composer stands out from all the rest. Mozart proved especially problematic. How

---

124. *VMS*, 1:100; *OMB*, 43.
125. *VMS*, 1:158; *OMB*, 75–76.

to explain away his indisputable achievements only half a generation before Beethoven?

In Brendel's account, Mozart is the "the representative of the classical," which is to say "the representative of the beautiful, in that the ideal and the real, the intellectual and the sensuous, interpenetrate to the utmost, so that both sides coincide." Mozart and Goethe "are artists in the narrower sense. Their first law is to satisfy the demands of art; for both, art is a closed-off realm; both are concerned with content primarily in so far as it lends itself to artistic presentation."[126] Beethoven's achievement was "the reorientation toward *Geist* over and against the sensuous tendency of Mozart." Beethoven is "the composer of the new spirit, brought forth through the [French] Revolution," the composer of "the new ideas of freedom and equality, the emancipation of peoples, classes, and individuals."[127] In the Ninth Symphony, "it is Beethoven the democrat who expresses himself at every moment." What differentiates Beethoven's music from that of his predecessors is its "striving for the greatest possible preciseness of expression, by which pure music, not connected to the word, is made capable of presenting very precise emotional states of the soul."[128] With Beethoven we arrive at last at the "dominance of a poetic idea, which elevates itself triumphantly above the merely technical in such a way that music emerges more and more out of its characteristic sphere, out of its own circle, and strives toward its sister art [of poetry] and its essence." Brendel further characterizes Beethoven's music by the "predominance of the ideal in contrast to the tendency of Mozart's music to pursue sensuousness and externality."[129] Not surprisingly, Brendel's history culminates with the achievements of Wagner, who continues along the path blazed by Beethoven.

---

126. Franz Brendel, *Geschichte der Musik in Italien, Deutschland und Frankreich, von den ersten christlichen Zeiten bis auf die Gegenwart* (Leipzig: B. Hinze, 1852), 502: "Mozart der Repräsentant des Schönen, in dem sich Ideales und Reales, Geistiges und Sinnliches auf das Innigste durchdringen, so dass beide Seiten sich decken." Ibid., 355: "Mozart und Göthe sind Künstler im engeren Sinne. Beiden ist erstes Gesetz, den Forderungen der Kunst Genüge zu leisten, Beiden ist die Kunst ein abgeschlossenes Gebiet, Beide interessirt ein Inhalt vorzugsweise insoweit, als er sich zu künstlerischer Darstellung eignet." On the Hegelian premises of Brendel's *Geschichte*, see Golan Gur, "Music and 'Weltanschauung': Franz Brendel and the Claims of Universal History," *M&L* 93 (2012): 350–73.

127. Brendel, *Geschichte der Musik* (1852), 502: "Beethoven's That war... die Rückwendung zum Geist—der zugleich sinnlichen Richtung Mozart's gegenüber." Ibid., 355: "Beethoven ist der Komponist des neuen, durch die Revolution hervorgerufenen Geistes, er ist der Komponist der neuen Ideen von Freiheit und Gleichheit, Emancipation der Völker, Stände und Individuen."

128. Brendel, *Geschichte der Musik* (1852), 367: "Es ist der Demokrat Beethoven, der sich überall ausspricht." Ibid., 338: "das Streben nach möglichster Bestimmtheit des Ausdrucks, wodurch die reine mit dem Worte nicht verbundene Tonkunst für die Darstellung ganz bestimmter Seelenzustände befähigt wurde."

129. Brendel, *Geschichte der Musik* (1852), 502: "endlich die Herrschaft einer poetischen Idee, welche sich über die blos technische Arbeit siegreich erhebt, so dass die Tonkunst mehr und mehr

Heinrich Adolf Köstlin (1846–1907), a professor of aesthetics at Tübingen, paints a remarkably similar picture of music's history but comes to very different conclusions. He opens his account with what amounts to a summary of the key ideas of *Vom Musikalisch-Schönen*:

Music is the presentation of the beautiful in tones. The content and object of music is therefore first and foremost the musically beautiful. The essence of this cannot be further explained or defined; it manifests itself directly to the human spirit [*Geist*] as beauty, in that it penetrates to the center of mind in sounding, tonal form, transmitted through the sense of hearing.[130]

But only after taking us through the entire history of music from the ancient Greeks through the middle of the eighteenth century does Köstlin arrive at what he calls the "free, beautiful style"—*der freie schöne Styl*—which he associates with the period 1750–1817.[131] This is the first moment in Köstlin's account in which the term "beautiful" figures as an attribute of any era: up to this point, he had used terms such as "strict" style or "declamatory" style, "Protestant" or "secular." But here, suddenly, with the period 1750–1817, we enter into an era whose style is characterized as both "free" and "beautiful":

Instrumental music, the favorite child of a time that subscribed one-sidedly to subjectivity, was by its very nature that form of music in which pure subjectivity achieved its richest and fullest unfolding. In the purely nonmaterial essence of instrumental music, accessible only to internal intuition, this period [1750–1817] recognizes... the mysterious revelation of the innermost human, its innermost essence—inaccessible to any kind of rational observation and not to be arrived at by any concept—which is at the same time identical with the hidden essence of the world. Tonal forms saturated in beauty are the finest counterpart of all "music" of the "soul" that reverberates through all being, that flows mysteriously through all forms and manifestations of the world.... Conceived in this way, instrumental music indeed manifests itself as music with the potential of being "music in music," and it is not unjustified to think that those masters called simply the "classicists of music" have given expression to the "musically beautiful" in classical forms in the realm of instrumental music: Haydn,

aus der ihr eigenthümlichen Sphäre, aus aus ihrem eigenen Kreis heraustritt, und der Schwesterkunst und ihrem Wesen zustrebt." Ibid., 509: "dieses Uebergewicht des Idealen im Gegensatz zu dem Auslaufen der Mozart'schen Richtung in Sinnlichkeit und Aeusserlichkeit, die poetische Richtung, das Streben nach Bestimmtheit des Ausdrucks." Brendel reiterates this point on p. 515 of his *Geschichte der Musik*.

130. Heinrich Adolf Köstlin, *Geschichte der Musik im Umriß* (Tübingen: H. Laupp, 1875), 1: "Die Tonkunst ist die Darstellung des Schönen in Tönen. Inhalt und Gegenstand der Tonkunst ist also zunächst das Musikalisch-Schöne. Dieses kann in seinem Wesen nicht weiter erklärt oder definirt werden; es gibt sich dem menschlichen Geiste als das Schöne unmittelbar kund, indem es in der tönenden Form, durch das Gehör vermittelt, in das Centrum des Geistes eindringt."

131. Köstlin, *Geschichte der Musik im Umriß*, 190.

Mozart, Beethoven. For it is here in instrumental music that composers are dealing with music and with nothing but music.[132]

Considered from a "purely musical perspective," even the best music from the period after Beethoven represents nothing more than an "aftergrowth of classical splendor."[133] The period since 1817, Köstlin maintains, reflects a closer connection between life and art: the same forces that have transformed social life are making their effects felt in the musical repertory as well. But this development comes at a cost: the demands of other arts, especially poetry and drama, have compromised the independence of music as an autonomous art. Content has come be favored over form.[134]

For most other writers, however, music history was not something to be considered from a "purely musical perspective." It was a cultural battleground, and the struggle for Beethoven's legacy stood at the center of this conflict. As early as 1834, Schumann had described the musical factions of the day in political terms: Liberal, Moderate, and Legitimist. "On the right sit the elders, the contrapuntists, the antiquarians and folklorists, the antichromaticists. On the left sit the youths, the Phrygian caps, the despisers of form, and the genially cheeky, among whom the Beethovenians stand out as a faction in their own right. In the *juste-milieu* waver young and old alike."[135] A decade later, the critic Herrmann Hirschbach observed that conservatives believe "in their Haydn, Mozart, and some Beethoven," while progressives "expect from the future a solution to the

---

132. Köstlin, *Geschichte der Musik im Umriß*, 193–94: "Das Schooßkind einer Zeit, welche einseitig dem Subjectivismus huldigte, war naturgemäß die Instrumentalmusik als diejenige Form der Musik, in welcher die reine Subjectivität zur reichsten und vollsten Entfaltung kommt. In dem rein unsinnlichen, nur der inneren Anschauung zugänglichen Wesen der Instrumentalmusik erkennt die Zeit... die geheimnißvolle Offenbarung des innersten Menschen, seines innersten, keiner Verstandesbetrachtung zugänglichen und von keinem Begriff zu erreichenden Wesens, das zugleich identisch ist mit dem verborgenen Wesen der Welt. Die schönheitsgesättigten Tonformen sind das feinste Gegenbild der alles Sein durchklingenden 'Musik' der 'Seele,' die alle Formen und Gestaltungen der Welt geheimnißvoll durchströmt.... So gefaßt erscheint allerdings die Instrumentalmusik als die Musik auf der Potenz, als die 'Musik in der Musik,' und es hat die Meinung nicht Unrecht, welche diejenigen Meister die 'Classiker der Musik' schlechtweg nennt, welche auf dem Gebiet der Instrumentalmusik das 'Musikalisch-Schöne' in classischen Formen zum Ausdruck gebracht haben: Haydn, Mozart, Beethoven. Denn hier in der Instrumentalmusik ist es dem Komponisten um Musik und um nichts als Musik zu thun."

133. Köstlin, *Geschichte der Musik im Umriß*, 268: "Nachblüte der classisichen Herrlichkeit."

134. Köstlin, *Geschichte der Musik im Umriß*, 267–71, 277–78. Köstlin has little to say about Beethoven's music after 1817.

135. Schumann, untitled review of two overtures by Kalliwoda, *NZfM* 1 (5 May 1834): 38: "Wie die politische [Gegenwart] kann man die musikalische in Liberale, Mittelmänner und Legitime oder in Romantiker, Moderne und Classiker theilen. Auf der Rechten sitzen die Alten, die Contrapunctler, die Alter- und Volksthümler, die Antichromatiker, auf der Linken die Jünglinge, die phrygischen Mützen, die Formenverächter, die Genialitätsfrechen, unter denen die Beethovener als Classe hervorstechen. Im Juste-Milieu schwankt Jung wie Alt vermischt." For further commentary on this passage, see Bonds, *Music as Thought*, 104.

challenge presented to music."[136] The Wagnerian Theodor Uhlig declared in 1851 that Beethoven's last four symphonies all express "socialistic principles" and that in the Ninth in particular the composer "reveals his socialistic conscience."[137] Oulibicheff, on the other hand, in his 1857 biography of Beethoven, lamented the "strange and disastrous fate" the composer had suffered at the hands of those commentators who had made him into a "precursor of a new era of humanity, an apostle of democratic socialism and atheism," whose works had inspired the dreams of the "German revolutionaries and rioters of 1848."[138]

Against this charged atmosphere, Hanslick's treatise can be read as an attempt to deny the force of history by ignoring it altogether. Hanslick's essentialism— his obsession with the idea of purity—is part of his broader effort to stave off what the literary critic Stanley Fish, in another context, has called "the invasion of the fortress of essence by the contingent, the protean, and the unpredictable."[139] The allure of essence is its immutability. By removing music from any and all connections with the other arts, and by treating it exclusively as an object and not as an experience, Hanslick radically altered discourse about the essence of the art. In the end, however—and quite literally at the end of his treatise—he was compelled to confront the implications of this conceptual isolation.

■ HANSLICK THE AMBIVALENT

Hanslick's self-assurance crumbles at the end of his treatise. His decision to delete what had been its final paragraph reflects a prolonged struggle with the most basic premise of the entire tract: that musical beauty can be defined only in terms of music. The original ending and its elimination betray his profound ambivalence toward his own argument.

In preparing a second edition 1858, Hanslick cut all but the first sentence of the last paragraph, and for the third edition of 1865, he struck that one remaining sentence. By the third edition, then, nothing of the original concluding paragraph remained: what had been the treatise's penultimate paragraph was now its conclusion. These three endings, at the close of the treatise's final chapter on the relationship between form and content, read as follows:

136. Herrmann Hirschbach, "Musikzustände der Gegenwart," *Musikalisch-kritisches Repertorium aller neuen Erscheinungen im Gebiete der Tonkunst* 1 (1844): 251: "Conservative und Progressive [stehen sich] feindlich einander gegenüber. Die Einen glauben an ihren Haydn, Mozart und etwas Beethoven....Die Progressiven dagegen...erwarten erst von der Zukunft die Lösung der Aufgabe, welche der Musik gestellt ist."

137. Uhlig, "Instrumentalmusik," 49, 51: "sozialistische Grundsätze"; "sozialistisches Bewußtsein."

138. Alexandre Oulibicheff, *Beethoven, ses critiques et ses glossateurs* (Leipzig: F. A. Brockhaus; Paris: Jules Gavelot, 1857), 316: "transformer en un précurseur d'une nouvelle ère de l'humanité, en apôtre du socialisme démocratique et de l'athéisme, en une idole symbolique, figurant les rêves les plus insensés et les plus criminelles tentatives des révolutionnaires et émeutiers allemands de 1848. Quelle étrange et fatale destinée, je le répète."

139. Stanley Fish, *Doing What Comes Naturally: Change, Rhetoric, and the Practice of Theory in Literary and Legal Studies* (Durham, NC: Duke University Press, 1989), 483.

1st edition (1854)	*2nd edition (1858)*	*3rd edition (1865)*
Contrary to the reproach that it lacks content, then, music has content, though it is musical content, which is no less a spark of divine fire than the beautiful in every other art. Only by relentlessly negating any and all other "content" of music, however, can one preserve its "substance." For no intellectual-spiritual meaning can be derived from the vague feeling that might somehow serve as the basis of these other kinds of content, whereas such spiritual-intellectual meaning can be derived from the specific configuration of tones as a free creation of *Geist* using nonconceptual materials capable of incorporating *Geist*.	Contrary to the reproach that it lacks content, then, music has content, though it is musical content, which is no less a spark of divine fire than the beautiful in every other art. Only by relentlessly negating any and all other "content" of music, however, can one preserve its "substance." For no intellectual-spiritual meaning can be derived from the vague feeling that might somehow serve as the basis of these other kinds of content, whereas such spiritual-intellectual meaning can be derived from the specific configuration of tones as a free creation of *Geist* using nonconceptual materials capable of incorporating *Geist*.	Contrary to the reproach that it lacks content, then, music has content, though it is musical content, which is no less a spark of divine fire than the beautiful in every other art. Only by relentlessly negating any and all other "content" of music, however, can one preserve its "substance." For no intellectual-spiritual meaning can be derived from the vague feeling that might somehow serve as the basis of these other kinds of content, whereas such spiritual-intellectual meaning can be derived from the specific, beautiful configuration of tones as a free creation of *Geist* from materials that are capable of incorporating *Geist*.[141]
In the psyche of the listener, furthermore, this intellectual-spiritual substance unites the beautiful in music with all other great and beautiful ideas. It is not merely and absolutely through its own intrinsic beauty that music affects the listener, but rather at the same time as a sounding image of the great motions of the universe. Through profound and secret connections to nature, the meaning of tones elevates itself high above the tones themselves, allowing us to feel at the same time the infinite in works of human talent. Just as the elements of music—sound, tone, rhythm, loudness, softness—are found throughout the entire universe, so does one find anew in music the entire universe.[140]	In the psyche of the listener, furthermore, this intellectual-spiritual substance unites the beautiful in music with all other great and beautiful ideas.	

140. *VMS*, 1:171:

> Gegenüber dem Vorwurf der Inhaltlosigkeit also hat die Musik Inhalt, allein musikalischen, welcher ein nicht geringerer Funke des göttlichen Feuers ist, als das Schöne jeder andern Kunst. Nur dadurch aber, daß man jeden andern 'Inhalt' der Tonkunst unerbittlich negirt, rettet man deren 'Gehalt.' Denn aus dem unbestimmten Gefühle, worauf sich jener Inhalt im besten Fall zurückführt, ist ihr eine geistige Bedeutung nicht abzuleiten, wohl aber aus der bestimmten Tongestaltung als der freien Schöpfung des Geistes aus geistfähigem, begriffslosem Material.
>
> Dieser geistige Gehalt verbindet nun auch im Gemüth des Hörers das Schöne der Tonkunst mit allen andern großen und schönen Ideen. Ihm wirkt die Musik nicht blos und absolut durch ihre eigenste Schönheit, sondern zugleich als tönendes Abbild der großen Bewegungen im Weltall. Durch tiefe und geheime Naturbeziehungen steigert sich die Bedeutung der Töne hoch über sie selbst hinaus und läßt uns in dem Werke menschlichen Talents immer zugleich das Unendliche fühlen. Da die Elemente der Musik: Schall, Ton, Rhythmus, Stärke, Schwäche im ganzen Universum sich finden, so findet der Mensch wieder in der Musik das ganze Universum.

Only the first of these two paragraphs appears in *OMB*, 83.

141. The original wording is slightly altered at two points for the third and all subsequent editions: (1) "aus der bestimmten Tongestaltung" becomes "aus der bestimmten schönen Tongestaltung";

The entire process resembles a series of amputations: Hanslick severed the original ending in 1858 but then in 1865 decided that he had not cut away enough of the offending text, and so he made a second cut. That one held: the double amputation of the ending remained unchanged from the third edition onward.

Amputation may seem like a violent term to use for this process, but in making these cuts Hanslick did real violence to his text and altered what remained in ways that are both obvious and subtle. The original ending has much to tell us about the remainder of the treatise: we cannot grasp the full breadth of Hanslick's argument without coming to terms with this suppressed conclusion. This is not an obscure passage buried in the middle of an internal chapter, nor is it a draft of something rejected before publication. It is—or at least was—the ringing peroration of his entire argument.

Accounts of Hanslick's original ending have focused almost entirely on his reasons for deleting it.[142] The standard rationalization begins and ends with the figure of Zimmermann, Hanslick's lifelong friend. The two grew up together in Prague and eventually became colleagues at the University of Vienna, Hanslick as professor of music aesthetics and history, Zimmermann as professor of philosophy.[143] In an otherwise highly favorable review of the first edition, Zimmermann took the author—his friend—to task on the grounds that the treatise's ending adopted the kind of speculative philosophy it had otherwise refuted. Zimmermann closes his review by quoting the treatise's original penultimate sentence about the "profound and secret connections to nature" and then glossing it:

> Yes, these connections to nature are indeed "secret," for are they there at all? What great motions of the universe are supposed to resonate in music? Celestial bodies, perhaps? Would music thus be a sounding astronomy? And would music then not in fact have a template in nature, something denied earlier [in the treatise]? Why does Hanslick at the end of his work cancel out his principal idea—this golden truth that the musically beautiful pleases by virtue of itself—by saying that it should please because it is a sounding reflection of the motions of the universe? It seems to me that at this point, the author has unintentionally allowed himself to be taken unaware by the same aesthetic he otherwise opposes so thoroughly and victoriously.[144]

(2) "als der freien Schöpfung des Geistes aus geistfähigem, begriffslosem Material" becomes "als der freien Schöpfung des Geistes aus geistfähigem Material."

142. Felix Printz was the first to discuss the deletions in any detail; see his *Zur Würdigung des musikästhetischen Formalismus Eduard Hanslicks*, 7–9. See also Schäfke, *Eduard Hanslick und die Musikästhetik*, 28–31; and Dahlhaus, *Die Idee der absoluten Musik*, 33–34 (*The Idea of Absolute Music*, 27–29). In the commentary volume to his edition of *VMS* (2:20–65), Strauß surveys the scholarship that addresses all of Hanslick's many revisions to the text as a whole, including the altered endings.

143. See Geoffrey Payzant, "On the Hanslick–Zimmermann Friendship," in Payzant, *Hanslick on the Musically Beautiful: Sixteen Lectures on the Musical Aesthetics of Eduard Hanslick* (Christchurch, N.Z.: Cybereditions, 2002), 129–42.

144. Robert Zimmermann, review of *VMS* in *Oesterreichische Blätter für Literatur und Kunst*, no. 47 (20 November 1854), 315: "Ja wohl sind diese Naturbeziehungen 'geheim,' denn sind sie denn überhaupt? Welche Bewegungen im Weltall sollen denn wiederklingen in der Musik? Etwa die

Zimmermann also took exception to another key passage Hanslick would delete for the second edition. It appears, significantly, just before he introduces the phrase *tönend bewegte Formen*:

> If we now ask what is to be expressed with this tone-material, then the answer is: *musical ideas*. But a musical idea presented in its entirety is already autonomous beauty; it is already an end in itself and in no way simply a medium or material for the representation of feelings and thoughts, even if it is capable of possessing, at the same time, a high degree of symbolic significance in its reflection of the great laws of the universe, which is something we find in all artistic beauty.
>
> *Tonally animated forms* are the sole and exclusive content and object of music.[145]

Zimmermann agreed wholeheartedly with the characterization of music as *tönend bewegte Formen*, but he could not understand why Hanslick had felt the need to "muddy immediately this correct insight through a superfluous concession to a false aesthetic" that viewed a musical idea as a reflection of universal laws.[146] For the second edition, Hanslick deleted the qualifying phrase about the great laws of the universe ("even if it is capable of possessing... all artistic beauty"), ending the sentence with "in no way simply a medium or material for the representation of feelings and thoughts." These two passages—the ending and the qualification that introduces the book's most famous phrase—are closely related, and if nothing else, Hanslick was entirely consistent in deleting both.

---

der Himmelskörper? Wäre die Musik eine tönende Astronomie? Und hätte denn nicht die Musik in der That ein Vorbild in der Natur, was doch vorher geleugnet worden? Warum hebt der Verfasser den Hauptsatz seiner Schrift: das Musikalisch-Schöne gefällt durch sich selbst, diese goldene Wahrheit am Schluß dadurch auf, daß es als 'tönendes Abbild der Bewegungen im Weltall' gefallen soll? Mich dünkt, hier hat der Verfasser sich unwillkürlich durch Reminiscenzen derselben Aesthetik überraschen lassen, die er sonst so schlagend und siegreich bekämpft." Zimmermann reissued this review, with minor changes, in Zimmermann, *Studien und Kritiken zur Philosophie und Aesthetik*, 2 vols. (Vienna: Wilhelm Braumüller, 1870), 2:239–53.

145. *VMS*, 1:75:

Frägt es sich nun, was mit diesem Tonmaterial ausgedrückt werden soll, so lautet die Antwort: *Musikalische Ideen*. Eine vollständig zur Erscheinung gebrachte musikalische Idee aber ist bereits selbstständiges Schöne, ist Selbstzweck und keineswegs erst wieder Mittel oder Material zur Darstellung von Gefühlen und Gedanken; wenn sie gleich in hohem Grad jene symbolische, die großen Weltgesetze wiederspiegelnde Bedeutsamkeit besitzen kann, welche wir in jedem Kunstschönen vorfinden.

Tönend bewegte Formen sind einzig und allein Inhalt und Gegenstand der Musik.

Emphasis in original. The translation in *OMB*, 28–29, is based on changes that had been made by the time of the eighth edition of 1891.

146. Zimmermann, review of *VMS*, 314: "Warum trübt der Verfasser diese richtige Erkentniß gleich wieder durch eine überflüssige Konzession an eine falsche Aesthetik?" Zimmermann was not the only reviewer to point out the apparent contradictions of the concluding paragraph with the rest of the treatise: see also the anonymous review in the *Leipziger Repertorium der deutschen und ausländischen Literatur* 13, no. 1 (1855): 36–39, and the review by "H.-L." in the *Neue Wiener Musik-Zeitung*, 24 May 1855, 81–82.

Zimmermann's critique hit close to home, and not only because of his personal relationship. On the surface, at least, there is some merit to the charge of inconsistency, for in both passages Hanslick seems to be contradicting his central argument that music is entirely self-contained and self-referential. There is, moreover, a striking contrast of tone between the original ending of *Vom Musikalisch-Schönen* and all that comes before: the closing paragraph, with its evocations of the cosmos and infinity, verges on the rhapsodic and differs markedly from the sharp, often acerbic prose that is otherwise so characteristic of his style. Some scholars have interpreted the fact that Hanslick could simply delete this paragraph and replace it with nothing at all as an indicator of the degree to which this original ending stood apart from the rest of the treatise, a "foreign body," as it were.[147] The conventional view of this change, in short, is that the final paragraph features inconsistencies of both substance and tone, that it carries no structural weight in the treatise as a whole, and that Hanslick's deletion of it makes good sense.

But why did Hanslick put this paragraph there in the first place? If his closing argument is so inconsistent with the rest of the treatise, why did he make it at all? To accept Zimmermann's explanation is to accept the idea that Hanslick had fallen asleep at the switch: even Homer nods from time to time, after all. But the very end of a treatise is an unlikely point for an author to doze off, especially an author as careful and sparing with words as Hanslick. The grandiosity of this original ending, with its reference to "the great motions of the cosmos," stands out too prominently for its content to be the product of neglect or a mere afterthought. Moreover, Hanslick did not cut the final paragraph all at once: for the second edition, at least, he retained its opening sentence, which leaves open a connection between musical beauty and "all other great and beautiful ideas." And most important of all, the final paragraph is not as inconsistent with the rest of the treatise as his critics would have it: it resonates, as noted, with the deleted passage that had immediately preceded the crucial pronouncement about *tönend bewegte Formen*. Hanslick, as we shall see, had good reasons for ending his treatise the way he did, not only for later editions but for the first one as well. His motivations for the original conclusion and its subsequent phased excision cast the whole of *Vom Musikalisch-Schönen* in a different light and compel us to rethink in fundamental ways the history of the construct we now think of as absolute music.

There is nothing particularly striking or novel about Hanslick's closing thoughts in and of themselves. The idea of the artwork as a vehicle of disclosure,

147. Wilhelm Seidel, for example, calls the original ending a superfluous "superstructure," proof that the idea of absolute music has no need of metaphysics ("Absolute Musik und Kunstreligion um 1800," in *Musik und Religion*, 2nd ed., ed. Helga de la Motte-Haber [Laaber: Laaber-Verlag, 2003], 135). Peter Kivy, in turn, sees this passage in *VMS* as a demonstration of Hanslick's "failure of nerve" to carry through with his theory of musical formalism (Kivy, *Antithetical Arts*, 67).

as a heterocosm, as a world unto itself and at the same time a reflection of the universe: these were well established ideas at the time (see chapter 7). What *is* striking about the original ending is that it appears at the conclusion of a text that has gone to such great lengths to isolate music from all other forms of art and for that matter all other forms of human expression. This original final paragraph represents Hanslick's attempt to resolve a dilemma he had created for himself, for by the time he reached the end of his treatise, he realized that he had painted himself into a philosophical corner. This peroration is his cryptic, awkward, and ultimately unsuccessful attempt to extricate himself from a difficulty of his own making.

This self-imposed dilemma can be traced back to the opening paragraph of the first edition of *Vom Musikalisch-Schönen*—also deleted for the second edition—which rejects speculative philosophy and lays the groundwork for a more "objective" aesthetics of music:

> The time of aesthetic systems in which the beautiful is considered only in regard to the "sensations" it has aroused has passed. The desire for an objective understanding of things, insofar as such is granted to human inquiry, had to topple a method that takes subjective sensation as its point of departure, one that strolls around the periphery of the phenomenon being investigated in order to come full circle back to sensation. No path leads into the center of things, even though every one of them should point in that direction. The fortitude and capacity to close in on things themselves, to investigate that which is permanent, objective, and unchangingly valid quite apart from the multiple thousands of impressions they make on humans: these characterize modern knowledge in all its various branches.[148]

For the second edition of his treatise, Hanslick replaced this paragraph with a different, less strident text. Like the deleted ending, this canceled opening provides important evidence for the roots of Hanslick's thought. Kant, in his *Kritik der reinen Vernunft*, had famously argued that we cannot know things in themselves directly but rather only through our mental representations of them. Hanslick objected to any epistemology that emphasized the constitutive role of the subject in aesthetic contemplation: he wanted to create an aesthetics of music in which beauty was a fixed and unchanging quality in the work itself, not

---

148. *VMS*, 1:21: "Die Zeit jener ästhetischen Systeme ist vorüber, welche das Schöne nur in Bezug auf die dadurch wachgerufenen 'Empfindungen' betrachtet haben. Der Drang nach objectiver Erkenntniß der Dinge, soweit sie menschlicher Forschung vergönnt ist, mußte eine Methode stürzen, welche von der subjectiven Empfindung ausging, um nach einem Spaziergang über die Peripherie des untersuchten Phänomens wieder zur Empfindung zurückzugelangen. Kein Pfad führt ins Centrum der Dinge, allein jeder muß dahin gerichtet sein. Der Muth und die Fähigkeit, den Dingen selbst an den Leib zu rücken, zu untersuchen, was losgelöst von den tausendfältig wechselnden Eindrücken, die sie auf den Menschen üben, ihr Bleibendes, Objectives, wandellos Giltiges sei,—sie charakterisiren die moderne Wissenschaft in ihren verschiedensten Zweigen." This passage does not appear in *OMB*. For a fuller discussion of the philosophical context of this deleted opening, see Landerer, "Ästhetik von oben?," 39–43.

a construct of the listener. The reference to "systems," in turn, is code for Hegel, whose thought was frequently described as a "system" in the middle decades of the nineteenth century and who, as we have seen, considered music the most subjective of all the arts, "the art of the psyche that addresses itself directly toward the psyche itself."[149]

This is the kind of thinking that Hanslick rejected as circular and unproductive. He believed it was possible to know things in themselves, and he wanted to get at the essence of music, which for him amounted to the essence of musical beauty. Beauty, to Hanslick's mind, is an intrinsic quality of objects and has nothing to do with perception. "The beautiful is and remains beautiful," he insisted, "even when it arouses no emotions, indeed when it is neither perceived nor contemplated. Beauty is thus only *for* the pleasure of a perceiving subject, not generated *through* that subject."[150] According to this line of thought, the effect of a musical work is simply not relevant to any account of music's essential nature. In order to create an objective aesthetics of music, then, Hanslick had to identify music's unchanging essence, which meant ignoring the listener, the act of listening, all issues of perception, and most important of all, anything having to do with music's effect. He did not deny that music could move us emotionally but insisted that such a response was little more than a by-product of beauty, that the musical work itself could not contain or express sadness or joy or any other emotion. Hanslick wanted to identify the essence of music, not its effect on listeners.

While this may seem like semantic hairsplitting, it is not a trivial point. Hanslick was correct to insist on the distinction between essence and effect, and the first two chapters of his treatise provide a much-needed corrective to a certain laxity in discourse about music. The essence of wine, as he points out, cannot be fathomed by getting drunk.[151] If we are trying to identify the essence of wine as an object, in other words, we cannot base our account on the effects it produces when we drink it. Drinking is an activity, not the thing itself; it is what we *do* to wine, and it is the *activity* that creates the effect. Hanslick makes this

149. Hegel, *Vorlesungen über die Ästhetik*, 3:135.

150. *VMS*, 1:26: "Das Schöne ist und bleibt schön, auch wenn es keine Gefühle erzeugt, ja wenn es weder geschaut noch betrachtet wird; also zwar nur *für* das Wohlgefallen eines anschauenden Subjekts, aber nicht *durch* dasselbe." Hanslick added this sentence to the second edition, and it remained in all subsequent editions; he took it almost verbatim and without acknowledgment from Robert Zimmermann's review of 1854, though Zimmermann's formulation is itself an unacknowledged sharpening of an assertion already present in the same paragraph in the first edition of *VMS* (1:26): "Das Schöne hat seine Bedeutung in sich selbst, es ist zwar schön nur *für* das Wohlgefallen eines anschauenden Subjects, aber nicht *durch* dasselbe." Payzant, in his translation (*OMB*, 3) of the sentence "Das Schöne ist und bleibt...nicht *durch* dasselbe," omits the final portion of that sentence (beginning with "also zwar") and justifies this omission (*OMB*, 105) on the grounds that these words are "apparently...vestigial," a bizarre claim, given Hanslick's obsessive attention to detail in every new edition of the treatise.

151. *VMS*, 1:31; *OMB*, 6. This particular analogy appears in a passage inserted into the sixth edition (1881) but it illustrates a point made throughout the treatise from the first edition onward.

same kind of distinction with respect to music. He does not deny the effect of music, but he rejects attempts to make this the basis of any account of music's essence, which compels him to his insist that musical beauty exists with or without a listener. In this respect Hanslick is very good at focusing our attention on what music *is*; but he dismisses the question of what it *does* on the grounds that our responses to it are subjective and variable and therefore inadmissible in the court of objective aesthetics.

This is where Hanslick paints himself into a corner. His reasoning is perfectly sound, but in limiting his efforts to defining music's essence, he limits the usefulness of his argument. Even if we accept his definition of music as "tonally animated forms," how does music then relate to the broader idea of beauty? In a way, Hanslick had made his case *too* well, isolating music not only from all other arts but from the concept of beauty in general, insisting that specifically musical beauty is its own separate category. (The title of his treatise, it should be recalled, is not *The Beautiful in Music*, as Cohen's translation renders it, but Payzant's more accurate *On the Musically Beautiful*. The hyphen between the two words in the German original brings them that much closer together.) This tendency to isolate music from all other arts is a point on which Hanslick's more thoughtful early critics would attack him, for beyond the final paragraph, Hanslick offers no explanation at all of just how music might relate to anything beyond itself.

The original ending reflects Hanslick's anticipation of that criticism; more important, it suggests that he formulated his ideas within a much broader framework than has been recognized to date. His comments here at the end do not in fact contradict what he has said before, for what Zimmermann perceived as an inconsistency goes to the heart of the issue Hanslick was struggling to resolve but had not confronted directly: the relationship of musical beauty to beauty in general. One of Hanslick's genuinely radical moves was to treat musical beauty in purely musical terms. The final paragraph suggests that he realized the circularity of this logic: if musical beauty could be defined only in terms of music, this begged the question of beauty itself, for if music consists of nothing more or less than *tönend bewegte Formen*, what is its broader significance? In what way do these "forms" amount to something more than a mere play with tones? Hanslick repeatedly asserts that music is imbued with spirit (*Geist*), but in the absence of any appeal to other arts or to a general concept of beauty—a move that would have contradicted his commitment to considering music in purely musical terms—it is not a particularly convincing argument. It is only here, at the eleventh hour, that Hanslick finally entertains the notion of beauty as a quality that goes beyond strictly musical beauty. Here at last—even if only on the way out the door, so to speak—Hanslick connects *das Musikalisch-Schöne* with *das Schöne*.

Zimmermann, too, seems to have recognized this problem, for his choice of words in his critique of the treatise's conclusion is striking: "Warum hebt Hanslick den Hauptsatz seiner Schrift: das Musikalisch-Schöne gefällt durch sich selbst, diese goldene Wahrheit, am Schluss dadurch auf, dass es als tönendes Abbild der Bewegungen im Weltall gefallen soll?" (see p. 184). The verb Zimmermann uses here is *aufheben*, a famously difficult word in mid-nineteenth-century German philosophy. In a literal sense it means "to lift"; metaphorically, it means to cancel or annul, as in the lifting of a siege, and this reading reflects Zimmermann's disappointment that Hanslick had "canceled" or "annulled" the leading argument of his book at the last moment. But as a professor of philosophy, Zimmermann knew well that Hegel had used the term to indicate a more complicated process of cancellation, preservation, and elevation all at the same time. In Hegelian thought, a thesis can be overturned by its antithesis even as it is preserved within an elevated synthesis. When an assertion is *aufgehoben* (often translated as "sublated"), it is at once negated, sustained, and subsumed within a higher reconfiguration.[152] Zimmermann had already taken Hanslick to task earlier in this review for using another term (*Phantasie*) in a specifically Hegelian sense, and we can read his critique of the treatise's closing paragraph just as easily in this way, as a gentle chiding to his friend for a last-minute Hegelian maneuver that extends the argument without closing it off.[153]

And this is indeed precisely what Hanslick had done. All the elements of sublation are in place in his original final paragraph: the intrinsic beauty of music unites in the psyche of the listener with "all other great and beautiful ideas," which in turn reflect the "great motions of the universe" and gives us an intimation of the infinite. The self-contained musically beautiful is *aufgehoben*: canceled, preserved, and elevated all at once. In this respect, Zimmermann's choice of verbs could not have been better, for Hanslick's maneuver is indeed a moment of *Aufhebung*. Without being negated, his argument is absorbed into a higher level of significance.

In his review of *Vom Musikalisch-Schönen*, Zimmermann also correctly identifies the principal source of Hanslick's misguided thinking. "Our physics today," he sniffs, "has moved beyond the music of the spheres. At most, this is something that goes through the heads of those same *Naturphilosophen* from whom that aesthetic derives. The musical idea has no need to reflect universal laws in order to be beautiful; it has nothing to do with metaphysics."[154]

Although of interest today primarily to historians of philosophy and science, *Naturphilosophie* was very much a part of mainstream thought in

---

152. For an overview of Hegel's use of the term, see the entries "Sublation" and "Dialectic" in Michael Inwood, *A Hegel Dictionary* (Oxford: Blackwell, 1992), 283–85 and 81–83.

153. Zimmermann, review of *VMS*, 313.

154. Zimmermann, review of *VMS*, 314: "Ueber die Sphärenmusik, dünkt uns, ist unsere heutige Physik hinaus. Sie geht höchstens noch in den Köpfen derselben Naturphilosophen um, von welchen auch jene Aesthetik herrührt. Die musikalische Idee braucht keine 'Weltgesetze widerzuspiegeln,' um schön zu sein, mit der Metaphysik hat sie nichts zu schaffen."

German-speaking lands during the first half of the nineteenth century. It resists easy definition but might best be described as an attempt to reconcile empirical science and metaphysics, using the one to justify the other. The *Naturphilosophen* to whom Zimmermann refers believed that common principles united organic and inorganic nature, energy and matter, and that the universe itself was, in effect, one enormous organism, imbued with spirit (*Geist*).[155] The harmony of the spheres served as a metaphor for this view of the universe as a coherent, quasi-organic whole; it was an image that suggested purposeful order without the necessity of any divine entity, even while accommodating the possibility of one.

At no time was *Naturphilosophie* a wholly coherent or stable body of thought. The historian of science Kenneth L. Caneva calls it a "congeries of like-spirited but specifically diverse systems," a "program for understanding and interpreting, not for producing new knowledge," while the historian of philosophy Frederick Beiser characterizes it as a search for "the first causes of nature, its deeper sources, and its inner activity," as opposed to empirical physics, which in the minds of *Naturphilosophen* limited itself to nature's "secondary causes, its external appearances, and the results or products of its activity."[156] *Naturphilosophie* offered a holistic paradigm of explanation in which mechanism functioned within a broader (and higher) organic whole. As Beiser notes, it grew out of the perceived failure of Kantian thought to explain the relationship between reason and the senses, even though Kant himself, in his *Metaphysische Anfangsgründe der Naturwissenschaft* (1786) had established the groundwork for a unified conception of the forces of nature.[157] Herbart and Lotze, two of the few philosophers with whom Hanslick openly aligned himself, both embraced *Naturphilosophie* as central to their metaphysics. Lotze in particular accorded special importance to the concept of motion, which he called "the most evolved of the cosmological forms."[158] In his *Ueber Bedingungen der Kunstschönheit* (1847), he posits the

155. The scholarly literature on *Naturphilosophie* is enormous. For concise introductions, see Barry Gower, "Speculation in Physics: The History and Practice of *Naturphilosophie*," *Studies in the History and Philosophy of Science* 3 (1973): 301–56; Kenneth L. Caneva, "Physics and *Naturphilosophie*: A Reconnaissance," *History of Science* 35 (1997), 35–106; Michael Heidelberger, "Naturphilosophie," in *The Routledge Encyclopedia of Philosophy*, 10 vols. (London and New York: Routledge, 1998), 6:737–43; and Frederick Beiser, *German Idealism: The Struggle against Subjectivism, 1781–1801* (Cambridge, MA: Harvard University Press, 2002), 483–90, 506–28.

156. Caneva, "Physics and *Naturphilosophie*," 40; Caneva, *Robert Mayer and the Conservation of Energy* (Princeton: Princeton University Press, 1993), 394 n. 4; and Beiser, *German Idealism*, 525.

157. Kant, *Metaphysische Anfangsgründe der Naturwissenschaft*, ed. Konstantin Pollok (Hamburg: Felix Meiner, 1997). See Frederick Beiser, *The Romantic Imperative: The Concept of Early German Romanticism* (Cambridge, MA: Harvard University Press, 2003), chapter 9 ("Kant and the *Naturphilosophen*"); and Michael Friedman and Alfred Nordmann, eds., *The Kantian Legacy in Nineteenth-Century Science* (Cambridge, MA: MIT Press, 2006), particularly the essay by Friedman, "Kant—*Naturphilosophie*—Electromagnetism," 51–79.

158. Herbart identifies *Naturphilosophie* as the basis of his metaphysics in the opening pages of the preface to his *Allgemeine Metaphysik, nebst den Anfängen der philosophischen Naturlehre*, 2 vols.

notion of art as a revelation of the structure of the universe, not on the basis of its material but rather on the basis of its form, in which all arts follow the same general laws that govern the universe as a whole. Beauty does not project a veiled outline of the universe, but it does incorporate the "eternal forms of the order of the universe that actually surround us."[159]

Zimmermann's implicit connection of *Naturphilosophie* to beauty and the universal laws of nature is particularly important for understanding his objections to—and the reasons behind—Hanslick's deleted ending. One need not have subscribed to the more speculative elements of *Naturphilosophie* to believe in a close relationship between beauty and the "great motions of the cosmos." Goethe, for example, had little sympathy for Schelling's metaphysics, yet both held a lifelong conviction that connected all the elements of the universe and their analogical manifestations in art and nature.[160] Beauty itself, as Goethe observed in an oft-quoted maxim, was "a manifestation of secret laws of nature that without its appearance would have remained forever hidden from us."[161] Hanslick's original conclusion, linking "the beautiful in music" to "profound and secret connections" of nature, reads like a paraphrase of Goethe's aphorism. Hanslick revered Goethe, and this aphorism alone would have been enough to encourage him, here at the end of his treatise, to broaden the scope of his argument about the nature of beauty.

Zimmermann was thus correct to link Hanslick's ending to *Naturphilosophie*, but he erred in assuming that this involved matter ("celestial bodies," not mentioned by Hanslick) as opposed to energy. The idea of music as *tönend bewegte Formen* conceives of the art in physical terms, emphasizing motion—the movement of vibrating air—as the force that produces musical tones. Hanslick does not in fact suggest that planets or any other objects in the heavens "resonate" (*widerklingen*), as Zimmermann would have it; he posits instead music as a sounding image (*tönendes Abbild*) of the *motions* of the cosmic bodies, not of the bodies themselves. This is an important distinction, for the concept of

(Königsberg: August Wilhelm Unzer, 1828–29), 1:iii–iv; see also 1:6–8. The same close connections between metaphysics and *Naturphilosophie* are evident throughout Herbart's *Kurze Encyklopädie der Philosophie* (1831), a work Hanslick cites explicitly in an extended addition he made to *Vom Musikalisch-Schönen* from the sixth edition (1881) onward; see p. 161. Hermann Lotze, *Metaphysik* (Leipzig: Weidmann, 1841), 218: "Die Bewegung ist die entwickeltste der kosmologischen Formen."

159. Lotze, *Ueber Bedingungen der Kunstschönheit*, 18: "die Züge der Schönheit...indem sie nicht den verhüllten Plan der Welt selbst darstellen, sondern nur die ewigen Formen der Weltordnung, die uns wirklich umgeben." Lotze, who may well have been working from the first edition Hanslick had sent him (see p. 147), specifically praised *Vom Musikalisch-Schönen* when he reiterated this point in his *Geschichte der Aesthetik in Deutschland* (Munich: J. G. Cotta, 1868), 482–87.

160. See the essays in Hans-Jürgen Schrader and Katharine Weder, eds., *Von der Pansophie zur Weltweisheit: Goethes analogisch-philosophische Konzepte* (Tübingen: Max Niemeyer, 2004).

161. Johann Wolfgang Goethe, "Maximen und Reflexionen," in Goethe, *Werke*, ed. Trunz, vol. 12, *Schriften zur Kunst*, 467: "Das Schöne ist eine Manifestation geheimer Naturgesetze, die uns ohne dessen Erscheinung ewig wären verborgen geblieben."

motion lies at the very heart of Hanslick's understanding of music, enshrined in the leading slogan of *tönend bewegte Formen*. It is easy to overlook the element of *Bewegung* in this phrase and focus instead on the more obviously difficult *Formen*. But however we understand *Formen*—and it is open to many interpretations—the concept of movement remains. Music may not have a model in nature—and Hanslick devotes the whole of his treatise's sixth chapter to driving this point home—but its motions do. In a comment added to the first chapter of the third edition, Hanslick emphasized the centrality of this idea: "In considering the essence and effect of music, the concept of *motion* has been strikingly neglected; it seems to us the most important and fruitful."[162]

Motion, in the form of energy, is what many *Naturphilosophen* perceived as the unifying element in the cosmos, manifested in such diverse forms as light, heat, magnetism, electricity, gravity, and sound. The essence of matter, according to this line of thought, lay not in the idea of extension—the taking up of space—but in force, and specifically the forces of attraction and repulsion. Kant had developed this idea in his *Metaphysische Anfangsgründe der Naturwissenschaft* (1786), and it was taken up with enthusiasm by Schelling and his followers in the early decades of the nineteenth century. Polarities of force were essential to Kant's dynamic physics: in a universe consisting only of attraction, all matter would be drawn to a single point; in a universe consisting only of repulsion, all matter would be scattered into infinity. Kant's system of dynamic physics offered an alternative to the Newtonian mechanistic-atomistic view of the universe by giving priority to energy over matter, moving forces (*bewegende Kräfte*) over objects. These forces are not necessarily convertible (though some *Naturphilosophen* held them to be), but they all share the basic principle of polarization.[163]

For Hanslick, *tönend bewegte Formen* were sounding manifestations of such polarities, and he explicitly connects these motions with forms in a key sentence early in chapter 3, in which he defines the nature of musical beauty:

> It is specifically musical. By this we mean a beauty that is independent and has no need of any content from outside, residing solely in tones and in their artistic concatenation. The meaningful connections among sounds, delightful in themselves, their coming together and their resistance against one another, their flight away from one another and their mutual arrival, their soaring and their subsiding—this is what presents itself in free forms to our intellectual-spiritual intuition and pleases us as beautiful.[164]

---

162. *VMS*, 1:47–48: "Der Begriff der *Bewegung* ist bisher in den Untersuchungen des Wesens und der Wirkung der Musik auffallend vernachlässigt worden; er dünkt uns der wichtigste und fruchtbarste." Emphasis in original. *OMB*, 11.

163. See Beiser, *German Idealism*, 513, 531–35; and Caneva, "Physics and *Naturphilosophie*," 41.

164. *VMS*, 1:74. "*Es ist ein specifisch Musikalisches.* Darunter verstehen wir ein Schönes, das unabhängig und unbedürftig eines von Außen her kommenden Inhaltes, einzig in den Tönen und

Although music, in Hanslick's view, could not embody emotions, it could embody the dynamics of emotions. This concept of motion—energy, force, movement—is central to his argument about the essence of music, and he emphasizes this point repeatedly in chapter 2 of *Vom Musikalisch-Schönen*.

Hanslick's familiarity with *Naturphilosophie* could have come from any number of sources, several of which he cites explicitly in his treatise. One of the most remarkable and unlikely of these is Schelling's *Ueber das Verhältniß der bildenden Künste zur Natur* (1807). Hanslick quotes with approval its characterization of beauty as "sublimely indifferent," and he no doubt also appreciated (though he did not quote) the sentence that immediately follows in Schelling's treatise: "The external side or the basis of all beauty is the beauty of form."[165] The fact that Hanslick would not only read but actually acknowledge a work by Schelling is surprising in its own right, given Hanslick's declared aversion to idealism in all its various guises. And while *Ueber das Verhältniß der bildenden Künste zur Natur* is by no means an obscure work, neither is it one of Schelling's best-known; as such, it offers an indication of the breadth and depth of Hanslick's philosophical readings. The choice is nevertheless consistent with *Vom Musikalisch-Schönen* as a whole, including its deleted ending, for, as René Wellek points out, Schelling posits in this oration a conception of art as "an analogue of nature and of nature's creative power," in which "art constitutes an active link between the soul and nature."[166] Schelling also downplays the role of imitation in the visual arts and emphasizes form as a "positive force," the creative basis of all art.[167]

Another passage in Schelling's tract that resonates with the original ending of *Vom Musikalisch-Schönen* occurs just before the "sublime indifference of beauty"

ihrer künstlerischen Verbindung liegt. Die sinnvollen Beziehungen in sich reizvoller Klänge, ihr Zusammenstimmen und Widerstreben, ihr Fliehen und sich Erreichen, ihr Aufschwingen und Ersterben,—dies ist, was in freien Formen vor unser geistiges Anschauen tritt und als schön gefällt." Emphasis in original. *OMB*, 28.

165. Friedrich Wilhelm Joseph Schelling, *Ueber das Verhältniß der bildenden Künste zur Natur* (Munich: Philipp Krüll, 1807), p. 29: "die erhabene Gleichgültigkeit der Schönheit. Die äußre Seite oder Basis aller Schönheit ist die Schönheit der Form." This work had also been re-issued more recently by the Berlin publisher G. Reimer in 1843. For a brief introduction to Schelling and *Naturphilosophie*, see Andrew Bowie, *Schelling and Modern European Philosophy* (London and New York: Routledge, 1993), chapter 2, "The Hermeneutics of Nature." A more extended study is Joseph L. Esposito, *Schelling's Idealism and Philosophy of Nature* (Lewisburg, PA: Bucknell University Press, 1977).

166. René Wellek, *A History of Modern Criticism, 1750–1950*, vol. 2, *The Romantic Age* (New Haven: Yale University Press, 1965), 75–76.

167. Schelling, *Ueber das Verhältniß der bildenden Künste zur Natur*, 13–14. On the idea of form as a "positive force," see Dieter Jähnig, *Der Weltbezug der Künste: Schelling, Nietzsche, Kant* (Freiburg and Munich: Karl Alber, 2011), 37–79. In his review of Ambros's *Die Grenzen der Musik und Poesie* and three other treatises, Moriz Carrière cites Schelling's *Ueber das Verhältnis der bildenden Künste zur Natur*, along with Schiller's *Aesthetische Briefe* and Lessing's *Laokoön*, as "exemplary" ("maßgebend") for the treatment of aesthetic issues; see his "Populäre Aesthetik," *Blätter für literarische Unterhaltung*, no. 23 (4 June 1857): 415.

quoted by Hanslick. In addressing the distinction between the characteristic and the sublime, Schelling evokes a process of sublation in which the former is *aufgehoben* in a synthesis with the latter in a way that preserves the integrity and force (*Kraft*) of both. "If we therefore cannot call this high and self-sufficient beauty characteristic, on the grounds of its limited or contingent manifestation, that which is characteristic in it nevertheless continues to work its effect indistinguishably, as in a crystal, which, even if it is transparent, nevertheless has its texture. Even if only very gently, every characteristic element contributes to and helps bring about the sublime indifference of beauty."[168]

Within the more specific realm of musical aesthetics, the acoustical figures (*Klangfiguren*) created by the scientist Ernst Chladni (1756–1827) provided a seemingly endless source of fascination for *Naturphilosophen* and those sympathetic to music as part of a broader web of natural laws. At no point does Hanslick actually cite him or his work by name, but Chladni looms large in the work of Nägeli, Goethe, and the Danish scientist Hans Christian Ørsted (1777–1851), three writers he does cite explicitly. Chladni's acoustic figures are also discussed at length (and illustrated) in the physics textbook by J. Ferdinand Hessler (1803–1865), who along with Exner was the second of the two non–music teachers from his Prague years that Hanslick mentions by name in his memoirs.[169]

Chladni caused a sensation in the 1780s when he made it possible to "see" acoustic vibrations for the first time by scattering a layer of very fine sand on a thin surface, usually glass, and then drawing a violin bow lightly along the outer edge of the surface. The vibrations produced not only sound but also geometric patterns of astonishing variety and design (see Figure 8). The symmetry of these nodal patterns gave new credence to the idea that music was in fact a sounding manifestation of number, just as Pythagorean thought had always insisted it was. Over the next three decades Chladni gave numerous lecture-demonstrations throughout Europe, and his work attracted the attention of leading scientists and philosophers of the time (see Figure 9).

For us today, accustomed as we are to oscilloscopes and similar instruments that make sound waves and other invisible forces visible, it may be difficult to appreciate just how momentous the idea of "seeing" sound for the first time really was. The experience made a deep impression not only on Nägeli, Goethe, and Ørsted, but also on the poet and philosopher Novalis, the physicist Johann

---

168. Schelling, *Ueber das Verhältniß der bildenden Künste zur Natur*, 28–29: "Wenn wir daher diese hohe und selbstgenügsame Schönheit nicht charakteristisch nennen können, inwiefern dabei an Beschränkung oder Bedingtheit der Erscheinung gedacht wird; so wirkte in ihr das Charakteristische dennoch auch ununterscheidbar fort, wie im Krystall, ist er gleich durchsichtig, die Textur nichtsdestoweniger besteht: jedes charakteristische Element wiegt, wenn auch noch so sanft mit, und hilf[t] die erhabene Gleichgültigkeit der Schönheit bewirken."

169. J. Ferdinand Hessler, *Lehrbuch der Physik. Nach den Bedürfnissen der Technik, der Künste und Gewerbe* (Vienna: Wilhelm Braumüller, 1852), 387–90. See Hanslick, *Aus meinem Leben*, 1:22.

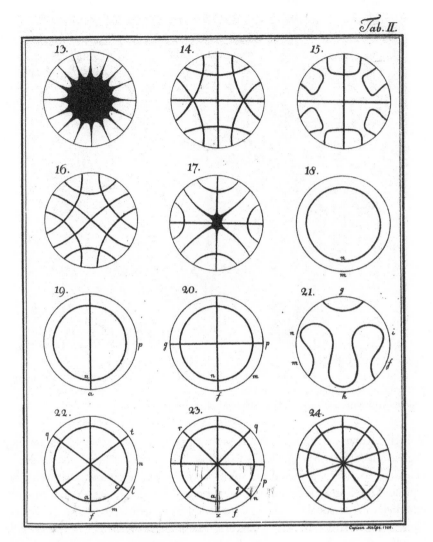

Figure 8. Chladni's "Acoustical Figures"
Hand-drawn renditions of Chladni's *Klangfiguren*, created by drawing a violin
bow across the edge of thin glass plates of various thicknesses strewn with sand.
Source: Ernst Chladni, *Entdeckungen über die Theorie des Klanges* (Leipzig: Weidmanns
Erben und Reich, 1787).

Figure 9. Ernst Chladni
Chladni demonstrates his *Klangfiguren* to an attentive audience during one of his many public lecture-demonstrations, ca. 1803.
Source: Anonymous drawing, Deutsches Museum, Munich.

Wilhelm Ritter, and the philosophers Schopenhauer and Hegel.[170] To varying degrees, all of these individuals saw Chladni's demonstrations as tangible evidence of a link between the material and spiritual worlds. In an aphorism that would be reprinted often in musical journals and copied by both Schumann and Brahms into their own personal notebooks years later, Jean Paul observed: "Through tones, Chladni builds structures with grains of sand, Amphion with stones, Orpheus with boulders, the musical genius with human hearts, and thus harmony builds the universe."[171] Perhaps nowhere is this connection more tellingly expressed than in

---

170. References to Chladni's acoustical figures appear in Ritter's *Fragmente aus dem Nachlasse eines jungen Physikers*, 2 vols. (Heidelberg: Mohr und Zimmer, 1810), 1:227; the opening paragraph of Novalis's *Die Lehrlinge zu Sais* (published posthumously in 1802); the first installment of Arthur Schopenhauer's *Die Welt als Wille und Vorstellung* (1819), ed. Arthur Hübscher, 4 vols. (Zurich: Diogenes, 1977), 1:334 (§52); and Hegel, *Encyklopädie der philosophischen Wissenschaften im Grundrisse*, 2nd ed., 284 (§301). Chladni's acoustical figures continued to fascinate throughout the nineteenth century and well into the twentieth: they are mentioned by Friedrich Nietzsche (*Über Wahrheit und Lüge im außermoralischen Sinne*), Thomas Mann (*Doktor Faustus*), Walter Benjamin (*Ursprung des deutschen Trauerspiels*), and Theodor Adorno ("Die Form der Schallplatte"), among others.

171. Jean Paul, "Die Tonkunst," in *Museum: Sedez-Aufsätze II* (1810), in Jean Paul, *Sämmtliche Werke*, 3rd ed., ed. Ernst Förster, 34 vols. (Berlin: Reimer, 1860–62), 28:50: "Chladni bauet mit

lectures Ralph Waldo Emerson (1803–1882) gave in the United States in the 1840s and '50s. He called Chladni's demonstrations "central" to understanding the nature of the universe and the connections between the phenomenal and noumenal:

> He strewed sand on glass and then drew musical tones from the glass, and the sand assumed symmetrical figures. With discords the sand was thrown about. Orpheus, then, is no fable: Sing, and the rocks will crystallize; Sing, and the plant will organize.[172]

Nägeli considered Chladni's demonstrations so important that he opened his *Vorlesungen über Musik* (1826) by recounting the excitement they had caused more than a decade earlier:

> Years ago the celebrated Chladni gave lectures on acoustics here in Zurich. He presented that experiment, now well-known, with plates of glass and grains of sand. With one stroke of the bow and a sound, the scattered grains of sand jumped up, quickly separated, and quickly conjoined into a mathematical figure. Those of us who were present were surprised, captivated, enthralled! A magical touch transformed for us the internal into the external, feeling into the visible, time into space. He allowed us to see tone and even to make it visibly recognizable, and he made its lawbound nature visible.[173]

Nägeli goes on to note that Chladni's demonstrations made visible the nature of the harmony that infuses the universe: "Like a ray of light, the ray of tone fills the entire world. Whether or not and how spheres can be carried by it—or whether

---

Tönen Gestalten aus Steinchen, Amphion aus Steinen, Orpheus aus Felsen, der Tongenius aus Menschenherzen, und so bauet die Harmonie die Welt." Joseph Fröhlich (writing under the cipher "F. L. B.") ends his "reflections on the essence of music" in the *AmZ* in 1815 by quoting Jean Paul's aphorism, after having discussed at length the harmony of the spheres and music as a "mirror of cosmic harmony"; see Fröhlich, "Reflexionen über das Wesen der Musik," *AmZ* 17 (22 November 1815), 785. The aphorism also appears as a motto at the head of the *NZfM* 7 (20 October 1837). On Schumann, see *Dichtergarten für Musik: Eine Anthologie für Freunde der Literatur und Musik*, ed. Gerd Nauhaus and Ingrid Bodsch (Frankfurt am Main: Stroemfeld, 2007), 262. On Brahms, see Johannes Brahms, *Des jungen Kreislers Schatzkästlein: Aussprüche von Dichtern, Philosophen und Künstlern*, ed. Carl Krebs (Berlin: Deutsche Brahmsgesellschaft, 1909), 109.

172. Ralph Waldo Emerson, *The Later Lectures of Ralph Waldo Emerson, 1843–1871*, 2 vols., ed. Ronald A. Bosco and Joel Myerson (Athens: University of Georgia Press, 2001), 1:120. See Sarah Ann Wider, "Chladni Patterns, Lyceum Halls, and Skillful Experimenters: Emerson's New Metaphysics for the Listening Reader," in *Emerson Bicentennial Essays*, ed. Ronald A. Bosco and Joel Myerson (Boston: Massachusetts Historical Society, 2006), 86–114.

173. Nägeli, *Vorlesungen über Musik*, 1: "Vor Jahren hielt einmal der bekannte Chladni auch in Zürich Vorlesungen über die Akustik. Er brachte jenes, nun bekannte Experiment vor mit Glasscheiben und Sandkörnchen. Auf einen Strich und Klang hüpften die hingestreuten Sandkörnchen auf, schnell sich sondernd, schnell sich fügend zur mathematischen Figur. Wie waren alle Anwesenden überrascht, ergriffen, entzückt! Ein Zauberschlag verwandelte ihnen Inneres in Aeusseres, Gefühl in Anschauung, Zeit in Raum. Er gab ihnen den Ton zu sehen, gab ihn sogar sichtbar zu erkennen, machte dessen Gesetzmässigkeit anschaulich." Chladni had lectured in Zurich in 1810: see Dieter Ullmann, *Chladni und die Entwicklung der Akustik von 1750–1860* (Basel: Birkhäuser, 1996), 119.

and how they carry it—we do not know. But a primordial myth, and indeed more than a myth, tells us that these spheres are brought into reciprocal action through it, and the myth designates this reciprocity with the beautiful-sounding word 'Harmony.'"[174] The speed with which Nägeli moves from a replicable experiment to speculation about the organization of the cosmos is typical of *Naturphilosophie* in general. His attention to parallels between the disparate phenomena of light and sound, as we shall see, is also characteristic of this mode of thought.

Hanslick's intellectual debt to Nägeli's lectures, as noted before, is far more extensive than the two brief citations in *Vom Musikalisch-Schönen* would indicate.[175] What is especially noteworthy here is that Nägeli uses Chladni's acoustical figures as a springboard from which to describe instrumental music as "pure" and "autonomous."[176]

Goethe too welcomed Chladni's work as tangible evidence for a connection among the forces of nature. During Chladni's visit to Weimar in 1803, Goethe wrote to Schiller:

> Doctor Chladni has arrived and brought with him his extensive study of acoustics, published in a quarto volume. I have already read half of it and will tell you more in person some rather pleasing things about its content, substance, method, and form. He belongs...to those fortunate souls who don't have the slightest inkling that there is such a thing as *Naturphilosophie* and who simply try to observe phenomena attentively so that afterward they can classify them and use them as much as they can be used and to the extent that these individuals' innate and practiced talent in and for the matter will allow them.[177]

Later, in his study of entoptic colors (1820), Goethe noted the striking parallels between Chladni's acoustical figures and the patterns of refracted light

174. Nägeli, *Vorlesungen über Musik*, 1–2: "Gleichwie der Lichtstrahl, so erfüllet auch der Tonstrahl die ganze Welt. Ob und wie die Sphären von ihm getragen werden,—oder, ob und wie sie ihn tragen, wissen wir nicht. Aber eine uralte Mythe, wohl mehr als Mythe, sagt uns, daß sie durch ihn in Wechselwirkung gebracht sind, und bezeichnet diese Wechselwirkung mit dem schönklingenden Worte: Harmonie."

175. *VMS*, 1:109 and 147. From the eighth edition onward, Hanslick dropped the first reference to Nägeli, and so this passage does not appear in Payzant's edition; the second of the two references is on p. 69 of *OMB*.

176. Nägeli, *Vorlesungen über Musik*, 187: "die 'reine' Musik, die selbständige Instrumentalmusik." See above, p. 117.

177. Goethe to Schiller, letter of 26 January 1803, in *Der Briefwechsel zwischen Schiller und Goethe*, ed. Emil Staiger and Hans-Georg Dewitz, rev. ed. (Frankfurt am Main: Insel Verlag, 2005), 978: "Doktor Chladni ist angekommen und hat seine ausgearbeitete Akustik in einem Quartbande mitgebracht. Ich habe sie schon zur Hälfte gelesen und werde Ihnen darüber mündlich, über Inhalt, Gehalt, Methode und Form manches Erfreuliche sagen können. Er gehört...unter die Glückseligen, welche auch nicht eine Ahndung haben, daß es eine Naturphilosophie gibt, und die nur, mit Aufmerksamkeit, suchen die Phänomene gewahr zu werden, um sie nachher so gut zu ordnen und zu nutzen, als es nur gehen will und als ihr angebornes, in der Sache und zur Sache geübtes Talent vermag." Two of Goethe's pencil-and-ink renditions of Chladni's tone figures are reproduced in Pascal Rousseau, "'Arabesques': Le formalisme

created by the physicist Thomas Johann Seebeck (1770–1821). Seebeck, with whom Goethe had been in close personal contact, used various configurations of prisms and mirrors to create refractions of polarized light that under certain conditions projected patterns remarkably similar to those made by Chladni using sound (see Figure 10).[178] For Goethe, such analogies provided "a handle, a lever by which to grasp and move nature." One should not be discouraged, he noted, if such analogies occasionally led the researcher astray, for "if we keep to our goal of a pure and methodical analogy," we can connect phenomena that are seemingly far apart, thereby allowing us gradually to perceive their "identity and the actual integrated life of nature" in a systematic, scientific fashion. Through such analogies, supported by experimental evidence, we can see that "everything in the universe hangs together, affects everything else, and responds to all else.... As soon as...the universality of each law is recognized, the identity of countless phenomena must readily come into play." At this point in his essay, Goethe turns to a discussion of Chladni's acoustical figures, laying out in parallel columns the similarities between the geometrical patterns Seebeck had discovered in light and those that Chladni had revealed in sound.[179] These were precisely the kinds of connections that Goethe, in his 1803 letter to Schiller, had found lacking in Chladni's work and person when he describes him as an intelligent individual who "doesn't have the slightest inkling that there is such a thing as *Naturphilosophie* and that such disparate phenomena might in fact be attributed to a common force."

Ørsted, best known for his discovery of electromagnetism, extended the implications of Chladni's discoveries still further. He too was committed to identifying underlying connections among the laws of nature. Using metal plates rather than glass and ultrafine metallic dust or pollen rather than sand,

---

musical dans les débuts de l'abstraction," in *Aux origines de l'abstraction, 1800–1914: Musée d'Orsay, 3 novembre 2003–22 février 2004* (Paris: Réunion des Musées Nationaux, 2003), 234.

178. For an account of Seebeck's experiments that produced these so-called entoptic figures, see Keld Nielsen, "Another Kind of Light: The Work of T. J. Seebeck and his Collaboration with Goethe," *Historical Studies in the Physical and Biological Sciences* 20 (1989), 107–78; 21 (1991), 317–97. Hanslick refers in passing to Goethe's study of color in *VMS*, 1:48; *OMB*, 12.

179. Goethe, "Entoptische Farben" (1820), in Goethe, *Schriften zur allgemeinen Naturlehre, Geologie und Mineralogie*, ed. Wolf von Engelhardt and Manfred Wenzel (Frankfurt am Main: Deutscher Klassiker Verlag, 1989), 710–11: "Hier dürfen wir also die Analogie als Handhabe, als Hebel die Natur anzufassen und zu bewegen gar wohl empfehlen und anrühmen. Man lasse sich nicht irre machen, wenn Analogie manchmal irre führt....Halten wir uns aber zu unserm Zweck an eine reine, methodische Analogie, wodurch Erfahrung erst belebt wird, indem das Abgesonderte und entfernt Scheinende verknüpft, dessen Identität entdeckt und das eigentliche Gesamtleben der Natur auch in der Wissenschaft nach und nach empfunden wird....Hieran finden wir abermals ein herrliches Beispiel, daß alles im Universen zusammenhängt, sich auf einander bezieht, einander antwortet....Sobald...die Allgemeinheit jenes Gesetzes anerkannt sein wird, so muß die Identität unzähliger Phänomene sich alsobald betätigen." Goethe's poem "Entoptische Farben" ("Laß dir von den Spiegeleien"), written in 1817, centers on the idea of the crystal as a microcosm of the universe and makes references to the shapes of Seebeck's figures.

Figure 10. Seebeck's "Entoptic Figures"
Thomas Seebeck created his "entoptic figures" by passing light through a series of prisms and mirrors. The similarity of the resulting patterns to Chladni's "acoustic figures" was immediately apparent to all, including Seebeck, Goethe, Chladni, and Ørsted.
Source: Seebeck, "Einige neue Versuche und Beobachtungen der Spiegelung und Brechung des Lichtes," *Journal für die Chemie, Physik und Mineralogie* 7(1813), Plate III.

Ørsted demonstrated in 1808 that the patterns created by the plates set in motion through sound were caused not only by mechanical forces, but by electrical ones as well (see Figure 11).[180]

180. Ørsted, "Versuche über die Klangfiguren," *Journal für die Physik, Chemie und Mineralogie* 8 (1809), 167–254. An English translation of the original Danish version (1808) is available as

Figure 11. Hans Christian Ørsted
This 1822 portrait, by C. W. Eckersberg, shows the scientist holding an acoustical figure; note the violin bow on the table to the right.
Source: Danish National Museum of Science and Technology, Helsingor.

Like Goethe, Ørsted postulated a connection between beauty and the laws of nature, and he wrote several essays and dialogues on the subject.[181] Hanslick refers to one of these at several points in *Vom Musikalisch-Schönen*, albeit misleadingly. In discussing the role of symmetry in musical beauty, he dismisses the idea that this quality alone might account for beauty in either melody or rhythm, and he takes Ørsted to task on this point:

> Most recently, Ørstedt has developed this Platonic outlook for music by using the example of the circle, to which he ascribes positive beauty. Has this esteemed individual never experienced the utter repulsiveness of an orbicular composition?[182]

"Experiments on Acoustic Figures," in *Selected Scientific Works of Hans Christian Ørsted*, ed. and trans. Karen Jelved, Andrew D. Jackson, Ole Knudsen (Princeton: Princeton University Press, 1998), 264–81.

181. On Ørsted's belief in the connections between science and beauty, see Dan Charly Christensen, "Ørsted's Concept of Force and Theory of Music," in *Hans Christian Ørsted and the Romantic Legacy in Science: Ideas, Disciplines, Practices*, ed. Robert M. Brain, Robert S. Cohen, Ole Knudsen (Dordrecht: Springer, 2007), 115–33; and Kristine Hays Lynning and Anja Skaar Jacobsen, "Grasping the Spirit in Nature: *Anschauung* in Ørsted's Epistemology of Science and Beauty," *Studies in History and Philosophy of Science (Part A)* 42 (2011), 45–57. Ørsted's aesthetic writings are summarized in Lorraine Daston, "Ørsted and the Rational Unconscious," in *Hans Christian Ørsted and the Romantic Legacy in Science*, 235–46.

182. *VMS*, 1:96: "Zuletzt hat für die Musik diese Platonische Ansicht Oerstedt an dem Beispiel des Kreises entwickelt, dem er positive Schönheit vindicirt. Sollte der Treffliche niemals die ganze

Aside from a poor attempt at humor, there are two problems here. The first is that Ørsted never made any such claim. Hanslick misrepresents the analogy of the circle by ignoring its context and then applying it in an overly literal manner. Ørsted goes out of his way to emphasize that his use of the circle as an image of rational beauty—geometric, mathematical—is intentionally simplistic.[183] His image of the circle is but one element in an extended and subtle discussion that advocates a dual approach to both nature and art from the perspectives of the phenomenal and noumenal, the same opposition Hanslick was trying to reconcile in the original final paragraph of *Vom Musikalisch-Schönen*. The second problem is that Hanslick himself evokes symmetry at several points in his treatise as a quality that can contribute to musical beauty: in his analysis of the main theme in Beethoven's overture to *The Creatures of Prometheus*; in his discussion of large- and small-scale rhythm; in his comparison of musical form to the images produced by turning a kaleidoscope; and as an element of musical form.[184]

The second reference to Ørsted, a few pages later, is even more obtuse. In dismissing mathematics as a basis of musical beauty, Hanslick claims not to understand what is meant or what is to be calculated when a character in one of Ørsted's dialogues asks (rhetorically) if "the lifetimes of multiple mathematicians" would "suffice to calculate all the beauties of a Mozartean symphony."[185] As presented by Hanslick—that is, stripped of all context—the question indeed makes little sense; but within the framework of Ørsted's dialogue, it serves as an illustration of how beauty, even though it defies rational explanation, resides in elements that are themselves rational, including the frequency of vibrations and the distance between pitches. The third and last of Hanslick's citations to Ørsted is the unkindest of all, for it attributes to him a statement posed by one of the dimmer characters in a dialogue, who relates a story that has been told to him about a dog trained to howl at a certain passage of music. The more intelligent

Entsetzlichkeit einer kreisrunden Composition an sich erlebt haben?" The reference is to Ørsted's "Ueber die Gründe des Vergnügens, welches die Töne hervorbringen," trans. K. L. Kannegiesser, in Ørsted's *Neue Beiträge zu dem Geist in der Natur* (Leipzig: Carl B. Lorck, 1851), 20–21. The translation in *OMB*, 41, is based on alterations Hanslick made to this passage in the fourth (1874) and seventh (1885) editions.

183. On Ørsted's use of geometrical figures as examples of beauty, see Lynning and Jacobsen, "Grasping the Spirit in Nature," pp. 50–51.

184. Beethoven: *VMS*, 1:50 (*OMB*, 12–13); rhythm: *VMS*, 1:74 (*OMB*, 28); kaleidoscope: *VMS*, 1:76 (*OMB*, 29); musical form: *VMS*, 1:167 (*OMB*, 81).

185. *VMS*, 1:97: "Wenn Oerstedt fragt: 'Sollte wohl die Lebenszeit mehrerer Mathematiker hinreichen, alle Schönheiten einer Mozart'schen Symphonie zu berechnen?' so bekenne ich, daß ich das nicht verstehe. Was soll denn oder kann berechnet werden?" *OMB*, 41. In a footnote, Hanslick cites at this point Ørsted's *Der Geist in der Natur*, vol. 3, p. 32, but the reference is slightly confusing, in that he cites the *Neue Beiträge zu dem Geist in der Natur* (1851) as if were the third volume of the two-volume *Der Geist in der Natur* (1850–51). The essay from which Hanslick quotes is once again "Ueber die Gründe des Vergnügens, welches die Töne hervorbringen."

interlocutors dismiss this account, but Hanslick conveys the story as if it Ørsted himself had related it and placed great stock in its veracity.[186]

Hanslick's misrepresentations of Ørsted's writings mask a deeper underlying debt, for in his aesthetic dialogues and essays Ørsted repeatedly returns to the connections that link the laws of nature to beauty and more specifically to musical beauty, the central concern of the deleted ending to *Vom Musikalisch-Schönen*. In another essay in the same volume quoted by Hanslick, Ørsted notes that Chladni's acoustical figures

> show us another remarkable confluence of natural effects that must seem worlds apart to the uninitiated, whereas in reality they have their origin in a single fundamental idea of nature. The dust-covered surface reveals to the eye divisions and shapes that follow laws [of nature], that is, figures stamped with thought. But only when vibrations produce figures that are pleasing to the eye do they create impressions that please us as well when transmitted through air. Even in our impressions of beauty, the one sense thus confirms the testimony of the other.[187]

Later in this same essay, Ørsted relates the vibrations of air that create sound to other kinds of vibrations—motion, movement, *Bewegung*—that create light, heat, electricity, and magnetism. He even uses the term *bewegte Formen* to describe the ripples created by a stone thrown into a pond and relates these visual manifestations of motion to Chladni's acoustical figures.[188] In another essay in the same volume, Ørsted aligns beauty with the infinite, the ugly with the finite. "That which is essentially beautiful," he says, "is eternal."[189] Still within the same volume cited by Hanslick, Ørsted sums up his argument about the relationship between the world of physical sound and the world of the spirit:

> If we choose external nature for our perspective, then the effects of music would seem to belong entirely to the physical world. If on the other hand we assume our

---

186. *VMS*, I:113–14; *OMB*, 51; Ørsted, "Ueber die Gründe des Vergnügens," 8–9.

187. Ørsted, "Zwei Kapitel der Naturlehre des Schönen," in Ørsted, *Neue Beiträge zu dem Geist in der Natur*, trans. K. L. Kannegiesser (Leipzig: Carl B. Lorck, 1851), 80–81: "Die Klangfiguren zeigen uns ein anderes merkwürdiges Zusammentreten von Naturwirkungen, die dem Unkundigen himmelweit verschieden scheinen müssen, während sie doch in der Wirklichkeit ihren Ursprung aus Einem Grundgedanken der Natur haben. Die bestäubte Platte zeigt dem Auge gesetzbestimmte Eintheilungen und Figuren, also Gestalten mit Gedankengepräge. Aber nur wenn die Schwingungen solche das Auge befriedigende Figuren hervorbringen, wird auch das Ohr durch die Eindrücke, die wir von ihnen durch die Luft empfangen, befriedigt. Der eine Sinn bestätigt so das Zeugniß des andern, auch was den Schönheitseindruck betrifft." My translations of Ørsted's texts are based on Kannegiesser's German renderings of the Danish originals on the grounds that these are the versions Hanslick would have known.

188. Ørsted, "Zwei Kapitel," 85, 79.

189. Ørsted, "Ueber das 'Unschöne' in der Natur," 142: "Ist seine Auffassung richtig, so wird das Häßliche, sowie in einer gewissen Bedeutung das Böse, ein Endlichkeitsverhältniß. Das Wesentlichschöne dagegen ist ewig."

perspective in the world of ideas, then their entire essence would seem to belong there. Having made this division, however, we must bring them together as one. The natural laws of the physical world are laws of reason....In other words: spirit and nature are one, viewed from two different sides. Thus we cease to be astonished at their harmony.[190]

In another volume of the same series quoted by Hanslick, Ørsted concludes his account of planetary motions by emphatically asserting that "*every well conducted investigation of a limited phenomenon reveals to us the eternal laws of the infinite Whole.*"[191] Pronouncements like these, coming from the pen of an "objective," empirical scientist of international renown, could not have failed to make an impression on Hanslick, and they help explain the source of his ideas in the final paragraph of the first edition of his treatise.

Nägeli, Goethe, Ørsted, and even Hanslick, at least in his earlier years, all believed that beauty, including musical beauty, could be explained according to the laws of nature, and that these laws could be reduced to the principle of motion, or, as Hanslick put it, "the great motions of the cosmos." While Hanslick's original ending may have struck Zimmermann as contradictory and superfluous, it had as much to do with physics as metaphysics. The final paragraph represents Hanslick's attempt to connect beauty with the inductive science of his time and without recourse to speculative philosophy.

Hanslick was determined to ground the laws of beauty in the immutable laws of nature, which in turn justified his conception of beauty as an objective quality not subject to the vagaries of individual perception.[192] The laws of nature offered a source of transcendent authority not to be found elsewhere. Even after Zimmermann's review had appeared in print, Hanslick observed in one of his journalistic essays that although music had no model in nature, its basic acoustical elements were firmly grounded in the "phenomena and laws" of nature, and he took explicit note of the work of Mersenne, Seebeck, and Chladni in the field

---

190. Ørsted, "Zwei Kapitel," 87: "Es zeigt sich also, daß, wenn wir unseren Standpunkt für die Betrachtung der Tonwirkungen in der äußeren Natur wählen, sie ganz der Körperwelt anzugehören scheinen müssen; wählen wir dagegen unseren Standpunkt in der Gedankenwelt, so scheint ihr ganzes Wesen dieser anzugehören. Aber nachdem wir diese Trennung bewerkstelligt haben, müssen Beide in Eins gefaßt werden. Die Naturgesetze in der Körperwelt sind Vernunftgesetze....Mit anderen Worten: Geist und Natur sind Eines, angesehen von zwei verschiedenen Seiten. Wir hören so auf, uns über ihre Harmonie zu wundern." For a detailed account of Ørsted's *Naturphilosophie*, see Dan Ch. Christensen, *Hans Christian Ørsted: Reading Nature's Mind* (Oxford: Oxford University Press, 2013).

191. Ørsted, "Ueber Geist und Studium der allgemeinen Naturlehre," in Ørsted, *Der Geist in der Natur*, 2:437–38: "daß eine jede wohlgeleitete Untersuchung eines beschränkten Gegenstandes uns einen Theil der ewigen Gesetzen des unendlichen Ganzen entdeckt." The statement is set in *Sperrdruck*, the equivalent of italics.

192. Among the references to laws (*Gesetze*) in *VMS* are 1:25 ("Naturgesetze"), 35 ("Gesetze [des] Organismus"), 48–49 ("höhere Gesetze"), 75 ("Weltgesetze"), 78–79 ("Naturgesetze"), and 84 ("allgemeine Gesetze").

of acoustics.[193] In the preface to the second edition of *Vom Musikalisch-Schönen*, Hanslick allowed that "the final value of beauty will always rest on the direct evidence of feeling" but insisted "that one cannot derive even a single musical law from an appeal to feeling."[194] For all the changes he made to subsequent editions, he never altered this remarkable sentence in the central third chapter: "All musical elements relate to one another in secret connections and elective affinities based on natural laws."[195] The idea of beauty as the manifestation of some kind of universal, eternal law was central to Hanslick's thought, even if he was reluctant to elaborate this point. If beauty was immutable, then its laws must similarly be immutable, no matter how obscure they might remain. This was an idea Hanslick seems to have harbored at least half a dozen years before the publication of *Vom Musikalisch-Schönen*. In an 1848 review of a work that contained parallel fifths, he argued that these could not be prohibited a priori, for "only the eternal laws of nature are inviolable," and the prohibition against parallel fifths could not be justified on the grounds of any natural law.[196] What is important here is not Hanslick's attitude toward parallel fifths—a hotly debated issue in his time—but his appeal to the authority of the laws of nature in general.

In sum, then, *Naturphilosophie* provided Hanslick the framework for what he thought of as an "objective" aesthetics, for it allowed him to align musical beauty with the unchanging laws of nature. In the original but later-to-be-deleted opening of *Vom Musikalisch-Schönen*, Hanslick had spoken hopefully of a time when the "inductive method of natural science" would supplant the "metaphysical principle" as a means of identifying the essence of musical beauty, thereby overcoming the "unscientific aesthetic of feeling" to arrive at an understanding of the beautiful in its "primordial, pure elements."[197] It seems almost inevitable

193. Hanslick, "Musikalische Briefe: Ueber musikalische Instrumente und deren Verhältniß zur Akustik," *Die Presse*, 15 July 1856, in Hanslick, *Sämtliche Schriften*, I/3, 263.

194. *VMS*, 1:10: "Ich theile vollkommen die Ansicht, daß der letzte Werth des Schönen immer auf unmittelbarer Evidenz des Gefühls beruhen wird. Aber ebenso fest halte ich an der Ueberzeugung, daß man aus all den üblichen Appellationen an das Gefühl nicht ein einziges musikalisches Gesetz ableiten kann." This passage does not appear in *OMB*.

195. *VMS*, 1:78–79: "Alle musikalischen Elemente stehen unter sich in geheimen, auf Naturgesetze gegründeten Verbindungen und Wahlverwandtschaften." *OMB*, 31. On the broader concept of "elective affinities" in music and its connection to Goethe's novel *Die Wahlverwandtschaften*, see Goehr, *Elective Affinities*. On Hanslick's use of the term and its resonances with the physical sciences, see Benjamin Steege, *Helmholtz and the Modern Listener* (Cambridge: Cambridge University Press, 2012), 160–63.

196. Hanslick, *Sämtliche Schriften*, I/1, 164; originally published in the *Wiener Zeitung*, 20 April 1848: "nur die ewigen Gesetze der *Natur* sind unantastbar. Ein solches ist aber das Quintenverboth nicht, kann es nicht sein, da eine Tonfolge *an sich*, allgemein nicht verbothen werden kann." Emphasis in original. Geoffrey Payzant offers a different translation and commentary in Payzant, "Eduard Hanslick and the 'geistreich' Dr. Alfred Julius Becher," *MR* 44 (1983): 104–15.

197. *VMS*, 1:21: "Sollte sich nun immerhin auch in Behandlung ästhetischer Fragen ein Umschwung in der Wissenschaft vorbereiten, welcher an der Stelle des metaphysischen Princips eine der inductiven naturwissenschaftlichen Methode verwandte Anschauung zu mächtigem Einfluß und wenigstens zeitlicher Oberhand verhälfe,—vor der Hand stehen die jüngsten Spitzen unsrer Wissenschaft noch

that having dropped most of the original final paragraph for the second edition of his treatise, Hanslick would drop this opening portion of his text as well.

Given Hanslick's motivations for saying what he said in his original final paragraph, we can now revisit the perennial question of why he deleted it. There are several possible answers here, none of which contradicts any of the others. Briefly:

(1) Zimmermann was more than a prominent critic who was chair of a philosophy department at a leading university; he was a close personal friend. Hanslick would dedicate the second, third, fifth, seventh, eighth, and ninth editions of *Vom Musikalisch-Schönen* to him.

(2) Hanslick probably realized that to argue his case about music's connections with the cosmos would have required a substantial expansion of his treatise. As he noted in his preface to the second edition, he had made what alterations he could without creating "an altogether different" work.[198] Even Hanslick's harshest critics had praised the brevity of the first edition.

(3) *Vom Musikalisch-Schönen* was part of a polemical attack against Liszt, Wagner, and the "Music of the Future," as Hanslick himself acknowledged in the preface to the second edition. This was a debate in which slogans were more important than subtleties. By 1858 it had become clear that the treatise's argument in favor of music's self-sufficient nature was finding a receptive audience, and there was no point in qualifying its principal thesis in ways that even allies like Zimmermann might misunderstand.

(4) The writings of Schopenhauer, which had languished in obscurity for decades, became extremely well-known in the middle of the 1850s (see chapter 12). It is entirely possible that someone—perhaps Zimmermann himself—pointed out to Hanslick in conversation that the original ending of *Vom Musikalisch-Schönen* seemed to echo certain passages from *Die Welt als Wille und Vorstellung*: we find in music not merely a simulacrum of the universe but the universe itself.

(5) Hanslick may have begun to entertain doubts about the wisdom of *Naturphilosophie*, which was beginning to fall out of fashion in the 1850s. Zimmermann's summary dismissal of it in his 1855 review suggests that this was the case.

Even in the face of all this, Hanslick did not capitulate entirely, at least not at once. Again, it was a two-stage amputation. He retained the first sentence of

---

unverdunkelt da und behaupten für alle Zeit das unvergängliche Verdienst, die Herrschaft der unwissenschaftlichen Empfindungs-Aesthetik vernichtet, und das Schöne in seinen ureigenen, reinen Elementen durchforscht zu haben." This passage does not appear in *OMB*.

198. *VMS*, 1:9. This passage does not appear in *OMB*.

his closing paragraph in the second edition, thereby preserving his assertion that there is indeed some sort of connection between musical beauty and "all other great and beautiful ideas." This seemed sufficiently vague as to be unexceptionable. He nevertheless removed it seven years later, in 1865, perhaps on the grounds that it raised more questions than it answered, much as the remainder of the closing paragraph had done.

The durability of *Naturphilosophie*, Zimmermann's dismissal of it notwithstanding, can be seen in Hermann von Helmholtz's *Die Lehre von den Tonempfindungen* (1863), a work that more than any other tried to put musical acoustics on a solidly empirical basis. Hanslick greeted Helmholtz's treatise enthusiastically, in part because it endorsed *Vom Musikalisch-Schönen*, in part because it promised renewed evidence of a link between beauty and the laws of nature.[199] Like Ørsted, Helmholtz emphasized that beauty, although based in the laws of nature, could not be calculated or prescribed and therefore remained beyond the grasp of human reason. At the very end of his treatise, in a section entitled "Connections to Aesthetics" ("Beziehungen zur Aesthetik"), Helmholtz deemed the musical artwork an image of the order of the universe, "governed in all its parts by law and reason."[200] It is, as the historian of science Lorraine Daston notes, "a piquant irony to find a transmogrified version of Schelling's *Naturphilosophie* nestled within a weighty scientific treatise by Helmholtz."[201]

* * *

The original ending of *Vom Musikalisch-Schönen* reflects a pivotal moment in the history of what would eventually come to be thought of as absolute music. In the transition from the first to the second edition, his *Contribution to a Revision of the Aesthetics of Music* manifests the shift from the transcendental idealism of a previous generation to the formalist realism that would come to dominate thinking about music from the second half of the nineteenth century until well into the twentieth century. In its original guise, the treatise embraces the concept of absolute music in the sense of "absolute" as that which is all-encompassing; from the second edition onward, it implicitly adopts the idea of "absolute" in the sense of music as an art wholly separate from and unrelated to anything outside itself. Hanslick's original, holistic conception of absolute music differs fundamentally from the harder-edged formalism that would emerge in subsequent editions of his treatise.

199. Hermann von Helmholtz, *Die Lehre von den Tonempfindungen als physiologische Grundlage für die Theorie der Musik* (Braunschweig: Vieweg & Sohn, 1863), 2–3, 386. Hanslick praised Helmholtz's work in the preface to the fourth edition (1874) of *VMS* (1:14), and in an extended passage revised for chapter 4 of the same edition (1:118–19; *OMB*, 54).

200. Helmholtz, *Die Lehre von den Tonempfindungen*, 555: "Wir lernen ... in dem Kunstwerk das Bild einer solchen Ordnung der Welt, welche durch Gesetz und Vernunft in allen ihren Theilen beherrscht wird, kennen und bewundern."

201. Daston, "Ørsted and the Rational Unconscious," 245.

10   Liszt's "Program" Music

The identification of absolute music with a specific repertory grew stronger still in the summer of 1855 with the first appearance—and almost immediate acceptance—of a term to describe works of purely instrumental music that were *not* absolute: program music. The term was coined by Franz Liszt in a long essay published serially in Brendel's *Neue Zeitschrift für Musik*.[1] Ostensibly a commentary on Berlioz's *Harold en Italie*, the essay in fact has little to say about that particular work and focuses instead on broader questions about the nature of instrumental music in general. And while Liszt never cites Hanslick or his treatise explicitly—in keeping with the tradition of polemics—his essay stands as one of the earliest extended responses to *Vom Musikalisch-Schönen*.[2]

What Liszt variously called *Programm-Musik* or *Programmmusik* literally changed the terms of the debate. In his "Harold" essay, he distinguishes between the "specifically musical composer," who places value only on "using material," and the composer driven by an overarching poetic image or narrative. He dismisses the first of these as a "formalist," a "mere musician" (*bloßer Musiker*) who is "capable of nothing better or cleverer than to use, propagate, arrange, and occasionally develop that which has already been achieved by others."[3] The composer of program music, by contrast, is a "tone-poet" (*Tondichter*) who draws on ever-new sources of inspiration.

---

1. Franz Liszt, "Berlioz und seine Haroldsymphonie," *NZfM* 43 (13 July, 20 July, 27 July, 17 August, 24 August 1855): 25–32, 37–46, 49–55, 77–84, 89–97.

2. Caroline zu Sayn-Wittgenstein's role in writing the text remains a matter of some dispute, and the genesis of the essay is altogether murky. Liszt had an early French-language draft of it ready in July 1854, i.e., before the appearance of *Vom Musikalisch-Schönen* in late September, but then altered it at some point in late 1854 or early 1855 before finally releasing it in a German translation (perhaps by Richard Pohl) in the summer of 1855. See Detlef Altenburg, "Vom poetisch Schönen: Franz Liszts Auseinandersetzung mit der Musikästhetik Eduard Hanslicks," in *Ars Musica, Musica Scientia: Festschrift Heinrich Hüschen*, ed. Detlef Altenburg (Cologne: Verlag der Arbeitsgemeinschaft für Rheinische Musikgeschichte, 1980), 1–10; James Deaville, "The Controversy Surrounding Liszt's Conception of Programme Music," in *Nineteenth-Century Music: Selected Proceedings of the Tenth International Conference*, ed. Jim Samson and Bennett Zon (Aldershot: Ashgate, 2002), 98–124; and Rainer Schmusch, *Der Tod des Orpheus: Entstehungsgeschichte der Programmusik* (Freiburg im Breisgau: Rombach, 1998), 271–74. On the many internal inconsistencies of Liszt's essay, see Vera Micznik, "The Absolute Limitations of Programme Music: The Case of Liszt's 'Die Ideale,'" *M&L* 80 (1999): 207–40.

3. Liszt, "Berlioz und seine Haroldsymphonie," *NZfM* 43 (27 July 1855): 51: "Der specifisch musikalische Componist, der gerade nur auf das Verbrauchen des Stoffes Werth legt, ist nicht fähig, ihm neue Formeln abzugewinnen, neue Kräfte einzuhauchen.... Die Formalisten [vermögen] nichts Besseres und Klügeres zu thun, als das von Jenen Errungene zu nutzen, zu verbreiten, einzutheilen und gelegentlich zu verarbeiten."

In program music, the recurrence, variation, alteration, and modulation of motifs are determined by their relationship to a poetic idea. Here one theme no longer begets another.... Though not ignored, all exclusively musical considerations are subordinated to the treatment of the subject at hand. Accordingly, the treatment and subject of this symphonic genre demand an engagement that goes beyond the technical treatment of the musical material. The vague impressions of the soul are elevated to definite impressions through an articulated plan, which is taken in by the ear in much the same manner in which a cycle of paintings is taken in by the eye. The artist who favors this kind of artwork enjoys the advantage of being able to connect with a poetic process all those affects which an orchestra can express with such great power.[4]

Liszt used the new term to identify a repertory of instrumental music which through an evocative title, a verbal program, or both, "draws the listener's attention in advance toward a specific object."[5] The practice itself, as he readily acknowledged, was not new: composers had been writing works of this kind in great quantity since the early decades of the eighteenth century. The idea that such works might constitute an intrinsically superior repertory was, however, altogether novel. Terms previously used to identify this kind of music had always suggested a modified or subordinate status, either as a subset of an existing genre (*symphonie à programme, charakteristische Symphonie*), or as a modified, more specialized category of music in general: depictional music, or, more literally, "music that paints" (*malende Musik*), characteristic music (*charakteristische Musik*), or representational music (*schildernde Musik*). Liszt's neologism was a compound noun, not a gerund- or adjective-noun pairing, and this helped reinforce the idea of *Programmmusik* as a category of music in its own right. The structural parallel encouraged a direct comparison with its implied opposite: absolute music.

Most critics were of the day were in any case perfectly willing to accept the idea that a work of music could project objects, events, or ideas lying outside the realm of sound, or that a composer might have such a "program" in mind when

---

4. Liszt, "Berlioz und seine Haroldsymphonie," *NZfM* 43 (17 August 1855): 81: "In der Programm-Musik ist Wiederkehr, Wechsel, Veränderung und Modulation der Motive durch ihre Beziehung zu einem poetischen Gedanken bedingt. Hier ruft nicht mehr ein Thema das andere hervor.... Alle ausschließlich musikalischen Rücksichten sind denen der Handlung des gegebenen Sujets untergeordnet, wenn auch nicht außer Acht gelassen. Handlung und Sujet nehmen also in dieser Symphonie ein über der technischen Handhabung des musikalischen Stoffes stehendes Interesse in Anspruch; die unbestimmten Eindrücke der Seele werden durch einen exponirten Plan zu bestimmten, der hier durch das Ohr vermittelt wird, wie er dem Auge durch eine Folge von Bildern mitgetheilt werden kann. Der Künstler, welcher diesem Genre von Kunstwerken den Vorzug giebt, genießt den Vortheil, alle Affecte, die das Orchester mit so großer Gewalt auszudrücken vermag, an einen poetischen Hergang anknüpfen zu können."

5. Liszt, "Berlioz und seine Harold-Symphonie," *NZfM* 43 (20 July 1855): 37–38: "ein...Hinweis, welcher...die Aufmerksamkeit im Voraus auf einen besonderen Gegenstand lenkt."

writing a work of purely instrumental music. The real question almost invariably centered on the extent to which such a program could or should be made known to an audience. In what was otherwise a favorable review of Berlioz's *Symphonie fantastique*, Schumann famously dismissed the work's prose program on the grounds that it was too detailed. Word of mouth or the descriptive movement titles alone, Schumann maintained, would have sufficed to convey the idea of the symphony. "Such guides," he declared, "always retain something unworthy and charlatanesque about them."[6] On another occasion, he declared: "Thus if a composer presents us with a program alongside his music, then I say: 'Let me first hear that you have written beautiful music; if so, your program will be agreeable to me afterward.'"[7] Schumann's comments reflect the broad consensus of his time that a programmatic work ultimately had to stand on its intrinsically musical merits.

On this point even Wagner and Hanslick agreed: extramusical elements remained outside the true essence of music. Wagner considered program music a stepping-stone in music's historical trajectory from its complete—absolute—isolation toward a more precise and fully articulate form of expression. Beethoven, he declared, had already written the last purely instrumental symphony, and subsequent works of this kind represented nothing more than an inadequate and superfluous preservation of a superseded genre, with or without programs. Followers such as Uhlig and Brendel concurred. Uhlig, as noted earlier, had belittled not only "pure" or "absolute music" but "depictional, representational, descriptive music" as well, noting that Beethoven had eventually recognized the futility of both when he turned to a sung text in the finale of the Ninth. For Brendel, the Ninth represented the "self-liquidation" (*Selbstauflösung*) of instrumental music. He proposed as its motto the famous line from Schiller's poem *Das Lied von der Glocke*:

Nun zerbrecht mir das Gebäude,   Now break the mold for me,
Seine Absicht hat's erfüllt.   It has fulfilled its purpose.[8]

All this called into question the very legitimacy of any kind of instrumental music, and Liszt's "Harold" essay can be read as much as a response to Wagner, Uhlig, and Brendel as it is was to Hanslick. The aesthetics of program music

---

6. Robert Schumann, "'Aus dem Leben eines Künstlers': Phantastische Symphonie in fünf Abtheilungen von Hector Berlioz," *NZfM* 3 (14 August 1835): 50: "Solche Wegweiser behalten immer etwas unwürdiges und Charlatanmäßiges."

7. Robert Schumann, "Symphonieen für Orchester," *NZfM* 18 (1 May 1843): 140: "Hält uns daher ein Komponist vor seiner Musik ein Programm entgegen, so sag' ich: 'vor allem laß mich hören, daß du schöne Musik gemacht, hinterher soll mir auch dein Programm genehm sein.'"

8. Brendel, *Geschichte* (1852), 517. Richard Pohl would quote Brendel's Schillerian motto with approval in 1884 as encapsulating the Ninth's achievement of having "liberated instrumental music from the restrictions of form"; see his *Hektor Berlioz: Studien und Erinnerungen* (Leipzig: Bernhard Schlicke, 1884), 21.

provided a philosophical justification by which instrumental music—or at least a certain type of instrumental music—could participate in the "Music of the Future." With "program music," *Zukunftsmusiker* now had a convenient short-hand—a label, a slogan, in effect—to distinguish their repertory of instrumental music from that of the past. The very novelty of the term operated to its advantage and helped distinguish new works shaped around a poetic idea from what in earlier times had been called *malende Musik* or *Tonmalerei*, terms that had always carried with them a faint odor of superficiality. Critics and composers alike had long been wary of instrumental works that claimed to depict storms, battles, pastoral scenes, and the like. No serious composer had ever championed this kind of music, and when composers engaged in it, they were held to account, as in the case of what many considered Haydn's overly literal depictions of nature in *The Seasons* and the whole of Beethoven's "battle symphony," *Wellingtons Sieg*. When Beethoven indicated that his *Pastoral* Symphony was "more the expression of feeling than its depiction," he was anticipating and protecting himself against wholly predictable criticisms of *Malerei* over and against *Ausdruck*. Liszt's neologism helped a new generation of composers justify an approach to composition that incorporated *Poesie*—conceptual content and not merely superficial representation—into purely instrumental music without the overtones of simplistic "tone-painting." Liszt hailed program music as "a new hemisphere of art," and his enthusiasm was shared by others who were desperate to emphasize a break with tradition.[9]

That break, however, was not nearly as pronounced as Liszt portrayed it, for the aesthetics of program music ultimately rested on the same premise of transcendence that had figured so large in the earlier aesthetics of idealism. Very much in line with that tradition, Liszt believed in the ability of all music, absolute or program, to elevate listeners to a higher realm of consciousness. He was a disciple of the Abbé Felicité de Lamennais (1782–1854), whose *Esquisse d'une philosophie* (1840) reads very much like a tract by Schopenhauer, albeit with heavily Christian overtones. In his quest for a unitary theory of art connected to the universe, Lamennais proposed that art introduces man "through the medium of his senses to the world of the ideal, the direct intuition of which will later enrapture his developing intellect."[10] Music's "foundations and laws" are "eternally fixed" and are the "product of the union of the laws of physical and intellectual order." Music deals in "infinite beauty" and as a result "tends

9. Liszt, "Berlioz und seine Haroldsymphonie," *NZfM* 43 (20 July 1855), 42: "Die Gegenfüßler dieser neuen Kunsthemisphäre." For an account of the ways in which Liszt was negotiating a theory of instrumental music compatible with Wagner's Zurich writings, see Winkler, "Der 'bestimmte Ausdruck.'"

10. Lamennais, *Esquisse d'une philosophie*, 4 vols. (Paris: Pagnerre, 1840–1846), 3:154: "Elle l'introduit par la sensation dans le monde idéal, dont la direct intuition ravira plus tard son intelligence progressive." Translation from Le Huray and Day, *Music and Aesthetics*, 519.

to represent the ideal model, the eternal essence of things, rather than things as they are."[11]

Liszt adopted this same approach in his writings on program music. Its power, he argued, lay less in its ability to depict a specific object than in its capacity to use that object to point toward a higher plane of ideality. He repeatedly emphasized the link between the tangible and the ideal in his writings on music. In the preface to his *Album d'un voyageur* (1842), he extolled transcendence as the means by which instrumental music might "free itself from its early fetters" and "bear the stamp of that ideality which marks the perfection of the plastic arts." With such advances, Liszt assured his readers, music would "cease to be a simple combination of tones and become a poetic language, one that, perhaps better than poetry itself, more readily expresses everything in us that moves beyond accustomed horizons, everything that eludes analysis, everything that stirs within the inaccessible depths of imperishable desires and presentiments of the infinite."[12] Transcendence plays a similarly central role in his later pronouncements on program music, including the essay on Berlioz's *Harold en Italie*, its more pointed tone notwithstanding. The purpose of a work's program is to guide the listener's mind not simply toward a specific idea, but rather through and beyond that idea to a state of transcendence. Without a program, the import of a work is left entirely to the fantasy of the individual listener. The program provides a frame of reference, a point of departure, but is not in itself a destination.

While Liszt's terminology was new, then, his argument was not, for its outlines had already been articulated on multiple occasions, most notably in a review-essay published shortly before by the composer, poet, and critic Peter Cornelius (1824–1874), Liszt's protégé in Weimar. Like other proponents of the "Music of the Future," Cornelius made history the basis of his aesthetics.[13] It was the destiny of the art, he declared, to move beyond the level of mere

---

11. Lamennais, *Esquisse d'une philosophie*, 3:135: "Ces lois résultant de l'union des lois de l'ordre physique et des lois de l'ordre intellectuel"; ibid., 3:310: "La musique a pour terme le Beau infini, et, dès-lors, ce qu'elle représente, ce qu'elle tend à reproduire, ce ne sont point les choses telles qu'elles sont, mais leur type éternel, le modèle idéal qu'elles recouvrent, en quelque manière." Translations from Le Huray and Day, *Music and Aesthetics*, 519, 520.

12. Franz Liszt, "Avant-propos" to *Album d'un voyageur* (1842), reproduced in facsimile in Liszt, *Album d'un voyageur I, III; Clochette et Carnaval de Venise*, ed. Adrienne Kaczmarczyk and Imre Mező (Budapest: Editio Musica, 2007), xlviii: "À mesure que la musique instrumentale progresse, se développe, se dégage des premières entraves, elle tend à s'empreindre de plus en plus de cette idéalité qui a marqué la perfection des arts plastiques, à devenir non plus une simple combinaison de sons, mais un langage poétique plus apte peut-être que la poésie elle-même à exprimer tout ce qui en nous franchit les horizons accoutumés; tout ce qui échappe à l'analyse; tout ce qui s'agite à des profondeurs inaccessibles de désirs impérissables, de pressentiments infinis."

13. On Cornelius's aesthetics in general, see James Deaville, "Peter Cornelius als Kritiker und Essayist," in Peter Cornelius, *Gesammelte Aufsätze: Gedanken über Musik und Theater, Poesie und bildende Kunst*, ed. Günter Wagner and James Deaville (Mainz: Schott, 2004), 17–50.

entertainment and convey unprecedented specificity in expressing thought and emotion. In the realm of instrumental music, this meant giving the listener some indication of the "poetic content" of a work, either through a distinctive title or a verbal program of some kind. Beethoven himself had at times specified this content, as in the *Coriolan, Leonore,* and *Egmont* Overtures. On other occasions, however, as in the Fifth Symphony, he had left it to the arbitrariness of listener's imagination as to what we might feel or think, even though such a work incorporated "the most complete logical sequence of ideas" (*der vollständigst logische Gedankengang*). The question of whether or not a composer should follow the technical conventions of form or give expression to a poetic idea, Cornelius maintained, divided the musical world into two camps.

> The first considers music a fantastical play of tones according to the rules of euphony and aesthetic laws derived from the specifically musical works of Haydn, Mozart, and Beethoven... such as unity in variety, clarity and proportion of forms and means, etc. According to this party, music achieves its effect through itself, without the mediation of accessory ideas; it elevates the soul out of the narrowness of life to ideal heights, rinsing away through its waves of tone, as it were, all the rot and triflings of life.... [The second camp] is no longer content to arouse vague feelings in the layperson.... It desires instead to take as its material the rich treasures of myth, of the Bible, of history, drawing on the inexhaustible source of one's own heart, the inner circumstances of its love, its passions, its struggles with the world.... It seeks to renounce the freedom of absolute music and its associated servitude to conventional forms in order to win a freedom of form by giving itself over to a specific poetic object. Even if the representation of a specific object runs the risk of remaining imperfect in certain respects... this camp considers such effort more beneficial than a constant refilling of superseded forms with vague feelings.[14]

14. Peter Cornelius, review of Richard Würst, *Preis-Sinfonie,* op. 21, *NZfM* 41 (8 December 1854): 258–59: "Diese Frage theilt noch heute die musikalische Welt in zwei Parteien. Der einen ist die Musik ein phantastisches Spiel in Tönen nach Regeln des Wohllautes und ästhetischen Gesetzen, die aus den specifisch-musikalischen Werken Haydn's, Mozart's und Beethoven's, so weit er ihrer Spur folgte, abgeleitet sind, als: Einheit in der Mannichfaltigkeit, Klarheit und Maaß in Formen und Mitteln usw. Nach ihr soll die Musik durch sich selbst wirken ohne vermittelnde Nebengedanken; sie soll die Seele aus dem engen Leben zu idealen Höhen emporheben, mit ihren Tonwellen gleichsam allen Moder und Quark des Lebens aus ihr wegspülen.... Die andere Partei... will sich nicht länger damit begnügen, unbestimmte Gefühle in dem Laien zu erregen.... Sie will aus dem reichen Schatz, dem Mythus, Bibel, Geschichte, und der unerschöpflichen poetischen Quelle, die das eigene Herz, die innerlichen Begebenheiten seiner Liebe, seiner Leidenschaften, seiner Kämpfe mit der Welt und dem Leben bietet, ihre Stoffe entnehmen.... Sie will der Freiheit absoluter Musik zugleich mit der Knechtschaft ihrer stehenden Formen entsagen, um dafür in einer Gefangengebung an einen bestimmten poetischen Gegenstand Freiheit der Form zu erringen. Selbst auf die Gefahr hin, in Darstellung dieses bestimmten Gegenstandes nach gewissen Seiten hin ebenso unvollkommen zu bleiben... halten sie ihr Bestreben für lohnender, als behufs einer Anregung unbestimmter Gefühle ausgelebte Formen immer wieder auf's Neue anzufüllen." For further commentary on this passage, see Gerhard J. Winkler, "Der 'bestimmte

Absolute music, according to Cornelius, offers more pleasure to the connoisseur than to the amateur. Those who understand the technicalities of music can appreciate the intricacies of harmony, orchestration, and counterpoint as they listen to a given work, but those who do not can sense little more than an arousal of vague feelings. (This had been one of Hegel's chief arguments about the limited reach of purely instrumental music.) In addition to being isolated, then, absolute music is also elitist—a charged accusation in the aftermath of the Revolutions of 1848-49. Liszt would make a similar point in his "Harold" essay: through festivals and public events, music has become more readily accessible to a wider audience, and composers and public alike felt the need for an Ariadne's thread that could lead them through the labyrinth of a work of music without a sung text.[15]

In spite of its length, the "Harold" essay adds little to Cornelius's basic argument. Liszt's novel contribution was to coin an antonym to Wagner's retronym, a new term to denote all music that was not absolute. In an age of slogans, every position needed its shorthand to proclaim its cause, and *Programmmusik* served its purpose well.[16]

Having earlier expressed their views on the limitations of instrumental music, Brendel and Wagner quickly accepted Liszt's new term and his philosophical justifications for it. (Uhlig had died in early January 1853 at the age of thirty.) In 1856 Brendel declared "modern program music" a "calling" (*Aufgabe*) of the present day, a "natural consequence" of music's development over time. History itself, he maintained, is a struggle of New and Old, and absolute music was very much a product of the Old, having achieved its high point in the music of Mozart.[17] In the third edition of his history of music (1860), Brendel would replace his earlier description of purely instrumental music as "superseded" with an enthusiastic account of Liszt's symphonic poems and the principles of program music in general.[18] Wagner,

---

Ausdruck': Zur Musikästhetik der Neudeutschen Schule," in *Liszt und die Neudeutsche Schule*, ed. Detlef Altenburg (Laaber: Laaber-Verlag, 2006), 39–53; and Garratt, *Music, Culture and Social Reform*, 179–80.

15. Liszt, "Berlioz und seine Haroldsymphonie," *NZfM* 43 (20 July 1855), 39. On the ensuing polemics between the followers of Liszt and Hanslick, see Markus Gärtner, *Eduard Hanslick versus Franz Liszt: Aspekte einer grundlegenden Kontroverse* (Hildesheim: Olms, 2005); idem, "Der Hörer im Visier: Hanslick und Liszt im Prinzipienstreit über die wahre Art, Musik zu verstehen," in Hanslick, *Sämtliche Schriften*, vol. 1, part 5, *Aufsätze und Rezensionen, 1859–1861*, ed. Dietmar Strauß (Vienna: Böhlau, 2005), 457–68.

16. On the importance of slogans in the polemics of the 1850s, including such phrases as *Zukunftsmusik* and *überwundener Standpunkt* (to which may be added *absolute Musik, tönend bewegte Formen*, and *Programmmusik*), see Christa Jost and Peter Jost, "'Zukunftsmusik': Zur Geschichte eines Begriffs," *Musiktheorie* 10 (1995), 133 n. 19. On slogans in German culture and politics in general during this same time, see Wulf Wülfing, *Schlagworte des Jungen Deutschland* (Berlin: Erich Schmidt, 1982).

17. Franz Brendel, "Programmmusik," *Anregungen für Kunst, Leben und Wissenschaft* 1 (1856): 86. See also Brendel's "Der Kampf des Alten und Neuen," *Anregungen* 1 (1856): 45–47, which cites Hanslick and his treatise by name. Brendel and Richard Pohl were coeditors of the *Anregungen*.

18. Brendel, *Geschichte der Musik*, 3rd ed. (Leipzig: Heinrich Matthes, 1860), 596–601; see Deaville, "Controversy," 105.

in turn, endorsed Liszt's terminology and his aesthetics of instrumental music in an open letter published in the *Neue Zeitschrift für Musik* in April 1857. He acknowledged that in the proper hands, poetic sources of inspiration such as "the deeds and sufferings of Orpheus, Prometheus, etc." could be transformed into "more highly individualized representations" (*höhere individualisirte Vorstellungen*), and he praised Liszt for having shown the possibilities of such an approach.[19] Wagner's change of heart can be traced in part to his personal loyalty to Liszt, in part to his recent discovery of the writings of Schopenhauer (see chapter 12).

Liszt's theory of program music found important additional support from the renowned philosopher Friedrich Theodor Vischer.[20] In his commentary on music in his *Ästhetik* (1857), Vischer quotes with approval Hanslick's observation that the union of words and music is like a morganatic marriage but then immediately adds that the emotional "purity" of instrumental music prevents it from achieving its fullest aesthetic potential. In listening to instrumental music, one has "the feeling of an unsolved riddle," something like a "progression through an Egyptian temple, from forecourt to forecourt, without ever arriving at a center." He compares the impression made by instrumental music to that made by a painting that overprivileges color: "one longs for the firm ground of line," a more specific delineation of an object. The depth of emotions reveals itself best through consciousness: "Only in connection with specific objects is the full richness of the world of emotions opened to us."[21]

19. Wagner, "Ein Brief von Richard Wagner über Franz Liszt," *NZfM* 46 (10 April 1857): 161. The letter was later published in Wagner's collected prose works under the title "Über Franz Liszts symphonische Dichtungen"; see *GSD*, 5:192.

20. On Vischer's aesthetics of music, see Titus, "Conceptualizing Music." On the relationship between Hanslick and Vischer specifically—the two were personal acquaintances—see Lothar Schneider, "Form versus Gehalt: Konturen des intellektuellen Feldes im späten 19. Jahrhundert," in *Eduard Hanslick zum Gedenken: Bericht des Symposions zum Anlass seines 100. Todestages*, ed. Theophil Antonicek, Gernot Gruber, and Christoph Landerer (Tutzing: Hans Schneider, 2010), 45–47.

21. Vischer, *Ästhetik*, vol. 3, part 1, *Die Kunstlehre*, 4. Heft, *Die Musik* (Stuttgart: Carl Mäcken, 1857), 830 (§764): "Ein Gefühl eines ungelösten Räthsels, ein Gang wie durch einen ägyptischen Tempel von Vorhof zu Vorhof ohne ein Anlangen bei einem Kerne.... Dieser Eindruck gleicht jenem, den die einseitige höchste Ausbildung des Colorits in der Malerei mit sich führt, die wir eine gefährliche Spitze genannt haben: man sehnt sich nach dem festen Boden der Zeichnung, der bestimmteren Geltung des Objects. Auch würden nimmermehr alle Tiefen des Gefühls sich entfalten ohne das begleitende Bewußtsein. An bestimmten Gegenständen erst schießt der ganze Reichthum der Gefühlswelt auf." Vischer's multivolume set appeared in installments between 1846 and 1858; on the work's complicated publication history, see Titus, "Conceptualizing Music," 15–16. Although Karl Köstlin wrote most of the section on music in Vischer's treatise, Vischer himself wrote the introductory section ("Vom Wesen der Musik") from which the passage quoted here is taken. Georg Gottfried Gervinus quotes portions of this passage approvingly in Gervinus, *Händel und Shakespeare: Zur Ästhetik der Tonkunst* (Leipzig: Wilhelm Engelmann, 1868), 171, just before launching into an attack on Vom Musikalisch-Schönen (172–73). On the ideological motivations behind Gervinus's account of Handel and later instrumental music, see James Garratt, "Composing Useful Histories: Music Historiography and the Practical Past," in *Konstruktivität von Musikgeschichtsschreibung: Zur Formation musikbezogenen Wissens*, ed. Sandra Danielczyk, Ina Knoth, and Lisbeth Suhrcke (Hildesheim: Olms, 2012), 123–39.

Hanslick took up the term "program music" as well. He used it often in his musical criticism, beginning as early as 1857, and even incorporated it into *Vom Musikalisch-Schönen* in a footnote added to the third edition (1865).[22] If a work of instrumental music evoked any sort of verbal program or evocative title, it was no longer a work of "pure" music but rather a hybrid manifestation of multiple arts, and the designation of "program music" indicated that hybrid status. Hanslick denied that such titles or programs could in any way affect a work's true content, which was audible and purely musical.[23] In the preface to the second edition of his treatise, he quietly introduced the term "extramusical" (*außermusikalisch*) as yet another means by which to identify implicitly "impure" elements in any work of music.[24]

By the end of the 1850s, the use of the terms "absolute" and "program" music to indicate contrasting repertories had become standard elements of discourse about the nature of music. It was a binary division accepted and used by most parties on both sides of the debate. No term ever emerged as a true counterpart to Wagner's original concept of absolute music as music of any kind—instrumental or vocal—that existed entirely for its own sake. But Wagner himself was inconsistent in his use of the term and more often than not used it as a synonym for purely instrumental music. It was in this sense that Liszt had proposed the new term, and it was in this sense that it proved most useful in the ideological struggle that followed.

---

22. Hanslick, "Oulibicheff über Beethoven," in Hanslick, *Sämtliche Schriften*, vol. 1, part 4, 113; originally published in *Die Presse* (Vienna), 17 June 1857. *VMS*, 1: 91; *OMB*, 38.

23. See *VMS*, 1:53: "Sogar Tonstücke mit bestimmten Ueberschriften oder Programmen müssen wir ablehnen, wo es sich um den 'Inhalt' der Musik handelt." *OMB*, 15.

24. *VMS*, 1:10; not in *OMB*. On the problematic nature of the term "extramusical" (*außermusikalisch*), see Lydia Goehr, *The Quest for Voice*, especially chapter 1 ("Secrecy and Silence").

11 Polemics

Armed with new nouns that aligned philosophical concepts with specific repertories, critics debated the superiority of absolute and program music in a spirit
of intense partisanship throughout the remainder of the nineteenth century. As
in ideological disputes of all kinds, each party tended to misrepresent the other's views. Self-styled progressives routinely described the "forms" of absolute
music as "rigid," "rulebound," and "outmoded," while self-styled traditionalists
dismissed program music as inherently "formless" and "unmusical." Such differences reflected more than simply a contrast of aesthetic outlooks, for the debate
about music was part of a larger culture war in a period of enormous social, political, and technological change. One side perceived the arts as an instrument of
reform, the other as a refuge from those very same forces of change.

Critical responses to *Vom Musikalisch-Schönen* occupied center stage in this
debate.[1] Within ten months of its publication in late September 1854, three substantial rebuttals had appeared in print: Franz Brendel's lengthy review, published
serially from mid-February through early March 1855 in the *Neue Zeitschrift für
Musik*; August Wilhelm Ambros's *Die Grenzen der Musik und Poesie*, issued in
May or June 1855; and Franz Liszt's "Harold" essay, also published serially in the
Neue Zeitschrift für Musik, in July and August 1855 (see chapter 10).

Brendel's review set the tone for the debate by mixing hostility with civility. He
welcomed Hanslick's text as the basis for a productive discussion of the issues and
to this end provided a detailed summary of its content. He praised the treatise's attempt to deal with aesthetics in a more "objective" fashion and lauded its acknowledgment of the difficulty of expressing specific concepts through purely musical
techniques. This pursuit of objectivity, however, implicitly endorsed a theory of
transcendence, whereas music's *Geist*, Brendel argued, is an immanent quality; indeed, the *Geist* of the composer himself resides in the notes.[2] The true content of
music is not *tönend bewegte Formen* but *Stimmungen der Seele* ("feelings of the soul").
Hanslick "is too little acquainted with the idiom of music; he steps forward here too

---

1. For an overview of the work's reception, see James Deaville, "Negotiating the 'Absolute': Hanslick's
Path Through Music History," in *Rethinking Hanslick: Music, Formalism, and Expression*, ed. Nicole
Grimes, Siobhán Donovan, and Wolfgang Marx (Rochester, NY: University of Rochester Press,
2013), 15–37, especially 17–21. See also the appendix of the present study, "Hanslick's *Vom
Musikalischen-Schönen*: Early and Selected Later Responses."
2. Franz Brendel, Review of Eduard Hanslick, *Vom Musikalisch-Schönen*, NZfM 42 (16 February
1855): 80–82.

much merely as a man of science, as a systematizer."[3] It is when Brendel shifts from a philosophical to a historical perspective that he abandons this relatively tempered tone: Hanslick completely misunderstands the most recent tendencies of musical aesthetics and is now, Brendel ominously concludes, "our opponent."[4]

A similar juxtaposition of philosophy and ideology characterizes *Die Grenzen der Musik und Poesie* by the critic and historian August Wilhelm Ambros (1816–1876), who happened to be one of Hanslick's lifelong friends. In the Prague of their early years, they had both belonged to what they called (after Schumann) a "Davidsbund" of artistically minded youth.[5] By the mid-1850s, however, the two had gone their separate aesthetic ways. Ambros maintains in his treatise that *Poesie*—which for him meant the creative imagination in general and verbal imagination in particular—is the motivating force of the arts at all times and in all places, and that it is the purpose of music to give expression to *Poesie*.[6] He rejects a retreat into the aesthetics of the past. No one, Ambros insists, could fail to recognize that music had reached a critical juncture, and he sees a fundamental division among contemporary composers:

> Among creative musicians, one faction (by far the smaller) has retreated into older perspectives and forms, where it cultivates its modest plot of land according to the principles of the so-called "classical" era. It would be presumptuous to disturb this idyllic happiness; but it is equally clear that everything such well-intentioned persons can tell us has already been said better by others before them. This stunted aftergrowth—barely noticed by the world, fortunately—asserts itself parasitically among genuine, naturally growing plants.[7]

The opposing and larger faction, as Ambros sees it, strives to introduce "a trove of great extramusical ideas" into the medium of music. Just how these composers might actually accomplish this is not altogether clear, but their efforts are certainly preferable to the attempts of those who go on making new contributions to

---

3. Brendel, review of Hanslick, *Vom Musikalisch-Schönen*, 99: "Der Inhalt der Tonkunst sind die Stimmungen der Seele." "Der Verf[asser] ist zu wenig mit dem musikalischen Sprachgebrauch vertraut, er tritt zu sehr nur als Mann der Wissenschaft, als Systematiker hervor."

4. Brendel, review of Hanslick, *Vom Musikalisch-Schönen*, 100: "unser Gegner."

5. See Bonnie Lomnäs, Erling Lomnäs, and Dietmar Strauß, *Auf der Suche nach der poetischen Zeit: Der Prager Davidsbund; Ambros, Bach, Bayer, Hampel, Hanslick, Helfert, Heller, Hock, Ulm*, 2 vols. (Saarbrücken: Pfau, 1999).

6. August Wilhlelm Ambros, *Die Grenzen der Musik und Poesie: Eine Studie zur Aesthetik der Tonkunst* (Leipzig: Heinrich Matthes, 1855; reprint, Hildesheim: Olms, 1976), 12–13.

7. Ambros, *Die Grenzen der Musik und Poesie*, i–ii: "Von den schaffenden Tonkünstlern hat sich ein Theil (der bei weitem kleinere) in ältere Anschauungen und Formen zurückgeflüchtet und baut dort seinen bescheidenen Acker nach den Prinzipien der sogenannten 'klassischen' Zeit. Es wäre unbescheiden, dieses idyllische Glück stören zu wollen, aber eben so sicher ist es, daß alles, was solche wohlmeinende Leute uns sagen können, von anderen vor ihnen schon besser gesagt worden ist— diese kümmerliche, zum Glück von der Welt kaum beachtete Nachblüte, drängt sich schmarotzerhaft zwischen die echten, naturwüchsigen Pflanzen."

a "museum of mummified abstractions" that "thanks to their mummification have an almost eternal existence but no life."[8] Ambros takes Hanslick to task for insisting that the effects of music are a product of form. To support his case, he cites the oft-repeated anecdote about the grizzled French veteran of the Napoleonic Wars, who, upon hearing the opening fanfare of the finale of Beethoven's Fifth Symphony in a performance at the Paris Conservatory, was moved to rise from his seat and shout: "Vive l'empereur!" Ambros points out that E. T. A. Hoffmann, Hector Berlioz, Wolfgang Robert Griepenkerl, and A. B. Marx had all responded to this same moment in a similar (if less colorful) fashion. The effect of a work of art, he concludes, can thus be said to have a "specific and individual physiognomy": no one has ever called the *Eroica* unheroic or the *Pastoral* unpastoral, but if the title pages of the two had somehow been reversed before their publication, there would have been a great outcry of confusion. "Whoever denies all content of music outside of *tönend bewegte Formen* would not be able to acknowledge this contradiction," for "there is no such thing as a heroic arabesque, a heroic kaleidoscope, a heroic triangle or square....Moreover, the three-four meter, the key of E-flat, the tempo of Allegro, and anything else belonging to absolute musical form is in and of itself neither heroic nor unheroic."[9] From a purely formal perspective, Ambros argues, Mozart's G-minor and Beethoven's C-minor Symphonies "are entirely the same" in their number of movements, their modulatory outlines, and their general structure. Yet Napoleon's veteran would not have stood up at the beginning of Mozart's finale. Any explanation of the effect of Beethoven's symphony that rests on "the formal moment alone is therefore unsatisfactory." Wherever there is a specific effect, a specific response to a work of music, he insists, there must be a satisfactory explanation for that effect, and form by itself is insufficient to account for this. In the end, Ambros rejects altogether the idea of music—or any other art, for that matter—as a *Sonderkunst* operating entirely according to its own unique principles. The boundaries between the various arts cannot be surveyed as precisely as the boundaries between nations, and it is pointless for *Kunstphilosophen* to demarcate such lines as if they were members of a "border commission."[10]

Ambros's narrow interpretation of Hanslick's notion of form would prove typical for those opposed to the aesthetics of *Vom Musikalisch-Schönen*. "Form" was

8. Ambros, *Die Grenzen der Musik und Poesie*, iii: "Die Tonsetzer wollen ihren großen außermusikalischen Ideenreichthum in die Musik hineintragen." Ibid., vii: "das Museum mumienhafter Abstraktionen...die zwar, kraft der Mumisirung, fast ewige Dauer aber kein Leben haben."

9. Ambros, *Die Grenzen der Musik und Poesie*, 46–47: "eine sehr bestimmte, individuelle Physiognomie....Wer jeden andern Inhalt der Musik läugnet als eben nur tönend bewegte Formen hätte durchaus kein Recht in diesen Wiederspruch mit einzustimmen. Es gibt keine heroische Arabeske, kein heroisches Kaleidoskopbild, kein heroisches Dreieck oder Viereck....Auch der Dreivierteltakt, die Tonart Es-dur, die Bewegung Allegro, und was sonst der absoluten Tonform angehört, ist an sich weder heroisch noch nicht-heroisch."

10. Ambros, *Die Grenzen der Musik und Poesie*, 49: "Die Erklärung der Wirkung aus dem bloßen formalen Moment ist also nicht genügend." Ibid., 48, 185 ("Gränzkommission").

and remains an ambiguous term (see p. 147), and because Hanslick himself never attempted to define it, critics such as Ambros defined it for him over the next fifty years in ways that almost invariably equate the term with the conventions of large-scale structure operating at the level of an entire movement or even an entire multimovement work. These kinds of form, in turn, would typically be associated with "rules" (often "strict rules") and supposedly inviolable conventions.

Aside from Hanslick's friend Robert Zimmermann (see p. 163), Ludwig Bischoff, editor of the conservatively inclined *Rheinische Musik-Zeitung* and later of the *Niederrheinische Musik-Zeitung*, was Hanslick's most vocal defender. As early as 1850 Bischoff had co-opted Wagner's pejorative neologism of "absolute music" and made it a positive. In a lengthy serialized review that appeared in his own journal between mid-February and mid-March 1855, Bischoff reprinted the entire last chapter of *Vom Musikalisch-Schönen* word for word and hailed it as "a sign of the revival of musical reason." He recognized the partisan nature of the text and called attention to the similarity of Hanslick's thesis with his own earlier defense of music that existed for no sake other than its own. *Vom Musikalisch-Schönen*, he assured his readers, could serve as a bulwark against the "scientific nonage and babbling lunacy of that guardian-swarm of realist propaganda. We greet this dawn with joyous shouts."[11]

One of the few early responses to *Vom Musikalisch-Schönen* to rise above partisanship confronted the polemical nature of the argument on both sides. Otto Jahn, in an unsigned review published in *Die Grenzboten* in April 1855, recognized the treatise as an anti-Wagnerian tract and in the process took both Wagner and Hanslick to task for their questionable a priori assumptions about the nature of music. Jahn praised Hanslick's text for its "unusual philosophical insight" but rejected the idea that music could not give voice—both literally and figuratively—to emotions. He saw no reason why composers should not give works of instrumental music descriptive titles; at the same time, he saw nothing that should compel them to do so.[12]

For Jahn, as for so many early reviewers, the sticking point remained Hanslick's rhetoric of exclusion, which denied emotion any role in either the

---

11. Ludwig Bischoff, "Eduard Hanslick," *Niederrheinische Musik-Zeitung* 3 (10 March 1855): 75: "Seine Schrift ist uns ein Zeichen des Auflebens der tonkünstlerischen Vernunft gegen die wissenschaftliche Unmündigkeit und den faselnden Wahnsinn der Scharwächter der realistischen Propaganda; wir begrüssen dieses Morgenroth mit freudigem Zurufe."

12. Otto Jahn, "Aesthetische Feldzüge," *Die Grenzboten* 14, 2nd ser. (April 1855): 201. I am grateful to James Garratt of the University of Manchester for identifying Jahn as the author of this unsigned essay (personal communication, 10 August 2011), based on the close similarity between the passage in this review that discusses Metastasio (pp. 211–12) and Jahn's treatment of the same topic in the first volume of his biography of Mozart, published the following year (*W. A. Mozart*, vol. 1 [Leipzig: Breitkopf & Härtel, 1856], 267–70).

content or the essence of music. Even the majority of those critics who agreed with Hanslick about the inseparability of music's form and content could not accept the corollary that music's essence had nothing to do with the expression of emotions. Many critics considered this position intellectually sound but ultimately too cold-blooded to explain the effect of music's essence in any satisfactory way. In what would appear to be the earliest public response to *Vom Musikalisch-Schönen* in North America, "J. H.," writing in *Dwight's Journal of Music* in mid-1855, agreed wholeheartedly with Hanslick's argument that the means of musical expression are strictly musical yet insisted that what music expresses is human feeling.[13] Two years later, the pro-Wagnerian critic Franz Gerstenkorn would dismiss Hanslick's theory of music as "applied mathematics in disguise."[14]

The emptiness of form is another theme that runs through the negative responses to *Vom Musikalisch-Schönen*. The anonymous reviewer in Wolfgang Menzel's *Literaturblatt* was one of many who pointed out that Hanslick's own examples of visual images without content—the kaleidoscope and the arabesque—are themselves empty and without meaning. "There is no such thing as music pure and simple and there has never been such a thing," the reviewer declared. Music is the "language of a higher state of being" and stands in relation to verbal language as sleepwalking does to ordinary wakefulness. "Music ennobles. Music elevates, as it were, from the everyday world into the world of the spirit."[15]

Nor did the tirades against *Vom Musikalisch-Schönen* soon diminish. Johann Christian Lobe issued an extended and at times openly sarcastic response in his *Fliegende Blätter für Musik* in 1857.[16] In an unusual postscript that appeared in the next issue of the journal, Lobe published the score to an original composition of his own, a four-voice fugue in C minor for keyboard under the heading "Once Again in Opposition to Dr. Hanslick—in Notes."[17] This may have been in response to Hanslick's claim that "an entire category of music lovers" concedes that "no one

13. J. H., "Music the Exponent of Emotion," *Dwight's Journal of Music*, 21 July 1855, 123–24.

14. Franz Gerstenkorn, "Dr. Hanslick und der 'Tannhäuser,'" *NZfM* 47 (30 October 1857): 193: "eine verkappte angewandte Mathematik."

15. Anonymous, "Ueber Musik," *Wolfgang Menzels Literaturblatt*, 25 April 1855, 131, 132: "Es gibt keine Musik schlechthin und hat nie eine gegeben.... [S]ie verhält sich zur gemeinen Sprache fast wie das magnetische Schlafwachen zum gemeinen Wachen. Es ist die Sprache höherer Wesen. Die Musik adelt. Die Musik erhebt gewissermaßen aus der gemeinen Welt in die Geisterwelt."

16. Johann Christian Lobe, "Gegen Dr. Eduard Hanslick's 'Vom Musikalisch-Schönen,'" *Fliegende Blätter für Musik* 2 (1857): 65–106. The review was reissued separately as a pamphlet under the same title later that year by Baumgärtner of Leipzig. On Lobe's aesthetics, see Torsten Brandt, *Johann Christian Lobe (1797–1881): Studien zu Biographie und musikschriftstellerischem Werk* (Göttingen: Vandenhoeck & Ruprecht, 2002).

17. Johann Christian Lobe, "Noch einmal gegen Dr. Hanslick—in Noten," *Fliegende Blätter für Musik* 2 (1857): 183–89.

can demonstrate an emotion" in any of the forty-eight preludes and fugues in Bach's *Well-Tempered Clavier.*[18]

The following year saw the publication of yet another book-length refutation of Hanslick's aesthetics, this time by the critic Adolph Kullak (1823–1862), co-editor of the *Berliner Musik-Zeitung.* So that there could be no mistake about the target of his attack, he called his treatise *Das Musikalisch-Schöne: Ein Beitrag zur Aesthetik der Tonkunst.* Like Hanslick, Kullak claimed to take a nonpartisan approach; but the claim was once again transparently untrue, for he clearly sympathized with the aesthetics (and the music) of Wagner and Liszt. Kullak opens his text with the declaration that "Musical beauty is a part of beauty in general," thereby confronting Hanslick's premise of music as a *Sonderkunst,* an art with its own specific kind of beauty unrelated to any other.[19] Kullak believes that music is capable of expressing a content, which is a mood (*Stimmung*). He accepts Hanslick's arguments about musical purity and about what instrumental music can and cannot "do" but uses this very point as a fulcrum with which to argue that every mode of human expression has its weaknesses and shortcomings and that for this reason every art stands in need of assistance. The deficiencies of any one art in isolation argue in favor of its combination with other arts into an integrated whole, and it is on these grounds that Kullak heartily endorses the idea of program music. His treatise's final, Hegelian sentence resonates with the first in both its brevity and content: "Nothing individual is the highest, only the whole."[20]

Philosophers were quick to weigh in as well. In a review of Ambros's *Die Grenzen der Musik und Poesie,* Moriz Carrière (1817–1895), professor of philosophy at the University of Munich, praised Ambros for having exposed the "empty formalism" of *Vom Musikalisch-Schönen.* There is no such thing as musical form in and of itself, Carrière argues: there must always be a content. "I would remind those enthusiasts of mere pleasure through the play of forms that tone is not merely an expression of our feeling, but is itself a feeling we have."[21] Carrière would attack *Vom Musikalisch-Schönen* even more forcefully two years later in his own treatise on aesthetics. It is clear from the very start, he observes, that "we are dealing here with an author who mostly ignores the Kantian critique or who considers its perspective superseded, not in the sense that others might have gone beyond them, but in the sense that it is considered false."[22] Carrière admits that he would not have given so much attention to *Vom Musikalisch-Schönen*

18. *VMS,* 2:21; *OMB,* 14.

19. Adolph Kullak, *Das Musikalisch-Schöne: Ein Beitrag zur Aesthetik der Tonkunst* (Leipzig: Heinrich Matthes, 1858), 1: "Das musikalisch-Schöne ist ein Theil des allgemeinen Schönen."

20. Kullak, *Das Musikalisch-Schöne,* 272: "Kein Einzelnes ist das Höchste, sondern das Ganze."

21. Carrière, "Populäre Aesthetik," 419: "Ich möchte die Anhänger des bloßen Ergötzens am Formenspiel daran erinnern, daß der Ton nicht blos Ausdruck unserer Empfindung, sondern überhaupt eine Empfindung von uns ist."

22. Carrière, *Aesthetik: Die Idee des Schönen,* 2 vols. (Leipzig: F. A. Brockhaus, 1859), 2:322: "Schon die ersten Zeilen zeigen daß wir es mit einem Schriftsteller zu thun haben welcher die Kantische Kritik

had it not been the object of so much praise. He sees the entire work as an over-reaction to the sobering events of 1848–49, which in turn had provided an overly fertile breeding ground for realism in place of the "empty dreams" of earlier years.[23]

It was also in 1857 that Friedrich Theodor Vischer, one of the most respected philosophers of his generation, issued the volume of his ongoing *Aesthetik* that included an account of music.[24] Vischer conceded that he had no technical understanding of music, and he delegated most of this portion of his text to Karl Reinhold von Köstlin (1819–1894), who taught theology, aesthetics, and art history at the University of Tübingen; Köstlin would later go on to write his own, entirely independent *Aesthetik*.[25] Vischer himself, however, wrote the extended introductory section titled "The Essence of Music in General," and it is here that he engages with *Vom Musikalisch-Schönen*.[26] He applauds Hanslick's insistence that form and content in music cannot be separated, but he maintains that this does not mean that the two concepts are identical. To call the ordering of tones "form," and to call "form" the "content of music," Vischer maintains, amounts to little more than a tautology. Tone and emotion must remain distinct if we are to argue for their unity. Instrumental music exists because words alone cannot always express emotions, and these sounding emotions are the content of music.[27]

Ambros was not the only friend of Hanslick's youth who would take issue with his treatise. Yet another book-length assault came from the pen of Graf Ferdinand Peter Laurencin (1819–1890), likewise a piano pupil of Tomášek in Prague and in later years also a critic. In a 227-page monograph published in 1859 and dedicated to Liszt, Laurencin praises Hanslick for his prose style but otherwise finds fault with almost every one of the many passages he quotes from the treatise. He accuses Hanslick at various points of tautology, contradiction, inconsistency, sophistry, general ignorance, gross materialism, and naïveté.[28] He dismisses the "materialistic" account of Beethoven's *Prometheus* overture as "hair-raising…the most

---

vornehm ignorirt oder für einen überwundenen Standpunkt hält, nicht in dem Sinne, daß man von demselben aus weiter gegangen wäre, sondern daß man ihn für falsch ansieht." Carrière was clearly responding to the first edition of the treatise.

23. Carrière, *Aesthetik*, 327, 328.

24. Vischer, *Aesthetik, oder Wissenschaft des Schönen*, part 3, *Die Kunstlehre*, sec. 2, *Die Künste*, vol. 4, *Die Musik* (Stuttgart: Carl Mäcken, 1857).

25. Tübingen: H. Laupp, 1869.

26. Vischer, *Aesthetik*, part 3, sec. 2, vol. 4, 775–840 (§746–66): "Das Wesen der Musik: α. Ueberhaupt."

27. Vischer, *Aesthetik*, part 3, sec. 2, vol. 4, 790–91; 829.

28. Ferdinand Peter Graf von Laurencin, *Dr. Eduard Hanslick's Lehre vom Musikalisch-Schönen: Eine Abwehr* (Leipzig: Heinrich Matthes, 1859). Laurencin was a frequent contributor to the *NZfM*; he became the journal's principal correspondent from Vienna in the 1860s, and his treatise, not surprisingly, received a highly favorably notice in the pages of that journal: see *NZfM* 52 (13 January 1860): 20–21. Selmar Bagge reviewed the work in highly negative terms in the *Deutsche Musik-Zeitung* 1 (11 February

ghastly thing I have ever encountered in the field of musical analysis."[29] Laurencin's core objection to *Vom Musikalisch-Schönen* is its author's penchant for separating thoughts and feelings too sharply, even while ascribing the powers of music to *Geist*, which as Laurencin argues, cannot be "atomized" into functionally distinct subunits: "*Geist* is the interpenetration, the inseparable reconciliation of understanding, feeling, imagination, reason.... Whenever *Geist* operates, then all its separate radii operate together."[30]

Wagner, for his part, attacked Hanslick openly in 1869 in a lengthy afterword to *Das Judenthum in der Musik*, where he added the critic's name to the list of those who had conspired against him, alongside Meyerbeer, Mendelssohn, and Offenbach. (Hanslick's mother had converted to Christianity from Judaism before her marriage.) Wagner compounded his anti-Semitic rant with factual error: he claims to have been told by Friedrich Theodor Vischer himself that it was Hanslick who had written the section of Vischer's *Aesthetik* dealing with music, though in fact it was Karl Reinhold von Köstlin.[31] Wagner condemns Vischer, "our thoroughly blond German aesthetician," for having granted "the musically Jewish-Beautiful" access "into the heart of a full-blooded Germanic system of aesthetics."[32] The "most singular and difficult questions of musical aesthetics," of which the "greatest philosophers" had always spoken with "conjectural uncertainty," had now become "complete dogma" through the concept of the "musically Jewish-Beautiful," propagated by a few "Jews and duped Christians."[33] Wagner's notion that the idea of autonomous musical beauty is somehow "Jewish" reflects his lifelong obsession with the belief that Jewish

1860): 53. Hanslick himself responded to the text in a slightly humorous and condescendingly benevolent notice in *Die Presse*, 24 January 1860, p. 2.

29. Laurencin, *Dr. Eduard Hanslick's Lehre vom Musikalisch-Schönen*, 53: "Nun aber kommt das Gräulichste, was mir je auf dem Felde musikalischer Analysis entgegengetreten. Ich meine die haarsträubende, materielle Art, in welcher Beethovens Prometheus-Ouvertüre zergliedert wird."

30. Laurencin, *Dr. Eduard Hanslick's Lehre vom Musikalisch-Schönen*, 15: "Der Geist ist das Ineinander, die untrennbarste Versöhnung von Verstand, Gemüth, Phantasie, Vernunft.... Wirkt der Geist, so wirken ihm vereint alle seine gesonderten Radien."

31. Vischer had in fact acknowledged the nature and extent of Köstlin's collaboration in print in 1857 in the preface to the final volume of his *Aesthetik*; see Vischer, *Aesthetik*, part 3, sec. 2., vol. 5, *Die Dichtkunst* (Stuttgart: Carl Mäcken, 1857), ix. This makes Wagner's assertion about Hanslick's participation in Vischer's treatise all the more puzzling. Hanslick himself refuted Wagner on this point (and many others) in his review of *Das Judenthum in der Musik* in the *Neue freie Presse*, 9 March 1869, 1–3.

32. Wagner, *Das Judenthum in der Musik* (Leipzig: J. J. Weber, 1869), 47: "einem gutartigen, durchaus blonden deutschen Aesthetiker, Herrn Vischer"; "die musikalische Judenschönheit mitten im Herzen eines vollblutig germanischen Systems der Aesthetik." This afterword, in the form of a letter to the dedicatee, Marie Muchanoff, was later published under the title "Aufklärungen über das Judentum in der Musik" in *GSD*; see 8:252–53. Wagner had originally issued the main portion of the essay under the pseudonym "Karl Freigedenk" in the *NZfM* in 1850.

33. Wagner, *Das Judenthum in der Musik*, 47: "die eigenthümlichsten und schwierigsten Fragen der Aesthetik der Musik, über welche die größten Philosophen... sich stets nur noch mit mutmaßender Unsicherheit geäußert hatten, wurden von Juden und übertölpelten Christen jetzt mit einer Sicherheit zur Hand genommen."

identity is unconnected to any specific national culture. The composer and violinist Alexander Ritter (1833–1896), the husband of one of Wagner's nieces, would expand on this line of thought in an essay that appeared in the *Bayreuther Blätter* in 1890 and that also cites Hanslick by name. Ritter distinguished between an "Aryan" view of music as expressive and metaphysical over and against a "Semitic" view based on dry technicalities.[34] Neither Wagner's nor Ritter's association of absolute music and Jewishness ever found much traction among musicians or the public at large, however. If anything, the absence of overt cultural markers in the repertory of nonprogrammatic instrumental music created what many Jewish musicians of the time, both amateur and professional, perceived to be a cultural space that transcended any one specific race, religion, or nationality, at least in theory.[35]

Wagner continued his rant against Hanslick a few years later in an open letter to the critic Friedrich Stade (1844–1928), published in the *Musikalisches Wochenblatt* in early 1871. Stade had recently issued a rebuttal to *Vom Musikalisch-Schönen*, and Wagner publicly thanked him for having recognized that even as "sophistic, flea-bitten a work... as that by Herr Hanslick" deserved refutation, given its "alarming" influence in the musical world.[36]

Histories of music, as we have seen (chapter 9), became yet another contested space for the advocates and opponents of Hanslick's theories. Brendel began to incorporate attacks on *Vom Musikalisch-Schönen* into his *Geschichte der Musik* as early as the second edition (1855), while Joseph Schlüter, in his *Allgemeine Geschichte der Musik in übersichtlicher Darstellung* (1863), praised Hanslick for demonstrating that music, like all other arts, has no end other than to "present pure beauty," that its "content and form are one in the same," and that "imagination" (*Phantasie*) is "the true organ of beauty."[37] Heinrich Adolf Köstlin, as noted earlier, pointedly opened his *Geschichte der Musik im Umriß* (1875) with what amounts to a two-sentence summary of Hanslick's treatise and structured his

34. Alexander Ritter, "Drei Kapitel: Von Franz Liszt, von der 'heiligen Elisabeth' in Karlsruhe, und von unserm ethischen Defekt," *Bayreuther Blätter* 12 (1890): 380.

35. See Nicholas Cook, *The Schenker Project: Culture, Race, and Music Theory in Fin-de-Siècle Vienna* (New York: Oxford University Press, 2007), 246–48.

36. Friedrich Stade, *Vom Musikalisch-Schönen: Mit Bezug auf Dr. E. Hanslick's gleichnamige Schrift* (Leipzig: C. F. Kahnt, 1871). Stade's text had originally appeared in serial form in the *Neue Zeitschrift für Musik* in the summer of 1870. Richard Wagner, "Offener Brief an Dr. phil. Friedrich Stade," *Musikalisches Wochenblatt* 13 January 1871; *SSD* 16:103–8: "Daß auch die philosophische Beurteilung der Musik von dieser Seite aus betrieben wurde, war beängstigend; aber wirklich geschah es, und mit welchem Erfolge, haben Sie selbst, geehrtester Herr, lebhaft erkannt, da Sie sich bemüssigt fühlten, einer sophistisch-flausenhaften Arbeit, wie der des Herrn Hanslick, eine tief und gründlich eingehende Beachtung zu schenken."

37. Joseph Schlüter, *Allgemeine Geschichte der Musik in übersichtlicher Darstellung* (Leipzig: Wilhelm Engelmann, 1863), 115: "Hanslick... beweist, daß die Musik wie jede andere Kunst nichts anderes darzustellen habe, als die reine Schönheit, daß bei ihr Inhalt und Form Eins und die Phantasie das eigentliche Organ des Schönen sei."

teleological narrative around the quest for the musically beautiful.[38] The confluence of history and aesthetics in opposition to Hanslick is on full display in Ludwig von Ganting's openly pro-Wagnerian *Die Grundzüge der musikalischen Richtungen in ihrer geschichtlichen Entwicklung* (1876), a thirty-six-page pamphlet that condenses the history of music since the Middle Ages into a series of events culminating in the opening of the Festspielhaus in Bayreuth. Ganting devotes two and a half pages—more than 10 percent of his text—to a denunciation of *Vom Musikalisch-Schönen*. The "artistic conflict of our time," he declares, stems from the inability of critics and theorists to keep up with the most recent developments in music, a tendency he traces throughout history. Hanslick, he points out, makes no mention at all of the many works with programmatic titles by such acknowledged masters as Mendelssohn and Schumann. Hanslick's ruthlessly "scientific" approach "throws out the baby with the bathwater."[39]

Even accounts limited to much earlier repertories could provoke ideological quarrels. In the first volume of his epochal biography of J. S. Bach (1870), for example, Philip Spitta attacked program music in his account of a lost work by Dietrich Buxtehude (ca. 1637–1707) that no one had seen for well over a century, a set of seven keyboard suites said to have depicted the "nature or quality of the planets."[40] Spitta rejected the idea that a composer of Buxtehude's stature might have thereby created "a paradigm of tasteless program music" and instead used the reported existence of these works to remind readers that the seven planets known at the time (which included the sun and moon) were believed to embody characteristic features that influenced the lives and fortunes of humans. In contrast to the superfluous titles François Couperin had added to his sarabandes and allemandes (Spitta cites as examples "La Majesteuse" and "La Tenebreuse"), Buxtehude's suites—even though they had long since disappeared—exhibit

> a much deeper understanding of the essence of pure instrumental music than the French ever possessed. From the time of antiquity down to the present day, the most profound intellects have been filled with the idea that the art of music is a reflected image of the harmonically ordered universe, and that there is a mysterious connection between pure tones, with their life and interweaving, and the eternal motion of universe with all its orbiting heavenly bodies through an infinite space permeated with life.[41]

38. Köstlin, *Geschichte der Musik im Umriß*, 1. See above, p. 181.

39. Ludwig von Ganting, *Die Grundzüge der musikalischen Richtungen in ihrer geschichtlichen Entwicklung* (Leipzig: Breitkopf & Härtel, 1876), 35–37.

40. The set (BuxWV 251) was never published and is known only through the report in Mattheson, *Der vollkommene Capellmeister*, 130: "Buxtehude...hat...auch mit gutem Beifall seiner Zeit zu Papier gebracht...die Natur oder Eigenschafft der Planeten, in sieben Clavier-Suiten, artig abgebildet."

41. Philipp Spitta, *Johann Sebastian Bach*, 2 vols. (Leipzig: Breitkopf & Härtel, 1873–80), 1:259: "Im Gegentheil verräth der Einfall ein viel tieferes Verständniß für das Wesen der reinen Instrumentalmusik,

In his own writings on Bach, Albert Schweitzer (1875–1965) explicitly rejected Spitta's deep-seated antipathy toward program music. Anti-Wagnerites like Spitta, Schweitzer observed in his memoirs, had turned Bach into the hero of "pure music," whereas Schweitzer, by his own account, had tried to present Bach as a "poet and painter in sound." A native of Alsace, Schweitzer called the original French version of his book *J. S. Bach, le musicien-poète* (1905), yet when he issued the expanded German-language version of it three years later, it appeared under the simpler title of *Johann Sebastian Bach*. Whether the change was Schweitzer's idea or his publisher's, the contrast reveals deep cultural differences on the issue of program music: the French were on the whole far more inclined to accept the idea of poetic content in instrumental music, while Germans were divided on this point. In any event, Schweitzer felt the need to add to the German edition a five-page critique of "Spitta's limited evaluation of tone-painting in Bach's music," along with an entirely new chapter titled "Poetic and Painterly Music" that addresses questions of "program" and "absolute" music head-on, arguing for the validity of a "musical language" that incorporates at least a certain degree of symbolism.[42]

As early as the 1860s Hanslick's ideas had established the parameters of the discourse so clearly that debates about "pure" or "absolute" music could go forward without any direct reference to him at all. In his study of music "in relation to the forms and developmental laws of all life of the spirit" (1869), Emil Naumann (1827–1888), a composer who had at one time studied with Mendelssohn, observes that music is absolute only when it is autonomous, and it is autonomous only in the realm of instrumental music unencumbered by a program or social function (as in a dance or march): this is the only kind of music that can match the power of other arts.[43] Charles Beauquier's *Philosophie de la musique* (1865), the first major French-language treatise to address the idea of absolute music at any length, similarly ignores Hanslick, in spite of obvious debts.[44] Beauquier (1833–1916) was a poet and critic who contributed frequently to *La revue et gazette musicale*; he later wrote the libretto for Édouard Lalo's *Fiesque* (1866) as well as a treatise on music and drama (1877). Hanslick's treatise would not be translated into French until 1877; in the meantime, Beauquier's account transmitted

als es die Franzosen je besaßen. Daß die musikalische Kunst ein Spiegelbild des harmonisch geordneten Universums sei, und ein geheimnißvoller Zusammenhang bestehe zwischen dem Leben und Weben der reinen Töne und der ewigen Bewegtheit des Weltalls mit all seinen kreisenden Himmelskörpern in den lebendurchgossenen unendlichen Räumen, dieser Gedanke hat von Alters her bis in die neueste Zeit die tiefsinnigsten Geister erfüllt."

42. Albert Schweitzer, *Aus meinem Leben und Denken* (Leipzig: Felix Meiner, 1931), 54; Schweitzer, *J. S. Bach, le musicien-poète* (Leipzig: Breitkopf & Härtel, 1905); Schweitzer, *Johann Sebastian Bach* (Leipzig: Breitkopf & Härtel, 1908).

43. Emil Naumann, *Die Tonkunst in ihren Beziehungen zu den Formen und Entwickelungsgesetzen alles Geisteslebens* (Berlin: B. Behr, 1869), 271, 294.

44. Charles Beauquier, *Philosophie de la musique* (Paris: Germer Baillière, 1865).

the central arguments of *Vom Musikalisch-Schönen* to a Francophone audience without once citing it or its author by name.[45] Beauquier equates what he calls *la musique pure*—Hanslick's *reine Musik*—with instrumental music, which is "pure, free, and without admixture" (*pure, libre, sans mélange*). Beauquier's thesis is, like Hanslick's, largely negative: music does not spring from nature or from language, nor does it express emotions. In his final chapter, titled "Ce qui constitue l'essence de la musique," he reviews and rejects the statements of numerous earlier critics and philosophers who maintain that music is an art of expression. It is a different cast of characters from that presented at the end of Hanslick's opening chapter—here we encounter the likes of Bossuet, Montesquieu, Thomas Reid, and Goethe—but the methodology and goal are the same: to show the repeated and consistent errors of past commentators. Beauquier even employs the images of the arabesque and kaleidoscope as visual analogues of music's abstract forms. He considers the symphony the highest of all musical genres and characterizes it as "an architectonic construction of tones, with forms in motion; it signifies absolutely nothing in the literary sense."[46] In his review of Beauquier's treatise, the German composer and critic Selmar Bagge would point out the similarity of the phrase *des formes en mouvement* to *tönend bewegete Formen* without bothering to identify the source of the latter in *Vom Musikalisch-Schönen*, so well-known had the phrase become by this time.[47] Beauquier considered this aesthetic something new: "It remains solely to our time to disengage the art of music from its selvedge, from its margins, and to present it in its pure and essential form in instrumental music. This development has been very slow, much slower than in all the other arts."[48]

The pro-Wagner critic Friedrich von Hausegger (1837–1899) published a major rebuttal to Hanslick in the mid-1880s with his widely read *Die Musik als Ausdruck*, a treatise that soon become the standard point of reference for those who subscribed to the belief that music could express specific content.[49] As a polemic, Hausegger's treatise does not mention Hanslick by name, but critics of the time immediately recognized its target.[50] Hausegger must also be credited with what may well be the

45. Hanslick, *Du beau dans la musique: Essai de reforme de l'esthetique musicale*, trans. Charles Bannelier (Paris: Brandus, 1877), translated from the fifth edition of 1876.

46. Beauquier, *Philosophie de la musique*, 159: "La symphonie est une construction architectonique de sons, avec des formes en mouvement, et ne signifie absolument rien dans le sens littéraire." The references to the arabesque and kaleidoscope are on pp. 196 and 197, respectively.

47. S[elmar] B[agge], "Eine französische Stimme über den Inhalt der Musik," *Leipziger allgemeine musikalische Zeitung* 1 (1866): 32.

48. Beauquier, *Philosophie de la musique*, 157: "Il était réservé seulement à notre temps de dégager l'art musical de ses langes, de ses lisières, et de le poser dans sa forme pure et essentielle, dans la musique instrumentale. Ce développement a été très-lent, plus lent que celui de tous les autres arts."

49. The text was originally published serially in the *Bayreuther Blätter* in 1884, then in a first edition by C. Konegen of Vienna in 1885, and finally in a revised edition by the same publisher in 1887.

50. On Hausegger's text as a response to Hanslick, see Schäfke, *Eduard Hanslick und die Musikästhetik*, 40–42; Ernst-Joachim Danz, *Die objektlose Kunst: Untersuchungen zur Musikästhetik*

one lighter moment in a decades-long debate of otherwise unrelenting earnestness. In a "Humoresque" published in the *Musikalisches Wochenblatt* in 1870, he recounts a recent dream he claims to have had after falling asleep while reading a reprint of Robert Zimmermann's review of *Vom Musikalisch-Schönen.*[51] In his dream the figure of an enormous Eduard Hanslick appears before Hausegger, shaking his fist and saying: "And yet she [i.e., music] nevertheless consists of nothing but *tönend bewegte Formen*, no matter how much makeup she puts on. I have seen her myself in the most gigantic negligée—nothing but *tönend bewegte Formen*, I assure you."[52]

Hanslick waged his own campaign against the aesthetics of emotion in his journalistic criticism, consistently praising those composers whose instrumental music remained free of any overt extramusical elements. Brahms repeatedly won his approbation on this count. After the premiere of the orchestral version of the *Variations on a Theme by Haydn* in 1873, Hanslick hailed the presence of a "rich, genuinely musical formative power, one that has no need to rely upon any printed or secret program and reveals its treasures unpretentiously."[53] Along the same lines, he lauded Brahms's Second Symphony five years later for being structured in "purely musical" terms (*rein musikalisch...gestaltet*) without the need of any "furtive glances" toward "foreign realms of art" such as poetry or painting and without "embarrassed or brazen begging" from them. All of this was a sure sign that it was indeed possible to write symphonies after Beethoven, even in the "old forms, on the old foundations."[54]

Brahms nevertheless provides a useful reminder of just how problematic the concept of the "purely musical" can be. In an age enamored of polarities,

Friedrich von Hauseggers (Regensburg: Bosse, 1981), 190–256; and Rudolf Flotzinger, "Hauseggers Verhältnis zu Hanslick," in *Eduard Hanslick zum Gedenken: Bericht des Symposions zum Anlass seines 100. Todestages*, ed. Theophil Antonicek, Gernot Gruber, and Christoph Landerer (Tutzing: Hans Schneider, 2010), 77–83.

51. Friedrich von Hausegger, "Ein Traum, ein Leben: Humoreske," *Musikalisches Wochenblatt* 1 (23 September 1870): 618. Hausegger does not identify the volume specifically, but it is almost certainly Zimmermann's recently published *Studien und Kritiken zur Philosophie und Aesthetik*, 2 vols. (Vienna: Wilhelm Braumüller, 1870), the second volume of which is dedicated to Hanslick and includes Zimmermann's 1854 review (pp. 239–53).

52. Hausegger, "Ein Traum, ein Leben," 619: "Und dennoch besteht sie aus Nichts, als aus tönend bewegten Formen, und da mag sie sich sonst aufputzen, wie sie will. Hab ich sie doch selbst gesehen in grösstem Negligée—nichts als tönend bewegte Formen, ich versichere Sie."

53. Hanslick, *Concerte, Componisten und Virtuosen der letzten fünfzehn Jahre, 1870–1885* (Berlin: Allgemeiner Verein für deutsche Litteratur, 1886), 72: "Eine reiche, echt musikalisch gestaltende Kraft, welche sich an kein gedrucktes oder verschwiegenes Programm zu lehnen braucht, breitet hier anspruchslos ihre Schätze aus."

54. Hanslick, *Concerte, Componisten und Virtuosen*, 225: "Dabei kein schielender Blick nach fremden Kunstgebieten, weder verschämtes noch freches Betteln bei der Poesie oder Malerei—Alles rein musikalisch empfangen und gestaltet, und ebenso rein musikalisch wirkend. Als ein unbesiegbarer Beweis steht dies Werk da, daß man (freilich nicht jedermann) nach Beethoven noch Symphonien schreiben kann, obendrein in den alten Formen, auf den alten Grundmauern." See also Hanslick's similar comments on the musical purity of Brahms's Second Piano Concerto (ibid., 302–3).

he became the paradigmatic counterpart to Wagner and Liszt, in spite of his reluctance to become involved in the aesthetic disputes of the day. Early in his
career Brahms had helped organize a petition to register opposition to the views
and activities "of a certain party whose organ is Brendel's *Zeitschrift für Musik.*"
Both the compositions and the prose of the New German School, the petition
claimed, "are contrary to the innermost essence of music."[55] But the petition had
been intercepted and published by a Berlin newspaper before its intended release, and the *Neue Zeitschrift für Musik* issued a biting parody of it in May 1860.
From that moment on Brahms avoided all public comment on aesthetics. This
did not, however, prevent more traditionally minded critics and music-lovers
from pointing to him as an example of how the "old forms, on the old foundations" could still provide the basis for vital new works of music. In reality neither
Brahms's compositions nor (so far as we can tell) his aesthetics were nearly as
"absolute" as either his supporters or opponents perceived them to be.[56]

For their part, critics who supported Liszt and Wagner were happy to have
in the person of Brahms a prominent and contemporary composer worthy of
attack. As late as the second half of the 1890s, Hausegger, author of *Die Musik
als Ausdruck,* noted that concerts of post-Beethovenian music still evoked partisanship. Whoever performs Beethoven, he noted, could be assured of universal
support, for here one "stands on neutral or even common ground. Classicists
and romantics alike consider him their own. Absolute music points to him as its
zenith; program music points to him as its origin. Wagner no less than Brahms
wants to qualify as his legitimate successor. No matter what their inclination,
all believe that they are his inheritors."[57] A symphony by Brahms, on the other
hand, steps forward in opposition to the symphonic poems of Liszt and Richard
Strauss, "fighting the fight for the supremacy of the priesthood of absolute tone."

55. See Max Kalbeck, *Johannes Brahms,* 4 vols. (Vienna and Leipzig: Wiener Verlag; Berlin: Deutsche
Brahms-Gesellschaft, 1904–14), 1:419: "dem innersten Wesen der Musik zuwider." The relevant documents are given in translation in David Brodbeck, "Brahms, the Third Symphony, and the New German
School," in *Brahms and His World,* rev. ed., ed. Walter Frisch and Kevin Karnes (Princeton: Princeton
University Press, 2009), 111–12.

56. Studies of the many secret—and occasionally not-so-secret—programmatic elements in
Brahms's music include Dillon Parmer, "Brahms, Song Quotation, and Secret Programs," *19CM* 14
(1995), 161–90; George S. Bozarth, "Brahms's *Lieder ohne Worte:* The 'Poetic' Andantes of the Piano
Sonatas," in *Brahms Studies,* ed. George S. Bozarth (Oxford: Clarendon Press, 1990), 345–78; and
Floros, *Johannes Brahms: "Free but Alone."*

57. Friedrich von Hausegger, "Die E-moll Symphonie von Joh. Brahms" (ca. 1896–99), in
Hausegger, *Gedanken eines Schauenden,* ed. Siegmund von Hausegger (Munich: F. Brückmann,
1903), 237: "Wer heute Beethoven bringt, kann der parteilosen Zustimmung Aller gewiss sein. Mit
ihm befindet man sich auf neutralem Boden oder vielmehr auf einem Boden, welcher Gemeingut ist.
Klassiker und Romantiker betrachten ihn als den Ihrigen, auf ihn weist die absolute Musik als auf ihren
Hochpunkt, die Programmmusik als auf ihren Ausgangspunkt hin; für seinen legitimen Nachfolger will
Richard Wagner nicht minder wie Brahms gelten. Alle, welcher Richtung sie immer angehören wollen,
glauben, damit sein Erbe angetreten zu haben."

Overzealous servants of his militant church call for inquisitions. We recently heard this call when the gifted tone poems of Richard Strauss, *Till Eulenspiegel* and *Also sprach Zarathustra*, triumphed in their victorious campaign through the concert halls of Germany. I do not feel called upon today to declare myself for the wisdom of Zarathustra or the Revelation of John. This is not about comparing personal capacities and accomplishments, it is about weighing formative and reformative forces in our cultural and artistic life, in order to determine the viability of what they bring forth.[58]

The cries for an "inquisition" into the works of Richard Strauss came most notably from the pen of Hanslick, who in his capacity as a journalist had ridiculed the composer's latest work without having seen or heard a single note of it.

Perhaps the composition itself is masterful; I do not yet know the work. But its title is plain nonsense. "Thus spake" can be followed only by a speech, brief or extended, but only by words, not by orchestral movements. Zarathustra did not speak in bassoon scales or clarinet trills. A sophisticated man like R. Strauss knows this as well as we do. But the desire to serve up at any cost the unusual, the unheard-of, leads him astray. It happens that Nietzsche is fashionable at the moment. Richard Strauss takes the most peculiar, unpopular book of his and names his newest symphonic poem after it (loosely based on "Nietzsche"). The example is contagious. Ibsen is also fashionable at present, and for this reason a very young composer from Munich has written a symphonic poem called "Rosmersholm." When he can summon up more courage, he will probably follow this up with a symphony called "Thus Spake Hedda Gabler:" (closely based on Ibsen).[59]

Hanslick clearly regarded Strauss as a lost cause, though he could still express hope for Antonín Dvořák, even after the composer's turn toward the genre of the

---

58. Hausegger, "Die E-moll Symphonie von Joh. Brahms," 238–39: "So tritt heute die Brahmssche Symphonie als Kämpferin der symphonischen Dichtung Liszts und der an diese anknüpfenden, in neuester Zeit am wirksamsten durch Richard Strauss vertretenen Richtung entgegen. Sie kämpft den Kampf um die Priesterherrschaft des absoluten Tones. Übereifrige Diener seiner streitenden Kirche rufen nach Ketzergerichten. Wir haben diesen Ruf vor Kurzem vernommen, als geniale Tondichtungen von Richard Strauss, *Till Eulenspiegel* und *Also sprach Zarathustra*, ihren Eroberungszug durch die Konzertsäle Deutschlands machten. Ich fühle mich heute nicht berufen, mich zu entscheiden für Zarathustras Weisheit oder die Offenbarung Johannis. Es handelt sich nicht um die Vergleichung persönlicher Fähigkeiten und Verdienste, es handelt sich um die Abwägung gestaltender und umgestaltender Kräfte in unserem Kunstleben, um eine Prüfung von Erscheinungen desselben auf ihre Lebensfähigkeit hin."

59. Eduard Hanslick, "E-moll Symphonie und 'Der Wassermann' von A. Dvořák," *Neue freie Presse*, 9 December 1896, republished in Hanslick, *Am Ende des Jahrhunderts* (Berlin: Allgemeiner Verein für deutsche Litteratur, 1899), 217–18: "Ich kenne die Komposition nicht, vielleicht ist sie meisterhaft, aber der Titel ist barer Unsinn. Auf 'also sprach:' kann nur eine Rede folgen, kurz oder ausführlich; nur gesprochene Worte, nicht Orchestersätze. Zarathustra sprach keine Fagottscalen oder Klarinett-Triller. Das weiß ein geistreicher Mann, wie R. Strauß, so gut wie wir. Allein die Sucht, um jeden Preis Absonderliches, Unerhörtes aufzutischen, sei es auch nur im Titel, verführt ihn. Nietzsche ist eben in der Mode. Richard Strauß nimmt das sonderbarste, unpopulärste Buch von ihm und benennt

symphonic poem in 1896 with *Vodník* ("The Water Goblin," or, in the German title used by Hanslick, *Der Wassermann*), based on a poem by the Czech poet Karel Jaromír Erben. "Dvořák," Hanslick concludes his review,

> is a genuine musician who has proven a hundred times that he needs no programs or descriptive titles to delight us with music that is pure and without an object. Dvořák has no need to ask before he starts on a new symphony: What Spake Nietzsche? What Spake Zarathustra? Perhaps he does not even know who these two bigshots were. But he does not need to know. He awakens in us thoughts and sentiments, showers of happiness and sadness, without the need of any swindle through false erudition. But after *Der Wassermann*, a gentle, friendly warning can perhaps do no harm.[60]

In his brief entry "Absolute Music" for the first edition of his musical dictionary in 1882, Hugo Riemann summed up these deeply polarized attitudes. The entry reads in its entirety:

> *Absolute music* (i.e., music in itself, without connections to other arts or to any representational object outside of itself) is a term that in recent times has become the watchword of a large party of musicians and music lovers. Absolute music stands in contrast to "depictional" or "representative" or "program" music, i.e., to music that is intended to express something definite. According to the view of a hypermodern minority, all music that does not express a poetic idea is empty play. Conversely, ultraconservative musicians deny altogether the capacity of music to represent an object.[61]

By 1896 Strauss had emerged as the leading composer among Riemann's "hypermoderns" who believed that "all music that does not express a poetic idea

danach (frei nach 'Nietzsche') seine neueste Symphonische Dichtung. Das Beispiel ist ansteckend. Ibsen ist gleichfalls in Mode; darum hat bereits ein blutjunger Münchener Komponist eine symphonische Dichtung 'Rosmersholm' komponiert. Wenn er mehr Kourage bekommt, so läßt er wohl eine Symphonie mit dem Titel folgen: 'Also sprach Hedda Gabler:' (streng nach Ibsen)."

60. Hanslick, "E-moll Symphonie und 'Der Wassermann' von A. Dvořák," 219: Dvořák...ist ein echter Musiker, der hundert Mal bewiesen hat, daß er keines Programms und keiner Aufschrift bedarf, um uns durch reine, gegenstandslose Musik zu entzücken. Dvořák braucht sich nicht vor einer neuen Symphonie erst zu fragen: Was sprach Nietzsche? Was sprach Zarathustra? Er weiß vielleicht gar nicht, wer diese beiden großen Tiere waren. Aber das hat er auch nicht nötig. Er weckt Gedanken und Empfindungen, Schauer des Glückes und der Wehmut in uns, ohne dazu des Schwindels mit falscher Gelehrsamkeit zu bedürfen. Aber eine leise freundschaftliche Warnung kann ihm nach dem 'Wassermann' vielleicht nicht schaden."

61. Hugo Riemann, "Absolute Musik," in Riemann, *Musik-Lexicon* (Leipzig: Bibliographisches Institut, 1882): "*Absolute Musik* (d.h. Musik an sich, ohne Beziehung zu andern Künsten oder zu irgend welchen außer ihr liegenden Vorstellungsobjekten) ist ein Terminus, der in neuerer Zeit das Losungswort einer großen Partei unter den Musikern und Musikfreunden bildet. Die a[bsolute] M[usik] steht im Gegensatz zur 'malenden' oder 'darstellenden' oder 'Programm'-Musik, d.h. zu der Musik, die etwas Bestimmtes ausdrücken soll. Nach der Ansicht einer hypermodernen Minorität ist alle Musik, die nicht einen poetischen Gedanken zum Ausdruck bringt, leere Spielerei. Umgekehrt sprechen ultrakonservative Musiker der Musik ganz und gar die Fähigkeit ab, etwas darzustellen."

is empty play." Strauss promoted the aesthetic and rhetoric of the New German School enthusiastically, dismissing absolute music as a relic of the past. In a letter of 1888 to the conductor Hans von Bülow, he declared that the inherited forms of earlier times were inadequate to express the "musical-poetic content" he wished to convey. The forms Beethoven had used to great effect sixty years before had long since become "formulas," and a composer of the present could achieve a unity of mood and a consistency of structure only "through the inspiration of a poetical idea," an idea which the composer might or might not choose to make explicit in a program. "Purely formalistic, Hanslickian music making is in any case no longer possible."[62] In another letter written the same year to the Slovak composer and conductor Ján Levoslav Bella (1843–1936), Strauss lamented "how few of our present-day musicians, wandering through the noble four-movement formulaic structure, have fully grasped the essence of our glorious music—of our 'Music as Expression,' not as a Hanslickian 'sounding form.'"[63] And in another letter to Bella, written from Weimar two years later, Strauss rhapsodized on the same topic, noting that

the representatives of music here divide themselves into two groups. The first considers music to be "expression" and which they use in a language as precise as verbal language, albeit for things to which the latter cannot give expression. The second considers music to be "sounding form," that is, they lay down some general mood beneath the work to be composed (retaining calmly and without thinking the form that is no longer the form but rather the formula of the classicists) and then develop the themes that have arisen out of this according to an entirely external musical logic for which I have absolutely no understanding, as I now acknowledge only a poetic logic.

Program music: real music!

Absolute music: with the help of a certain routine and craftsmanship, its rigidification is within the grasp of anyone who is even only moderately musical.

The first: true art!

The second: artistic skill!

Remarkably, our present-day music takes the second of these as its point of departure and became fully conscious of its true calling only through Wagner and Liszt.

We musicians of the present thus always begin with No. 2 and pursue it until we come to the realization that this is not really music at all, but rather that the

---

62. Strauss to Hans von Bülow, 24 August 1888, in Richard Strauss and Hans von Bülow, "Briefwechsel," ed. Willi Schuh and Franz Trenner, *Richard Strauss Jahrbuch 1954*, 70: "Ein rein formales Hanslicksches Musizieren ist dabei allerdings nicht mehr möglich."

63. Richard Strauss to Johann Levoslav Bella, 2 December 1888, quoted in Willi Schuh, *Richard Strauss: Jugend und frühe Meisterjahre; Lebenschronik, 1864–1898* (Zurich: Atlantis, 1976), 153: "Wie wenige unserer heutigen, in edlem viersätzigem Formelwesen sich herumtreibenden Musiker haben das Wesen unserer herrlichen Musik ganz begriffen. Unserer 'Musik als Ausdruck,' nicht als Hanslick'sche 'tönende Form.'"

foundational requirement of a musical work is "the most precise expression of a musical idea," which must create its own form and with every new idea its own new form.[64]

As the end of the century approached, such charged rhetoric was becoming a thing of the past, however. Hausegger died in 1899, Hanslick in 1904. Strauss, only thirty-six in 1900, would prove to be something of an outlier among his contemporaries. In the early decades of the new century, the idea of absolute music would undergo a remarkable transformation: associated for more than a generation with the music of the past, it would soon become the watchword of musical modernism.

64. Strauss to Johann Levoslav Bella, 13 March 1890, quoted in Schuh, *Richard Strauss*, 154:

Die Vertreter der hiesigen Musik teilen sich doch in zwei Gruppen, die einen, denen Musik "Ausdruck" ist und die sie als eine ebenso präcise Sprache behandeln wie die Wortsprache, aber allerdings für Dinge, deren Ausdruck eben der letzteren versagt ist. Die anderen, denen die Musik "tönende Form" ist, d.h. sie legen dem zu componierenden Werke (die Form, d.h. nicht mehr Form, sondern Formel der Classiker ruhig gedankenlos beibehaltend) irgend eine allgemeine Grundstimmung unter und entwickeln diese entsprungenen Themen nach einer ganz äußerlichen musikalischen Logik, für die mir heute, da ich nunmehr eine dichterische Logik anerkenne, schon jedes Verständnis fehlt.

    Programm-Musik: eigentliche Musik!

    Absolute Musik:—ihre Verfestigung mit Hilfe einer gewissen Routine und Handwerkstechnik jedem nur einigermaßen musikalischen Menschen möglich.

    Erstere:—wahre Kunst!

    Zweite:—Kunstfertigkeit!

    Nun hat ja merkwürdigerweise unsere heutige Musik ihren Ausgangspunkt von No. II genommen und ist erst durch Wagner und Liszt voll bewußt ihrer wahren Bestimmung zugeführt worden.

    Wir heutigen Musiker beginnen daher noch immer mit No. II, bis wir dahinter kommen, daß dies noch gar nicht Musik ist, sondern "der präciseste Ausdruck einer musikalischen Idee," die sich dann ihre Form selbst schaffen muß, jede neue Idee ihre eigene neue Form, die Grundbedingung eines musikalischen Werkes ist.

    For a different translation, see Willi Schuh, *Richard Strauss: A Chronicle of the Early Years, 1864–1898*, trans. Mary Whittall (Cambridge: Cambridge University Press, 1982), 148–49.

12 Reconciliation

During the last quarter of the nineteenth century, the polemics between advocates of absolute and program music began to lose steam. The two sides continued to clash, but without the fervor that had characterized the debate in earlier decades. A new generation of composers and critics was inclined to accept the legitimacy of absolute and program music alike. The rhetoric of exclusion gradually gave way to one of tolerance. At the end of the century, relatively few subscribed to the idea that one repertory belonged to the past and the other to the future. Those who began their careers after 1880 tended to adopt a less polarizing attitude to explain the relationship between music's essence and its effect. Hanslick continued to fulminate against program music, and Hausegger railed against absolute music, but their views reflected the perspectives of a generation that had come of age in the 1850s. By 1896 the composer and critic Carl Raphael Hennig (1845–1914) could propose a synthesis of the aesthetics of Hanslick and Hausegger even while the two were still active.[1] The distinction between absolute and program music remained an important topic of debate, to be sure, as Sandra McColl's cross-sectional examination of Viennese musical criticism during the 1896–97 season demonstrates with exceptional clarity.[2] But the tone of the discourse was now far less strident and the issue itself no longer nearly so divisive. Such composers as Gustav Mahler (b. 1860) and Arnold Schoenberg (b. 1874), as we shall see, could accommodate both perspectives in their work, and even Richard Strauss (b. 1864) would eventually acknowledge the common ground between programmatic and absolute repertories.

Oddly enough, the initial phase of this process of reconciliation played itself out in the writings of the dispute's two chief protagonists, Hanslick and Wagner. Their changing views after the mid-1850s reflect the shifting ground of the debate as a whole. At some point, perhaps as early as the 1860s, Hanslick began to entertain private doubts about his own treatise. In his memoirs, published in 1894, he claimed that he had intended *Vom Musikalisch-Schönen* as a nothing

---

1. Carl Raphael Hennig, *Die Aesthetik der Tonkunst* (Leipzig: Johann Ambrosius Barth, 1896), 93–98. See the summary of Hennig's treatise in Paul Moos, *Moderne Musikästhetik in Deutschland: Historisch-kritische Uebersicht* (Leipzig: Hermann Seemann Nachfolger, 1902), 326–27. For an overview of the lessening of tensions at the turn of the twentieth century, see Charles Youmans, *Richard Strauss's Orchestral Music and the German Intellectual Tradition: The Philosophical Roots of Musical Modernism* (Bloomington: Indiana University Press, 2005), 3–15.

2. Sandra McColl, *Music Criticism in Vienna, 1896–1897: Critically Moving Forms* (Oxford: Clarendon Press, 1996), 185–98.

more than a "sketch," the "foundation" of a larger future work. He acknowledged that the "negative, polemical" portion of his treatise far outweighed its "positive, systematic" portion in both scope and clarity. He also confessed to having grown weary of philosophy and of "working with abstract concepts." The history of music, on the other hand, now filled him with an "inexhaustible delight," all the more so after his appointment at the University of Vienna, first as a *Privatdozent* in 1856, then as an *außerordentlicher Professor* (1861), and then ultimately (1870) as the institution's first and only full professor (*Ordinarius*) of the "history and aesthetics of music."[3] His enriched historical perspective led him to question one of the fundamental premises of *Vom Musikalisch-Schönen*, that musical beauty is an immutable quality independent of time or place. In the preface to an anthology of his criticisms of contemporary opera published in 1875, Hanslick noted that music, as a "human product," is necessarily permeated by elements subject to mortality. And in his memoirs, he reflected even more openly on this point:

> What is beautiful in music? Indeed, different times, different peoples, and different schools have answered this question quite differently. The more I immersed myself in the study of the history of music, the more the abstract aesthetics of music fluttered away from my sight, ever more vaguely, ever more vaporously, almost like a mirage.[4]

Hanslick thus confessed—though not in any later edition of his treatise—that aesthetics could be approached in terms of history after all and that beauty might be contingent rather than absolute. It is a stunning acknowledgment. By the 1870s, however, his views on the nature of the art were too well-known for him to retract his position explicitly or reformulate it in any sort of systematic fashion, and as late as the 1890s, as we have seen, he was still casting public aspersions on the basic premise of program music.

Wagner was far more open in acknowledging his changing attitudes toward purely instrumental music. By coincidence, he discovered the works of Schopenhauer in September 1854, just at the moment when Hanslick was putting the finishing touches on the first edition of *Vom Musikalisch-Schönen*. The experience caused Wagner to rethink in fundamental ways the relationship of music to the other arts.[5] Schopenhauer valued music's disclosive capacities

---

3. Hanslick, *Aus meinem Leben*, 1:242. On the university's deliberations over these appointments, see Karnes, *Music, Criticism, and the Challenge of History*, 21–37.

4. Hanslick, *Die moderne Oper: Kritiken und Studien* (Berlin: A. Hofmann, 1875), vi–vii. Hanslick, *Aus meinem Leben*, 1:243: "Was ist schön in der Musik? Ja, das haben verschiedene Zeiten, verschiedene Völker, verschiedene Schulen ganz verschieden beantwortet. Je mehr ich mich in historisches Musikstudium vertiefte, desto vager, luftiger zerflatterte die abstrakte Musikästhetik, fast wie eine Luftspiegelung, vor meinen Augen."

5. On Wagner's discovery of Schopenhauer, see Grey, *Wagner's Musical Prose*, 38–42; Bryan Magee, *The Philosophy of Schopenhauer* (Oxford: Clarendon Press, 1997), 326–78; and Magee, *Wagner and Philosophy* (London: Allen Lane, 2000), 126–73.

above those of any other art, not in spite of its nonconceptual nature but because of it. Music, he argued, is not simply another reflection of the idea of the Will (his term for the irreducible, subjective, inner aspect of things, including ourselves), but a reflection of the Will itself: "We could just as well call the world embodied music as embodied Will; this is the reason music makes every picture, indeed every scene from real life and from the world, at once appear in enhanced significance."[6] The real world of particular things consists of *universalia in re*, and concepts are *universalia post rem*, but music presents *universalia ante rem*, the "innermost kernel preceding the shaping of all form." The "effect of music" is more "more powerful and penetrating" than that of the other arts, for "these others speak only of the shadow, but music of the essence.[7]

By positing music as a direct reflection of the Will, Schopenhauer had no need to distinguish between vocal and instrumental manifestations of the art: additional forms of mediation, such as a sung text, an accompanying verbal program, or an evocative title, were to his mind altogether secondary. He pointed to Rossini's arias as exemplars of melody: from a philosophical perspective, their words and dramatic context are of no consequence. They neither enhance nor inhibit the music.

Schopenhauer's philosophy allowed Wagner to continue writing music dramas, but within a new hierarchy of priorities in which music governed all else. It connected music to the phenomenal world even while elevating music above that world by eliminating the need for mediation through concepts or language, even while accommodating additional layers of mediation. Schopenhauer was adamant about the connections between the world of phenomena and the world of ideas. "My philosophy," he declared to a follower in 1852, "is never concerned with cloud-cuckoo-land, but rather with *this* world, which is to say, it is *immanent*, not transcendent. It deciphers the world before us."[8] "Despite the dualistic description," observes Lydia Goehr, "there is only one world—the world is truly a *universe* and music is part of it." Schopenhauer's method of philosophizing by

6. Schopenhauer, *Die Welt als Wille und Vorstellung*, 1:330: "Man könnte demnach die Welt eben so wohl verkörperte Musik, als verkörperten Willen nennen; daraus also ist es erklärlich, warum Musik jedes Gemälde, ja jede Scene des wirklichen Lebens und der Welt, sogleich in erhöhter Bedeutsamkeit hervortreten lässt." Translation from Schopenhauer, *The World as Will and Representation*, 2 vols. (New York: Dover, 1966), trans. E. F. J. Payne, 1:262–63.

7. Schopenhauer, *Die Welt als Wille und Vorstellung*, 1:330-31: "die Musik hingegen den innersten aller Gestaltung vorhergängigen Kern, oder das Herz der Dinge giebt." Ibid., 1:324: "Die Musik ist also keineswegs, gleich den andern Künsten, das Abbild der Ideen, sondern *Abbild des Willens selbst*, dessen Objektität auch die Ideen sind: deshalb eben ist die Wirkung der Musik so sehr viel mächtiger und eindringlicher, als die der andern Künste: denn diese reden nur vom Schatten, sie aber vom Wesen." Translation from Schopenhauer, *The World as Will and Representation*, trans. E. F. J. Payne, 1:257.

8. Schopenhauer to Julius Frauenstädt, letter of 21 August 1852, in Schopenhauer, *Gesammelte Briefe*, ed. Arthur Hübscher (Bonn: Bouvier, 1978), 291: "Meine Philosophie redet nie von Wolkenkukuksheim, sondern von *dieser* Welt, d.h., sie ist *immanent*, nicht transscendent. Sie liest die vorliegende Welt ab." Emphasis in original.

analogy, as Goehr goes on to point out, "helps inexpressible languages be *understood* even if they are not adequately (philosophically) *explained*."[9]

The influence of Schopenhauer is already evident in Wagner's open letter of 1857 on Liszt's symphonic poems. "Hear my creed," he implored: "Music can never cease to be the highest, most redemptive art, regardless of any alliance into which it might enter. Its essence lies in this: what all other arts merely suggest becomes, in and through music, the most unassailable certainty, the most immediately determinant of all truths."[10] Wagner would express this conviction repeatedly in subsequent writings. Purely instrumental music, far from lacking the "fertilizing seed" of the word, was now a vehicle of metaphysical disclosure in its own right. Through "purely musical expression that captivates the listener in the most unimaginably varied nuances," Wagner asserted in 1860, Beethoven had been able to create works that appear as "a revelation from another world," opening up to listeners "all the various coherence among worldly phenomena in such a way that logic and reason are upended and disarmed."[11]

Wagner's most extended account of the disclosive capacity of purely instrumental music is his "Beethoven" essay of 1870, written on the occasion of the composer's centennial. It opens with an extended meditation on the essence of music as revelation (*Offenbarung*), a force that both drives and reflects all. Music subsumes drama, which is "a counterpart of music given visible form." Instrumental music constitutes nothing less than a bridge between the conscious, rational world, and the higher realm of the spirit that can otherwise be intuited only through dream.[12] As a window on the universe, music can accommodate any text. In a passage uncannily reminiscent of Hanslick's observations in chapter 2 of *Vom Musikalisch-Schönen*, Wagner observes that a melody loses nothing of its character when set to a different text: the relationship of poetry and music is thus "entirely illusory," for in any union of the two the former must

9. Lydia Goehr, "Schopenhauer and the Musicians: An Inquiry into the Sounds of Silence and the Limits of Philosophizing about Music," in *Schopenhauer, Philosophy, and the Arts*, ed. Dale Jacquette (Cambridge: Cambridge University Press, 1996), 208, 222. Emphasis in the original.

10. Wagner, "Über Franz Liszts symphonische Dichtungen," *GSD*, 5:191: "Hören Sie meinen Glauben: die Musik kann nie und in keiner Verbindung, die sie eingeht, aufhören die höchste, die erlösendste Kunst zu sein. Es ist dies ihr Wesen, daß, was alle anderen Künste nur andeuten, durch sie und in ihr zur unbezweifeltsten Gewißheit, zur allerunmittelbarst bestimmenden Wahrheit wird." *PW*, 3:246.

11. Wagner, "Zukunftsmusik," *GSD*, 7:110: "So muß uns die Symphonie geradesweges als eine Offenbarung aus einer anderen Welt erscheinen; und in Wahrheit deckt sie uns einen von dem gewöhnlichen logischen Zusammenhang durchaus verschiedenen Zusammenhang der Phänomene der Welt auf, von welchem das eine zuvörderst unleugbar ist, nämlich, daß er mit der überwältigendsten Überzeugung sich uns aufdrängt und unser Gefühl mit einer solchen Sicherheit bestimmt, daß die logisierende Vernunft vollkommen dadurch verwirrt und entwaffnet wird." *PW*, 3:318.

12. Wagner, "Beethoven," *GSD*, 9:105 and 112. Klaus Kropfinger, *Wagner and Beethoven: Richard Wagner's Reception of Beethoven*, trans. Peter Palmer (Cambridge: Cambridge University Press, 1991), 136–41, makes the case for anti-Hanslickian elements in the "Beethoven" essay.

defer to the latter.[13] At another point, Wagner argues strenuously that music adheres to "aesthetic laws different from those of any other art."[14]

One wonders what Hanslick must have made of such astonishing concessions. Did he trouble himself to come to terms with Schopenhauer's philosophy? Probably not. But others who subscribed to Hanslick's rhetoric of musical purity found in Schopenhauer's thought a prestigious legitimation of their beliefs. It acknowledged the unique nature of music and its material autonomy. It allowed for but crucially did not require the mediation of other arts. More than any other single development, Schopenhauer's philosophy of music helped dissipate the toxic atmosphere that had been building up since the aesthetic-ideological collisions of the 1850s.

This is not to say that Wagner and Hanslick themselves ever publicly agreed on the nature of the art. Personal animosities prevented them from acknowledging any such common ground. The original ending of the first edition of *Vom Musikalisch-Schönen*, with its dual appeal to music as an autonomous art and as a reflection of the cosmos, might at one time have provided a basis for some kind of reconciliation between the two. Wagner conceived of music in relation to the universe as whole even before his confrontation with Schopenhauer and still more so after it. Hanslick, by contrast, became increasingly committed to the idea of music as a *Sonderkunst*, an art unrelated to anything but itself.

With the passage of time, more and more observers began to realize that the two sides were really not as far apart as they had once seemed. By 1889 even as ardent a Wagnerian as Alois John (1860–1935) could count absolute music as one of three "elemental components" of Wagner's art.[15] John even went so far as to praise absolute music as "the truly revolutionary, the reformational" feature of Wagner's art, a "new language" born of "necessity," capable of expressing "endless longing" and that which cannot be articulated in words. Wagner's absolute music, John hastened to add, was free of "all rules and schools" and of "every authority and conventional manner." His music went beyond "the old style, the pious melody, the pleasant play" that had degenerated into "caricature" and no longer sufficed for the "powerful domain of ideas of the new work of art." The need for an art imbued with "power, heroism, and passion" had brought forth from Wagner "a new musical language, an absolute music."[16]

13. Wagner, "Beethoven," *GSD*, 9:103–4; see *VMS*, 1:55–56; *OMB*, 16–17.

14. Wagner, "Beethoven," *GSD*, 9:71–72: "daß diese ganz anderen ästhetischen Gesetzen unterworfen sein muß, als jede andere Kunst."

15. Alois John, *Richard Wagner-Studien: Sieben Essays über Richard Wagner's Kunst und seine Bedeutung im modernen Leben* (Bayreuth: Carl Gießel, 1889), 39–40. John's work won enthusiastic praise from an anonymous reviewer in the pro-Wagnerian English journal *The Meister* 5 (21 July 1892): 94–95.

16. John, *Richard Wagner-Studien*, 39: "eine so ureigene, selbstherrliche Kraft ist die absolute Musik, ein Freisein, ein Losgewordensein von aller Regel und Schule, jeder Autorität und conventionellen Sitte. Der alte Stil, die fromme Melodie, das gefällige Spiel reichte nicht mehr aus oder wäre zur Carricatur

Other Wagnerians experienced Schopenhauerian epiphanies of their own. In his *Richard Wagner and the Music of the Future*, published in 1874, the German-born music critic of *The Times*, Francis (Franz) Hueffer (1845–1889) refers repeatedly to absolute music in disparaging tones for its "strict forms" and "dead formalism" and speaks glowingly of the "victory of poetical over absolute music—of the 'Future' over the 'Past.'" "The possibility of music for the sole sake of sonorous beauty has virtually ceased to exist," Hueffer declares, "and any composer with higher aspirations than those of a *genre* painter, without subject or artistic purpose, has to consider it his task to express a preconceived poetical idea by means of his sound. It is the part of music to receive this idea, and to bring it forth again idealised and raised to its own sphere of pure passion."[17] Fifteen years later Hueffer expressed a very different view. In relating a conversation he had had recently with an unnamed young English composer of promise, Hueffer reported the was

> exceedingly struck by the emphatic manner in which my young friend held forth against so-called "absolute" music. The Symphony, the Sonata, and other classical forms appear to him to be the effete types of a bygone age. A piece of music without a subject, he thought, was as meaningless as a picture without a subject. In short, he expressed the most unqualified allegiance to that "poetic idea in music" which Wagner, Liszt, and Berlioz have proclaimed in their various ways.
>
> With this thorough-going revolutionism I was, of course, unable to agree in all its bearings. Ripe experience has taught me that in the house of music there are many habitations, that the classical form created by Haydn, and imbued with infinite varieties and depths of beauty by Mozart, Beethoven, Schumann, Mendelssohn, and many others, is by no means obsolete; that in the hands of genius it may still bring forth rich and noble fruit. Neither can I admit that music must necessarily deal with an extraneous subject; even painting may to a certain extent dispense with such a subject, may become a vague and delightful harmony of colour, as Turner and Mr. Whistler have taught us. Much more so is this the case in the art of sounds. There are some thoughts that lie too deep for words, too deep even for definite realisation; and it is just in expressing these inexpressible things that music shows its most specific power, and ascends from the world of appearances to the world of realities, from the phenomenon to the noumenon, as Plato has it.[18]

As in the case of Wagner, we can trace this change of mind to an exposure to the writings of Schopenhauer, which Hueffer seems to have discovered at some

geworden für die gewaltigen Gedankenkreise des neuen Kunstwerkes, für diese von Kraft, Heroismus und Leidenschaft durchglühten Gestalten. Dieselbe Nothwendigkeit, die eine neue Sprache erzeugte, mußte auch eine neue musikalische, eine absolute Musik erzeugen."

17. Francis Hueffer, *Richard Wagner and the Music of the Future: History and Aesthetics* (London: Chapman & Hall, 1874), 106, 223, 190, 46.

18. Francis Hueffer, *Half a Century of Music in England, 1837–1887: Essays towards a History* (London: Chapman & Hall, 1889), 235–36.

point between 1874, when he had dismissed absolute music, and 1876, when he published an essay on the philosopher in the *Fortnightly Review* of Edinburgh.[19] Hueffer's enthusiasm for the "Music of the Future" would not diminish in the slightest, but his acceptance of absolute music as viable repertory reflects the influence of Schopenhauer not only on Wagner but on an entire generation of Wagnerians, including the critic Wilhelm Tappert (1830–1907). Writing shortly after the premiere of *Parsifal*, Tappert observed that it remained to be seen whether the "Music of the Future" or absolute music would win out, but he noted that the two were by no means mutually exclusive and even complemented each other.[20] A decade later, in 1892, the critic Paul Schneider proposed a reconciliation of feeling and form through the philosophy of Schopenhauer: beauty resides in form, but music can reflect the Will.[21] The ongoing rehabilitation of absolute music among a still later generation of Wagnerians is evident in the writings of the eminent English critic Ernest Newman (1868–1959), who in 1899 pointed out the inconsistencies in Wagner's Zurich writings, the longer-term development of the composer's thought between the early 1850s and 1870 (the date of the "Beethoven" essay), and the incongruities between the composer's proclaimed theory and actual works. "It is curious," Newman wryly observed, "how Wagner's mere statement of his badly thought-out theories should prevent so many acute readers from noticing their radical contradiction with most of his practice." Newman expressed the hope that his account of these inconsistencies would "afford a basis of compromise between the Wagnerians and the anti-Wagnerians."[22]

The most extended and systematic attempt to reconcile the aesthetics of Wagner and Hanslick came from the pen of Ottokar Hostinský (1847–1910), a student of Smetana who would eventually become professor of aesthetics in his native Prague. In his *Das Musikalisch-Schöne und das Gesammtkunstwerk vom Standpunkte der formalen Aesthetik* (1877), Hostinský accepts Hanslick's premise that every art has its own parameters of beauty, but he rejects the associated rhetoric of purity, arguing that while instrumental music is a *reine Kunst*, vocal music is superior as a *Kunstverein* or "union of the arts."[23] He quotes no fewer than three

19. Francis Hueffer, "Arthur Schopenhauer," *Fortnightly Review* 20 (1876): 773–92. Hueffer published an expanded version of this essay, with additional remarks dealing specifically with music, in Hueffer, *Musical Studies: A Series of Contributions* (Edinburgh: Adam & Charles Black, 1880), 85–129.

20. Wilhelm Tappert, *Für und Wider: Eine Blumenlese aus den Berichten über die Aufführungen des Bühnenweihfestspieles Parsifal* (Berlin: Theodor Barth, 1882), 7.

21. Paul Schneider, *Über das Darstellungsvermögen der Musik: Eine Untersuchung an der Hand von Prof. Ed. Hanslick's Buch "Vom Musikalisch-Schönen"* (Oppeln and Leipzig: Eugen Frank, 1892), 124–25.

22. Ernest Newman, *A Study of Wagner* (London: Bertram Dobell, 1899), 129, 255.

23. Ottokar Hostinský, *Das Musikalisch-Schöne und das Gesammtkunstwerk vom Standpuncte der formalen Aesthetik: Eine Studie* (Leipzig: Breitkopf & Härtel, 1877), 147. The treatise was Hostinský's *Habilitationsschrift* in philosophy at the University of Prague. Excerpts in an English translation by Martin Cooper are available in *Music in European Thought, 1851–1912*, ed. Bojan Bujić (Cambridge: Cambridge

times Hanslick's observation that the union of poetry and music "extends the power of music but not its boundaries" and uses this to argue that the joining of the arts can create something more powerful than any one art alone. Hostinský was well aware of the audacity of blending the theories of Hanslick and Wagner, and he defended Hanslick's treatise as having been "more attacked than comprehended, more condemned than understood."[24] His treatise offers the most dispassionate review of the dispute up to that time, taking note of the positions put forward by Ambros, Kullak, Laurencin, Stade, and others. Hanslick himself remained unconvinced. In the sixth edition (1881) of *Vom Musikalisch-Schönen*, he took note of Hostinský's ideas, calling them "interesting and diligent" but confused, in that the first half of the treatise seemed to agree with the position of *Vom Musikalisch-Schönen*, while the second did not.[25]

The very fact that someone would even attempt to reconcile the positions of Hanslick and Wagner while both were still alive was significant enough in its own right. The noted historian and theorist Hugo Riemann (1849–1919) made similarly overt if less systematic efforts in this direction on more than one occasion when he sought to bring a degree of "equilibrium" to the opposition between the advocates of program and absolute music.[26] In his essay "Das formale Element in der Musik" (1880), he does not deny the capacity of music to represent but insists that this does not belong to the fundamental essence of the art. Music is first and foremost a "spontaneous expression of feeling" and only secondarily an art of beauty, and form is what makes expression comprehensible.[27]

After Wagner's death in 1883, commentators began to treat the polemics of the previous generation with a growing sense of critical and historical distance. Richard Wallaschek's account in his *Ästhetik der Tonkunst* (1886) is remarkably balanced. A pioneer in the field of comparative musicology, Wallaschek (1860–1917) takes Hanslick to task for his overly formalistic approach, which ignores

University Press, 1988), 132–58. For further commentary on Hostinský, see Dahlhaus, *Die Idee der absoluten Musik*, 40–42; Schneider, "Form versus Gehalt," 47–49; and Felix Wörner, "Otakar Hostinský, the Musically Beautiful, and the *Gesamtkunstwerk*," in *Rethinking Hanslick: Music, Formalism, and Expression*, ed. Nicole Grimes, Siobhán Donovan, and Wolfgang Marx (Rochester, NY: University of Rochester Press, 2013), 70–87.

24. Hostinský, *Das Musikalisch-Schöne*, 71, 80, 134, citing VMS, 1:53: "Die Vereinigung mit der Dichtkunst erweitert die Macht der Musik, aber nicht ihre Gränzen." Hostinský, *Das Musikalisch-Schöne*, 5: "das ihr zu Grunde liegende Princip [wurde] mehr bekämpft, als begriffen, mehr verdammt, als verstanden."

25. VMS, 1:15; this passage is not in *OMB*.

26. Hugo Riemann, "Programmmusik, Tonmalerei und musikalischer Kolorismus," *Die Grenzboten* 41, no. 3 (1882): 76: "was ich thun will, nämlich einen Beitrag liefern zur Ausgleichung des Gegensatzes zwischen den Verfechtern der Programmmusik und denen der absoluten Musik." Riemann republished the essay in his *Präludien und Studien*, 3 vols. (Leipzig: Hermann Seemann Nachfolger, 1895–1901), 1:54–64.

27. Riemann, "Das formale Element in der Musik," *Die Grenzboten* 39 (1880): 203–4: "in erster Linie spontaner Empfindungsausdruck."

issues of perception, and for failing to define beauty at any point in a treatise whose title includes that very word. He cites with special disapproval Hanslick's assertion, added from the second edition onward, that "the beautiful is and remains beautiful, even when it arouses no emotions, indeed when it is neither perceived nor contemplated. Beauty is thus only *for* the pleasure of a perceiving subject, not generated *through* that subject."[28] Wallaschek nevertheless praises Hanslick for having taken on the "uncertain gropings" of "swooning idealists" and the "pronounced partisans of a certain school" at a time when the rest of the world would have "walked through fire" to defend their positions.[29]

Advances in the fields of psychology and physiology also helped make the distinction between different repertories of music less important than they had once seemed. By approaching art through issues of perception rather than form or content, psychologists such as Moritz Lazarus could agree with Hanslick that music cannot represent anything other than itself. In his *Das Leben der Seele* (1856–57), Lazarus observed that his differences with *Vom Musikalisch-Schönen* stemmed from a contrast between his focus on psychology and Hanslick's on aesthetics. Hanslick "attends primarily to the content of music, I to the effect of it." This distinction, Lazarus points out, "is far greater in music than in any other art."[30] Lazarus was in fact pursuing aesthetics in the original sense as proposed by Baumgarten and understood by Kant and others in the eighteenth century: the science of sensory cognition.

The acoustical and physiological discoveries of Hermann von Helmholtz also helped move the discussion beyond the binary opposition of absolute and program music. Early on in his epochal *Lehre von den Tonempfindungen als physiologische Grundlage für die Theorie der Musik* (1863), Helmholtz praises Hanslick for having made "unmistakable progress" in the aesthetics of music through his emphasis on the role of physical motion (*Bewegung*) in the art. But Helmholtz goes on to note that such advances must remain "fragmentary and uncertain" as long as we lack clarity about "their actual origin and foundation... in the scientific justification for the elementary rules for the construction of the scale, chords, and keys." In contrast to the visual arts, music "strives for no verisimilitude with nature; tones and the perception of tones exist entirely for their own sake and affect us quite independently of any connection to external objects."[31]

---

28. Richard Wallaschek, *Ästhetik der Tonkunst* (Stuttgart: W. Kohlhammer, 1886), 139, quoting *VMS*, 1:26. On the sources and implications of this passage in *VMS*, see above, p. 189.

29. Wallaschek, *Ästhetik der Tonkunst*, 146: "das unsichere Tappen schwärmerischer Idealisten und prononcierter Parteigänger einer gewissen Schule"; "wo alle Welt für solche Lehren ins Feuer gegangen ware."

30. Lazarus, *Das Leben der Seele*, 2:314: "weil...er auf den Inhalt, ich auf die Wirkung derselben vorzüglich achte; ein Unterschied, welcher bei der Musik weitaus größer ist als bei jeder anderen Kunst."

31. Hermann von Helmholtz, *Die Lehre von den Tonempfindungen als physiologische Grundlage für die Theorie der Musik* (Braunschweig: Vieweg & Sohn, 1863), 2–4: "Inzwischen hat die Aesthetik

From this "objective" perspective, then, the question of whether or not a given work of music might attempt to associate itself in some way with "external objects" becomes moot.

Gustav Mahler summed up the growing sense of reconciliation between absolute and program music in a letter to Arthur Seidl in 1897, in which he affirmed the critic's earlier distinction between his own working methods and those of Richard Strauss. "You have accurately characterized my goals in contrast to those of Strauss," Mahler wrote. "You are right that my 'music finally arrives at a program as the last, ideal clarification, whereas with Strauss the program stands as a given task.' "[32] Mahler went on to add: "Schopenhauer somewhere uses the image of two miners who dig a tunnel from opposite sides and then meet on their subterranean ways. That seems fittingly to characterize my relationship with Strauss."[33]

Mahler was famously ambivalent about supplying programs for his own music. Scholars have interpreted his contradictory statements and actions on this count in a variety of ways, but his vacillation was more than merely personal: it reflects an era that was itself ambivalent on the issue.[34] In the summer of 1904, he wrote to his friend the conductor Bruno Walter:

> That our music involves in some way the "purely human" (everything that belongs to it, including therefore the "mental") certainly cannot be denied. As in all art, it depends on the pure medium of expression, etc. etc. If one wants to make music, one may not paint, versify, or describe as well. But the music one creates is nevertheless the *whole* (and thus the feeling, thinking, breathing, suffering, etc.) human. There would really be nothing to say against a "program" (even if it is not the

der Musik...unverkennbare Fortschritte gemacht, namentlich dadurch, dass man den Begriff der Bewegung bei der Untersuchung der musikalischen Kunstwerke betont hat....Aber alle diese Untersuchungen...müssen lückenhaft und unsicher bleiben, so lange ihnen ihr eigentlicher Anfang und ihre Grundlage fehlt, nämlich die wissenschaftliche Begründung der elementaren Regeln für die Construction der Tonleiter, der Accorde, der Tonarten....In der Musik...wird gar keine Naturwahrheit erstrebt, die Töne und Tonempfindungen sind ganz allein ihrer selbst wegen da und wirken ganz unabhängig von ihrer Beziehung zu irgend einem äusseren Gegenstande."

32. Gustav Mahler to Arthur Seidl, letter of 17 February 1897, in Mahler, *Briefe*, 2nd ed., ed. Herta Blaukopf (Vienna: Paul Zsolnay, 1996), 222: "Sie haben recht, daß meine Musik schließlich zum Programm als letzter ideeller Verdeutlichung gelangt, währenddem bei Strauss das Programm als gegebenes Pensum daliegt." Translation from Stephen E. Hefling, "Miners Digging from Opposite Sides: Mahler, Strauss, and the Problem of Program Music," in *Richard Strauss: New Perspectives on the Composer and His Work*, ed. Bryan Gilliam (Durham, NC: Duke University Press, 1992), 41.

33. Mahler to Seidl, 17 February 1897, in Mahler, *Briefe*, 224: "Schopenhauer gebraucht irgendwo das Bild zweier Bergleute, die von entgegengesetzten Seiten in einen Schacht hineingraben und sich dann auf ihrem unterirdischen Wege begegnen. So kommt mir mein Verhältnis zu Strauss treffend gezeichnet vor." Translation from Hefling, "Miners," 41. Seidl later published this portion of Mahler's letter in his *Moderner Geist in der deutschen Tonkunst* (Berlin: Verlagsgesellschaft für Literatur und Kunst "Harmonie," 1901), 61.

34. On the many problems associated with ascribing any one particular point of view to Mahler in regard to program music, see Vera Micznik, "Music and Aesthetics: The Programmatic Issue," in *The*

highest rung on the ladder)—but a *musician* must speak in that case, and not a literary figure, a philosopher, or a painter (all of whom are incorporated within the musician).[35]

Particularly revealing here is Mahler's "etc. etc." The debate about the purity of expression is clearly old hat for Mahler and Walter alike. Program music has in any case ceded its midcentury status as the most progressive branch of the art: it is no longer "the highest rung on the ladder."

In France, Gabriel Fauré (1845–1924) could advocate and create models of *musique pure* and yet also lavish praise on a work such as Strauss's *Ein Heldenleben*.[36] The English composer Edward Elgar (1857–1934), who had written numerous programmatic works earlier in his career, repressed the programs of his two symphonies (1908, 1911) and of his Violin Concerto (1910) and promoted the aesthetics of absolute music in lectures he delivered in Birmingham in 1905.[37] Even Strauss, late in his life, would acknowledge (if only privately) that the aesthetic polarities of his earlier years—the very polarities he had helped intensify—had been exaggerated:

> Our learned music scholars—I will name the two principal ones: Friedrich von Hausegger ("music as expression") and Eduard Hanslick ("music as tonally moving form")—gave us formulations that ever since have been considered antagonistic opposites. This is false. These are the two forms of musical construction, and they complement each other.[38]

Cambridge Companion to Mahler, ed. Jeremy Barham (Cambridge: Cambridge University Press, 2007), 35–49. For an interpretation of Mahler's symphonies that emphasizes their programmatic elements, see Constantin Floros, *Gustav Mahler*, 3 vols. (Wiesbaden: Breitkopf & Härtel, 1977–85).

35. Mahler to Bruno Walter, letter of summer 1904, from Mahler, *Briefe*, 316: " Daß unsere Musik das 'rein Menschliche' (alles was dazu gehört, also auch das 'Gedankliche') in irgendeiner Weise involviert, ist ja doch nicht zu leugnen. Es kommt wie in aller Kunst, eben auf die reinen Mittel des Ausdrucks an, etc. etc. Wenn man musizieren will, darf man nicht malen, dichten, beschreiben wollen. Aber *was* man musiziert, ist doch immer der *ganze* (also fühlende, denkende, atmende, leidende etc.) Mensch. Es wäre ja auch weiter nichts gegen ein 'Programm' einzuwenden (wenn es auch nicht gerade die höchste Staffel der Leiter ist)—aber ein *Musiker* muß sich da aussprechen und nicht ein Literat, Philosoph, Maler (alle die sind im Musiker enthalten)." Emphasis in original.

36. See Carlo Caballero, *Fauré and French Musical Aesthetics* (Cambridge: Cambridge University Press, 2001), 48–53, 250–56.

37. See Edward Elgar, *A Future for English Music and Other Lectures*, ed. Percy M. Young (London: Dennis Dobson, 1968), 105–8. See also Ernest Newman, *Elgar* (London: John Lane, 1922), "Appendix: Elgar and Programme Music," 176–85.

38. Quoted in Willi Schuh, *Richard Strauss: Jugend und frühe Meisterjahre: Lebenschronik 1864–1898* (Zurich: Atlantis, 1976), 155: "Unsere Musikgelehrten—ich nenne die beiden Hauptnamen: Friedrich von Hausegger ('Musik als Ausdruck') und Eduard Hanslick ('Musik als tönend bewegte Form')— haben Formulierungen gegeben, die seither als feindliche Gegensätze gelten. Dies ist falsch. Es sind die beiden Formen musikalischen Gestaltens, die sich gegenseitig ergänzen." Strauss's comments appear in a memoir believed to have been written in the late 1930s, although it was not published until 1949, the year of his death.

By 1909 the debate about the nature of absolute and program music had changed so fundamentally since the time of Wagner, Hanslick, and Liszt that Hugo Riemann saw fit to revise his entry on absolute music for his *Musik-Lexikon* for the first time since its original publication in 1882. From the first through the sixth (1905) edition of the work, Riemann had defined absolute music in terms of its partisans: the "hypermoderns," who believed that "all music that does not express a poetic idea is empty play," and the "ultraconservatives," who "deny altogether the capacity of music to represent an object" (see p. 234). For the seventh edition of 1909, he dropped all reference to partisanship and defined absolute music partly in opposition to program music but also partly in conjunction with it. The revised entry reads in its entirety:

> *Absolute music* (i.e., music in itself, without connections to other arts or to any representational object outside of itself) in contrast to "depictional" or "representative" or "program" music, i.e., to music that is intended to express something definite. When music turns to symbolism, i.e., to the intentional arousal of specific associational ideas through certain formulas or to the stylized imitations of noises, it leaves its intrinsic sphere and moves into the realm of poetry or the visual arts. For the essence of poetry consists of arousing and linking specific representations through conventional formulas (words); the essence of the visual arts does the same through the direct imitations of external appearances; both thus achieve the same final goal of all art, to move the soul, through an indirect path of which music has no need, as it is in itself freely flowing sentiment that transforms itself back into sentiment without the mediation of reason by the performer and listener.[39]

The polemical debate has lost its edge by this point: program music is now part of the musical mainstream, and absolute music is no longer associated with an "ultraconservative party." Riemann's emphasis in 1909 is on the common goals of these two varieties of instrumental music: even though their paths differ, they lead to the same destination. The route of absolute music is more direct and thus implicitly superior, for it has no need of any detour (*Umweg*—literally,

---

39. Riemann, "Absolute Musik," in Riemann, *Musik-Lexikon*, 7th ed. (Leipzig: Max Hesse, 1909): "*Absolute Musik* (d.h. Musik an sich, ohne Beziehung zu andern Künsten oder zu irgendwelchen außer ihr liegenden Vorstellungsobjekten) im Gegensatz zur 'malenden' oder 'darstellenden' oder 'Programm'-Musik, d.h. zu der Musik, die etwas Bestimmtes ausdrücken soll. Die Musik tritt, wenn sie zur Symbolik, d.h. zur absichtlichen Erweckung bestimmter Ideenassoziationen durch gewisse Formeln oder zur stilisierten Nachahmung von Geräuschen greift, aus ihrem eigensten Gebiet heraus und in das der Poesie oder darstellenden Kunst über. Denn das Wesen der Poesie besteht darin, durch konventionelle Formeln (die Worte) bestimmte Vorstellungen zu wecken und zu verketten, das der darstellenden Kunst in der direkten Nachbildung der äußeren Erscheinungen; beide erreichen also das Endziel aller Kunst, die Seele zu bewegen, auf Umwegen, deren die Musik nicht bedarf, da sie selbst frei ausströmende Empfindung ist und ohne Vermittlung des Verstandes beim Spieler und Hörer sich wieder in Empfindung umsetzt."

a "way around") to reach its goal. But this is only a question of means; the end both seek is the same.

A similar sense of reconciliation is evident in Rudolf Louis's 1909 survey of contemporary German music. Louis (1870–1914) was both a critic and a composer: he had published studies of Wagner, Liszt, and Berlioz, and his *Proteus*, a "symphonic fantasy, after Hebbel" for orchestra and organ, had been performed in 1903 at the festival of the Allgemeiner Deutscher Musikverein in Basel. His credentials as an heir to the tradition of the New German School were, in short, impeccable. Louis's account of the current musical scene is nevertheless sympathetic to a wide range of composers. He calls the division of the musical world into two "wholly separate and adversarial camps" that began shortly after the middle of the nineteenth century an "unholy schism" and even acknowledges that his own earlier monograph on Liszt (1900) had been overly one-sided, a work of "propaganda and apology."[40] Louis announces that as far as program music is concerned, he is now prepared to distinguish between Liszt's historical importance and his artistic achievements, particularly now that more and more composers are turning away from program music. In the same account Louis also deplores the New German School's deprecation of Brahms in the last third of the nineteenth century as a product of prejudice and "party dogma." This polarity had led the "progressives" to "crucify" Brahms as a formalist instead of learning from his art. Brahms's supporters, in turn, had contributed to the "unholy schism" by failing to learn from the achievements of the New Germans and by making Brahms the "idol" of those who worshipped at the altar of academicism. With the benefit of historical distance, Louis maintains, we can now see that composers of the nineteenth century worked through the problems of program music more thoroughly than at any time before, and the gradual turn away from it at the present should not be understood to indicate that this repertory had been based on a false principle. If nothing else, he argues, program music had emancipated composers from the unthinking adherence to conventional schemata that had been handed down from one generation to the next. Louis warns against an over-reaction against program music, which would simply move the musical world from one extreme to the other.[41]

As it turns out, however, this is precisely what would happen. In a swing of the aesthetic pendulum, some of the most prominent composers active at the turn of the century chose to turn their backs on program music and embrace the aesthetics of purity offered by absolute music.

40. Rudolf Louis, *Die deutsche Musik der Gegenwart* (Munich and Leipzig: Georg Müller, 1909), 130: "zwei vollständig geschiedene feindliche Lager…dieses unheilvolle Schisma." Ibid., 136: "Propaganda und Apologie."

41. Louis, *Die deutsche Musik der Gegenwart*, 136–40, 152, 157, 206, 208, 313.

13 Qualities Recast

The reification of absolute music as a repertory in the middle of the nineteenth century compelled writers to recast the qualities that had for so long dominated discussions about the relationship between music's essence and effect. Expression, beauty, form, autonomy, and disclosiveness would remain basic to this discourse but in new configurations.

- **Expression.** Until the 1920s, debates about expression tended to center on *what* music expressed, not *whether* it could express anything. In the years after World War I, however, a variety of "hard" formalism arose in part as a backlash against what many perceived to be the overwrought expressivity of works from the pre-War decades. The aesthetics of "New Objectivity" conceived of the musical work as a construct, not as an outpouring of expression; the more radical formalists of the time downplayed or even denied altogether the expressive capacities of music.
- **Beauty.** The role of beauty in all the fine arts declined precipitously from the closing decades of the nineteenth century onward. It remained an important quality in the minds of many but was no longer the defining element of art. Aesthetics, once considered the philosophy of beauty, came to be thought of as the philosophy of art.
- **Form.** In the ongoing debate about the relationship of form and content, form gained the upper hand. For centuries critics had regarded music as different from (and for the most part inferior to) all other arts because of its lack of objective content. With the gradual acceptance of abstraction in the visual arts around the turn of the twentieth century, critics came to see form as the central element of the visual arts. By the early 1900s the newfound prestige of abstraction in painting and sculpture would enhance the status of form in music.
- **Autonomy.** The renewed emphasis on form in the early twentieth century emphasized the abstract nature of music, which in turn reinforced conceptions of its autonomy. Purity became an ideal of unprecedented importance, and the aesthetic prestige of absolute music, conceived as a repertory, grew enormously as a result. However, the fact that even supposedly autonomous works could be used to serve ideological purposes of their own eventually called into question the most basic premises of aesthetic autonomy.
- **Disclosiveness.** For many critics, the disclosive capacity to disclose higher truths became music's most distinctive quality, and absolute music,

conceived as a repertory, was uniquely positioned to reveal truths in ways that other arts—representational, conceptual, spatial, material—could not. Through Wagner, Schopenhauer's view of music—itself a continuation of a longer tradition of idealist thought—became a paradigm of Western thought about both the nature and the power of music.

■ EXPRESSION

Most of the responses to *Vom Musikalisch-Schönen*, as we have seen, took issue with its views on expression, often ignoring or misrepresenting Hanslick's repeated and explicit affirmation of music's power not only to arouse feelings but even to project the dynamic—the motion, the *Bewegung*—of those feelings. Hanslick held that while music could not convey the specific "whispering of longing" or the "violence of bellicosity," it could convey the dynamic of whispering or violence.[1] This subtlety seems to have been lost on many commentators, however, including at least some who were for the most part sympathetic to the treatise's broader arguments.

The notion that purely instrumental music could be expressive was really never in question. As Karl Grunsky argued in his *Musikästhetik* of 1907, the differences between absolute, program, and vocal music were ultimately minimal: all music is expressive.[2] Grunsky's treatise captures the paradoxical fact that by the beginning of the twentieth century Hanslick's thought, dismissed as old-fashioned, was so deeply engrained in discourse that the ideas he had promoted were no longer necessarily associated with him. Grunsky notes that "it is conceded, maintained, and expected that music is the expression of the soul's life," because "hardly anyone pays attention to Hanslick anymore," The account of musical expression that follows, however, is deeply indebted to *Vom Musikalisch-Schönen*. Grunsky encourages his readers to think about musical expression in terms of its dynamic, not in terms of representation or emotion: "Music provides only the moving tones, not the motivational foundations behind them."[3] Yet Grunsky never cites Hanslick by name. In a similar fashion, Eugen Schmitz began his *Musikästhetik* of 1915 by outlining the history of the opposition between the aesthetics of form (as represented by Hanslick) and the aesthetics of content (as represented by Wagner), accused both of parties

---

1. *VMS*, 1:43: "Das *Flüstern*? Ja;—aber keineswegs der 'Sehnsucht'; das *Stürmen*? Allerdings, doch nicht der Kampflust." Payzant's translation of this passage (*OMB*, 9) obscures Hanslick's point by ignoring the repetition of the noun implied by the genitive case.

2. Karl Grunsky, *Musikästhetik* (Leipzig: G. J. Göschen, 1907), 31–32, 146–47.

3. Grunsky, *Musikästhetik*, 22: "Daß Musik Ausdruck seelischen Lebens sei, wird heutzutage, da man Hanslick kaum mehr beachtet, fast von allen Seiten zugegeben, verfochten, verlangt." Ibid., 24: "Die Musik gibt nur die bewegten Töne, aber nicht die begründenden Ursachen."

of one-sidedeness, and then described their fusion in the aesthetic thought of more recent times.[4]

Hanslick's more narrow conceptualization of music as a play of motion in tones—*tönend bewegte Formen*—would be pursued by such critics and theorists as August Halm (1869–1929), Heinrich Schenker (1868–1935), Ernst Kurth (1886–1946), and Hans Mersmann (1891–1971), each of whom placed central importance on energy and motion in identifying the essence of the art. In the 1930s the musicologist Rudolf Schäfke coined the term *Energetik*— "energetics"—to describe these analytical perspectives and methodologies.[5] Halm, for example, talked about musical themes as "the material into which motion is introduced," which produces a "drama of forces...but not a drama of persons or personifications."[6] As Lee Rothfarb observes, "rather than emotionalizing musical events," Halm "*dynamicized* them."[7] Schenker, in turn, called music the "animated motion of tones in naturally given space," the "composing-out...of the sounds present in nature. Man brings motion, the law of all life, into this sound, which nature has prefigured in his ear....Everything in music depends on this motion, on this creation."[8]

After the Music of the Future

Since at least the end of the eighteenth century, every generation of composers has worked to differentiate itself from the one before: the imperative of originality weighs on cohorts as well as on individuals. At some point around the turn of the twentieth century, the New German School began to grow old. The idea of basing an orchestral work on a literary model, as the Viennese critic Richard Kralik noted in 1897, had lost its freshness and novelty. The

---

4. Eugen Schmitz, *Musikästhetik* (Leipzig: Breitkopf & Härtel, 1915), 1–6.

5. See Lee Rothfarb, "Hermeneutics and Energetics: Analytical Alternatives in the Early 1900s," *JMT* 36 (1992): 43–68; idem, "Energetics," in *The Cambridge History of Western Music Theory*, ed. Thomas Christensen (Cambridge: Cambridge University Press, 2002), 927–55. On the nineteenth-century antecedents of these theories, see Köhler, *Natur und Geist*. On the surprisingly close connection of energetics and hermeneutics, see Matthew Pritchard, " 'A Heap of Broken Images'? Reviving Austro-German Debates over Musical Meaning, 1900–36," *JRMA* 138 (2013): 129–74.

6. August Halm, *Von Zwei Kulturen der Musik* (Munich: Georg Müller, 1913), 50: "Das Thema ist das Material, in das eine Bewegung hineinfährt....Ein Drama von Kräften haben wir vor uns; nicht aber ein Drama von Personen oder Personifikationen."

7. Rothfarb, "Hermeneutics and Energetics," 56; emphasis in original.

8. Heinrich Schenker, "Die Kunst der Improvisation," *Das Meisterwerk in der Musik* 1 (1925): 12: "Musik ist lebendige Bewegung von Tönen im naturgegebenen Raum, Auskomponierung...des in der Natur gegebenen Klanges. Das Gesetz alles Lebens, die Bewegung,...trägt der Mensch auch in den Klang hinein, den die Natur in seinem Ohr vorgezeichnet hat. Alles in der Musik kommt auf diese Bewegung, auf diese Zeugung an." Cook, *The Schenker Project*, 48–62, makes a strong case for the influence of Hanslick's thought on Schenker. On the implications of the concept of motion in music theory, see Steve Larson, *Musical Forces: Motion, Metaphor, and Meaning in Music* (Bloomington: Indiana University Press, 2012).

"moderns" who were striving to "clamber higher and farther up the proud paths of Berlioz and Liszt" had fallen into an epigonism that by its very nature was "untrue, affected, stilted, and transitory. They think they are still making music of the future, but all they are making is the music of the past, of the forties and fifties. What was true and alive then is no longer so."[9] In the early decades of the twentieth century, program music relinquished its position as the leading "progressive" aesthetic. The reasons for this decline have never been adequately explained and are beyond the scope of the present study. But there can be no doubt that the simultaneous rise in the prestige of absolute music during this time contributed to these changing perceptions.[10] The turn away from program music and toward absolute music is evident in the output of three of the period's most celebrated composers, all of whom had written major programmatic works earlier in their careers. Claude Debussy (1862–1918), Arnold Schoenberg (1874–1951), and Igor Stravinsky (1882–1971) exemplify a broader turn toward the repertory of absolute music and an acceptance of the aesthetic principles behind it.

Debussy cultivated program music throughout most of his professional life, and to great critical acclaim. He had won praise for such works as the *Prélude à l'après-midi d'un faune* (1894), based on—and in certain respects structurally related to—Mallarmé's poem of the same name, and *La mer* (1905), whose three movements bear the titles "De l'aube à midi sur la mer," "Jeux de vagues," and "Dialogue du vent et de la mer."[11] In the last three years of his life, however, Debussy turned toward what he and his French contemporaries called *musique pure*. As he wrote to Stravinsky in October 1915, he had recently composed "nothing except pure music: twelve etudes for piano; two sonatas for various instruments, in our old form, which graciously did not impose tetralogical efforts on auditory faculties."[12] The reference to "tetralogical efforts" is of course a dig at Wagner's *Ring* cycle: conciseness, clarity, and transparency were among the

9. Richard Kralik, "Musik," *Das Vaterland: Zeitung für die österreichische Monarchie*, 1 January 1897, 1: "Diese Modernen sehen nicht, daß auch sie…einem Epigonenthum des Genies verfallen, das wie jedes Epigonenthum unwahr, gespreizt, aufgestelzt, vergänglich ist. Sie glauben noch Zukunftsmusik zu machen, und machen doch nur die Vergangenheitsmusik der Vierziger- und Fünfziger-Jahre. Was damals wahr und lebendig war, ist es jetzt nicht mehr." Sandra McColl, *Music Criticism in Vienna, 1896–1897*, 220, identifies Kralik as the author of this unsigned piece.

10. Constantin Floros, *Musik als Botschaft* (Wiesbaden: Breitkopf & Härtel, 1989), 84–89, surveys the decline under the rubric "Das Unbehagen gegenüber der Programmusik" but offers no explanation for this "discomfort" beyond appealing to the long-standing suspicions about overly pictorial music, reservations that were already being articulated quite forcefully as early as the eighteenth century.

11. See David J. Code, "Hearing Debussy Reading Mallarmé: Music *après Wagner* in the *Prélude à l'après-midi d'un faune*," *JAMS* 54 (2001): 493–554.

12. Debussy to Stravinsky, letter of 24 October 1915, in Debussy, *Correspondance, 1884–1918*, ed. François Lesure (Paris: Hermann, 1993), 362: "Je n'ai d'ailleurs écrit que de la musique pure: douze *Études* pour le piano; deux *Sonates* pour divers instruments, dans notre vieille forme, qui gracieusement

characteristic features of *musique pure*.[13] As Debussy's jibe suggests, *musique pure* was at least in part a French response against Wagner and *Wagnerisme*. On a still broader scale, it exemplified the idea of music as music, as opposed to music as metaphysics. In a 1909 interview published under the title "The Music of Today and the Music of Tomorrow"—yet another allusion to Wagner—Debussy expressed disdain for composers who attempted to use music as a vehicle of philosophical ideas: "One combines, constructs, and imagines themes that seek to express ideas; one develops them, modifies them when they encounter other themes that represent other ideas, one puts forth metaphysics, but one does not put forth music."[14]

In an essay published in 1909, the same year as Debussy's interview, Schoenberg characterized the contemporary "flowering of so-called absolute music" as a "natural reaction against Wagner, the theatre-musician." The partisans of Wagner, Liszt, Wolf, and Bruckner, Schoenberg observed, had grown "old," particularly in relation to art, "which is constantly self-renewing. But then simply senile, too. And they thus formed a closed block, more overbearing, more opposed to developments than their predecessors had been. For these former revolutionaries took their past as the present, destined to suppress the future."[15] Three years later, Schoenberg opened another essay with this pronouncement:

> There are relatively few people who are capable of understanding purely musically what music has to say. The assumption that a piece of music must arouse representations of some kind, and that a work has not been understood or amounts to nothing if it does not do this, is as widespread as only that which is false and banal can be.[16]

---

n'imposait pas aux facultés audivites des efforts tétralogiques." In his English translation of this passage in Debussy's correspondence, Roger Nichols places quotation marks around "pure" and renders *forme* as "style"; see Debussy, *Letters*, ed. François Lesure and Roger Nichols, trans. Roger Nichols (Cambridge, MA: Harvard University Press, 1987), 309. On Debussy's shift to purely instrumental genres around 1914, see Marianne Wheeldon, *Debussy's Late Style* (Bloomington: Indiana University Press, 2009).

13. For a contemporary characterization of *musique pure*, see Gaston Carraud, "La musique pure dans l'école française contemporaine," *S.I.M. Revue musicale mensuelle* 6 (1910): 483–505.

14. Claude Debussy, "La musique d'aujourd'hui et celle de demain" (1909), in *Monsieur Croche et autres écrits*, 2nd ed., ed. François Lesure (Paris: Gallimard, 1987), 296: "On combine, on construit, on imagine des thèmes qui veulent exprimer des idées; on les développe, on les modifie à la rencontre d'autres thèmes qui représent d'autres idées, on fait de la métaphysique, mais on ne fait pas de la musique."

15. Arnold Schoenberg, "Über Musikkritik," *Der Merker* 1 (1909): 60: "Aber die Vorkämpfer Wagners, Liszts, Hugo Wolfs, Bruckners wurden alt. Alt vor Allem im Verhältnis zur Kunst, die sich stets erneut. Dann aber auch: einfach senil. Und so bildeten sie einen geschlossenen Block, der entwicklungsfeindlicher und hochfahrender war als der seiner Vorgänger. Denn die ehemaligen Revolutionäre hielten ihre Vergangenheit für die Gegenwart, die bestimmt ist, die Zukunft zu unterdrücken....Die natürliche Reaktion auf Wagner, den Theatermusiker, hatte ein Aufblühen der sogenannten absoluten Musik hervorgebracht." Translation from "About Music Criticism," in Schoenberg, *Style and Idea: Selected Writings of Arnold Schoenberg*, ed. Leonard Stein (Berkeley and Los Angeles: University of California Press, 1975), 192–93.

16. Schoenberg, "Das Verhältnis zum Text" (1912), in Schoenberg, *"Stile herrschen, Gedanken siegen": Ausgewählte Schriften*, ed. Anna Maria Morazzoni (Mainz: Schott, 2007), 67: "Es gibt relativ wenig Menschen, die imstande sind, rein musikalisch zu verstehen, was Musik zu sagen hat. Die Annahme,

This association of program music with the "banal" is one that Schoenberg, like so many other composers of his generation, had made only recently. His turn away from program music is overshadowed by his more obvious break with tonality around this same time,. Neither move came easily to him, and he struggled with the idea of program music in one way or another throughout his life. When Henri Hinrichsen, chief of the Leipzig publishing firm C. F. Peters, agreed in 1912 to publish the *Fünf Orchesterstücke*, op. 16, he asked that the composer supply titles for the individual movements. In his diary we can see Schoenberg wrestling with this request: he thought he "might give in," on the grounds that he already had possible titles in mind for the generically entitled "five pieces for orchestra" he had finished three years before. Still, he found himself

> in general not sympathetic to the idea. For one of the wonderful things about music is that one can say everything in such a way that anyone who is knowledgeable understands everything, and yet one still has one's secrets that one doesn't admit even to oneself and doesn't blab about. But a title blabs. Besides: what was to be said was said by the music. Why words on top of it? If words were needed, they would be in the music. But the music says more than words. The titles that I might use don't give away anything because they are in part quite obscure, in part technical. Namely: I. Premonitions (everyone has them), II. Past (everyone has them, too), III. Chord colorations (technical), IV. Peripeteia (is certainly general enough), V. The obbligato (or perhaps better: "extended" or "endless") recitative. In any case with the comment that this is a technical matter of publication, not an indication of "poetic content."[17]

The titles did not appear in the first edition of 1912, but Schoenberg included them later (in a slightly different form) in the concert program of a performance he conducted in Amsterdam in 1914; furthermore, the second edition, published by Peters in 1922, included the titles (altered slightly once again); and for a different orchestral arrangement in 1949, he changed one of the titles yet again.[18] Schoenberg later claimed not to have been opposed to program music

ein Tonstück müsse Vorstellungen irgendwelcher Art erwecken, und wenn solche ausbleiben, sei das Tonstück nicht verstanden worden oder es tauge nichts, ist so weit verbreitet, wir nur das Falsche und Banale verbreitet sein kann."

17. Schoenberg, *Berliner Tagebuch*, ed. Josef Rufer (Frankfurt am Main: Propyläen, 1974), 13–14 (entry for 28 January 1912): "Im ganzen die Idee nicht sympathisch. Denn Musik ist darin wunderbar, daß man alles sagen kann, so daß der Wissende alles versteht, und trotzdem hat man seine Geheimnisse, die, die man sich selbst nicht gesteht, nicht ausplaudert. Titel aber plaudert aus. Außerdem: Was zu sagen war, hat die Musik gesagt. Wozu dann noch das Wort. Wären Worte nötig, wären sie drin. Aber die Musik sagt doch mehr als Worte. Die Titel, die ich vielleicht geben werde, plaudern nun, da sie teils höchst dunkel sind, teils Technisches sagen, nichts aus. Nämlich: I. Vorgefühle (hat jeder), II. Vergangenheit (hat auch jeder), III. Akkordfärbungen (Technisches), IV. Peripetie (ist wohl allgemein genug), V. Das obligate (vielleicht besser das 'ausgeführte' oder das 'unendliche') Rezitativ. Jedenfalls mit der Anmerkung, daß es sich um Verlagstechnische und nicht um 'poetischen Inhalt' handelt."

18. For a detailed account of Schoenberg's various changes to the titles, see Michael Mäckelmann, *Arnold Schönberg: Fünf Orchesterstücke op. 16* (Munich: Wilhelm Fink, 1987), 49–53.

per se and said as much in a 1933 radio interview, maintaining that the source of a composer's inspiration is irrelevant. When asked if he would describe his music as "absolute—pure music," the composer responded: "No, I do not prefer to call it that. Fancy is the dominant force which drives the artist, and it is not of great difference [*sic*] to me, whether it is a poetical idea or a musical idea. A musician can always only see music, and the cause is of no importance. I am not against what you call 'program music.'"[19]

Schoenberg nevertheless repressed programmatic elements in his later works, including most notably his String Trio, op. 45 (1946). According to several independent accounts from friends, students, and associates, the work reflects events related to his treatment for and recovery from a recent heart attack.[20] He confided to Thomas Mann, for example, that he had "secretly woven" certain experiences of his life into the work, including his illness, medical care, and the novel experience of male nurses in a hospital. But Schoenberg never divulged the autobiographical side of this work publicly, and the verb Mann used in transmitting the composer's account (*hineingeheimnissen*) emphasizes the furtive, almost clandestine nature of the enterprise.[21] More revealing still is Schoenberg's response, in 1950, to the challenge of writing program notes for a recording of his early and openly programmatic *Verklärte Nacht*, op. 4, a work for string sextet he had written in 1899, more than half a century before. Here he went through extraordinary contortions to justify and at the same time distance himself from the aesthetics of program music. Realizing that he could not wholly disavow the influence of Richard Dehmel's poem, he opened his commentary by explaining that

> after Brahms' death, many young composers followed the example of Richard Strauss by composing "program" music. This explains the origin of *Verklärte Nacht*. It *is* program music, illustrating and giving musical expression to the poem "Weib und Welt" of Richard Dehmel.[22]

Buried in this acknowledgment is a falsehood: *Weib und Welt* is the name of the collection in which Schoenberg found the poem *Verklärte Nacht*.[23] Whether this

19. Interview with William Lundell, 19 November 1933; see *Schoenberg and His World*, ed. Walter Frisch (Princeton: Princeton University Press, 1999), 295.

20. For a summary of these accounts, including repressed programs for other works as well, see Walter B. Bailey, *Programmatic Elements in the Works of Schoenberg* (Ann Arbor: UMI Research Press, 1984), 129–57.

21. Thomas Mann, *Die Entstehung des Doktor Faustus: Roman eines Romans* (Frankfurt am Main: Suhrkamp, 1949), 190: "er [erzählte] mir von seinem neuen...Trio und den Lebenserfahrungen,...die er in die Komposition hineingeheimnist habe, deren Niederschlag das Werk gewissermaßen sei." See Mann, *The Story of a Novel: The Genesis of Doctor Faustus*, trans. Richard and Clara Winston (New York: Knopf, 1961), 217.

22. Arnold Schoenberg, liner notes to *Verklaerte Nacht*, op. 4; Hollywood String Quartet with Alvin Dinkin, viola, and Kurt Reher, violoncello; Capitol L8118, 1950. Emphasis in original.

23. Richard Dehmel, *Weib und Welt: Gedichte* (Berlin: Schuster & Loeffler, 1896). The poem "Verklärte Nacht" appears on p. 61–63.

misstatement is the product of false memory or conscious deception, its effect is to create yet one more layer of separation between the composer and the poem by making it appear that Dehmel's poem and Schoenberg's work bear different titles.[24] But this is the least of the odd twists and turns in Schoenberg's account.

Dehmel's poem tells the story of two lovers walking through a forest at night: the woman confesses to the man that she "walks in sin" next to him, for she is carrying the unborn child of her husband, whom she does not love. The man tells the woman that the child "should be no burden to your soul," and he pledges that the radiance of their love, reflected in nature, will "transfigure" all. In his program notes, Schoenberg insists that

> because it does not illustrate any action or drama, but was restricted to portray nature and to express human emotions, it seems that, due to this attitude, my composition has gained qualities which can also satisfy even if one does not know what it illustrates; or in other words, it offers the possibility to be appreciated as "pure" music. Thus, perhaps, it can make you forget the poem.
>
> Nevertheless, much of the poem deserves appreciation because of its highly poetic presentation of the emotions provoked by the beauty of nature, and for the distinguished moral attitude in dealing with a staggeringly difficult human problem.

The claim that the music "does not illustrate any action or drama" is stupefyingly disingenuous, particularly in the context of Schoenberg's account, which maps out precise correspondences between the poetic narrative and the music, complete with musical notation of the relevant motifs as they relate to Dehmel's poem. The composer's sixteen musical examples, presented in double columns, occupy most of the second page of a two-page flyer inserted into the LP recording. His method replicates the leitmotif guides to Wagnerian music dramas:

> Promenading in a park (Ex. 1), in a clear, cold moonlight night (Ex. 2 and 3), the wife confesses a tragedy to the man in a dramatic outburst (Ex. 4)....A climactic ascension, elaborating the motif (Ex. 8), expresses her self-accusation of her great sin....But "the voice of a man speaks, a man whose generosity is as sublime as his love" (Ex. 10).

Schoenberg's justification for this precise alignment of poetic and musical events is that "much of the poem deserves appreciation" for *its* "presentation of the emotions provoked by the beauty of nature, and for the distinguished moral attitude in dealing with a staggeringly difficult human problem." Schoenberg

24. The program of the premiere performance, in Vienna on 18 March 1902, identifies the work as "Sextett nach Richard Dehmels Gedicht 'Die verklärte Nacht,'" and the program for a performance in Prague in 1904 calls it "'Verklärte Nacht,' nach dem gleichnamigen Gedichte DEHMELS in dessen 'WEIB UND WELT' für sechs Streichinstrumente." Both programs are reproduced in Albrecht Dümling, "Public Loneliness: Atonality and the Crisis of Subjectivity in Schönberg's Opus 15," in *Schönberg and Kandinsky: An Historic Encounter*, ed. Konrad Boehmer (Amsterdam: Harwood, 1997), 103–4.

thereby associates dramatic content with the poem but not with his music, at least not in any direct way; it is as if the two function on altogether separate planes. He could not have seriously entertained this view of course, and at least some of the confusion may be ascribed to the composer's non-native English. Yet the motivation behind all these rationalizations and their attendant contradictions goes back to an underlying sense of embarrassment that this *is* a work of program music. His defense of *Verklärte Nacht*, in the end, resonates with long-standing attitudes toward this kind of music as expressed by Mahler ("not the highest rung on the ladder") and Schumann long before ("Let me first hear that you have written beautiful music"): that if a work of program music cannot stand on its own, without a program, then it is deficient as a work of music.

Stravinsky was equally anxious to brush away evidence linking at least some of his earlier works with programmatic content. He went to great lengths to repress the connections between his *Scherzo fantastique* of 1908 and Maurice Maeterlinck's *La vie des abeilles* (1901), a socio-philosophical essay that takes as its point of departure the "life of bees." Stravinsky insisted decades later that he had written the work "as a piece of 'pure' symphonic music," attributing the idea of bees to "a choreographer." He conceded that had always been "fascinated by bees" but insisted that he had "never attempted to evoke them in my work (as, indeed, what pupil of the composer of the *Flight of the Bumblebee* would?)."[25] Richard Taruskin has shown in detail that this is a "patent fib," providing as evidence a letter from the composer written in June 1907 to none other than Rimsky-Korsakov, in which Stravinsky says that he has been "captivated" by Maeterlinck's account of the life of bees and that he is now at work on an orchestral piece to be called "'The Bees' (after Maeterlinck): Fantastic Scherzo." "When we see each other," Stravinsky added, "I'll show you the spots I've taken for the program; in a letter I can't give you a complete idea."[26] Stravinsky's "deception," as Taruskin notes, was not cynical so much as "principled," for the composer "badly needed to dissociate himself" in his Parisian and American years "from an artistic milieu that put such stock in program music that one could not so much as begin writing a scherzo without having some definite 'subject' in mind."[27] Taruskin has also pointed to other instances of Stravinsky's attempts to cover up his programmatic tracks, most notably in the ballet *Le sacre*

---

25. Igor Stravinsky and Robert Craft, *Conversations with Igor Stravinsky* (Garden City, NY: Doubleday, 1959), 40.

26. Richard Taruskin, *Stravinsky and the Russian Traditions: A Biography of the Works through "Mavra,"* 2 vols. (Berkeley and Los Angeles: University of California Press, 1996), 1:6–7. The translation is by Taruskin.

27. Taruskin, *Stravinsky and the Russian Traditions*, 1:8. For further commentary on the *Scherzo fantastique* and on the broader tradition of depicting insects, fairies, and other small creatures in music, see Francesca Brittan, "On Microscopic Hearing: Fairy Magic, Natural Science, and the *Scherzo fantastique*," *JAMS* 64 (2011): 527–600.

du printemps, which was, the composer repeatedly claimed, from the 1920s onward, a "purely musical" work.[28]

Stravinsky's turn toward the aesthetics of absolute music had already begun by December 1915, as is evident in an interview he gave in French to the American journalist C. Stanley Wise. In a somewhat garbled translation whose meaning is nevertheless clear enough, Stravinsky declared that "programme music...has been obviously discontinued as being distinctly an uncouth form which already has had its day; but music, nevertheless, still drags out its life in accordance with these false notions and conceptions. Without absolutely defying the programme, musicians still draw upon sources foreign to their art. As a consequence, inspiration is not found in matter purely musical, but in subjects which have nothing to do with music." And in a sentence fortunately left in its original French, the composer concluded: "La musique est trop bête pour exprimer autre chose[s] que la musique."[29]

Stravinsky's most pointed rejection of program music came in a lecture he gave in Paris in December 1935, in which he apologized for not having sufficient time to give a technical analysis of his new Concerto for Two Pianos. He said that he would be "embarrassed" to provide any "extramusical commentary" on the work.[30] He then went on to distinguish between two types of listening, the first of which he compares to "self-interested love, wherein one demands from music emotions of a general sort—joy, sorrow, sadness, a subject for dreaming on, forgetfulness of ordinary existence." But this attitude "devalues music by assigning it a utilitarian end."

> Why not love it for its own sake? Why not love it as one loves a picture, for the sake of the beautiful painting, the beautiful design, the beautiful composition? Why not admit that music has an intrinsic value, independent of the sentiments or images that it may evoke by analogy, and that can only corrupt the hearer's judgment? Music needs no help. It is sufficient unto itself. Don't look for anything else in it beyond what it already contains.[31]

---

28. Taruskin, *Defining Russia Musically,* 370.

29. C. Stanley Wise, "American Music Is True Art, Says Stravinsky," *New York Tribune,* 16 January 1916, 3. I am grateful to William Robin for calling my attention to this interview and for sharing with me a typescript of his essay "Formalizing a 'Purely Acoustic' Musical Objectivity: Revisiting a 1915 Interview with Stravinsky," in *Reassessing Stravinsky's "Le sacre du printemps," 1913/2013,* ed. Severine Neff, Maureen A. Carr, and Gretchen Horlacher (Bloomington: Indiana University Press, forthcoming).

30. Igor Stravinsky, "Quelques confidences sur la musique" (1935), in Eric Walter White, *Stravinsky: The Composer and His Works,* 2nd ed. (Berkeley and Los Angeles: University of California Press, 1979), 585: "Quant à des commentaires extramusicaux, de moi, vous n'en attendez pas, j'espère. Je serais vraiment bien embarrassé de vous en fournir."

31. Stravinsky, "Quelques confidences sur la musique," 585: "Il y a différentes manières d'aimer et d'apprécier la musique. Il y a, par exemple, la manière que j'appellerai l'amour intéressé, cell où l'on demande à musique des émotions d'ordre général, la joie, la douleur, la tristesse, un sujet de rêve, l'oubli

Composers were not the only ones to de-program music history. When the prestige of program music began to decline around the turn of the twentieth century, critics sympathetic to the idea of music as a wholly self-referential art minimized and in some cases simply dismissed extramusical elements in the works of earlier composers. Accounts of Beethoven are particularly revealing in this regard. The distinguished English critic Donald Francis Tovey (1875–1940) struggled to hide his prejudice against program music in his entry on the subject for the eleventh edition of the *Encyclopedia Britannica* (1911). Beethoven, he asserts, "recorded his theory of programme music on the title-page" of the *Pastoral* Symphony "by calling it 'rather the expression of feeling than tone-painting.'" Tovey then goes on to claim that

> there is not a bar...that would have been otherwise if its "programme" had never been thought of.... The nightingale, cuckoo and quail have exactly the same function in the coda of the slow movement as dozens of similar non-thematic episodes at the close of other slow movements.... The "merry meeting of country folk" is a subject that lends itself admirably to Beethoven's form of *scherzo* (q.v.); and the thunderstorm, which interrupts the last repetition of this scherzo, and forms an introduction to the finale, is nonetheless purely musical for being, like several of Beethoven's inventions, without any formal parallel in other works.[32]

By this account, programmatic elements that conform to formal conventions are first and foremost formal conventions, while structurally unconventional elements manifest the composer's proclivity to create forms that follow no established pattern. The notion that a poetic program might in any way have shaped the music is to Tovey's mind simply not plausible.

A similar line of argumentation is evident in Walter Riezler's Beethoven monograph of 1936. Riezler (1878–1965) was a critic with strong modernist sympathies and a member of the Deutscher Werkbund, an organization of artists, architects, and designers who counted among its members Ludwig Mies van der Rohe, Peter Behrens, and Josef Hoffmann. In his Beethoven monograph of 1936, Riezler announces at the outset that his ideas are founded on "a profound

---

de la vie prosaïque. Ce serait déprécier la musique que de lui assigner un pareil but utilitaire. Pourquoi ne pas l'aimer pour elle-même? Pourquoi ne pas l'aimer comme on aime un tableau, pour la belle peinture, le beau dessin, la belle composition? Pourquoi ne pas admettre la musique comme une valeur en soi, indépendante des sentiments et des images que, par analogie, elle pourrait évoquer, et qui ne sauraient que fausser le jugement de l'auditeur? La musique n'a pas besoin d'adjuvant. Elle se suffit à elle-même. N'y cherchons donc pas autre chose que ce qu'elle comporte." Translation in Richard Taruskin, "Myth," 4; also in *Defining Russia Musically*, 366.

32. Donald Francis Tovey, "Programme Music," in *The Encyclopaedia Britannica*, 11th ed. (Cambridge: At the University Press, 1911). Tovey would revise this and other entries for later editions of the *Encyclopedia Britannica*, but the essence of this particular passage would remain intact throughout; see Tovey, *Musical Articles from the Encyclopaedia Britannica*, ed. Hubert J. Foss (London: Oxford University Press, 1944), 168.

conviction of music's autonomy."[33] He rejects the position of his contemporary Paul Bekker, who had based his own study of Beethoven (1910) on the idea that the composer was "first and foremost a thinker and poet, and only secondarily a musician."[34] Throughout his lengthy chapter titled "Beethoven and Absolute Music," Riezler downplays and at times simply explains away the programmatic elements in the composer's music. In his treatment of the Piano Sonata in E-flat Major, op. 81a (*Les adieux*), for example, he says that the movement titles ("Das Lebewohl," "Abwesenheit," "Das Wiedersehen") merely clarify "what the attentive performer or listener will notice in any event: that the dialogical outer movements contrast with the monological interior movement, that the tension-filled accents of the first movement contrast with the relaxed jubilation of the last movement."[35] Likewise, Riezler is certain that listeners will hear a sense of "otherworldly religiosity" in the slow movement of the String Quartet in A Minor, op. 132, even without knowing the composer's descriptive title for it ("Heiliger Dankgesang eines Genesenen an die Gottheit, in der lydischen Tonart").[36] Riezler consistently avoids associating Beethoven's instrumental music with ideas and emphasizes instead the gestalt of each work, its structure and organic wholeness.

Hans Mersmann's Beethoven monograph of 1922 also minimizes the importance of programmatic elements, acknowledging their presence in earlier works but arguing that the composer eventually "outgrew" this approach to his art.[37] Fritz Cassirer's *Beethoven und die Gestalt* (1925) is even more rigorous in its concentration on the score and the score alone, emphasizing the processes of growth and transformation of motivic ideas.[38] Beethoven, hailed in the middle of the nineteenth century as the figure who had rescued instrumental music from empty formalism by infusing it with poetic content, had now been recast into the composer who preserved and extended the integrity of music as a timeless, universal art, an art whose most important element was form.

---

33. Walter Riezler, *Beethoven* (Berlin and Zurich: Atlantis, 1936), 11: "Das ganze Buch ruht auf dem Grunde einer tiefen Überzeugung von der Autonomie der Musik."

34. Paul Bekker, *Beethoven* (Berlin: Schuster & Loeffler, 1910), 560: "Beethoven ist in erster Linie Denker und Dichter, in zweiter Linie erst Musiker." Riezler does not, however, cite Bekker's important qualification in the two sentences that immediately follow: "Er trägt nie Bedenken, die Forderungen der Idee denen des Klanges unterzuordnen. Sein ganzes Schaffen ist ein Ringen der Idee mit der Klangmaterie." On the polemics between Riezler and Bekker, see Pritchard, "'A Heap of Broken Images'?," 170–71.

35. Riezler, *Beethoven*, 88: "Die allgemeinen Überschriften sind brauchbarer, wenn sie auch nur das deutlicher machen, was der aufmerksame Spieler oder Hörer ohenhin merkt: den dialogischen Ecksätzen steht der Monolog des Mittelsatzes gegenüber, den spannungsreichen Akzenten des ersten der gelöste Jubel des letzten."

36. Riezler, *Beethoven*, 87.

37. Hans Mersmann, *Beethoven: Die Synthese der Stile* (Berlin: Julius Bard, 1922), 31.

38. Fritz Cassirer, *Beethoven und die Gestalt* (Berlin and Leipzig: Deutsche Verlags-Anstalt, 1925).

These more structurally oriented accounts of Beethoven's music reflect broader changes in the scholarly study of music altogether. Guido Adler, Hanslick's successor at the University of Vienna, emphasized the history of musical style in a way that accorded analysis central importance. He did not ignore biography, institutional histories, or cultural settings, but in his *Der Stil in der Musik* (1911) and *Methode der Musikgeschichte* (1919), he placed unprecedented emphasis on the works themselves and their formal attributes. He encouraged historians to think of the history of music not so much as a series of works by great composers (Bach, Haydn, Mozart, Beethoven, et al.) but rather as an unfolding of musical styles through their hands. This was in keeping with Adler's efforts to place the still-young discipline of musicology on a more objective, "scientific" basis. "Purely musical" analysis, he maintained, both by word and by example, would help musicology establish its credentials as a legitimate field of study within the academy, comparable in its "objective" methods to the only slightly older field of art history.[39] Analysis, long associated with the pedagogy of composition, was now a means by which to enhance the understanding of a given work. By confining itself to the notes on the page, analysis lent itself to a more dispassionate approach to the study of music.

Objectivity

The turn to an aesthetics of objectivity in the 1920s has long been recognized as a reaction against what many perceived as the overwrought, overblown idioms of previous decades. A significant number of composers rejected the enormous orchestras, advanced chromatic harmony, and extreme expressionism that had characterized much of the early twentieth century's musical avant-garde. The aesthetics of objectivity proved especially attractive to the new generation of composers and listeners coming of age after the Great War.[40] What German writers called *Neue Sachlichkeit* (the "New Objectivity") emphasized a detached perspective toward all the arts; this resonated with Hanslick's brief against the immanence of emotion in music, even if no writer of the time cared to invoke his name. In any event, the protean concept of absolute music provided commentators with a ready-made term that helped characterize this new approach.

Purity and an attitude of emotional detachment were central to this new aesthetic. As the German critic Adolph Weissmann (1873–1929) noted in 1925:

---

39. Guido Adler, *Der Stil in der Musik*, 20, 68, 97; ibid., *Methode der Musikgeschichte* (Leipzig: Breitkopf & Härtel, 1919), 17–18, 58–59, 109, 121. On Adler's efforts to put musicology on a "scientific" basis, see Karnes, *Music, Criticism, and the Challenge of History*, part 3, "Guido Adler and the Problem of Science."

40. For an overview of the aesthetics of objectivity in the 1920s and '30s, see Lippman, *A History of Western Musical Aesthetics*, chapter 13, "Conceptions of Objectivity."

One of the chief tenets in the doctrine of the new music is evolution toward the absolute,—in other words toward pure music, or better still, pure counterpoint.... The tendency, it is obvious, has been developed in opposition to the music of the nineteenth century. It is in conflict with the romantic, the emotional and the naturalistic. It demands of music the abolition of everything realistic, everything human, so that the art may emerge in its native purity.[41]

The conviction that art should distance itself from "everything human" is also central to the Spanish philosopher and essayist José Ortega y Gasset's *La deshumanización del arte*, another work issued in 1925. The "new sensibility" advocated by Ortega y Gasset (1883–1955) was a turn against personal expression. "From Beethoven to Wagner," he complained, music had been tantamount to an art of "confession," with each composer creating "great structures of sound to accommodate his autobiography." Our experience of this art, in turn, can be only passive and vague: aesthetic pleasure amounts to a kind of "contagion." But this contagion is an "unconscious phenomenon," and art must instead "be full clarity, high noon of the intellect," not "blind." For this reason, the arts "had to be relieved of private sentiments and purified in an exemplary objectification." Debussy was the first to achieve this in music. His turn toward objectivity now makes it "possible to listen to music serenely, without swoons and tears.... Debussy dehumanized music," and "that is why he marks a new era in the art of music."[42] Ortega y Gasset's condemnation of emotional "contagion" through musical experience is eerily similar to Hanslick's dismissal of "pathological" listening. He even uses Hanslick's example of the lottery winner to distinguish aesthetic joy from joy in general.[43] The average person responds to the expression of emotion, but it is precisely the *absence* of such expression in Debussy's music that compels the listening mind to engage with it as a work of art. More than one critic during Debussy's lifetime had taken the composer to task on just these grounds. As Raphaël Cor observed in 1909, "One will in

41. Adolph Weissmann, "The Tyranny of the Absolute," *Modern Music* 2, no. 2 (1925): 17.

42. José Ortega y Gasset, *La deshumanización del arte* (1925), ed. Valeriano Bozal (Madrid: Espasa-Calpe, 1987), 68: "Desde Beethoven a Wagner el tema de la música fue la expresión de sentimientos personales. El artista mélico componía grandes edificios sonoros para alojar en ellos su autobiografía. No había otra manera de goce estético que la contaminación.... El arte no puede consistir en el contagio psíquico, porque éste es un fenómeno inconsciente y el arte ha de ser todo plena claridad, mediodía de intelección." Ibid., 71: "Era forzoso extirpar de la música los sentimientos privados, purificarla en una ejemplar objetivación. Esta fue la hazaña de Debussy. Desde él es posible oír música serenamente, sin embriaguez y sin llantos.... Debussy deshumanizó la música y por ello data de él la nueva era del arte sonoro." Translation from *The Dehumanization of Art and Other Essays on Art, Culture, and Literature*, 2nd ed., trans. Helen Weyl (Princeton, NJ: Princeton University Press, 1968), 26, 29–30.

43. Ortega y Gasset, *La deshumanización del arte*, 69; *The Dehumanization of Art*, 27; VMS, 1:37; OMB, 7. This passage suggests that Ortega y Gasset, who studied philosophy in Germany in 1905–8, may well have been familiar with *Vom Musikalisch-Schönen*. The treatise had been translated into Spanish in 1865 in any case.

truth have said almost everything there is to say about M. Debussy's music when you say what it is not. His originality is eminently negative. Take away rhythm, melody, and emotion, and you will just about have it."[44] Sixteen years later, this same absence of personal expression is what Ortega y Gasset would find so refreshing. For him, true art cannot appeal to the masses because "true artistic pleasure" is incompatible with "human content." Works expressing emotion require only an everyday sense of emotional empathy and a "willingness to sympathize with our neighbor's joys and worries. No wonder that nineteenth-century art has been so popular; it is made for the masses inasmuch as it is not art but an extract from life."[45]

Four years earlier the Italian-German pianist and composer Ferruccio Busoni (1866–1924) had called for "the renunciation of subjectivity" in a renewal of earlier values through what he called Young Classicism (*junge Klassizität*). In his idiosyncratically punctuated manifesto of that name from 1920, he advocated a musical style that would include a

> casting off of the *"sensuous"* and the *renunciation of subjectivity* (the path to objectivity—the author stepping back from his work—a purifying path, a hard road, a trial by fire and water), the reconquest of cheerfulness (*Serenitas*): not the corners of Beethoven's mouth, and also not the "liberating laughter" of Zarathustra, but the smile of the wise, of the godhead and—*absolute* music. Not profundity and disposition and metaphysics; but rather:—music through and through, distilled, never under the mask of figures and concepts borrowed from other realms.[46]

44. Raphaël Cor, "M. Claude Debussy et le snobisme contemporain" (1909), in *Le cas Debussy*, ed. C-Francis Caillard and José de Bérys (Paris: H. Falque, 1910), 16: "A la vérité, on en a presque tout dit, quand on a dit ce qu'elle n'est pas. Son originalité est éminemment négative. Enlevez à la musique le rythme, la mélodie, l'émotion, et vous serez bien près de l'avoir définie."

45. Ortega y Gasset, *La deshumanización del arte*, 53, 55: "Basta con poseer sensibilidad humana y dejar que en uno repercutan las angustias y alegrías del prójimo. Se comprende, pues, que el arte del siglo XIX haya sido tan popular: está hecho para la masa indiferenciada en la proporción en que no es arte, sino extracto de vida." Translation from *The Dehumanization of Art*, 9–10, 11–12.

46. Ferruccio Busoni, "Junge Klassizität" (1920), in Busoni, *Von der Einheit der Musik*, ed. Martina Weindel (Wilhelmshaven: Florian Noetzel, 2006), 95: "die Abstreifung des 'Sinnlichen' und die *Entsagung gegenüber dem Subjektivismus*, (der Weg zur Objektivität—das Zurücktreten des Autors gegenüber dem Werke—ein reinigender Weg, ein harter Gang, eine Feuer- und Wasserprobe), die Wiedereroberung der Heiterkeit (Serenitas): nicht die Mundwinkel Beethovens, und auch nicht das 'befreiende Lachen' Zarathustras, sondern das Lächeln des Weisen, der Gottheit und—*absolute* Musik. Nicht Tiefsinn und Gesinnung und Metaphysik; sondern:—Musik durchaus, destilliert, niemals unter der Maske von Figuren und Begriffen, die anderen Bezirken entlehnt sind." On the association of *serenitas* and formalism in music, see Andreas Eichhorn, "Annäherung durch Distanz: Paul Bekkers Auseinandersetzung mit der Formalästhetik Hanslicks," *AfMw* 54 (1997): 205–6. Busoni's earlier pronouncements on absolute music in his *Entwurf einer neuen Ästhetik der Tonkunst* (1907) explicitly equate "form" with the conventional structures like sonata form, theme and variations, and the like. On Busoni's aesthetics of absolute music in general, see Erinn E. Knyt, "Ferruccio Busoni and the Absolute in Music: Form, Nature and Idee," *JRMA* 137 (2012): 35–69.

Few took up Busoni's terminology, but many endorsed his attitude. Edgard Varèse announced in 1925 that music (including his own) can "express nothing but itself."[47] A similar aesthetic is evident in the writings and compositions of Paul Hindemith.[48] But no composers in the 1920s promoted the idea of music as an objective art with greater zeal than Igor Stravinsky. He described his own Octet in this way in a 1924 essay published under his name in the New York journal *The Arts*. He opens his account with a series of short, clipped, declarative statements.

My Octuor is a musical object.

This object has a form and that form is influenced by the musical matter with which it is composed.

The differences of matter determine the differences of form. One does not do the same with marble that one does with stone. . . .

My Octuor is not an "emotive" work but a musical composition based on objective elements which are sufficient in themselves. . . .

My Octuor, as I said before, is an object that has its own form. Like all other objects it has weight and occupies a place in space, and like all other objects it will necessarily lose part of its weight and space in time and through time. The loss will be in quantity, but it can not lose in quality as long as its emotive basis has objective properties and as long as this object keeps its "specific weight" One cannot alter the specific weight of an object without destroying the object itself.[49]

The quasi-scientific jargon ("objective elements," "specific weight") underscores the importance of considering the work in a detached manner, in the way one might examine a natural phenomenon or laboratory sample of some kind. The composer and educator Nadia Boulanger (1887–1979), Stravinsky's close associate at this time, adopted this kind of rhetoric in her review of an early performance of the Octet in Paris in November 1923. "In this work," she observed, "Stravinsky reveals himself as a constructivist, a geometer. . . . No transpositions, everything is music, purely."[50]

Other critics joined in the chorus to sing the praises of purity and the attendant quality of impersonality in Stravinsky's music. In 1925 the Russian

47. Louise Varèse, *Varèse: A Looking-Glass Diary* (New York: Norton, 1972), 228, quoting program notes her husband had written for a performance of his *Intégrales* in New York City in 1925.

48. See Stephen Hinton, "Aspects of Hindemith's *Neue Sachlichkeit*," *Hindemith-Jahrbuch* 14 (1985): 22–80.

49. Igor Stravinsky, "Some Ideas about My Octuor," *Arts*, January 1924, quoted in White, *Stravinsky: The Composer and his Works*, 574–75.

50. Nadia Boulanger, "Concerts Koussevitsky," *Le monde musical*, November 1923, 365: "Dans cette oeuvre, Stravinsky apparaît sous son jour de constructeur, de géomètre. . . . Nulle transposition, toute est musique, purement." For a translation of the complete portion of the review dealing with the Octet, see Scott Messing, *Neoclassicism in Music: From the Genesis of the Concept through the Schoenberg/Stravinsky Polemic* (Rochester: University of Rochester Press, 1996), 133.

émigré Boris de Schloezer (1881–1969) summed up the composer's recent production:

> The classicism of Stravinsky consists precisely in this: since Bach and Mozart there has been no music that is purer, more unobscured by extramusical elements. Psychologism, which makes our musical art impure just as it corrodes our logical thought, is completely absent in Stravinsky's production, which appears just as impersonal, just as objective, as the great creations of Classicism in painting, sculpture, and poetry. The personality of the composer is absent in his music, just as Homer is absent in the Iliad and Phidias in the frieze of the Parthenon.[51]

Stravinsky did not think much of de Schloezer as a critic of his works, but the composer himself incorporated these same basic ideas in his autobiography of 1935.[52]

> For I consider that music is, by its very nature, essentially powerless to *express* anything at all, whether a feeling, an attitude of mind, a psychological mood, a phenomenon of nature, etc. ... *Expression* has never been an inherent property of music. That is by no means the purpose of its existence. If, as is nearly always the case, music appears to express something, this is only an illusion and not a reality. It is simply an additional attribute which, by tacit and inveterate agreement, we have lent it, thrust upon it, as a label, a convention—in short, an aspect which, unconsciously or by force of habit, we have often come to confuse with its essential being.[53]

It is unlikely (though not impossible) that Stravinsky or his ghostwriter, Walter Nouvel (1871–1949), an associate of the Ballets Russes, had read *Vom*

---

51. Boris de Schloezer, "Igor Strawinksy," in *Von neuer Musik*, ed. H. Grues, E. Kruttge, E. Thalheimer (Cologne: F. J. Marcan, 1925), 132: "Gerade darin besteht der Klassizismus Strawinskys: seit Bach und Mozart gab es keine reinere, von außermusikalischen Elementen ungetrübtere Musik. Der Psychologismus, der unsere musikalische Kunst verunreinigt, wie er unser logisches Denken zerfrißt, fehlt völlig in Strawinskys Schaffen, das uns ebenso unpersönlich, ebenso objektiv erscheint wie die größten Schöpfungen der Klassik in Malerei, Skulptur und Poesie. Die Persönlichkeit des Komponisten fehlt seiner Musik wie die Homers der Ilias, wie die des Phidias dem Parthenonfries." The translation of all but the last sentence is from Edward Lippman, *A History of Western Musical Aesthetics*, 408–09.

52. On Stravinsky's opinion of de Schloezer, see Valérie Dufour, *Stravinski et ses exégètes (1910–1940)* (Brussels: Éditions de l'Université de Bruxelles, 2006), 107–34. For further evocations of "purity" in Stravinsky's music of the 1920s, see Messing, *Neo-Classicism in Music*, 99, 104.

53. Stravinsky, *Chroniques de ma vie*, 2 vols. (Paris: Denoël et Steele, 1935), 1:116–17: "Car je considère la musique, par son essence, impuissante à *exprimer* quoi que ce soit: un sentiment, une attitude, un état psychologique, un phénomène de la nature, etc. ... *L'expression* n'a jamais été la propriété immanente de la musique. La raison d'être de celle-ci n'est d'aucune façon conditionnée par celle-là. Si, comme c'est presque toujours le cas, la musique paraît exprimer quelque chose, ce n'est qu'une illusion et non pas une réalité. C'est simplement un élément additionnel que, par une convention tacite et invétérée, nous lui avons prêté, imposé, comme une étiquette, un protocole, bref, une tenue et que, par accoutumance ou inconscience, nous sommes arrivée à confondre avec son essence." The ellipses and emphases are in the original. The translation is from the authorized but unattributed English translation, published as *An Autobiography* (New York: Simon & Schuster, 1936), 83–84.

Musikalisch-Schönen. Certain passages of the autobiography resonate in any case with the logic and even the language of Hanslick's treatise. What is particularly striking in the passage quoted above is the attempt to define the essence of music through the rhetoric of negation, by denying the presence of expression as an immanent quality (*propriété immanente*) of the art. Like Hanslick, Stravinsky treats any emotional response to music as a secondary consideration (*une élément additionnel*), a reaction shaped largely by convention and wrongly attributed to qualities within the musical work itself. When asked many years later if he still believed that "music is, by its very nature, essentially powerless to express anything at all," Stravinsky replied that he stood by his statement, "though today I would put it the other way around: music expresses itself."[54]

The qualities of purity and impersonality, combined with the absence of personal self-expression, extended the range of meanings associated with the term "absolute music." The negation of self-expression carried decidedly political overtones. Hanns Eisler (1898–1962), a pupil of Schoenberg and a committed Marxist, argued in 1928 that the "turn away from romanticism" had led to a conviction that "the sentiment of one individual was no longer sufficient to express something of more general validity, and so one wanted to make music absolutely, without feeling, without expression, only a play in tones."[55] That same year the composer and critic Heinz Tiessen (1887–1971) proposed a distinction between "I-Music" and "It-Music" (*Ich-Musik* and *Es-Musik*), the former centered on personal expression, the latter on the "unfolding of the musical substance from within itself."[56] The idea that absolute music, by virtue of its presumed impersonality, might represent a conception centered more on the collective than on the individual is similarly evident in Colin McPhee's report of his musical experiences on the island of Bali. In "The Absolute Music of Bali," an essay published in *Modern Music* in 1935, McPhee (1900–1964) describes the ceremonial music used there as music that is "*not to be listened to in itself*"—the italics are McPhee's—and ends with the hope that this "might inspire the longing for a similar condition in our own country, one in which music might play a more vital role in the life of the people."

Here is a music which has successfully achieved the absolute,—impersonal and non-expressive, with a beauty that depends upon form and pattern and a vigor that

54. Igor Stravinsky and Robert Craft, *Expositions and Developments* (Garden City, NY: Doubleday, 1962), 115.

55. Eisler, "Zur Situation der modernen Musik" (1928), in Eisler, *Musik und Politik: Schriften, 1924–1948*, ed. Günter Mayer (Munich: Rogner & Bernhard, 1973), 89: "Auch die Abkehr von der Romantik ist darauf zurückzuführen. Man spürte, daß die Empfindung des einzelnen nicht mehr ausreichte, um etwas allgemein Gültigeres zu sagen, und so wollte man absolut musizieren, ohne Gefühl, ohne Ausdruck: nur ein Spiel in Tönen."

56. Heinz Tiessen, *Zur Geschichte der jüngsten Musik (1913–1928): Probleme und Entwicklungen* (Mainz: Melosverlag, 1928), 60: "die musikalische Substanz um ihre Entfaltung aus sich selbst."

springs from a rhythmic vitality both primitive and joyous.... Modest and unassuming, [the musicians] nevertheless take great pride in their art, an art which, however, is so impersonal that the composer himself has lost his identity.... The original nature of music reveals itself with ever greater clarity as a phenomenon of sound rather than of language, as something springing from the urge to rhythmic expression, spontaneous and physical, rather than as a means for unembarrassed self-revelation.[57]

McPhee's use of the term never caught on. Yet in an odd way it captures the sense of "absolute" as that which is before and above all things, primordial and unconditioned, a sublation of individual expression into a larger whole.

■ BEAUTY

Not even the harshest of Hanslick's early critics questioned his decision to make beauty central to his "revision of musical aesthetics." Aesthetics, after all, had long been thought of as the philosophy of the beautiful, and the essence of the fine arts resided in their capacity to incorporate and convey beauty. In the final quarter of the nineteenth century, however, beauty lost its leading role in aesthetics, which was reconceived as the philosophy of art, of which beauty was simply one of many possible qualities—a special one, to be sure, but no longer indispensable, no longer the one that defined art. With each passing decade, critics came to see beauty more and more as a superficial quality, a mere appearance behind which lay the true essence of the artwork. Schopenhauer's philosophy of music—and, crucially, Wagner's promulgation of it—hastened the abandonment of beauty as the sine qua non of the art of sound. Music's power to disclose, its capacity to reflect the Will, had little or nothing to do with the quality of beauty. That the listening public continued to clamor for beauty served only to demonstrate beauty's intrinsically superficial nature. The essence of music was to be explained through other qualities.[58]

Carl Fuchs (1838–1922), an organist, critic, and friend of Nietzsche, was one of the first aestheticists of music to articulate this new outlook. In his *Präliminarien zu einer Kritik der Tonkunst* (1871), Fuchs explicitly rejects the role of beauty in aesthetics on the grounds that it is not a criterion of truth. He takes Schopenhauer's philosophy as his point of departure and attacks as sterile Hanslick's emphasis on form. He identifies three levels of musical pleasure, ranging, in order of lowest to highest, from physiological to intellectual to

---

57. Colin McPhee, "The 'Absolute' Music of Bali," *Modern Music* 12 (1935): 163–64. On McPhee's musical experiences in Bali and their influence on his own works, see Carol J. Oja, *Colin McPhee: Composer in Two Worlds* (Urbana: University of Illinois Press, 2004).

58. On the gradual decline of beauty as an aesthetic category, see Jerome Stolnitz, "'Beauty': Some Stages in the History of an Idea," *JHI* 22 (1961): 185–204; Prettejohn, *Beauty and Art*; and Nehamas, *Only a Promise of Happiness*, chapter 1.

metaphysical.[59] Subsequent writers' confrontations with Hanslick simply ignore the category of beauty. Even Paul Bekker, who recognized that musical modernism's allegiance to the centrality of form owed much to the aesthetics of Hanslick, rarely mentions beauty in his writings from the 1910s and '20s.[60]

Another factor that contributed to beauty's decline was the growing tendency to regard it more as matter of perception than as an inherent quality of the artwork itself. Friedrich Theodor Vischer came to this conclusion in 1866, eight years after the tenth and final installment of his *Aesthetik* had gone to press. "Beauty is an act," he declared, "the contact between an object and a perceiving subject, and because the truly active entity in this contact is the subject, it is therefore an act…a specific kind of perception."[61] The philosopher George Santayana (1863–1952) took a similar position, maintaining that "beauty is an emotional element, a pleasure of ours, which nevertheless we regard as a quality of things."[62]

This reconceptualization of beauty as a subjective response rather than as an objective quality seriously undercut its prestige in aesthetic thought (see Figure 12). It did not, however, compromise the importance of form and autonomy. To the contrary: these two qualities took on unprecedented importance in the generations after Hanslick.

■ FORM

"Form" was a polarizing term throughout the second half of the nineteenth century. Self-styled progressives equated it with the aesthetics of an earlier time that had reached its zenith in the works of Haydn and Mozart but was no longer adequate as a foundation for the content-laden "Music of the Future." Aesthetic conservatives, by contrast, thought of form as a timeless quality and rejected as "formless" new instrumental works based on elements from outside the realm of music. During the first decade of the twentieth century, this polarization reversed itself: composers seeking to position themselves on the leading edge of change proclaimed the primacy of form over content, and in so doing embraced

---

59. Carl Fuchs, *Präliminarien zu einer Kritik der Tonkunst* (Leipzig: E. W. Fritzsch, 1871), 12, 135–40.

60. See Eichhorn, "Annäherung durch Distanz"; idem, *Paul Bekker: Facetten eines kritischen Geistes* (Hildesheim: Olms, 2002), 484–86.

61. Friedrich Theodor Vischer, "Kritik meiner Ästhetik," in Vischer, *Kritische Gänge: Neue Folge*, 5. Heft (Stuttgart: Cotta, 1866), 6: "Das Schöne…ist Contact eines Gegenstands und eines auffassenden Subjects und, da das wahrhaft Thätige in diesem Contacte das Subject ist, so ist es ein Act. Kurz das Schöne ist einfach eine bestimmte Art der Anschauung." On Vischer's acknowledgment of his own changing views on aesthetics, see Sandra Richter, *A History of Poetics: German Scholarly Aesthetics and Poetics in International Context, 1770–1960* (Berlin: de Gruyter, 2010), 115–16.

62. George Santayana, *The Sense of Beauty, Being The Outlines of Æsthetic Theory* (New York: Charles Scribner's Sons, 1896), 47–48. See also p. 49: "Beauty is pleasure regarded as the quality of a thing."

MODERN ÆSTHETICS.

(*Ineffable Youth goes into ecstacies over an extremely Old Master—say,* FRA PORCINELLO BABARAGIANNO, A.D. 1266—1281?)

Matter-of-Fact Party. "BUT IT'S SUCH A REPULSIVE *SUBJECT!*"
Ineffable Youth. " 'SUBJECT' IN ART IS OF NO MOMENT! THE *PICKTCHAH* IS BEAUTIFUL!"
Matter-of-Fact Party. "BUT YOU 'LL OWN THE *DRAWING'S* VILE, AND THE *COLOUR'S* BEASTLY!"
Ineffable Youth. "I'M CULLAH-BLIND, AND DON'T P'OFESS TO UNDERSTAND D'AWING! THE *PICKTCHAH* IS BEAUTIFUL!"
Matter-of-Fact Party (getting warm). "BUT IT'S ALL OUT OF *PERSPECTIVE,* HANG IT! AND SO ABOMINABLY *UNTRUE TO NATURE!*"
Ineffable Youth. "I DON'T CARE ABOUT NAYTCHAH, AND HATE PERSPECTIVE! THE *PICKTCHAH* IS *MOST* BEAUTIFUL!"
Matter-of-Fact Party (losing all self-control). "BUT, DASH IT ALL, MAN! WHERE THE *DICKENS* IS THE *BEAUTY,* THEN?"
Ineffable Youth (quietly). "IN THE PICKTCHAH!"   [*Total defeat of Matter-of-Fact Party.*]

Figure 12. Ineffable, intrinsic beauty.
The admiring women resemble the "love-sick maidens" of Gilbert and Sullivan's
Patience, who scorn noblemen and military officers in favor of aesthetes.
Source: George Du Maurier, "Modern Aesthetics," *Punch,* 10 February 1877.

the principles of absolute music. It was composers of program music who now
seemed to represent the aesthetic of an earlier time.

So powerful was the allure of form by the 1920s that the Austrian musicologist
Alfred Lorenz (1868–1939) could make it the focus of his monumental study of
Wagner's music.[63] In a series of volumes devoted to the *Ring* (1924), *Tristan und
Isolde* (1926), *Die Meistersinger* (1930), and *Parsifal* (1933), Lorenz revealed
what he called the "secret of form" in these works, which he treated essentially
as exemplars of absolute music, examining the ways in which melody, harmony,
and rhythm—independent of any text—contributed to the construction of each

---

63. Alfred Lorenz, *Das Geheimnis der Form bei Richard Wagner,* 4 vols. (Berlin: Max Hesse, 1924–33).

work's constituent units, from the smallest to the largest.[64] Lorenz's approach did not quarrel with Wagner's theories about the connections between music and drama, and many of the units he describes map neatly onto the text and actions on the stage, but the focus on purely musical form in an account of Wagner's dramatic works is telling indeed.

The rehabilitation of form's prestige in the aesthetics of music owes much to changing attitudes in the visual arts and literature. Painters (Whistler, Gauguin), art critics (Worringer, Bell, Fry), and poets (Mallarmé, Wilde, Hofmannsthal, George) who insisted on the priority of form over content made it easier for a new generation of composers (Schoenberg, Busoni, Webern, Stravinsky) to embrace absolute music. By the outbreak of World War I, the primacy of form had become central to the aesthetics of musical modernism.

Painting

What Theodor Adorno called the convergence of music and painting around the turn of the twentieth century has long been recognized. From at least the 1870s onward, a number of prominent painters and art critics had been looking to music for parallels that would help explain the relationship between form and content in the visual arts. The move away from representation and the conventions of perspective, as has often been pointed out, coincided with advanced chromaticism and the eventual elimination of a tonal center in the works of such composers as Schoenberg, Webern, and Berg.[65] Equally significant but largely ignored to date was the effect that contemporary accounts about form in art had on the status of form in music. Once modernist painters had accepted the principles of abstraction and thus, by extension, the primacy of form in their art, it became far easier for modernist composers to argue for the primacy of form in music.

Accounts that trace the long and gradual move toward abstraction routinely cite—and often begin with—Walter Pater's celebrated pronouncement from 1877 that "all art constantly aspires towards the condition of music." And with good reason: Pater's dictum was invoked repeatedly by his own contemporaries. It resonated with those who sought to find a model by which to integrate form and content in the visual arts and was widely regarded as an important step on the road to abstraction and nonrepresentation in the arts, elements basic to the

64. See Stephen McClatchie, *Analyzing Wagner's Operas: Alfred Lorenz and German Nationalist Ideology* (Rochester, NY: University of Rochester Press, 1998).

65. Theodor W. Adorno, "Über einige Relationen zwischen Musik und Malerei" (1965), in Adorno, *Gesammelte Schriften*, vol. 16, ed. Rolf Tiedemann (Frankfurt am Main: Suhrkamp, 1978), 628–42; translated by Susan Gillespie as "On Some Relationships between Music and Painting," *MQ* 79 (1995): 66–79. For further commentary and references to additional literature, see Walter Frisch, *German Modernism: Music and the Arts* (Berkeley and Los Angeles: University of California Press, 1995), chapter 3: "Convergences: Music and the Visual Arts."

aesthetics of modernism.[66] This makes it all the more paradoxical that Pater's conception of form and content in music owes so much to Hanslick, a writer whose supporters in his own time perceived him as deeply conservative and whose detractors dismissed him as hopelessly outmoded.

Because Pater's aphorism has been quoted so often in isolation, then as now—rather like Hanslick's *tönend bewegte Formen*—it is worth considering its original context in some detail. The phrase appears in "The School of Giorgione," an essay Pater wrote for the *Fortnightly Review* in 1877 and incorporated (with minor revisions) into the third edition of his monograph *The Renaissance: Studies in Art and Poetry* (1888). Pater opens by criticizing the idea that poetry, music, and painting are "but translations into different languages of one and the same fixed quantity of imaginative thought." Each art, he insists, "has its own special mode of reaching the imagination, its own special responsibilities to its material," and it is a function of criticism to

> define these limitations, to estimate the degree in which a given work of art fulfils its responsibilities to its special material: to note in a picture that true pictorial charm which is neither a mere poetical thought or sentiment on the one hand, nor a mere result of communicable technical skill in colour or design on the other; to define in a poem that true poetical quality which is neither descriptive nor meditative merely, but comes of an inventive handling of rhythmical language, the element of song in the singing; to note in music the musical charm, that essential music which presents no words, no definable matter of sentiment or thought, separable from the special form in which it is conveyed to us.
>
> ...*All art constantly aspires towards the condition of music.* For while in all other works of art it is possible to distinguish the matter from the form, and the understanding can always make this distinction, yet it is the constant effort of art to obliterate it. That the mere matter of a poem, for instance, its subject, its given incidents or situation; that the mere matter of a picture, the actual circumstances of an event, the actual topography of a landscape, should be nothing without the form, the spirit of the handling; that this form, this mode of handling, should become an end in itself, should penetrate every part of the matter;—this is what all art constantly strives after, and achieves in different degrees.
>
> ...Art, then, is thus always striving to be independent of the mere intelligence, to become a matter of pure perception, to get rid of its responsibilities to its subject or material; the ideal examples of poetry and painting being those in which the constituent elements of the composition are so welded together that the material or subject no longer strikes the intellect only; nor the form, the eye or the ear only; but form and matter, in their union or identity, present one single effect to the imaginative reason,

---

66. See Patricia Herzog, "The Condition to Which All Art Aspires: Reflections on Pater and Music," *British Journal of Aesthetics* 36 (1996): 122–34; and Prettejohn, *Beauty and Art*, 144–45.

that complex faculty for which every thought and feeling is twin-born with its sensible analogue or symbol.

It is the art of music which most completely realises this artistic ideal, this perfect identification of form and matter, this strange chemistry, uniting, in the integrity of pure light, contrasted elements. In its ideal, consummate moments, the end is not distinct from the means, the form from the matter, the subject from the expression; they inhere in and completely saturate each other; and to it, therefore, to the condition of its perfect moments, all the arts may be supposed constantly to tend and aspire. Music, then, not poetry, as is so often supposed, is the true type or measure of consummate art. Therefore, although each art has its incommunicable element, its untranslateable order of impressions, its unique mode of reaching the imaginative reason, yet the arts may be represented as continually struggling after the law or principle of music, to a condition which music alone completely realises; and one of the chief functions of aesthetic criticism, dealing with the concrete products of art, new or old, is to estimate the degree in which each of those products approaches in this sense to musical law.[67]

We have no evidence that Pater had read *Vom Musikalisch-Schönen*, but on the basis of passages like this (among others), it seems reasonable to assume that he was familiar with the gist of the treatise.[68] When Pater says "music," he clearly has in mind music that is instrumental and nonprogrammatic, and he places great weight on the need of each art to find its distinct mode of expression and follow its own "special responsibilities to its material."

The challenge for Pater was to describe a visual art in which form and content could not be separated. This necessarily entailed a high degree of abstraction, and critics were reluctant to accept an art that would be the visual counterpart to Pater's (absolute) music. Twenty years earlier Vischer had explained instrumental music's inability to express concepts by comparing it to painting that relied too much on color, without reference to any identifiable object.[69] More recently still, Vischer had ridiculed the idea that a painting might somehow be constructed on the basis of color alone. An artist committed to formalism who wished to paint a fox, he pointed out, would use the animal as a mere "scaffold" on which "to hang certain shades of red, yellow, gray, and white!"[70] Vischer's

---

67. Walter Pater, "The School of Giorgione," *Fortnightly Review* 22 (October 1877): 526, 528, 530. Emphasis in the original. The version in the third edition of Pater's *The Renaissance: Studies in Art and Poetry* (London: Macmillan, 1888) differs slightly but not significantly.

68. Hanslick is not among the many German-language authors whose works are cited in Billie Andrew Inman, *Walter Pater's Reading: A Bibliography of His Library Borrowings and Literary References, 1858–1873* (New York: Garland, 1981), though Inman acknowledges that what can be documented likely represents only a small fraction of what Pater actually read.

69. Vischer, *Aesthetik*, 3:830; see above, p. 217.

70. Vischer, "Kritik meiner Ästhetik," in Vischer, *Kritische Gänge: Neue Folge*, 6. Heft (Stuttgart: J. G. Cotta, 1873), 6: "ein Rechen, dessen der Maler sich bedient hat, um gewisse Schattirungen von Roth, Gelb, Grau und Weiß daran zu hängen!"

exclamation point captures what he perceived to be the absurdity of such an idea: he simply could not imagine a painting that did not depict *something*. He was by no means extreme in this regard. The philosopher Gustav Theodor Fechner (1801–1887) used a very different example to make essentially the same point in his *Vorschule der Aesthetik* (1876), observing that if one were to remove all representational associations from Raphael's *Sistine Madonna*, one would be left with a "variegated color-chart that outdoes any carpet pattern as far as pleasure is concerned."[71] For Vischer, Fechner, and other critics of their time, the act of representation was basic to painting. One *could* look at a painting without regard to the object, event, or person it portrayed—in other words, from a purely formal perspective—but to view a painting exclusively in this way would be quite literally laughable.[72]

Wallpaper and arabesques were one thing; real painting was another. Few critics of the time could imagine a visual form without reference to content operating at an aesthetic level equivalent to that of representational art. One of the first to do so was Sidney Colvin (1845–1927), who in 1867 defined beauty as "the perfection of forms and colours." In a review of an exhibition of recent English paintings, he divides the nation's artists into two groups, one of which strives for realism, the other for "beauty without realism." Colvin's second group consists of such artists as Frederic Leighton, Albert Moore, and James MacNeill Whistler. He notes of Moore that "with him form goes for nearly everything, expression for next to nothing."[73]

Of these, Whistler would minimize the representational content of his paintings more than any other artist of his generation. The relation between form and content in his work would in fact become a legal issue when he sued the critic John Ruskin for libel in 1877, and analogies between musical and depictional form would play an important role in the case. In his review of an exhibition of paintings selected by Sir Coutts Lindsay of Balcarres, owner and proprietor of the Grosvenor Gallery, London, Ruskin had written of Whistler's *Nocturne in Black and Gold: The Falling Rocket* (1875):

---

71. Gustav Theodor Fechner, *Vorschule der Aesthetik*, 2 vols. (Leipzig: Breitkopf & Härtel, 1876), 1:118: "In der That, was von der sixtinischen Madonna nach Abzug aller Association noch übrig bleibt, ist eine kunterbunte Farbentafel, der es jedes Teppichmuster an Wohlgefälligkeit zuvor thut." The adjective *kunterbunt* suggests elements of randomness or disorder, whereas a *Farbentafel* (color-chart) is systematic and comprehensive. The juxtaposition of these two words underscores what Fechner considers to be the absurdity of seeing Raphael's painting from a purely and exclusively formal perspective.

72. On the history of formal analysis in painting, see Hubert Locher, "Towards a Science of Art: The Concept of 'Pure Composition,'" in *Pictorial Composition from Medieval to Modern Art*, ed. Paul Taylor and François Quiviger (London: Warburg Institute, 2000), 217–51. On earlier theories, see Thomas Puttfarken, *The Discovery of Pictorial Composition: Theories of Visual Order in Painting, 1400–1800* (New Haven: Yale University Press, 2000).

73. Sidney Colvin, "English Painters and Painting in 1867," *Fortnightly Review*, n.s., 2 (1867): 464–76. See Prettejohn, *Beauty and Art*, 139.

For Mr. Whistler's own sake, no less than for the protection of the purchaser, Sir Coutts Lindsay ought not to have admitted works into the gallery in which the ill-educated conceit of the artist so nearly approached the aspect of wilful imposture. I have seen and heard much of Cockney impudence before now, but never expected to hear a coxcomb ask 200 guineas for flinging a pot of paint in the public's face.[74]

Throughout the trial, the distinction between painting (implicitly understood as a representational art) and wallpaper (understood as nonrepresentational, consisting of line and color alone) came up repeatedly. Kant, dead for more than seventy years by this point, would no doubt have been pleased that his exemplars of "fine" and "agreeable" art were still in circulation. Albert Moore testified on Whistler's behalf and called his colleague's work "beautiful" and worth the price for which it had sold. Edward Burne-Jones, called by the defense, disagreed but conceded under cross-examination that Whistler "had an almost unrivalled appreciation of atmosphere, and his colour was beautiful, especially in moonlight scenes." In support of his own suit, Whistler testified that by calling the painting in question a "nocturne" he had "wished to indicate an artistic interest alone, divesting the picture of any outside anecdotal interest which might have been otherwise attached to it. A nocturne is an arrangement of line, form, and color first." Whistler had begun giving paintings "musical" titles in 1867, with the *Symphony in White No. 2* and *No. 3*.[75] Such titles allowed Whistler to call attention to the form of his paintings and at the same time draw attention away from their content, identified only in the subtitle if at all. The jury ultimately found in favor of Whistler but awarded him damages of exactly one farthing.

More enlightening than the testimony of the trial itself were the comments Whistler gave in an interview with the *World* on 22 May 1878.

Why should not I call my works "symphonies," "arrangements," "harmonies," and "nocturnes"?

... The vast majority of English folk cannot and will not consider a picture as a picture, apart from any story which it may be supposed to tell.

My picture of a "Harmony in Grey and Gold" is an illustration of my meaning—a snow scene with a single black figure and a lighted tavern. I care nothing for the past,

---

74. This and the following quotations from the trial are from the summary based on reporting by the *Times* and reproduced as "Report of the Trial: Whistler v. Ruskin," in John Ruskin, *The Works of John Ruskin*, 39 vols. (London: G. Allen, 1903–12), 29:580–84. For a more recent account, see Linda Merrill, *A Pot of Paint: Aesthetics on Trial in Whistler v. Ruskin* (Washington, DC: Smithsonian Institution Press, 1992).

75. The portrait of a young woman dressed in white standing on top of a bearskin, now known as *Symphony No. 1: The White Girl*, was given its title retrospectively and may in fact have been suggested by an early reviewer, who in 1863 praised the painting as a "symphony in white." See Locher, "Towards a Science of Art," 218–19.

present, or future of the black figure, placed there because the black was wanted at that spot. All that I know is that my combination of grey and gold is the basis of the picture. Now this is precisely what my friends cannot grasp.

Whistler justifies the human figure at this spot on the canvas not for its part in any "story" the image might have to tell but entirely for reasons of composition, of form, "because the black was wanted at that spot."

As music is the poetry of sound, so is painting the poetry of sight, and the subject-matter has nothing to do with harmony of sound or of colour.

The great musicians knew this. Beethoven and the rest wrote music—simply music; symphony in this key, concerto or sonata in that.

On F or G they constructed celestial harmonies—as harmonies—as combinations, evolved from the chords of F or G and their minor correlatives.

This is pure music as distinguished from airs—commonplace and vulgar in themselves, but interesting from their associations, as, for instance, "Yankee Doodle," or "Partant pour la Syrie."

Art should be independent of all clap-trap—should stand alone, and appeal to the artistic sense of eye or ear, without confounding this with emotions entirely foreign to it, as devotion, pity, love, patriotism, and the like. All these have no kind of concern with it; and that is why I insist on calling my works "arrangements" and "harmonies."

Take the picture of my mother, exhibited at the Royal Academy as an "Arrangement in Grey and Black." Now that is what it is. To me it is interesting as a picture of my mother; but what can or ought the public to care about the identity of the portrait?[76]

As Linda Merrill observes in her account of *Whistler v. Ruskin*, there was simply no word in the lexicon in 1878 to identify what we now think of as abstract art.[77] The best Whistler could do at the time was to compare his paintings to works of music, and specifically to works of "absolute" music like symphonies and nocturnes that conveyed no "anecdotal" meaning in their titles. In this way he could present his art as works whose representational qualities were at best secondary to their form and whose form, in the shape of lines and colors, was paramount.[78]

---

76. Whistler republished the interview under the title "The Red Rag" in his *The Gentle Art of Making Enemies* (London and Edinburgh: Ballantyne Press, 1892), 126–28. The *Harmony in Grey and Gold* would later become known as the *Nocturne in Grey and Gold*. "Partant pour la Syrie" was the unofficial anthem of Third Empire France. As Elizabeth Prettejohn notes in *Beauty and Art*, 149, Whistler's *Arrangement in Grey and Black* had in fact been exhibited at the Royal Academy with its subtitle: *Portrait of the Painter's Mother*. For further commentary on Whistler's musical imagery, see Peter Dayan, *Art as Music, Music as Poetry, Poetry as Art, from Whistler to Stravinsky and Beyond* (Farnham, Surrey: Ashgate, 2011), 9–32.

77. Merrill, *A Pot of Paint*, 6.

78. On musical imagery in nineteenth-century writings on art, see Karl Schawelka, *Quasi una musica: Untersuchungen zum Ideal des "Musikalischen" in der Malerei ab 1800* (Munich: Mäander, 1993); and Christian Thorau, "*Symphony in White*: Musik als Modus der Referenz," in *Musik—Zu Begriff und*

Whistler was not the only artist of his time to use musical imagery to describe his paintings. Paul Gauguin (1848–1903) claimed in an interview in 1895 that "by arranging lines and colors," using only a "pretext of an arbitrary subject borrowed from life or nature," he obtained "symphonies, harmonies that represent nothing absolutely *real* in the vulgar sense of the word since they do not express directly any idea." These "symphonies," however, "compel us to reflect, as music compels us to reflect, without the aid of ideas or images, simply by means of the mysterious affinities that exist between our brain and those arrangements of colors and lines."[79]

The sense of painting as an art primarily of form rather than of representation won growing acceptance toward the end of the nineteenth century. The French painter and writer Maurice Denis (1870–1943) pointed out in 1890 that "it is well to remember that a picture—before being a battle horse, a nude woman, or some anecdote—is essentially a plane surface covered with colors assembled in a certain order."[80] In lectures delivered at Harvard in the 1890s, Santayana speculated on the possibility of a "new abstract art" that would "deal with colors as music does with sound."[81] Along similar lines, the German architect August Endell (1871–1925) spoke in 1898 about "the beginning of a totally new art, an art with forms that mean nothing and represent nothing and remind one of nothing; yet that will be able to move our souls so deeply, as before only music has been able to do with tones."[82]

The writings of the German art historian Wilhelm Worringer (1881–1965) lent further prestige to the aesthetics of abstraction. In his influential *Abstraktion und Einfühlung: Ein Beitrag zur Stilpsychologie* (1908), he asserted that throughout

Konzepten: Berliner Symposion zum Andenken an Hans Heinrich Eggebrecht, ed. Michael Beiche and Albrecht Riethmüller (Wiesbaden: Franz Steiner, 2006), 135–50.

79. Eugène Tardieu, "La peinture et les peintres: M. Paul Gauguin," *Echo de Paris*, 13 May 1895, 2: "J'obtiens par des arrangements de lignes et de couleurs, avec le prétexte d'un sujet quelconque emprunté à la vie ou à la nature, des symphonies, des harmonies ne représentant rien d'absolument *réel* au sens vulgaire du mot, n'exprimant directement aucune idée, mais qui doivent faire penser comme la musique fait penser, sans le secours des idées ou des images, simplement par les affinités mystérieuses qui sont entre nos cerveaux et tels arrangements de couleurs et de lignes." Emphasis in original.

80. Maurice Denis, writing under the pseudonym Pierre-Louis, "Définition du Néo-traditionisme," *Art et critique* 2 (30 August 1890): 540: "Se rappeler qu'un tableau—avant d'être un cheval de bataille, une femme nue ou une quelconque anecdote—est essentiellement une surface plane recouverte de couleurs dans un certain ordre assemblées." Translation from *Theories of Modern Art: A Source Book by Artists and Critics*, ed. Herschel B. Chipp (Berkeley and Los Angeles: University of California Press, 1968), 94.

81. Santayana, *The Sense of Beauty*, 75.

82. August Endell, "Formenschönheit und dekorative Kunst," *Dekorative Kunst* 1 (1898): 75: "dass wir nicht nur im Anfang einer neuen Stilperiode, sondern zugleich im Beginn der Entwicklung einer ganz neuen Kunst stehen, der Kunst, mit Formen, die nichts bedeuten und nichts darstellen und an nichts erinnern, unsere Seele so tief, so stark so erregen, wie es nur immer die Musik mit Tönen vermag." Three essays by the art historian David Morgan are particularly helpful in tracing the gradual valorization of abstraction in the late nineteenth and early twentieth centuries: "Concepts of Abstraction in French Art Theory from the Enlightenment to Modernism," *JHI* 53 (1992): 669–85; "The Idea of Abstraction in German Theories of the Ornament from Kant to Kandinsky," *JAAC* 50 (1992): 231–42; and "The

history nonrepresentational art—whether in the forms of Gothic architecture or in the stylized designs of ancient Egypt or Byzantium—reflected a society's distrust of materiality and a correspondingly greater attraction to the world of the spirit: stylized art is by its very nature imbued with a higher degree of spirituality. The urge to abstraction reflects a "primal artistic impulse" that "has nothing to do with the rendering of nature." Through "instinctive necessity," it "creates geometric abstraction from within itself." It is for humankind "the complete and sole conceivable expression of emancipation from all contingency and temporality."[83] Abstract art thus operates at a higher metaphysical level than representational art. In its refusal to engage with the material world, it is superior.[84]

Proponents of formalism in music, as we have seen, had always been vulnerable to the charge of bloodlessness. But visual abstraction could no longer be equated with an absence of emotion. The Symbolist painter, poet, and critic Albert Aurier (1865–1892) put the matter even more forcefully in his 1891 essay on Gauguin: the true artist must possess the gift of emotivity [émotivité]—"not the sentimentality of the popular café singers or the makers of popular prints," but the "transcendental emotivity" that is "so grand and precious that it makes the soul tremble before the pulsating drama of the abstractions. Oh, how rare are those [artists] who move body and soul to the sublime spectacle of Being and pure Ideas!"[85] The Russian painter Wassily Kandinsky (1866–1944) likewise insisted that "the content [of a painting]...is not a literary narrative...but the sum of the emotions aroused by *purely pictorial* means."[86] Artists who made

Enchantment of Art: Abstraction and Empathy from German Romanticism to Expressionism," *JHI* 57 (1996): 317–41.

83. Wilhelm Worringer, *Abstraktion und Einfühlung: Ein Beitrag zur Stilpsychologie* (Munich: Piper, 1908), 44: "Der Urkunsttrieb hat mit der Wiedergabe der Natur nichts zu tun. Er sucht nach reiner Abstraktion als der einzigen Ausruh-Möglichkeit innerhalb der Verworrenheit und Unklarheit des Weltbildes und schafft mit instinktiver Notwendigkeit aus sich heraus die geometrische Abstraktion. *Sie ist der vollendete und dem Menschen einzig denkbare Ausdruck der Emancipation von aller Zufälligkeit und Zeitlichkeit des Weltbildes.*" Emphasis in the original. Worringer's treatise is based on his Zurich dissertation of 1907 of the same name. The translation here is adapted from Worringer, *Abstraction and Empathy*, trans. Michael Bullock (New York: International Universities Press, 1953), 44.

84. On Worringer's influence on modernist aesthetics, see the essays in Neil H. Donahue, ed., *Invisible Cathedrals: The Expressionist Art History of Wilhelm Worringer* (University Park: Pennsylvania State University Press, 1995).

85. G. Albert Aurier, "Le symbolisme en peinture: Paul Gauguin," *Mercure de France,* série moderne 2 (1891): 164: "non point.... cette émotivité que savent les chansonniers de café-concert et les fabricants de chromo—mais cette transcendental émotivité, si grande et si précieuse, qui fait frissoner l'âme devant le drame ondoyant des abstractions. Oh! combien sont rares ceux dont s'émeuvent les corps et les coeurs au sublime spectacle de l'Etre et des Idées pures!" Translation slightly modified from that by H. R. Rookmaaker and Herschel B. Chipp in Chipp, *Theories of Modern Art,* 93.

86. Wassily Kandinsky, untitled essay in *Cahiers d'art* 10 (1935): 56: "Mais ce contenu n'est pas...un récit littéraire...mais la somme des émotions provoquées par les moyens *purement picturaux.*" Emphasis in original. Translation from Kandinsky, *Complete Writings on Art,* 2 vols., ed. K. Lindsay and P. Vergo (London: Faber & Faber, 1982), 2:771.

form a guiding principle were in effect turning inward, away from the material world and toward a world of pure essences.[87]

The English art critic Clive Bell (1881–1964) proposed an even stronger connection between form—or "significant form," to use the catchphrase he introduced in 1914—and expression. Form, he maintained, was the quality that distinguished works of art from all other objects, and in his influential *Art* (1914), he defined it as the product of "lines and colours combined in a particular way" in a particular way such that they "stir our aesthetic emotions." He conceded that a reader could substitute the word "beauty" for "significant form" if desired, provided that beauty is defined as "combinations of lines and colours that provoke aesthetic emotion." Bell considered representation in art "not baneful" though often a symptom of "weakness" in an artist.[88] This resembled a comparable weakness Bell described in himself when listening to purely instrumental music.

The form of a musical composition must be simple indeed, if I am to grasp it. My opinion about music is not worth having. Yet, sometimes, at a concert, though my appreciation of the music is limited and humble, it is pure. Sometimes, though I have a poor understanding, I have a clean palate. Consequently, when I am feeling bright and clear and intent, at the beginning of a concert for instance, when something that I can grasp is being played, I get from music that pure aesthetic emotion that I get from visual art. It is less intense, and the rapture is evanescent; I understand music too ill for music to transport me into the world of pure aesthetic ecstasy. But at moments I do appreciate music as pure musical form, as sounds combined according to the laws of a mysterious necessity, as pure art with a tremendous significance of its own and no relation whatever to the significance of life; and in those moments I lose myself in that infinitely sublime state of mind to which pure visual form transports me. How inferior is my normal state of mind at a concert. Tired or perplexed, I let slip my sense of form, my aesthetic emotion collapses, and I begin weaving into the harmonies that I cannot grasp the ideas of life. Incapable of feeling the austere emotions of art, I begin to read into the musical forms human emotions of terror and mystery, love and hate, and spend the minutes, pleasantly enough, in a world of turbid and inferior feeling. At such times, were the grossest pieces of onomatopoeic representation—the song of a bird, the galloping of horses, the cries of children, or the laughing of demons—to be introduced into the symphony, I should not be offended. Very likely I should be pleased; they would afford new points of departure for new trains of romantic feeling or heroic thought. I know very well what has happened. I have been using art as a means to the emotions of life and reading into it the ideas of life.... I have tumbled from the superb peaks of aesthetic exaltation to the snug

87. On the connections between abstraction and purity, see Mark A. Cheetham, *The Rhetoric of Purity: Essentialist Theory and the Advent of Abstract Painting* (Cambridge: Cambridge University Press, 1994).

88. Clive Bell, *Art* (London: Chatto & Windus, 1914), 8, 12, 28.

foothills of warm humanity. It is a jolly country. No one need be ashamed of enjoying himself there. Only no one who has ever been on the heights can help feeling a little crestfallen in the cosy valleys.[89]

Like representation in painting, representation in music—or more specifically, the *perception* of representation—is "not baneful," but it falls short of the highest ideals of art because it is not "pure." Although couched in personal terms, Bell's description of the listening process reflects part of a broader change in attitudes toward music during the early decades of the twentieth century: program music was not scorned, but it was no longer exalted in the way it had been by the New German School and its followers. It was no longer "the highest rung on the ladder," to invoke Mahler's image once again. Bell's aesthetic of form differs from Hanslick's or Zimmermann's, however, in that it is grounded in emotion, and specifically in the emotional response of the beholder: "The starting point for all systems of aesthetics must be the personal experience of a peculiar emotion."[90] In Bell's aesthetics, the ideals of emotion, form, and purity all converge.

Purity was especially important in the aesthetics of the painter and critic Roger Fry (1866–1934). He described three paintings by Kandinsky in a 1913 London exhibition as "pure visual music," noting that he could "no longer doubt the possibility of emotional expression by such abstract visual signs."[91] Like Pater before him, Fry assumed that his readers would understand his reference to music as absolute music, a term Fry would in fact use on at least one occasion in his later criticism.[92]

Schoenberg recognized these parallel developments in art and music around this same time. A painter of no small talent in his own right, he contributed an essay on the relationship of text and music to *Der blaue Reiter* (1912), an anthology of avant-garde writings edited by Kandinsky and Franz Marc, in which he mused on the converging arts of music and painting:

> When...W. Kandinsky and Oskar Kokoschka paint pictures whose material, external subject is little more than an excuse to fantasize in colors and forms and thereby express themselves in such a way as only the musician has until now—these are symptoms of a gradually expanding recognition of the true essence of art. And with great joy I read Kandinsky's book *On the Spiritual in Art*, in which the path for painting is pointed out and hope aroused that those who ask about the text, about the subject matter, will quickly run out of questions.[93]

89. Bell, *Art*, 31–32.

90. Bell, *Art*, 6.

91. Roger Fry, "The Allied Artists," *Nation* (2 August 1913), republished in *A Roger Fry Reader*, ed. Christopher Reed (Chicago: University of Chicago Press, 1996), 153.

92. Fry, "The Double Nature of Painting," a lecture delivered in 1933 but not published until 1969; see Fry, *A Roger Fry Reader*, 386.

93. Schoenberg, "Das Verhältnis zum Text," 70: "Wenn...W. Kandinsky und Oskar Kokoschka Bilder malen, denen der stoffliche äußere Gegenstand kaum mehr ist, als ein Anlaß, in Farben und

Schoenberg's comments are as much about music as they are about painting. Earlier in the same essay, he had expressed embarrassment at his sudden realization, a few years before, that he had "no idea" about the text of several well-known songs by Schubert. But his shame soon turned to pride, for he quickly realized that "without knowing the poem, I had grasped the content, the real content, perhaps even more profoundly than if I had clung to the surface of the mere thoughts expressed in words."[94] In the end, Schoenberg found it *better* to analyze lieder without regard to their poetry. The point of contact here with the "Blue Rider" exhibition is that the composer who grasps the "true essence" of music will think purely in tones and without regard to representation—in this case, the representation of a verbal text in music. For Schoenberg, the "true essence" of music lies in its fundamentally abstract nature, its refusal to represent or suggest anything outside of itself.

Abstraction was not a function of atonality. In a radio talk delivered in 1932, Schoenberg's pupil and, later, colleague Anton Webern called Bach's *Die Kunst der Fuge*—a work firmly rooted in tonality—"the most abstract music we know" and as such an antecedent of twelve-tone serialism. "Perhaps we are all on the way to writing so abstractly," he added in an aside.[95] In another radio talk a year later, he returned to this idea, calling *Die Kunst der Fuge*

> a work that leads to the abstract, a music in which everything is missing that is normally indicated in notation: whether for voices or instruments, no performance indications, there is nothing at all there. It really is almost an abstract object—or as I would rather put it: *the highest reality!*—All these fugues are created on the basis of one single theme that is constantly transformed: a thick book of musical ideas, whose entire content derives from one single thought![96]

Another of Schoenberg's pupils, Egon Wellesz (1885–1974), blamed the "chaotic development of music in recent generations" on a "lack of a feeling for

---

Formen zu phantasieren und sich so auszudrücken, wie sich bisher nur der Musiker ausdrückte, so sind das Symptome für eine allmählich sich ausbreitende Erkenntnis von dem wahren Wesen der Kunst. Und mit großer Freude lese ich Kandinskys Buch *Über das Geistige in der Kunst*, in welchem der Weg für die Malerei gezeigt wird und die Hoffnung erwacht, daß jene, die nach dem Text, nach dem Stofflichen fragen, bald ausgefragt haben werden." For a different translation, see Schoenberg, "The Relationship to the Text," in *Style and Idea*, 144–45.

94. Schoenberg, "Das Verhältnis zum Text," 69: "Es zeigte sich mir, daß ich, ohne das Gedicht zu kennen, den Inhalt, den wirklichen Inhalt, sogar vielleicht tiefer erfaßt hatte, als wenn ich an der Oberfläche der eigentlichen Wortgedanken haften geblieben wäre." Translation from Schoenberg, "The Relationship to the Text," in *Style and Idea*, 144.

95. Anton Webern, "Der Weg zur Komposition in zwölf Tonen," in Webern, *Wege zur neuen Musik*, ed. Willi Reich (Vienna: Universal, 1960), 47: "Es ist die abstrakteste Musik, die wir kennen. (Wir sind vielleicht alle auf dem Wege, so abstrakt zu schreiben.)"

96. Webern, "Der Weg zur neuen Musik," in Webern, *Wege zur neuen Musik*, 36: "Ein Werk, das völlig ins Abstrakte führt, eine Musik, der alles fehlt, was sonst durch die Notierung gekennzeichnet wird: ob für Gesang oder Instrumente, keine Vortragszeichen, gar nichts steht da. Es ist wirklich fast ein Abstraktum—oder ich möchte lieber sagen: *die höchste Realität!*—Alle diese Fugen sind geschaffen auf Grund eines einzigen Themas, das immer wieder abgewandelt wird: ein dickes Buch von musikalischen

form" inherited from "romanticism and its epigonal currents."[97] Romanticism, Wellesz maintained, had placed too much emphasis on content and originality. The greatest challenge of the present was not to create new forms that might replace genres such as the symphony, but rather to "restore a compelling, cogent relationship between form and content."[98] Wellesz stopped short of using the epithet of formlessness, but his lament is otherwise strikingly similar to the complaints voiced by the critics of the New German School in the middle of the nineteenth century. As such, Wellesz, the archmodernist, was advocating—probably without being aware of it—an aesthetic most closely associated several generations before with Eduard Hanslick.

Wellesz's comments appeared in 1925, Hanslick's centenary, and at least one critic of the day recognized the debt of modernist aesthetics to *Vom Musikalisch-Schönen*. In an essay entitled "Hanslick and the Present," Alfred Heuss (1877–1934), editor of the *Zeitschrift für Musik*, called attention to the extent to which modern composers had committed themselves to a "specifically musical" perspective that owed much to Hanslick's theories. Heuss was no friend of musical modernism, nor was he an apologist for Hanslick: he took the earlier critic to task for any number of assumptions, conclusions, and contradictions.[99] But his recognition of a common emphasis on form by Hanslick and modernists points to an irony of aesthetic history that few if any others were prepared to acknowledge publicly.

Literature

Literary critics also took up the nexus of form and content around the turn of the twentieth century in ways that helped shift modernist musical aesthetics. The idea of the verbal arts as an art of pure form was not entirely new: a hundred years before, Novalis had mused about the possibility of "poems—simply *euphonious* and full of beautiful words—but also without any sense or coherence—at most one or two isolated strophes comprehensible."[100] Poetry at this

---

Gedanken, dessen ganzer Inhalt von einem einzigen Gedanken ausgeht!" In this radio address of 3 April 1933, Webern elaborates on the same technique Schoenberg had discussed in a radio talk two months earlier in the music of Brahms. Schoenberg's radio address would eventually become the basis for his essay "Brahms the Progressive."

97. Egon Wellesz, "Das Problem der Form," in *Von neuer Musik*, ed. H. Grues, E. Kruttge, E. Thalheimer (Cologne: F. J. Marcan, 1925), 35: "Es war der Mangel an Formgefühl, der an der chaotischen Entwicklung der Musik der letzten Generationen Schuld trägt, und dieser Mangel ist ein Erbe der Romantik mit ihren epigonalen Strömungen."

98. Wellesz, "Das Problem der Form," 36: "Form und Inhalt wieder in eine zwingende Beziehung zu bringen."

99. Alfred Heuss, "Eduard Hanslick und die Gegenwart," *Zeitschrift für Musik* 92 (1925): 501–5. On Heuss's antimodernist aesthetics, see Joel Sachs, "Some Aspects of Musical Politics in Pre-Nazi Germany," *Perspectives of New Music* 9 (1970): 75–87.

100. Novalis, *Schriften*, 3:572: "Gedichte—blos *wohlklingend* und voll schöner Worte—aber auch ohne allen Sinn und Zusammenhang—höchstens einzelne Strofen verständlich." Emphasis in original.

level of abstraction would not become a reality until much later, however, in the *poésie pure* of Stéphane Mallarmé (1842–1898), and in the poetry of Paul Valéry (1871–1945), who spoke of *poésie absolue*. In his 1896 essay "Crise de vers," Mallarmé used musical imagery to convey the nature of a new kind of thought that is "no longer expressed merely in common language" but instead more closely approximates "that modern meteor, the symphony," which "approaches thought with the consent or ignorance of the musician."[101]

What is striking here, once again, is the assumed superiority of a music that functions without reference to external objects or ideas. Statements such as this helped bolster the prestige of absolute music and made it not only acceptable but desirable for the new generation of musicians eager to challenge the traditions of the past.[102]

Nor was it only French writers who gave renewed prestige to form. In his essay "The Critic as Artist" (1890), Oscar Wilde argued that the "real artist" is the one who proceeds "not from feeling to form, but from form to thought and passion":

> He does not first conceive an idea, and then say to himself, "I will put my idea into a complex metre of fourteen lines," but, realising the beauty of the sonnet-scheme, he conceives certain modes of music and methods of rhyme, and the mere form suggests what is to fill it and make it intellectually and emotionally complete. From time to time the world cries out against some charming artistic poet, because, to use its hackneyed and silly phrase, he has "nothing to say." But if he had something to say, he would probably say it, and the result would be tedious. It is just because he has no new message, that he can do beautiful work. He gains his inspiration from form, and from form purely, as an artist should. A real passion would ruin him. Whatever actually occurs is spoiled for art. All bad poetry springs from genuine feeling.[103]

Six years later another writer with strong modernist inclinations, the Austrian poet and dramatist Hugo von Hofmannsthal (1874–1929), cited with approval an anonymous observation that identified the value of any literary work as residing in its "form, not in its content or sense (for in that case it would be something more like wisdom or scholarship)." Form has nothing to do with the

---

101. Stephane Mallarmé, "Crise de vers," in Mallarmé, *Oeuvres complètes*, ed. Henri Mondor and G. Jean-Aubry (Paris: Gallimard, 1965), 365: "Le moderne des météores, la symphonie, au gré ou à l'insu du musicien, approche la pensée; qui ne se réclame plus seulement de l'expression courante." Translation from Mallarmé, *Selected Prose, Poems, Essays, and Letters*, ed. and trans. Bradford Cook (Baltimore: Johns Hopkins University Press, 1956), 39.

102. Recent studies of the French Symbolist poets and music include David Hertz, *The Tuning of the Word: The Musico-Literary Poetics of the Symbolist Movement* (Carbondale: Southern Illinois University Press, 1987); Louis Marvick, *Waking the Face That No One Is: A Study in the Musical Context of Symbolist Poetics* (Amsterdam: Rodopi, 2004); and Joseph Acquisto, *French Symbolist Poetry and the Idea of Music* (Aldershot: Ashgate, 2006).

103. Oscar Wilde, "The True Function of Criticism," *Nineteenth Century* 28 (1890): 452.

superficial: it is that which "in its dimension and sound is deeply moving" and which "in all times has separated masters from their descendents, the primordial from those of lesser rank."[104]

■ AUTONOMY

Disputes about music's material autonomy had largely ceased by the end of the nineteenth century. Those who accepted the aesthetics of Schopenhauer—which included all Wagnerians—considered music to be a direct reflection of the Will and therefore too elemental to be affected by any connection (or lack of connection) to any other art. Music could accommodate other forms of expression but had no need of any of them. Those who believed that music's power lay in its purity, on the other hand, like Hanslick, continued to insist on music's autonomy. Autonomy thus remained vital to one side of the debate even as it became irrelevant to the other; and so, despite their differences, these two conceptualizations of music coexisted with little friction. Issues that had occupied center stage in the middle of the century were largely moot fifty years later.

Purity

In the second half of the nineteenth century, purity was an enormously attractive quality for those many critics opposed to the "Music of the Future." Much of its appeal lay in its implicit superiority: mixtures, hybrids, and half-breeds did not carry the cachet of purity. Vocal music on the whole was largely exempt from this debate, in part because it made up so much of the performed repertory of the day, in part because it represented the continuation of a long and venerable tradition. But as far as instrumental music was concerned, critics in thrall to purity looked down on program music as a mongrel breed.

The ideal of purity also made it easy for critics to reduce complex issues to simple binaries. In his 1871 survey of German composers since the time of Bach, Emil Naumann, a former pupil of Mendelssohn, declared that anyone who interpreted Beethoven's symphonies as in any way programmatic denied the power of

---

104. Hugo von Hofmannsthal, "Poesie und Leben," *Die Zeit*, 16 May 1896: 105: "Den Wert der Dichtung... entscheidet nicht der Sinn (sonst wäre sie etwa Weisheit, Gelahrtheit), sondern die Form, d.h. durchaus nichts äußerliches, sondern jenes tief Erregende in Maß und Klang, wodruch zu allen Zeiten die Ursprünglichen, die Meister sich von den Nachfahren, den Künstlern zweiter Ordnung unterschieden haben." The author of the aphorism would later be revealed as the poet Stefan George (1868–1933). George himself advocated a highly abstract approach to poetry; see Martin Stern, "'Poésie pure' und Atonalität in Österreich: Stefan Georges Wirkung auf Jung-Wien und Schönberg," in *Die österreichische Literatur: Ihr Profil von der Jahrhundertwende bis zur Gegenwart (1880–1980)*, ed. Herbert Zeman, 2 vols. (Graz: Akademische Druck- und Verlagsanstalt, 1989), 2:1457–69; and Jürgen Brokoff, *Geschichte der reinen Poesie: Von der Weimarer Klassik biz zur historischen Avantgarde* (Göttingen: Wallstein, 2010), 445–506.

Beethoven as a composer, for it is only in the realm of purely instrumental music that a composer can demonstrate his abilities to the highest degree.[105] Florence May's 1905 biography of Brahms is only slightly more nuanced. May (1845–1923) was an English pianist who had studied piano with Brahms briefly in the early 1870s but who admired the music of Wagner as well. Her book includes an appendix entitled "Musical Form—Absolute Music—Programme Music—Berlioz and Wagner," in which she attempts to explain "how it was that Brahms, an uncompromising champion of musical tradition, whose very existence as an artist was staked on the vitality of Absolute music, could deeply respect the art of Wagner."[106] She accepts the premise of Wagner's efforts to create an art that synthesizes verbal and musical expression on the grounds that music and drama both operate within the domain of sound. But she has nothing good to say about Berlioz's attempts at program music:

> If it be said that the object of the programme is to be a sort of guide-post to the emotions or sentiments to which the music is addressed, the position becomes worse, for the incapacity of the musician as such stands confessed. The union of poetry and music in the sense of the instrumental Programme composer is, from the point of view of the creator of Absolute music, fatal, not only to the dignity, but to the vital force, of both arts. The poem becomes a phantom, the music a conundrum; the listener wastes his time and fancy in trying to fit them together, and is without means of knowing how far he has been successful, and the product of these processes is something which, in the words of Wagner, is neither fish nor fowl.... The art of sound, the art of music, is and remains the special art divine because it is capable of reaching beyond the limited impressions of which words are the symbols, and of suggesting the infinite.[107]

This line of thought would be taken to its logical extreme by the Viennese critic and theorist Heinrich Schenker.[108] Like Hanslick, he saw performance not as the realization of a musical work but as a source of ontological corruption. Purity, for Schenker, was to be found in the score, scrupulously edited to reflect the composer's will. "A composition does not require a performance in order to exist," he maintained: a silent reading of the score is not only sufficient to assess a given work but preferable to any performance of it, for once a performance takes place, "one must realize that thereby new elements are added to a complete work of art: the nature of the instrument that is played; properties of the hall, the room, the audience; the mood of the performer, technique, et cetera. Now,

---

105. Emil Naumann, *Deutsche Tondichter von Sebastian Bach bis auf die Gegenwart* (Berlin: Robert Oppenheim, 1871), 161–62.

106. Florence May, *The Life of Johannes Brahms*, 2 vols. (London: Edward Arnold, 1905), 1:286.

107. May, *The Life of Johannes Brahms*, 1:287, 290.

108. As noted earlier (p. 252), Cook, *The Schenker Project*, 48–62, makes a persuasive case for Hanslick's influence on Schenker.

if the composition is to be inviolate, kept as it was prior to the performance, it must not be compromised by these elements (which after all are entirely foreign to it)."[109]

Over the course of his career, Schenker became increasingly committed to explaining the logic of music in purely musical terms through the kind of technical exegesis Hanslick had not been equipped to carry out. Schenker accepted the idea of describing music in metaphorical terms through at least the 1890s, but in the following decade began to criticize poetic interpretations with asperity.[110] He had little patience for program music, noting in 1897 that the "older composers"—by which he meant Haydn, Mozart, and Beethoven—"spoke words in the shape of music," while "the 'New Germans' only paint the words. If these 'painted words' have an effect, then this is a contemporary act of self-deception."[111] Composers of program music, he maintained, try to force "a foreign logic on the work at the expense of musical logic."[112] It is the study of counterpoint that "most securely liberates the disciple of art from the lunacy that tones, aside from their absolute effect, might also be able to point toward something else, something tangible and external."[113] Schenker denounced Wagner's

109. Heinrich Schenker, *Die Kunst des Vortrags*, §1: "Im Grunde bedarf die Komposition durchaus nicht erst der Ausführugg [sic] damit es heißt, daß sie existent sei." §2: "Tritt aber die Ausführung dennoch hinzu, so hat man zu verstehen, daß sich an das an sich schon fertige Kunstwerk neue Elemente herandrängen; so z.B. Gesetze des Instrumentes, auf dem gespielt wird, Gesetze des Saales, des Zimmers, des Publikums, der persönlichen Stimmung des Vortragenden, der Technik u.s.w. Soll nun die erste Unantastbarkeit der Komposition gewahrt werden, und soll die Komposition das bleiben, was sie schon vor der Ausführung gewesen, so darf sie durch die erwähnten, neuen Ingredienzen, die ihr ja von Haus aus ganz fremd sind, nicht kompromittiert werden." Schenker's text, begun in 1911, has not yet been published in the original German; I am grateful to Dr. Nicholas Marston, Cambridge University, for providing a transcription of the relevant passages from one of the text's surviving sources. The translation, by Irene Schreier Scott, is from Schenker, *The Art of Performance*, ed. Heribert Esser (New York: Oxford University Press, 2000), 3.

110. See Pritchard, "'A Heap of Broken Images'?," 129–32.

111. Heinrich Schenker, "Unpersönliche Musik," originally published in *Neue Revue* 8 (1897), republished in *Heinrich Schenker als Essayist und Kritiker: Gesammelte Aufsätze, Rezensionen und kleinere Berichte aus den Jahren 1891–1901*, ed. Hellmut Federhofer (Hildesheim: Olms, 1990), 218: "Die älteren redeten in Tönen Worte, die 'Neudeutschen' malen nur die Worte. Wenn die gemalten Worte wirken, so ist es Selbsttäuschung der Gegenwart." For a slightly different translation within an English-language version of the entire essay, see Schenker, "Impersonal Music," trans. Horst B. Loeschmann, *Music Analysis* 7 (1988): 135–38. Schenker's "impersonal music," it should be noted, is very different from the "objectivity" later advocated by Busoni, Stravinsky, and others (see p. 262); Schenker in fact emphasizes the presence of the composer's persona in the music, even if the anecdotal sources of these experiences are irrelevant to any evaluation of the finished product, the work.

112. Heinrich Schenker, "Über den Niedergang der Kompositionskunst: Eine technisch-kritische Untersuchung," typescript (ca. 1905–9) transcribed by William Drabkin, *Music Analysis* 24 (2005): 168: "Er…zwingt auf Kosten der musikalischen Logik dem Kunstwerk eine fremde Logik auf." The translation, by William Drabkin, is from Schenker, "The Decline of the Art of Composition: A Technical-Critical Study," *Music Analysis* 24 (2005): 72.

113. Heinrich Schenker, *Kontrapunkt*, 2 vols. (Vienna: Universal, 1910–22), 1:21: "Die Kontrapunktslehre…lehrt die eigenste Wirkung der Töne, man möchte sagen deren Eigenbewegung,

interpretation of the Ninth Symphony as an allegory of absolute music yearning for the redemption of words, maintaining that even after Beethoven had introduced Schiller's text into the finale, he remained loyal to the "primordial law of all absolute music."[114]

Schenker's insistence on the purity of music, including even the vocal finale of the Ninth Symphony, is symptomatic of the broader trend in analysis toward an autonomous manner of contemplating music, outside the parameters of biography, history (social, cultural, political, institutional), performance, reception, or anything beyond the notes on the page. In Schenker's world, purity, autonomy, and essentialism are mutually reinforcing. The title of his 1930 essay on the *Eroica*—"Beethovens 3. Sinfonie zum erstenmal in ihrem wahren Inhalt dargestellt" (Beethoven's Third Symphony, Presented for the First Time in Its True Content)— reflects more than its author's estimation of his own originality or analytical prowess. It testifies a faith, shared by many of his more modest contemporaries, that an analysis of work's formal structure, without regard for any other considerations, was the key to understanding the true nature, the essence of any given work of music.[115]

Applied Autonomy

Its claims to functional isolation notwithstanding, autonomy had its uses. It is no small irony that many of those writers who endorsed the superiority of "pure" music evoked these same qualities to assert the superiority of specifically German music— and by extension, German culture—over that of any other nation. Throughout the nineteenth century, German writers viewed instrumental music as the special province of their land, in part to compensate for the relatively underdeveloped genres of German vocal music, particularly opera, when compared against the traditions of Italy and France.[116] Triest, in his 1800 survey of German music over the previous hundred years, proudly pointed out that Johann Sebastian Bach, "the greatest, most profound musical harmonist of all times, who surpassed everything that Italy, France, and England had done for *pure* music...was a German!"[117]

und befreit den Kunstjünger dadurch am sichersten von dem Wahn, als müßten die Töne außer eben ihrer absoluten Wirkung auch noch was anderes, Gegenständliches, Äußerliches zu bedeuten haben."

114. Heinrich Schenker, *Beethovens Neunte Sinfonie* (Vienna and Leipzig: Universal-Edition, 1912), 247: "das Urgesetz aller absoluten Musik."

115. Heinrich Schenker, "Beethovens Dritte Sinfonie zum erstenmal in ihrem wahren Inhalt dargestellt," *Das Meisterwerk in der Musik* 3 (1930): 25–101.

116. Sanna Pederson, "A. B. Marx, Berlin Concert Life, and German National Identity," *19CM* 18 (1994): 87–107; Celia Applegate, "How German Is It? Nationalism and the Idea of Serious Music in the Early Nineteenth Century," *19CM* 21 (1998): 274–96; and Celia Applegate and Pamela Potter, "Germans as the 'People of Music': Genealogy of an Identity," in *Music and German National Identity*, ed. Celia Applegate and Pamela Potter (Chicago: University of Chicago Press, 2002), 1–35.

117. Triest, "Bemerkungen über die Ausbildung der Tonkunst in Deutschland im achtzehnten Jahrhundert," *AmZ* 3 (14 January 1801): 259: "Welche Freude für einen patriotischen Bewohner

Five years later, no less a figure than Goethe observed that while the Italians had brought vocal music to its present state, it was the Germans who had perfected the technical aspects of instrumental music and "applied it in the most lively fashion, almost without regard for its effect on the psyche." Their "more profound treatment of harmony"—and by this Goethe no doubt meant what we now think of as counterpoint—was "more fitting" for Germans, who had thereby raised instrumental music to "a level paradigmatic for all peoples."[118] The symphony, as the most prestigious of all instrumental genres, was widely hailed as a distinctly German invention that had flourished at the hands of Haydn, Mozart, and above all Beethoven. August Kahlert, writing in 1834, declared music in general to be a legacy of Christianity and instrumental music in particular a legacy of German *Geist*.[119] In his later *System der Aesthetik*, Kahlert noted that German composers had won international acclaim far surpassing that of German poets, for music is an international language immediately accessible to all, without need of translation. These composers, accordingly, had "prescribed laws not just for the Fatherland, but for the world."[120]

These sentiments grew more virulent after the Revolutions of 1848–49. In an essay on the "the place of Germans in the history of music," the composer Joachim Raff observed that "whatever forms of absolute music are cultivated in France are either of German origin or carry the unambiguous stamp of such origin." The universality of German music, he informed his readers, assured its superiority over the music of all other nations.[121]

Not all such assertions of national superiority were quite so blunt. Most, in fact, took a more subtle form by arguing that absolute music—which happened to have been cultivated more intensively in German-speaking lands than anywhere else—was the most cosmopolitan and therefore *least* nationalist form

unsers Vaterlandes, zu wissen, dass der grösste, tiefsinnigste Harmonist aller bisherigen Zeiten, der alles, was Italien, Frankreich und England für die *reine* Musik gethan hatte, übertraf...ein Deutscher war!" Emphasis in original. Translation by Susan Gillespie in Triest, "Remarks," 334.

118. Goethe, "Anmerkungen" to *Rameau's Neffe* (1805), his translation of Diderot's *Le neveu de Rameau*, in Goethe, *Sämtliche Werke*, vol. 11, *Leben des Benvenuto Cellini; Übersetzungen I*, ed. Hans-Georg Dewitz and Wolfgang Proß (Frankfurt am Main: Deutscher Klassiker Verlag, 1998), 771: "Wie der Italiener mit dem Gesang, so verfuhr der Deutsche mit der Instrumentalmusik. Er...vervollkommnete ihr Technisches und übte sie, fast ohne weitern Bezug auf Gemütskräfte, lebhaft aus, da sie denn bei einer, dem Deutschen wohl gemäßen, tiefern Behandlung der Harmonie zu einem hohen, für alle Völker musterhaften Grade gelangt ist." Friedrich Rochlitz republished these comments under the heading "Göthe über Musik," *AmZ* 7 (22 May 1805): 543–44.

119. August Kahlert, "Ueber die Bedeutung des Romantischen," 244: "Die Tonkunst ist ein Erzeugnis des Christentums; die Instrumentalmusik ein Erzeugnis des deutschen Geistes."

120. Kahlert, *System der Aesthetik* (Leipzig: Breitkopf & Härtel, 1846), 365: "die...größten deutschen Tonmeister, welche nicht ihrem Vaterlande sondern der Welt Gesetze vorschrieben." For further similar citations, see Bonds, *Music as Thought*, 88–91.

121. Joachim Raff, "Die Stellung der Deutschen in der Geschichte der Musik: Kunsthistorische Skizze," *Weimarisches Jahrbuch für deutsche Sprache, Literatur und Kunst* 1 (1854): 211: "Was von

of music. As the critic Richard Wallaschek put it in his *Ästhetik der Tonkunst* (1889), German music has no "national characteristic element" at all; its distinguishing feature is "pure beauty."[122] Schenker's writings, in particular, are laden with a strong sense of German national superiority based on the quality of universality.[123] In an era that still believed in the ideal of music as a "universal language," this was no trivial matter. Nineteenth-century German critics and composers shaped the nature of discourse about music so profoundly that even today, "Germanness," as Richard Taruskin astutely observes, "is transparent. It must be dyed if it is to be tracked."[124]

Autonomy might also function as a useful dye by which to make distinctions among social classes: the more removed an artwork is from the society around it, the more prestigious its cultural status.[125] This was certainly the case with the repertory of absolute music in the nineteenth and twentieth centuries. Without words, gesture, or any overt symbolic significance to provide listeners with a point of reference, absolute music stood out as the most culturally abstract—and therefore remote—category of the art. And among instrumental genres, chamber music reigned supreme; not coincidentally, this was the repertory least affected by the aesthetics of the New German School, and while the occasional string quartet might bear a programmatic title (as in the case of Smetana's "Z mého života" [From My Life]), such works were the exception and not the rule. To endorse the aesthetics of absolute music was to endorse an attitude that treated music as separate from society, free from any broader meaning or direct function.

Yet an art completely removed from society's needs and interests remained a deeply problematic concept. The artistic movement known as aestheticism illustrates this with special clarity. It applied the doctrine of *l'art pour l'art* to an extreme degree, making the pursuit of beauty the highest activity in life. Its origins lie in the Epicurianism of antiquity; in its modern form, it is generally traced to Victorian England and is associated most closely with Walter Pater (1839–1904), Algernon Charles Swinburne (1837–1909), and Oscar Wilde (1854–1900). The contemporaneous French manifestation of this movement counted among its advocates Théophile Gautier (1811–1872) and Leconte de Lisle (1818–1894). Swinburne, for one, vigorously opposed any use of art as means of social engagement, effectively absolving art of its moral and ethical dimensions:

Kunstformen der absoluten Musik in Frankreich gepflegt wird, ist entweder deutscher Abkunft, oder trägt den unzweideutigen Stempel derselben." Ibid., 205.

122. Wallaschek, *Ästhetik der Tonkunst*, 249: "Die deutsche Musik hat in ihren Kunstwerken in der That kein national-charakteristisches Element, es ist reine Schönheit."

123. See Leon Botstein, "Schenker the Regressive: Observations on the Historical Schenker," *MQ* 86 (2002): 239–47.

124. Richard Taruskin, "Speed Bumps," *19CM* 29 (2005): 198.

125. See Pierre Bourdieu, *Distinction: A Social Critique of the Judgement of Taste*, trans. Richard Nice (Cambridge, MA: Harvard University Press, 1984).

Once let art humble herself, plead excuses, try at any compromise with the Puritan principle of doing good, and she is worse than dead. Once let her turn apologetic, and promise or imply that she really will now be "loyal to fact" and useful to men in general (say, by furthering their moral work or improving their moral nature), she is no longer of any human use or value. The one fact for her which is worth taking account of is simply mere excellence of verse or colour, which involves all manner of truth and loyalty necessary to her well-being. That is the important thing; to have her work supremely well done, and to disregard all contingent consequences.[126]

Yet even this amounted to a program of individual self-improvement (whether "moral" or not), giving art a social function in the end after all. It was for this reason that T. S. Eliot identified Pater's attitude toward art, no matter how detached, as a prescribed approach to life and thus a "theory of ethics."[127] Indeed, aestheticism eventually came to be accepted as a means of elevating the lives of all individuals at all levels of society.[128]

■ DISCLOSIVENESS

For those who accepted Schopenhauer's aesthetics, disclosiveness became the central quality by which to explain the relationship between music's essence and effect. Schopenhauer's own views on the matter come remarkably close to Pythagoreanism, for he saw music and the cosmos as unmediated representations of the Will. We can "regard the phenomenal world, or nature, and music," he maintained, "as two different expressions of the same thing."[129] If we

cast a glance at purely instrumental music, a symphony of Beethoven presents us with the greatest confusion which yet has the most perfect order as its foundation; with the most vehement conflict which is transformed the next moment into the most beautiful harmony. It is *rerum concordia discors* [the concord of things through discord], a true and complete picture of the nature of the world, which rolls on in the boundless confusion of innumerable forms, and maintains itself by constant

---

126. Algernon Charles Swinburne, *William Blake: A Critical Essay* (London: John Camden Hotten, 1868), 92. For further commentary on aestheticism, see Leon Chai, *Aestheticism: The Religion of Art in Post-Romantic Literature* (New York: Columbia University Press, 1990); Elizabeth Prettejohn, ed., *After the Pre-Raphaelites: Art and Aestheticism in Victorian England* (New Brunswick, NJ: Rutgers University Press, 1999); and Elizabeth Prettejohn, *Art for Art's Sake: Aestheticism in Victorian Painting* (New Haven: Yale University Press, 2007).

127. T. S. Eliot, "Arnold and Pater" (1930), in Eliot, *Selected Essays* (New York: Harcourt, Brace, 1950), 390.

128. See Diana Maltz, *British Aestheticism and the Urban Working Classes, 1870–1900: Beauty for the People* (New York: Palgrave Macmillan, 2006).

129. Schopenhauer, *Die Welt als Wille und Vorstellung*, ed. Hübscher, 1:329: "Diesem allen zufolge können wir die erscheinende Welt, oder die Natur, und die Musik als zwei verschiedene Ausdrücke der selben Sache ansehen." Translation from Schopenhauer, *The World as Will and Representation*, trans. E. F. J. Payne, 1:262.

destruction. But at the same time, all the human passions and emotions speak from this symphony; joy, grief, love, hatred, terror, hope, and so on in innumerable shades, yet all, as it were, only in the abstract and without any particularization; it is their pure form without the material, like a pure spirit world without matter. We certainly have an inclination to reify it while we listen, to clothe it in the imagination with flesh and bone, and to see in it all the different scenes of life and nature. On the whole, however, this does not promote an understanding or enjoyment of it, but rather gives it a strange and arbitrary addition. It is therefore better to interpret it purely and in its immediacy.[130]

Schopenhauer acknowledged the Pythagorean nature of his thought on several occasions without ever going into the parallels in detail. "The entire essence of the world, both as a microcosm and macrocosm," he noted in his *Parerga und Paralipomena* of 1851, "may certainly be expressed by numerical relations alone and at the same time to a certain extent be reduced to these relations. On these grounds, Pythagoras was right to ascribe the true essence of things to number. But what are numbers? Successive relations whose possibility is based on time."[131] The idea of music as number and number as the essence of all things is also implicit in Schopenhauer's variation on Leibniz's dictum: "Music is an unconscious exercise in metaphysics in which the mind does not know it is philosophizing."[132]

---

130. Schopenhauer. *Die Welt als Wille und Vorstellung*, ed. Hübscher, 2:529: "Werfen wir jetzt einen Blick auf die bloße Instrumentalmusik; so zeigt uns eine Beethoven'sche Symphonie die größte Verwirrung, welcher doch die vollkommenste Ordnung zum Grunde liegt, den heftigsten Kampf, der sich im nächsten Augenblick zur schönsten Eintracht gestaltet: es ist ein *rerum concordia discors*, ein treues und vollkommenes Abbild des Wesens der Welt, welche dahin rollt, im unübersehbaren Gewirre zahlloser Gestalten und durch stete Zerstörung sich selbst erhält. Zugleich nun aber sprechen aus dieser Symphonie alle menschlichen Leidenschaften und Affekte: die Freude, die Trauer, die Liebe, der Haß, der Schrecken, die Hoffnung u.s.w. in zahllosen Nüancen, jedoch alle gleichsam nur *in abstracto* und ohne alle Besonderung: es ist ihre bloße Form, ohne den Stoff, wie eine bloße Geisterwelt, ohne Materie. Allerdings haben wir den Hang, sie, beim Zuhören, zu realisiren, sie, in der Phantasie, mit Fleisch und Bein zu bekleiden und allerhand Scenen des Lebens und der Natur darin zu sehen. Jedoch befördert Dies, im Ganzen genommen, nicht ihr Verständniß, noch ihren Genuß, giebt ihr vielmehr einen fremdartigen, willkürlichen Zusatz: daher ist es besser, sie in ihrer Unmittelbarkeit und rein aufzufassen." Translation slightly modified from Schopenhauer, *The World as Will and Representation*, trans. E. F. J. Payne, 2:450: I have changed *realisieren* from Payne's "to realize," to "to reify," and I have rendered *bloß* throughout as "pure"; Payne's "mere" for the second and third occurrences of this word suggests a sense of deprecation not implied in the original. I have also changed Payne's translation of Horace's Latin.

131. Schopenhauer, *Parerga und Paralipomena: Kleine philosophische Schriften*, 2 vols. (Berlin: A. W. Hayn, Berlin 1851), 1:37: "eine Auslegung der Pythagorischen Zahlenphilosophie....Hienach also ist das ganze Wesen der Welt, sowohl als Mikrokosmos, wie als Makrokosmos, allerdings durch bloße Zahlenverhältnisse auszudrücken, mithin gewissermaßen auf sie zurückzuführen: in diesem Sinne hätte dann Pythagoras Recht, das eigentliche Wesen der Dinge in die Zahlen zu setzen.—Was sind nun aber Zahlen?—Successionsverhältnisse, deren Möglichkeit auf der Zeit beruht."

132. Schopenhauer, *Welt als Wille und Vorstellung*, ed. Hübscher, 1:332: "Musica est exercitium metaphysices occultum nescientis se philosophari animi." Translation from Schopenhauer, *The World as Will and Representation*, trans. E. F. J. Payne, 1:264.

Leibniz's observation about music as the unconscious "counting" or "calcula-tion" of the soul is true enough on a lower level, Schopenhauer points out; but his revision of this often-quoted aphorism brings out the metaphysical import of music's basis in number.

Those who did not openly accept Schopenhauer's philosophy, insisting in-stead that musical beauty was a thing unto itself, had to confront at some point the same question with which Hanslick had struggled—reluctantly, briefly, intensely, and unsuccessfully—at the end of the first edition of *Vom Musikalisch-Schönen*: if music is a wholly self-contained art, then how can it rise above the level of a pleasing "play with tones" (as the charge was so often for-mulated), lacking deeper significance? Hanslick's original inclination, evident in the suppressed ending of the first edition of his treatise, was to evoke the tran-scendental nature of music and its broader connections to the structure of the universe. As partisan positions hardened over the course of the 1850s and '60s, Hanslick turned away from the issue altogether, paring away those few but cru-cial portions of his original text that had addressed or at least alluded to this challenge. In the end he was left to confess his own inability to offer an adequate solution and fell back repeatedly, as we have seen, on an appeal to the element of *Geist* that resided in music's material as well as its form.

But others, particularly those born after 1840, recognized that the question could not be deferred indefinitely, and they did not share Hanslick's aversion to notions of transcendence. Once again, theories of visual art helped pave the way for music. Doctrines of self-reflexive purity, as Mark Cheetham has pointed out in connection with the early history of abstract painting, must be augmented by some sort of transcendental model if an art is to avoid the danger of sealing itself off from everything around it.[133] Significance, after all, is a relative concept: an object takes on meaning only in relation to something else outside of itself. The same holds true for the inherently abstract art of absolute music.

From the third quarter of the nineteenth century onward, most critics accepted the premise of transcendence in music in one way or another, some openly, some tacitly. The notion that music might function as a portal to higher truths was by this point a commonplace, no longer reserved to a small coterie of philosophers. In 1870 the general-circulation *Atlantic Monthly* published "The Intellectual Influence of Music," which amounts to a creed of musical transcendentalism, penned by none other than the noted critic and editor John Sullivan Dwight (1813–1893). Dwight had been a member of the Brook Farm community at one point and a close associate of Emerson. "The highest kind of music," Dwight declared,

> is *pure* music, that which lives and moves in purely musical ideas.... The highest def-inition of music, its full significance and worth, is to be sought mainly in the highest

133. Cheetham, *The Rhetoric of Purity*, 35–37.

kind of music; that is to say, *pure music*, dealing in purely musical ideas, conscious of no outward purpose, content in its own world, preoccupied with its own peculiar mission, which is too divine to need the justification of any end to serve. This, indeed, is the first principle of truth in art of any kind.

In this we find the intellectuality of music. For music, in this view, is the most abstract, pure embodiment and type of universal law and movement. It is a key to the divine method throughout all the ordered distribution of the worlds of matter and of spirit. It is the most fluid, free expression of form, in the *becoming* (what the Germans call *das Werden*); form developing according to intrinsic and divine necessity. There is nothing arbitrary in music; no acquiring any power in it except by patient, reverent study and mastering of divine proportions and the eternal laws of fitness.[134]

Nor were such views restricted to New England transcendentalists. The London reviewer writing under the rubric of "The Popular Concerts" for the *Musical World* in 1883 clearly assumed that the journal's readers were familiar with the concept of music as a vehicle of metaphysical insight. The critic ("D. T.") hailed the slow movement of Beethoven's String Quartet in E Minor, op. 59 no. 2, as an exemplar of music that asserts the art's "highest power and glorious qualities more convincingly than anything else" and reported this of the work's performance, led by the violinist Joseph Joachim:

The composer who has just gone from us [i.e., Wagner] taught that Beethoven, longing, in his Ninth Symphony, for a fuller expression, attained it by connecting music with the poetic word. We cannot subscribe to this. The word, poetic or not, fetters music. That subtle art goes where language cannot follow, and conveys impressions that elude speech. Amateurs had reason to think of this on Monday evening, when the crowded hall lay under the spell of Beethoven's enchanting discourse, and listened with breathless attention to a delivery almost as remarkable as the theme. It is not hyperbole to say that some, at least, among the audience might have borrowed Pauline language, and declared that, whether in the body or out of the body they could not tell, but that they were conscious of marvelous things. This is the pure delight of music, abstracted entirely from mundane matters, and partaking in no measure of their imperfections and grossness. Few will readily forget the thunder of applause which followed the last note of Beethoven's music. It burst from every part of the hall with a spontaneousness that showed how deep and general had been the feelings excited during the performance of the work.[135]

---

134. John Sullivan Dwight, "The Intellectual Influence of Music," *Atlantic Monthly*, November 1870, 620. On the phenomenon of "becoming" in music, see Janet Schmalfeldt, *In the Process of Becoming: Analytic and Philosophical Perspectives on Form in Early Nineteenth-Century Music* (New York: Oxford University Press, 2011).

135. D.T., "The Popular Concerts," *Musical World* 61, no. 9 (March 3, 1883): 131.

The "marvelous things" made accessible by music often included a glimpse into the secrets of nature itself. Music, as Carrière pointed out in his *Aesthetik* (1859), is no mere aggregate of successive tones, but rather "an ideal of the movement of life." The idea that music puts forward in tones is "the principle of becoming" and thus reveals in time "the developmental law of life that governs all things."[136] Or, as Hausegger put it in his *Die Musik als Ausdruck* (1885), tones are the language by which nature reveals herself to humankind in an immaterial manner, thereby disclosing herself "from a new angle, undermining that which we had been accustomed to recognizing as our world, loosening its rigidity, drawing us magically through our senses into its life in a newly achieved activity of becoming in such a way that the external truth of this world represents a mere appearance compared to its vital truth."[137] What makes music the most revealing of all the arts is its combination of immateriality and temporality.

Conceptions of music as a reflection of the cosmos are common throughout the last quarter of the nineteenth century and well into the twentieth, both in writings about music and in compositions themselves. Karl Grunsky observed in his *Musikästhetik* of 1907 that "the primal essence of music" is the "struggle and strife of different forces in a cosmic state of motion, liberated from matter." Composers can best replicate this struggle through polyphony.[138] August Halm declared in 1913 that the ideal theme is "nothing less than a piece of the order of the world" that carries out a "cosmically necessary task."[139] Halm and other critics associated with the theory of energetics saw meaningful congruences between the motions of the cosmos and the dynamic of emotions (see p. 252).

Composers discussed their music in similar terms. Mahler commented on more than one occasion about the cosmic nature of the symphony as a genre, with its full instrumentarium and range of sonic possibilities. "To me, a symphony means this: to construct a world with all the available technical means," he told his confidante Natalie Bauer-Lechner in 1895. Six years later, during a rehearsal of his Fourth Symphony, he declared that "a symphony must have

---

136. Carrière, *Aesthetik*, 312: "Die Musik…stellt das Ideal der Lebensbewegung dar…" Ibid., 311: "Sie erfasst die Idee als das Princip des Werdens"; "sie offenbart das Entwickelungsgesetz des Lebens wie es alle Dinge beherrscht."

137. Hausegger, *Die Musik als Ausdruck*, 150: "Von neuer Seite enthüllt sie sich, dasjenige, was wir als unsere Welt zu erkennen gewohnt waren, zersetzend, ihre Erstarrung lösend, in neu gewonnener Werdethätigket eine neue Welt vor unsere Sinne zaubernd und uns in ihr Leben mit hineinziehend, so daß vor der lebensvollen Wahrheit dieser Welt die äußere sich als bloßer Schein darstellt." For a different translation, see *Music in European Thought*, ed. Bujić, 109.

138. Karl Grunsky, *Musikästhetik* (Leipzig: G. J. Göschen, 1907), 75–76: "Was den Tondichter immer wieder zur Mehrstimmigkeit hinzieht, ist die Aussicht, im kontrapunktischen Widerspiel dem Urwesen der Musik am nächsten zu kommen, insofern diese den Kampf und Streit verschiedener Kräfte in kosmischer Bewegtheit, losgelöst vom Stofflichen, auskämpfen läßt."

139. Halm, *Von zwei Kulturen der Musik*, 251: "ein Stück Weltordnung: das, und nichts Geringeres, ist ein solches Thema bester Art; es leistet eine kosmisch notwendige Arbeit."

something cosmic about it; it must be inexhaustible like the world and life, if it is not to make a mockery of its name."[140] On another occasion, he compared the composer who writes a work "so *enormous* that it reflects the *entire cosmos*" to "an instrument on which the universe plays."[141] And while at work on his Eighth Symphony (the *Symphony of a Thousand*, for an enormous orchestra, soloists, and multiple choruses), he wrote to the conductor Willem Mengelberg: "Imagine the universe beginning to sound and resound. These are no longer human voices, but rather planets and suns in orbit."[142]

Paul Hindemith (1895–1963) made Johannes Kepler the central character of his opera *Die Harmonie der Welt* (1956–57) and entitled the three movements of his symphony *Die Harmonie der Welt* (1951), based on musical ideas that would find their way into the opera, "Musica instrumentalis," "Musica humana," and "Musica mundana." The connections between music and the cosmos are also evident toward the end of Hindemith's introduction to his treatise on composition, the *Unterweisung im Tonsatz* (1937), where he muses on the nature of the material with which composers work. The intervals, he observes, were perceived in ancient times as "witnesses from the first days of creation. Mysterious, like number, and of the same essence as the fundamental concepts of surface and space, a standard, as it were, by which to measure the audible as well as the visible world; elements of the universe, which expands in the same proportions as the intervals of the overtone series so that measure, music, and the cosmos melt into one." Hindemith urges every aspiring composer to develop some sort of understanding about the nature of music's basic materials. "We cannot conjure up past times," he concedes, but the goal of his treatise will have been achieved if it succeeds in transmitting "a spark of the old spirit toward our views of tonal material and its application."[143] In all of these instances, Hindemith was demonstrably influenced by the writings of Hans Kayser (1891–1964), a pupil of Schoenberg,

140. Natalie Bauer-Lechner, *Erinnerungen an Gustav Mahler* (Leipzig: E. P. Tal, 1923), 18: "Symphonie heißt mir eben: mit allen Mitteln der vorhandenen Technik eine Welt aufbauen." Ibid., 171: "Sie muß etwas Kosmisches an sich haben, muß unerschöpflich wie die Welt und das Leben sein, wenn sie ihres Namens nicht spotten soll." In both instances, "Welt" can be understood as either "world" or "cosmos."

141. Mahler, letter of 28 (?) June 1896 to Anna von Mildenburg, in Mahler, *Briefe*, 187: "Nun aber denke Dir so ein *großes* Werk, in welchem sich in der Tat die *ganze Welt* spiegelt—man ist, sozusagen, selbst nur ein Instrument, auf dem das Universum spielt." Emphasis in original.

142. Mahler, letter of 18 August 1906 to Willem Mengelberg, in Mahler, *Briefe*, 335: "Denken Sie sich, daß das Universum zu tönen und zu klingen beginnt. Es sind nicht mehr menschli[che] Stimmen, sondern Planeten und Sonnen, welche kreisen." For further citations of a similar nature from Mahler's pen, see Christian Wildhagen, *Die Achte Symphonie von Gustav Mahler: Konzeption einer universalen Symphonik* (Frankfurt am Main: Peter Lang, 2000), 195–233.

143. Hindemith, *Unterweisung im Tonsatz*, vol. 1, *Theoretischer Teil* (Mainz: B. Schott's Söhne, 1937), 27: "Zeugnisse aus den Urtagen der Weltschöpfung. Geheimnisvoll wie die Zahl, gleichen Wesens mit den Grundbegriffen der Fläche und des Raumes, Richtmaß gleicherweise für die hörbare wie die sichtbare Welt; Teile des Universums, das in gleichen Verhältnissen sich ausbreitet wie die Intervalle der Obertonreihe, so daß Maß, Musik und Weltall in eins verschmolzen....Wir können vergangene

who had spearheaded a revival of Pythagoreanism in the 1920s and with whom Hindemith carried on an extended correspondence.[144]

Other twentieth-century composers were similarly attracted to the idea of translating the order of the cosmos into music. We can find traces of such thought in Charles Ives's unfinished *Universe Symphony*, Karlheinz Stockhausen's *Sternklang* (1971), George Crumb's *Makrokosmos I* and *II* (1973), John Cage's *Etudes Australes* (1974/75), and Iannis Xenakis's *Pléiades* (1979).[145]

Not everyone was thrilled with the annexation of music as a branch of metaphysics. Nietzsche, for one, rejected Platonism, all forms of idealism, and the very notion of "disinterested interestedness."[146] In his *Zur Genealogie der Moral* (1887), he spoke disparagingly of Wagner's conversion to Schopenhauerian philosophy, which had led to a wider attitude of asceticism, an over-intellectualization of music that deprives it of pleasure and physical immediacy:

> With this extraordinary increase in the market value of music (which seemed to arise out of Schopenhauer's philosophy), the musician's stock rose all at once to unprecedented heights: he was now an oracle, a priest, indeed more than a priest—a kind of mouthpiece of the intrinsic in-and-of-itself nature of all things, a telephone to the Beyond. From now on, he was no longer speaking only music, this ventriloquist of God—he was speaking metaphysics.[147]

As he was so often in life, however, Nietzsche was in the minority on this point. His contemporaries—and generations since—have for the most part embraced the idea of music as a disembodied art of disclosure.

Zeiten nicht heraufzaubern....Daß aber ein Funken des alten Geistes auf unsere Anschauungen vom Tonmaterial und seiner Anwendung bei allen, die sich damit beschäftigen, zündend überspringe, möge mit dieser Arbeit erreicht werden." Arthur Mendel's English translation in Hindemith, *The Craft of Musical Composition*, book 1, *Theoretical Part* (New York: Associated Music Publishers, 1942), 12–13, renders *ein Funken des alten Geistes* as "a kindling spark from the spirit of the old masters," which obscures Hindemith's connection of *Geist* with the Pythagorean concept of number, music, and universe.

144. Among Kayser's many writings on the subject, see his *Orpheus vom Klang der Welt: Morphologische Fragmente einer allgemeinen Harmonik* (Potsdam: G. Kiepenheuer, 1926), and *Vom Klang der Welt: Ein Vortragszyklus zur Einführung in die Harmonik* (Zurich: M. Niehans, 1937). On Hindemith's cosmological leanings in general, see Bruhn, *The Musical Order of the World*.

145. On the influence of American transcendentalism on Ives and, later, Cage, see Frank Mehring, *Sphere Melodies: Die Manifestation transzendentalistischen Gedankenguts in der Musik der Avantgardisten Charles Ives und John Cage* (Stuttgart and Weimar: J. B. Metzler, 2003). On Ives's *Universe Symphony*, see Larry Austin, "The Realization and First Complete Performances of Ives's 'Universe Symphony'" and Philip Lambert, "Ives' Universe," both in *Ives Studies*, ed. Philip Lambert (Cambridge: Cambridge University Press, 1997), 179–232, and 233–59. On Xenakis and Stockhausen, see Helga de la Motte-Haber, *Musik und Natur: Naturanschauung und musikalische Poetik* (Laaber: Laaber-Verlag, 2000), 108–12.

146. See Ekbert Faas, *The Genealogy of Aesthetics* (Cambridge: Cambridge University Press, 2002).

147. Nietzsche, *Zur Genealogie der Moral* (1887), in Nietzsche, *Sämtliche Werke*, 15 vols., ed. Giorgio Colli and Mazzino Montinari (Munich: Deutscher Taschenbuch Verlag, 1980), 5:346: "Mit dieser ausserordentlichen Werthsteigerung der Musik, wie sie aus der Schopenhauer'schen Philosophie zu erwachsen schien, stieg mit Einem Male auch der Musiker selbst unerhört im Preise: er wurde nunmehr ein Orakel, ein Priester, ja mehr als ein Priester, eine Art Mundstück des 'An-sich' der Dinge, ein Telephon des Jenseits,—er redete fürderhin nicht nur Musik, dieser Bauchredner Gottes,—er redete Metaphysik."

Epilogue: Since 1945

The idea of absolute music became so central to Western aesthetics after World War II that its development from that point onward cannot be traced apart from the broader sweep of musical aesthetics in general. Both as a repertory and as a philosophical concept, it enjoyed its greatest prestige in the period between roughly 1945 and 1970. Its abstract nature appealed to composers and audiences who had lived through a period when music and all the arts had been co-opted by national, social, and political ideologies to an unprecedented degree. Partly in response to this, Western artists actively promoted an approach to music that favored material autonomy, which was the surest guarantor of ethical autonomy. The Soviet Union's repeated denunciations of art for art's sake helped make the aesthetics of absolute music all the more attractive in the West. Eastern bloc regimes, echoing Wagner, denounced as "formalist" any art that was not socially engaged. Nikita Krushchev, for one, attacked serial composition publicly on more than one occasion.[1] Western governments, by contrast, absolved their artists from task of building a new society. Freed from the distasteful servitude of politics, composers embraced the aesthetics of absolute music as never before, for it offered them the prospect of a truly cosmopolitan art, one that transcended national boundaries and ideological differences.

Or so it seemed. In retrospect, we can now see that music's autonomy had many useful applications for the West during the Cold War. The very absence of overt ideological elements was itself inspired by the ideologies of purity and individual freedom. We know, moreover, that Western governments actively (and at times covertly) supported many important artists of this era who helped advance the aesthetics of absolute music and its correlative, the detached, independent—and for this reason superior—artist who lives only for the sake of art. Organizations like the Congress for Cultural Freedom, funded by the Central Intelligence Agency, actively promoted avant-garde music as an exemplar of artistic "freedom." The political and ideological implications of abstract music, particularly serial music, have been examined in a number of recent insightful studies.[2]

---

1. See Peter J. Schmelz, *Such Freedom, If Only Musical: Unofficial Soviet Music During the Thaw* (New York: Oxford University Press, 2009), 5.

2. See in particular Amy Beal, "Negotiating Cultural Allies: American Music in Darmstadt, 1946-56," *JAMS* 53 (2000), 105-139; Anne Shreffler, "Ideologies of Serialism: Stravinsky's *Threni* and the

Competing Cold War perspectives played themselves out in the field of musicology as well, perhaps most pointedly in the writings of scholars working in a divided Germany. Carl Dahlhaus, from his vantage point in West Berlin, produced an account of absolute music that in retrospect reads very much like a veiled attack on the aesthetics of his counterpart in East Berlin, Georg Knepler, who approached music as a form of expression, and more specifically, as a form of social expression.[3] Most scholars, however, including Dahlhaus, recognized that the conceptual dichotomy of absolute and program music was unsustainable; over time, the two extremes came to be seen more and more as opposite ends of a conceptual spectrum.[4]

The prestige of absolute music began to decline around 1970 with the turn toward postmodernism. In this more recent era of eclecticism, the rhetoric of purity has taken a back seat to the rhetoric of diversity. Purity, once lauded as an aesthetic ideal, has become deeply suspect as a concept. Composers, performers, and critics are today far more open to the potential advantages of hybridity. A growing understanding of musical repertories and practices outside the Western tradition has further undermined claims of pre-eminence or universality for any one particular aesthetic or repertory. The fact that we now speak routinely of "musics" is a useful reminder of the art's culturally constructed nature. It may well be that the notion of absolute music itself, in any generally accepted sense of the term, is a uniquely Western concept.[5] The long-cherished belief of music as a universal language has in any case given way to a broader conception of music as a social construct whose significance and function derive from and reflect cultural conventions. The idea of a wholly autonomous art, free from all contingencies, finds relatively few adherents today, and the belief that we can think about music exclusively in terms of "the music itself," independent

Congress for Cultural Freedom," in *Music and the Aesthetics of Modernity*, ed. Karol Berger and Anthony Newcomb (Cambridge, MA: Harvard University Department of Music, 2005), 217-45; Elizabeth Janik, *Recomposing German Music: Politics and Tradition in Cold War Berlin* (Leiden and Boston: Brill, 2005); Mark Carroll, *Music and Ideology in Cold War Europe* (Cambridge: Cambridge University Press, 2006); Jennifer DeLapp-Birkett, "Aaron Copland and the Politics of Twelve-Tone Composition in the Early Cold War United States," *Journal of Musicological Research* 27 (2008): 31-62. See also the bibliography of writings in the appendix to Peter J. Schmelz, "Introduction: Music in the Cold War," *JM* 26 (2009): 14–16.

3. Dahlhaus, *Die Idee der absoluten Musik*; Georg Knepler, *Geschichte als Weg zum Musikverständnis: Zur Theorie, Methode und Geschichte der Musikgeschichtsschreibung*, 2nd ed. (Leipzig: Philipp Reclam jun., 1982). See James Hepokoski, "The Dahlhaus Project and its Extra-musicological Sources," *19CM* 14 (1991): 221-246; Shreffler, "Berlin Walls"; Nina Noeske and Matthias Tischer, eds., *Musikwissenschaft und Kalter Krieg: Das Beispiel DDR* (Cologne: Böhlau, 2010).

4. The two most important contributions in this regard are Walter Wiora, "Zwischen absoluter und Programmusik," in *Festschrift Friedrich Blume zum 70. Geburtstag*, ed. Anna Amalie Abert and Wilhelm Pfannkuch (Kassel: Bärenreiter, 1963), 381-88; and Anthony Newcomb, "Once More 'Between Absolute and Program Music': Schumann's Second Symphony," *19CM* 7 (1984): 233-50.

5. See Alan P. Merriam, *The Anthropology of Music* (Evanston, IL: Northwestern University Press, 1964), chapter 13: "Aesthetics and the Interrelationships of the Arts."

of any and all broader contexts, is not one to which many still subscribe. Claims of superiority have receded in an atmosphere of increasing artistic diversity and tolerance.

The idea of absolute music will neverthelesss continue to shape our attempts to identify and comprehend the essence of music, even if only as a regulative concept. Whether the construct's attendant quality of isolation amounts to purity or sterility will always be a point of contention. Yet the history of the idea makes it clear that absolute music will always play a role in our attempts to explain an art whose essence remains as elusive as its effect remains real.

■ APPENDIX

Hanslick's Vom Musikalisch-Schönen: *Early and Selected Later Responses*

Reviews and commentaries are arranged chronologically whenever a precise date of publication is available, otherwise alphabetically by the name of the author within each year. Responses to later editions, from the second onward, are cited more selectively, limited to those that are reasonably substantive. Items discussed in the text are cross-referenced with relevant page numbers.

■ 1854 4 November
"Wiener Briefe." *Niederrheinische Musikzeitung* 2, no. 44 (4 November 1854): 348–49.

Highly enthusiastic; signed by "-r-." Praises the author's clarity of style as well as the substance of his argument.

■ 1854 20 November
Zimmermann, Robert. "Vom Musikalisch-Schönen." *Oesterreichische Blätter für Literatur und Kunst*, 20 November 1854, 313–15. Republished with minor changes in Zimmermann, *Zur Aesthetik: Studien und Kritiken*, 2 vols. (Vienna: Wilhelm Braumüller, 1870), 2:239–53.

→ p. 185–87. The first and most detailed of Zimmermann's several largely positive reviews.

■ 1854 25 November
Kuh, Emil. Untitled review. *Der Humorist* (Vienna), nos. 305, 306, 309 (25, 26, and 29 November 1854), pp. 1219, 1223, 1235.

Highly positive. Kuh (1828–1876), a Viennese author and literary critic, praises Hanslick's synthesis of a "poetic perspective" and a "relentless dialectic." Recognizes the polemical nature of the work and welcomes it as a counterweight to Wagner's writings. Predicts that it will arouse passionate debate from critics on all sides.

■ 1855 1 January
Anonymous. "Aus Wien." *NZfM* 42 (1 January 1855): 5–8.

A single sentence at the very end of this report (signed "Cs" and dated "end of December") notes that Hanslick's "first-rate brochure" (*treffliche Brochüre*) has elicited "considerable attention" (*großes Aufsehen*) in Vienna.

■ **1855   5 January**

Anonymous. "Wissenschaft und Kritik." *Die Grenzboten* 14 (5 January 1855): 479.

A single paragraph, highly enthusiastic; identifies *tönend bewegte Formen* as a central concept.

■ **1855 January**

Anonymous. "Correspondenz: Aus Wien, 16 December 1854." *Deutsches Museum* 5 (1855): 39–42.

Mentions *VMS* briefly but very positively (p. 41).

■ **1855 January**

Anonymous. Untitled review. *Leipziger Repertorium der deutschen und ausländischen Literatur* 13, no. 1 (1855): 36–39.

Negative. Argues for the expressive capacity of music, without which this art would not speak to us. Points out the contradiction of the final paragraph with rest of treatise; agrees that music reflects universal laws (*Weltgesetze*).

■ **1855   16 February**

Brendel, Franz. Untitled review. *NZfM* 42 (16 February, 23 February 23, 2 March 1855): 77–82, 89–91, 97–100.

→ pp. 219–20. A lengthy summary of the treatise's contents; welcomes the work as a basis for future debate but rejects its central premises.

■ **1855   17 February**

Bischoff, Ludwig. "Eduard Hanslick." *Niederrheinische Musik-Zeitung* 3 (1855), nos. 7 (17 February), 8 (24 February), 9 (3 March), and 10 (10 March).

→ p. 222. Highly positive; reinforces arguments Bischoff points out he had made himself several years before.

■ **1855   24 March**

Bischoff, Ludwig. "Stimmen der Kritik über Richard Wagner. II." *Niederrheinische Musik-Zeitung* 3 (24 March 1855): 89–91.

Uses *VMS* as the basis from which to attack Wagner's theory of the music drama.

■ **1855   12 April**

Anonymous. Untitled review. *Blätter für literarische Unterhaltung*, no. 15 (12 April 1855): 277–78.

Sees *VMS* as the foundational work for a new approach to the aesthetics of music. The treatise navigates a position between extreme realism, in which music must present concrete ideas, and a world of vague dreams. Signed with the cipher "53."

■ **1855 17 April**
Anonymous. "Tagesneuigkeiten." *Die Presse* (Vienna), 17 April 1855, p. 4.

Includes a paragraph noting that *VMS* has attracted considerable attention abroad. Literary and musical journals alike recognize it as "epoch-making" in its field. Notes with regret that the two Viennese music journals may well be the only ones not to have reviewed the treatise. (The *Neue Wiener Musik-Zeitung* would review *VMS* in its issue of 24 May 1855; the *Blätter für Musik, Theater und Kunst*, more generally sympathetic to the aesthetics of Wagner and Liszt, did not run a notice of any kind.)

■ **1855 25 April**
Anonymous. "Ueber Musik." *Wolfgang Menzels Literaturblatt*, 25 April 1855, 129–32.

→p. 223. Highly negative; rejects the treatise's formalist approach.

■ **1855 April**
[Jahn, Otto.] "Aesthetische Feldzüge." *Die Grenzboten* 14, 2nd ser. (April 1855): 201–12.

→ pp. 222–23. Criticizes both Wagner and Hanslick for their unexamined premises about the nature of music. Praises *VMS* for its "unusual philosophical insight" but rejects the idea that music cannot give voice—both literally and figuratively—to emotions.

■ **1855 April**
Schladebach, Julius, ed. *Neues Universal-Lexikon der Tonkunst.* Volume 1. Dresden: Robert Schaefer, 1856.

→ p. 172. The preface, dated April 1855, includes a brief comment that Hanslick's views are "not nearly as new as one might be tempted to believe."

■ **1855 24 May**
H. L. Untitled review under the rubric "Literarische Anzeige." *Neue Wiener Musik-Zeitung*, 24 May 1855, 81–82.

The book's "rich and substantive content" has already garnered much praise in Germany and is warmly recommended to the music-loving public. The treatise offers profound insight into the essence of music. The reviewer nevertheless finds the work's references to "universal laws" and the "great motions of the universe" inconsistent with its principal ideas.

■ **1855 May**
Zeising, Adolf. *Ästhetische Forschungen.* Frankfurt am Main: Meidinger Sohn, 1855.

Brief references in support of Hanslick (pp. 248, 488, 563–64). Argues that there is no real model for music in nature; each art must strive to realize its fullest potential on its own terms, not in conjunction with other arts.

■ **1855 May or June**
Ambros, August Wilhelm. *Die Grenzen der Musik und Poesie: Eine Studie zur Aesthetik der Tonkunst.* Leipzig: Heinrich Matthes, 1855.

→ pp. 220–22. A book-length response to *VMS* by one of Hanslick's lifelong friends. Rejects any precise demarcation between different manifestations of human expression, such as verbal and musical.

■ **1855 June**
Brendel, Franz. *Geschichte der Musik in Italien, Deutschland und Frankreich.* 2nd ed. Leipzig: Heinrich Matthes, 1855.

Similar to his comments in his earlier review in the *NZfM* but much briefer (p. 340).

■ **1855 5 July**
Lotze, Hermann. Untitled review. *Göttingische Gelehrte Anzeigen* 117 (5 and 7 July 1855): 1049–65, 1065–68.

Agrees with some of Hanslick's premises and conclusions, disagrees with others. Praises the treatise's "scientific" approach but rejects the idea that subjectivity relegates the listener to a subordinate position in aesthetics.

■ **1855 13 July**
Liszt, Franz. "Berlioz und seine Haroldsymphonie." *NZfM* 43 (13 July, 20 July, 27 July, 17 August, 24 August 1855): 25–32, 37–46, 49–55, 77–84, 89–97.

→ pp. 210–11. A lengthy manifesto on the nature of program music. Does not mention Hanslick or his treatise by name but argues against many of its premises.

■ **1855 21 July**
"Music the Exponent of Emotion." *Dwight's Journal of Music*, July 21, 1855, 123–24.

→ p. 223. Agrees that while music's means of expression are strictly musical, they nevertheless convey emotion. Signed "J. H."

■ **1855 September**
Anonymous. Untitled review. *Unterhaltungen am häuslichen Herd*, 3, no. 43 (1855), 688.

A brief (three paragraphs) but extremely favorable notice that praises the work for its clarity of style. Aligns Hanslick's thought with Leibniz's dictum that music is a secret counting and calculation of the soul.

■ **1855 17 October**

Lange, O[tto]. Untitled review. *Neue Berliner Musikzeitung* 9 (17 October 1855): 331.

Brief but highly enthusiastic; cites *tönend bewegte Formen* as the treatise's key concept. The work's brevity will recommend it to a wide readership.

■ **1855 November**

Zamminer, Friedrich Georg Karl. *Die Musik und die musikalischen Instrumente in ihrer Beziehung zu den Gesetzen der Akustik*. Gießen: J. Ricker, 1855.

Short but very positive reference to *VMS* (p. 172), citing it in support of the argument that music's content lies in its substance, not in any external object of expression.

■ **1855 3 December**

Zimmermann, Robert. Review of August Wilhelm Ambros, *Die Grenzen der Musik und Poesie*. *Oesterreichische Blätter für Literatur und Kunst*, 2 December 1855, 369–70.

Includes numerous positive references to *VMS*, contrasting Hanslick's views favorably against those of Hand.

■ **1855 6 December**

Ambros, August Wilhelm. "Musik." *Prager Zeitung*, 6 December 1855. Republished in Bonnie Lomnäs, Erling Lomnäs, and Dietmar Strauß, eds., *Auf der Suche nach der poetischen Zeit: Der Prager Davidsbund; Ambros, Bach, Bayer, Hampel, Hanslick, Helfert, Heller, Hock, Ulm*. 2 vols. (Saarbrücken: Pfau, 1999), 2:135–38.

Concludes with observations similar to those Ambros had made in his earlier *Die Grenzen der Musik und Poesie*.

■ **1856 August**

Bayer, Josef. *Aesthetik in Umrissen*. 2 vols. Prague: Heinrich Mercy, 1856–63.

Includes mixed commentary on *VMS* at various points in volume 1 (pp. 140, 235, 313–25, 329, 332). Bayer, one of the *Davidsbund* of Hanslick's youth in Prague, agrees with the assertion that form constitutes music's content but maintains that music can nevertheless give expression to certain moods and states of mind.

■ **1856 10 December**

Anonymous. "Nachrichten: Berlin." *Neue Berliner Musikzeitung* 10 (10 December 1856): 397–98.

Reports on a recent lecture by Adolph Kullak surveying the "current state of the debate on aesthetic positions in music." Includes comments on Hanslick, Marx, Brendel; calls Hanslick a realist and aligns him with Hegel.

■ **1856**

Sieber, Ferdinand. *Vollständiges Lehrbuch der Gesangkunst.* Magdeburg: Heinrichshofen, 1856.

Is instrumental music capable of evoking specific images in the mind of the listener? This is the "burning question of our time" (p. 427). Sieber offers no opinion of his own on this point but summarizes the perspectives of several contemporaneous writers, including Hanslick, Vischer, Zeising, Brendel, and Kullak.

■ **1857   1 May**

Brendel, Franz. "Die Aesthetik der Tonkunst." *NZfM* 46 (1 May 1857): 185–86.

Reiterates his opposition to *VMS*, even while repeating his praise for its clear style of presentation and for moving the focus of aesthetics away from emotions and toward concepts.

■ **1857   June**

Carrière, Moriz. "Populäre Aesthetik." *Blätter für literarische Unterhaltung*, no. 23 (4 June 1857): 415–19.

Praises Ambros's *Die Grenzen der Musik und Poesie* for having successfully refuted *Vom Musikalisch-Schönen* by exposing the "empty formalism" of Hanslick's treatise.

■ **1857   30 October**

Gerstenkorn, Franz. "Dr. Hanslick und der 'Tannhäuser.'" *NZfM* 47 (30 October 1857): 192–93.

Links Hanslick's recent review of *Tannhäuser* to the aesthetic ideas set forward in *VMS*. Calls Hanslick's philosophy a manifestation of the "long-since antiquated 'realistic' philosophy." Hanslick's theory of music, moreover, is "applied mathematics in disguise."

■ **1857**

Kullak, Adolph. "Ueber das musikalisch Schöne." *Anregungen für Kunst, Leben und Wissenschaft* 2 (1857): 183–88.

Surveys the debate and summarizes the views of Hanslick, Hand, Zeising, Zamminer, Vischer, and others. Devotes the greatest amount of attention to Vischer but intersperses his commentary with numerous negative comments about *VMS*, which Kullak interprets as a decidedly partisan attack on the aesthetics of Wagner.

■ **1857**

Lazarus, Moritz. *Das Leben der Seele in Monographien über seine Erscheinungen und Gesetze.* 2 vols. Berlin: Heinrich Schindler, 1856–57.

→ p. 245. Largely positive, though acknowledging that Hanslick's emphasis on music's content comes at the expense of any concern with its effect.

■ 1857

Lobe, Johann Christian. "Gegen Dr. Eduard Hanslick's 'Vom Musikalisch-Schönen.'" *Fliegende Blätter für Musik* 2 (1857): 65–106. Also published as a monograph (Leipzig: Baumgärtner, 1857).

→ p. 223. Highly negative and at times openly sarcastic.

■ 1857

Lobe, Johann Christian. "Noch einmal gegen Dr. Hanslick—in Noten." *Fliegende Blätter für Musik* 2 (1857): 183–89.

→ p. 223. The score of an original four-voice fugue in C minor for keyboard. Lobe provides no verbal commentary beyond the title: "Once Again in Opposition to Dr. Hanslick—in Notes."

■ 1857

Vischer, Friedrich Theodor. *Aesthetik, oder Wissenschaft des Schönen*. 3 vols. Reutlingen and Leipzig: C. Mäcken, 1846–57.

→p. 225. Applauds Hanslick's insistence that form and content in music cannot be separated, but this does not mean that the two concepts are identical. To call the ordering of tones "form" and "form" the "content of music" amounts to little more than a tautology.

■ 1858

Anonymous. Untitled review of second edition (1858). *Monatsschrift für Theater und Musik* 4 (1858): 81–82.

Highly positive review from a journal published in Vienna. Notes in the first sentence that in the second edition Hanslick has deleted "a few things" that had led to "misunderstandings" or might have "appeared to have carried matters too far." Recommends the treatise to younger composers in particular, who might then be in a better position to avoid "fruitless dreaming."

■ 1858

B[ischoff], L[udwig]. Untitled review of second edition (1858). *Niederrheinische Musik-Zeitung* 6 (13 November 1858): 363–64.

Highly positive and in the same vein as Bischoff's earlier (1855) and longer review of the first edition.

■ 1858

Elterlein, Ernst von [i.e., Ernst Gottschald]. *Beethoven's Symphonien nach ihrem idealen Gehalt*. 2nd ed. Dresden: Adolph Brauer, 1858.

A brief but mildly positive reference (p. 2) to *VMS*.

■ **1858**

Kullak, Adolph. *Das Musikalisch-Schöne: Ein Beitrag zur Aesthetik der Tonkunst.* Leipzig: Heinrich Matthes, 1858.

→ p. 224. An expansion of the views Kullak had expounded in his 1857 essay "Ueber das musikalisch Schöne." In his review of Kullak's book in the *NZfM* 50 (13 and 20 May and 1859): 217–19, 229–31, Julius Schäffer drew close parallels between the theories of Hanslick and Kullak, to which the latter objected in the next volume of the same journal: see Kullak, "Ueber musikalische Aesthetik," *NZfM* 51 (5, 12, and 19 August 1859):45–46, 53–55, 61–62.

■ **1859**

Carrière, Moriz. *Aesthetik: Die Idee des Schönen*, vol. 2, *Die bildende Kunst; Die Musik; Die Poesie.* Leipzig: F. A. Brockhaus, 1859.

→ p. 224. Highly negative; expands on his earlier comments (June 1857). Concedes that the work has won wide praise but dismisses *VMS* as an overreaction to the sobering events of 1848–49, which in turn had provided an overly fertile breeding ground for realism in place of the "empty dreams" of earlier years.

■ **1859**

Laurencin, Ferdinand Peter, Graf von. *Dr. Eduard Hanslick's Lehre vom Musikalisch-Schönen: Eine Abwehr.* Leipzig: Heinrich Matthes, 1859.

→pp. 225–26. The most thoroughly negative of all commentaries on *VMS*.

■ **1860**

Brendel, Franz. "Vorstudien zur Aesthetik der Tonkunst." *NZfM* 53 (1860): 105–8, 141–44.

Similar in tone to Brendel's earlier comments on *VMS*. Praises the treatise's attention to the technical side of music but disputes the idea that it marks an end of the discussion. In the second installment, Brendel develops his own theory of an isomorphic relationship between emotion and form.

■ **1860**

Kossmaly, C[arl]. "Zur Verständigung über einige Fragen der musikalischen Aesthetik. Vorstudien zur Aesthetik der Tonkunst." *Neue Berliner Musikzeitung* 14 (22 February 1860): 57–58.

Extremely negative. Rejects as "eccentric" the premise that music has nothing to do with emotion and praises Laurencin's recent critique of Hanslick's "sophisms."

■ **1861**

Ehrlich, H[einrich]. "Die musikalisch-ästhetische Literatur der letzten zehn Jahre." *Neues Frankfurter Museum: Beiblatt der "Zeit,"* nos. 81-88, 90-94, and 103 (7–14 July, 16 July, 18-21 July, 23 July, and 3 September 1861), 637–39, 645–47,

657–59, 663–66, 672–74, 680–83, 689–90, 696–97, 711–13, 719–22, 727–29, 733–36, 746–47, 1029–31.

A lengthy review of writings on musical aesthetics of the previous ten years, but focused largely on Wagner's Zurich writings, *VMS*, and Laurencin's *Dr. Eduard Hanslick's Lehre vom Musikalisch-Schönen: Eine Abwehr* (1859). Summarizes and discusses the arguments of *VMS* in great detail. Ehrlich's attitude toward the treatise is sympathetic but not entirely positive: he praises the work for its many insights but points out its inconsistencies and shortcomings as well. Ehrlich's views in his *Die Musik-Aesthetik in ihrer Entwickelung von Kant bis auf die Gegenwart* (1882) remain essentially the same.

■ **1862**

Anonymous. Untitled review of second edition (1858). *Zeitschrift für exacte Philosophie im Sinne des neuen philosophischen Realismus* 2 (1862): 359–60.

Sees *VMS* as attack on current aesthetics, not the aesthetics of the past. Highly positive.

■ **1863**

Helmholtz, Hermann von. *Die Lehre von den Tonempfindungen als physiologische Grundlage für die Theorie der Musik*. Braunschweig: Vieweg & Sohn, 1863.

→ pp. 245–46. Praises Hanslick for his emphasis on the role of physical motion (*Bewegung*) in music.

■ **1863**

Schlüter, Joseph. *Allgemeine Geschichte der Musik in übersichtlicher Darstellung*. Leipzig: Wilhelm Engelmann, 1863.

→ p. 227. Endorses Hanslick's views wholeheartedly.

■ **1864**

Daumer, Georg Friedrich. "Musikalischer Katechismus." *Deutsche Vierteljahrs-Schrift* 27, no. 3 (1864): 43–89.

Rejects the idea that music has no roots in nature; accuses Hanslick of having made *Phantasie* his "goddess." There is no criterion for beauty other than the pleasure it gives. Hanslick is at war with realism, substantivism, and music itself.

■ **1864**

Eckardt, Ludwig. *Die Zukunft der Tonkunst, namentlich mit Bezug auf die Symphonie, die Kirchenmusik, das Oratorium und die Oper: Vortrag an der dritten Versammlung deutscher Tonkünstler zu Carlsruhe, 1864*. Leipzig: C. F. Kahnt, 1864.

Eckardt (1827–1871), an Austrian poet and playwright, dedicated the published version of his address to Liszt. Accuses Hanslick of materialism, concerned only with sound for its own sake, without regard to the world beyond music.

■ **1865**

Anonymous. Untitled review of third edition (1865). *Recensionen und Mittheilungen über Theater und Musik* 11 (13 May 1865): 304.

> Brief but positive notice.

■ **1865**

Daumer, Georg Friedrich. "Was braucht die Musik nicht, um ihre Wirkungen zu thun!" *Niederrheinische Musik-Zeitung* 13 (1 July 1865): 201–5.

> Reiterates points made in his 1864 commentary on *VMS*.

■ **1865**

Eckardt, Ludwig. *Vorschule der Aesthetik*. 2 vols. Karlsruhe: A. Bielefeld, 1865.

> Says that Hanslick believes music to be nothing more than a "play of tones" and rejects this view (2:15–17). "Has Hanslick never heard Beethoven?" (2:16).

■ **1865**

Beauquier, Charles. *Philosophie de la musique*. Paris: Germer Baillière, 1865.

> → pp. 229–30. Never mentions Hanslick by name but is clearly indebted to *VMS*.

■ **1865**

Vogt, Theodor. *Form und Gehalt in der Aesthetik: Eine kritische Untersuchung über Entstehung und Anwendung dieser Begriffe*. Vienna: Carl Gerold's Sohn, 1865.

> An account of musical form (pp. 134–48) highly sympathetic to the perspective of *VMS*.

■ **1866**

Krüger, Eduard. *System der Tonkunst*. Leipzig: Breitkopf & Härtel, 1866.

> → p. 178. Calls Hanslick's equation of form and content tautological: if music is only music, then we can never really say anything about it. "A thing," Krüger points out, "is not merely an 'it'; it is also a 'something.'"

■ **1867**

Bensey, Rudolf. "Die Mittel des Tonreiches nach Inhalt und Form." *NZfM* 63 (5 and 12 July 1867): 241–43, 250–55.

> Derides Hanslick's account of music's "pathological" effects; argues that love (*eros*) is the driving force of music.

■ **1868**

von Kirchmann, Julius Hermann. *Aesthetik auf realistischer Grundlage*. 2 vols. Berlin: Julius Springer, 1868.

> Refutes many of the treatise's points (1:208–20) and classifies Hanslick as an idealist.

■ **1868**

Lotze, Hermann. *Geschichte der Aesthetik in Deutschland*. Munich: J. G. Cotta, 1868.

Includes a slightly revised republication of his 1855 review of *VMS* (pp. 479–87). Notes that his opinion of the work has not changed since that time. Republished in his *Kleine Schriften*, vol. 3 (Leipzig: Breitkopf & Härtel, 1891), 200–14.

■ **1869**

Wagner, Richard. *Das Judenthum in der Musik*. Leipzig: J. J. Weber, 1869.

→ pp. 226–27. Mistakenly ascribes the musical portion of Vischer's *Ästhetik* to Hanslick and condemns the "the musically Jewish-Beautiful" as lacking any grounding in national identity.

■ **1870**

Stade, Friedrich. "Vom Musikalisch-Schönen. Mit Bezug auf Dr. E. Hanslick's gleichnamige Schrift." *NZfM* 66: 241–43 (24 June 1870); 253–55 (1 July); 261–64 (8 July); 269–71 (15 July); 277–79 (22 July). Also published separately as a monograph (Leipzig: C. F. Kahnt, 1871).

→ p. 227. An attack on *VMS* from the pen of a youthful Wagnerian.

■ **1870**

Hausegger, Friedrich. "Ein Traum, ein Leben: Humoreske." *Musikalisches Wochenblatt* 1 (23 September 1870): 618–20.

→ p. 231. A humorous piece relating Hanslick's unflattering appearance in one of Hausegger's dreams.

■ **1871**

Wagner, Richard. "Offener Brief an Dr. phil. Friedrich Stade." *Musikalisches Wochenblatt*, 13 January 1871. Republished in Wagner, 16:103–8.

→ p. 227. Thanks Stade for having recognized that even as "sophistic, flea-bitten a work... as that by Herr Hanslick" deserved refutation, given its "alarming" influence in the musical world.

■ **1871**

Fuchs, Carl. *Präliminarien zu einer Kritik der Tonkunst*. Leipzig: E. W. Fritzsch, 1871.

→ pp. 268–69. One of the first aesthetics of music to embrace Schopenhauer's views; attacks Hanslick's emphasis on form as sterile.

■ **1874**

Anonymous. Untitled review of fourth edition (1874). *AmZ* 9 (25 February 1874): 116.

A brief notice that acknowledges the importance of the work but asks why its author has not yet delivered the more expansive treatment of his subject promised in the treatise's first edition.

▪ 1874

Ambros, August Wilhelm. "Schriften über Musik. I." *Wiener Abendpost*, 24 June 1874, p. 1132.

A review of the fourth (1874) edition. Ambros summarizes the polarizing effect of the treatise since its first appearance and notes the continuing public discussion of this "widely read" and "well-known" work. The new edition is so "fundamentally improved, that it barely resembles earlier ones, particularly the first." As in his initial responses to *VMS* (1855), Ambros takes issue with many of the treatise's arguments but in the end concedes that Hanslick's contribution has been to show "with a firm hand" that there are other ways of approaching music other than through the "beloved antechamber of feeling" (*die beliebte Gefühls-Antichambre*).

▪ 1875

Köstlin, Heinrich Adolf. *Geschichte der Musik im Umriß*. Tübingen: H. Laupp, 1875.

→ pp. 227–28. A history of music that openly endorses Hanslick's conception of the art.

▪ 1876

Ganting, Ludwig von. *Die Grundzüge der musikalischen Richtungen in ihrer geschichtlichen Entwicklung*. Leipzig: Breitkopf & Härtel, 1876.

→ p. 228. A pro-Wagnerian synopsis of music history that devotes more than 10 percent of its content to a denunciation of *VMS*.

▪ 1876

Klengel, Paul. *Zur Aesthetik der Tonkunst*. Leipzig: O. Mutze, 1876.

An extended rebuttal of Hanslick's treatise (pp. 22–40) which rejects the notion that form and content in music are inseparable. Takes Hanslick to task for his terminological vagueness, e.g., using *Form, Inhalt, Gehalt,* and *Idee* more or less interchangeably.

▪ 1876

Liebmann, Otto. *Zur Analysis der Wirklichkeit: Philosophische Untersuchungen*. Strassburg: Karl J. Trübner, 1876.

A brief but concentrated attack on the premises of *VMS* (pp. 567–69). Considers music to be an essentially expressive art.

▪ **1877**

Hostinský, Ottokar. *Das Musikalisch-Schöne und das Gesammtkunstwerk vom Standpuncte der formalen Aesthetik: Eine Studie.* Leipzig: Breitkopf & Härtel, 1877.

→ pp. 243–44. An attempt to synthesize the aesthetic theories of Wagner and Hanslick.

▪ **1877**

Lessmann, Otto. Review of fifth edition (1876). *Allgemeine Deutsche Musik-Zeitung* 4 (24 August 1877): 266–67.

Concedes the importance of the treatise but argues that aesthetics should be dictated by the musical repertory of the day, not by supposedly immutable principles.

▪ **1877**

Riemann, Hugo. "Vom Musikalisch-Schönen." *Allgemeine Deutsche Musik-Zeitung* 4 (1877): 69–70, 77–78, 85–86, 93–94, 101–02, 110, 119–20, 129–30, 137–38, 145–46, 154–55, 179–80.

An expanded version of a lecture delivered in Bielefeld on 14 February 1877. The title notwithstanding, Riemann mentions Hanslick only occasionally, developing instead his own theories of musical beauty, which is contingent upon the listener and performer(s) as well as the work, and which varies across time.

▪ **1878**

Anonymous. Review of Charles Bannelier's translation of the fifth edition (1876) as *Du beau dans la musique: Essai de réforme de l'esthétique musicale* (Paris: Brandus, 1877), *Revue philosophique de la France et de l'Étranger* 6 (1878): 426–30.

The most substantial of the French-language reviews to appear in response to Bannelier's translation. The reviewer ("Ch.B.") praises the work of the translator but questions many of the treatise's most basic assertions and points out that the arguments are frequently contradictory. Hanslick exercises "scholastic subtlety" more often than "true scientific logic."

▪ **1879**

Breakspeare, Eustace J. "Musical Æsthetics." *Proceedings of the Musical Association,* 6th session (1879–80): 59–77.

Includes an introduction to *VMS* "to English readers." Emphasizes Hanslick's concept of "pure contemplation" and the "attentive observation of the changes and manifold combinations of tonal forms." Disagrees with his views on the relationship between the senses and mind, arguing that there must be something between Hanslick's ideal listener on the one hand, and "the emotional savage or the sentimental dreamer" on the other. On the whole sympathetic to *VMS* but critical of the treatise's many inconsistencies, caused by its author's "desire to regard the work of musical art as something purely objective."

■ **1882**

Doempke, Gustav. "Das Problem der musikalischen Aesthetik." *Musik-Welt* 2 (7 and 14 January 1882): 17–20, 29–32.

A largely favorable review of the sixth edition, with extended excerpts. Concludes that the treatise, although written in response to the theories of the New German School, makes arguments that have nothing to do with specific repertory. Doempke (1853–1923) was at one time a music critic for the *Wiener allgemeine Zeitung*, a position secured in part through a recommendation from Hanslick.

■ **1882**

Ehrlich, Heinrich. *Die Musik-Aesthetik in ihrer Entwickelung von Kant bis auf die Gegenwart: Ein Grundriss.* Leipzig: F. E. C. Leukhart, 1882.

A sympathetic but not wholly positive account of *VMS* (pp. 66–70).

■ **1882**

Lessmann, Otto. Review of sixth edition (1881). *Allgemeine Deutsche Musik-Zeitung* 9 (6 January 1882): 3–4.

Similar in substance to Lessmann's 1877 review of the fifth edition but more openly negative and sharper in its tone.

■ **1884**

Hausegger, Friedrich von. "Die Musik als Ausdruck." *Bayreuther Blätter* 7 (1884): 9–15, 37–48, 78–82, 107–13, 142–52, 175–84, 214–19, 242–53, 305–16, 356–67, 381–93. Republished as a monograph under the same title (Vienna: Carl Konegen, 1885; 2nd ed., 1887).

→ pp. 230–31. A defense of music as an art of expression; does not mention *VMS* explicitly but refutes the basic thrust of Hanslick's treatise, dismissing the notion of music as *tönend bewegte Formen*.

■ **1884**

Jungmann, Joseph. *Aesthetik.* Freiburg im Breisgau: Herder, 1884.

An extended (pp. 842–60) and fairly neutral summary and critique. This is a revised and expanded version of the author's *Die Schönheit und die schöne Kunst* (Innsbruck: Wagnersche Universitäts-Buchhandlung, 1866), which does not mention *VMS*.

■ **1885**

Zimmermann, Robert. Untitled review of seventh edition (1885). *Vierteljahrsschrift für Musikwissenschaft* 1 (1885): 251–52.

A brief and but predictably favorable review from the dedicatee of the seventh edition.

■ **1886**

Hartmann, Eduard von. "Zur Aesthetik des Tonkunst." *Deutsche Rundschau* 46 (January–March 1886): 72–94. Republished as "Idealismus und Formalismus in der Musik-Aesthetik," in Hartmann, *Die Deutsche Aesthetik seit Kant* (Berlin: C. Dunker, 1886), 484–509.

Generally positive, though with serious qualifications. Concludes that *VMS* is a one-sided but a useful counterweight to the correspondingly one-sided approach of Vischer. Hanslick "is in complete agreement with aesthetic idealism."

■ **1886**

Wallaschek, Richard. *Ästhetik der Tonkunst*. Stuttgart: W. Kohlhammer, 1886.

→ pp. 244–45. Praises Hanslick for having objected to the "uncertain gropings" of "swooning idealists" but takes issue with the treatise's overly formalistic approach, its refusal to address issues of perception, and its failure to define beauty in spite of the presence of that word in its title.

■ **1887**

Seidl, Arthur. *Vom Musikalisch-Erhabenen: Prolegomena zur Aesthetik der Tonkunst*. Leipzig: C. F. Kahnt Nachfolger, 1887.

A book-length rebuttal to *VMS* that plays on the title of Hanslick's treatise by emphasizing the "musically sublime" rather than the "musically beautiful." Seidl criticizes *VMS* early and often. The publisher brought out a second, expanded edition of this work in 1907.

■ **1892**

Schneider, Paul. *Über das Darstellungsvermögen der Musik: Eine Untersuchung an der Hand von Prof. Ed. Hanslick's Buch "Vom Musikalisch-Schönen."* Oppeln and Leipzig: Georg Frank, 1892.

→ p. 243. Proposes a reconciliation of feeling and form through the philosophy of Schopenhauer: beauty resides in form, but music can reflect the Will.

■ **1893**

Bellaigue, Camille. *Psychologie musicale*. Paris: Delagrave, 1893.

Equates musical beauty with expression and in its introduction refutes *VMS* at length (pp. vi–xvii).

■ WORKS CITED

Abbate, Carolyn. "Music—Drastic or Gnostic?" *Critical Inquiry* 30 (2004): 505–36.

Abegg, Werner. *Musikästhetik und Musikkritik bei Eduard Hanslick.* Regensburg: Bosse, 1974.

Abert, Hermann. *Die Musikanschauung des Mittelalters und ihre Grundlagen.* Halle: Niemeyer, 1905.

Abrams, M. H. "Art as Such: The Sociology of Modern Aesthetics." In *Doing Things with Texts,* 163–227. New York: W. W. Norton, 1989.

——. "From Addison to Kant: Modern Aesthetics and the Exemplary Art." In *Studies in Eighteenth-Century British Art and Aesthetics,* 16–48. Edited by Ralph Cohen. Berkeley and Los Angeles: University of California Press, 1985.

——. *The Mirror and the Lamp: Romantic Theory and the Critical Tradition.* London: Oxford University Press, 1953.

Acquisto, Joseph. *French Symbolist Poetry and the Idea of Music.* Aldershot: Ashgate, 2006.

Adler, Guido. *Methode der Musikgeschichte.* Leipzig: Breitkopf & Härtel, 1919.

——. *Der Stil in der Musik.* Leipzig: Breitkopf & Härtel, 1911.

Adlung, Jakob. *Anleitung zu der musikalischen Gelahrtheit.* Erfurt: J. D. Jungnicol, 1758.

Adorno, Theodor. "Über einige Relationen zwischen Musik und Malerei" (1965). In *Gesammelte Schriften,* vol. 16, edited by Rolf Tiedemann, 628–42. Frankfurt am Main: Suhrkamp, 1978. Translated by Susan Gillespie as "On Some Relationships between Music and Painting," *MQ* 79 (1995): 66–79.

Alberti, Leon Battista. [*De re aedificatoria.* English.] *On the Art of Building* (1485). Translated by Joseph Rykwert, Neil Leach, and Robert Tavernor. Cambridge, MA: MIT Press, 1988.

Albrechtsberger, Johann Georg. *Gründliche Anweisung zur Composition.* Leipzig: J. G. I. Breitkopf, 1790.

d'Alembert, Jean Lerond. "De la liberté de la musique" (1758). In *Oeuvres,* 5 vols. 1:515–46. Paris: Belin, 1821–22.

——. *Discours préliminaire de l'Encyclopédie et articles de l'Encyclopédie* (1751). Edited by Martine Groult. Paris: Champion, 2011.

——. [*Discours préliminaire de l'Encyclopédie.* English.] *Preliminary Discourse to the Encyclopedia of Diderot.* Translated by Richard N. Schwab. Chicago: University of Chicago Press, 1995.

Altenburg, Detlef. "Vom poetisch Schönen: Franz Liszts Auseinandersetzung mit der Musikästhetik Eduard Hanslicks." In *Ars Musica, Musica Scientia: Festschrift Heinrich Hüschen,* 1–10. Edited by Detlef Altenburg. Cologne: Verlag der Arbeitsgemeinschaft für Rheinische Musikgeschichte, 1980.

Ambros, August Wilhelm. *Die Grenzen der Musik und Poesie: Eine Studie zur Aesthetik der Tonkunst.* Leipzig: Heinrich Matthes, 1855; reprint, Hildesheim: Olms, 1976.

Ammann, Peter J. "The Musical Theory and Philosophy of Robert Fludd." *Journal of the Warburg and Courtauld Institutes* 30 (1967): 198–227.

Anderson, Robert Michael. "Polemics or Philosophy? Musical Pathology in Eduard Hanslick's *Vom Musikalisch-Schönen.*" *Musical Times* 154, no. 1924 (Autumn 2013): 65–76.

Anderson, Warren D. "Damonian Theory in Plato's Thought." *Transactions and Proceedings of the American Philological Association* 86 (1955): 88–102.

———. *Ethos and Education in Greek Music: The Evidence of Poetry and Philosophy.* Cambridge, MA: Harvard University Press, 1966.

André, Yves Marie. *Essai sur le beau.* Paris: Guerin, 1741.

Anonymous. Review of Eduard Hanslick, *Vom Musikalisch-Schönen*, 1st ed. (1854). *Leipziger Repertorium der deutschen und ausländischen Literatur* 13, no. 1 (1855): 36–39.

Anonymous. Review of Ferdinand Hand, *Ästhetik der Tonkunst.* In *Blätter für literarische Unterhaltung*, nos. 146–48 (26–28 May 1838): 593–95, 597–98, 601–02.

Anonymous. "Ueber Musik." *Wolfgang Menzels Literaturblatt*, no. 33 (25 April 1855): 129–32.

Applegate, Celia. "How German Is It? Nationalism and the Idea of Serious Music in the Early Nineteenth Century." *19CM* 21 (1998): 274–96.

Applegate, Celia, and Pamela Potter. "Germans as the 'People of Music': Genealogy of an Identity." In *Music and German National Identity*, 1–35. Edited by Celia Applegate and Pamela Potter. Chicago: University of Chicago Press, 2002.

Aquinas, Thomas, Saint. *The "Summa Theologica."* 2nd ed. Translated by Fathers of the English Dominican Province. 22 vols. New York: Benziger Brothers, 1920–25.

Aristotle. *Politics, Books VII and VIII.* Edited and translated by Richard Kraut. Oxford: Clarendon Press, 1997

Augustine, Bishop of Hippo, Saint. [*De Civitate Dei.* English.] *Concerning the City of God against the Pagans.* Translated by Henry Bettenson. London: Penguin Books, 2003.

———. [*Confessiones.* English.] *The Confessions.* Edited by Temple Scott. Translated by Edward B. Pusey. New York: E. P. Dutton, 1900.

Aurier, G. Albert. "Le symbolisme en peinture: Paul Gauguin." *Mercure de France*, série moderne 2 (1891): 155–65.

Austin, Larry. "The Realization and First Complete Performances of Ives's *Universe Symphony*." In *Ives Studies*, 179–232. Edited by Philip Lambert. Cambridge: Cambridge University Press, 1997.

Avins, Styra, ed. *Johannes Brahms: Life and Letters.* New York: Oxford University Press, 1997.

Bach, Carl Philipp Emanuel. *Versuch über die wahre Art das Clavier zu spielen.* 2 vols. Berlin: C. F. Henning (vol. 1) and G. L. Winter (vol. 2), 1753–62.

Bach, Johann Sebastian. *Schriftstücke von der Hand Johann Sebastian Bachs.* Edited by Werner Neumann and Hans-Joachim Schulze. Bärenreiter: Kassel, 1963. (*Bach-Dokumente* 1).

Bagge, Selmar. "Eine französische Stimme über den Inhalt der Musik." *Leipziger allgemeine musikalische Zeitung* 1 (1866): 21–22, 32–34.

Bailey, Walter B. *Programmatic Elements in the Works of Schoenberg.* Ann Arbor: UMI Research Press, 1984.

Baker, Nancy Kovaleff, and Thomas Christensen, eds. and trans. *Aesthetics and the Art of Musical Composition in the German Enlightenment: Selected Writings of Johann Georg Sulzer and Heinrich Christoph Koch.* Cambridge: Cambridge University Press, 1995.

Barker, Andrew, ed. and trans. *Greek Musical Writings.* 2 vols. Cambridge: Cambridge University Press, 1984–89.

———. "Mathematical Beauty Made Audible: Musical Aesthetics in Ptolemy's *Harmonics*." *Classical Philology* 105 (2010): 403–20.

Bartel, Dietrich. *Musica poetica: Musical-Rhetorical Figures in German Baroque Music.* Lincoln: University of Nebraska Press, 1997.

Batteux, Charles. *Les beaux-arts réduits à un même principe.* Paris: Durand, 1746.

———. [*Les beaux-arts réduits à un même principe. German.*] *Einschränkung der schönen Künste auf einen einzigen Grundsatz.* 3rd ed. 2 vols. Edited and translated by Johann Adolf Schlegel. Leipzig: Weidmanns Erben und Reich, 1770; reprint, Hildesheim: Olms, 1976.

Bauer, Roger. *Der Idealismus und seine Gegner in Österreich*. Heidelberg: C. Winter, 1966.

Bauer-Lechner, Natalie. *Erinnerungen an Gustav Mahler*. Leipzig: E. P. Tal, 1923.

Baumgarten, Alexander Gottlieb. *Aesthetica*. 2 vols. Frankfurt am Main: Johann Christian Kleyb, 1750–58.

Beattie, James. "An Essay on Poetry and Music, as They Affect the Mind" (1762). In *Essays*, 349–580. Edinburgh: William Creech, 1776.

Beauquier, Charles. *Philosophie de la musique*. Paris: Germer Baillière, 1865.

Becker, Carl Ferdinand. "Die zu frühe Rezension." *NZfM* 13 (14 November 1840): 158–59.

Beierwaltes, Werner. "Augustins Interpretation von Sapientia 11, 21." *Révue des études Augustiniennes* 15 (1969): 51–61.

Beiser, Frederick. *Diotima's Children: German Aesthetic Rationalism from Leibniz to Lessing*. New York: Oxford University Press, 2009.

———. *German Idealism: The Struggle against Subjectivism, 1781–1801*. Cambridge, MA: Harvard University Press, 2002.

———. *The Romantic Imperative: The Concept of Early German Romanticism*. Cambridge, MA: Harvard University Press, 2003.

Bekker, Paul. *Beethoven*. Berlin: Schuster & Loeffler, 1910.

Bell, Clive. *Art*. London: Chatto & Windus, 1914.

Bell-Villada, Gene H. *Art for Art's Sake and Literary Life: How Politics and Markets Helped Shape the Ideology & Culture of Aestheticism, 1790–1990*. Lincoln: University of Nebraska Press, 1996.

Bennett, William Sterndale. *Lectures on Musical Life*. Edited by Nicholas Temperley. Woodbridge: Boydell Press, 2006.

Berg, Darrell M. "C. P. E. Bach's Character Pieces and His Friendship Circle." In *C. P. E. Bach Studies*, 1–32. Edited by Stephen L. Clark. Oxford: Clarendon Press, 1988.

Berger, Karol. "Concepts and Developments in Music Theory." In *European Music, 1520–1640*, 303–28. Edited by James Haar. Woodbridge: Boydell, 2006.

———. "Musicology According to Don Giovanni, or: Should We Get Drastic?" *JM* 22 (2005): 490–501.

———. *Theories of Chromatic and Enharmonic Music in Late 16th-Century Italy*. Ann Arbor: UMI Research Press, 1980.

Berghahn, Klaus L. "German Literary Theory from Gottsched to Goethe." In *The Cambridge History of Literary Criticism*, vol. 4, *The Eighteenth Century*, 522–45. Edited by H. B. Nisbet and Claude Rawson. Cambridge: Cambridge University Press, 1997.

Berkeley, George. *Alciphron: or, The Minute Philosopher*. 2nd ed. 2 vols. London: J. Tonson, 1732.

Bernstein, J. M. *The Fate of Art: Aesthetic Alienation from Kant to Derrida and Adorno*. University Park: Pennsylvania State University Press, 1992.

Birke, Joachim. *Christian Wolffs Metaphysik und die zeitgenössische Literatur- und Musiktheorie: Gottsched, Scheibe, Mizler*. Berlin: de Gruyter, 1966.

Bischoff, Ludwig. "Eduard Hanslick." *Niederrheinische Musik-Zeitung* 3 (1855): 49–53, 57–60, 65–66, 73–75.

———. "Joseph Haydn's Musik." *Rheinische Musik-Zeitung* 1 (23 November 1850 and 1 February 1851): 161–64, 253–56.

Bitter, C. H. *Carl Philipp Emanuel und Wilhelm Friedemann Bach und deren Brüder*. 2 vols. Berlin: Wilhelm Müller, 1868.

Blankenburg, Walter. "Der Harmonie-Begriff in der lutherisch-barocken Musikanschauung." *AfMw* 16 (1959): 44–56.

Blanning, T. C. W. [Tim]. *The Culture of Power and the Power of Culture: Old Regime Europe, 1660–1789*. Oxford: Oxford University Press, 2002.

——. *The Triumph of Music: The Rise of Composers, Musicians, and Their Art*. Cambridge, MA: Harvard University Press, 2008.

Blaukopf, Kurt. "Im Geiste Bolzanos und Herbarts: Ansätze empiristischer Musikforschung in Wien und Prag." In *Bolzano und die österreichische Geistesgeschichte*, 237–64. Edited by Heinrich Ganthaler and Otto Neumaier. Sankt Augustin: Academia, 1997 (Beiträge zur Bolzano Forschung, 6).

——. "Kunstforschung als exacte Wissenschaft." In *Elemente moderner Wissenschaftstheorie: Zur Interaktion von Philosophie, Geschichte und Theorie der Wissenschaften*, 177–211. Edited by Friedrich Stadler. Vienna and New York: Springer, 2000.

——. *Pioniere empiristischer Musikforschung: Österreich und Böhmen als Wiege der modernen Kunstsoziologie*. Vienna: Hölder-Pichler-Tempsky, 1995.

Boethius, Anicius Manlius Severinus. [*De institutione arithmetica*. English.] *Boethian Number Theory*. Edited and translated by Michael Masi. Amsterdam: Rodopi, 1983.

——. [*De institutione musica*. English.] *Fundamentals of Music*. Edited by Claude V. Palisca. Translated by Calvin M. Bower. New Haven: Yale University Press, 1989.

Boisits, Barbara. "Formalismus als österreichische Staatsdoktrin? Zum Kontext musikalischer Formalästhetik innerhalb der Wissenschaft Zentraleuropas." *Muzikološki zbornik/Musicological Annual* 40 (2004): 129–36.

Bonaventure, Saint. [*Itinerarium mentis in Deum*. English.] *The Journey to the Mind of God*. Edited by Stephen F. Brown. Translated by Philotheus Boehner. Indianapolis: Hackett, 1993.

Bonds, Mark Evan. *Music as Thought: Listening to the Symphony in the Age of Beethoven*. Princeton: Princeton University Press, 2006.

——. *Wordless Rhetoric: Musical Form and the Metaphor of the Oration*. Cambridge, MA: Harvard University Press, 1991.

Borchmeyer, Dieter. *Richard Wagner: Theory and Theatre*. Translated by Stewart Spencer. Oxford: Clarendon Presss, 1991.

Botstein, Leon. "Schenker the Regressive: Observations on the Historical Schenker." *MQ* 86 (2002): 239–47.

Boyd, John. *The Function of Mimesis and its Decline*. 2nd ed. New York: Fordham University Press, 1980.

Boulanger, Nadia. "Concerts Koussevitsky." *Le monde musical*, November 1923, 365, 367.

Bourdieu, Pierre. *Distinction: A Social Critique of the Judgement of Taste*. Translated by Richard Nice. Cambridge, MA: Harvard University Press, 1984.

Bower, Calvin. "*Adhuc ex parte et in enigmate cernimus*...: Reflections on the Closing Chapters of *Musica Enchiriadis*." In *Music in the Mirror: Reflections on the History of Music Theory and Literature for the 21st Century*, 21–44. Edited by Andreas Giger and Thomas J. Mathiesen. Lincoln: University of Nebraska Press, 2002.

——. "From Alleluia to Sequence: Some Definitions of Relations." In *Western Plainchant in the First Millennium: Studies in the Medieval Liturgy and Its Music*, 351–98. Edited by Sean Gallagher. Aldershot: Ashgate, 2003.

Bowie, Andrew. *Aesthetics and Subjectivity from Kant to Nietzsche*. 2nd ed. Manchester: Manchester University Press, 2003.

——. *From Romanticism to Critical Theory: The Philosophy of German Literary Theory*. London: Routledge, 1997.

——. *Music, Philosophy, and Modernity*. Cambridge: Cambridge University Press, 2007.

———. *Schelling and Modern European Philosophy*. London and New York: Routledge, 1993.

Bozarth, George S. "Brahms's *Lieder ohne Worte*: The 'Poetic' Andantes of the Piano Sonatas." In *Brahms Studies*, 345–78. Edited by George S. Bozarth. Oxford: Clarendon Press, 1990.

Brahms, Johannes. *Des jungen Kreislers Schatzkästlein: Aussprüche von Dichtern, Philosophen und Künstlern*. Edited by Carl Krebs. Berlin: Deutsche Brahmsgesellschaft, 1909.

Brandt, Torsten. *Johann Christian Lobe (1797–1881): Studien zu Biographie und musikschriftstellerischem Werk*. Göttingen: Vandenhoeck & Ruprecht, 2002.

Brendel, Franz. *Geschichte der Musik in Italien, Deutschland und Frankreich, von den ersten christlichen Zeiten bis auf die Gegenwart: Zweiundzwanzig Vorlesungen gehalten zu Leipzig im Jahre 1850*. Leipzig: B. Hinze, 1852; reprint,, Vaduz: Sändig, 1985.

———. *Geschichte der Musik in Italien, Deutschland und Frankreich, von den ersten christlichen Zeiten bis auf die Gegenwart: Zweiundzwanzig Vorlesungen gehalten zu Leipzig im Jahre 1850*. 3rd ed. Leipzig: Heinrich Matthes, 1860.

———. "Der Kampf des Alten und Neuen." *Anregungen für Kunst, Leben und Wissenschaft* 1 (1856): 45–47.

———. "Programmmusik." *Anregungen für Kunst, Leben und Wissenschaft* 1 (1856): 82–92.

———. Review of Eduard Hanslick, *Vom Musikalisch-Schönen*. *NZfM* 42 (1855): 77–82, 89–91, 97–100.

Brittan, Francesca. "On Microscopic Hearing: Fairy Magic, Natural Science, and the *Scherzo fantastique*." *JAMS* 64 (2011): 527–600.

Brodbeck, David. "Brahms, the Third Symphony, and the New German School." In *Brahms and His World*, 95–116. Revised ed. Edited by Walter Frisch and Kevin Karnes. Princeton: Princeton University Press, 2009.

Brokoff, Jürgen. *Geschichte der reinen Poesie: Von der Weimarer Klassik biz zur historischen Avantgarde*. Göttingen: Wallstein, 2010.

Bruchhagen, Paul. "Hanslick und die spekulative Ästhetik." *Zeitschrift für Ästhetik und allgemeine Kunstwissenschaft* 30 (1936): 270–76.

Bruhn, Siglind. *The Musical Order of the World: Kepler, Hesse, Hindemith*. Hillsdale, NY: Pendragon Press, 2005.

Buelow, George J. "Mattheson and the Invention of the *Affektenlehre*." In *New Mattheson Studies*, 393–407. Edited by George J. Buelow and Hans Joachim Marx. Cambridge: Cambridge University Press, 1983.

Bujić, Bojan, ed. *Music in European Thought, 1851–1912*. Cambridge: Cambridge University Press, 1988.

Burbach, Hermann-Josef. *Studien zur Musikanschauung des Thomas von Aquin*. Regensburg: Gustav Bosse, 1966.

Burke, Edmund. *A Philosophical Enquiry into the Origins of Our Ideas of the Sublime and Beautiful* (1756). Rev. ed. Edited by James T. Boulton. Oxford: Basil Blackwell, 1987.

Burkert, Walter. *Greek Religion: Archaic and Classical*. Translated by John Raffan. Oxford: Basil Blackwell, 1985.

———. *Lore and Science in Ancient Pythagoreanism*. Translated by Edwin L. Minar, Jr. Cambridge, MA: Harvard University Press, 1972.

Burmeister, Joachim. [*Musica poetica*. English.] *Musical Poetics*. Translated by Benito V. Rivera. New Haven: Yale University Press, 1993.

Busoni, Ferruccio. *Von der Einheit der Musik*. Edited by Martina Weindel. Wilhelmshaven: Florian Noetzel, 2006.

Butler, Christopher. *Number Symbolism*. London: Routledge, 1970.

Butler, E. M. *The Saint-Simonian Religion in Germany: A Study of the Young German Movement.* Cambridge: Cambridge University Press, 1926.

Caballero, Carlo. *Fauré and French Musical Aesthetics.* Cambridge: Cambridge University Press, 2001.

Caccini, Giulio. *Le nuove musiche.* Florence: Marescotti, 1601; reprint, Florence: Studio per edizioni scelte, 1983.

———. *Le nuove musiche.* Edited by H. Wiley Hitchcock. 2nd ed. Madison, WI: A-R Editions, 2008.

Caneva, Kenneth L. "Physics and *Naturphilosophie*: A Reconnaissance." *History of Science* 35 (1997): 35–106.

———. *Robert Mayer and the Conservation of Energy.* Princeton: Princeton University Press, 1993.

Carraud, Gaston. "La musique pure dans l'École française contemporaine." *S.I.M. Revue musicale mensuelle* 6 (1910): 483–505.

Carrière, Moriz. *Aesthetik: Die Idee des Schönen.* 2 vols. Leipzig: F. A. Brockhaus, 1859.

———. "Populäre Aesthetik." *Blätter für literarische Unterhaltung,* no. 23 (4 June 1857): 415–19.

Carroll, Mark. *Music and Ideology in Cold War Europe.* Cambridge: Cambridge University Press, 2006.

Carter, Tim. "Artusi, Monteverdi, and the Poetics of Modern Music." In *Musical Humanism and Its Legacy: Essays in Honor of Claude V. Palisca,* 171–94. Edited by Nancy Kovaleff Baker and Barbara Russano Hanning. Stuyvesant, NY: Pendragon Press, 1992.

Cassirer, Ernst. *The Philosophy of the Enlightenment.* Translated by Fritz C. A. Koelln and James P. Pettegrove. Princeton: Princeton University Press, 1951.

Cassirer, Fritz. *Beethoven und die Gestalt.* Berlin and Leipzig: Deutsche Verlags-Anstalt, 1925.

Chabanon, Michel-Paul Guy de. *De la musique considérée en elle-même et dans ses rapports avec la parole, les langues, la poésie, et le théatre.* Paris: Pissot, 1785.

Chai, Leon. *Aestheticism: The Religion of Art in Post-Romantic Literature.* New York: Columbia University Press, 1990.

Cheetham, Mark A. *The Rhetoric of Purity: Essentialist Theory and the Advent of Abstract Painting.* Cambridge: Cambridge University Press, 1994.

Chipp, Herschel B., ed. *Theories of Modern Art: A Source Book by Artists and Critics.* Berkeley and Los Angeles: University of California Press, 1968.

Chladni, Ernst Florens Friedrich. *Entdeckungen über die Theorie des Klanges.* Leipzig: Weidmanns Erben & Reich, 1787.

Christensen, Dan Charly. *Hans Christian Ørsted: Reading Nature's Mind.* Oxford: Oxford University Press, 2013.

———. "Ørsted's Concept of Force and Theory of Music." In *Hans Christian Ørsted and the Romantic Legacy in Science: Ideas, Disciplines, Practices,* 115–33. Edited by Robert M. Brain, Robert S. Cohen, and Ole Knudsen. Dordrecht: Springer, 2007.

Christensen, Thomas. *Rameau and Musical Thought in the Enlightenment.* Cambridge: Cambridge University Press, 1993.

Chua, Daniel K. L. *Absolute Music and the Construction of Meaning.* Cambridge: Cambridge University Press, 1999.

———. "Vincenzo Galilei, Modernity and the Division of Nature." In *Music Theory and Natural Order from the Renaissance to the Early Twentieth Century,* 17–29. Edited by Suzannah Clark and Alexander Rehding. Cambridge: Cambridge University Press, 2001.

Cicero. [*De oratore.* English.] *On the Ideal Orator.* Translated by James M. May and Jakob Wise. New York: Oxford University Press, 2001.

Cloot, Julia. *Geheime Texte: Jean Paul und die Musik.* Berlin: de Gruyter, 2001.

Code, David J. "Hearing Debussy Reading Mallarmé: Music *après Wagner* in the *Prélude à l'après-midi d'un faune.*" *JAMS* 54 (2001): 493–554.

Collier, Jeremy. *Essays upon Several Moral Subjects.* 3rd ed. London: R. Sare and H. Hindmarch, 1698.

Colvin, Sidney. "English Painters and Painting in 1867." *Fortnightly Review*, n.s., 2 (1867): 464–76.

Coen, Deborah R. *Vienna in the Age of Uncertainty: Science, Liberalism, and Private Life.* Chicago: University of Chicago Presss, 2007.

Cook, Nicholas. *The Schenker Project: Culture, Race, and Music Theory in Fin-de-siècle Vienna.* New York: Oxford University Press, 2007.

Copleston, Frederick Charles. *A History of Philosophy,* vol. 7, *Modern Philosophy: From the Post-Kantian Idealists to Marx, Kierkegaard, and Nietzsche.* New York: Doubleday, 1994.

Cor, Raphaël. "M. Claude Debussy et le snobisme contemporain" (1909). In *Le Cas Debussy,* 7–47. Edited by C-Francis Caillard and José de Bérys. Paris: H. Falque, 1910.

Cornelius, Peter. Review of Richard Würst, *Preis-Sinfonie,* op. 21. *NZfM* 41 (8 December 1854): 257–59.

Cornford, Francis Macdonald. *Plato's Cosmology: The Timaeus of Plato.* London: Kegan Paul, 1937.

Couperin, François. *Pièces de clavecin: Première livre.* Paris: Author; Boivin, 1713.

Cranefield, Paul F. "On the Origin of the Phrase 'Nihil est in intellectu quod non prius fuerit in sensu.'" *Journal of the History of Medicine and Allied Sciences* 25 (1970), 77–80.

Crocker, Richard L. "*Musica rhythmica* and *Musica metrica* in Antique and Medieval Theory." *JMT* 2 (1958): 2–23.

——. "Pythagorean Mathematics and Music." *JAAC* 22 (1963–64): 189–98, 325–35.

Dahlhaus, Carl. "Eduard Hanslick und der musikalische Formbegriff." *Die Musikforschung* 20 (1972): 145–53.

——. *Die Idee der absoluten Musik.* Kassel: Bärenreiter, 1978.

——. [*Die Idee der absoluten Musik.* English.] *The Idea of Absolute Music.* Translated by Roger Lustig. Chicago: University of Chicago Press, 1989.

——. "Schoenberg and Programme Music." In *Schoenberg and the New Music,* 94–104. Translated by Derrick Puffett and Alfred Clayton. Cambridge: Cambridge University Press, 1987.

Dalberg, Johann Friedrich Hugo von. *Blicke eines Tonkünstlers in die Musik der Geister.* Mannheim: Neue Hof- und akademische Buchhandlung, 1787.

——. *Vom Erfinden und Bilden.* Frankfurt am Main: Johann Christian Hermann, 1791.

Dambeck, Johann Heinrich. *Vorlesungen über Aesthetik.* 2 vols. Edited by Joseph Adolf Hanslik. Prague: Carl Wilhelm Enders, 1822–23.

Danz, Ernst-Joachim. *Die objektlose Kunst: Untersuchungen zur Musikästhetik Friedrich von Hauseggers.* Regensburg: Bosse, 1981.

Daston, Lorraine. "Ørsted and the Rational Unconscious." In *Hans Christian Ørsted and the Romantic Legacy in Science: Ideas, Disciplines, Practices,* 235–46. Edited by Robert M. Brain, Robert S. Cohen, and Ole Knudsen. Dordrecht: Springer, 2007.

Daumer, Georg Friedrich. "Musikalischer Katechismus." *Deutsche Vierteljahrs-Schrift* 27, no. 3 (1864): 43–89.

Daverio, John. "Sounds without the Gate: Schumann and the Dresden Revolution." *Il saggiatore musicale* 4 (1997): 87–112.

Dayan, Peter. *Art as Music, Music as Poetry, Poetry as Art, from Whistler to Stravinsky and Beyond*. Farnham, Surrey: Ashgate, 2011.

Deaville, James. "The Controversy Surrounding Listzt's Conception of Programme Music." In *Nineteenth-Century Music: Selected Proceedings of the Tenth International Conference*, 98–124. Edited by Jim Samson and Bennett Zon. Aldershot: Ashgate, 2002.

——. "Negotiating the 'Absolute': Hanslick's Path through Music History." In *Rethinking Hanslick: Music, Formalism, and Expression*, 15–37. Edited by Nicole Grimes, Siobhán Donovan, and Wolfgang Marx. Rochester, NY: University of Rochester Press, 2013.

——. "Die neudeutsche Musikkritik: Der Weimarer Kreis." In *Liszt und die Neudeutsche Schule*, 55–76. Edited by Detlef Altenburg. Laaber: Laaber-Verlag, 2006.

——. "Peter Cornelius als Kritiker und Essayist." In Peter Cornelius, *Gesammelte Aufsätze: Gedanken über Musik und Theater, Poesie und bildende Kunst*, 17–50. Edited by Günter Wagner and James Deaville. Mainz: Schott, 2004.

Debussy, Claude. *Correspondance, 1884–1918*. Edited by François Lesure. Paris: Hermann, 1993.

——. *Letters*. Edited by François Lesure and Roger Nichols. Translated by Roger Nichols. Cambridge, MA: Harvard University Press, 1987.

——. *Monsieur Croche et autre écrits*. 2nd ed. Edited by François Lesure. Paris: Gallimard, 1987.

Dehmel, Richard. *Weib und Welt: Gedichte*. Berlin: Schuster u. Loeffler, 1896.

DeLapp-Birkett, Jennifer. "Aaron Copland and the Politics of Twelve-Tone Composition in the Early Cold War United States." *Journal of Musicological Research* 27 (2008): 31–62.

Dell'Antonio, Andrew. *Listening as Spiritual Practice in Early Modern Italy*. Berkeley and Los Angeles: University of California Press, 2011.

——. *Syntax, Form and Genre in Sonatas and Canzonas, 1621–35*. Lucca: Libreria musicale italiana, 1997

Descartes, René. *Compendium musicae*. Utrecht: G. Zijll, 1650.

——. [*Compendium musicae*. English.] *Compendium of Music*. Edited by Charles Kent. Translated by Walter Robert. S.l.: American Institute of Musicology, 1961.

——. *Traité des passions de l'âme* (1649). Edited by Geneviève Rodis-Lewis. Paris: J. Vrin, 2010.

——. [*Traité des passions de l'âme*. English.] *The Passions of the Soul*. Translated by Stephen H. Voss. Indianapolis: Hackett, 1989.

Dickreiter, Michael. *Der Musiktheoretiker Johannes Kepler*. Bern: Francke, 1973.

Diderot, Denis. "Lettre au sujet des observations du Chevalier de Chastellux sur le Traité du mélodrame" (1771). In *Oeuvres completes*, 20 vols., 8:506–10. Edited by J. Assézat. Paris: Garnier frères, 1875–77.

——. *Mémoires sur différents sujets de mathématiques* (1748). Edited by Jean Mayer. In *Diderot, Œuvres complètes: Édition critique et annotée*, edited by Herbert Dieckmann, Jean Fabre, and Jacques Proust, vol. 2, *Philosophie et mathématique: Idées I*, 231–338. Edited by Arthur M. Wilson. Paris: Hermann, 1975.

——. *Mémoires sur différens sujets de mathématiques*. Amsterdam: n.p., 1772.

Dodds, E. R. *The Greeks and the Irrational*. Berkeley and Los Angeles: University of California Press, 1951.

Donahue, Neil H., ed. *Invisible Cathedrals: The Expressionist Art History of Wilhelm Worringer*. University Park: Pennsylvania State University Press, 1995.

Dorn, Heinrich. "G. Schilling." *NZfM* 14 (1841): 9–11, 13–14, 17–20, and 21–26.

Drabkin, William. "Schenker's 'Decline': An Introduction." *Music Analysis* 24 (2005): 3–31.

Dreyfus, Laurence. *Bach and the Patterns of Invention.* Cambridge, MA: Harvard University Press, 1996.

Dubos, Jean Baptiste. *Réflexions critiques sur la poésie et sur la peinture.* 2 vols. Paris: Jean Mariette, 1719.

Dufour, Valérie. *Stravinski et ses exégètes (1910–1940).* Brussels: Éditions de l'Université de Bruxelles, 2006.

Dümling, Albrecht. "Public Loneliness: Atonality and the Crisis of Subjectivity in Schönberg's Opus 15." In *Schönberg and Kandinsky: An Historic Encounter,* 101–38. Edited by Konrad Boehmer. Amsterdam: Harwood, 1997.

Duncan, David Allen. "Persuading the Affections: Rhetorical Theory and Mersenne's Advice to Harmonic Orators." In *French Musical Thought, 1600–1800,* 149–75. Edited by Georgia Cowart. Ann Arbor: UMI Research Press, 1989.

Dürer, Albrecht. *Schriftlicher Nachlass.* 3 vols. Edited by Hans Rupprich. Berlin: Deutscher Verein für Kunstwissenschaft, 1956–69.

Dwight, John Sullivan. "The Intellectual Influence of Music." *Atlantic Monthly,* 19 November 1870, 614–25.

Dyck, Martin. *Novalis and Mathematics.* Chapel Hill: University of North Carolina Press, 1959.

Dyer, Joseph. "The Place of *Musica* in Medieval Classifications of Knowledge." *JM* 24 (2007): 3–71.

Edler, Arnfried. " 'Die Macht der Töne': Über die Bedeutung eines antiken Mythos im 19. Jahrhundert." In *Musik in Antike und Neuzeit,* 51–65. Edited by Michael von Albrecht and Werner Schubert. Frankfurt am Main: Peter Lang, 1987.

———. *Studien zur Auffassung antiker Musikmythen im 19. Jahrhundert.* Kassel: Bärenreiter, 1970.

Edwards, Warwick. "Text Treatment in Motets around 1500: The Humanistic Fallacy." In *The Motet around 1500: On the Relationship of Imitation and Text Treatment,* 113–38. Edited by Thomas Schmidt-Beste. Turnhout: Brepols, 2012.

Eggebrecht, Hans Heinrich. *Zur Geschichte der Beethoven-Rezeption.* 2nd ed. Laaber: Laaber-Verlag, 1994.

Eichhorn, Andreas. "Annäherung durch Distanz: Paul Bekkers Auseinandersetzung mit der Formalästhetik Hanslicks." *AfMw* 54 (1997): 194–209.

———. *Paul Bekker: Facetten eines kritischen Geistes.* Hildesheim: Georg Olms, 2002.

Einfalt, Michael. "Autonomie." In *Ästhetische Grundbegriffe: Historisches Wörterbuch,* 1:431–79. 7 vols. Edited by Karlheinz Barck. Stuttgart: Metzler, 2000–2005.

Eisler, Hanns. *Musik und Politik: Schriften, 1924–1948.* Edited by Günter Mayer. Munich: Rogner & Bernhard, 1973.

Eliot, T. S. "Arnold and Pater" (1930). In *Selected Essays,* 382–93. New York: Harcourt, Brace, 1950.

Elgar, Edward. *A Future for English Music and Other Lectures.* Edited by Percy M. Young. London: Dennis Dobson, 1968.

Emerson, Ralph Waldo. *The Later Lectures of Ralph Waldo Emerson, 1843–1871.* 2 vols. Edited by Ronald A. Bosco and Joel Myerson. Athens: University of Georgia Press, 2001.

Endell, August. "Formenschönheit und dekorative Kunst." *Dekorative Kunst* 1 (1898): 75–77.

Engel, Johann Jakob. *Über die musikalische Malerei.* Berlin: Christian Friedrich Voss und Sohn, 1780.

Esposito, Joseph L. *Schelling's Idealism and Philosophy of Nature.* Lewisburg, PA: Bucknell University Press, 1977.

Faas, Ekbert. *The Genealogy of Aesthetics*. Cambridge: Cambridge University Press, 2002.

Fechner, Gustav Theodor. *Vorschule der Aesthetik*. 2 vols. Leipzig: Breitkopf & Härtel, 1876.

Fend, Michael. "The Changing Function of *Senso* and *Ragione* in Italian Music Theory of the Late Sixteenth Century." In *The Second Sense: Studies in Hearing and Musical Judgment from Antiquity to the Seventeenth Century*, 199–221. Edited by Charles Burnett, Michael Fend, and Penelope Gouk. London: Warburg Institute, 1991.

Fish, Stanley. *Doing What Comes Naturally: Change, Rhetoric, and the Practice of Theory in Literary and Legal Studies*. Durham, NC: Duke University Press, 1989.

Floros, Constantin. *Gustav Mahler*. 3 vols. Wiesbaden: Breitkopf & Härtel, 1977–85.

——. *Johannes Brahms: "Frei aber einsam": Ein Leben für eine poetische Musik*. Zurich and Hamburg: Arche, 1997.

——. [*Johannes Brahms*. English.] *Johannes Brahms: "Free but Alone": A Life for Poetic Music*. Translated by Ernest Berhard-Kabisch. Frankfurt am Main: Peter Lang, 2010.

——. *Musik als Botschaft*. Wiesbaden: Breitkopf & Härtel, 1989.

Flotzinger, Rudolf. "Hauseggers Verhältnis zu Hanslick." In *Eduard Hanslick zum Gedenken: Bericht des Symposions zum Anlass seines 100. Todestages*, 77–83. Edited by Theophil Antonicek, Gernot Gruber, and Christoph Landerer. Tutzing: Hans Schneider, 2010.

Forbes, Elliot. *Thayer's Life of Beethoven*. Rev. ed. Princeton: Princeton University Press, 1967.

Forkel, Johann Nicolaus. *Allgemeine Geschichte der Musik*. 2 vols. Leipzig: Schwickert, 1788–1801; reprint,, Graz: Akademische Druck- u. Verlagsanstalt, 1967.

——. *Ueber die Theorie der Musik, insofern sie Liebhabern und Kennern nothwendig und nützlich ist: Eine Einladungsschrift zu musikalischen Vorlesungen*. Göttingen: Wittwe Vandenhoeck, 1777.

Foucault, Michel. *The Order of Things: An Archaeology of the Human Sciences*. New York: Vintage, 1994.

——. "What is an Author?" In *Textual Strategies: Perspectives in Post-Structuralist Criticism*, 141–60. Edited by Josué V. Harari. Ithaca, NY: Cornell University Press, 1979.

Fowler, Alastair. *Spenser and the Numbers of Time*. New York: Barnes & Noble, 1964.

Friedman, John Block. *Orpheus in the Middle Ages*. Cambridge, MA: Harvard University Press, 1970.

Friedman, Michael, and Alfred Nordmann, eds. *The Kantian Legacy in Nineteenth-Century Science*. Cambridge, MA: MIT Press, 2006.

Frisch, Walter. *German Modernism: Music and the Arts*. Berkeley and Los Angeles: University of California Press, 2005.

——, ed. *Schoenberg and His World*. Princeton: Princeton University Press, 1999.

Frisch, Walter, and Kevin Karnes, eds. *Brahms and His World*. Rev. ed. Princeton: Princeton University Press, 2009.

F. L. B. [Fröhlich, Joseph.] "Reflexionen über das Wesen der Musik." *AmZ* 17 (15 and 22 November 1815): 761–67, 777–85.

Fry, Roger. *A Roger Fry Reader*. Edited by Christopher Reed. Chicago: University of Chicago Press, 1996.

Fubini, Enrico, ed. *Music & Culture in Eighteenth-Century Europe: A Source Book*. Translated by Wolfgang Freis, Lisa Gasbarrone, and Michael Louis Leone. Edited by Bonnie J. Blackburn. Chicago: University of Chicago Press, 1994.

Fuchs, Carl. *Präliminarien zu einer Kritik der Tonkunst*. Leipzig: E. W. Fritzsch, 1871.

Fuller, David. "Of Portraits, 'Sapho' and Couperin: Titles and Characters in French Instrumental Music of the High Baroque." *M&L* 78 (1997): 149–74.

Galilei, Vincenzo. *Dialogo della musica antica, et della moderna.* Florence: Giorgio Mareschotti, 1581.

——. [*Dialogo della musica antica.* English.] *Dialogue on Ancient and Modern Music.* Translated by Claude V. Palisca. New Haven: Yale University Press, 2003.

Ganassi, Silvestro. *Opera intitolata Fontegara.* Venice: n.p., 1535; reprint, Bologna: Forni, 1969.

Ganting, Ludwig von. *Die Grundzüge der musikalischen Richtungen in ihrer geschichtlichen Entwicklung.* Leipzig: Breitkopf & Härtel, 1876.

Garratt, James. "Composing Useful Histories: Music Historiography and the Practical Past." In *Konstruktivität von Musikgeschichtsschreibung: Zur Formation musikbezogenen Wissens,* 123–39. Edited by Sandra Danielczyk, Ina Knoth, and Lisbeth Suhrcke. Hildesheim: Olms, 2012.

——. "Inventing Realism: Dahlhaus, Geck, and the Unities of Discourse." *M&L* 84 (2003): 456–68.

——. *Music, Culture and Social Reform in the Age of Wagner.* Cambridge: Cambridge University Press, 2010.

Gärtner, Markus. *Eduard Hanslick versus Franz Liszt: Aspekte einer grundlegenden Kontroverse.* Hildesheim: Olms, 2005.

——. "Der Hörer im Visier: Hanslick und Liszt im Prinzipienstreit über die wahre Art, Musik zu verstehen." In Eduard Hanslick, *Sämtliche Schriften,* vol. 1, part 5, *Aufsätze und Rezensionen 1859–1861,* 457–68. Edited by Dietmar Strauß. Vienna: Böhlau, 2005.

Gautier, Théophile. "Du beau dans l'art." *Revue des deux mondes* 19 (1847): 887–908.

Gebauer, Gunter, and Christoph Wulf. *Mimesis: Culture, Art, Society.* Translated by Don Reneau. Berkeley and Los Angeles: University of California Press, 1995.

Geck, Martin. *Zwischen Romantik und Restauration: Musik im Realismus-Diskurs der Jahre 1848 bis 1871.* Stuttgart: Metzler, 2001.

Gerhard, Anselm. "Leonhard Euler, die Französische Gemeinde zu Berlin und die ästhetische Grundlegung der 'absoluten Musik.' " *Schweizer Jahrbuch für Musikwissenschaft, Neue Folge* 17 (1997): 15–28.

——. *London und der Klassizismus in der Musik: Die Idee der "absoluten" Musik und Muzio Clementis Klavierwerk.* Stuttgart: Metzler, 2002.

Gervinus, Georg Gottfried. *Händel und Shakespeare: Zur Ästhetik der Tonkunst.* Leipzig: Wilhelm Engelmann, 1868.

Godwin, Joscelyn, ed. *The Harmony of the Spheres: A Sourcebook of the Pythagorean Tradition in Music.* Rochester, VT: Inner Traditions International, 1993.

Goehr, Lydia. "*Doppelbewegung*: The Musical Movement of Philosophy and the Philosophical Movement of Music." In *Sound Figures of Modernity: German Music and Philosophy,* 19–63. Edited by Jost Hermand and Gerhard Richter. Madison: University of Wisconsin Press, 2006.

——. *Elective Affinities: Musical Essays on the History of Aesthetic Theory.* New York: Columbia University Press, 2008.

——. *The Quest for Voice: On Music, Politics, and the Limits of Philosophy.* Berkeley and Los Angeles: University of California Press, 1998.

——. "Schopenhauer and the Musicians: An Inquiry into the Sounds of Silence and the Limits of Philosophizing about Music." In *Schopenhauer, Philosophy, and the Arts,* 200–228. Edited by Dale Jacquette. Cambridge: Cambridge University Press, 1996.

Goethe, Johann Wolfgang. "Entoptische Farben" (1820). In *Schriften zur allgemeinen Naturlehre, Geologie und Mineralogie,* 682–728. Edited by Wolf von Engelhardt and Manfred Wenzel. Frankfurt am Main: Deutscher Klassiker Verlag, 1989.

——. "Über Wahrheit und Wahrscheinlichkeit der Kunstwerke: Ein Gespräch" (1798). In *Werke: Hamburger Ausgabe*, 14 vols. Edited by Erich Trunz. Vol. 12, *Schriften zur Kunst, Schriften zur Literatur, Maximen und Reflexionen*, 67–73. Edited by Erich Trunz and Hans Joachim Schrimpf. Munich: Beck, 1981.

——. "Maximen und Reflexionen." In *Werke: Hamburger Ausgabe*, 14 vols. Edited by Erich Trunz. Vol. 12, *Schriften zur Kunst, Schriften zur Literatur, Maximen und Reflexionen*, 365–547. Edited by Erich Trunz and Hans Joachim Schrimpf. Munich: Beck, 1981.

——. *Wilhelm Meisters Wanderjahre*. In *Werke: Hamburger Ausgabe*, 14 vols. Edited by Erich Trunz. Vol. 8, *Romane und Novellen III*, 7–486. Edited by Erich Trunz. Munich: Beck, 1981.

Goldschmidt, Hugo. *Die Musikästhetik des 18. Jahrhunderts und ihre Beziehungen zu seinem Kunstschaffen*. Zurich and Leipzig: Rascher, 1915.

Gooley, Dana. "The Battle against Instrumental Virtuosity in the Early Nineteenth Century." In *Franz Liszt and His World*, 75–111. Edited by Christopher H. Gibbs and Dana Gooley. Princeton: Princeton University Press, 2006.

Gottschald, Ernst. *Beethoven's Symphonien nach ihrem idealen Gehalt*. Dresden: Adolph Brauer, 1854.

Gottsched, Johann Christoph. *Versuch einer critischen Dichtkunst*. 3rd ed. Leipzig: Bernhard Christoph Breitkopf, 1742.

Gouk, Penelope. "Music and the Sciences." In *The Cambridge History of Seventeenth-Century Music*, 132–57. Edited by Tim Carter and John Butt. Cambridge: Cambridge University Press, 2005.

——. "The Role of Harmonics in the Scientific Revolution." In *The Cambridge History of Western Music Theory*, 223–45. Edited by Thomas Christensen. Cambridge: Cambridge University Press, 2002.

Gower, Barry. "Speculation in Physics: The History and Practice of *Naturphilosophie*." *Studies in the History and Philosophy of Science 3* (1973): 301–56.

Gozza, Paolo. "A Renaissance Mathematics: The Music of Descartes." In *Number to Sound: The Musical Way to the Scientific Revolution*, 155–72. Edited by Paolo Gozza. Dordrecht: Kluwer, 1999.

Grey, Thomas S. "Masters and Their Critics: Wagner, Hanslick, Beckmesser, and *Die Meistersinger*." In *Wagner's "Meistersinger": Performance, History, Representation*, 165–89. Edited by Nicholas Vazsonyi. Rochester, NY: University of Rochester Press, 2003.

——. *Wagner's Musical Prose: Texts and Contexts*. Cambridge: Cambridge University Press, 1995.

Grillparzer, Franz. *Sämmtliche Werke*. 4th ed. 16 vols. Stuttgart: Cotta, 1887.

Grimes, Nicole. "In Search of Absolute Inwardness and Spiritual Subjectivity? The Historical and Ideological Context of Schumann's 'Neue Bahnen.'" *International Review of the Aesthetics and Sociology of Music 39* (2008): 139–63.

Grimm, Ines. *Eduard Hanslicks Prager Zeit: Frühe Wurzeln seiner Schrift "Vom Musikalisch-Schönen."* Saarbrücken: Pfau, 2003.

Grunsky, Karl. *Musikästhetik*. Leipzig: G. J. Göschen, 1907.

Gumprecht, Otto. "Geist und Musik." *Deutsches Museum: Zeitschrift für Literatur, Kunst und öffentliches Leben 2* (1852): 597–609, 801–14.

Gur, Golan. "Music and 'Weltanschauung': Franz Brendel and the Claims of Universal History." *M&L 93* (2012): 350–73.

Guthrie, Kenneth Sylvan, and David R. Fideler, eds. *The Pythagorean Sourcebook and Library*. Grand Rapids, MI: Phanes Press, 1987.

Guthrie, W. K. C. *Orpheus and Greek Religion: A Study of the Orphic Movement*. Rev. ed. New York: W. W. Norton, 1966.

Guyer, Paul. "Free Play and True Well-Being: Herder's Critique of Kant's Aesthetics." *JAAC* 65 (2007): 353–68.

——. *Kant and the Experience of Freedom: Essays on Aesthetics and Morality.* Cambridge: Cambridge University Press, 1993.

——. *Values of Beauty: Historical Essays in Aesthetics.* Cambridge: Cambridge University Press, 2005.

H.-J. "Music the Exponent of Emotion." *Dwight's Journal of Music*, 21 July 1855, 123–24.

Halm, August. *Von zwei Kulturen der Musik.* Munich: Georg Müller, 1913.

Hand, Ferdinand Gotthelf. *Aesthetik der Tonkunst.* 2 vols. Leipzig: Hochhausen und Fournes; Jena: Carl Hochhausen, 1837–41.

Hanslick, Eduard. *Aus meinem Leben.* 2 vols. Berlin: Allgemeiner Verein für deutsche Litteratur, 1894.

——. *Concerte, Componisten und Virtuosen der letzten fünfzehn Jahre, 1870–1885.* Berlin: Allgemeiner Verein für deutsche Litteratur, 1886.

——. "E-moll Symphonie und 'Der Wassermann' von A. Dvorak." *Neue Freie Presse*, 9 December 1896. Republished in Hanslick, *Am Ende des Jahrhunderts*, 213–19. Berlin: Allgemeiner Verein für deutsche Litteratur, 1899.

——. *Die moderne Oper: Kritiken und Studien.* Berlin: A. Hofmann, 1875.

——. *Musikalische Stationen.* Berlin: A. Hofmann, 1880.

——. "Richard Wagner über das Hofoperntheater." *Die Presse*, 18 October 1863, 1–3.

——. *Sämtliche Schriften: Historisch-kritische Ausgabe.* Edited by Dietmar Strauß. Vienna and Cologne: Böhlau, 1993–.

——. *Vom Musikalisch-Schönen: Ein Beitrag zur Revision der Ästhetik der Tonkunst* (1854). 2 vols. Edited by Dietmar Strauß. Mainz: Schott, 1990.

——. [*Vom Musikalisch-Schönen*. English. 1891.] *The Beautiful in Music.* Translated by Gustav Cohen. London: Novello, 1891.

——. [*Vom Musikalisch-Schönen*. English. 1986.] *On the Musically Beautiful: A Contribution towards the Revision of the Aesthetics of Music.* Edited and translated by Geoffrey Payzant. Indianapolis: Hackett, 1986.

Hanus, I. J. *Zusätze und Inhalts-Verzeichnisze* [sic] *zu Hanslik's Geschichte und Beschreibung der k. k. Prager Universitäts-Bibliothek.* Prague: Hanuś, 1863.

Harrán, Don. *Word-Tone Relationships in Musical Thought from Antiquity to the Seventeenth Century.* Neuhausen-Stuttgart: Hänssler, 1986.

Hausegger, Friedrich von. "Die E-moll Symphonie von Joh. Brahms." In *Gedanken eines Schauenden*, 237–39. Edited by Siegmund von Hausegger. Munich: F. Brückmann, 1903.

——. *Die Musik als Ausdruck.* 2nd ed. Vienna: C. Konegen, 1887.

——. "Ein Traum, ein Leben: Humoreske." *Musikalisches Wochenblatt* 1 (23 September 1870): 618–20.

Hawkins, John. *A General History of the Science and Practice of Music.* 5 vols. London: T. Payne and Son, 1776.

Haydn, Joseph. *Gesammelte Briefe und Aufzeichnungen.* Ed. Dénes Bartha. Kassel: Bärenreiter, 1965.

Hefling, Stephen E. "Miners Digging from Opposite Sides: Mahler, Strauss, and the Problem of Program Music." In *Richard Strauss: New Perspectives*, 41–53. Edited by Bryan Gilliam. Durham, NC: Duke University Press, 1992.

Hegel, Georg Friedrich Wilhelm. *Encyklopädie der philosophischen Wissenschaften im Grundrisse*, 2nd ed. Heidelberg: August Oßwald, 1827.

———. *Phänomenologie des Geistes* (1807). Edited by Eva Moldenhauer and Karl Markus Michel. Frankfurt am Main: Suhrkamp, 1970.

———. *Vorlesungen über die Ästhetik* (1835). Edited by Eva Moldenhauer and Karl Markus Michel, 3 vols. Frankfurt am Main: Suhrkamp, 1970.

Heidelberger, Michael. "Naturphilosophie." In *The Routledge Encyclopedia of Philosophy*, 6:737–43. 10 vols. London and New York: Routledge, 1998.

Heilmann, Anja. *Boethius' Musiktheorie und das Quadrivium: Eine Einführung in den neuplatonischen Hintergrund von "De institutione musica."* Göttingen: Vandenhoeck & Ruprecht, 2007.

Heine, Heinrich. "Musikalische Saison von 1844." In *Werke, Briefwechsel, Lebenszeugnisse: Säkularausgabe.* Vol. 11, *Lutezia: Berichte über Politik, Kunst und Volksleben*, 247–63. Edited by Lucienne Netter. Berlin: Akademie-Verlag; Paris: Editions du CNRS, 1974.

———. *Die romantische Schule.* Hamburg: Hoffmann und Campe, 1836.

Heinse, Wilhelm. *Hildegard von Hohenthal* (1795–96). In *Sämmtliche Werke*, vols. 5–6. Edited by Carl Schüddekopf. Leipzig: Insel-Verlag, 1903.

Helmholtz, Hermann von. *Die Lehre von den Tonempfindungen als physiologische Grundlage für die Theorie der Musik.* Braunschweig: Vieweg & Sohn, 1863.

Heninger, S. K., Jr. *Touches of Sweet Harmony: Pythagorean Cosmology and Renaissance Poetics.* San Marino, CA: Huntington Library, 1974.

Henneberg, Gudrun. *Idee und Begriff des musikalischen Kunstwerks im Spiegel des deutschsprachigen Schrifttums der ersten Hälfte des 19. Jahrhunderts.* Tutzing: Schneider, 1983.

Hennig, C. R. *Die Aesthetik der Tonkunst.* Leipzig: Johann Ambrosius Barth, 1896.

Hentschel, Frank. *Bürgerliche Ideologie und Musik: Politik der Musikgeschichtsschreibung in Deutschland, 1776–1871.* Frankfurt am Main: Campus, 2006.

———. *Sinnlichkeit und Vernunft in der mittelalterlichen Musiktheorie: Strategien der Konsonanzwertung und der Gegenstand der musica sonora um 1300.* Stuttgart: Franz Steiner, 2000.

Hepokoski, James. "The Dahlhaus Project and its Extra-musicological Sources." *19CM* 14 (1991): 221–46.

Herbart, Johann Friedrich. *Allgemeine Metaphysik, nebst den Anfängen der philosophischen Naturlehre.* 2 vols. Königsberg: August Wilhelm Unzer, 1828–29.

———. *Allgemeine praktische Philosophie.* Göttingen: Justus Friedrich Danckwerts, 1808.

———. *Kurze Encyklopädie der Philosophie.* Halle: C. A. Schwetschke und Sohn, 1831.

———. Review of Carl Ludwig Seidel, *Charinomos: Beiträge zur allgemeinen Theorie und Geschichte der schönen Künste*, vol. 1 (Magdeburg, 1825). First published in *Leipziger Literatur-Zeitung* 1826, No. 316; republished in Herbart's *Sämtliche Werke*, 12:339–46. Edited by Otto Flügel. Langensalza: Hermann Beyer & Söhne, 1907.

Herder, Johann Gottfried. *Werke.* 10 vols. Edited by Martin Bollacher. Frankfurt am Main: Deutscher Klassiker Verlag, 1985–2000.

Hertz, David. *The Tuning of the Word: The Musico-Literary Poetics of the Symbolist Movement.* Carbondale: Southern Illinois University Press, 1987.

Herzog, Patricia. "The Condition to Which All Art Aspires: Reflections on Pater and Music." *British Journal of Aesthetics* 36 (1996): 122–34.

Hessler, J. Ferdinand. *Lehrbuch der Physik. Nach den Bedürfnissen der Technik, der Künste und Gewerbe.* Vienna: Wilhelm Braumüller, 1852.

Heuss, Alfred. "Eduard Hanslick und die Gegenwart." *Zeitschrift für Musik* 92 (1925): 501–5.

Hindemith, Paul. *Unterweisung im Tonsatz*, vol. 1, *Theoretischer Teil*. Mainz: B. Schott's Söhne, 1937. Translated by Arthur Mendel as *The Craft of Musical Composition*, book 1, *Theoretical Part*. New York: Associated Music, 1942.

Hinrichs, Friedrich. *Richard Wagner und die neuere Musik: Eine kritische Skizze aus der musikalischen Gegenwart*. Halle Schrödel u. Simon 1854.

Hinton, Stephen. "Aspects of Hindemith's Neue Sachlichkeit." *Hindemith-Jahrbuch* 14 (1985): 22–80.

Hirschbach, Herrmann. "Musikzustände der Gegenwart." *Musikalisch-kritisches Repertorium aller neuen Erscheinungen im Gebiete der Tonkunst* 1 (1844): 251–54.

Hoeschen, Andreas. "Gegenstand, Relation und System im 'ästhetischen Formalismus.'" In *Herbarts Kultursystem: Perspektiven der Transdisziplinarität im 19. Jahrhundert*, 297–316. Edited by Andreas Hoeschen and Lothar Schneider. Würzburg: Königshausen & Neumann, 2001.

Hoffmann, E. T. A. Review of Beethoven's Fifth Symphony. *AmZ* 12 (4 and 11 July 1810): 630–42, 652–59.

Hofmannsthal, Hugo von. "Poesie und Leben." *Die Zeit* (Vienna), 16 May 1896, 104–6.

Holsinger, Bruce W. *Music, Body, and Desire in Medieval Culture: Hildegard of Bingen to Chaucer*. Palo Alto, CA: Stanford University Press, 2001.

Hooper, Giles. "An Incomplete Project: Modernism, Formalism and the 'Music Itself.'" *Music Analysis* 23 (2004): 311–29.

Hoplit. *See* Pohl, Richard.

Hostinský, Ottokar. *Das Musikalisch-Schöne und das Gesammtkunstwerk vom Standpuncte der formalen Aesthetik: Eine Studie*. Leipzig: Breitkopf & Härtel, 1877.

Hudson, Nicholas. "Theories of Language." In *The Cambridge History of Literary Criticism*, vol. 4, *The Eighteenth Century*, 335–48. Edited by H. B. Nisbet and Claude Rawson. Cambridge: Cambridge University Press, 1997.

Hueffer, Francis. "Arthur Schopenhauer." *Fortnightly Review* 20 (1876): 773–92.

———. "Arthur Schopenhauer." In *Musical Studies: A Series of Contributions*, 85–129. Edinburgh: Adam & Charles Black, 1880.

———. *Half a Century of Music in England, 1837–1887: Essays towards a History*. London: Chapman & Hall, 1889.

———. *Richard Wagner and the Music of the Future: History and Aesthetics*. London: Chapman & Hall, 1874.

Hume, David. "Of the Standard of Taste" (1757). In *Selected Essays*, 133–54. Edited by Stephen Copley and Andrew Edgar. New York: Oxford University Press, 1993.

———. "The Sceptic" (1742). In *Selected Essays*, 95–113. Edited by Stephen Copley and Andrew Edgar. New York: Oxford University Press, 1993.

———. *A Treatise of Human Nature* (1739–40). Edited by L. A. Selby-Bigge. Revised by P. H. Nidditch. Oxford: Clarendon Press, 1978.

Inman, Billie Andrew. *Walter Pater's Reading: A Bibliography of His Library Borrowings and Literary References, 1858–1873*. New York: Garland, 1981.

Inwood, Michael. *A Hegel Dictionary*. Oxford: Blackwell, 1992.

Jäger, Georg. "Die Herbartianische Ästhetik—ein österreichischer Weg in die Moderne." In *Die österreichische Literatur: Ihr Profil im19. Jahrhundert (1830–1880)*, 195–219. Edited by Herbert Zeman. Graz: Akademische Druck- u. Verlagsanstalt, 1982.

Jähnig, Dieter. *Schelling: Die Kunst in der Philosophie*, 2 vols. Pfullingen: Neske, 1966–69.

——. *Der Weltbezug der Künste: Schelling, Nietzsche, Kant*. Freiburg and Munich: Karl Alber, 2011.

Janik, Elizabeth. *Recomposing German Music: Politics and Tradition in Cold War Berlin*. Leiden and Boston: Brill, 2005.

Jean Paul [Johann Paul Friedrich Richter]. *Sämmtliche Werke*. Edited by Ernst Förster. 3rd ed. 34 vols. Berlin: Reimer, 1860–62.

John, Alois. *Richard Wagner-Studien: Sieben Essays über Richard Wagner's Kunst und seine Bedeutung im modernen Leben*. Bayreuth: Carl Gießel, 1889.

Johnson, James H. *Listening in Paris: A Cultural History*. Berkeley and Los Angeles: University of California Press, 1995.

Johnston, William M. *The Austrian Mind: An Intellectual and Social History, 1848–1938*. Berkeley and Los Angeles: University of California Press, 1972.

Joost-Gaugier, Christiane L. *Measuring Heaven: Pythagoras and His Influence on Thought and Art in Antiquity and the Middle Ages*. Ithaca, NY: Cornell University Press, 2006.

——. *Pythagoras and Renaissance Europe: Finding Heaven*. Cambridge: Cambridge University Press, 2009.

Jordan, William. "Galileo and the Demise of Pythagoreanism." In *Music and Science in the Age of Galileo*, 129–39. Edited by Victor Coelho. Dordrecht: Kluwer Academic Publishers, 1992.

Jost, Christa, and Peter Jost. "'Zukunftsmusik': Zur Geschichte eines Begriffs." *Musiktheorie* 10 (1995): 119–35.

Kahlert, August. *System der Aesthetik*. Leipzig: Breitkopf & Härtel, 1846.

——. "Ueber den Begriff der klassischen und romantischen Musik." *AmZ* 50 (3 May 1848): 289–95.

——. "Ueber die Bedeutung des Romantischen." *Cäcilia* 16 (1834): 235–44.

Kalbeck, Max. *Johannes Brahms*. 4 vols. Vienna and Leipzig: Wiener Verlag; Berlin: Deutsche Brahms-Gesellschaft, 1904–14.

Kaltenecker, Martin. *L'oreille divisée: Les discours sur l'écoute musicale aux XVIIIe et XIXe siècles*. Paris: MF, 2010.

Kandinsky, Wassily. *Complete Writings on Art*. 2 vols. Edited by Kenneth C. Lindsay and Peter Vergo. Boston: G. K. Hall, 1982.

——. [Untitled essay.] *Cahiers d'art* 10 (1935): 53–54, 56.

Kant, Immanuel. *Kritik der Urteilskraft* (1790). Edited by Heiner F. Klemme. Hamburg: Felix Meiner, 2001.

——. [*Kritik der Urteilskraft*. English.] *Critique of the Power of Judgment*. Edited by Paul Guyer. Translated by Paul Guyer and Eric Matthews. Cambridge: Cambridge University Press, 2000.

——. *Metaphysische Anfangsgründe der Naturwissenschaft* (1786). Edited by Konstantin Pollok. Hamburg: Felix Meiner, 1997.

——. "Reflexionen zur Ästhetik, als Randbemerkungen zu A. G. Baumgartens *Psychologia empirica*." In *Schriften zur Ästhetik und Naturphilosophie*, 57–138. Edited by Manfred Frank and Véronique Zanetti. Frankfurt am Main: Deutscher Klassiker Verlag, 1996.

Kapp, Reinhard. "Orpheus Settings." In *Talismane: Festschrift Klaus Heinrich zum 70. Geburtstag*, 425–57. Edited by Sigrun Anselm and Caroline Neubaur. Basel: Stroemfeld, 1998.

Karnes, Kevin. *Music, Criticism, and the Challenge of History: Shaping Modern Musical Thought in Late Nineteenth-Century Vienna*. New York: Oxford University Press, 2008.

Katz, Ruth. *A Language of Its Own: Sense and Meaning in the Making of Western Art Music*. Chicago: University of Chicago Press, 2009.

Kayser, Hans. *Akróasis: Die Lehre von der Harmonik der Welt*. Basel: Benno Schwabe, 1946.

———. *Orpheus vom Klang der Welt: Morphologische Fragmente einer allgemeinen Harmonik*. Potsdam: G. Kiepenheuer, 1926.

———. *Vom Klang der Welt: Ein Vortragszyklus zur Einführung in die Harmonik*. Zurich: M. Niehans, 1937.

Kennaway, James. *Bad Vibrations: The History of the Idea of Music as a Cause of Disease*. Aldershot: Ashgate, 2012.

Kennedy, George A. *Classical Rhetoric and its Christian and Secular Tradition from Ancient to Modern Times*. 2nd ed. Chapel Hill: University of North Carolina Press, 1999.

Kepler, Johannes. *The Harmony of the World*. Translated by E. J. Aiton, A. M. Duncan, and J. B. Field. Philadelphia: American Philosophical Society, 1997.

Kerényi, Karl. *Pythagoras und Orpheus: Präludien zu einer zukünftigen Geschichte der Orphik und des Pythagoreismus*. 3rd ed. Zurich: Rhein-Verlag, 1950.

Kircher, Athanasius. *Musurgia universalis*. 2 vols. Rome, 1650; reprint, Hildesheim: Olms, 1999.

Kivy, Peter. *Antithetical Arts: On the Ancient Quarrel between Literature and Music*. Oxford: Clarendon Press, 2009.

———. *Music Alone: Reflections on the Purely Musical Experience*. Ithaca, NY: Cornell University Press, 1990.

———. *The Possessor and the Possessed: Handel, Mozart, Beethoven, and the Idea of Musical Genius*. New Haven: Yale University Press, 2001.

Klengel, Paul. *Zur Aesthetik der Tonkunst*. Leipzig: O. Mutze, 1876.

Knepler, Georg. *Geschichte als Weg zum Musikverständnis: Zur Theorie, Methode und Geschichte der Musikgeschichtsschreibung*. 2nd ed. Leipzig: Philipp Reclam jun., 1982.

Knyt, Erinn E. "Ferruccio Busoni and the Absolute in Music: Form, Nature and *Idee*." *JRMA* 137 (2012): 35–69.

Koch, Heinrich Christoph. *Kurzgefasstes Handwörterbuch der Musik für praktische Tonkünstler und für Dilettanten*. Leipzig: Johann Friedrich Hartknoch, 1807; reprint, Hildesheim: G. Olms, 1981.

Koen, Benjamin D., ed. *The Oxford Handbook of Medical Ethnomusicology*. New York: Oxford University Press, 2008.

Köhler, Louis. *Die Melodie der Sprache in ihrer Anwendung besonders auf das Lied und die Oper*. Leipzig: J. J. Weber, 1853.

Köhler, Rafael. *Natur und Geist: Energetische Form in der Musiktheorie*. Stuttgart: Franz Steiner, 1996.

Köstlin, Heinrich Adolf. *Geschichte der Musik im Umriß*. Tübingen: H. Laupp, 1875.

Köstlin, Karl. *Aesthetik*. Tübingen: H. Laupp, 1869.

Kralik, Richard. "Musik." *Das Vaterland: Zeitung für die österreichische Monarchie*, 1 January 1897, 1.

Kramer, Lawrence. "The Mysteries of Animation: History, Analysis and Musical Subjectivity." *Music Analysis* 20 (2001): 153–78.

———. "Oracular Musicology; or, Faking the Ineffable." *AfMw* 69 (2012): 101–9.

Krause, Karl Christian Friedrich. *Anfangsgründe der allgemeinen Theorie der Musik nach Grundsätzen der Wesenlehre*. Edited by Victor Strauss. Göttingen: Dieterich, 1838.

Kretschmann, Carl. "Romantik in der Musik." *NZfM* 29 (1 and 4 July 1848): 1–6, 9–11.

Kristeller, Paul Oskar. "The Modern System of the Arts: A Study in the History of Aesthetics." *JHI* 12 (1951): 496–527; 13 (1952): 17–46.

Kropfinger, Klaus. *Wagner and Beethoven: Richard Wagner's Reception of Beethoven*. Translated by Peter Palmer. Cambridge: Cambridge University Press, 1991.

Krüger, Eduard. *Beiträge für Leben und Wissenschaft der Tonkunst.* Leipzig: Breitkopf & Härtel, 1847.

———. *System der Tonkunst.* Leipzig: Breitkopf & Härtel, 1866.

Kuhnau, Johann. *Musikalische Vorstellung einiger Biblischer Historien.* Leipzig: Immanuel Tietzen, 1700; reprint, Florence: Studio per Edizioni Scelte, 2000.

Kullak, Adloph. *Das Musikalisch-Schöne: Ein Beitrag zur Aesthetik der Tonkunst.* Leipzig: Heinrich Matthes, 1858.

Lafont, Cristina. *The Linguistic Turn in Hermeneutic Philosophy.* Translated by José Medina. Cambridge, MA: MIT Press, 1999.

Lambert, Philip. "Ives' Universe." In *Ives Studies,* 233–59. Edited by Philip Lambert. Cambridge: Cambridge University Press, 1997.

Lamennais, Hughes Félicité Robert de. *Esquisse d'une philosophie.* 4 vols. Paris: Pagnerre, 1840–46.

Landerer, Christoph. "Ästhetik von oben? Ästhetik von unten? Objektivität und 'naturwissenschaftliche' Methode in Eduard Hanslicks Musikästhetik." *AfMw* 61 (2004): 38–53.

———. *Eduard Hanslick und Bernard Bolzano: Ästhetisches Denken in Österreich in der Mitte des 19. Jahrhunderts.* Sankt Augustin: Academia, 2004.

———. "Eduard Hanslick und die österreichische Geistesgeschichte." In *Eduard Hanslick zum Gedenken: Bericht des Symposions zum Anlass seines 100. Todestages,* 55–63. Edited by Theophil Antonicek, Gernot Gruber, and Christoph Landerer. Tutzing: Hans Schneider, 2010.

———. "Eduard Hanslicks Ästhetikprogramm und die österreichische Philosophie der Jahrhundertmitte." *Österreichische Musikzeitschrift* 54, no. 9 (1999): 6–20.

Larson, Steve. *Musical Forces: Motion, Metaphor, and Meaning in Music.* Bloomington: Indiana University Press, 2012.

Laurencin, Ferdinand Peter, Graf von. *Dr. Eduard Hanslick's Lehre vom Musikalisch-Schönen: Eine Abwehr.* Leipzig: Heinrich Matthes, 1859.

Lazarus, Moritz. *Das Leben der Seele in Monographien über seine Erscheinungen und Gesetze.* 2 vols. Berlin: Heinrich Schindler, 1856–57.

Le Huray, Peter, and James Day, eds. *Music and Aesthetics in the Eighteenth and Early-Nineteenth Centuries.* Cambridge: Cambridge University Press, 1981.

Leibniz, Gottfried Wilhelm. *Epistolae ad diversos.* 4 vols. Leipzig: Bernhard Christoph Breitkopf, 1734–42.

Leisinger, Ulrich. *Leibniz-Reflexe in der deutschen Musiktheorie des 18. Jahrhunderts.* Würzburg: Königshausen & Neumann, 1994.

Levinson, Jerrold. *Music, Art, & Metaphysics: Essays in Philosophical Aesthetics.* New York: Oxford University Press, 2011.

Lichtenthal, Peter. *Der musikalische Arzt: Abhandlung von dem Einflusse der Musik auf den Körper, und von ihrer Anwendung in gewissen Krankheiten; Nebst einigen Winken, zur Anhörung einer guten Musik.* Vienna: Christian Friedrich Wappler und Beck, 1807.

Linforth, Ivan M. *The Arts of Orpheus.* Berkeley and Los Angeles: University of California Press, 1941.

Lippius, Johannes. *Synopsis of New Music (Synopsis musicae novae).* Translated by Benito V. Rivera. Colorado Springs: Colorado College Music Press, 1977.

Lippman, Edward A. *A History of Western Musical Aesthetics.* Lincoln: University of Nebraska Press, 1992.

———. *Musical Thought in Ancient Greece.* New York: Columbia University Press, 1964.

——, ed. *Musical Aesthetics: A Historical Reader.* 3 vols. Stuyvesant, NY: Pendragon Press, 1985–90.

Liszt, Franz. "Avant-propos," *Album d'un voyageur* (1842). In *Album d'un voyageur I, III; Clochette et Carnaval de Venise.* Edited by Adrienne Kaczmarczyk and Imre Mező. Budapest: Editio Musica, 2007.

——. "Berlioz und seine Haroldsymphonie." *NZfM* 43 (13 July, 20 July, 27 July, 17 August, 24 August 1855): 25–32, 37–46, 49–55, 77–84, 89–97.

——. "Marx und die Musik des neunzehnten Jahrhunderts." *NZfM* 42 (11 and 18 May 1855): 213–21, 225–30.

Lobe, Johann Christian. "Briefe über Richard Wagner an einen jungen Komponisten." *Fliegende Blätter für Musik* 1 (1855): 411–29.

——. "Gegen Dr. Eduard Hanslick's 'Vom Musikalisch-Schönen.'" *Fliegende Blätter für Musik* 2 (1857): 65–106.

——. "Noch einmal gegen Dr. Hanslick—in Noten." *Fliegende Blätter für Musik* 2 (1857): 183–89.

Locher, Hubert. "Towards a Science of Art: The Concept of 'Pure Composition.'" In *Pictorial Composition from Medieval to Modern Art,* 217–51. Edited by Paul Taylor and François Quiviger. London: Warburg Institute, 2000.

Locke, Ralph P. *Music, Musicians, and the Saint-Simonians.* Chicago: University of Chicago Press, 1986.

Lockwood, Lewis. *Beethoven: The Music and the Life.* New York: W. W. Norton, 2003.

Lomnäs, Bonnie, Erling Lomnäs, and Dietmar Strauß. *Auf der Suche nach der poetischen Zeit: Der Prager Davidsbund; Ambros, Bach, Bayer, Hampel, Hanslick, Helfert, Heller, Hock, Ulm.* 2 vols. Saarbrücken: Pfau, 1999.

Lorenz, Alfred. *Das Geheimnis der Form bei Richard Wagner.* 4 vols. Berlin: Max Hesse, 1924–33.

Lotze, Hermann. *Briefe und Dokumente.* Edited by Reinhardt Pester. Würzburg: Königshausen & Neumann, 2003. (Studien und Materialien zum Neukantianismus, 20)

——. *Geschichte der Aesthetik in Deutschland.* Munich: J. G. Cotta, 1868.

——. *Medicinische Psychologie, oder, Physiologie der Seele.* Leipzig: Weidmann, 1852; reprint, Amsterdam: E. J. Bonset, 1966.

——. *Metaphysik.* Leipzig: Weidmann, 1841.

——. *Ueber Bedingungen der Kunstschönheit.* Göttingen: Vandenhoeck und Ruprecht, 1847.

Louis, Rudolf. *Die deutsche Musik der Gegenwart.* Munich and Leipzig: Georg Müller, 1909.

Lynning, Kristine Hays, and Anja Skaar Jacobsen. "Grasping the Spirit in Nature: *Anschauung* in Ørsted's Epistemology of Science and Beauty." *Studies in History and Philosophy of Science (Part A)* 42 (2011): 45–57.

Maaß, Johann Gebhard Ehrenreich. "Ueber die Instrumentalmusik." *Neue Bibliothek der schönen Wissenschaften* 48 (1792): 3–40.

Mace, Dean T. "Marin Mersenne on Music and Language." *JMT* 14 (1970): 2–34.

Mäckelmann, Michael. *Arnold Schönberg: Fünf Orchesterstücke op. 16.* Munich: Wilhelm Fink, 1987.

Magee, Bryan. *The Philosophy of Schopenhauer.* Oxford: Clarendon Press, 1997.

——. *Wagner and Philosophy.* London: Allen Lane, 2000.

Mahler, Gustav. *Briefe.* Edited by Herta Blaukopf. 2nd ed. Vienna: Paul Zsolnay, 1996.

Maier, Franz Michael. "Lotze und Zimmermann als Rezensenten von Hanslicks *Vom Musikalisch-Schönen.*" *AfMw* 70 (2013): 209–26.

Malek, James S. "Adam Smith's Contribution to Eighteenth-Century British Aesthetics." *JAAC* 31, no. 1 (1972): 49–54.

———. *The Arts Compared: An Aspect of Eighteenth-Century British Aesthetics.* Detroit: Wayne State University Press, 1974.

Mallarmé, Stephane. "Crise de vers" (1896). In *Oeuvres complètes*, 360–68. Edited by Henri Mondor and G. Jean-Aubry. Paris: Gallimard, 1945.

———. *Selected Prose Poems, Essays, and Letters.* Edited and translated by Bradford Cook. Baltimore: Johns Hopkins University Press, 1956.

Maltz, Diana. *British Aestheticism and the Urban Working Classes, 1870–1900: Beauty for the People.* New York: Palgrave Macmillan, 2006.

Maniates, Maria Rika. " '*Sonate, que me veux-tu?*' The Enigma of French Musical Aesthetics in the 18th Century." *Current Musicology* 9 (1969): 117–40.

Mann, Thomas. *Die Entstehung des Doktor Faustus: Roman eines Romans.* Frankfurt am Main: Suhrkamp, 1949.

———. [*Die Entstehung des Doktor Faustus.* English.] *The Story of a Novel: The Genesis of Doctor Faustus.* Translated by Richard and Clara Winston. New York: Knopf, 1961.

Marais, Marin. *Pièces de viole*, Book 5. In *The Instrumental Works*, vol. 5, *Pièces de viole: Cinquème livre* (1725). Edited by John Hsu. New York: Broude Trust, 2000.

Marchenkov, Vladimir L. *The Orpheus Myth and the Powers of Music.* Hillsdale, NY: Pendragon Press, 2009.

Marpurg, Friedrich Wilhelm. "Anmerkungen über vorhergehendes Schreiben." *Historisch-kritische Beyträge zur Aufnahme der Musik* 1 (1754): 23–46.

Marvick, Louis. *Waking the Face That No One Is: A Study in the Musical Context of Symbolist Poetics.* Amsterdam: Rodopi, 2004.

Marx, Adolph Bernhard. *Die alte Musiklehre im Streit mit unserer Zeit.* Leipzig: Breitkopf & Härtel, 1841.

———. *Die Musik des 19. Jahrhunderts und ihre Pflege.* Leipzig: Breitkopf & Härtel, 1855.

Mason, Laura. *Singing the French Revolution: Popular Culture and Politics, 1787–1799.* Ithaca, NY: Cornell University Press, 1996.

Mathiesen, Thomas. *Apollo's Lyre: Greek Music and Music Theory in Antiquity and the Middle Ages.* Lincoln: University of Nebraska Press, 1999.

———. "Problems of Terminology in Ancient Greek Theory: ΑΡΜΟΝÍΑ." In *Festival Essays for Pauline Alderman: A Musicological Tribute*, 3–17. Edited by Burton L. Karson. Provo, UT: Brigham Young University Press, 1976.

Mattheson, Johann. *Das forschende Orchestre.* Hamburg: Schillers Wittwe, 1721.

———. *Kern melodischer Wissenschaft.* Hamburg: Herold, 1737.

———. *Der vollkommene Capellmeister.* Hamburg: Herold, 1739; reprint, Kassel: Bärenreiter, 1954.

May, Florence. *The Life of Johannes Brahms.* 2 vols. London: Edward Arnold, 1905.

McArthur, Tom, ed. *The Concise Oxford Companion to the English Language.* Oxford: Oxford University Press, 2005.

McClain, Ernest G. *The Pythagorean Plato: Prelude to the Song Itself.* Stony Brook, NY: N. Hays, 1978.

McClary, Susan. *Conventional Wisdom.* Berkeley and Los Angeles: University of California Press, 2000.

———. "Music, the Pythagoreans, and the Body." In *Choreographing History*, 82–104. Edited by Susan Leigh Foster. Bloomington: Indiana University Press, 1995.

——. "Narrative Agendas in 'Absolute' Music: Identity and Difference in Brahms's Third Symphony." In *Musicology and Difference: Gender and Sexuality in Music Scholarship*, 326–44. Edited by Ruth Solie. Berkeley and Los Angeles: University of California Press, 1993.

McClatchie, Stephen. *Analyzing Wagner's Operas: Alfred Lorenz and German Nationalist Ideology*. Rochester, NY: University of Rochester Press, 1998.

McColl, Sandra. *Music Criticism in Vienna, 1896–1897: Critically Moving Forms*. Oxford: Clarendon Press, 1996.

McCreless, Patrick. "Music and Rhetoric." In *The Cambridge History of Western Music Theory*, 847–79. Edited by Thomas Christensen. Cambridge: Cambridge University Press, 2002.

McKinnon, James W. "Jubal vel Pythagoras, quis sit inventor musicae?" *MQ* 64 (1978): 1–28.

——. "The Patristic Jubilus and the Alleluia of the Mass." In *Cantus Planus: Papers Read at the Third Meeting, Tihany, Hungary, 19–24 September 1988*, 61–70. Edited by László Dobszay. Budapest: Hungarian Academy of Sciences, 1990.

——, ed. *Music in Early Christian Literature*. Cambridge: Cambridge University Press, 1987.

McPhee, Colin. "The 'Absolute' Music of Bali." *Modern Music* 12 (1935): 163–69.

McWilliam, Neil. *Dreams of Happiness: Social Art and the French Left, 1830–1850*. Princeton: Princeton University Press, 1993.

Mehring, Frank. *Sphere Melodies: Die Manifestation transzendentalistischen Gedankenguts in der Musik der Avantgardisten Charles Ives und John Cage*. Stuttgart and Weimar: J. B. Metzler, 2003.

Mendelssohn, Felix. *Sämtliche Briefe*. Edited by Helmut Loos and Wilhelm Seidel. Kassel: Bärenreiter, 2008-.

Mendelssohn, Moses. "Über die Hauptgrundsätze der schönen Künste und Wissenschaften" (1757). In *Schriften zur Philosophie, Aesthetik und Apologetik*, 2:142–68. 2 vols. Edited by Moritz Brasch. Leipzig: Leopold Voss, 1880.

Merriam, Alan P. *The Anthropology of Music*. Evanston, IL: Northwestern University Press, 1964.

Merrill, Linda. *A Pot of Paint: Aesthetics on Trial in Whistler v. Ruskin*. Washington, DC: Smithsonian Institution Press, 1992.

Mersenne, Marin. *Harmonie universelle, contenant la théorie et la pratique de la musique*. 3 vols. Paris, 1636–37; reprint, Paris: CNRS, 1963.

Mersmann, Hans. *Beethoven: Die Synthese der Stile*. Berlin: Julius Bard, 1922.

Messing, Scott. *Neoclassicism in Music: From the Genesis of the Concept through the Schoenberg/ Stravinsky Polemic*. Rochester, NY: University of Rochester Press, 1996.

Meyer-Baer, Kathi. *Music of the Spheres and the Dance of Death: Studies in Musical Iconology*. Princeton: Princeton University Press, 1970.

Michaelis, Christian Friedrich. "Ueber das Idealische in der Tonkunst." *AmZ* 10 (1808): 449–52.

——. *Ueber den Geist der Tonkunst*. 2 vols. Leipzig: Schäfer, 1795–1800; reprint, Brussels: Culture et Civilisation, 1970.

——. *Ueber den Geist der Tonkunst und andere Schriften*. Edited by Lothar Schmidt. Chemnitz: Gudrun Schröter Verlag, 1997.

——. "Ein Versuch, das innere Wesen der Tonkunst zu entwickeln." *AmZ* 8 (23 and 30 July 1806): 673–83, 691–96.

Micznik, Vera. "The Absolute Limitations of Programme Music: The Case of Liszt's 'Die Ideale,' " *M&L* 80 (1999): 207–40.

——. "Music and Aesthetics: The Programmatic Issue." In *The Cambridge Companion to Mahler*, 35–49. Edited by Jeremy Barham. Cambridge: Cambridge University Press, 2007.

Migne, J.-P., ed. *Patrologiae cursus completus: Series Latina.* 221 vols. Paris: Migne, 1844–55.

Minturno, Antonio. *De Poeta.* Venice: Franciscus Rampazetus, 1559.

Mizler, Lorenz Christoph. "Gesetze der correspondirenden Societät der musikalischen Wissenschaften in Deutschland." *Neu-eröffnete musikalische Bibliothek* 3 (1746): 348–62.

——. "Vorrede." *Neu-eröffnete musikalische Bibliothek* 1 (1736), fols. 2–8.

Moos, Paul. *Moderne Musikästhetik in Deutschland: Historisch-kritische Übersicht.* Leipzig: Hermann Seemann Nachfolger, 1902.

Morgan, David. "Concepts of Abstraction in French Art Theory from the Enlightenment to Modernism." *JHI* 53 (1992): 669–85.

——. "The Enchantment of Art: Abstraction and Empathy from German Romanticism to Expressionism." *JHI* 57 (1996): 317–41.

——. "The Idea of Abstraction in German Theories of the Ornament from Kant to Kandinsky." *JAAC* 50 (1992): 231–42.

Moritz, Karl Philipp. *Über die bildende Nachahmung des Schönen* (1788). In *Werke*, 2 vols., 1:958–91. Edited by Heide Holmer and Albert Meier. Frankfurt am Main: Deutscher Klassiker Verlag, 1997.

Morrow, Mary Sue. *German Music Criticism in the Late Eighteenth Century: Aesthetic Issues in Instrumental Music.* Cambridge: Cambridge University Press, 1997.

de la Motte-Haber, Helga. *Musik und Natur: Naturanschauung und musikalische Poetik.* Laaber: Laaber-Verlag, 2000.

Moyer, Ann E. *Musica Scientia: Musical Scholarship in the Italian Renaissance.* Ithaca, NY: Cornell University Press, 1992.

Mozart, Wolfgang Amadeus. *Briefe und Aufzeichnungen.* Edited by Wilhelm A. Bauer and Otto Erich Deutsch. 7 vols. Kassel: Bärenreiter, 1962–75.

——. *The Letters of Mozart and His Family.* Edited and translated by Emily Anderson. New York: W. W. Norton, 1989.

Mueller-Vollmer, Kurt. "Romantic Language Theory and the Art of Understanding." In *The Cambridge History of Literary Criticism*, vol. 5, *Romanticism*, 162–84. Edited by Marshall Brown. Cambridge: Cambridge University Press, 2000.

Müller, Wilhelm Christian. *Aesthetisch-historische Einleitungen in die Wissenschaft der Tonkunst.* 2 vols. Leipzig:Breitkopf & Härtel, 1830.

Mundt, Theodor. *Aesthetik: Die Idee der Schönheit und des Kunstwerks im Lichte unserer Zeit.* Berlin: M. Simion, 1845.

Nägeli, Hans Georg. *Vorlesungen über Musik, mit Berücksichtigung der Dilettanten.* Stuttgart and Tübingen: Cotta, 1826.

Nattiez, Jean-Jacques. "Hanslick: The Contradictions of Immanence." In *The Battle of Chronos and Orpheus: Essays in Applied Musical Semiology*, 105–26. Translated by Jonathan Dunsby. New York: Oxford University Press, 2004.

Naumann, Emil. *Deutsche Tondichter von Sebastian Bach bis auf die Gegenwart.* Berlin: Robert Oppenheim, 1871.

——. *Die Tonkunst in ihren Beziehungen zu den Formen und Entwickelungsgesetzen alles Geisteslebens.* Berlin: B. Behr, 1869.

Nehamas, Alexander. *Only a Promise of Happiness: The Place of Beauty in a World of Art.* Princeton: Princeton University Press, 2007.

Neubauer, John. *The Emancipation of Music from Language: Departure from Mimesis in Eighteenth-century Aesthetics*. New Haven: Yale University Press, 1986.

Newcomb, Anthony. "Once More 'Between Absolute and Program Music': Schumann's Second Symphony." *19CM* 7 (1984): 233–50.

Newman, Ernest. *Elgar*. London: John Lane, 1922.

——. *A Study of Wagner*. London: Bertram Dobell, 1899.

Nielsen, Keld. "Another Kind of Light: The Work of T. J. Seebeck and His Collaboration with Goethe." *Historical Studies in the Physical and Biological Sciences* 20 (1989): 107–78; 21 (1991): 317–97.

Nietzsche, Friedrich. *Zur Genealogie der Moral* (1887). In *Sämtliche Werke*, 15 vols., 5:245–412. Edited by Giorgio Colli and Mazzino Montinari. Munich: Deutscher Taschenbuch Verlag, 1980.

Noeske, Nina, and Matthias Tischer, eds. *Musikwissenschaft und Kalter Krieg: Das Beispiel DDR*. Cologne: Böhlau, 2010.

Nolan, Catherine. "Music Theory and Mathematics." In *The Cambridge History of Western Music Theory*, 272–304. Edited by Thomas Christensen. Cambridge: Cambridge University Press, 2002.

Novalis [Friedrich von Hardenberg]. *Schriften*. Edited by Paul Kluckhohn and Richard Samuel. 3rd ed. Stuttgart: W. Kohlhammer, 1977–.

Oesterle, Günter. "Arabeske." In *Ästhetische Grundbegriffe: Historisches Wörterbuch*, 1:272–86. 7 vols. Edited by Karlheinz Barck. Stuttgart: Metzler, 2000–2005.

Oja, Carol J. *Colin McPhee: Composer in Two Worlds*. Urbana: University of Illinois Press, 2004.

O'Meara, Dominic J. *Pythagoras Revived: Mathematics and Philosophy in Late Antiquity*. Oxford: Clarendon Press, 1989.

Ørsted, Hans Christian. *Der Geist in der Natur*. 2 vols. Translated by K. L. Kannegiesser. Munich: J. G. Cotta, 1850–51.

——. "Ueber das 'Unschöne' in der Natur in seinem Verhältniß zur Schönheitsharmonie des Ganzen." In *Neue Beiträge zu dem Geist in der Natur*, 127–42. Translated by K. L. Kannegiesser. Leipzig: Carl B. Lorck, 1851.

——. "Ueber die Gründe des Vergnügens, welches die Töne hervorbringen." Translated by K. L. Kannegiesser. In *Neue Beiträge zu dem Geist in der Natur*, 1–38. Leipzig: Carl B. Lorck, 1851.

——. "Versuche über die Klangfiguren." *Journal für die Chemie, Physik und Mineralogie* 8 (1809): 223–54.

——. "Zwei Kapitel der Naturlehre des Schönen." In *Neue Beiträge zu dem Geist in der Natur*, 71–125. Translated by K. L. Kannegiesser. Leipzig: Carl B. Lorck, 1851.

Ortega y Gasset, José. *La deshumanización del arte* (1925). In *La deshumanización del arte y otros ensayos de estética*. Edited by Valeriano Bozal. Madrid: Espasa-Calpe, 1987.

——. [*La deshumanización del arte*. English.] *The Dehumanization of Art and Other Essays on Art, Culture, and Literature*. 2nd ed. Translated by Helen Weyl et al. Princeton: Princeton University Press, 1968.

Ossi, Massimo. *Divining the Oracle: Monteverdi's Seconda Prattica*. Chicago: University of Chicago Press, 2003.

Oulibicheff, Alexandre [Ulybyshev, Aleksandr Dmitrievich]. *Beethoven, ses critiques et ses glossateurs*. Leipzig: F. A. Brockhaus; Paris: Jules Gavelot, 1857.

——. *Nouvelle biographie de Mozart*. 3 vols. Moscow: Auguste Semen, 1843.

Ozuf, Mona. *Festivals and the French Revolution.* Translated by Alan Sheridan. Cambridge, MA: Harvard University Press, 1988.

Palisca, Claude V. "Aristoxenus Redeemed in the Renaissance." In *Studies in the History of Italian Music and Music Theory,* 189–99. Oxford: Clarendon Press, 1994.

——. "The Artusi–Monteverdi Controversy." In *Studies in the History of Italian Music and Music Theory,* 54–87. Oxford: Clarendon Press, 1994.

——. "Harmonies and Disharmonies of the Spheres." In *Humanism in Italian Renaissance Musical Thought,* 161–90. New Haven: Yale University Press, 1986.

——. "A Natural New Alliance of the Arts." In *Humanism in Italian Renaissance Musical Thought,* 333–68. New Haven: Yale University Press, 1986.

——. "*Ut oratoria musica*: The Rhetorical Basis of Musical Mannerism." In *Studies in the History of Italian Music and Music Theory,* 282–311. Oxford: Clarendon Press, 1994.

——, ed. *Hucbald, Guido, and John on Music: Three Medieval Treatises.* Translated by Warren Babb. New Haven: Yale University Press, 1978.

——, ed. and trans. *The Florentine Camerata: Documentary Studies and Translations.* New Haven: Yale University Press, 1989.

Panofsky, Erwin. *Galileo as a Critic of the Arts.* The Hague: Nijhoff, 1954.

Parmer, Dillon. "Brahms, Song Quotation, and Secret Programs." *19CM* 14 (1995), 161–90.

Pater, Walter. "The School of Giorgione." *Fortnightly Review* 22 (October 1877): 526–38.

——. *The Renaissance: Studies in Art and Poetry.* 3rd ed. London: Macmillan, 1888.

Payzant, Geoffrey. "Eduard Hanslick and Bernhard Gutt." *MR* 50 (1989): 124–33.

——. "Eduard Hanslick and the 'geistreich' Dr. Alfred Julius Becher." *MR* 44 (1983): 104–15.

——. "Hanslick, Sams, Gay, and 'Tönend bewegte Formen.'" *JAAC* 40 (1981): 41–48.

——. "On the Hanslick-Zimmermann Friendship." In *Hanslick on the Musically Beautiful: Sixteen Lectures on the Musical Aesthetics of Eduard Hanslick,* 129–42. Christchurch, N.Z.: Cybereditions, 2002.

Pederson, Sanna. "A. B. Marx, Berlin Concert Life, and German National Identity." *19CM* 18 (1994): 87–107.

——. "Defining the Term 'Absolute Music' Historically." *M&L* 90 (2009): 240–62.

——. "*On the Musically Beautiful* and 'Absolute Music.'" Paper presented at the annual meeting of the American Musicological Society, Philadelphia, 2009.

——. "Romantic Music under Siege in 1848." In *Music Theory in the Age of Romanticism,* 57–74. Edited by Ian Bent. Cambridge: Cambridge University Press, 1996.

Pelosi, Francesco. *Plato on Music, Soul and Body.* Translated by Sophie Henderson. Cambridge: Cambridge University Press, 2010.

Pesïc, Peter. "Earthly Music and Cosmic Harmony: Johannes Kepler's Interest in Practical Music, Especially Orlando di Lasso." *Journal of Seventeenth-Century Music,* 11, no. 1 (2005), http://www.sscm-jscm.org/v11/no1/pesic.html.

Pico della Mirandola, Giovanni. [*Oratio de hominis dignitate.* English.] *On the Dignity of Man.* Translated by Charles Glenn Wallis, Paul J. W. Miller, and Douglas Carmichael. Indianapolis: Hackett, 1998.

Planche, Gustave. "Histoire et philosophie de l'art. VI: Moralité de la poésie." *Revue des deux mondes* 19 (1835): 241–63.

Plato. *Complete Works.* Edited by John M. Cooper. Indianapolis: Hackett, 1997.

Plutarch. *De musica.* In *Moralia,* 17 vols., 14:343–455. Translated by B. Einarson and P. H. De Lacy. Cambridge, MA: Harvard University Press; London: William Heinemann, 1967.

Podro, Michael. *The Manifold in Perception: Theories of Art from Kant to Hildebrand.* Oxford: Clarendon Press, 1972.

Pohl, Richard. *Hektor Berlioz: Studien und Erinnerungen.* Leipzig: Bernhard Schlicke, 1884.

———. *Das Karlsruher Musikfest im Oktober 1853.* Leipzig: Bruno Hinze, 1853.

Powers, Harold S. "Language Models and Musical Analysis." *Ethnomusicology* 24 (1980): 1–60.

Prettejohn, Elizabeth. *Art for Art's Sake: Aestheticism in Victorian Painting.* New Haven: Yale University Press, 2007.

———. *Beauty and Art, 1750–2000.* Oxford: Oxford University Press, 2005.

———, ed. *After the Pre-Raphaelites: Art and Aestheticism in Victorian England.* New Brunswick, NJ: Rutgers University Press, 1999.

Prihonsky, Franz. *Neuer Anti-Kant, oder: Prüfung der Kritik der reinen Vernunft nach den in Bolzano's Wissenschaftslehre niedergelegten Begriffen.* Bautzen: Weller, 1850.

Printz, Felix. *Zur Würdigung des musikästhetischen Formalismus Eduard Hanslicks.* Borna-Leipzig: R. Noske, 1918.

Pritchard, Matthew. "'A Heap of Broken Images'? Reviving Austro-German Debates over Musical Meaning, 1900–36." *JRMA* 138 (2013): 129–74.

Puttfarken, Thomas. *The Discovery of Pictorial Composition: Theories of Visual Order in Painting, 1400–1800.* New Haven: Yale University Press, 2000.

Quantz, Johann Joachim. *Versuch einer Anweisung die Flöte traversiere zu spielen.* Berlin: J. F. Voss, 1752.

Raff, Joachim. "Die Stellung der Deutschen in der Geschichte der Musik: Kunsthistorische Skizze." *Weimarisches Jahrbuch für deutsche Sprache, Literatur und Kunst* 1 (1854): 171–214.

———. *Die Wagnerfrage.* Braunschweig: Vieweg und Sohn, 1854.

Raftery, Paul K. "Amalar of Metz on the Mass: A Translation of Book III, Chapters 1–18 of the *Liber officialis.*" Licentiate in Sacred Theology, Jesuit School of Theology at Berkeley, 1988.

Rameau, Jean-Philippe. *Code de musique pratique.* Paris: Imprimerie royale, 1760.

———. *Traité de l'harmonie réduits à ses principes naturels.* Paris: Ballard, 1722.

———. [*Traité de l'harmonie.* English.] *Treatise on Harmony.* Edited and translated by Philip Gossett. New York: Dover, 1971.

Rampley, Matthew. "The Idea of a Scientific Discipline: Rudolf von Eitelberger and the Emergence of Art History in Vienna, 1847–1873." *Art History* 34 (2011): 54–79.

Reckow, Fritz. "'Wirkung' und 'Effekt': Über einige Voraussetzungen, Tendenzen und Probleme der deutschen Berlioz-Kritik." *Die Musikforschung* 33 (1980): 1–36.

———. "Zwischen Ontologie und Rhetorik: Die Idee des *movere animos* und der Übergang vom Spätmittelalter zur frühen Neuzeit in der Musikgeschichte." In *Traditionswandel und Traditionsverhalten,* 145–78. Edited by Walter Haug and Burghart Wachinger. Tübingen: Max Niemeyer, 1991.

Reiss, Timothy J. *Knowledge, Discovery, and Imagination in Early Modern Europe: The Rise of Aesthetic Rationalism.* Cambridge: Cambridge University Press, 1997.

Reynolds, Joshua. *Discourses on Art* (1769–90). Edited by Robert R. Wark. New Haven: Yale University Press, 1975.

Richter, Sandra. *A History of Poetics: German Scholarly Aesthetics and Poetics in International Context, 1770–1960.* Berlin: de Gruyter, 2010.

Riedel, Friedrich Just. *Theorie der schönen Künste und Wissenschaften: Ein Auszug aus den Werken verschiedener Schriftsteller.* Jena: Cuno, 1767.

Riedweg, Christoph. *Pythagoras: His Life, Teaching, and Influence*. Translated by Steven Rendall. Ithaca, NY: Cornell University Press, 2005.

Riemann, Hugo. *Die Elemente der musikalischen Aesthetik*. Berlin and Stuttgart: W. Spemann, 1901.

———. "Das formale Element in der Musik." *Die Grenzboten* 39 (1880): 228–41.

———. *Musik-Lexikon*. Leipzig: Bibliographisches Institut, 1882.

———. *Musik-Lexikon*. 7th ed. Leipzig: Max Hesse, 1909.

———. "Programmmusik, Tonmalerei und musikalischer Kolorismus." *Die Grenzboten* 41 (1882): 75–84. Republished in Riemann's *Präludien und Studien*, 1:54–64. 3 vols. Leipzig: Hermann Seemann Nachfolger, 1895–1901.

Riezler, Walter. *Beethoven*. Berlin and Zurich: Atlantis, 1936.

Riley, Matthew. "Johann Nikolaus Forkel on the Listening Practices of 'Kenner' and 'Liebhaber.' " *M&L* 84 (2003): 414–33.

———. *Musical Listening in the German Enlightenment: Attention, Wonder and Astonishment*. Aldershot: Ashgate, 2004.

Ritter, Alexander. "Drei Kapitel: Von Franz Liszt, von der 'heiligen Elisabeth' in Karlsruhe, und von unserm ethischen Defekt." *Bayreuther Blätter* 12 (1890): 380.

Robin, William. "Formalizing a 'Purely Acoustic' Musical Objectivity: Revisiting a 1915 Interview with Stravinsky." In *Reassessing Stravinsky's "Le sacre du printemps," 1913/2013*. Edited by Severine Neff, Maureen A. Carr, and Gretchen Horlacher. Bloomington: Indiana University Press, forthcoming.

Robinson, Jenefer. *Deeper than Reason: Emotion and its Role in Literature, Music, and Art*. Oxford: Clarendon Press, 2005.

[Rochlitz, Friedrich.] "Göthe über Musik." *AmZ* 7 (22 May 1805): 541–44.

Rothfarb, Lee. "Energetics." In *The Cambridge History of Western Music Theory*, 927–55. Edited by Thomas Christensen. Cambridge: Cambridge University Press, 2002.

———. "Hermeneutics and Energetics: Analytical Alternatives in the Early 1900s." *JMT* 36 (1992): 43–68.

Rothstein, Edward. *Emblems of the Mind: The Inner Life of Music and Mathematics*. New York: Random House, 1995.

Rousseau, Jean-Jacques. *Dictionnaire de musique*. Paris: Veuve Duchesne, 1768.

———. *Essai sur l'origine des langues*. Edited by Jean Starobinski. Paris: Gallimard, 1990.

———. [*Essai sur l'origine des langues*. English.] *Essay on the Origin of Language*. Translated by John H. Moran. In *On the Origin of Language*, 1–83. Edited by John H. Moran and Alexander Gode. New York: Frederick Ungar, 1966.

Rousseau, Pascal. " 'Arabesques': Le formalisme musical dans les débuts de l'abstraction." In *Aux origines de l'abstraction, 1800–1914: Musée d'Orsay, 3 novembre 2003–22 février 2004*, 230–45. Paris: Réunion des Musées Nationaux, 2003.

Ruskin, John. *The Works of John Ruskin*. 39 vols. London: G. Allen, 1903–12.

Sachs, Joel. "Some Aspects of Musical Politics in Pre-Nazi Germany." *Perspectives of New Music* 9 (1970): 74–95.

Santayana, George. *The Sense of Beauty, Being the Outlines of Æsthetic Theory*. New York: Charles Scribner's Sons, 1896.

Schäfke, Rudolf. *Eduard Hanslick und die Musikästhetik*. Leipzig: Breitkopf & Härtel, 1922.

Schawelka, Karl. *Quasi una musica: Untersuchungen zum Ideal des "Musikalischen" in der Malerei ab 1800*. Munich: Mäander, 1993.

Schelling, Friedrich Wilhelm Joseph. *Philosophie der Kunst* (1802–03). Edited by K. F. A. Schelling. Stuttgart: Cotta, 1859; reprint, Darmstadt: Wissenschaftliche Buchgesellschaft, 1976.

———. *System des transzendentalen Idealismus* (1800). Edited by Horst D. Brandt and Peter Müller. Hamburg: Felix Meiner, 1992.

———. *Ueber das Verhältniß der bildenden Künste zur Natur.* Munich: Philipp Krüll, 1807.

———. *Die Weltalter: Fragmente in den Urauffassungen von 1811 und 1813.* Edited by Manfred Schröter. Munich: Beck, 1966.

Schenker, Heinrich. "Beethovens Dritte Sinfonie zum erstenmal in ihrem wahren Inhalt dargestellt." In *Das Meisterwerk in der Musik* 3 (1930): 25–101.

———. *Beethovens Neunte Sinfonie.* Vienna and Leipzig: Universal Edition, 1912.

———. "The Decline of the Art of Composition: A Technical-Critical Study." Edited and translated by William Drabkin. *Music Analysis* 24 (2005): 33–129.

———. *Kontrapunkt.* 2 vols. Vienna: Universal Edition, 1910–22.

———. "Die Kunst der Improvisation." *Das Meisterwerk in der Musik* 1 (1925): 9–40.

———. [*Die Kunst des Vortrags.* English.] *The Art of Performance.* Edited by Heribert Esser. Translated by Irene Schreier Scott. New York: Oxford University Press, 2000.

———. "Unpersönliche Musik." *Neue Revue* 8 (1897): 464–68. Republished in *Heinrich Schenker als Essayist und Kritiker: Gesammelte Aufsätze, Rezensionen und kleinere Berichte aus den Jahren 1891–1901,* 216–21. Edited by Hellmut Federhofer. Hildesheim: Olms, 1990.

———. ["Unpersönliche Musik." English.] "Impersonal Music." Translated by Horst B. Loeschmann. In Heinrich Schenker, "Three Essays from the 'Neue Revue' (1894–7)." *Music Analysis* 7 (1988): 135–38.

Schiller, Friedrich. *Der Briefwechsel zwischen Schiller und Goethe.* Edited by Emil Staiger and Hans-Georg Dewitz. Rev. ed. Frankfurt am Main: Insel Verlag, 2005.

———. [*Über die ästhetische Erziehung des Menschen.* German and English.] *On the Aesthetic Education of Man.* Edited and translated by Elizabeth Wilkinson and L. A. Willoughby. Oxford: Clarendon Press, 1967.

———. *Werke und Briefe.* Edited by Klaus Harro Hilzinger. 12 vols. Frankfurt am Main: Deutscher Klassiker Verlag, 1988–2004.

Schilling, Gustav. *Geschichte der heutigen oder modernen Musik.* Karlsruhe: Christian Theodor Groos, 1841.

———. *Versuch einer Philosophie des Schönen in der Musik, oder Aesthetik der Tonkunst.* 2 vols. Mainz: B. Schott's Söhne, 1838.

Schladebach, Julius, ed. *Neues Universal-Lexikon der Tonkunst.* Volume 1. Dresden: Robert Schaefer, 1855.

Schlegel, August Wilhelm. *Vorlesungen über Ästhetik I (1798–1803).* Edited by Ernst Behler. Paderborn: Ferdinand Schöningh, 1989.

Schlegel, Friedrich. *Kritische Friedrich-Schlegel-Ausgabe.* Edited by Ernst Behler Munich: Ferdinand Schöningh, 1958–.

de Schloezer, Boris. "Igor Strawinsky." In *Von neuer Musik,* 124–40. Edited by H. Grues, E. Kruttge, E. Thalheimer. Cologne: F. J. Marcan, 1925.

Schlüter, Joseph. *Allgemeine Geschichte der Musik in übersichtlicher Darstellung.* Leipzig: Wilhelm Engelmann, 1863.

Schmalfeldt, Janet. *In the Process of Becoming: Analytic and Philosophical Perspectives on Form in Early Nineteenth-Century Music.* New York: Oxford University Press, 2011.

Schmelz, Peter J. "Introduction: Music in the Cold War." *JM* 26 (2009): 3–16.

——. *Such Freedom, If Only Musical: Unofficial Soviet Music During the Thaw*. New York: Oxford University Press, 2009.

Schmidt, Julian. *Geschichte der deutschen Nationallitteratur im neunzehnten Jahrhundert*. 2 vols. Leipzig: Herbig, 1853.

Schmidt, Lothar. "Arabeske. Zu einigen Voraussetzungen und Konsequenzen von Eduard Hanslicks musikalsichem Formbegriff." *AfMw* (1989): 91–120.

Schmitz, Eugen. *Musikästhetik*. Leipzig: Breitkopf & Härtel, 1915.

Schmusch, Rainer. *Der Tod des Orpheus: Entstehungsgeschichte der Programmusik*. Freiburg im Breisgau: Rombach, 1998.

Schneider, Lothar. "Form versus Gehalt: Konturen des intellektuellen Feldes im späten 19. Jahrhundert." In *Eduard Hanslick zum Gedenken: Bericht des Symposions zum Anlass seines 100. Todestages*, 39–54. Edited by Theophil Antonicek, Gernot Gruber, and Christoph Landerer. Tutzing: Hans Schneider, 2010.

——. "Realismus und formale Ästhetik: Die Auseinandersetzung zwischen Robert Zimmermann und Friedrich Theodor Vischer als poetologische Leitdifferenz im späten neunzehnten Jahrhundert." In *Herbarts Kultursystem: Perspektiven der Transdisziplinarität im 19. Jahrhundert*, 259–81. Edited by Andreas Hoeschen and Lothar Schneider. Würzburg: Königshausen & Neumann, 2001.

Schneider, Paul. *Über das Darstellungsvermögen der Musik: Eine Untersuchung an der Hand von Prof. Ed. Hanslick's Buch "Vom Musikalisch-Schönen."* Oppeln and Leipzig: Georg Frank, 1892.

Schoenberg, Arnold. *Berliner Tagebuch*. Edited by Josef Rufer. Frankfurt am Main: Propyläen, 1974.

——. "Über Musikkritik." *Der Merker* 1 (1909): 59–64.

——. ["Über Musikkritik." English.] "About Music Criticism" (1909). In *Style and Idea: Selected Writings of Arnold Schoenberg*, 191–97. Edited by Leonard Stein. Berkeley and Los Angeles: University of California Press, 1975.

——. "Das Verhältnis zum Text" (1912). In *"Stile herrschen, Gedanken siegen": Ausgewählte Schriften*, 67–71. Edited by Anna Maria Morazzoni. Mainz: Schott, 2007.

——. ["Das Verhältnis zum Text." English.] "The Relationship to the Text" (1912). In *Style and Idea: Selected Writings of Arnold Schoenberg*, 141–45. Edited by Leonard Stein. Berkeley and Los Angeles: University of California Press, 1975.

——. *Verklärte Nacht*, op. 4. Liner notes to the recording by the Hollywood String Quartet, with Alvin Dinkin, viola, Kurt Reher, violoncello. Capitol Classics L-8118, 1950.

Scholar, Richard. *The Je-Ne-Sais-Quoi in Early Modern Europe: Encounters with a Certain Something*. New York: Oxford University Press, 2005.

Schopenhauer, Arthur. *Gesammelte Briefe*. Edited by Arthur Hübscher. Bonn: Bouvier, 1978.

——. *Parerga und Pariplomena: Kleine philosophische Schriften*. 2 vols. Berlin: A. W. Hayn, Berlin 1851.

——. *Die Welt als Wille und Vorstellung* (1819, 1844). Edited by Arthur Hübscher. 4 vols. Zurich: Diogenes, 1977.

——. [*Die Welt als Wille und Vorstellung*. English.] *The World as Will and Representation*. Translated by E. F. J. Payne. 2 vols. New York: Dover, 1966.

Schrader, Hans-Jürgen, and Katharine Weder, eds. *Von der Pansophie zur Weltweisheit: Goethes analogisch-philosophische Konzepte*. Tübingen: Max Niemeyer, 2004.

Schubart, Christian Friedrich Daniel. *Ideen zu einer Ästhetik der Tonkunst*. Edited by Ludwig Schubart. Vienna: J. V. Degen, 1806.

——. *Ideen zu einer Ästhetik der Tonkunst*. Edited by Ludwig Schubart. Stuttgart: J. Scheible, 1839.

Schueller, Herbert M. "Correspondences Between Music and the Sister Arts, According to 18th Century Aesthetic Theory." *JAAC* 11 (1953): 334–59.

Schuh, Willi. *Richard Strauss: Jugend und frühe Meisterjahre: Lebenschronik 1864–1898*. Zurich: Atlantis, 1976. Translated by Mary Whittall as *Richard Strauss: A Chronicle of the Early Years, 1864–1898*. Cambridge: Cambridge University Press, 1982.

Schumann, Clara, and Johannes Brahms. *Clara Schumann und Johannes Brahms: Briefe aus den Jahren 1853–1896*. Edited by Berthold Litzmann. 2 vols. Leipzig: Breitkopf & Härtel, 1927.

Schumann, Robert. "'Aus dem Leben eines Künstlers': Phantastische Symphonie in fünf Abtheilungen von Hector Berlioz." *NZfM* 3 (1835): 1–2, 33–35, 37–38, 41–44, 45–48, 49–51.

——. *Briefe: Neue Folge*. Edited by F. Gustav Jansen. Leipzig: Breitkopf & Härtel, 1904.

——. *Dichtergarten für Musik: Eine Anthologie für Freunde der Literatur und Musik*. Edited by Gerd Nauhaus and Ingrid Bodsch. Frankfurt am Main: Stroemfeld, 2007.

——. *Gesammelte Schriften und Dichtungen*. 5th ed. Edited by Martin Kreisig. 2 vols. Leipzig: Breitkopf & Härtel, 1914.

——. [Untitled review of two overtures by Kalliwoda.] *NZfM* 1 (5 May 1834): 38.

——. "Symphonieen für Orchester." *NZfM* 18 (1 and 15 May 1843): 139–41, 155–56.

Schweitzer, Albert. *Aus meinem Leben und Denken*. Leipzig: Felix Meiner, 1931.

——. *J. S. Bach, le musicien-poète*. Leipzig: Breitkopf & Härtel, 1905.

——. *Johann Sebastian Bach*. Leipzig: Breitkopf & Härtel, 1908.

Scruton, Roger. "Absolute Music." *The New Grove Dictionary of Music and Musicians*. 2nd ed. Edited by Stanley Sadie. London: Macmillan, 2001.

Seebass, Tilman. "Lady Music and Her Protégés, from Musical Allegory to Musicians' Portraits." *Musica Disciplina* 42 (1988): 23–61.

Seebeck, Thomas Johann. "Einige neue Versuche und Beobachtungen der Spiegelung und Brechung des Lichtes." *Journal für die Chemie, Physik und Mineralogie* 7 (1813): 259–98, 382–384.

Seidel, Carl. *Charinomos: Beiträge zur allgemeinen Theorie und Geschichte der schönen Künste*. 2 vols. Magdeburg: Ferdinand Rubach, 1825–28.

Seidel, Wilhelm. "Absolute Musik." In *Die Musik in Geschichte und Gegenwart*. 2nd ed. 27 vols. Kassel: Bärenreiter, 1994–2008.

——. "Absolute Musik und Kunstreligion um 1800." In *Musik und Religion*, 129–54. 2nd ed. Edited by Helga de la Motte-Haber. Laaber: Laaber-Verlag, 2003.

——. "Zählt die Musik zu den imitativen Künsten? Zur Revision der Nachahmungsästhetik durch Adam Smith." In *Die Sprache der Musik: Festschrift Klaus Wolfgang Niemöller zum 60. Geburtstag*, 495–511. Edited by Jobst Peter Fricke. Regensburg: G. Bosse, 1989.

Serauky, Walter. *Die musikalische Nachahmungsästhetik im Zeitraum von 1700 bis 1850*. Münster: Helios-Verlag, 1929.

Shaftesbury, Anthony Ashley Cooper, third Earl of. *Characteristics of Men, Manners, Opinions, Times* (1713). Edited by Lawrence Klein. Cambridge: Cambridge University Press, 1999.

Shiner, Larry. *The Invention of Art: A Cultural History*. University of Chicago Press, 2001.

Shreffler, Anne. "Berlin Walls: Dahlhaus, Knepler, and Ideologies of Music History." *JM* 20 (2003): 498–525.

———. "Ideologies of Serialism: Stravinsky's *Threni* and the Congress for Cultural Freedom." In *Music and the Aesthetics of Modernity*, 217–45. Edited by Karol Berger and Anthony Newcomb. Cambridge, MA: Harvard University Department of Music, 2005.

Smith, Adam. "Of the Nature of that Imitation which Takes Place in What are Called the Imitative Arts." In *Essays on Philosophical Subjects*, 131–84. London: T. Cadell and W. Davies, 1795.

Spate, Virginia. *Orphism: The Evolution of Non-figurative Painting in Paris, 1910–1914*. Oxford: Clarendon Press, 1979.

Spitta, Philipp. *Johann Sebastian Bach*. 2 vols. Leipzig: Breitkopf & Härtel, 1873–80.

Sponheuer, Bernd. *Musik als Kunst und Nicht-Kunst: Untersuchungen zur Dichotomie von "hoher" und "niederer" Musik im musikästhetischen Denken zwischen Kant und Hanslick*. Kassel: Bärenreiter, 1987.

Stade, Friedrich. *Vom Musikalisch-Schönen. Mit Bezug auf Dr. E. Hanslick's gleichnamige Schrift*. Leipzig: C. F. Kahnt, 1871.

Steblin, Rita. *A History of Key Characteristics in the Eighteenth and Early Nineteenth Centuries*. 2nd ed. Rochester, NY: University of Rochester Press, 2002.

Steege, Benjamin. *Helmholtz and the Modern Listener*. Cambridge: Cambridge University Press, 2012.

Stephenson, Bruce. *The Music of the Heavens: Kepler's Harmonic Astronomy*. Princeton: Princeton University Press, 1994.

Stern, Martin. " 'Poésie pure' und Atonalität in Österreich: Stefan Georges Wirkung auf Jung-Wien und Schönberg." In *Die Österreichische Literatur: Ihr Profil von der Jahrhundertwende bis zur Gegenwart (1880–1980)*, 2:1457–69. Edited by Herbert Zeman. 2 vols. Graz: Akademische Druck- und Verlagsanstalt, 1989.

Sternfeld, F. W. *The Birth of Opera*. Oxford: Clarendon Press, 1993.

Stevens, John. *Words and Music in the Middle Ages: Song, Narrative, Dance, and Drama, 1050–1350*. Cambridge: Cambridge University Press, 1986.

Stolnitz, Jerome. " 'Beauty': Some Stages in the History of an Idea." *JHI* 22 (1961): 185–204.

———. "On the Origins of 'Aesthetic Disinterestedness.' " *JAAC* 20 (1961–62): 131–43.

Strauß, Dietmar. "Eduard Hanslick und die Diskussion um die Musik der Zukunft." In Eduard Hanslick, *Sämtliche Schriften*, vol. 1, part 4, *Aufsätze und Rezensionen, 1857–1858*, 407–25. Edited by Dietmar Strauß. Vienna: Böhlau, 2002.

Strauss, Richard, and Hans von Bülow. "Briefwechsel." Edited by Willi Schuh and Franz Trenner. In *Richard Strauss Jahrbuch 1954*, 7–88.

Stravinsky, Igor. *Chroniques de ma vie*. 2 vols. Paris: Denoël et Steele, 1935.

———. [*Chroniques de ma vie*. English.] *An Autobiography*. New York: Simon and Schuster, 1936.

———. "Quelques confidences sur la musique" (1935). In Eric Walter White, *Stravinsky: The Composer and His Works*, 581–85. 2nd ed. Berkeley and Los Angeles: University of California Press, 1979.

———. "Some Ideas about my Octuor" (1924). In Eric Walter White, *Stravinsky: The Composer and His Works*, 574–77. 2nd ed. Berkeley and Los Angeles: University of California Press, 1979.

Stravinsky, Igor, and Robert Craft. *Conversations with Igor Stravinsky*. Garden City, NY: Doubleday, 1959.

———. *Expositions and Developments*. Garden City, NY: Doubleday, 1962.

Strohm, Reinhard. "*De plus en plus*: Number, Binchois, and Ockeghem." In *Citation and Authority in Medieval and Renaissance Musical Culture: Learning from the Learned*,

160–73. Edited by Suzannah Clark and Elizabeth Eva Leach. Woodbridge, UK: Boydell Press, 2005.

Strunk, Oliver, and Leo Treitler, eds. *Source Readings in Music History*. Revised ed. New York: W. W. Norton, 1998.

Sullivan, Blair. *The Classical Analogy between Speech and Music and its Transmission in Carolingian Music Theory*. Tempe: Arizona Center for Medieval and Renaissance Studies, 2011.

Sulzer, Johann Georg. *Allgemeine Theorie der schönen Künste*. 2 vols. Leipzig: M. G. Weidemanns Erben und Reich, 1771–74.

Summers, David. "'Form,' Nineteenth-Century Metaphysics, and the Problem of Art Historical Description." *Critical Inquiry* 15 (1989): 372–93.

Swinburne, Algernon Charles. *William Blake: A Critical Essay*. London: John Camden Hotten, 1868.

T., D. "The Popular Concerts." *The Musical World* 61, no. 9 (3 March 1883): 131.

Tadday, Ulrich. *Das schöne Unendliche: Ästhetik, Kritik, Geschichte der romantischen Musikanschauung*. Stuttgart and Weimar: J. B. Metzler, 1999.

Tappert. Wilhelm. *Für und Wider: Eine Blumenlese aus den Berichten über die Aufführungen des Bühnenweihfestspieles Parsifal*. Berlin: Theodor Barth, 1882.

Tardieu, Eugène. "La peinture et les peintres: M. Paul Gauguin." *Echo de Paris*, 13 May 1895, 2.

Taruskin, Richard. "Afterword: *Nicht blutbefleckt?*" *JM* 26 (2009): 274–84.

——. "Back to Whom? Neoclassicism as Ideology." In *The Danger of Music*, 382–405. Berkeley and Los Angeles: University of California Press, 2009.

——. "Is There a Baby in the Bathwater?" *AfMw* 63 (2006): 163–85, 309–27.

——. "A Myth of the Twentieth Century: The Rite of Spring, the Tradition of the New, and 'The Music Itself.'" *Modernism/Modernity* 2 (1995): 1–26. Republished in *Defining Russia Musically: Historical and Hermeneutical Essays*, 360–88. Princeton: Princeton University Press, 1997.

——. "Speed Bumps." *19CM* 29 (2005): 185–207.

——. *Stravinsky and the Russian Traditions: A Biography of the Works through "Mavra."* 2 vols. Berkeley and Los Angeles: University of California Press, 1996.

——. *Text and Act: Essays on Music and Performance*. New York: Oxford University Press, 1995.

Tatarkiewicz, Władysław. *A History of Six Ideas: An Essay in Aesthetics*. Translated by Christopher Kasparek. Warsaw: Polish Scientific Publishers, 1980.

Taylor, Charles. *Human Agency and Language*. Cambridge: Cambridge University Press, 1985.

Thomas, Downing. *Music and the Origins of Language: Theories from the French Enlightenment*. Cambridge: Cambridge University Press, 1995.

Thompson, Verne Waldo. "Wenzel Johann Tomaschek: His Predecessors, His Life, His Piano Works." Ph.D. diss., University of Rochester, 1955.

Thorau, Christian. "*Symphony in White*: Musik als Modus der Referenz." In *Musik—Zu Begriff und Konzepten: Berliner Symposion zum Andenken an Hans Heinrich Eggebrecht*, 135–50. Edited by Michael Beiche and Albrecht Riethmüller. Wiesbaden: Franz Steiner, 2006.

Tieck, Ludwig. "Die Töne." In *Phantasien über die Kunst, für Freunde der Kunst* (1799). In Wilhelm Heinrich Wackenroder, *Sämtliche Werke und Briefe: Historisch-kritische Ausgabe*, 1:233–39. Edited by Silvio Vietta and Richard Littlejohns. 2 vols. Heidelberg: Carl Winter, 1991.

Tiessen, Heinz. *Zur Geschichte der jüngsten Musik (1913–1928): Probleme und Entwicklungen.* Mainz: Melosverlag, 1928.

Tischer, Matthias. *Ferdinand Hands Aesthetik der Tonkunst: Ein Beitrag zur Inhaltsästhetik der ersten Hälfte des 19. Jahrhunderts.* Sinzig: Studio, 2004.

Titus, Barbara. "Conceptualizing Music: Friedrich Theodor Vischer and Hegelian Currents in German Music Criticism, 1848–1887." Ph.D. diss., Oxford University, 2005.

——. "The Quest for Spiritualized Form: (Re)positioning Eduard Hanslick." *Acta musicologica* 80 (2008): 67–97.

Tomaschek, Wenzel. "Selbstbiographie." *Libussa: Jahrbuch für 1846,* 321–76.

Tomlinson, Gary. *Music in Renaissance Magic: Toward a Historiography of Others.* Chicago: University of Chicago Press, 1993.

——. "Vico's Songs: Detours at the Origins of (Ethno)musicology." *MQ* 83 (1999): 344–77.

Tovey, Donald Francis. *Musical Articles from the Encyclopaedia Britannica.* Edited by Hubert J. Foss. London: Oxford University Press, 1944.

——. "Programme Music." In *The Encyclopaedia Britannica,* 11th ed. Cambridge: At the University Press, 1911.

Trautmann-Waller, Céline, and Carole Maigné, eds. *Formalismes esthétiques et héritage herbartien: Vienne, Prague, Moscou.* Hildesheim: Olms, 2009.

Treitler, Leo. "The Historiography of Music: Issues of Past and Present." In *Rethinking Music,* 356–77. Edited by Nicholas Cook and Mark Everist. Oxford: Oxford University Press, 1999.

Triest, Johann Karl Friedrich. "Bemerkungen über die Ausbildung der Tonkunst in Deutschland im achtzehnten Jahrhundert." *AmZ* 3 (1801): 225–35, 241–49, 257–064, 273–86, 297–308, 321–32, 369–79, 389–401, 405–10, 421–32, 437–45. Translated by Susan Gillespie as "Remarks on the Development of the Art of Music in Germany in the Eighteenth Century." In *Haydn and His World,* 321–394. Edited by Elaine Sisman. Princeton: Princeton University Press, 1997.

Uhlig, Theodor. "Die Instrumentalmusik." *Deutsche Monatsschrift für Politik, Wissenshaft, Kunst und Leben* 2 (1851): 40–53, 173–82.

——. "Zur Kritik des Liedes." *NZfM* 36 (4 June 1852): 253–55.

Ullmann, Dieter. *Chladni und die Entwicklung der Akustik von 1750–1860.* Basel: Birkhäuser, 1996.

Ulybyshev. *See* Oulibicheff.

Varèse, Louise. *Varèse: A Looking-Glass Diary.* New York: W. W. Norton, 1972.

Vicentino, Nicola. *L'antica musica ridotta alla moderna prattica.* Rome: Antonio Barre, 1555; reprint, Kassel: Bärenreiter, 1959. Edited by Claude V. Palisca and translated by Maria Mika Maniates as *Ancient Music Adapted to Modern Practice.* New Haven: Yale University Press, 1996.

Vischer, Friedrich Theodor. *Aesthetik, oder Wissenschaft des Schönen.* 3 vols. Reutlingen and Leipzig: C. Mäcken, 1846–57.

——. "Kritik meiner Ästhetik." In *Kritische Gänge: Neue Folge,* 5:1–156. Stuttgart: Cotta, 1866.

Wackenroder, Wilhelm Heinrich. "Das eigentümliche innere Wesen der Tonkunst, und die Seelenlehre der heutigen Instrumentalmusik." In *Phantasien über die Kunst, für Freunde der Kunst* (1799). In *idem, Sämtliche Werke und Briefe: Historisch-kritische Ausgabe,* 1: 216–23. Edited by Silvio Vietta and Richard Littlejohns. 2 vols. Heidelberg: Carl Winter, 1991.

Wagner, Richard. "Ein Brief von Richard Wagner über Franz Liszt." *NZfM* 46 (10 April 1857): 157–63.

——. *Gesammelte Schriften und Dichtungen.* Edited by Wolfgang Golter. 11 vols. Berlin: Bong, 1913.

——. *Das Judenthum in der Musik.* Leipzig: J. J. Weber, 1869.

——. *Mein Leben (1870–80).* 2 vols. Munich: F. Bruckmann, 1911.

——. *Prose Works.* Translated by William Ashton Ellis. 8 vols. London: K. Paul, Trench, Trübner, 1893–99.

——. *Sämtliche Briefe.* Edited by Gertrud Strobel and Werner Wolf. Leipzig, Deutscher Verlag für Musik, 1967–.

Walden, Joshua S. "Composing Character in Musical Portraits: Carl Philipp Emanuel Bach and *L'Aly Rupalich.*" *MQ* 91 (2008): 379–411.

Walker, D. P. "Kepler's Celestial Music." *Journal of the Warburg and Courtauld Institutes* 30 (1967): 228–50.

Walker, John. "Two Realisms: German Literature and Philosophy, 1830–1890." In *Philosophy and German Literature, 1700–1900,* 102–49. Edited by Nicholas Saul. Cambridge: Cambridge University Press, 2002.

Wallaschek, Richard. *Ästhetik der Tonkunst.* Stuttgart: W. Kohlhammer, 1886.

Walter, Horst. "Haydn gewidmete Streichquartette." In *Joseph Haydn: Tradition und Rezeption,* 17–53. Edited by Georg Feder, Heinrich Hüschen, and Ulrich Tank. Regensburg: Gustav Bosse, 1985.

Walther, Johann Gottfried. *Praecepta der musicalischen Composition* (1708). Edited by Peter Benary. Leipzig: Breitkopf & Härtel, 1955.

Walton, Kendall L. "Listening with Imagination: Is Music Representational?" *JAAC* 52 (1994): 47–61.

——. "What is Abstract About the Art of Music?" *JAAC* 46 (1988): 351–64.

Warden, John, ed. *Orpheus: Metamorphoses of a Myth.* Toronto: University of Toronto Press, 1982.

Watkins, Holly. *Metaphors of Depth in German Musical Thought: From E. T. A. Hoffmann to Arnold Schoenberg.* Cambridge: Cambridge University Press, 2011.

Webb, Daniel. *Observations on the Correspondence between Poetry and Music.* London: J. Dodsley, 1769.

Weber, William. "Did People Listen in the 18th Century?" *Early Music* 25 (1997): 678–91.

——. *The Great Transformation of Musical Taste: Concert Programming from Haydn to Brahms.* Cambridge: Cambridge University Press, 2008.

Webern, Anton. *Wege zur neuen Musik.* Edited by Willi Reich. Vienna: Universal Edition, 1960.

Weisse, Christian Hermann. *System der Ästhetik als Wissenschaft von der Idee der Schönheit.* 2 vols. Leipzig: E. H. F. Hartmann, 1830.

Weissmann, Adolph. "The Tyranny of the Absolute." *The League of Composers' Review* 2, no. 2 (1925): 17–20.

Wellbery, David. *Lessing's Laocoon: Semiotics and Aesthetics in the Age of Reason.* Cambridge: Cambridge University Press, 1984.

——. "The Transformation of Rhetoric." In *The Cambridge History of Literary Criticism,* vol. 5, *Romanticism,* 185–202. Edited by Marshall Brown. Cambridge: Cambridge University Press, 2000.

Wellek, René. *A History of Modern Criticism: 1750–1950,* vol. 2, *The Romantic Age.* New Haven: Yale University Press, 1965.

Wellesz, Egon. "Das Problem der Form." In *Von neuer Musik,* 35–38. Edited by H. Grues, E. Kruttge, and E. Thalheimer. Cologne: F. J. Marcan, 1925.

Wend, Julius. "Berlioz und die moderne Symphonie: Ein Beitrag zu einer Philosopie der Musik." *Wiener allgemeine Musik-Zeitung* 6 (1846): 157–58, 161–62, 169–70.

Werckmeister, Andreas. *Erweiterte und vermehrte Orgel-Probe*. Quedlinburg, 1698; reprint, Kassel: Bärenreiter, 1970.

——. *Musicalische Paradoxal-Discourse*. Quedlinburg, 1707; reprint, Hildesheim: Olms, 1970.

Werner, Eric. "The Last Pythagorean Musician: Johannes Kepler." In *Aspects of Medieval and Renaissance Music: A Birthday Offering to Gustave Resse*, 867–92. Edited by Jan LaRue. New York: W. W. Norton, 1966.

Wheeldon, Marianne. *Debussy's Late Style*. Bloomington: Indiana University Press, 2009.

Whistler, James McNeill. *The Gentle Art of Making Enemies*. London and Edinburgh: Ballantyne Press, 1892.

White, Eric Walter. *Stravinsky: The Composer and His Works*. 2nd ed. Berkeley and Los Angeles: University of California Press, 1979.

Whitehead, Alfred North. *Science and the Modern World*. New York: Macmillan, 1925.

Wider, Sarah Ann. "Chladni Patterns, Lyceum Halls, and Skillful Experimenters: Emerson's New Metaphysics for the Listening Reader." In *Emerson Bicentennial Essays*, 86–114. Edited by Ronald A. Bosco and Joel Myerson. Boston: Massachusetts Historical Society, 2006.

Wiesenfeldt, Christiane. "Johannes Brahms im Briefwechsel mit Eduard Hanslick." In *Musik und Musikforschung: Johannes Brahms im Dialog mit der Geschichte*, 275–348. Edited by Wolfgang Sandberger and Christiane Wiesenfeldt. Kassel: Bärenreiter, 2007.

Wiesing, Lambert. "Formale Ästhetik nach Herbart und Zimmermann." In *Herbarts Kultursystem: Perspektiven der Transdisziplinarität im 19. Jahrhundert*, 283–96. Edited by Andreas Hoeschen and Lothar Schneider. Würzburg: Königshausen & Neumann, 2001.

Wilcox, John. "The Beginnings of l'Art pour l'Art." *JAAC* 11 (1952): 360–77.

Wilde, Oscar. "The True Function of Criticism." *The Nineteenth Century* 28 (1890): 123–47, 435–59.

Wildhagen, Christian. *Die Achte Symphonie von Gustav Mahler: Konzeption einer universalen Symphonik*. Frankfurt am Main: Peter Lang, 2000.

Will, Richard. *The Characteristic Symphony in the Age of Haydn and Beethoven*. Cambridge: Cambridge University Press, 2002.

Wille, Günther. *Akroasis: Der akustische Sinnesbereich in der griechischen Literatur bis zum Ende der klassischen Zeit*. 2 vols. Tübingen: Attempto, 2001.

Wilson, Blake McDowell. "*Ut oratoria musica* in the Writings of Renaissance Music Theorists." In *Festa Musicologica: Essays in Honor of George J. Buelow*, 341–68. Edited by Thomas J. Mathiesen and Benito V. Rivera. Stuyvesant, NY: Pendragon Press, 1995.

Winkler, Gerhard. J. "Der 'bestimmte Ausdruck': Zur Musikäshtetik der Neudeutschen Schule." In *Liszt und die Neudeutsche Schule*, 39–53. Edited by Detlef Altenburg. Laaber: Laaber-Verlag, 2006.

Winter, Eduard, ed. *Robert Zimmermanns philosophische Propädeutik und die Vorlagen aus der Wissenschaftslehre Bernard Bolzanos: Eine Dokumentation zur Geschichte des Denkens und der Erziehung in der Donaumonarchie*. Vienna: Österreichische Akademie der Wissenschaften, 1975.

Wiora, Walter. "Herders Ideen zur Geschichte der Musik." In *Im Geiste Herders*, 73–128. Edited by Erich Keyser. Kitzingen: Holzner, 1953.

——. "Zwischen absoluter und Programmusik." In *Festschrift Friedrich Blume zum 70. Geburtstag*, 381–88. Edited by Anna Amalie Abert and Wilhelm Pfannkuch. Kassel: Bärenreiter, 1963.

Wise, C. Stanley. "American Music is True Art, Says Stravinsky." *New York Tribune*, 16 January 1916, 3.

Wolff, Christoph. *Bach: Essays on His Life and Music.* Cambridge, MA: Harvard University Press, 1991.

Woodmansee, Martha. "The Interests in Disinterestedness: Karl Philipp Moritz and the Emergence of the Theory of Aesthetic Autonomy in Eighteenth-Century Germany." *Modern Language Quarterly* 45 (1984): 22–47.

Wörner, Felix. "Otakar Hostinský, the Musically Beautiful, and the *Gesamtkunstwerk.*" In *Rethinking Hanslick: Music, Formalism, and Expression*, 70–87. Edited by Nicole Grimes, Siobhán Donovan, and Wolfgang Marx. Rochester, NY: University of Rochester Press, 2013.

Worringer, Wilhelm. *Abstraktion und Einfühlung: Ein Beitrag zur Stilpsychologie.* Munich: Piper, 1908. Translated by Michael Bullock as *Abstraction and Empathy: A Contribution to the Psychology of Style.* New York: International Universities Press, 1953.

Wülfing, Wulf. *Schlagworte des Jungen Deutschland.* Berlin: Erich Schmidt, 1982.

Yearsley, David. *Bach and the Meanings of Counterpoint.* Cambridge: Cambridge University Press, 2002.

Youmans, Charles. *Richard Strauss's Orchestral Music and the German Intellectual Tradition: The Philosophical Roots of Musical Modernism.* Bloomington: Indiana University Press, 2005.

Zaminer, Frieder. "Über die Herkunft des Ausdrucks 'Musik verstehen.'" In *Musik und Verstehen: Aufsätze zur semiotischen Theorie, Ästhetik und Soziologie der musikalischen Rezeption*, 314–19. Edited by Peter Faltin and Hans-Peter Reinecke. Cologne: Arno Volk, 1973.

Zangwill, Nick. "Against Emotion: Hanslick was Right About Music." *British Journal of Aesthetics* 44 (2004): 29–43.

——. *The Metaphysics of Beauty.* Ithaca, NY: Cornell University Press, 2001.

Zarlino, Gioseffo. *Dimostrationi harmoniche.* Venice: Francesco dei Franceschi Senese, 1571; reprint, Ridgewood, NJ: Gregg Press, 1966.

——. *Le istitutione harmoniche.* Venice: [F. de Franceschi], 1558.

Zimmermann, Robert. "Abwehr." *Zeitschrift für exacte Philosophie im Sinne des neuern philosophischen Realismus* 4 (1864): 199–206.

——. *Aesthetik.* 2 vols. Vienna: Wilhelm Braumüller, 1858–65.

——. Review of Eduard Hanslick, *Vom Musikalisch-Schönen* (Leipzig, 1854). *Oesterreichische Blätter für Literatur und Kunst*, no. 47 (20 November 1854), 313–15.

——. "Die spekulative Aesthetik und die Kritik." *Oesterreichische Blätter für Literatur und Kunst*, no. 6 (6 February 1854), 37–40.

——. "Über den wissenschaftlichen Charakter und die philosophische Bedeutung Bernhard [sic] Bolzanos. Gastvortrag in der Sitzung vom 17. Oktober 1849." *Sitzungsberichte der kaiserlichen Akademie der Wissenschaften: Philosophisch-historische Classe. Jahrgang 1849*, 2. Abteilung, 163–74. Vienna: Hof- und Staatsdruckerei, 1849.

■ INDEX

Abbate, Carolyn, 16n, 30n
Abegg, Werner, 158n
Abert, Hermann, 47n
Abrams, M. H., 69n, 79n, 105n
"absolute" (term), 132–33, 135, 137,
     218, 268
Absolute, the, 135, 144, 145–46, 150
absolute art, 133, 135, 137, 177
absolute music, 1–2, 3, 5, 6, 7, 9, 11, 12–16,
     40, 106n, 111, 127, 128, 131–40,
     146, 153, 156, 187, 209, 211,
     212, 215–16, 219, 221, 227, 229,
     232, 234, 235, 236, 237, 241–49
     passim, 251, 253–54, 255, 259,
     261, 262–63, 264, 267, 268, 270,
     271, 273, 276, 280, 283, 285,
     287, 288–89, 292, 297, 298–99
  definitions, 1, 4, 13, 144, 248
  as regulative concept, 6, 16, 299
  as repertory, 13–14, 135, 136, 210,
     250–51, 253, 289, 297
absolute Musik (term), 131, 133, 135, 139,
     143, 144, 146n, 156n, 172n,
     216n, 232n, 234n, 236n, 241n,
     242n, 248n, 264n
absolute Tonkunst (term), 143, 144n, 146
abstract art & music, 2, 3, 13, 127, 250, 276,
     277, 278, 280, 281, 292, 293, 297
abstraction, 4, 10, 30, 34, 90, 135, 221, 250,
     271, 273, 277–78, 279n, 281,
     283, 291
acoustical figures. See Klangfiguren.
acoustics, 24, 69, 70, 94, 95, 98, 199, 200,
     207, 209, 245
Acquisto, Joseph, 283n
Addison, Joseph (1672–1719), 81
Adler, Guido (1855–1941), 172, 262
Adlung, Jakob (1699–1762), 94
Adorno, Theodor W. (1903–1969),
     198n, 271
Aeschylus, 10
aestheticism, 289–90

aesthetics, 3, 6, 9, 12, 15, 16, 23, 61, 70, 79,
     80, 81, 82, 84n, 88n, 98, 103,
     129, 137, 139, 148, 150, 151,
     156, 160, 162, 163–64, 174, 176,
     177, 181, 188, 191, 207, 212–13,
     214, 219, 220, 221, 226, 228,
     230, 232, 237, 243, 245, 250,
     268, 280, 282, 297, 298, 306,
     309, 313
aesthetics, musical, 1, 9, 13, 14, 16, 45, 79,
     84, 106, 108, 120, 125, 126, 141,
     150, 155, 161, 164, 171, 185,
     188–89, 196, 217n, 226, 238,
     241, 245, 268, 271, 282, 297,
     302, 305, 309, 311
Affektenlehre, 71, 168
agreeable, the, 82, 87, 88, 101, 105–106,
     150, 275
akroasis, 122
Alberti, Leon Battista (1404–1472), 82
Albertus Magnus (ca. 1206–1280), 38
Albrechtsberger, Johann Georg
     (1736–1809), 161
Alembert, Jean Leronde d'
     (1717–1783), 75–76
Alexander the Great (356–323 BCE), 21
Alleluia, 44, 45
Allgemeine musikalische Zeitung, 116,
     151, 170
Allgemeiner Deutscher Musikverein, 249
Altenburg, Detlef, 210n
Amalar of Metz, Archbishop of Lyon
     (d. ca. 850), 44
Ambros, August Wilhelm (1816–1876),
     159, 195n, 219, 220–22, 224,
     225, 244, 304, 305, 306, 312
Ambrose, Saint, Bishop of Milan
     (d. 397), 26, 29
Ammann, Peter J., 92n
Amphion, 19, 55, 198
analysis, musical, 3, 68, 262, 286, 287
anatomy, 94

Anaximander, 29
ancient/modern music (debate), 56–57, 60
Anderson, Robert Michael, 23n
Anderson, Warren D., 22n
André, Yves Marie (1675–1704), 84–85
anima, 148
antiquity, 9, 19, 31, 34, 47, 54, 55, 56, 59,
        70, 80, 92, 99, 289
anti-Semitism, 226–27
Apollo, 34–35, 106
Apollonius Rhodius (3rd cent. BCE), 10
Applegate, Celia, 287n
Aquinas, Thomas. *See* Thomas Aquinas.
arabesque(s), 165, 171, 221, 223, 230, 274
architecture, 82, 98, 165, 277, 278
Arion, 19, 55
Aristeus, 45–46
Aristides Quintilianus (3rd or 4th cent.), 23
Aristotelianism, 38, 53, 67n
Aristotle (384–322 BCE), 22, 23, 25, 29, 31,
        37, 38, 47, 54n, 55, 69, 81, 95, 107
Aristoxenus (b. ca. 375/360 BCE),
        31, 39, 49
arithmetic, 8, 10, 24, 25, 26, 31, 32, 39, 45,
        96. *See also* mathematics.
Arnim, Achim von (1781–1831), 163
art(s), 2, 3, 8, 11, 22, 69, 71, 72, 79, 82, 86,
        97, 98, 100, 103, 107, 109–10,
        116, 118, 119–21, 130, 133, 134,
        135, 137, 143, 145, 148, 150,
        154, 160–63, 165–67, 170, 180,
        184, 187, 193, 195, 204, 213,
        220, 224, 243, 248, 262, 263,
        264, 268, 272–73, 279, 280,
        293, 304. *See also* absolute art;
        abstract art; *and under* music.
    autonomy, 108–11, 135, 167, 180, 221,
        276, 298
    democratization, 109, 110
    history, 82, 156, 225, 262, 277
    socio-political aspects, 3, 109, 110, 111,
        129–31, 134, 135, 174, 182, 219,
        289–90, 297
art(s), fine, 11, 71, 79–80, 81, 86, 88, 89, 103,
        108, 118, 124, 151, 250, 268, 275
art(s), verbal, 127, 166, 282. *See also* drama;
        literature; poetry.
art(s), visual, 12–13, 87, 99, 103, 104, 118,
        165, 166, 195, 245, 248, 250,

271, 273, 279, 292. *See also*
        painting; sculpture.
art pour l'art, l' (ideology), 82, 110–111,
        134, 136, 289, 297
Artusi, Giovanni Maria (ca. 1540–1613),
        51–52, 58
"Aryan" (concept), 227
asceticism, 296
Asclepiades of Bithynia (130–40 BCE), 21
astronomy, 8, 26, 31, 39, 50, 91–92, 185
Athanasius, Saint, Patriarch of Alexandria
        (d. 373), 42, 43
atheism, 183
Athens (Greece), 26n, 131, 137, 177, 266
atonality, 271, 281
attention, 9, 81, 176
Auber, Daniel François Esprit
        (1782–1871), 153
audience(s), 41, 62, 65, 77, 149, 212, 216,
        285, 293, 297. *See also* listeners.
aufheben (verb), 133, 191, 196
Augustine, Saint, Bishop of Hippo
        (354–430), 22, 26, 42, 43–44,
        46, 93, 95, 102
Aurelian of Réôme (fl. mid 9th c.), 34
Aurier, Albert (1865–1892), 278
Austin, Larry, 296n
Austria, 158–59, 162, 270, 283
autobiography, 256, 263
autonomy (concept), 2, 3–4, 5, 6, 9, 11, 13,
        15, 40, 103, 106, 107, 108, 110,
        135, 176, 221, 250, 269, 287,
        289. *See also under* art; music.
avant-garde music, 262, 297

Bach, Carl Philipp Emanuel (1714–1788),
        68, 74, 170
Bach, Johann Sebastian (1685–1750), 1, 4,
        5, 21, 73, 93, 94, 100, 149, 154,
        157, 177, 178, 179, 229, 262,
        266, 281, 287
Bagge, Selmar (1823–1896), 225n, 230
Bailey, Walter B., 256n
Baillet de Latour, Theodor, Graf
        (1780–1848), 154
Bali Island (Indonensia), 267–68
Ballets Russes, 266
banality, 254–55
Bannelier, Charles (1840–1899), 313

Bardi, Giovanni de' (1534–1612),
    55–56, 127
Barker, Andrew, 23n, 32n, 47n
Bartel, Dietrich, 71n
Basel (Switzerland), 249
Basil, Saint, Bishop of Caesarea (ca.
    329–379), 21
basso continuo, 50, 60, 73
Batteux, Charles (1713–1780), 71–72,
    103–104
Bauer, Roger, 158n, 162n
Bauer-Lechner, Natalie (1858–1921), 294
Baumgarten, Alexander Gottlieb (1714–
    1762), 80, 83, 245
Bayer, Josef (1827–1910), 305
Beal, Amy, 297n
Beattie, James (1735–1803), 104–105
Beauquier, Charles (1833–1916),
    229–30, 310
beauty, 3, 8, 11, 22, 29, 40, 78, 79–87, 90,
    95, 98, 99, 100–101, 103, 108,
    111, 116–20, 124, 127, 141, 148,
    150, 160–169 *passim*, 176, 178,
    180, 181, 184, 186, 188, 189,
    190, 193, 195, 196, 203–204,
    205, 206, 207, 209, 224, 227,
    242, 243, 244, 245, 250, 259,
    267–69, 274, 289, 309, 315
    definitions, 82–83, 84, 120–21, 274,
        279, 315
    indifference of, 195–96
    moral aspects, 108–109
beauty, musical, 9, 64, 79, 84–85, 108, 112,
    123, 127, 141, 142, 143, 145, 157,
    168, 170, 176–78, 179, 181, 183,
    184, 185, 189–91, 193, 194, 204,
    205, 206, 207, 209, 213–14, 224,
    226–27, 228, 238, 292, 313, 315
beaux-arts. See arts, fine.
Becher, Alfred Julius (1803–1848),
    152–153
Becker, Carl Ferdinand (1804–1877), 124n
becoming (*das Werden*), 293, 294
Beethoven, Ludwig van (1770–1827), 15,
    112, 114, 116, 117, 134, 137,
    139, 153, 154, 157, 173, 177,
    178, 179–80, 182, 183, 212, 215,
    232, 235, 240, 242, 260–62, 263,
    264, 276, 284–85, 286, 288, 310

    early works, 6–7
    overtures, 204, 215, 225–226
    Quartet, strings, op. 59, no. 2: 293
    Quartet, strings, op. 132: 261
    Sonata, piano, op. 81a: 261
    symphonies, 117, 124, 183, 284, 290–91
        no. 3: 221, 287
        no. 5: 106n, 116, 136–37, 144,
           215, 221
        no. 6: 138, 143, 170, 179, 213,
           221, 260
        no. 9: 6, 7, 131–32, 133, 136, 137, 138,
           139, 178–79, 180, 212, 287, 293
    Wellingtons Sieg, 213
Behrens, Peter (1868–1940), 260
Beierwaltes, Werner, 95n
Beiser, Frederick, 96n, 97n, 192, 194n
Bekker, Paul (1882–1937), 261, 269
Bell, Clive (1881–1964), 271, 279–80
Bell-Villada, Gene H., 110–11
Bella, Ján Levoslav (1843–1936), 235
Bellaigue, Camille (1858–1930), 315
Bellini, Fermo (1804–1865), 170
Benjamin, Walter (1892–1940), 198n
Bennett, William Sterndale
    (1816–1875), 100n
Bensey, Rudolf, 310
Berg, Alban (1885–1935), 271
Berg, Darrell M., 74n
Berger, Karol, 23n, 52n, 56n
Berghahn, Klaus L., 105n
Berkeley, George (1685–1753), 81, 83
Berlin (Germany), 15n, 88n, 112, 232, 298
Berlioz, Hector (1803–1869), 1, 152–153,
    154, 171, 210, 212, 221, 242,
    249, 253, 285
Bernsdorf, Eduard (1825–1901), 172n
Bernstein, Jay M., 109n
Bible, 59, 215
    Genesis, 105
    Psalms, 42, 43–44, 59
    Wisdom 11:21, 95
    I Corinthians 13, 45, 47
    II Corinthians 12:2, 293
    Revelation, 233
Billroth, Theodor (1829–1894), 178
birdsong, 72, 142, 146, 147, 167, 169,
    179, 279
Birke, Joachim, 96n

Bischoff, Ludwig (1794–1867), 139–40, 222, 302, 307
Bitter, C. H., 68n
Blankenburg, Walter, 95n
Blanning, Timothy C. W., 109n
Blaue Reiter, Der, 280, 281
Blaukopf, Kurt, 159n, 162n
body, 101, 122
    and mind, 16, 22, 23, 30, 31, 32, 34, 42, 56, 70, 80, 82, 83, 90, 119, 149, 180, 192. *See also* spiritual/material.
Boethius, Anicius Manlius Severinus (ca. 480-ca. 524), 8, 25, 26, 32, 35, 36, 47, 48, 49, 92, 93
Boisits, Barbara, 159n, 162n
Bolzano, Bernard (1781–1848), 157, 158, 159, 160, 162
Bonaventure, Saint (ca. 1217–74), 29
Bonds, Mark Evan, 15n, 68n, 114n, 116n, 119n, 136n, 144n, 182n, 288n
Borchmeyer, Dieter, 131n, 135n
Bossuet, Jacques-Bénigne (1627–1704), 230
Botstein, Leon, 289n
Boulanger, Nadia (1887–1979), 265
Bourdieu, Pierre, 289n
Bower, Calvin, 34, 45n, 47
Bowie, Andrew, 62n, 112n, 113, 114n, 195n
Boyd, John, 105n
Bozarth, George S., 232n
Brahe, Tycho (1546–1601), 38
Brahms, Johannes (1833–1897), 173, 174–75, 178, 198, 231–32, 249, 256, 282n, 285
Brandt, Torsten, 223n
Breakspeare, Eustace J. (b. 1854), 313
Brendel, Franz (1811–1868), 130, 131, 151, 156, 165, 174, 179–80, 210, 212, 216, 219–20, 227, 232, 302, 304, 305, 306, 308
Brentano, Clemens (1778–1842), 163
Brittan, Francesca, 258n
Brodbeck, David, 232n
Brokoff, Jürgen, 284n
Brook Farm (community), 292
Bruchhagen, Paul, 145n
Bruckner, Anton (1824–1896), 254
Bruhn, Siglind, 92n, 296n

Buelow, George J., 71n
Bülow, Hans von (1830–1894), 235
Burbach, Hermann-Josef, 45n
Burke, Edmund (1729–1797), 81, 115
Burkert, Walter, 23n, 34n, 95n
Burmeister, Joachim (ca. 1564–1629), 54–55
Burne-Jones, Edward (1833–1898), 275
Busnoys, Antoine (ca. 1430–1492), 36
Busoni, Feruccio (1866–1924), 12, 264–265, 271, 286n
Butler, Christopher, 36n
Butler, E. M., 110n
Buxtehude, Dietrich (ca. 1637–1707), 228
Byzantium, 278

Caballero, Carlo, 247n
Caccini, Giulio (1551–1618), 57–58
cadences, 53, 54, 178
Cage, John (1912–1992), 296
Caneva, Kenneth L., 192, 194n
cantor (term), 34, 36
Carraud, Gaston, 254n
Carrière, Moriz (1817–1895), 195n, 224–25, 294, 306, 308
Carroll, Mark, 298n
Carter, Tim, 52n
Cassiodorus, Flavius Magnus Aurelius (ca. 490–526), 21
Cassirer, Ernest, 80n
Cassirer, Fritz (1871–1926), 261
Castiglione, Baldassarre, conte, (1478–1529), 77
Catholicism, 158
Central Intelligence Agency (U.S.), 297
Chabanon, Michel Paul Gui de (1730–1792), 63, 65
Chai, Leon, 290n
chamber music, 14, 289
chant. *See* plainchant.
Cheetham, Mark A., 279n, 292
Chladni, Ernst Florens Friedrich (1756–1827), 196–200, 201, 202, 205, 206
Chopin, Frédéric (1810–1849), 153
Christensen, Dan Charly, 203n
Christensen, Thomas, 97n
Christianity, 26, 29, 42, 59, 93, 213, 226, 288
chromaticism, 57, 173, 182, 262, 271

Chrysostom, Saint, Bishop of
    Constantinople (d. 407), 26
Chua, Daniel K. L., 6n, 15, 39n
Cicero, Marcus Tullius (106–43 BCE), 25,
    35, 54, 62, 65
Cigoli, Lodovico (1559–1613), 61n
circle (image), 84
"Classical" era (music) & classicism, 6,
    14–15, 177, 180, 181–82, 220,
    232, 235, 242, 266
Claudius Ptolemy. See Ptolemy.
Clement of Alexandria, Saint (ca. 150-ca.
    215), 26
Cloot, Julia, 123n
Code, David J., 253n
Coen, Deborah R., 159n
Cohen, Gustav, 8n, 190
Cold War, 3, 13, 297, 298
Collier, Jeremy (1650–1726), 37
color(s), 13, 72, 87, 123, 200, 217, 273, 274,
    275–76, 277, 279, 280, 290
Colvin, Sidney (1845–1927), 274
composers, 21, 41, 45, 50, 51–52, 55, 62,
    67–68, 76, 77, 114, 117, 136,
    142, 145, 153, 170, 171, 174,
    178, 210, 212, 213, 215, 220,
    235, 242, 249, 254, 256, 260,
    268, 269–270, 271, 276, 285,
    288, 289, 294, 295, 297, 298, 307
  biography, 115, 256, 263, 286n, 287
  as oracles, 112, 114–15, 116, 296
composition, 4, 41, 52, 58, 68, 142, 152–53,
    161, 177–78, 211, 213, 247, 262.
    See also serial composition.
concepts. See ideas.
concerts, 77, 109, 166, 279
concinnitas, 82
Condillac, Étienne Bonnot de
    (1715–1780), 63
Congress for Cultural Freedom, 297
consciousness, 113, 114, 119, 121,
    133, 145, 213, 217. See also
    self-consciousness.
conservatism & conservatives, 7, 95, 111,
    129, 135, 137, 139, 140, 173,
    219, 220, 222, 232, 248, 269,
    272, 285
consonance & dissonance, 29, 39, 46, 47n,
    52, 53, 58, 61, 67, 82

Constant, Benjamin (1767–1830), 110
contemplation & reflection, 9, 10, 22, 66,
    79, 80, 81, 82, 84, 85, 87, 88, 90,
    106, 108, 118, 119, 129, 142,
    166, 168, 188, 189, 245, 313
content, 88, 99, 101, 133, 141, 142, 148,
    170, 172, 180, 184, 186, 213, 215,
    218, 221, 223, 224, 245, 250, 251,
    261, 281, 282, 305, 307. See also
    meaning; subject matter; and
    under form.
Cook, Nicholas, 227n, 252n
Cooper, Anthony Ashley (1671–1713). See
    Shaftesbury.
Copernicus, Nicolaus (1473–1543), 38, 95
Copleston, Frederick Charles, 160n
Cor, Raphäel (b. 1882), 263–64
Corax of Syracuse (5th cent. BCE), 56
Corelli, Arcangelo (1653–1713), 104
Cornelius, Peter (1824–1874), 139, 214–16
Cornford, Francis Macdonald, 8n
cosmos, 8, 10, 25, 26, 30, 40, 56, 91, 121,
    122, 126, 143, 187, 290, 291,
    295. See also motions; universe;
    and under harmony; music.
Cotton, John. See Johannes Afflighemensis.
counterpoint, 4, 52, 55, 56–57, 125, 161,
    182, 216, 263, 286, 288
Couperin, François (1668–1733),
    73–74, 228
Cousin, Victor (1792–1867), 110
Craft, Robert, 258n, 267n
Cranefield, Paul F., 67n
Crete (Nebraska), 125n
critics & criticism, 2, 3, 7, 61, 109, 119, 121,
    132–33, 137, 149, 150, 152, 155,
    163, 164, 174, 211, 225, 230,
    237, 260, 268, 271, 272, 273,
    274, 284, 287, 289, 292, 294, 298
Crocker, Richard L., 25n, 47
Crumb, George (b. 1929), 296
Cudworth, Ralph (1617–1688), 29

Dahlhaus, Carl (1928–1989), 6n, 13–14,
    15, 185n, 244n, 298
Dalberg, Johann Friedrich Hugo von
    (1760–1812), 121
Dambeck, Johann Heinrich
    (1774–1820), 152

Damon of Athens, 21, 22n
dance, 76
Danz, Ernst-Joachim, 230n
Daston, Lorraine, 203n, 209
Daumer, Georg Friedrich (1800–1875), 309, 310
Daverio, John, 130n
David, King of Israel, 21, 22, 26, 55, 73
Davidsbund (Prague), 220, 305
Dayan, Peter, 276n
Deaville, James, 139n, 210n, 214n, 216n, 219n
Debussy, Claude (1862–1918), 253–54, 263–64
deformity, 84
Dehmel, Richard (1863–1920), 256–58
DeLapp-Birkett, Jennifer, 298n
delight. See pleasure.
Dell'Antonio, Andrew, 60n, 61, 77n-78n
democracy, 137, 177
Demodocus, 55
Denis, Maurice (1870–1943), 277
Descartes, René (1596–1650), 62, 70–71
desire, 81, 82, 97
Deutscher Werkbund, 260
Dickreiter, Michael, 92n
Diderot, Denis (1713–1784), 75, 78, 98
disclosiveness & disclosure, 11, 40, 65, 112, 113, 114, 116, 118–21, 127, 141, 145, 187–88, 238–39, 240, 250–51, 268, 290, 293, 294, 296
disinterestedness, 81, 296
dissonance. See consonance.
diversity, 298, 299
Dodds, E. R., 34n
Doempke, Gustav (1853–1923), 314
Dorn, Heinrich (1804–1892), 125n
Dowland, John (1563?-1626), 21
drama, 2, 57, 61, 64, 88, 127, 131, 182, 229, 240, 252, 271, 285
Dreyfus, Laurence, 5n
Dryden, John (1631–1700), 21
Dubos, Jean-Baptiste (1670–1742), 63
Dufour, Valérie, 266n
Dukas, Paul (1865–1935), 1, 2
Du Maurier, George, 270
Dümling, Albrecht, 257n
Duncan, David Allen, 62n
Dürer, Albrecht (1471–1528), 83

Dvořák, Antonín (1841–1904), 233–234
Dwight, John Sullivan (1813–1893), 100n, 292–93
Dyck, Martin, 123n
Dyer, Joseph Henry, 38
dynamics (music), 8, 54, 184

ear. See hearing.
Eckart, Ludwig (1827–1871), 309, 310
Eckersberg, Christoffer Wilhelm (1783–1853), 203
economics, 4–5, 15
Edler, Arnfried, 21n
Edwards, Warwick, 49n, 60n
Eggebrecht, Hans Heinrich, 118n
egoism, 110, 163
Egypt (ancient), 278
Ehrlich, Heinrich (1822–1899), 308–309, 314
Eichhorn, Andreas, 264n, 269n
Einfalt, Michael, 108n
Eisler, Hanns (1898–1962), 267
Eitelberger, Rudolf von (1817–1885), 156
electromagnetism, 201, 202
Elgar, Sir Edward (1857–1934), 247
Eliot, T. S. (1888–1965), 290
elitism, 216
Ellis, William Ashton (1852–1919), 2n
Elterlein, Ernst von. See Gottschald, Ernst.
Emerson, Ralph Waldo (1803–1882), 199, 292
emotion(s), 2, 5, 9, 16, 22, 23, 40, 41, 54, 57, 62, 63, 65–66, 69, 70, 71, 72, 76, 87, 90, 99, 101, 112, 113, 115, 119, 127, 131, 136, 141–42, 153, 157, 162, 166, 167, 168–69, 180, 189, 195, 215, 217, 222–23, 224, 225, 230, 231, 245, 251, 257, 259, 262, 263, 264, 265, 267, 269, 276, 278, 279, 280, 285, 291, 294, 304, 306, 308. See also feeling; passion.
emotivity, 278
Endell, August (1871–1925), 277
energetics, 252, 294
energy, 63, 64, 192, 193, 194, 195, 252
Engel, Johann Jakob (1741–1802), 62n
England, 15, 21, 242, 247, 260, 274, 275, 279, 285, 287, 289

Enlightenment, the, 11, 66, 73, 81, 82, 96n, 107

entertainment, 37, 82, 108, 130, 215

Epicureanism, 289

Epicurus (341–270 BCE), 29

epistemology, 10, 32, 40, 47, 80, 113, 136, 162, 188

Er, 25

Erben, Karel Jaromír (1811–1870), 234

Esposito, Joseph L., 195n

essentialism, 176–78, 183, 287

ethics. *See* morality.

ethnomusicology, 4, 298

Euclid (fl. ca. 300 BCE), 84

Eumenides, 106

Euridice, 19, 45–46

Euripides (ca. 485-ca. 406 BCE), 10

Exner, Franz Serafin (1802–1853), 159, 196

expression, 5, 6, 11, 40, 41, 43, 45, 48, 49, 50, 51–53, 57–58, 60, 61, 63, 65, 66, 67, 69, 75, 79, 82, 88, 90, 96, 97, 101–102, 103, 105, 112, 113, 119, 121, 124, 127, 131, 132, 136, 141, 148, 153, 154, 155, 156, 157, 161, 166, 167, 168, 170, 171, 180, 212, 213, 214, 215, 219, 222–23, 224, 227, 230, 234, 235–36, 242, 244, 246–47, 248, 250, 251, 260, 263–67, 273, 274, 279, 284, 293, 298, 302, 304, 305, 312, 314, 315

expressionism, 262

extramusical elements & ideas, 218, 220, 231, 259, 260, 266, 269

Faas, Ekbert, 296n

fall of man, the, 63, 131

fathers, church, 26, 43

Fauré, Gabriel (1845–1924), 247

Fechner, Gustav Theodor (1801–1887), 274

feeling(s), 9, 13, 45, 53, 63, 72, 101, 102, 113–14, 121, 122, 131, 136, 141, 150, 153, 154, 155, 156, 160, 161, 166, 167–68, 170, 184, 186, 207, 213, 215, 216, 219, 223, 224, 226, 243, 244, 251, 260, 273, 279, 283, 293, 312, 315. *See also* emotion; passion.

Fend, Michael, 93n

Feuerbach, Ludwig (1804–1872), 133, 134, 174

Fichte, Johann Gottlieb (1762–1814), 125, 163

Ficino, Marsilio (1433–1499), 11, 29, 50

fine art. *See* art, fine.

finite, the, 205

Fish, Stanley, 183

Florentine Camerata, 55, 56n, 58

Floros, Constantin, 173n, 232n, 247n, 253n

Flotzinger, Rudolf, 231n

Fludd, Robert (1574–1637), 25, 27, 28, 92

Fontenelle, Bernard Le Bovier de (1657–1757), 74–77, 78

Forbes, Elliot, 170n

force (physics), 194, 195, 196

Forkel, Johann Nicolaus (1749–1818), 68, 77–78, 86–87, 89, 96, 115, 146

form(s), 2, 11, 13, 40, 66, 71, 84, 90, 95, 98, 99–100, 102, 111, 112, 120, 121, 126, 127, 130, 139, 141, 143, 147–48, 149, 150, 152, 154, 159, 164, 165, 166, 168, 177, 181, 182, 190, 195, 204, 212n, 215, 219, 221–22, 223, 224, 229, 230, 235–36, 239, 242, 243, 244, 250, 251, 261, 264n, 265, 267, 268, 269–71, 274, 275, 278–79, 280, 282, 283–84, 285, 293, 308, 310, 311, 313, 315. See also *tönend bewegte Formen.*

and content, 2, 3, 98–99, 100, 143, 154–55, 162, 164–65, 167, 170–71, 172, 182, 223, 224, 225, 227, 245, 250, 269, 271–72, 273–74, 275–76, 277, 279, 282, 283, 305, 307, 310, 312

and material, 90, 99, 167, 193, 265, 272–73, 291, 292

pure, 1, 2, 3, 166, 167, 168, 179, 282, 291

formalism, 3, 90, 98, 100, 101, 111, 139, 150, 159n, 162, 167, 176, 179, 209, 210, 224, 242, 244, 249, 250, 261, 264n, 273, 278, 297, 303, 306, 315

Formen (term), 147–48, 165, 194

formlessness, 173, 269, 282

Foucault, Michel (1926–1984), 12, 113

France, 21, 74, 109, 110, 111, 134, 177, 228, 229–30, 247, 253, 254, 276n, 277, 283, 287, 288, 289

Franz Joseph I, Emperor of Austria (1830–1916), 159, 174
Frauenstädt, Julius (1813–1879), 239n
freedom, 99, 106, 121, 129–30, 135, 180, 181, 215, 297
French Revolution, 109, 110, 180
Friedman, John Block, 19n
Friedman, Michael, 192n
Frisch, Walter, 271n
Fröhlich, Joseph (1780–1862), 199n
Fry, Roger (1866–1934), 271, 280
Fuchs, Carl (1838–1922), 268–69, 311
fugue, 149–50, 161
Fuller, David, 73n

Galilei, Vincenzo (late 1520s-1591), 39, 56–57, 58–59, 60, 93, 127
Galileo (Galileo Galilei, 1564–1642), 38, 60–61, 95
Ganassi, Silvestro di (b. 1492), 59–60
Ganting, Ludwig von, 228, 312
Garratt, James, 102, 109n, 129n, 216n, 217n, 222n
Gärtner, Markus, 216n
Gauguin, Paul (1848–1903), 271, 277, 278
Gautier, Théophile (1811–1872), 111, 289
Gebauer, Gunter, 69n
Geck, Martin, 129n
Gehalt, 100, 151. See also substance.
Geist, 79, 82, 85–86, 88, 99, 101, 118, 120, 124, 125, 142, 143, 146, 147, 148–50, 157, 166, 167, 169, 179, 180, 181, 184, 190, 192, 219, 226, 292, 296n. See also spirit.
Gemüt (Gemüth), 97, 150–51, 168. See also psyche.
genius, 105, 114, 136, 242
geometry, 8, 26, 31, 95, 204, 278
George, Stefan (1868–1933), 271, 284n
Gerhard, Anselm, 14, 15
German language, 100, 144, 147, 148, 150, 190, 205n
German music, 107, 249, 284, 287–89. See also New German School.
Germany, 16, 21, 74, 110, 129, 132, 139, 149, 151, 154, 158, 192, 229, 233, 263n, 277, 287–88, 298, 303
Gerstenkorn, Franz, 223, 306

Gervinus, Georg Gottfried (1805–1871), 129, 217n
Gesamtkunstwerk, 137, 285
Gesner, Johann Matthias (1691–1761), 21
gesture, 54, 89, 104, 106, 131, 144, 289
Gilbert, Sir William S. (1836–1911), 270
Gill, André (1840–1885), 174
Gillespie, Susan, 271n
God, 22, 32, 44, 45, 59, 67, 81, 91, 92, 95–96, 97, 112, 133, 192, 264, 296
Goehr, Lydia, 5, 147n, 218n, 239–40
Goethe, Johann Wolfgang (1749–1832), 98, 100, 105, 111, 118, 148, 151, 154, 180, 193, 196, 200–201, 202, 203, 206, 230, 288
Goldbach, Christian (1690–1764), 96n
golden age (myth), 163
Goldschmidt, Hugo (1859–1920), 104n
good, the, 108, 109
Gooley, Dana, 149n
Gothic style, 165, 278
Gottschald, Ernst (b. 1826), 139n, 307
Gottsched, Johann Christoph (1700–1766), 95, 96
Gouk, Penelope, 25n, 62n
Gower, Barry, 192n
Gozza, Paolo, 70n
"great man" school, 179–180, 262
"Great Theory," 82, 83
Greece (ancient), 23, 26n, 35, 56, 57, 71, 122, 127, 131, 137, 177, 181
Grey, Thomas S., 12n, 129n, 131n, 135n, 173n, 238n
Griepenkerl, Wolfgang Robert (1810–1868), 221
Grillparzer, Franz (1791–1872), 113
Grimes, Nicole, 165n
Grimm, Ines, 152n, 159n, 170n
Grocheo, Johannes de (fl. ca. 1300), 47
Grunsky, Karl (1871–1943), 251, 294
Guido of Arezzo (ca. 991/2-after 1033), 34
Gumprecht, Otto, 172
Gur, Golan, 180n
Guthrie, W. K. C., 19n
Gutt, Bernhard (d. 1849), 152
Guyer, Paul, 80, 81n, 109

Halm, August (1869–1929), 252, 294
Hamann, Johann Georg (1730–1788), 113

Hammerschmidt, Andreas (1611 or
    12–1675), 21
Hand, Ferdinand Gotthelf (1786–1851),
    120–21, 123–24, 126, 157, 164,
    166–69, 170, 305, 306
Handel, George Frideric (1685–1759), 21,
    149, 154, 179, 217n
Hanslick, Eduard (1825–1904), 6–8,
    11–12, 15, 23, 36, 52, 82, 123n,
    124–25, 126, 127–28, 140, 146,
    147, 150, 152–56, 158n, 159–60,
    161–62, 164, 166, 167, 171,
    173–79, 195, 196, 200, 206, 208,
    210, 212, 216n, 217, 218, 226n,
    231, 233–34, 236, 237, 241, 243,
    244, 245, 247, 248, 251–52, 262,
    263, 268–69, 272, 280, 282, 284,
    285, 286, 292, 311, 314
  mean-spiritedness, 165, 168–69, 171,
    178, 203–205
  prose style, 187, 189n, 225, 301, 304,
    306, 312
  Aus mein Leben, 152, 154, 155, 159, 166,
    196, 237
  Vom Musikalisch-Schönen, 2, 3, 5, 8–9, 12,
    68–69, 79, 101, 108, 127, 128,
    139, 141–57, 159–61, 164–79,
    181, 183–91, 194, 195, 200,
    203–209, 210, 216n, 217n, 237–
    38, 240, 245, 251, 266–67, 273
    editions, 7, 144, 208
      first (1854), 9, 123n, 126, 141n,
        143, 151, 156, 184, 188, 189n,
        193n, 208, 209, 210n, 225n, 312
      second (1858), 145, 156, 157, 177,
        183, 184, 185, 186, 187, 188, 189n,
        207, 208, 209, 218, 245, 307, 309
      third (1865), 127, 183, 184, 185,
        194, 208, 209, 218, 310
      fourth (1874), 204n, 209n, 311–12
      fifth (1876), 208, 230n, 313
      sixth (1881), 108, 161, 189n, 193n,
        244, 314
      seventh (1885), 204n, 208, 314
      eighth (1891), 164n, 200n, 208
      ninth (1896), 208
      tenth (1901), 7
    ending, 9, 112, 143, 145–46, 151,
        183–88, 190–91, 193, 195–96,
        204, 205, 206, 208–209, 241,
        292, 302
    opening, 188, 207–208
    responses to, 7, 140, 148n, 159–60,
        178, 185–87, 190–91, 208, 210,
        219–31, 244–45, 251, 268,
        282, 301–15
    translations, 7, 8n, 229, 263n, 313
Hanslik, Joseph Adolf (1785–1859), 152
Hanuš, I. J. (1812–1869), 152n
Hardenberg, Friedrich von. See Novalis.
harmony, 10, 11, 22, 25, 26, 29, 32, 36, 37,
    49, 50–51, 55, 57, 59, 62, 64, 67,
    70, 85, 91, 93, 105, 106, 108–109,
    120, 123n, 125, 142, 162, 172,
    178, 198, 206, 216, 262, 270, 288
  cosmic, 11, 26, 29, 43, 56, 70, 124, 125,
    199–200, 276
  of the spheres, 25, 32, 47, 50n, 91–92, 96,
    123, 125, 191, 192, 199n
Harrán, Don, 49n
Hartmann, Eduard von (1842–1906), 315
Hasse, Johann Adolph (1699–1783), 21
Hausegger, Friedrich von (1837–1899),
    230–31, 232, 236, 237, 247, 294,
    311, 314
Hawkins, Sir John (1719–1789), 95–96
Haydn, Joseph (1732–1809), 6–7, 15,
    21, 112, 114, 116, 136, 139,
    143, 157, 161, 173, 179, 181,
    182, 213, 215, 242, 262, 269,
    286, 288
hearing, 4, 5, 8, 10, 30, 31, 32, 43, 58, 67, 70,
    93, 96, 122–23, 125, 127, 181,
    211. See also listening.
heart, 44, 62, 64, 76, 85, 86, 87, 102, 119,
    198, 215
Hebbel, Christian Friedrich, 249
Hebenstreit, Wilhelm (1774–1854), 162
Hefling, Stephen E., 246n
Hegel, Georg Wilhelm Friedrich (1770–
    1831), 88, 110n, 120, 125, 131,
    133, 134, 145, 148–49, 150, 157,
    158–59, 162, 163, 165, 170, 171,
    174, 180n, 189, 191, 198, 216,
    224, 305
Heidelberger, Michael, 192n
Heilmann, Anja, 26n
Heine, Heinrich (1797–1856), 22–23, 111

Heinse, Wilhelm (1746–1803),
    113, 121–22
Helmholtz, Hermann von (1821–1894),
    209, 245, 309
Heninger, S. K., Jr., 26n, 29n
Hennig, Carl Raphael (1845–1914), 237
Hentschel, Frank, 48n, 86n
Hepokoski, James, 15, 298n
Herbart, Johann Friedrich (1776–1841),
    157, 158–62, 164, 165, 192
Herder, Johann Gottfried (1744–1803),
    37n, 82, 83, 105, 106–107,
    113, 122–23
heroic, the, 117, 221, 241, 279
Hertz, David, 283n
Herzog, Patricia, 272n
Hesiod (8ᵗʰ cent. BCE), 55
Hessler, J. Ferdinand (1803–1865), 196
Heuss, Alfred (1877–1934), 282
Hindemith, Paul (1895–1963), 3,
    265, 295–96
Hinrichs, Friedrich (1820–1892), 138n
Hinrichsen, Henri (1868–1942), 255
Hinton, Stephen, 265n
Hirschbach, Herrmann
    (1812–1888), 182–83
history & historiography, 15–16, 136, 139,
    164, 177, 178, 183, 214, 215,
    216, 228, 287
Hoeschen, Andreas, 158n
Hoffmann, E. T. A. (1776–1822), 44, 106n,
    116, 119, 136, 144, 221
Hoffmann, Josef (1870–1956), 260
Hofmannsthal, Hugo von (1874–1929),
    271, 283–84
Holsinger, Bruce W., 30n, 42n
Holzbauer, Ignaz (1711–1783), 121
Homer, 19, 266
homophony, 50
Hooper, Giles, 16n
Hoplit. See Pohl, Richard.
Hostinský, Ottokar (1847–1910),
    243–44, 313
Hudson, Nicholas, 62n
Hueffer, Francis (1843–1889), 242–43
Hugh of Saint Victor (1096?-1141), 45
humanism, 10, 39, 48
humankind, 26, 93, 111, 125, 134, 135, 146,
    149, 150, 167, 169, 181, 184,
    246, 263, 264, 278, 294

Humboldt, Wilhelm von (1767–1835), 113
Hume, David (1711–1776), 81,
    83–84, 88–89
Hutcheson, Francis (1694–1746), 81, 109

I-Music/It-Music, 267
Iamblichus of Chalcis (ca. 250-ca.
    330), 34–35
Ibsen, Henrik (1828–1906), 233
idea(s), 2, 23, 40, 41, 63, 69, 87, 90, 115,
    120, 127, 131, 142, 145, 151,
    157, 168, 169, 181, 206, 214,
    215, 219, 239, 254, 277, 278,
    283, 306. See also poetic idea.
  musical, 68, 71, 142, 145, 172, 186, 191,
    256, 261, 281, 292–93, 295
ideal, the, 180, 213, 214
idealism, 11, 16, 31, 119n, 123, 136, 158,
    160, 195, 209, 213, 245, 251,
    296, 310, 315
images, 64, 93, 103, 153, 209, 210, 223, 277,
    306. See also sounding image.
imagination, 64, 77, 78, 79, 80, 104, 115,
    138, 142, 145, 165, 215, 220,
    226, 227, 272, 273. See also
    Phantasie.
imitation, 61, 62, 63, 64, 65, 69, 71–72,
    101–102, 104–105, 107, 195,
    248. See also mimesis.
immateriality, 294
immutability, 9, 10, 26, 38, 56, 83, 86, 90,
    96, 157, 183, 188, 207, 313
impersonality, 265–66, 267, 268
individualism, 129, 163, 297
ineffable, the, 100. See also under music.
infinite & infinity, 112, 115, 120, 121, 124,
    184, 187, 191, 205, 214, 285
Ingres, Jean-Auguste-Dominique
    (1780–1867), 111
Inman, Billie Andrew, 273n
inspiration, 73, 114, 116, 132, 173, 210,
    217, 235, 256, 259, 283
instinct, 65
intellect, 9, 22, 34, 36, 59, 97, 119, 148,
    150, 162, 213, 263, 272, 293. See
    also mind.
intervals, 8, 24, 25, 27, 28, 29, 30, 31, 39, 45,
    46, 48, 66, 92, 123, 295
Inwood, Michael, 191n
Isidore of Seville, Saint (ca. 599–636), 26

Isocrates (436–338 BCE), 56
isomorphic resonance, 30, 38, 39, 41, 45,
    47–48, 90, 96
Italy, 21, 287, 288
Ives, Charles (1874–1954), 296

Jacobsen, Anja Skaar, 203n, 204n
Jäger, Georg, 158n
Jahn, Otto (1813–1869), 222–23, 303
Jähnig, Dieter, 120n, 195n
Janik, Elizabeth, 298n
Jean Paul (Jean Paul Friedrich Richter,
    1763–1825), 123, 198
Jeitteles, Ignaz (1783–1843), 162
Jerome, Saint (ca. 347–420), 26, 59
Jews & Judaism, 26n, 29, 226–27, 311
Joachim, Joseph (1831–1907), 293
Johannes Afflighemensis (John Cotton, fl.
    ca. 1100), 41, 53–54
John, Alois (1860–1935), 241
Johnson, James H., 77n
Johnston, William M., 158n, 162n
Jommelli, Niccolò (1714–1774), 21
Joost-Gaugier, Christiane L., 26n
Jordan, William, 39n
Jost, Christa, 216n
Jost, Peter, 216n
Jubal, 26
jubilus, 44, 45
judgment, 80–81, 87, 88, 89
Jungmann, Joseph (1830–1885), 314
just intonation, 39

Kahlert, August (1807–1864), 125n,
    129–30, 146, 151, 171, 288
Kalbeck, Max, 232n
kaleidoscope, 142, 171, 204, 221, 223, 230
Kalliwoda, Johann Wenzel
    (1801–1866), 182n
Kaltenecker, Martin, 77n
Kandinsky, Wassily (1866–1944), 278, 280
Kannegiesser, K. L. (1781–1864), 205n
Kant, Immanuel (1724–1804), 15, 22, 23,
    36, 79, 80–81, 82, 83, 84, 87–88,
    100–101, 107, 109, 110, 120,
    148, 150, 152, 157, 158–59, 162,
    163, 171, 188, 192, 194, 224,
    245, 275
Kapp, Reinhard, 58n
Karlsruhe Music Festival (1853), 139

Karnes, Kevin, 159n, 162n, 262n
Katz, Ruth, 6n
Kayser, Hans (1891–1964), 122n, 295–96
Kennaway, James, 23n
Kennedy, George A., 54n
Kent, Charles, 71n
Kepler, Johannes (1571–1630), 25, 38,
    91–92, 96, 120, 295
Kerényi, Karl, 34n
Kircher, Athanasius (1601–1680), 24,
    25, 70, 95
Kirchmann, Julius Hermann von
    (1802–1884), 310
Kivy, Peter, 5, 117n, 187n
Klagenfurt (Austria), 155
Klangfiguren, 196–200, 201–202, 203,
    205
Klengel, Paul (1854–1935), 312
Knepler, Georg (1906–2003), 298
knowledge, 10, 26, 32, 34, 36, 38, 46, 80, 94,
    95, 115, 116, 133, 136. *See also*
    epistemology.
Knyt, Erinn E., 264n
Koch, Heinrich Christoph (1749–1816),
    107–108
Köhler, Louis (1820–1886), 138n
Köhler, Rafael, 165n, 252n
Kokoschka, Oskar (1886–1980), 280
Kossmaly, Carl (1812–1893), 308
Köstlin, Heinrich Adolf (1846–1907), 179,
    181–82, 227–28, 312
Köstlin, Karl Reinhold von (1819–1894),
    217n, 225, 226
Kralik, Richard (1852–1934), 252–53
Kramer, Lawrence, 44n, 112n
Krause, Karl Christian Friedrich (1781–
    1832), 125, 126, 146
Kraut, Richard, 69n
Kretschmann, Carl (1826–1897), 129
Kristeller, Paul Oskar, 69n
Kropfinger, Klaus, 240n
Krüger, Eduard (1807–1885), 117,
    178, 310
Kruschev, Nikita (1894–1971), 297
Kuh, Emil (1828–1876), 301
Kuhnau, Johann (1660–1722),
    73, 96
Kullak, Adolph (1823–1862), 224, 244,
    305, 306, 308
Kurth, Ernst (1886–1946), 252

Lafont, Cristina, 113n
Lalo, Édouard (1823–1892), 229
Lambert, Philip, 296n
Lamennais, Felicité Robert de
    (1782–1854), 213–14
Landerer, Christoph, 158n, 162n, 188n
Lange, Otto, 305
language, 7, 14, 19, 41, 43, 44, 45, 48,
    49–50, 53–54, 58, 60, 61–64, 65,
    71, 88, 89, 94, 106, 112–13, 114,
    125, 131, 132, 168, 223, 230,
    235, 239, 240, 268, 272, 283,
    293. See also text; words; and
    under music.
Larson, Steve, 252n
Lassus, Orlande de (1530 or
    32–1594), 54, 92
laudes musicae, 21
Laurencin, Ferdinand Peter, Graf von (1819–
    1890), 225–26, 244, 308, 309
Lazarus, Moritz (1824–1903), 159, 245,
    306–307
Leconte de Lisle, Charles Marie
    (1818–1894), 289
Leibniz, Gottfried Wilhelm (1646–1716),
    11, 95, 96–97, 121, 126, 162,
    291, 292, 304
Leighton, Frederick (1830–1896), 274
Leisinger, Ulrich, 95n, 97n
Lessing, Gotthold Ephraim (1729–1781),
    103, 105, 195n
Lessmann, Otto (1844–1918), 313, 314
Levinson, Jerrold, 5
Liebmann, Otto (1840–1912), 312
light, 116, 132, 154, 194, 199, 200–201,
    202, 205, 273
Lindsay, Sir Coutts, of Balcarres
    (1824–1913), 274–75
Linforth, Ivan M., 19n
Lippius, Johannes (1585–1612), 91
Lippman, Edward A., 22n, 25n, 69n, 104n,
    122n, 266n
listening & listeners, 5, 6, 23, 42, 69, 71,
    73, 74, 77–78, 88, 89, 93, 97,
    114–15, 122–23, 141, 142, 145,
    168, 176, 189, 190, 191, 213,
    214, 215, 248, 259, 261, 263,
    267, 268, 279–80, 285, 289, 293,
    304, 306, 313

Liszt, Franz (1811–1886), 7, 12, 23, 127,
    128, 130n, 134n, 137, 139, 151,
    155, 157, 173, 174, 208, 210–14,
    216, 219, 224, 225, 232, 235,
    240, 242, 248, 249, 253, 254,
    303, 304, 309
literature, 87, 88, 110n, 247, 271, 282
Lobe, Johann Christian (1797–1881),
    139n, 223–24, 307
Locher, Hubert, 274n, 275n
Locke, John (1632–1704), 63
Locke, Ralph P., 110n
Lockwood, Lewis, 170n
logic, 80, 116, 162, 235, 240, 286
Logier, Johann Bernhard (1777–1846),
    124n–25n
Lomnäs, Bonnie, 220n
Lomnäs, Erling, 220n
longing, 81, 136–37, 144, 169, 241, 251
Lorenz, Alfred (1868–1939), 270–271
Lotze, Hermann (1817–1881), 147–48,
    165, 192–93, 304, 311
Louis, Rudolf (1870–1914), 249
love, 71, 81, 215, 259, 276, 279, 291, 310
Lully, Jean-Baptiste (1632–1687), 21
Lundell, William, 256n
Luther, Martin (1483–1546), 93
Lynning, Kristine Hays, 203n, 204n
lyre, 19, 20, 106

Maaß, Johann Gebhard Ehrenreich
    (1766–1823), 100–101
Mace, Dean T., 62n, 70n
Mäckelmann, Michael, 255n
macrocosm. See microcosm.
madness, 116, 130
madrigal, 50, 52
Maeterlinck, Maurice (1862–1949), 258
Magee, Bryan, 238n
Mahler, Gustav (1860–1911), 237, 246–47,
    258, 280, 294–95
Maier, Franz Michael, 148n
Malek, James S., 103n, 106n
Mallarmé, Stéphane (1842–1898), 253,
    271, 283
Maltz, Diana, 290n
Maniates, Maria Rika, 74n
Mann, Thomas (1875–1955), 198n, 256
Mannheim (Germany), 121

Marais, Marin (1656–1728), 73
Marc, Franz (1880–1916), 280
Marcello, Benedetto (1686–1739), 68
Marchenkov, Vladimir L., 35n
Marpurg, Friedrich Wilhelm
 (1718–1795), 74
Marston, Nicholas, 286n
Marvick, Louis, 283n
Marx, Adolph Bernhard (1795–1866), 130,
 131n, 149, 221, 305
Marxism, 267
Mason, Laura, 109n
Mass (liturgy), 61
material & matter, 2, 24, 33, 67, 90, 98,
 99, 100, 120, 125, 151, 165,
 193, 194, 278, 293, 294. See also
 under form.
materialism, 309
mathematics, 14, 29, 31, 37, 38, 47, 48, 49,
 50, 53, 63, 66, 70, 72, 81, 91,
 93–94, 95, 96, 97, 100, 107, 123,
 126, 162, 204, 223, 306. See also
 arithmetic; geometry; number
Mathiesen, Thomas J., 25n, 31n
Mattheson, Johann (1681–1764), 66–68,
 94, 114, 170, 228n
Matthisson, Friedrich von (1761–1831), 99
May, Florence (1845–1923), 285
McClain, Ernest G., 8n
McClary, Susan, 4n, 13, 15, 16, 30n
McClatchie, Stephen, 271n
McColl, Sandra, 237, 253n
McCreless, Patrick, 55n
McKinnon, James W., 26n, 44n, 45n
McPhee, Colin (1900–1964), 267–68
McWilliam, Neil, 110n
meaning, 8, 41, 45, 49, 57, 63, 68, 72, 74,
 89, 90, 105, 161, 166, 171,
 184, 223, 292. See also content;
 subject matter.
Mehring, Frank, 296n
melismas, 44, 45
melody, 31, 36, 39, 41, 43, 45, 46, 52, 54, 60,
 62, 64, 71, 104, 105, 106, 107,
 117, 120, 135, 142, 145, 147,
 166, 172, 178, 203, 239, 240,
 241, 264, 270
melos, 10–11, 50
Mendel, Arthur, 296n

Mendelssohn, Felix (1809–1847), 100, 157,
 178, 226, 228, 229, 242, 284
Mendelssohn, Moses (1729–1786), 62n,
 63, 118
Mengelberg, Willem (1871–1951), 295
Menzel, Wolfgang (1798–1873), 223
Merriam, Alan P., 298n
Merrill, Linda, 275n, 276
Mersenne, Marin (1588–1648), 62–63,
 69, 206
Mersmann, Hans (1891–1971), 252, 261
Messing, Scott, 265n, 266n
metaphysics, 40, 67, 69, 117, 159, 160,
 187n, 191, 192, 193, 206, 207,
 227, 240, 254, 264, 269, 278,
 291, 292, 293, 296
Metastasio, Pietro (1698–1782), 222n
Meyer-Baer, Kathi, 59n
Meyerbeer, Giacomo (1791–1864),
 153, 226
Michaelis, Christian Friedrich
 (1770–1834), 101–102,
 116, 170
microcosm/macrocosm, 9, 25, 26, 28, 43,
 46, 47, 90, 92, 93, 201n, 291. See
 also isomorphic resonance.
Micznik, Vera, 210n, 246n
Middle Ages, 8, 21, 26, 29, 31, 34, 38, 41,
 45, 47, 49
Mies van der Rohe, Ludwig
 (1886–1969), 260
Mildenburg, Anna von (1872–1947), 295n
mimesis, 69, 71–75, 78, 103–105. See also
 imitation.
mind, 8, 10, 23, 30, 31, 40, 42, 44–45, 54,
 67, 69, 75, 79, 80, 82, 84, 85, 87,
 90, 92, 96–97, 105, 119, 122–23,
 125, 142n, 143, 146, 148, 150,
 181, 313. See also intellect; and
 under body.
Minturno, Antonio, Bishop of Crotona
 (d. ca. 1574), 35–36
Mizler, Lorenz Christoph (1711–1778),
 93–94, 95
moderation, 65, 91
modernism, 3, 12, 14, 236, 260, 269,
 271–72, 282, 283
modes (music), 35, 41, 42–43, 45, 71
monochord, 27, 28, 67, 96, 122

monody, 60
monophony, 39
monotheism, 29
Montesquieu, Charles de Secondat, baron
    de (1689–1755), 230
Monteverdi, Claudio (1567–1643), 50,
    51–52, 57, 58, 60
Monteverdi, Giulio Cesare (1573–1630 or
    31), 52, 60
mood(s), 224, 235, 305
Moore, Albert (1841–1893), 274, 275
Moos, Paul, 237n
morality, 81, 98, 109, 110, 111, 257,
    289–90. See also under music.
Morgan, David, 277n
Moritz, Karl Philipp (1756–1793), 118
Morrow, Mary Sue, 74n
Moses, 29
motet, 54, 61, 92
motion & movement, 31, 36, 48, 59, 66, 69,
    70, 105, 120, 124, 125, 126, 164,
    166, 167, 172, 192, 193–95, 205,
    206, 230, 245, 251, 252, 293,
    294, 309. See also tönend bewegte
    Formen.
"motions of the cosmos," 8, 9, 92, 104, 120,
    124, 126, 184, 185, 187, 191,
    193, 206, 228, 294, 303
Motte-Haber, Helga de la, 296n
Moyer, Ann E., 25n
Mozart, Wolfgang Amadeus (1756–1791),
    1, 4–5, 6–7, 15, 21, 114, 116,
    136, 154, 157, 173, 177, 178,
    179–80, 182, 204, 215, 216, 221,
    242, 262, 266, 269, 286, 288
Muchanoff, Marie, 226n
Mueller-Vollmer, Kurt, 113n
Müller, Wilhelm Christian
    (1752–1831), 150–51
Mundt, Theodor (1808–1861), 125–26,
    146, 176
muses, 36, 106, 116
music, 14–15, 26, 31, 34, 36, 41, 43, 49, 53,
    77, 78, 79, 89, 90, 91, 93–94, 96,
    97, 98–99, 112–14, 119, 125, 131,
    146, 149, 152, 153–54, 166, 196,
    220, 239, 273, 292–93. See also
    absolute music; program music.
 "applied," 107, 108, 171

and other arts, 2, 3, 8, 9, 40, 88, 98–100, 102,
    103, 106, 107, 114, 126, 127, 144,
    148, 165, 167, 172, 179, 182, 183,
    188, 190, 229, 231, 234, 238, 239,
    241, 243–44, 246–47, 250, 251, 271,
    272–73, 274, 275, 277, 280, 284, 294
autonomy, 1, 2, 7, 11, 14, 15, 40, 102,
    104–11, 112, 125, 127, 134, 139,
    141, 142, 144, 145, 149, 152,
    154, 157, 166, 171, 176, 182,
    183, 187, 190, 208, 209, 221,
    222, 224, 229, 241, 245, 250,
    259, 260, 261, 264, 281, 284,
    289, 292, 297, 298–99, 310
context, 4–5, 16, 177, 229, 287, 289, 298
cosmic aspects, 8, 9, 10, 25, 30, 34, 35, 37,
    43, 48, 53, 93n, 98, 120, 121–26,
    143, 184, 185, 193, 208, 228,
    241, 290, 294–95, 296. See also
    isomorphic resonance.
danger of, 3, 21–22, 36–37, 42
definitions, 1, 67, 93, 96, 120, 152, 166,
    169, 170, 181, 291, 292
essence & effect, 1, 6, 7, 8, 9–10, 11–12, 16,
    17, 30, 31, 34, 35, 38, 39–40, 41,
    42, 45, 46, 47, 48, 52, 53, 57, 58,
    61, 63, 66, 71, 82, 88, 90, 92–93,
    94, 96, 99–100, 101, 102, 108,
    125n, 126, 127–28, 140, 141–42,
    143, 144–45, 150, 155, 156, 160,
    161, 164, 166, 168, 170, 171, 176,
    181, 183, 189–90, 194, 195, 199n,
    205, 212, 213, 215, 221, 223, 225,
    232, 237, 239, 240, 244, 245, 250,
    252, 266–67, 268, 281, 287, 290,
    294, 299, 303, 307
ethical/moral aspects, 22, 36, 42–43, 47,
    59, 67, 103, 297
history, 7, 131, 136, 155, 178, 179, 181, 182,
    185, 227–28, 238, 262, 288, 312
ineffability, 44, 45, 46, 47
as language, 7, 41, 55, 60, 61–64, 66,
    68–69, 71, 72, 73, 75, 76, 77,
    85, 87, 106, 112–14, 136, 139,
    168, 214, 223, 229, 235, 286,
    288, 289, 294, 298
and number, 8, 23, 29, 31, 39, 46, 47,
    48, 50, 56, 66, 90, 91, 122, 126,
    291–92, 295. See also sounding
    number.

power of, 11, 19, 21, 23, 30, 37, 39, 40,
    41–42, 45, 47, 48, 65, 66, 70, 96,
    97, 106, 144, 145, 149, 226, 242,
    244, 251, 284
pure/purity, 4, 7–8, 12, 14, 15, 45, 102,
    107–108, 122, 125, 126, 128,
    146, 154, 164, 171–72, 180, 217,
    218, 223, 224, 229, 230, 231, 234,
    241, 247, 253–54, 256, 257, 258,
    259, 263, 265–66, 276, 284, 287,
    289, 293. *See also* absolute music.
socio-political aspects, 3, 15, 16, 21–22,
    103, 109, 111, 127, 131, 134, 135,
    174, 176, 177, 179, 182, 183, 229,
    289, 297–298
music, instrumental, 1, 2, 6, 12, 13, 14–15,
    20, 32, 44, 57, 58–62, 65, 66,
    67–68, 71–78, 87–89, 101, 103,
    107, 112–13, 114, 115, 116, 120,
    126, 127, 128, 131–32, 134,
    135, 136, 138, 139, 140, 141–42,
    143–45, 146, 148, 149, 153, 157,
    164–68, 171, 172, 178, 181–82,
    210, 212–18, 222, 224, 225, 227,
    228, 229, 230, 231, 238, 239, 240,
    243, 248, 251, 261, 269, 273, 279,
    284, 285, 287, 288, 289, 290
    autonomy, 65, 105–106, 117, 164, 200, 287
music, vocal, 7, 57, 58, 59–60, 61, 65, 67, 71, 76,
    107, 134–35, 138, 140, 143, 144, 164,
    166, 239, 243, 251, 284, 287, 288
"music itself," 3–4
"Music of the Future," 7, 139, 151, 156–57, 173,
    177, 208, 213, 214, 243, 269, 284
musica (term), 34
Musica enchiriadis (treatise), 45–47, 53
musica humana, 32, 33, 48, 50, 67, 92,
    121, 295
musica instrumentalis, 32, 33, 48, 92, 295
musica mundana, 32, 33, 48, 50, 67, 92, 295
musica pathetica, 70
"Musical Left," 174
musicians. *See* performers.
musicology, 162n, 244, 262, 298
musicus (term), 34, 36
mythology, 19, 23, 25, 215

Nägeli, Hans Georg (1773–1836), 117,
    157, 164–65, 167, 168, 196,
    199–200, 206

Napoleon I, Emperor of the French
    (1769–1821), 221
nationalism, 287–89, 297, 311
Nattiez, Jean-Jacques, 3
nature, 8, 36, 59, 63, 65, 71, 72, 92, 105, 107,
    118, 120, 123, 124, 125, 134, 139,
    142–43, 146, 149, 166, 167, 169,
    172, 184, 185, 192, 193, 194, 195,
    200, 204, 230, 245, 252, 257, 277,
    290, 294, 304, 309
    laws of, 37, 95, 96, 186, 192, 193, 196,
    201, 203, 205–206, 207, 209,
    213, 302, 303
Naturphilosophie, 191–93, 194, 195, 196,
    200, 201, 207, 208, 209
Naumann, Emil (1827–1888), 229, 284
Nehamas, Alexander, 81n, 268n
Neoplatonism, 31, 34, 69
Neubauer, John, 14–15, 107n, 122n
Neue Zeitschrift für Musik, 129, 151, 165,
    174, 210, 217, 219, 225n, 232
New German School, 135, 151, 232, 235,
    249, 252, 280, 282, 286, 289, 314
"New Objectivity," 3, 250, 262
Newcomb, Anthony, 298n
Newmann, Ernest (1868–1959), 243, 247n
Newton, Sir Isaac (1642–1727), 123, 194
Nichols, Roger David Edward, 254n
Nicomachus of Gerasa (2nd cent.), 23
Nielsen, Keld, 201n
Nietzsche, Friedrich (1844–1900), 198n,
    233, 268, 296
noise, 74, 75, 248
Nolan, Catherine, 29n
notation, 71
noumenal, 199, 204, 242
Nouvel, Walter (1871–1949), 266
Novalis (Friedrich von Hardenberg, 1772–
    1801), 15, 123, 196, 198n, 282
novelty, 117, 134, 213, 252. *See also*
    originality.
number, 8, 10, 11, 23–24, 25, 26, 29, 30, 31–
    32, 35–36, 39–40, 46, 47, 53, 55,
    56, 58, 60, 82, 93, 95–96, 97, 122,
    291, 295. *See also under* music.

objective philosophy, 141, 162, 163, 188
objectivity, 88, 148, 156, 163, 219,
    246, 262–63, 264, 265, 266,
    286n, 313

obscurity, 115, 116, 117, 151
Ockeghem, Johannes (ca. 1410–1497), 36
Odysseus, 19, 37, 43
Oesterle, Günter, 165n
Offenbach, Jacques (1819–1880), 226
Oja, Carol J., 268n
O'Meara, Dominic J., 35n
opera, 1, 57, 64, 77, 107, 134, 146, 153, 155,
        171–72, 177, 287, 302
oracles, 114, 116. See also under composers.
oration & orators, 11, 50–51, 54, 55, 57, 62,
        65, 67, 72, 74, 78, 89, 114–15.
        See also rhetoric.
orchestra, 64, 84, 125, 211, 262, 294
orchestration, 149, 216
Orcus, 106
originality, 105, 172, 252, 264, 282, 283,
        287, 303. See also novelty.
Orpheus, 10, 17, 19–21, 22, 23, 30, 34–36,
        37, 45–46, 55, 57, 58, 70, 106,
        198, 199, 217
Orpheus, New, 21, 36
Ørsted, Hans Christian (1777–1851), 196,
        201–206, 209
Ortega y Gasset, José (1883–1955),
        263, 264
Ossi, Massimo, 52n
Österreichische Blätter für Literatur und
        Kunst, 155–56
Ostrolenka, Battle of, 153
Oulibicheff, Alexandre (1794–1858),
        171–72, 183
overtone series, 295
Ovid (Publius Ovidius Nasso, 43 BCE-17
        or 18 CE), 10, 19
Ozouf, Mona, 109n

painting(s), 2, 3, 13, 60, 71, 72, 88, 98, 105,
        115, 120, 176, 211, 217, 231,
        242, 247, 250, 259, 271, 272,
        273, 274, 275–77, 278, 280, 292
Palestrina, Giovanni Pierluigi da (1525?-
        1594), 138, 178
Palisca, Claude V., 25n, 39n, 48n, 49, 52n,
        54n, 55n, 56n
Pan, 106
Panofsky, Erwin, 61n
parallel fifths, 207
Parmer, Dillon, 232n

"Partant pour la Syrie" (song), 276
passion(s), 2, 31, 37, 53, 54, 60, 61, 62, 63,
        65, 67, 69, 70, 71, 75, 77, 81, 97,
        101, 102, 115, 124, 154, 170,
        215, 241, 242, 283, 291. See also
        emotion.
Pater, Walter (1839–1904), 3, 271–72, 280,
        289, 290
pathology/"pathological," 22–23, 36, 87,
        102, 142, 167, 263, 310
Paul, Saint (apostle), 45, 47, 293
Pavlov, Ivan Petrovich (1849–1936), 71
Payne, E. F. J., 291n
Payzant, Geoffrey, 8n, 147n, 161n, 164n,
        168, 185n, 189n, 190, 200n,
        207n, 251n
Pederson, Sanna, 1n, 14n, 129n, 146n, 287n
Pelosi, Francesco, 8n
perception, 26, 70, 80–81, 84, 85, 88–89,
        106, 112, 113, 120–21, 122, 133,
        142, 164, 165, 176, 189, 206,
        245, 269, 272, 280, 315
performance, 4, 142, 164, 281, 285–86, 287,
        293. See also concerts.
performers, 17, 32, 50, 60, 77, 94, 170, 176,
        248, 261, 285, 298, 313
Peri, Jacopo (1561–1633), 57
periodicals, 115, 116
Pesic, Peter, 92n
Peters, C. F. (firm), 255
Phantasie, 79, 102n, 142, 145n, 165, 191,
        226n, 227, 291n, 309. See also
        imagination.
Phidias (ca. 500-ca. 430 BCE), 266
philosophy & philosophers, 2, 5, 7, 10, 15,
        17, 35, 40, 49, 61, 83, 84, 98,
        100, 101, 104, 113, 116, 118,
        119, 120, 121, 125, 129, 135,
        139, 144, 151, 152, 153–54, 157,
        158, 159, 160, 162, 163, 164,
        165, 166, 171, 185, 188, 191,
        206, 219, 220, 222, 224, 225,
        226, 230, 238, 239–40, 247, 254,
        263n, 268, 274, 291, 292, 303
physics, 69, 70, 91, 95, 191, 192, 194, 206
physiology, 69, 70–71, 142, 245, 268
Pico della Mirandola, Giovanni
        (1463–1494), 29, 35
Pindar (522?-443 BCE), 10, 19, 55

pitch(es), 25, 31, 36, 48, 54, 55, 58, 91, 204
plainchant, 39, 41, 44, 45, 47, 53
Planche, Gustave (1808–1857), 110
planets, 25, 50, 91, 193, 206, 228, 295
Plato (427?-347 BCE), 3, 8, 10–11, 21, 23,
    25, 26, 31, 36, 38, 41, 42, 50,
    55, 58, 59, 69, 81, 91, 93, 95,
    116, 242
Platonism, 203, 296. *See also*
    Pythagorean-Platonic cosmos.
pleasure & delight, 22, 29, 36, 37, 42, 43,
    58–59, 64, 66, 70, 72, 75, 81, 82,
    84, 85, 86, 87, 94, 96–97, 98,
    101–102, 103, 104, 106, 114, 118,
    123, 124, 125, 127, 130, 149, 150,
    167, 185, 189, 194, 205, 224, 245,
    263, 268–69, 293, 296, 309
Plutarch (ca. 45–120), 23, 30
Plutarch (pseudo), 48
Podro, Michael Isaac, 158n
Poesie, 151, 213, 220
poet-musician(s), 19, 55, 229, 261
poetic idea, 143, 180, 210, 211, 213, 215,
    234–35, 242, 248, 256, 261, 272
poetry & poets, 2, 12, 19, 49, 50, 55, 57, 64,
    65, 67, 71, 73, 80, 88, 96n, 98,
    99, 105, 107, 110, 116, 118, 131,
    144, 145, 152, 180, 182, 214,
    217, 231, 240, 248, 271, 272–73,
    282–83, 284n, 285, 288
Pohl, Richard (1826–1896), 138–39, 140,
    210n, 212n, 216n
polarization, 194, 231, 237, 312
politics, 3, 15, 111, 129–130, 134, 135, 153,
    154, 163, 164, 173, 177, 179,
    180, 267, 297. *See also under* art;
    music.
polyphony, 32, 39, 50, 138, 149, 294
Porphyrius (ca. 234-ca. 305), 31n
postmodernism, 44n, 298
Potter, Pamela, 287n
Powers, Harold S., 53n
Prague, 125, 150, 152, 159, 162, 163,
    171, 185, 196, 220, 225, 243,
    257n, 305
Prettejohn, Elizabeth, 111n, 268n, 274n,
    276n, 290n
Prihonsky, Franz (1788–1859), 158
prima pratica, 52

Printz, Felix, 164n, 185n
Pritchard, Matthew, 252n, 261n, 286n
program music, 1, 12, 40, 73–74, 104, 107,
    127, 128, 134, 144, 152–53, 155,
    157, 172, 173, 179, 210–18, 219,
    224, 228–39 *passim*, 244–49,
    251, 253, 255–56, 258–61, 270,
    280, 284, 285, 286, 298
progressives, 7, 129, 135, 140, 182, 219,
    220, 249, 253, 269
Prometheus, 112, 114, 217
proportion(s), 10, 25, 26, 27, 28, 30, 34, 38,
    43, 66, 72, 82, 83, 85, 91, 93, 95,
    97, 98, 108, 295. *See also* ratios.
propriety, 85
Protestantism, 158, 165, 181
Proudhon, Pierre-Joseph (1809–1865),
    134
psyche, 150, 184, 189, 288. See also *Gemüt*.
Psalms. *See under* Bible.
psychologism, 266
psychology, 142, 245
Ptolemy, Claudius (after 83–161), 23, 25,
    31–32, 49
Puchberg, Michael, 4–5
Purcell, Henry (1659–1695), 21
purity, 3–4, 6, 12, 120, 128, 154, 166, 183,
    243, 249, 250, 262–63, 264,
    265–66, 267, 279n, 280, 284,
    285, 287, 292, 297, 298, 299. *See
    also under* music.
Puttfarken, Thomas, 274n
Pythagoras, 7, 10, 16, 17, 23–24, 26, 29, 30,
    34–36, 42–43, 55, 66, 70, 82, 93,
    95, 98, 120, 122, 142, 291
Pythagorean-Platonic cosmos, 26, 29,
    37–38, 39, 42, 48, 93
Pythagoreanism, 8, 9, 11, 14, 24–26, 29,
    30, 31, 39, 47, 49, 66–67, 90, 91,
    93, 94, 96, 97, 98, 121, 125, 126,
    196, 290, 291, 296

quadrivium, 8, 26, 32, 53
Quantz, Johann Joachim (1697–1773), 68
Quintilian (Marcus Fabius Quintilianus, ca.
    35-ca. 100), 35, 54, 62, 65

Raff, Joachim (1822–1882), 138, 139, 156, 288
Raftery, Paul K., 45n

Rameau, Jean-Philippe (1683–1764), 11, 21, 52, 97, 170
Rampley, Matthew, 156n
Raphael (Raffaello Sanzio, 1483–1520), 274
rationalism, 70
ratios, 8, 24, 29, 30, 31, 36, 39, 45, 46, 47, 49, 92. *See also* proportions.
realism, 129, 135, 209, 222, 263, 274, 302, 305, 306, 308, 309
reason & rationality, 16, 22, 23, 30, 37, 39, 42, 43, 48, 49, 53, 58, 59, 65, 80, 82, 83, 85, 86, 93, 96, 97, 114, 116, 167, 181, 192, 204, 206, 209, 222, 226, 240, 248, 272
recitative, 50, 60
Reckow, Fritz, 45n, 149n
reflection. *See* contemplation.
Reid, Thomas (1710–1796), 230
reification, 13–14, 291
reine Musik. See music: pure.
Reinhold, Karl (1758–1823), 101
Reiss, Timothy J., 95n
relationship. *See* proportion.
religion, 29, 111, 153–54, 163, 169
Renaissance, the, 21, 26n, 29, 35, 49, 54, 92n
representation, 2, 13, 61, 69, 71–72, 75, 96, 101, 102, 134, 138, 142, 154, 166, 186, 188, 212, 213, 215, 234, 244, 245, 248, 251, 254, 271, 274, 275, 277, 278, 279, 280, 281. *See also* content; expression; imitation.
revelation, 45, 114, 117, 123, 126, 146, 181, 193, 240
revolution, 3, 164
Revolutions of 1848–49, 3, 129, 130, 153, 154, 158, 173, 183, 216, 225, 288, 308
Reynolds, Sir Joshua (1723–1792), 107
rhetoric, 49, 53–55, 56, 65, 68, 71, 72, 100, 114, 122
rhythm, 8, 11, 36, 42, 48, 50–51, 55, 58, 59, 62, 64, 69, 70, 71, 120, 142, 168, 184, 203, 204, 264, 268, 270
Richter, Jean Paul Friedrich. *See* Jean Paul.
Richter, Sandra, 269n

Riedel, Friedrich Justus (1742–1785), 104
Riedweg, Christoph, 23n, 34n
Riemann, Hugo (1849–1919), 6n, 234, 244, 248, 313
Riezler, Walter (1878–1965), 260–61
Riley, Matthew, 77n
Rimsky-Korsakov, Nikolay (1844–1908), 258
Ritter, Alexander (1833–1896), 227
Ritter, Johann Wilhelm (1776–1810), 197–98
Robin, William, 259n
Robinson, Jenefer, 5
Rochlitz, Friedrich (1769–1842), 116, 288n
romanticism, 15, 16, 61, 116, 119, 121, 129, 139, 154, 163, 177, 232, 263, 267, 279, 282
Romberg, Bernhard (1767–1841), 21
Rossini, Gioachino (1792–1868), 125, 135, 177, 239
Rothfarb, Lee, 252
Rothstein, Edward, 29n
Rousseau, Jean-Jacques (1712–1788), 52, 63, 64, 74–76, 131, 146, 171
Rousseau, Pascal, 200n
Rudolph, Archduke of Austria (1788–1831), 117n
Ruge, Arnold (1802–1880), 129
Ruskin, John (1819–1900), 274–75

Sachs, Joel, 282n
Saint-Simonian movement, 110, 134
Santayana, George (1863–1952), 269, 277
Saul, King of Israel, 21, 22
Sayn-Wittgenstein, Caroline zu (1819–1887), 210n
scale(s), 29, 30, 123, 245
Scarlatti, Domenico (1685–1757), 154
Schäffer, Julius (1823–1902), 308
Schäfke, Rudolf, 158n, 185n, 230n, 252
Schawelka, Karl, 276n
Schelling, Friedrich Wilhelm Joseph (1775–1854), 119–120, 125, 133, 134, 163, 193, 194, 195–96, 209
Schenker, Heinrich (1868–1935), 252, 285–87, 289
Schiller, Friedrich (1759–1805), 15, 81, 98–100, 101, 102, 119, 195n, 200, 201, 212n, 287

Schilling, Gustav (1805–1880), 124–25, 126, 150, 171
Schladebach, Julius (1810–1872), 172, 303
Schlegel, August Wilhelm (1767–1845), 15, 104n, 118
Schlegel, Friedrich (1772–1829), 15, 104n, 113
Schlegel, Johann Adolf (1721–1793), 103, 104n
Schlegel, Johann Elias (1719–1749), 104n
Schleiermacher, Friedrich Daniel Ernst (1768–1834), 113
Schloezer, Boris de (1881–1969), 266
Schlüter, Joseph, 227, 309
Schmalfeldt, Janet, 293n
Schmelz, Peter J., 297n, 298n
Schmidt, Julian (1818–1886), 117
Schmidt, Lothar, 101n, 165n
Schmitz, Eugen (1882–1959), 251–52
Schmusch, Rainer, 210n
Schneider, Lothar, 158n, 217n, 244n
Schneider, Paul, 243, 315
Schoenberg, Arnold (1874–1951), 3, 12, 237, 253, 254–58, 267, 271, 280–81, 282n, 295
Scholar, Richard, 83n
Schopenhauer, Arthur (1788–1860), 125, 198, 208, 213, 217, 238–43, 246, 251, 268, 284, 290–92, 296, 311, 315
Schubart, Christian Friedrich Daniel (1739–1791), 123, 126
Schubert, Franz Peter (1797–1828), 153, 281
Schueller, Herbert M., 103n
Schuh, Willi, 235n, 236n, 247n
Schumann, Clara (1819–1896), 175
Schumann, Robert (1810–1856), 108, 130, 177, 178, 182, 198, 212, 228, 242, 258
Schütz, Heinrich (1585–1672), 178
Schweitzer, Albert (1875–1965), 229
science(s), 10, 37, 38, 95, 97, 98, 106, 192, 201, 206, 207, 265
Scruton, Roger, 6n, 14
sculpture, 2, 3, 60–61, 71, 88, 176, 250
seconda pratica, 52, 53, 60
Seebass, Tilman, 32n
Seebeck, Thomas Johann (1770–1821), 201, 202, 206

seeing, 36, 83, 122, 199, 205, 211
Seidel, Carl (1788–1844), 124n, 160
Seidel, Wilhelm, 6n, 106n, 187n
Seidl, Arthur (1863–1928), 246, 315
self-consciousness, 82, 113, 125–26, 133
self-expression, 105, 267, 268
"Semitic" (concept), 227
Senfl, Ludwig (ca. 1486–1542 or 43), 21
sense(s) & sensation(s), 8, 10, 22, 26, 30, 31, 32, 39, 40, 42, 43, 48, 49, 59, 66, 67, 70, 75, 80–90 passim, 93, 95, 97, 119, 145, 188, 192, 213, 245, 313
sensualism, 36, 43, 70, 79, 85, 97, 99, 120, 150, 162, 180, 188, 264
sentiment(s), 63, 64, 75, 84, 86, 87, 88–89, 97, 101, 152, 170, 248, 263, 267, 272, 285
sentimentality, 278
Serauky, Walter, 69n
serenitas, 264
serial composition, 3, 281, 297
Shaftesbury, Anthony Ashley Cooper, Earl of (1671–1713), 81, 89, 108–109
Shiner, Larry, 79n, 109n
Shreffler, Anne, 15, 297n, 298n
Sieber, Ferdinand (1822–1895), 306
sight. See seeing.
signification & signs, 59, 62, 63, 64, 72, 89, 101, 105, 161, 172, 186, 230, 292. See also symbolism.
singing, 1, 19, 35, 41, 42, 43, 44, 46, 50, 53, 54, 57, 59, 127, 142, 146, 272. See also music, vocal.
skepticism, 154
slogans, 208, 213, 216, 234, 236
smell (sense), 88
Smetana, Bedřich (1824–1884), 243, 289
Smith, Adam (1723–1790), 105
socialism, 183
Societät der musicalischen Wissenschaften, 93–94
society, 3, 15, 129, 134, 135, 164, 219, 267–68, 289, 290, 297, 298. See also under art; music.
Socrates, 3, 21–22, 29, 116
sonata, 14, 61, 74, 75, 76, 90, 242, 253
Sonderkunst, 221, 224, 241. See also autonomy.

song(s), 35, 41, 46, 48, 61, 62–63, 67, 116,
    272. *See also* singing.
soul, 22, 25, 31, 32, 35, 36, 37, 42, 46, 48,
    59, 69, 70, 75, 85, 91, 101, 118,
    120, 121, 124, 125, 145, 148, 149,
    168, 180, 195, 211, 215, 219, 248,
    278, 304
sound, 8, 24, 30, 31, 36, 37, 38, 39, 46, 47,
    48, 53, 55, 62, 63, 66, 67, 69, 70,
    72, 77, 85, 88, 91, 93, 97, 105,
    120, 125, 142, 146, 169, 184,
    194, 200, 205–206, 252, 268,
    279, 309. *See also* tone.
"sounding forms." See *tönend bewegte
    Formen.*
"sounding image," 8, 9, 184, 185, 193
"sounding number," 45, 50, 56, 85, 91, 92,
    95, 196
Soviet Union, 297
speech, 11, 41, 42, 43, 44, 51, 54, 58, 59,
    63, 64, 67, 131, 132, 136, 233,
    293. *See also* language; oratory;
    rhetoric.
spirit, 79, 82, 124, 145, 148, 150, 205–
    206, 223, 229, 240, 293. See
    also *Geist.*
spiritual/material, 16, 120, 124, 198,
    278, 279, 291. *See also* body
    and mind.
Spitta, Philipp (1841–1894), 228–29
Sponheuer, Bernd, 149n
Spontini, Gaspare (1774–1851), 177
Stade, Friedrich (1844–1928), 227,
    244, 311
Staël, Madame de (1766–1817), 110
Stamitz, Johann (1717–1757), 123n
Stattler, Benedikt (1728–1797), 158
Steblin, Rita, 71n
Steege, Benjamin, 207n
Stephenson, Bruce, 92n
Stern, Martin, 284n
Sternfeld, F. W., 57n
Stevens, John, 45n
Stockhausen, Karlheinz (1928–2007), 296
Stolnitz, Jerome, 81n, 268n
Strato of Lampsacus (fl. 3rd cent. BCE), 29
Strauß, Dietmar, 156n, 185n, 220n
Strauss, Richard (1864–1949), 232–36,
    237, 246, 247, 256

Stravinsky, Igor Fedorovich (1882–1971),
    3, 12, 253, 258–59, 265–67,
    271 286n
string quartet, 173, 178, 289
Strohm, Reinhard, 36n
style, 4, 15, 52, 60, 91, 99, 181, 262, 264
subject/object, 81, 83–84, 133, 163, 164,
    188, 189–90, 206, 269
subject matter, 127, 242, 258, 272, 273–74,
    276, 277, 280. *See also* content;
    meaning.
subjectivity, 113, 149, 163, 181, 188–90,
    264, 304
sublation, 191, 196. See also *aufheben.*
sublime, the, 116, 118, 168, 196, 279, 315
substance (*Gehalt*), 100, 151, 184, 305
Sullivan, Sir Arthur (1842–1900), 270
Sullivan, Blair, 41n
Sulzer, Johann Georg (1720–1779), 64, 104
Summers, David, 84n
Swinburne, Algernon Charles
    (1837–1909), 289–90
symbolism & symbols, 109, 169, 179, 186,
    229, 248, 273, 285, 289. *See also*
    signification.
Symbolists, 278, 283n
symmetry, 203–204
symphony (genre), 6, 14, 64, 74, 78,
    136, 155, 171, 173, 212, 221,
    230, 242, 276, 277, 282, 283,
    288, 294–95

Tadday, Ulrich, 14n
Tappert, Wilhelm (1830–1907), 243
Tardieu, Eugène, 277n
Tartini, Giuseppe (1692–1770), 75
Taruskin, Richard, 4, 14, 15, 16, 108,
    258–59, 289
taste, 80–81, 83, 84, 89, 150, 163, 164
Tatarkiewicz, Władysław (1886–1980), 82
Taylor, Charles, 113n
tempo, 41, 74, 170, 221
temporality, 278, 294
Terpander (fl. ca. 675 BCE), 55
text, 1, 19, 41, 49, 65, 68, 71, 107, 127, 135,
    142, 148, 157, 161, 171, 239,
    240, 270–71, 281
text-setting, 41, 45, 46, 49–58 *passim*, 60
text underlay, 49–50

theology, 26, 29, 35, 81, 165, 225
Theophrastus (ca. 371–287 BCE), 31, 48
theory (music), 29, 47, 54, 71, 94, 108, 123
theory/practice, 10, 49, 94
Thomas Aquinas (ca. 1225–1274), 29, 38, 45, 59, 81, 82, 102
Thomas, Downing A., 62n, 63n, 64n
Thompson, Verne Waldo, 125n, 152n
Thorau, Christian, 276n
thought, 9, 23, 31, 34, 45, 65, 66, 79, 88, 90, 97, 101, 113, 114, 115, 120, 133, 136, 170, 186, 205, 215, 226, 272–73, 283
Tieck, Ludwig (1773–1853), 13n, 15, 44, 107, 119
Tiessen, Heinz (1887–1971), 267
timbre, 31, 42, 54, 142
Timotheus (fl. 324 BCE), 19, 21
Tinctoris, Johannes (ca. 1435–1511), 47
Tischer, Matthias, 166n
title(s), 1, 73–74, 127, 211, 212, 215, 218, 222, 228, 234, 239, 255, 261, 275, 276, 289
Titus, Barbara, 126n, 217n
toccata, 61
Tomášek, Václav (1774–1850), 125, 126, 150, 152, 171, 225
Tomlinson, Gary, 64n, 92n
tonality, 71, 245, 255, 281
tone(s), 8, 54, 101, 103, 113, 114, 119, 120, 122, 131, 142–43, 144, 146–48, 149, 152, 165, 166, 168, 169, 170, 176, 181, 184, 190, 193, 194, 214, 215, 225, 228, 230, 232, 245, 251, 267, 277, 281, 286, 294
    and sound, 142, 146–47
tone painting, 102, 211, 213, 229, 260
tone poems, 154, 210, 233
tönend bewegte Formen, 141, 142, 147–48, 149, 167, 172, 186, 187, 190, 193–94, 219, 221, 230, 231, 235, 247, 252, 272, 302, 305, 314
Tovey, Donald Francis (1875–1940), 260
transcendence, 11, 145–46, 213, 214, 219, 239, 292
transcendentalism, 292, 293, 296n
Treitler, Leo, 16
Triest, Johann Karl Friedrich, 107, 287

Trinity, Holy, 29
trivium, 53
truth(s), 11, 26, 32, 40, 65, 89, 109, 112, 118, 127, 162, 163, 167, 240, 268, 290, 292, 293, 294
tuning, 29, 39
Turner, Joseph Mallord William (1775–1851), 242

Uhlig, Theodor (1822–1853), 138, 172n, 183, 212, 216
Ullmann, Dieter, 199n
universe, 8, 10, 23, 26, 27, 30, 38, 82, 116, 118, 122, 123, 184, 186, 188, 192, 193, 198, 201, 208, 209, 239, 295. See also cosmos.
    laws of. See under nature.
utility, 79–80, 81, 111, 127, 138, 259, 289, 290

Valéry, Paul (1871–1945), 283
Valgulio, Carlo (d. 1498), 48
Varèse, Edgard (1883–1965), 265
Varèse, Louise, 265n
Verdi, Giuseppe (1813–1901), 150
vibration(s), 125, 204, 205
Vicentino, Nicola (1511-ca. 1576), 48–49, 57
Vico, Giambattista (1668–1744), 63
Vienna (Austria), 5, 15, 104, 112, 126n, 152, 154, 155, 156, 173, 225n, 237, 252, 257n, 285, 301, 303, 307
    University, 156n, 159, 163, 172, 185, 238, 262
Virgil (Publius Virgilius Maro, 70–19 BCE), 10, 19, 46n
virtue, 67, 81, 109
virtuosity, 146, 149
Vischer, Friedrich Theodor (1807–1887), 126, 171, 217, 225, 226, 269, 273–74, 306, 307, 311, 315
vision. See seeing.
visual arts. See arts, visual.
Vivaldi, Antonio (1678–1741), 73
Vogt, Theodor, 310
voice, 42, 46, 54, 60, 61, 63, 107, 117, 132, 164, 179, 303. See also speech.
voice-leading, 53

Wackenroder, Wilhelm Heinrich (1773–1798), 13n-14n, 15, 44, 119

Wagner, Richard (1813–83), 1–2, 3, 5, 6–7, 12, 14, 15, 52, 107, 111, 127–28, 130–146 *passim*, 151, 152, 156–57, 172n, 173, 174, 177, 178, 179, 180, 208, 212, 216–17, 222, 224, 226–27, 232, 235, 237, 238–39, 240–44, 248, 249, 251, 254, 257, 263, 268, 270–71, 284, 285, 286–87, 293, 296, 297, 301, 302, 303, 306, 311, 312, 313
  operas, 139, 153, 155, 156, 173, 243, 253, 270, 306
  Zurich writings, 111, 129, 213n, 243, 309
Walden, Joshua S., 74n
Walker, D. P., 91n
Walker, John, 110n
Wallascheck, Richard (1860–1917), 244–45, 289, 315
wallpaper, 87, 274, 275
Walter, Bruno (1876–1962), 246–47
Walter, Horst, 21n
Walther, Johann Gottfried (1684–1748), 93, 95
Walton, Kendall, 5
Watkins, Holly, 123n, 149n
Webb, Daniel (1718 or 19–1798), 65–66
Weber, William, 77n, 109n
Webern, Anton (1883–1945), 12, 271, 281
Weigel, Rudolph, 156
Weisse, Christian Hermann (1801–1866), 157, 164, 165–66, 168
Weissmann, Adolph (1873–1929), 262–63
Wellbery, David E., 103n, 114n
Wellek, René, 195
Wellesz, Egon (1885–1974), 281–82
Wend, Julius, 171
Werckmeister, Andreas (1645–1706), 92–93, 95, 97
Werner, Eric, 91n
Western culture & thought, 16, 17, 22, 29, 30, 43, 82, 90, 98, 123, 251, 298
Wheeldon, Marianne, 254n
Whistler, James MacNeill (1834–1903), 242, 271, 274–76, 277
White, Eric Walter, 259n
Whitehead, Alfred North (1861–1947), 14, 95
Wider, Sarah Ann, 199n
Wiesenfeldt, Christiane, 176n
Wiesing, Lambert, 158n

Wilcox, John, 110n
Wilde, Oscar (1854–1900), 271, 283, 289
Wildhagen, Christian, 295n
Will, Richard, 134n
Will, the, 42, 239, 243, 268, 284, 290, 315
Willaert, Adrian (1490?-1562), 48
Wille, Günther, 122n
Wilson, Blake McDowell, 54n
Winkler, Gerhard J., 213n, 215n
Winter, Eduard, 159n
Wiora, Walter, 123n, 298n
wisdom, 29, 46, 112, 283
Wise, C. Stanley, 259
Wolf, Hugo (1860–1903), 254
Wolff, Christian (1679–1754), 96, 158
Wolff, Christoph, 21n
Woodmansee, Martha, 108n 109n
words, 19, 41, 42, 43, 44, 49, 58, 60, 62, 63, 67, 71, 78, 83, 89, 103, 104, 106, 112, 113, 114, 143, 144, 168, 225, 233, 289. *See also* language; text.
  and music, 42, 43, 45, 46, 49, 52, 53, 54, 55, 57, 64, 66, 67, 70, 73, 75–76, 107, 108, 125, 127, 131, 138, 142, 145, 146, 166, 217, 239, 240–41, 255, 272, 280–81, 285, 286, 293. *See also* text setting.
World Soul, 11, 25
World War I, 250, 262, 271
World War II, 297
Wörner, Felix, 244n
Worringer, Wilhelm (1881–1965), 271, 277–78
Wulf, Christoph, 69n
Wülfing, Wulf, 216n
Würst, Richard, 215n

Xenakis, Iannis (1922–2001), 296

"Yankee Doodle" (song), 276
Yearsley, David, 93n
Youmans, Charles, 237n
Young Classicism, 264

Zaminer, Frieder, 115n
Zamminer, Friedrich Georg Karl (1817–1858), 305, 306
Zangwill, Nick, 5
Zarathustra (Zoroaster), 233, 264

Zarlino, Gioseffo (1517–1590), 25, 50–51, 52, 53, 55, 90–91, 127
Zeising, Adolf (1810–1876), 303–304, 306
Zelter, Carl Friedrich (1758–1832), 100n, 112

Zimmermann, Robert (1824–1898), 157, 159–60, 162–64, 185–87, 189n, 190–93, 206, 208, 209, 222, 231, 280, 301, 305, 314
Zukunftsmusik. See "Music of the Future."